THE ARDEN SHAKESPEARE

THIRD SERIES
General Editors: Richard Proudfoot,
David Scott Kastan and

ROMEO AND JULIET

THE ARDEN SHAKESPEARE

* Second series

THE ARDEN SHAKESPEARE

ROMEO AND JULIET

Edited by
RENÉ WEIS

Arden Shakespeare

1 3 5 7 9 10 8 6 4 2

This edition of *Romeo and Juliet* edited by René Weis, first published
2012 by the Arden Shakespeare

Editorial matter copyright © 2012 René Weis

Arden Shakespeare is an imprint of Bloomsbury Publishing Plc

Methuen Drama
Bloomsbury Publishing Plc
49-51 Bedford Square
London WC1B 3DP
www.methuendrama.com
www.ardenshakespeare.com

A CIP catalogue record for this book is available from the British Library
Hardback ISBN: 9781903436905
Paperback ISBN: 9781903436912

Available in the USA from Bloomsbury Academic & Professional,
175 Fifth Avenue/3rd Floor, New York, NY10010.
www.BloomsburyAcademicUSA.com

The general editors of the Arden Shakespeare have been
W.J. Craig and R.H. Case (first series 1899-1944)
Una Ellis-Fermor, Harold F. Brooks, Harold Jenkins and
Brian Morris (second series 1946-82)

Present general editors (third series)
Richard Proudfoot, Ann Thompson, David Scott Kastan and H.R. Woudhuysen

Typeset by DC Graphic Design Ltd, England
Printed in India

The Editor

René Weis is Professor of English Literature at University College London (UCL) where he has taught for many years. He is the editor of a parallel text of *King Lear* (1993, rev. edn 2010) and of *Henry IV Part 2* (1997), and he has a longstanding research interest in *Antony and Cleopatra*. He is the author of *Shakespeare Revealed: A Biography* (2007), *Criminal Justice: The True Story of Edith Thompson* (1988) and *The Yellow Cross: The Story of the Last Cathars* (2000), which has been translated into seven languages. In 2009 he was awarded a three-year Major Leverhulme Trust Research Fellowship for a book on the genesis of Verdi's opera *La Traviata*. He is the University of London Trustee of the Shakespeare Birthplace Trust and a Governor of Goodenough College in Bloomsbury.

For Ross and Marion Woodman

CONTENTS

LIST OF
ILLUSTRATIONS

GENERAL EDITORS' PREFACE

The earliest volume in the first Arden series, Edward Dowden's *Hamlet*, was published in 1899. Since then the Arden Shakespeare has been widely acknowledged as the pre-eminent Shakespeare edition, valued by scholars, students, actors and 'the great variety of readers' alike for its clearly presented and reliable texts, its full annotation and its richly informative introductions.

In the third Arden series we seek to maintain these well-established qualities and general characteristics, preserving our predecessors' commitment to presenting the play as it has been shaped in history. Each volume necessarily has its own particular emphasis which reflects the unique possibilities and problems posed by the work in question, and the series as a whole seeks to maintain the highest standards of scholarship, combined with attractive and accessible presentation.

Newly edited from the original Quarto and Folio editions, texts are presented in fully modernized form, with a textual apparatus that records all substantial divergences from those early printings. The notes and introductions focus on the conditions and possibilities of meaning that editors, critics and performers (on stage and screen) have discovered in the play. While building upon the rich history of scholarly activity that has long shaped our understanding of Shakespeare's works, this third series of the Arden Shakespeare is enlivened by a new generation's encounter with Shakespeare.

THE TEXT

On each page of the play itself, readers will find a passage of text supported by commentary and textual notes. Act and scene divisions (seldom present in the early editions and often the product of eighteenth-century or later scholarship) have been retained for ease of reference, but have been given less prominence than in previous series. Editorial indications of location of the action have been removed to the textual notes or commentary.

In the text itself, unfamiliar typographic conventions have been avoided in order to minimize obstacles to the reader. Elided forms in the early texts are spelt out in full in verse lines wherever they indicate a usual late twentieth-century pronunciation that requires no special indication and wherever they occur in prose (except where they indicate non-standard pronunciation). In verse speeches, marks of elision are retained where they are necessary guides to the scansion and pronunciation of the line. Final -ed in past tense and participial forms of verbs is always printed as -ed, without accent, never as -'d, but wherever the required pronunciation diverges from modern usage a note in the commentary draws attention to the fact. Where the final -ed should be given syllabic value contrary to modern usage, e.g.

> Doth Silvia know that I am banished?
>
> (*TGV* 3.1.214)

the note will take the form

> 214 **banished** banishèd

Conventional lineation of divided verse lines shared by two or more speakers has been reconsidered and sometimes rearranged. Except for the familiar *Exit* and *Exeunt*, Latin forms in stage directions and speech prefixes have been translated into English and the original Latin forms recorded in the textual notes.

COMMENTARY AND TEXTUAL NOTES

Notes in the commentary, for which a major source will be the *Oxford English Dictionary*, offer glossarial and other explication of verbal difficulties; they may also include discussion of points of interpretation and, in relevant cases, substantial extracts from Shakespeare's source material. Editors will not usually offer glossarial notes for words adequately defined in the latest edition of *The Concise Oxford Dictionary* or *Merriam-Webster's Collegiate Dictionary*, but in cases of doubt they will include notes. Attention, however, will be drawn to places where more than one likely interpretation can be proposed and to significant verbal and syntactic complexity. Notes preceded by * discuss editorial emendations or variant readings from the early edition(s) on which the text is based.

Headnotes to acts or scenes discuss, where appropriate, questions of scene location, Shakespeare's handling of his source materials, and major difficulties of staging. The list of roles (so headed to emphasize the play's status as a text for performance) is also considered in the commentary notes. These may include comment on plausible patterns of casting with the resources of an Elizabethan or Jacobean acting company and also on any variation in the description of roles in their speech prefixes in the early editions.

The textual notes are designed to let readers know when the edited text diverges from the early edition(s) or manuscript sources on which it is based. Wherever this happens the note will record the rejected reading of the early edition(s), in original spelling, and the source of the reading adopted in this edition. Other forms from the early edition(s) recorded in these notes will include some spellings of particular interest or significance and original forms of translated stage directions. Where two or more early editions are involved, for instance with *Othello*, the notes also record all important differences between them. The textual notes take a form that has been in use since the nineteenth century. This comprises, first: line reference, reading adopted in the text and closing square bracket; then: abbreviated reference, in italic, to the earliest edition to adopt the accepted reading, italic semicolon and noteworthy alternative reading(s), each with abbreviated italic reference to its source.

Conventions used in these textual notes include the following. The solidus / is used, in notes quoting verse or discussing verse lining, to indicate line endings. Distinctive spellings of the basic text (Q or F) follow the square bracket without indication of source and are enclosed in italic brackets. Names enclosed in italic brackets indicate originators of conjectural emendations when these did not originate in an edition of the text, or when the named edition records a conjecture not accepted into its text. Stage directions (SDs) are referred to by the number of the line within or immediately after which they are placed. Line numbers with a decimal point relate to centred entry SDs not falling within a verse line and to SDs more than one line long, with the number after the point indicating the line within the SD: e.g. 78.4 refers to the fourth line of the SD following line 78. Lines of SDs at the start of a scene are numbered 0.1, 0.2, etc. Where only a line number precedes a square bracket, e.g. 128], the note relates to the whole line; where SD is added to the number, it relates to the whole of a SD within or immediately following the line. Speech prefixes (SPs) follow similar conventions, 203 SP] referring to the speaker's name for line 203. Where a SP reference takes the form e.g. 38+ SP, it relates to all subsequent speeches assigned to that speaker in the scene in question.

Where, as with *King Henry V*, one of the early editions is a so-called 'bad quarto' (that is, a text either heavily adapted, or reconstructed from memory, or both), the divergences from the present edition are too great to be recorded in full in the notes. In these cases, with the exception of *Hamlet*, which prints an edited text of the quarto of 1603, the editions will include a reduced photographic facsimile of the 'bad quarto' in an appendix.

INTRODUCTION

Both the introduction and the commentary are designed to present the plays as texts for performance, and make appropriate reference to stage, film and television versions, as well as introducing the reader to the range of critical approaches to the plays. They discuss the history of the reception of the texts within the theatre and scholarship and beyond, investigating the interdependency of the literary text and the surrounding 'cultural text' both at the time of the original production of Shakespeare's works and during their long and rich afterlife.

PREFACE

My greatest debt is to George Walton Williams, mentor and friend. His voluminous notes on my drafts, followed by letters, emails and postcards about 'our' play from Charleston, Venice, Florence, Hellas and Troy, were a constant source of instruction and pleasure. Ann Thompson of King's College London read all my materials with characteristic acuity, and time and again caused me to rethink notes, collations and ideas. I could not have hoped for more generous and erudite general editors. Henry Woudhuysen advised on the choice of the facsimile of Q1 reproduced in the edition, as did Richard Proudfoot, whose detailed comments, at first proof, once again demonstrated his passion for accuracy and an incomparable ear for Shakespeare's words and rhythms. My intellectual debts and bonds of friendship to David Scott Kastan of Yale stretch back to gilded times at Dartmouth and UCL.

The Arden inhouse team were wonderfully efficient and supportive. It is a particular pleasure to thank Margaret Bartley, who commissioned the edition and allowed me to benefit from her commitment, sound judgement and extensive experience. I am deeply grateful to Jane Armstrong whose meticulous critical intelligence turned being copyedited into a delightful learning curve. Anna Brewer dealt with all the picture permissions with good humour and cheering emails about opera.

With extraordinary generosity, David Crystal recorded the whole of *Romeo and Juliet* for me in Old Pronunciation, thus enabling me to internalize every line of the play through the sounds used and heard by Shakespeare and his contemporaries. Shortly after my appointment to the edition, John Snelson of the Royal Opera House Covent Garden invited me to write about *Romeo and Juliet* 'without words', an undertaking which prompted me to reconsider ideas I had taken for granted.

At UCL, I owe much to Michael Worton, whose literary gifts, idealism and unwavering sense of duty continue to inspire. In my Department, Rosemary Ashton has long set the highest standards for her colleagues to emulate; my debt to her is considerable. It was my good fortune to be taught Shakespeare by David Daniell, the Arden editor of *Julius Caesar* and one of the foremost Shakespeareans of his generation. I am grateful to current and former colleagues for their support and friendship; and particularly to Tim Langley, whose glorious mind and big heart made working with him an honour.

My students at UCL have over the years included some of the most talented young men and women in the country and beyond. It has been a privilege discussing literature with them, and with Kate Mossman, Rivka Jacobson, Chris Laoutaris and Tom Rutter.

It is a pleasure to acknowledge debts of learning and friendship to Jim Shapiro of Columbia and to David Bevington of Chicago. Greg Wyatt's magnificent Shakespeare sculptures have added immeasurably to my enjoyment of the plays and poems. Bill Hamilton of A.M. Heath reminded me time and again, by example, how much literature really matters in our daily lives. I have profited repeatedly from Katherine Duncan-Jones's research and lectures, and I owe a major debt to Brian Vickers's valuable surveys of Shakespeare's critical heritage.

I learnt much from others who have edited *Romeo and Juliet* – George Walton Williams, as mentioned above, and Brian Gibbons, G.B. Evans, John Jowett, Jill Levenson and Lukas Erne. Fleur Rothschild's outstanding 1997 King's College London doctoral thesis on *Romeo and Juliet* was a mine of information.

The research for this edition was carried out in the UCL library, in Senate House, the British Library, the Maughan

Library of KCL and the Garrick Club. On the steps of the CIEM library in Hanoi a young woman, one of our Vietnamese hosts, archly suggested that, as editor, I might consider giving *Romeo and Juliet* a happier ending since Shakespeare's was too heart-breaking. The power to move of the greatest teenage love story ever told clearly knows no frontier.

I wish to thank my fellow trustees of the Shakespeare Birthplace Trust for their wisdom and advice on much ado about Shakespeare.

Ross Woodman of the University of Western Ontario and I first met many years ago in London House and instantly became fast friends; in Montaigne's words, 'Parce que c'estoit luy, parce que c'estoit moy'. I owe a long-range intellectual debt to Goodenough College and particularly to its current Director, Andrew Ritchie, and to Roger de H. Llewellyn and Mark Lewis.

To Jean I owe even more than I could say in the parlour of Susanna Shakespeare's home in Stratford-upon-Avon.

I am of course alone responsible for any errors in the edition.

René Weis
University College London

INTRODUCTION

WRITING LOVE

Shakespeare's play about Romeo and Juliet of Verona is probably the most famous story of doomed young love ever written. In defying parental authority invested in hatred, Romeo and Juliet have become emblems of adolescent innocence, idealism and transcending romance. The play's prologue squarely blames the stars and an insensate 'ancient grudge' between their families (Prologue, 3), as ancient as the two lovers are young. To the extent that they are victims of fate rather than shapers of their destiny, the lovers are hardly lofty tragic heroes as defined by Aristotle in the *Poetics*.[1] Nevertheless, the two early quartos of 1597 and 1599 proudly advertise *Romeo and Juliet* as a tragedy, and William Hazlitt, one of Shakespeare's most intelligent critics, boldly remarked that 'Romeo is Hamlet in love. There is the same rich exuberance of passion and sentiment in the one that there is of thought and sentiment in the other' (Hazlitt, 254). Whatever *Romeo and Juliet* may lack in philosophical range, its imaginative achievements are multiple and impressive. Frank Kermode acclaims it as 'a masterpiece, the virtuosities of the language matched by the subtlety of the plotting', noting further that by using a modern novella and a contemporary setting Shakespeare 'called for new thinking about tragic experience, now less remote from ordinary life' (Kermode, 58–9). In popular culture *Romeo and Juliet* has been brilliantly distilled to its sheer essentials of *amor vincit omnia*, that is, love triumphs over everything. What the play's richly creative afterlife reveals further is the importance of its storyline, a narrative that Shakespeare did

---

1 Nor was the play granted the accolade of inclusion by A.C. Bradley in his hugely influential study *Shakespearean Tragedy* (1904), which enshrined *Hamlet*, *Othello*, *King Lear* and *Macbeth* as the pinnacles of Shakespeare's creative achievement.

not invent but one which he shaped, structured and mediated. It comes as a surprise to realize that several of the best-known recent adaptations of the play do not contain a single word by Shakespeare. The play's magnetism does not reside exclusively in its language, even though it exhibits some of Shakespeare's most expressive rhetorical fugues before *Hamlet*: it has many affinities with *Love's Labour's Lost* and particularly with *A Midsummer Night's Dream*, two maverick comedies revelling in myriads of verbal games. While Shakespeare inherited the story of Romeo and Juliet, mostly from a single source, Arthur Brooke's poem *The Tragical History of Romeus and Juliet* (1562), he created an iconic work, fashioning literary gold from dross.[1] His version above all others lies at the root of the almost universal appeal of the story. Ever since its first performances in the London of the late 1590s, it has been one of Shakespeare's best loved works, in the theatre as well as in the study. The reason for this is partly Shakespeare's Juliet.

'All the daughters of my father's house'

At thirteen, Juliet is the youngest Juliet by far in the Romeo and Juliet line of stories; at the same time, she has the third-longest speaking part among Shakespeare's women.[2] By reducing her age to thirteen from sixteen in Brooke, Shakespeare turns her into a barely pubescent bride (see List of Roles, 1n.). Although her extreme youth is commented on solicitously by her father when talking to her suitor Paris – he would prefer her to be fifteen or sixteen (1.2.9–11), echoing Brooke – such considerations play a part no longer when, in a 'desperate tender' (3.4.12), he cedes her hand in marriage after Tybalt's

1 Shakespeare had earlier used Brooke's poem in *TGV*; see Carroll, 77.
2 Only Cleopatra (693, *AC*) and Rosalind (686, *AYL*) speak more lines than Juliet (571), who is ahead of Portia (557, *MV*), Helena (451, *AW*) and Isabella (426, *MM*); see Juliet Dusinberre (ed.), *As You Like It* (2006), 362.

death.¹ The word 'thirteen' never occurs in the play, but Juliet speaks thirteen lines in Act 5, one line for every year of her life, with the thirteenth ending on 'die' (5.3.170). Such evident self-awareness in the dramatist about the unlucky number thirteen may be connected to Juliet's status as his first tragic heroine. We learn more biographical details about Juliet's history than we do with any other character in Shakespeare, mostly through Nurse's affectionate, if embarrassing, banter. Behind Nurse's story of Juliet lies a somewhat lurid passage in Brooke in which Nurse tells Romeo about her girlhood: 'And thus of Juliet's youth began this prating Nurse' (659).² Juliet's age is mentioned no fewer than five times with reference to 'fourteen'. One of these (1.3.15–18) spells out that she will be fourteen in little over a fortnight, on 31 July. Fourteen is of course also the line-count of the sonnet, the play's most distinctive literary form. While the play gives Juliet's age and birthday (her star sign is Leo, fittingly for her undaunted mettle), it says nothing about her appearance, whether she is tall or short (cf. Helena and Hermia in *A Midsummer Night's Dream*) or the perfect height for a thirteen-year-old girl, what colour her eyes are, or whether her hair is blonde, as it appears to be in Brooke when 'with cruel hand she tare her golden hairs' (2389) just as Brooke's Romeus tears 'his golden locks' (1291) on hearing news of his banishment. Also, she remains an English 'Juliet'. This allows Shakespeare to sidestep the potential pitfalls of Italian 'Giulietta' in English verse, and furthermore would have enabled an English audience of the 1590s to perceive Juliet as one of their own, someone with whom they could have ready empathy.

---

1 In *Shakespeare, Law, and Marriage* (Cambridge, 2003), B.J. and Mary Sokol note that 'It is evident that Paris as well as Juliet's father and mother expect her to cohabit immediately following the arranged marriage, having no plans for the young couple to live apart for several years as was common in aristocratic marriages.' The authors concede that Juliet 'is indeed over the legal minimum age of twelve' and observe that her mother expects her to conceive shortly afterwards.

2 Nurse's use of 'dug', 'a signifier Shakespeare uses rarely and usually to refer to the bodies of female animals or old women', Juliet's late weaning and the repercussions in the play of her parents' absence from her rearing are discussed by Gail Kern Paster in 'Quarreling with the dug' (Paster, 215–31).

She is anchored in her family in ways that are recognizably gendered. Whereas Romeo can roam the streets at night with other young men from Verona without being answerable to parents, and even woo his first love, Rosaline, with rich gifts (1.1.212), such freedoms are unimaginable for Juliet. The extent of her containment by family and father is evident from the clash in 3.5, the timing of which is crucial because by then she is Romeo's wife, owing her primary loyalty to her husband and no longer to her father. Two of her father's remarks indicate how high the stakes are: in conversation with Paris he notes that Juliet is 'the hopeful lady of my earth' (1.2.14).[1] Most editions follow Q2 here and reproduce 'Earth hath swallowed all my hopes but she, / She is the hopeful lady of my earth', which would seem to imply that Juliet once had brothers and sisters. But Capulet apparently contradicts this later with:

> Wife, we scarce thought us blessed
> That God had lent us but this only child,
> But now I see this one is one too much,
> And that we have a curse in having her.
>
> (3.5.164–7)

Juliet is an only child and, young though she is, she has no Celia or Nerissa in whom to confide – only Nurse, whose capricious pragmatism about the new reality of Paris over Romeo elicits from Juliet the apostrophe 'Ancient damnation' (3.5.236). Shakespeare moreover ensures that her mother and father are dramatically developed as parents, hence their substantive roles: Capulet's is the fourth-longest part in the play, after Romeo's, Juliet's and the Friar's, and his wife's is the eighth-longest. Her age, like her daughter's, is tantalizingly open to interpretation: 'By my count, / I was your mother much upon these years / That you are now a maid' (1.3.72–4), she tells Juliet reassuringly, aligning herself with other esteemed ladies of Verona who were made mothers at

---

1   It may not be by coincidence that this occurs at line 14, given the repeated play on thirteen and fourteen here.

the age of thirteen or even younger. At the same time, towards the end of the play, the sight of the families' dead children prompts her to say that it 'warns my old age to a sepulchre' (5.3.207).

Capulet's Wife's lines about herself as a teenage mother may well be spoken in jest; hence perhaps 'By my count', which may be teasing and insinuating, trying to woo Juliet on Paris' behalf and to allay her anxieties about her youth. Since Capulet seems to be at least in his fifties (1.5.30–9; see also List of Roles, 2n.*)*, a director might want to cast Juliet as the daughter of elderly parents; doing so would agree too with their apparent grief over having only one child and therefore being singularly protective of her.

Nurse's age is similarly problematic. Brooke calls her an 'ancient dame' (344), whence Juliet's 'Ancient' when spurning Nurse's bigamous suggestion that she should marry Paris while being Romeo's wife. Nurse's nearly toothless presence (1.3.13–14) may indicate an older woman, as may her raucous sense of humour, though she is hardly the Wife of Bath or an old bawd. At the same time, the dialogue here also suggests that she could be much younger, since her dead daughter Susan was exactly Juliet's age and Nurse suckled Juliet. We are probably to imagine Nurse and Juliet's mother as fairly close in age, in which case 1.3 becomes emblematic of the core tensions between young and old in the play, underlining the scale of Juliet's isolation (see Fig. 1).

How extensive Juliet's family and connections are becomes clear from the invitations to the ball, from which we learn, among other things, that Rosaline is Juliet's cousin (1.2.69). Since Tybalt is Capulet's nephew by marriage, the son of his wife's brother (3.1.148), is he Rosaline's brother? If he is, that might account for Tybalt's smouldering resentment of Romeo Montague while raising the question why Romeo was already courting a member of the Capulet household.[1]

As she prepares to swallow the draught in 4.3, Juliet speaks an anguished soliloquy about waking up among the dead and

---

1   H.B. Charlton comments that 'It is odd that Romeo's love for [Rosaline], since she was a Capulet, had given him no qualms on the score of the feud' (Bryant, 193).

1 Juliet (Dorothy Tutin) and Nurse (Edith Evans), in the 1961 RSC production of *Romeo and Juliet*, directed by Peter Hall

going mad: 'My dismal scene I needs must act alone' (19), she declares, after first calling Nurse before realizing at once that this prop is forever lost to her. She is alone and full of fear, at the mercy of the Friar whom she suddenly doubts: could he be poisoning her to save himself from being exposed for marrying them clandestinely? Worse still, what if his potion should not last until Romeo comes, if instead of waking up in Romeo's arms she should wake alone among the dead and be asphyxiated by the foul air of the Capulet tomb, contaminated further by the recently dead Tybalt lying there festering in his shroud? 'The horrible conceit of death and night, / Together with the terror of the place' (37–8), as she puts it, would surely rob her of her reason. Her small knife will, she pledges, rescue her if all else fails (23).

Compared to Juliet, Romeo is almost a cipher, at least as far as family and past life are concerned. We know nothing about him other than his infatuation with Rosaline. He grows rhetorically in stature at his first sight of Juliet, as smitten, inspired and elevated as Dante was by Beatrice.[1] Of his life apart from Juliet we see only his interactions with Benvolio and Mercutio and with the Friar. The fact is that, the play's double title notwithstanding, its focus rests squarely on Juliet. Its final couplet, with a strategically placed possessive pronoun, says as much: 'For never was a story of more woe / Than this of Juliet and her Romeo' (5.3.309–10). The play may have started as 'Romeo and Juliet' but it ends as 'Juliet and Romeo', a hierarchy more truly reflective of the essence of the drama. Its closing rhyme of Romeo and woe is possible only because Shakespeare restored his hero's Italian name.

Love's young sweet song: 'an excellent conceited tragedy'[2]
The dramatic trajectory of *Romeo and Juliet* follows Romeo's progress through the physical spaces in Capulet's house, a land of

---

1 See Dante's *La Vita Nuova* and *La Divina Commedia*.
2 The play is thus described on the title-page of the first printed text of *Romeo and Juliet*, Q1 (1597). Two years later, Q2 (1599) advertises the play as 'the most excellent and lamentable tragedy of Romeo and Juliet'.

Colchis through which he journeys questing for the golden fleece of love's perfection. The Capulets' home, though dangerous to him, is a hospitable place, with halls that can be turned into ballrooms, with kitchens and pantry – a festive world of comedy, fun, good cheer, music, food and cooking. Although the house stands in a city, it reassuringly boasts an orchard, a place laden with rich symbolic associations of fruit and birdsong. Above all the house contains an inner sanctum, Juliet's bedroom, where she and Romeo eventually consummate their marriage.[1]

Romeo's first sight of Juliet at her parents' ball draws from him a spontaneous rhapsodic response:

> O, she doth teach the torches to burn bright.
> It seems she hangs upon the cheek of night
> As a rich jewel in an Ethiop's ear,
> Beauty too rich for use, for earth too dear.
> So shows a snowy dove trooping with crows
> As yonder lady o'er her fellows shows.
>
> (1.5.43–8)

These contrapuntal conceits inaugurate a rhetorical register vastly richer than Romeo's callow attempts to describe his devotion to Rosaline, a passion that has frequently troubled romantic sensibilities because Juliet is not Romeo's first love (though she never loves anyone other than him). Romeo is persuaded to join his friends at the feast as a diversion, to 'Examine other beauties' (1.1.226), to catch 'some new infection' (1.2.48). He agrees to do so because Rosaline will 'sup' there (84) and because there

---

1 Coppélia Kahn develops this further by reading Romeo's death in the Capulets' tomb as his ultimate submersion in Juliet's being, in defiance of patriarchal norms: 'Romeo's death in the tomb of the Capulets rather than in that of his own fathers reverses the traditional passage of the female over to the male house in marriage and betokens his refusal to follow the code of his fathers. And it is Juliet, not Romeo, who boldly uses his dagger, against herself' (Kahn, 190). See also Rothschild, ch. 6, and Gayle Whittier, who argues that Tybalt's blood-stained shroud might evoke 'the blood-stained sheets of a consummated wedding . . . Such a reading enhances the tomb scene as a consummation of the marriage . . . The fact that Juliet's body is found still bleeding in death when it has so recently bled in love further emphasizes this connection' (Whittier, 39, n. 23).

can be no earthly chance of any young woman prettier than her existing: 'One fairer than my love! The all-seeing sun / Ne'er saw her match since first the world begun', he says, and then asserts confidently that at the festivities he will 'rejoice in splendour of mine own' (93–4, 102). Rosaline, he vows, will be as admired by his friends as she is by him. Although no entry is given for Rosaline in the text, there is a clear expectation that Romeo will encounter her at the Capulets' entertainment. The audience is bracing itself for this even as the young men prepare to gatecrash the party: they will be masked but the women of the house of Capulet, including Juliet and Rosaline, will not be. Directors have to decide whether or not Rosaline should be identified and, if so, how she should look alongside Juliet. In the text she is eclipsed by Romeo's rhetoric in response to Juliet. Up to the moment where he sees Juliet, Romeo's language of love consists of strings of self-conscious oxymorons, lifeless clichés incapable of expressing true emotion, mere verbiage of melancholy suitable for moping in groves of sycamores (appropriate behaviour for lovesick – 'sick amor' – young men). Compare Romeo's first glimpse of Juliet with his response to the remnants of the fight in Act 1:

> O me, what fray was here?
> Yet tell me not, for I have heard it all.
> Here's much to do with hate, but more with love.
> Why then, O brawling love, O loving hate,
> O anything of nothing first create,
> O heavy lightness, serious vanity,
> Misshapen chaos of well-seeming forms,
> Feather of lead, bright smoke, cold fire, sick health,
> Still-waking sleep that is not what it is.
> This love feel I that feel no love in this.
> Dost thou not laugh?
>
> (1.1.171–81)

He seems to be practising his poetic scales for Benvolio's sake. These are parodied by Mercutio's 'Now is he for the numbers that Petrarch flowed in' (2.4.38–9); they are the 'Taffeta phrases, silken terms precise, / Three-piled hyperboles, spruce affectation, / Figures pedantical' that were mocked for their lack of candour in *Love's Labour's Lost* (5.2.406–8).

Romeo's initial response to Juliet is grounded in the visual contrasts of the feast, the *pénombre* that the torches are trying to dispel (Capulet three times calls for 'More light'). His first conceit exalts Juliet's luminosity, a seminal step towards casting her as a star on the cheek of personified night, a radiant ornament that naturally turns into the jewel of 'Jule'. The young women at the ball had earlier been called 'Earth-treading stars that make dark heaven light' (1.2.24) by Capulet in a brilliant conceit that prepares the way for tying sublunary romance to heaven's constellations. As much as wielding planetary influence, stars stand in for young women, and particularly Juliet's eyes. Romeo's 'for earth too dear' (1.5.46) also echoes her father's 'She is the hopeful lady of my earth' (1.2.14), but adds to it the ominous hyperbole that Juliet may be too precious for earth. This motif too, of the heavens and earth vying for Juliet's eyes, recurs later and in the end marks the finale of the play. The last couplet here, contrasting Juliet as a 'snowy dove' with a throng of crows (1.5.47–8), continues the play on light and dark that is one of the distinctive features of the poetic dynamic of the tragedy. Setting key scenes such as 1.5 or 2.2 at night, or at dawn, the play's favourite, and final, time of day (see 1.1.116ff.), artfully grounds the text's luminous metaphors in an evocative chiaroscuro.

The conceits initiated by Romeo's first sight of Juliet resonate throughout the play, particularly in the so-called balcony scene. His second sight of her, strategically placed just before dawn, links her to the rising sun by contrast to the fading 'vestal' moon (2.2.8). Juliet's eyes – 'eye' (10x) and 'night' (12x) are the two most rhymed words in the play – trade places with 'two of the fairest stars' in heaven so that 'Her eyes in heaven / Would through the airy region stream so bright / That birds would sing and think it were not night' (2.2.20–2). S.T. Coleridge perspicaciously noted that there were 'in *Romeo and Juliet* passages where the poet's whole excellence is evinced, so that nothing superior to them can be met with in the production of his after years' (Coleridge, 140). 'The 'cheek of night' from 1.5 now becomes Juliet's cheek, touched by her hand, as Romeo watches her from the orchard below her window, yearning to be a glove on that hand. The play's dazzling metaphors dare us to *experience*, not just witness, the lovers' beauty and courting. (See Fig. 2.)

One of the distinctive strategies of *Romeo and Juliet* is 'unmetaphoring', Shakespeare's trick of sinking conventional images back into 'reality'.[1] Thus he dramatically recreates afresh the traditional love-at-first-sight conceit in the second encounter between Romeo and Juliet in the balcony scene. The orchard is a *hortus conclusus*, an enclosed garden which, according to Colie,

> a virgin is, and where also pure love dwells, according to the Song of Songs and a host of subsequent poems and romances. Juliet's balcony simply opens upon such an orchard . . . The virgin is, and is in, a walled garden: the walls of that garden are to be breached by a true lover, as Romeo leaps into the orchard.[2]

Written into the lovers' courtship almost from the start is a significant role for their bodies. Eyes, cheeks, hands and above all lips and kissing give physical sustenance to their love and ground the lofty strain of idealization that permeates Romeo's cosmic conceits in particular. After all, one of Mercutio's roles in the play is to expose the sham of courtly love and its pre-Freudian pretence that a lover is fuelled by sentiment alone. On the contrary, Mercutio proclaims, what interests rampant young men above all are quivering thighs, raised spirits in mistresses' circles, open-arses and and poperin pears: when Romeo is truly Romeo he is lusty and priapic. There is no room for a dejected, gloomy

---

1 Rosalie L. Colie, '*Othello* and the problematic of love', in Bloom, 87–115.
2 Colie, in Bloom (96). Whittier (31) notes a similar transfiguring of Petrarchan convention in Romeo's 'cheek of night . . . jewel' image.

2   Juliet (Olivia Hussey) on the balcony embracing Romeo (Leonard Whiting), in Franco Zeffirelli's film version, 1968

fellow to worry about a 'pale, hard-hearted wench' (2.4.4) when his friends are to hand to help chase girls. Mercutio's lubricious jokes refer to Rosaline; he dies before Romeo can tell him that he has just married Tybalt's cousin and that therefore he will not accept Tybalt's challenge. The play bristles with sexual jokes, swords, daggers and spears, and the opening scene sets this otherwise archi-romantic play in a key of sex and violence through the predatory raillery of the swashbuckling Samson and Gregory. Marianne Novy notes that Romeo's reason for not confiding in either Mercutio or Benvolio about his love for Juliet is because it constitutes 'not only a challenge to the feud but also a challenge to associations of masculinity and sexuality with violence' (Novy, 106). It is also the case that the love plot is too precipitate for Romeo to commune with his friends before he and Juliet marry.

Arguably more than Juliet, Romeo stays in the realm of idealizing love, his friendship with Mercutio notwithstanding, whereas she is more aware of a less gentle side of love. Hence her use of hawking imagery (2.2.158–60) and her desire to hold on to Romeo the way a 'wanton' toys with a bird reined in on a string (177ff.). Above all, her pining for night in 3.2, because it will bring her young husband to her bed, shows a Juliet full of physical longing. These lines do not originate in Brooke; they are Shakespeare's invention.[1] Juliet's first line in the scene, 'Gallop apace, you fiery-footed steeds', sets the tone for a speech driven by passion, in which she openly desires to lose her virginity: 'And learn me how to lose a winning match, / Played for a pair of stainless maidenhoods. / Hood my unmanned blood, bating in my cheeks' (3.2.12–14). Her sense of her body and blood could hardly be more explicit as she in turn imagines Romeo in metaphors of night and day that he used about her: he will be her 'day in night' and 'lie upon the wings of night / Whiter than new snow upon a raven's back' (17, 18–19). At the feast she had trooped like a white dove

---

1 Sasha Roberts has argued that cultural ambiguities surround Juliet's candour in this scene, suggesting that her desire for sex and her dominating role during the lovers' encounter in the balcony scene are at odds with Elizabethan notions of womanhood. She may exhibit 'the sexual proclivities of a hot-blooded Italian . . . rather than representing a feminine ideal Juliet evokes the problematic figure of the unruly woman; the woman who challenges patriarchal dictates and social convention' (Roberts, 52–3). Stephen Greenblatt counters that 'few readers or spectators come away from *Romeo and Juliet* with the conviction that it would be better to love moderately. The intensity of the lovers' passion seems to have its own compelling, self-justifying force, which quietly brushes away all social obstacles and moralizing warnings' (Norton Shakespeare introduction to *Romeo and Juliet*, New York, 1997, 870).

among crows in his imagination and here she, who did not overhear his trope, unconsciously echoes it, as if to underline their essential merged oneness which the imminent night will irrevocably turn into physical union.[1]

Juliet's next few lines move the play and her to a different plane by their sheer sexual candour:

> Come, gentle night, come, loving black-browed night,
> Give me my Romeo, and when I shall die
> Take him and cut him out in little stars,
> And he will make the face of heaven so fine
> That all the world will be in love with night
> And pay no worship to the garish sun.
> O, I have bought the mansion of a love
> But not possessed it, and though I am sold,
> Not yet enjoyed. So tedious is this day
> As is the night before some festival
> To an impatient child that hath new robes
> And may not wear them.
>
> (3.2.20–31)

This eroticized language has sometimes in the past caused consternation and unease.[2] Rather than being offended by her sexuality, one might want to pause instead over her readiness to take her own life: three times in moments of crisis she refers to her knife as a means to freedom out of the impasse of marriage to Paris (4.1.54, 62; 4.3.23), and it is by stabbing herself that she dies a suicide.

---

1 Cf. *Macbeth* and *Antony and Cleopatra*, two plays in which the couples' echoes of each other are used to underscore their mutuality; see Ernest Schanzer, *The Problem Plays of Shakespeare* (1963), 133ff.

2 Bowdler sanitized Juliet's speech but left in the dying and little stars, both of which are open to innocent readings. One of the most memorable airings of 21–5 in modern times occurred at the 1964 US Democratic Party Convention, when Robert Kennedy closely paraphrased them in tribute to his murdered brother: 'When I think of President Kennedy, I think of what Shakespeare said in *Romeo and Juliet*: "When he shall die take him and cut him out in little stars and he shall make the face of heaven so fine that all the world will be in love with night and pay no worship to the garish sun"' (transcribed from YouTube).

Romeo launches their shared sonnet at 1.5.92 with a string of words that are connected to religious doctrine ('profane . . . shrine . . . sin . . . pilgrims'), to which she, gently teasing perhaps, replies with 'devotion . . . saints . . . holy palmers'. These are of course above all romantic hyperboles. Nevertheless, the extent to which courtly rhetoric blurs the boundaries of romance and doctrine can be gathered from Romeo's emphatic response to Benvolio's challenge that at the Capulets' ball he will show him young women of such beauty that 'I will make thee think thy swan a crow' (which, ironically, is exactly what happens, with Romeo even recalling the image on seeing Juliet, though substituting 'snowy dove' for Benvolio's 'swan'). Romeo replies:

> When the devout religion of mine eye
> Maintains such falsehood, then turn tears to fires,
> And these who, often drowned, could never die,
> Transparent heretics, be burnt for liars.
> One fairer than my love! The all-seeing sun
> Ne'er saw her match since first the world begun.
>
> (1.2.89–94)

Such rhetoric, reminiscent of John Donne's 'Canonization', forms part of Romeo's Rosaline register, in which hyperbole and assertion usurp the place of reality and expression.[1] Inasmuch as the issue of religion arises in the play at all, it may do so not primarily through words and phrases, however charged they may seem, but because a Friar plays a hugely important part in it and, above all, because Romeo and Juliet both commit suicide. When her parents, Nurse and Paris inconsolably wail for Juliet (4.5.43–64), the Friar fiercely comforts them with

---

1   Alison Shell also compares Romeo and Juliet to the lovers of Donne's poem, noting that the last two lines of the poem ('Countries, towns, courts: beg from above / A pattern of your love') 'exactly describe what is happening at the end of *Romeo and Juliet*, when the grieving Montagues and Capulets . . . vow to raise the statues of the lovers in pure gold as a civic example' (Shell, 64). To Donne's lovers too, 'love was peace, that now is rage'.

the traditional Christian view of death as set out by St Paul in 1 Corinthians, 15 and by Donne in his poem starting 'Death be not proud'. Arguing that Juliet has been 'advanced' to the highest honour and goal of all humankind, to join her maker: 'She's not well married that lives married long, / But she's best married that dies married young' (77–8), he remonstrates with them while granting that 'fond nature' is bound to 'lament' her loss. The Friar calls both Romeo and Juliet 'desperate' as, at different times, they each threaten to take their own life in his cell. It is often argued that in his plays Shakespeare's view of suicide is doctrinally Christian: that it constitutes a mortal sin. The punishment under Elizabethan law for attempting 'self-slaughter' was death; suicides were buried in unhallowed ground at crossroads, with stakes driven through their hearts. Hamlet is acutely conscious of the Everlasting's canon fixed against suicide, as is Imogen when she resists the temptation to take her life because prohibition divine 'cravens my weak hand' (*Cym* 3.4.79).[1]

One might expect Romeo and Juliet to be similarly aware of the deadly sin of suicide because the 'fair Verona' of the play, unlike the unimagined city of *The Two Gentlemen of Verona*, is as emphatically Catholic as Italian. Alongside orchards groaning with pomegranates and sunbaked streets bursting with prowling hot-heads, it possesses an abbey garden in which a friar, friend and confidant of both families, gathers herbs (in Bogdanov's production the repeated peals of church bells appropriately conjured up Italian piazzas). Laurence, moreover, is a follower of St Francis, pantheist, poet and patron saint of birds, including the lark and nightingale, nature's herald of the morn and night's troubadour. Shakespeare knew the Catholic orders well enough to

---

1 Othello, a convert to Christianity, about to kill himself, catches an imaginary glimpse of the hereafter: 'When we shall meet at compt / This look of thine will hurl my soul from heaven / And fiends will snatch at it' (5.2.271–3). His suicide adds another mortal sin to murder. *Othello* too is set in an Italian context (Venice and its imperial outpost Cyprus), though one in which religion hardly features; or only inasmuch as, on the margins of the play, a battle with historical resonances is fought between Christians and Turks (Saracens) for hegemony in the Mediterranean.

realize that some were stricter than others: the reason why Isabella in *Measure for Measure* is a novice of the Clares, the sister order of the Franciscans, is because the Clares were famously austere and enforced a vow of silence. The Franciscans themselves were traditionally more liberal and less institutional than other orders; they were dedicated to poverty and the worship of God's immanence in nature (in Bogdanov, Friars Laurence and John met on bicycles). Friar Laurence has more in common with Giovanni Guareschi's hands-on village priest Don Camillo than with orthodox Church doctrine, ready though he is to evoke it when Juliet has 'died' in Act 4 (a more militantly Protestant view of friars is given by Brooke; see p. 46). But he of course knows that she is alive, that her coma is a subterfuge to protect her marriage, so his exhortation to the family to observe the commandments of Christian consolation is essentially feigned. Once Romeo and Juliet are dead all the Friar can do is to report the true version of events to the Prince of Verona and the others who are present. No one comments on the theological implications of suicide when Montague and Capulet decide to commemorate their dead children in pure gold, when all of Verona will pay homage to 'true and faithful Juliet' (5.3.302) and Romeo. The play skates over sanctions against suicide on a tailwind of grief, perhaps taking its moral compass from Juliet's words in Brooke. Immediately before stabbing herself, Brooke's Juliet addresses the spirit of Romeus, pledging him her everlasting love: 'That so our parted sprites, from light that we see here, / In place of endless light and bliss, may ever life yfere [together]. / These said, her ruthless hand through girt her valiant heart' (2787–9).[1]

---

1   Northrop Frye dismisses the notion that Romeo might be damned for suicide: 'the question is tedious, and Shakespeare avoids tedium' (Bloom, 159). He argues instead that *Romeo and Juliet* subscribes to a different 'religion' altogether, love, which operates according to its own particular codes, boasting its own saints and martyrs, and in ways that do not interfere with Romeo confessing to a friar. On more conservative, ideological interpretations of the play by e.g. Roy Battenhouse (*Shakespearean Tragedy: Its Art and Its Christian Premises*, 1969) and Francis Fergusson (*Trope and Allegory: Themes Common to Dante and Shakespeare*, Georgia, 1977), see Rothschild, 74–9 ('The authority of theology').

It has been argued that Shakespeare nowhere condones suicide except in the Roman plays, where self-murder is the ultimate act of freedom – 'a Roman by a Roman / Valiantly vanquished' (*AC* 4.15.59–60) – a deed worthy of Brutus, and in *Antony and Cleopatra* the road to apotheosis. The Roman world is not subject to Judaeo–Christian sanctions; perhaps surprisingly, a similar indulgence regarding canon law is extended to Romeo and Juliet in Catholic Verona. Unlike Hamlet and Imogen, they never engage with suicide as a mortal sin, even though they freely use the rhetoric of divinity as part of their exchanges of love. The audience is not meant to imagine Romeo and Juliet among the *lussuriosi* in the second circle of hell in the company of Paolo and Francesca da Rimini, whose calamitous fate so affected Dante that he fainted and 'fell like a corpse'.[1]

Shakespeare is bending the rules with his lovers, and he can do so partly by setting the play away from home. Catholic Italy was just distant enough to be a place where things happened that were not possible in England, even though Shakespeare must have known that Christian sanctions against suicide applied equally in the Catholic and English churches. He and his contemporaries were very familiar with basic Catholic tenets, since as recently as the lifetime of Shakespeare's grandfather Catholicism had been the common religion of the English people. As well as reading about Italy, Shakespeare probably learned about the country and culture of Giulio Romano (who appears in *The Winter's Tale*) and Michelangelo Buonarroti (who died the year Shakespeare was born) from Italian acquaintances in London, including John Florio, the Earl of Southampton's tutor and the translator of Montaigne, and perhaps too from the 'half-Italian Marston' (Duncan-Jones, *Ungentle*, 155). Moreover, Emilia Bassano, of the family of Venetian musicians at court, had been the mistress of Henry Carey, Lord Hunsdon, until she became pregnant and married Alfonso Lanier in 1594. Whether or not she was the so-called dark lady of the sonnets, as many have argued over the years, the players must

1   *La Divina Commedia*, *Inferno*, 5.142.

have known her through Hunsdon, who was their patron in his capacity as Lord Chamberlain. Within a year of setting a play in Verona Shakespeare returned to Italy in *The Merchant of Venice*.

At the end of *Romeo and Juliet* young love triumphs, it seems, unconditionally in the teeth of doctrinal sanctions against self-murder. The defiant words of the Duchess of Malfi (sister of a cardinal) when she flouts the Church with a hugger-mugger love-match come to mind: 'How can the church build faster? / We now are husband and wife, and 'tis the church / That must but echo this' (*Duchess of Malfi*, 1.1.481–3).[1] The challenges to authority in *Romeo and Juliet* are less ideological than in Webster's tragedy of mature love. Rather, the imaginative conception of the young Veronese lovers is as much aesthetic as it is sentimental: Romeo and Juliet cannot grow old, their beauty can never fade.

Love and literary form

Foremost among imaginative strategies in *Romeo and Juliet* is the exploration of the lovers' relationship through selfconscious verbal play; M.M. Mahood identifies no fewer than 175 puns and related word-games in the text. The poetics of love and the writing of sonnets were in ferment just then. A contemporary who undoubtedly left his mark on *Romeo and Juliet* is Sir Philip Sidney, particularly through his cycle of poems *Astrophil and Stella* (see Ard[2], 43–7). Sidney's songs and sonnets rank as the most formally experimental love poems before Shakespeare's own, untitled, sonnets and the similarly untitled sequence of songs and sonnets by John Donne. That literary form is part of the imaginative texture of *Romeo and Juliet* is clear from its opening chorus, which charts the main plot of the play in the form of an English sonnet, the classic *abab cdcd efef gg* pattern pioneered by

---

1   *John Webster: The Duchess of Malfi and Other Plays*, ed. René Weis, 1996. Catherine Belsey notes that Juliet, like other women in Shakespeare (e.g. Portia, Cleopatra) and near-contemporaries such as the Duchess of Malfi, Beatrice-Joanna (*The Changeling*) and Annabella ('*Tis Pity She's a Whore*), exhibits 'an intensity of passion which is not evidently exceeded by that attributed to the men they love. These women are shown as subjects and agents of their own desire, able to speak of it and to act on the basis of it' (Belsey, 127).

Henry Howard, Earl of Surrey, in 'Tottel's Miscellany' (1557).[1] Sidney's sequence weaves in and out of Italian forms (usually an octave, *abba abba*, followed by a sestet, *cde cde*) and the English one, but Shakespeare stays resolutely English in the three complete sonnets in the play: the two choruses that open Acts 1 and 2 respectively, and the core sonnet which conjoins Romeo and Juliet (1.5.92–105). Romeo speaks eight lines to Juliet's six in the kissing sonnet. While Shakespeare might have followed Brooke and deployed an Italian paradigm in the opening chorus (Brooke's 'Argument' rhymes *abba abba cdcdcd*), perhaps in deference to the play's setting in Verona, this option is not available in the lovers' shared sonnet if they are to kiss on a couplet. Only the structure of the English sonnet provides the harmony of rhyme that turns the lovers' kiss into a teasing union of sound and symbol.

Rhyme plays a crucial role in the rhetorical texture of a play which attributes extraordinary power of control to language (see pp. 418–20). Benvolio's first full line in the play is in verse, as he tries to impose order on chaos, something the Prince too attempts to achieve. When at the start of Act 3 Benvolio warns Mercutio of the dangers of the combined effects of heat and brawling, he again uses verse. Mercutio jauntily replies in prose, and does the same to Tybalt when the latter addresses him and Benvolio with mock courtesy. Tybalt counters with prose, at which point Benvolio once more tries to keep the peace in verse (3.1.49–52). But the die is cast and within minutes Mercutio and Tybalt are both dead. Throughout this scene Romeo, who earlier happily traded prose volleys with Mercutio and Nurse (2.4), speaks verse. Romeo and Juliet speak verse to each other, and while he slips into prose in the company of his friends, she only ever does so once, in her first line in the play (1.3.5).[2]

1 The collection's actual title is *Songs and Sonnets*.
2 Shakespeare was just then writing some of the greatest prose in English drama in the two *Henry IV* plays, which probably preceded *Romeo and Juliet* by a few months and were therefore sandwiched between *A Midsummer Night's Dream* and *Romeo and Juliet* (see pp. 33–43). The next play after *Romeo and Juliet* was (again probably) *Merry Wives*, written for the investiture at Windsor on 23 April 1597 of the next patron of the company.

It would be tidier if the lovers' kiss on the couplet marked the end of their first exchange. But they carry on beyond the closure of the sonnet, with yet another English quatrain, as if Shakespeare wished to suggest that theirs is a love that will grow and evolve, that it cannot be contained by form:

ROMEO

   . . . Thus from my lips by thine my sin is purged.

JULIET

   Then have my lips the sin that they have took.

ROMEO

   Sin from my lips? O trespass sweetly urged!

   Give me my sin again.   [*Kisses her.*]

JULIET   You kiss by th' book.

                             (1.5.106–9)[1]

By the late 1580s the sonnet, through the influence of Sidney, Spenser (*Amoretti*) and Samuel Daniel (*Delia*), had established itself as the structure *par excellence* of love poetry. Its prominence in *Romeo and Juliet* should be seen in that context, even if its very artifice would seem to run counter to the expressive needs of dramatic dialogue. Can the intensity and integrity of love be truly tested by means of a highly patterned language, a vehicle more obviously suited to rhetorical fireworks than soul-searching poetry, the exploring of genuine sentiment? As it is, many of Shakespeare's sonnets, however contrived, are intensely dramatic and confront similar psychomachias to the tragedies. By the time of *Romeo and Juliet* Shakespeare may well already

---

1   Sonnet fragments were used earlier in Benvolio's English sestet at 1.2.44–9, and notably in the highly artificial twenty-line exchange about Rosaline at 1.2.83–102, which ends with Romeo's 'shown/own' rhyme. The next line is 'Nurse, where's my daughter? Call her forth to me'. The counterpoint of rhetorical artifice and a domestic question about Juliet's whereabouts is effective and immediate.

have written the bulk of his sonnets (Riv[2], 1839).[1] They are mentioned in 1598 in *Palladis Tamia* by Francis Meres, who also refers to *Romeo and Juliet*, thus confirming the play's existence by then.

Like Shakespeare's sonnets, *Romeo and Juliet* explores the range and potential of conceits and tropes. Thus, when Romeo starts to evoke 'yonder blessed moon' (2.2.107) Juliet stops him, because the moon is changeable and because he waxes self-consciously lyrical about the moon tipping 'with silver all these fruit-tree tops'. This is the same romantic light that decks with 'liquid pearl the bladed grass' during the enchanted night in a wood near Athens (*MND* 1.1.211), or sleeps 'sweet' upon a bank in Belmont (*MV* 5.2.54) on such a night as lovers keep their trysts. However evocative and romantic the moon may be, it belongs to the wooing world of Romeo and Rosaline. This is why Juliet asks him to swear instead by his 'gracious self / Which is the god of my idolatry' (2.2.113–14), a phrase that distils spirituality, idealism, love and worship in a metaphysical conceit.[2] Through such 'reciprocal idolatry' Shakespeare sets out 'to reveal the nature of love rather than to create, as male idolatry does, preconceptions about the nature of women . . . Shared idolatry can grow into equality, as with Romeo and Juliet' (Dusinberre, *Women*, 157). She wants his essential self without a name, the quintessence of Romeo, the Platonic ideal of the uncontaminated self. Arguably the most famous lines in the play, the ones which more than any others speak of the

1 Katherine Duncan-Jones, however, tentatively distinguishes four possible periods of composition up to 1609 (Duncan-Jones, ed., *Sonnets*, 13). Don Paterson concedes that 'Most commentators still argue that the poems were written in a six- or seven-year span in the mid-1590s' because of Meres's reference, but believes that not all were written then (Paterson, xii). Edmondson and Wells are agnostic about dating the sonnets, not least because at least four of them may have been revised.

2 See similarly Miranda's 'Do you love me?' (*Tem* 3.1.67) in answer to Ferdinand's wooing by the courtly book. The ingenuousness of her reply provokes a torrent of adulatory protestations from him. For Shakespeare, directness and simplicity in the language of love equate with sincerity. Commenting on the repeated exchange of religious language and secular love in the play, Shell (62) detects in Juliet's exhortation to Romeo an echo from the Sermon on the Mount (Matthew, 5.34): 'But I say unto you, Swear not at all'.

idealism of love, are uttered by Juliet in her window. Carefully calibrated, they befit the play's charismatic, spirited heroine. In their own way they are as radical as anything in *Hamlet* or *King Lear* regarding human selfhood and moral being:

JULIET
    O Romeo, Romeo, wherefore art thou Romeo?
    Deny thy father and refuse thy name,
    Or if thou wilt not, be but sworn my love,
    And I'll no longer be a Capulet.
ROMEO
    Shall I hear more, or shall I speak at this?
JULIET
    'Tis but thy name that is my enemy.
    Thou art thyself, though not a Montague.
    What's Montague? It is nor hand nor foot,
    Nor arm nor face nor any other part
    Belonging to a man. O be some other name!
    What's in a name? That which we call a rose
    By any other word would smell as sweet;
    So Romeo would, were he not Romeo called,
    Retain that dear perfection which he owes
    Without that title. Romeo, doff thy name,
    And for thy name, which is no part of thee,
    Take all myself.
ROMEO   I take thee at thy word.
    Call me but love and I'll be new baptized.
    Henceforth I never will be Romeo.

                              (2.2.33–51)

These lines, spoken by a Juliet philosophically sophisticated beyond her years, assert the need to see through to the core of things, past outward trappings.[1] Juliet fell in love (almost literally

---

1   Rothschild (255) notes that 'The novelty of allowing Juliet so articulate and pervasive a voice has yet to be appreciated fully in the criticism of the play. The atmosphere of shared admiration creates an equality between the lovers unparalleled in any other relationship in the play.'

in a *coup de foudre*: 'Too like the lightning which doth cease to be / Ere one can say "it lightens"' 2.2.119–20) with a masked young man, and he is the one she will marry, whoever he is. In a reading of the play that affirms the power of desire to subvert signifiers, Belsey notes that Juliet is 'a Saussurean *avant la lettre*, but in drawing the inference that Romeo can arbitrarily cease to be a Montague, she simply affirms what her own desire dictates' (Belsey, 133).

Time's winged chariot

The single most distinctive feature of *Romeo and Juliet* may be its treatment of time. Its calendar is the most tightly controlled of any of the plays, including the only two works which are technically, and for Shakespeare exceptionally, neoclassical with regard to the unities of time, place and action, *The Comedy of Errors* and particularly *The Tempest*, a work determined to synchronize its action and real-life playing time. The reference by the Chorus of *Romeo and Juliet* to 'two hours' traffic' has attracted a good deal of scrutiny. Almost all edited texts of the play are based on the Second Quarto (1599), which is about 3,052 lines long, well in excess of two hours' playing time even in a production without intervals. The opening chorus therefore sets up an immediate tension between text and performance.[1] The plotting of time in *Romeo and Juliet* is singularly specific while remaining elusive in the theatre. G. Blakemore Evans notes that the 'play is unusually full, perhaps more so than any

---

1 At 2,364 lines (MSR, ix), Q1 *Romeo and Juliet* (1597) is 688 lines shorter than Q2 (3,052 lines) and can comfortably be acted in two hours without interval. Ben Jonson refers to 'two short hours' for *The Alchemist* and suggests moreover that *Bartholomew Fair*, which is nearly 1,000 lines longer than Q2 *Romeo and Juliet*, could be played in 'the space of two hours and a half, and somewhat more'; see Gurr, *Playing*, 81–3. In the most wide-ranging recent study of the evidence, Michael J. Hirrel concludes that 'The time available for theatrical events could, and regularly did, approach four hours' and that the 'the longer plays of Jonson and Shakespeare', including *Romeo and Juliet*, 'were performed essentially as written'. He estimates that the 'maximum time available for a play' would have been 'about three hours and a quarter', a time-span able to accommodate scripts of up to 3,900 lines, that is, works longer even than Q2 *Hamlet* (3,668) (Hirrel, 181).

other Shakespearean play, of words like *time*, *day*, *night*, *today*, *tomorrow*, *years*, *hours*, *minutes* and specific days of the week, giving us a sense of events moving steadily and inexorably in a taut temporal framework' (Cam², 10). What an attentive audience will undoubtedly pick up is the pressure on Juliet from her father's proposed move forward of her wedding to Paris from Thursday. There are fourteen references to that day in the play, one for each year of Juliet's life were she to reach her next birthday. It comes to be lodged firmly in our minds, a wedding day intended to wrench a happy ending from the death of Tybalt when in fact it ironically triggers the tragedy. When Capulet, flush with joy at Juliet's apparent change of heart, advances the day to Wednesday ('tomorrow') in 4.2.24 and 37, his wife holds out briefly for Thursday instead (36), trying to protect her daughter from a precipitate arrangement, having witnessed her reluctance in 3.5. Capulet had earlier proposed Wednesday (3.4.17), but when Paris reminded him of the fact that it was already Monday – Tybalt had died a few hours earlier – Capulet suggested Thursday (20). The uses of Monday (2x), Wednesday (3x) and Thursday (14x) and other references to the time of the action – there are 103 in total[1] – show how precipitate the action is. The play is set during the second half of July; it starts on a Sunday morning and ends at dawn the following Thursday.

Sunday

Morning	1.1: a street mêlée, the Prince, the families, Romeo and Benvolio
Afternoon	1.2: Paris and Capulet, then Romeo, Benvolio, an illiterate Capulet servant
Evening	1.3: Juliet, Nurse and her mother discuss Juliet's readiness for marriage
Night	1.4: Mercutio and the masquers
	1.5: Romeo and Juliet kiss at the ball

---

1 Tom F. Driver, 'The Shakespearian clock: time and the vision of reality in *Romeo and Juliet* and *The Tempest*', *SQ*, 15 (1964), 363–70.

Monday

Before dawn	2.1: Mercutio and Benvolio outside the Capulets' home
	2.2: The 'balcony' scene
After dawn	2.3: Friar Laurence in his garden agrees to marry Romeo and Juliet
9 a.m.	[Juliet sends Nurse to meet Romeo]
Around noon	2.4: Mercutio, Benvolio and Romeo with Nurse
	2.5: Juliet quizzes Nurse
Afternoon	2.6: The Friar, Romeo and Juliet; the lovers marry offstage at the end of the scene
	3.1: Tybalt kills Mercutio, Romeo slays Tybalt
Evening	3.2: Juliet is longing for night; Nurse brings news of Tybalt's death
	3.3: Romeo, the Friar and Nurse in the Friar's cell
Later	3.4: The Capulet parents and Paris

Tuesday

Dawn	3.5: Romeo parts from Juliet; she defies her father
Afternoon	4.1: The Friar with Paris and Juliet
Evening	4.2: The Capulet household prepare for the wedding
Night	4.3: Juliet's soliloquy while swallowing the Friar's philtre

Wednesday

3 a.m.	4.4: Capulet, his wife, Nurse and servants prepare the wedding breakfast
Dawn	4.5: Juliet is found unconscious and is presumed dead
Afternoon	5.1: Romeo in Mantua hears of Juliet's 'death' and decides to join her; the apothecary's shop is shut because Wednesday is a holiday

Late evening	5.2: The Friar learns that his letter to Romeo could not be delivered
After midnight	5.3.1–187: In the cemetery and Capulet vault in Verona

Thursday

| Dawn | 5.3.188–310: The Prince, the Capulet parents and Montague |

Nothing could be further from comedy than such a tightly plotted and exiguous time-scheme. 'There's no clock in the forest', Jaques tells Touchstone in Arden (*AYL* 3.2.295–6), meaning that the topsy-turvy green worlds of inversions and comedy have no need of time, the concept by which human beings measure the course of life towards death. And even when time does rear its head in comedy, as it does in *A Midsummer Night's Dream*, a play with close links to *Romeo and Juliet*, the wood near Athens proves as impervious to time as the forest of Arden. In *A Midsummer Night's Dream* a notional time-frame for the play's action is established early on when Theseus tells Hippolyta that 'Four days will quickly steep themselves in night; / Four nights will quickly dream away the time' (1.1.8–9). As in *Romeo and Juliet*, so here too a young woman, Hermia, refuses to marry the man chosen for her by her father. The penalty, if she persists, is either the frigid virginal life of a nun, or death. The fairies save Hermia but they do not come to Juliet's rescue, even though much of *Romeo and Juliet* also takes place at night, a time when reason is suspended in dreams and the fairy world may rule. The only fairy in *Romeo and Juliet* exists in Mercutio's Queen Mab speech, from which it appears that Mab would hardly be a benign Titania. That in *A Midsummer Night's Dream* and *Romeo and Juliet*, plays which at times seem obverse sides of the same coin, the time-scale should be comparable is in itself interesting, suggesting that Shakespeare may have been working along similar structural templates. In *A Midsummer Night's Dream* the period of four days and nights is tied vaguely to the lunar cycle.

No days of the week are mentioned, but the play is precise about the night in the 'wood' near Athens, the night before May Day. May Day is one of the most recognizable carnival holidays in the English calendar, a fact acknowledged in the play by jokes about the tall Helena as a painted Maypole (*MND* 3.2.296; see also Bullough, 1.367). Its prominence among rural festivals and its sexual connotations may be why Shakespeare chose it, even though May Day hardly counts as a midsummer holiday. The play's title promises a midsummer setting when in fact the night in the wood is that of 30 April/1 May. In Shakespeare's English, 'wood' meant 'mad' as well as 'forest', a rich semantic seam mined extensively in the course of this English folklore Walpurgisnacht, with additional puns on wooing (the folly of love), wooed and wood.

Romeo and Juliet is as particular as *A Midsummer Night's Dream* about its season, the 'dog days' of high summer, leading up to Juliet's birthday on 31 July. Unlike May in *A Midsummer Night's Dream*, July is not mentioned in the text. Instead, Lammastide, 1 August, and Lammas Eve, 31 July, situate the action of the play in time when Juliet's mother answers Nurse's question 'How long is it now / To Lammastide?' with 'A fortnight and odd days' (see 1.3.16, 18, 22). Shakespeare's use of the heat of summer drives a plot in which excitable young men repeatedly collide in sudden, convulsive sprees of violence: it is just too hot to remain sane and patient in Verona during late afternoon (3.1.1–4).[1] July, of course, fits with Juliet's name (she is called 'Jule' by Nurse's husband; 1.3.44, 48, 58) and may be one of the reasons why Shakespeare did not call her 'Giulietta', while happily, and shrewdly, Italianizing the Romeus of his main source to Romeo (see List of Roles, 13n.). It is the 'odd days'

---

1 On the role played by July as 'a season of extremes, and so a particularly appropriate choice by the stars for the imposition of their malevolent design', see Ard[2], 60. Commenting on the 'calendrical associations of July with passion and madness', Alison Findlay notes that these are 'conjured up even more powerfully in the case of the tragic heroine Juliet' because her birthday on Lammas Eve 'marked the official end of summer' (Findlay, 217).

of Juliet's mother's reply that seem intriguing in the light of the single-mindedness of the four- to five-day calendar which demonstrably provides a supporting frame to the love story, one moreover not present in a source to which it otherwise closely adheres.

Quite how literal one dare be when dealing with a Shakespeare play is a moot point. It is not necessarily helpful to ponder 'double time' too deeply in *Othello* or to be unduly exercised by the curious topography of *King Lear*. The exchange between Nurse and her mistress takes place on Sunday evening, not long before the Capulets' ball. Three days later is Wednesday, the intended wedding day of Paris and Juliet, which then turns into the day of her 'death' and funeral. It is also, Romeo tells us, a 'holiday', hence the apothecary's closed shop (5.1.56). Given the play's awareness of seasonal holidays like Lammastide, it may be legitimate to wonder whether a middle-of-July holiday, 'odd days' after our first views of Juliet, may not lie beneath the text, namely St Swithin's Day on 15 July. This is probably alluded to in the 'Swithold' of *King Lear* (3.4.17), in a passage that moreover echoes Mercutio's Queen Mab speech.[1] Rain on St Swithin's Day reputedly augured forty days of wet weather, hence perhaps the 'glooming peace' at the end of the play when 'The sun for sorrow will not show his head' (5.3.306).

The telescoped time-scheme and strategically placed pointers to it in the shape of named weekdays and, perhaps, specific holidays too, suggest that Shakespeare carefully structured this part of the play almost to the point of being novelistic about it.[2] It is the more surprising, then, that one of the most important time-markers, the Friar's instructions to Juliet about his herbal narcotic, seems curiously mistaken about the timing of the plot:

---

1   See *Lear* 3.4.112–20, particularly 'he gives the web and the pin, squinies the eye and makes the harelip; mildews the white wheat and hurts the poor creature of earth'.
2   In his essay on *Romeo and Juliet* in *Henry V: War Criminal?* (ed. John Sutherland and Cedric Watts, 2000), John Sutherland highlights startling aspects of the play's treatment of time, including Nurse's apparently precocious loss of her virginity (1.3.2) and Juliet's mother's age when she had Juliet (72–4).

Each part, deprived of supple government,
Shall stiff and stark and cold appear like death,
And in this borrowed likeness of shrunk death
Thou shalt continue two-and-forty hours,
And then awake as from a pleasant sleep.
                                                    (4.1.102–6)

The 'two-and-forty hours' here are at odds with the wider
plotting of the action; the Friar calculates that Juliet will be in a
coma for forty-two hours from Wednesday night, which would
allow time for her to be 'buried' and for Romeo to join her from
Mantua in the course of Friday night. When Capulet advances
her wedding to Wednesday (4.2.24) at short notice, she swallows
the draught on Tuesday night instead. But the potion's effect
lasts only twenty-four hours, and Juliet wakes in the Capulet
tomb on Wednesday night. Evans (Cam[2], 160–1) suggests that
William Painter's claim that Juliet would 'abide in such extasie
the space of xl. houres at the least' (Painter, 2.237) coloured
Shakespeare's sense of time. Brooke's Friar does not specify a
duration when passing the sleeping draught to Juliet, although,
as Gibbons (Ard[2], 54, 200) points out, the implication seems to
be that it will last for twenty-four hours: 'The next night after
that [Juliet's 'death' and burial] he willeth him to come / To help
to take his Juliet out of the hollow tomb, / For by that time the
drink, he saith, will cease to work' (Brooke, 2479–81).

Why Shakespeare would fine-tune Painter's 'forty' to 'two-and-
forty' without otherwise, it seems, considering the implications
of this for the dramatic narrative is hard to determine.[1] Jill L.
Levenson notes that the incongruous, yet oddly precise, time-
scale may serve to foreground the Friar's loss of control over
events (Oxf[1], 307). Throughout the play he has acted as a *deus
ex machina* figure trying to help the young lovers, aiding and

---

1   Gibbons notes the anomaly in Shakespeare's time-scheme but points out that 'in the
    theatre Shakespeare's specific references to time will give an audience a continuous
    sense of firm location and urgent haste, and they will not notice a problem only
    shown up by close attention in the study' (Ard[2], 54n.).

abetting their clandestine marriage in the hope that it will restore harmony to Verona by means of a dynastic union (2.3.87–8). It will do so, but at the cost of both their lives. That fate, and not the Friar, is in charge is clear in 5.2 when Laurence's all-important letter to Romeo has not been delivered because of a sudden bout of plague (5.2.6–12). Assuming that in this play at least Shakespeare meant to be consistent and structured about his time-scheme, one ought not to discount a more mundane explanation for the curious forty-two hours, namely that 'four-and-twenty' in Shakespeare's manuscript was unconsciously transposed to 'two-and-forty' by the compositor. Metathesis is a common source of error in slips of the tongue and one of the drivers of historical linguistic change.[1]

The Friar's role is, remarkably, the third-longest in the play after the lovers', with 346 lines compared to Juliet's 571 and Romeo's 615 (King). Given the tactical pressures of time elsewhere in the play, the Friar's expansiveness would seem to be a luxury that the 3,052 lines of Q2 could ill afford. Although he is an indispensable cog in the narrative – he is needed to marry the lovers, to drug Juliet to escape a union to Paris, to keep in touch with Romeo in Mantua – his lines are frequently homiletic beyond the needs of the plot and come moreover in substantial chunks. This is the case particularly in 3.3.107ff. ('Hold thy desperate hand', to Romeo), 4.1.89ff. ('Hold then: go home', to Juliet) and in the long final speech at 5.3.229ff. ('I will be brief'), where he reveals to the other players the truth about Romeo and Juliet and his own part in the plot. The latter speech is often cut. Shakespeare's main source influenced his portrayal of the Friar to the point where Laurence's longer speeches correspond to extended stretches in the source. It is as if Shakespeare were passively soaking up the source rather than harnessing its raw material in the service of his art. On at least two occasions he may even be tripped up by its fourteeners: at

---

1 But in da Porto, when Giulietta asked for poison, the Friar gave her a narcotic draught that was meant to last forty-eight hours (Ard[2], 35).

2.4.173 and 2.5.58–9 (see Commentary) he seems unconsciously to reproduce his source's metre, as if spellbound by it.

The Friar's speeches are not the only ones to afford pauses or even relief from the intensity of the lovers' conceits. County Paris' hired musicians, who are first heard at 4.4.22 (they enter at 4.5.95.1), find themselves in a curious predicament: they were Juliet's aubade to speed her along on her way to church, but now they find everything turned upside down. Just before their entry Capulet announces that 'Our instruments to melancholy bells, / Our wedding cheer to a sad burial feast, / Our solemn hymns to sullen dirges change' (86–8). Rather than leaving, the musicians stay behind in a curiously introspective scene that seems so detached from the rest of the play that it may have been written separately.[1] The friars and the musicians are interlopers in this tragedy without a subplot, a tragedy which not only features comic misrule but has all the structural makings of a comedy, including the marriage of the two protagonists, up to 3.1 when Mercutio and Tybalt die.[2] In his last scene before that, 2.4, Mercutio challenged Romeo to a duel of wits until Nurse appeared with Peter to draw their verbal fire. The scene is sandwiched between Romeo's visit to the Friar and Juliet impatiently awaiting Nurse's return from her visit to Romeo. Comically, what should have taken only a short time takes six times longer: 'The clock struck nine when I did send the Nurse; / In half an hour she promised to return', Juliet complains at noon (2.5.1–2). The scene with Nurse, Mercutio and Romeo (Benvolio and Peter too get a look-in briefly) helps to reinforce the audience's sense of Mercutio as fun-loving, effervescent, besotted with his own wit, horsing about with his friends: 'Why, is not this better now than groaning for love?', he asks, since

---

1   George Walton Williams suggests that the scene may have been written in as an after-thought to provide a chance for Will Kemp/Peter to shine (private communication).

2   Ann Thompson sees the use of comedy as one of the defining thematic links between *Romeo and Juliet* and Chaucer's *Troilus and Criseyde*. Both works frame their narratives by announcing their tragic outcomes from the start while maintaining 'a comic or affirmative tone much of the time' (Thompson, 99).

Romeo is no longer moping about after some wench: 'now art thou Romeo, now art thou what thou art, by art as well as by nature, for this drivelling love is like a great natural that runs lolling up and down to hide his bauble in a hole' (2.4.85–9). The scene displays the young men as a dashing *jeunesse dorée*, bursting with wit, sex and swagger, only to knock them down the next time we see them later the same day. By then Romeo is married to Juliet.

Ovid's famous dictum *tempus edax rerum* ('time the devourer of things') occurs in his *Metamorphoses*, a poem that Shakespeare used extensively in *Love's Labour's Lost* and *A Midsummer Night's Dream*, and whose Book 15 is the source of Sonnet 60, 'Like as the waves make towards the pebbled shore' (Ovid, *Met.*, 15.181–4). *Romeo and Juliet* is acutely self-conscious of the destructiveness of time. When Capulet sees his dead daughter he exclaims, 'Uncomfortable time, why cam'st thou now / To murder, murder our solemnity?' (4.5.60–1). By embedding the lovers' relationship in a countdown of four days, Shakespeare tightens the dramatic screw. When the film director Alfred Hitchcock was asked how long he could make a kiss last, he replied 'twenty to twenty-five minutes . . . but I would put a bomb under the bed first'. The equivalent for Romeo and Juliet of a time bomb is Paris' desire to marry the daughter of the rich Capulet, which elicits first the prospect of an unwanted wedding, then a day for it, ratcheting up the pressure by providing an end date beyond which the story cannot go.

THE DATES OF FIRST PERFORMANCE AND PUBLICATION

Lord Hunsdon's servants and Will Kemp at the Curtain (1596–7?)

Edmond Malone trusted the title-page of the 1597 First Quarto of *Romeo and Juliet*, which announced that this play had often been 'played publicly by the right Honourable the

L. of Hunsdon his Servants'. Q1 puts the writing and first performances of the play in a relatively narrow window between 22 July 1596 and 14 April 1597, because that was the only period during which Shakespeare's company was named after Hunsdon. Before that they had been the Lord Chamberlain's Men, which they became again when George Carey, 2nd Baron Hunsdon, succeeded his father in that office on 14 April 1597. Between the Hunsdons lay the seven-month tenure of the office of Lord Chamberlain by the nearly septuagenarian Sir William Brooke Cobham of the Oldcastle family. It had proved a disaster for the company when Shakespeare offended the family with Falstaff, who had at first been named Oldcastle.[1] There was much in that name, and the famous retraction in the Epilogue of *2 Henry IV*, publicly disassociating Falstaff from Oldcastle, is evidence of the company's most serious brush up to that point with the authorities. Brooke died on 5 March 1597 and Hunsdon succeeded him as Lord Chamberlain a few weeks later.

On 22 July 1596 the Privy Council closed the London theatres to stop the spreading of the plague. As a result Lord Hunsdon's servants toured away from London, performing among other places at Rye in August and at Dover and Bristol in September. Given the bibliographical characteristics of Q1, as a shortened version of the play, one that was long surmised to be a memorially reconstructed text and that required a smaller cast than Q2, the manuscript situation of *Romeo and Juliet* would seem to tally with the timing of real-life events outside the play. In September 1596 the pamphleteer, poet and playwright Thomas Nashe complained in a letter to William Cotton, of the Hunsdon household, that the players 'are piteously persecuted by the L. Mayor & the aldermen, & however in their old Lord's time [Henry Carey, the previous

---

1   For one of the most astute, least partisan, accounts of the Falstaff/Oldcastle *débâcle*, see David Scott Kastan (ed.), *1 Henry IV* (2003), 51–62.

Lord Chamberlain] they thought their state settled, it is now so uncertain they cannot build upon it' (Chambers, 4.319).[1]

A latest date for the composition of *Romeo and Juliet* is easy enough to establish because in March 1597 the house that was printing Q1, John Danter's in Hosier Lane in Holborn (his name is on Q1's title-page), was raided and the presses impounded. Danter was also the printer of Nashe's polemical *Have With You to Saffron Walden*, which was published in September 1596 (it appears to have been circulating in manuscript by late spring or early summer) and which left a significant trace in *Romeo and Juliet*.[2] Shakespeare's play is moreover alluded to in John Marston's 1598 satire 'The Scourge of Villainy':

> Luscus, what's played to-day? Faith now I know
> I set thy lips abroach from whence doth flow
> Naught but pure Juliet and Romeo.
> Say who acts best? Drusus or Roscio?
> Now I have him, that ne'er of ought did speak
> But when of plays or players he did treat –
> H'ath made a common-place book out of plays,
> And speaks in print: at least what e'er he says
> Is warranted by Curtain plaudities,
> If e'er you heard him courting Lesbia's eyes
> Say (courteous sir), speaks he not movingly
> From out some new pathetic tragedy?[3]

These lines consolidate the testimony of Q1 about the latest date of *Romeo and Juliet*. They suggest too that it was playing in London by the time Marston wrote his satire, that it may

1 Nashe was hardly an objective observer, as the Carey family were his most supportive patrons. According to Joan Ozark Holmer, 'given both Shakespeare's and Nashe's patronage from the Careys, Shakespeare's interest in Nashe's writing was probably not far removed from the man himself' (Holmer, 'Nashe', 68).

2 See Cam², 3–4, and J.J.M. Tobin, 'Nashe and *Romeo and Juliet*', *N&Q*, 27 (1980), 161–2. In the light of Shakespeare and Nashe sharing Danter in 1596–7 it is worth noting that Q2 *Romeo and Juliet* was printed in 1599 by Thomas Creede for the same Cuthbert Burby to whom Nashe's *Lenten Stuff* was entered on 11 January 1599.

3 Satire 11, 37–48 (*Humours*), in Marston, vol. 3.

have done so at the Curtain in Shoreditch, which Shakespeare's company used after they stopped playing at the nearby Theatre in 1597, and that it was popular.[1] There is little doubt about the cut-off point for the writing of *Romeo and Juliet*; opinion diverges mostly about the earliest possible date. That it is unlikely to have been written before 1594 is suggested by the demonstrable presence in the company only by then of Will Kemp; and Kemp the actor is listed instead of 'Peter' (the role) in the Q2 stage direction at 4.5.95. Kemp joined the Lord Chamberlain's Men in the second half of 1594, when the companies were being reconstituted after the two-year plague closure. He played for the Lord Chamberlain's Men at court during the 1595/6 Christmas season and took on the roles of several of Shakespeare's most famous clowns (Costard, Bottom, Lancelot Gobbo, Dogberry) as well as Nurse's man Peter. There is wide agreement, too, that he acted Falstaff in the *Henry IV* plays and in *Merry Wives*.

Earth tremors and thirteen-year-old children

A tantalizing clue about the date of the play, one which would seem to link a line of dialogue to a real-life event, occurs when Nurse claims that Juliet was weaned 'since the earthquake now eleven years' (1.3.24). There is no mention of an earthquake in Brooke, but Nashe refers to 1580 as 'the year when the earthquake was' (Nashe, 3.69), and this was also the year in which Gabriel Harvey published 'four notable famous letters' on that event.[2] Since Thomas Tyrwhitt first noted in *Observations and Conjectures upon some passages of Shakespeare* (1766) that the reference in *Romeo and Juliet* might refer to a real earthquake, historians have searched for tremors that might bear out Nurse's claim. The likeliest may be the one at Mottingham in Kent, not

---

1   That *Romeo and Juliet* should have been staged at the Curtain need not be surprising. One of the few recorded facts about Shakespeare's career as actor is that he played at the Curtain as a member of the Lord Chamberlain's in Jonson's *Every Man in his Humour* in 1598.

2   Harvey's publication was called '*Three proper, and wittie, familiar letters: lately passed betwene two universitie men* [Spenser and Harvey], *touching the earthquake in Aprill last, and our English refourmed versifying*'.

far from London.[1] It was recorded on 4 August 1585, close to the imagined time of the play's action in late July and a mere four days after Juliet's birthday. If Mottingham was indeed at the back of Shakespeare's mind, then Nurse's 'eleven years' firmly situate *Romeo and Juliet* in July or August 1596 – one of the most trying times in Shakespeare's life, because on 11 August 1596 his son Hamnet was buried in Stratford-upon-Avon. It would mean that Shakespeare wrote *Romeo and Juliet* in the wake of Hamnet's death. In a thought-provoking essay, Julia Kristeva wonders whether the death of Hamnet may not have been the catalyst for the play: 'I might also advance the hypothesis . . . that Hamnet's death triggered within Shakespeare the nostalgia for a couple that would have been in love.' She detects in *Romeo and Juliet* an 'idyllic tinge' that turns it into 'a dirge for the son's death' so that the play becomes 'the father's gift to the son's tomb'.[2]

Hamnet and his twin sister Judith were born in 1585, eleven years before the likely date for *Romeo and Juliet*, while Juliet and her 'twin', Susan, were weaned eleven years before the action of the play takes place. Could the 'eleven years' since the earthquake in *Romeo and Juliet* mark another Richard Field moment, one in which art and real life briefly seem to coalesce? When *Cymbeline*'s heroine, Imogen, a 'female page' who goes by the name of 'Fidele', is asked who her master is, she replies that he is 'Richard du Champ' (*Cym* 4.2.377). Not only does 'du Champ' mean 'of the field', but Imogen's adopted male name, 'Fidele', is virtually an anagram of Field. Richard Field was a friend of Shakespeare's and a fellow Stratfordian, and was the printer

---

1   See Ard[2], 26–7, and Cam[2], 2; Sarah Dodson, *MLN*, 65 (1950), 144, draws attention to the closeness in time of this landslip to Lammas Eve.

2   Julia Kristeva, '*Romeo and Juliet*: love-hatred in the couple', in John Drakakis (ed.), *Shakespearean Tragedy* (1992), 304. While acknowledging the originality of Kristeva's argument and its roots in Denis de Rougemont's *L'amour et l'Occident* (1970), with *Tristan und Isolde* as the archetype of transgressive love, Rothschild (190) offers a fair critique of Kristeva's 'transhistorical' and psychoanalytical approach to the play at the expense of its literary qualities which, among others, involve carefully calibrated uses of verse and prose.

of Shakespeare's *Venus and Adonis* and *Lucrece*. He published a number of works in Spanish under the name of 'Ricardo del Campo' (Shapiro, 150). Field's barely submerged presence in *Cymbeline* suggests that Shakespeare may have harboured few qualms about crossing aesthetic boundaries between life and art. The chorus to Act V of *Henry V* likewise hails the Earl of Essex as a conquering hero returning from Ireland, and Titania's forgeries of jealousy speech (*MND* 2.1.81–117) alludes to the spoiled summers of the mid-1590s that impacted so badly on the harvests.[1] Again, in *Pericles* Shakespeare brings on the poet Gower, whose tomb he must have seen at his brother's funeral, as Gossett points out in her Arden edition of the play, noting further that the birth and death scenes in *Pericles* may have been influenced by his daughter Susanna's giving birth around the time the play was written.[2]

As a literary monument to the beauty and innocence of youth, *Romeo and Juliet* may connect with the bereaved poet's family. Two further aspects of the play point in that direction: reducing Juliet's age to thirteen from the source's sixteen and inventing a double for Juliet, Nurse's deceased daughter Susan, whom Nurse bore at the same time as Capulet's Wife did Juliet. Marjorie Garber sees in the latter a variant of a

> twinning pattern, in which the specter of an offstage 'twin' or 'sister' offers a strong contrast to the onstage protagonist and acts as an index of her progress . . . Susan is almost forgotten as the play unfolds, but her alternative fate is instructive in our observation of Juliet's growth to maturity.
>
> (Garber, 37)

Was Susanna the inspiration for the spirited Juliet, so quick off the mark, so undaunted even in the face of death? We will never

---

1 See Emmanuel Le Roy Ladurie, *Histoire humaine et comparée du climat* (Paris, 2004), 244–54.
2 Suzanne Gossett (ed.), *Pericles* (2004), 60–1; see also Weis, *Revealed*, 322–5.

know. The fact remains that her name features in *Romeo and Juliet*, the play which asks the most poignant question in all of Shakespeare about the essence of names; and if Nurse's Susan had lived, she too, like Susanna, would have been thirteen in a play in which the 'eleven' years of the real-life Susanna's younger brother Hamnet are mentioned. This may help consolidate the idea that *Romeo and Juliet* was written eleven years after 1585, or thirteen years after 1583, in the autumn of 1596, hard on the heels of Nashe's *Have With You to Saffron Walden*, to which it seems indubitably indebted.

Nashe's Have With You to Saffron Walden *(1596) and* Romeo and Juliet

A number of unusual readings or ideas in *Romeo and Juliet* engage with Nashe's pamphlet dialogue *Have With You*. They include several of Mercutio's more suggestive phrases, including 'Prince of Cats' (2.4.19; 'not Tibault or Isegrim, Prince of Cattes, were ever endowed with the like Title', Nashe, 3.51), 'rat-catcher' (3.1.74; another Nashe word) and Nurse's 'dishclout' (3.5.220; 'dishclout for a relic', Nashe, 3.54). Nurse's reference to Mercutio's 'ropery' (2.4.140) and her attempt at comical play on the letter 'R' and a dog's 'arr' (201–2) may be further borrowings from Nashe. Behind 'ropery' appears to lie a dig in *Have With You* at Gabriel Harvey's father, a rope-maker who, Nashe alleges, chose the first letters of his sons' names from 'the chief marts of his . . . profession and occupation: as Gabriel . . . beginning with a G for gallows, John with a J for jail, Richard with an R for rope maker' (3.56–8). This passage may have prompted Nurse's odd musings on the first letter of Romeo's name (2.4.198–9, 201–4), a parody of Juliet's meditation on 'What's in a name?'. Romeo's 'single-soled jest' (64) echoes Nashe's 'single-soled pumps', while the alligator at the apothecary's (5.1.43) is borrowed from *Have With You*, and is the only occurrence of the word in Shakespeare. Shakespeare had used other Nashe texts before, most recently *Summer's Last Will and Testament* in

2 Henry IV. Silence's 'Do me right, / And dub me knight – / Samingo' probably echoes a drinking song from *Summer's Last Will*: 'Monsieur Mingo for quaffing doth surpass, / In cup, in can, or glass. / God Bacchus, do me right, / And dub me knight Domingo' (3.264), with Silence's 'Samingo' a version of 'Sir Mingo'. *2 Henry IV* may have been written shortly before the assumption of the office of Lord Chamberlain by Cobham and thus immediately precede *Romeo and Juliet*.[1] With *Romeo and Juliet* a height-of-summer play set around Lammastide, it need not come as a surprise that Shakespeare would remember the conversation between Summer and Harvest in Nashe's text if he had recently drawn on the same text in another play. As it is, 'put up' in the First Musician's 'Faith, we may put up our pipes and be gone' (4.5.96) recalls *Summer's Last Will*, which reads 'We were as good even put up our pipes, and sing merry, merry, for we shall get no money' (3.263); on the following page occurs the 'knight Domingo' passage echoed in *2 Henry IV*.

Two contested readings in *Romeo and Juliet* may originate in *Have With You*: Juliet's 'cunning' in 'But trust me, gentleman, I'll prove more true / Than those that have more cunning to be strange' (2.2.100–1) – *Have With You* has 'coying' – and the 'fantasticoes' in Mercutio's 'The pox of such antic, lisping, affecting fantasticoes, these new tuners of accent!' (2.4.28–9). To 'have more cunning' here means to 'have more knowledge how to do a thing' (*OED* cunning *sb.*[3]); the word had not yet accrued intrinsic moral opprobrium. Q2, based on Shakespeare's papers, has 'coying', Q4 has 'more coying', while Q1 has 'more cunning'. To use 'coying' in conjunction with 'strange' (i.e. reserved, stand-offish) would seem self-contradictory, as the two words are virtually synonymous – a gloss of Q2 would read 'Than those that are more reticent to be reticent'. It is for this reason that Q1's 'cunning' is adopted here even though 'coying' is supported

---

1   On a late 1596 date for the play, see René Weis (ed.), *2 Henry IV* (Oxford, 1997), 8–16.

by Q4 and by its occurrence in *Have With You* ('cockering and coying himself', Nashe, 3.116).

With regard to 'fantasticoes', the reading of Q1 (Q2 has 'phantacies'), *OED* lists it as the first of only two recorded usages (the other is in Dekker's 1600 comedy *Old Fortunatus*), overlooking *Have With You*, which has: 'follow some of these new-fangled *Galiardos* [galliards] and *Senior Fantasticos*, to whose amorous *Villanellas* and *Quipassas* I prostitute my pen in hope of gaine' (Nashe, 3.31). Q1's reading has the merit of contemporary authority and is supported by Nashe. In both these instances textual decisions are affected, if not necessarily influenced, by an awareness of Shakespeare's indebtedness to *Have With You*.

A Midsummer Night's Dream

That *Romeo and Juliet* and *A Midsummer Night's Dream* share some common ground is widely accepted. The word diptych has been applied to them (Ard², 31), as if they formed different sides of the same coin, tragedy and comedy, Romeo and Juliet/Pyramus and Thisbe as burlesque first cousins. Bullough (1.374) quotes George Pettie's claim from *A Petite Pallace of Pettie his Pleasure* (1576) that the tyranny of parents 'brought Pyramus and Thisbe to a woeful end, Romeo and Julietta to untimely death'. While the Ovidian story of Pyramus and Thisbe (Ovid, *Met.*, 4) may be the most obvious parallel between the two plays, they also share a keen interest in the scope and limits of poetic rhetoric, in common with *Love's Labour's Lost* and *Richard II*. Both plays too appear to be profoundly influenced by Apuleius' *The Golden Ass*, which had been translated by William Adlington in 1566. The debt Bottom owes to Apuleius' intensely eroticized, rampant ass, is widely accepted (see Hackett, liv–lv), while Garber sees in Romeo's 'It is my soul that calls upon my name' (2.2.164) an allusion to the nocturnal love story of Cupid and Psyche from Book 4 of the novella: 'In both there are an unseen lover and a love relationship which is possible only in darkness' (Garber, 170).

41

There is no firm agreement about the date of *A Midsummer Night's Dream* or whether it came before or after *Romeo and Juliet*, but the marriage comedy fits well with 19 February 1596, the date of the wedding of Elizabeth Carey, daughter of George Carey, 2nd Baron Hunsdon (for whose instauration into the Garter on 23 April 1597 Shakespeare probably wrote *Merry Wives*).[1] The bride's grandfather was the Lord Chamberlain, the patron of Shakespeare's company; her father would accede to the same office within little over a year while in the meantime acting as the company's protector during the intervening period. *A Midsummer Night's Dream* and *Romeo and Juliet* both deal with the madness of love on moonlit nights and both, as has already been noted, play at specific times in the calendar, one in spring, the other in high summer. Both, to varying degrees, involve famous dreams: one of them is the most dazzling dream vision in the language and features Bottom, who wants his dream expounded; the other has Mercutio relate the parable of Queen Mab, the fairies' midwife who presides over dreams and nightmares. The Mab speech may help date *Romeo and Juliet*, because Mercutio's claim that Mab 'driveth o'er a soldier's neck, / And then dreams he of cutting foreign throats, / Of breaches, ambuscados, Spanish blades, / Of healths five fathom deep' (1.4.82–5) may allude to Essex's Cadiz

1 In 'Tragical mirth: from *Romeo* to *Dream*' (Porter, 100–6), Amy J. Riess and George Walton Williams, after conceding that editors such as Gibbons (Ard²), Evans (Cam²) and Stanley Wells and Gary Taylor (Oxf) put *Romeo and Juliet* later than *A Midsummer Night's Dream*, argue instead, with reference to the mechanicals' playlet, for the reverse: 'The language and context of passages concerning the wall in the playlet betray the fact that Shakespeare had these fatal "orchard walls" of *Romeo and Juliet* in mind when he fashioned the "witty partition" of "Pyramus and Thisbe"' (101), as there are no walls in either the *Dream* or the playlet. Helen Hackett (xliii) tentatively supports the Carey union as the most likely of the eleven court weddings proposed for *A Midsummer Night's Dream*, while also noting that, if *Romeo and Juliet* did come after the *Dream*, 'themes and motifs of the tragedy . . . seem to have been gestating in his imagination during the composition of a comedy' (Hackett, xxx). It is also conceivable that Puck's 'We will make amends ere long' in the epilogue (*MND* 5.1.420) could be a sly reference to the forthcoming *Romeo and Juliet*, 'as amends for the botched perform- ance of Pyramus and Thisbe' (Hackett, private communication). In his 1994 edition of *A Midsummer Night's Dream* for Oxf¹, Peter Holland remains agnostic about the dates of the two plays, noting instead that 'in the final analysis, all that matters is that the two plays were clearly being worked on at roughly the same moment' (110).

expedition and the looting of the city in June 1596; news of this event had reached London by the end of July, and on 8 August 'a great triumph was made at London'.[1] Shakespeare probably alludes to it again in *The Merchant of Venice*.[2] If *Romeo and Juliet* does indeed refer to the sack of Cadiz, then a date of autumn 1596 for the play would become fairly secure. This date may be further consolidated by a curious entry in the Stationer's Register for 5 August 1596 of 'a new ballad of ROMEO AND JULIET', printed by Edward White, a lost poem that may have prompted renewed interest in the story. It is worth noting that the names of the lovers 'appear together in this form *only* in the title of this ballad and Shakespeare's play' (Holmer, 'Nashe', 72). It is not impossible that the ballad reflects the impact of Shakespeare's play; we would only know if it turned up one day. In the light of Shakespeare's debt to Nashe, however, and the dates suggested for performances of Q1 by Lord Hunsdon's Men, it is more likely that the ballad preceded the play, thus placing the likely composition of *Romeo and Juliet* firmly in late summer to early autumn of 1596.[3]

SOURCES

The story of Romeo and Juliet boasts a pedigree that reaches back ultimately into fairy tale, as its affinities with the tale of Pyramus and Thisbe also suggest. Its particular Italian city state setting may have been around as early as the thirteenth century, for Dante refers to the Montagues and Capulets as examples of civil strife that the new (1298) Holy Roman Emperor Albert I of Habsburg needs to be aware of: '*Vieni a veder Montecchi e Cappelletti*', Dante writes in the sixth canto of the *Purgatorio*; the Montecchi were a Ghibelline family of Verona (supporters

1 John Stow, *Annales*; see also Cam², 3.
2 See Weis, *Revealed*, 201–2.
3 *OED* cites four different dates for *Romeo and Juliet*, with a range of seven years: 1592 (e.g. confusion), 1597 (e.g. plantain), 1598 (e.g. charge 9 *fig.*), and 1599 (e.g. pined 6 *intr.*). There are no reasons for believing that Shakespeare revisited the play, as he may have done with *King Lear* and probably did with *Love's Labour's Lost*, so only one of these can be right.

of the emperor), the Cappelletti Guelfs (of the papal faction) from Cremona. The story of Giulietta Cappelletti and Romeo Montecchi, as told by Luigi da Porto (*Istoria . . . di due nobile amanti, c.* 1530) and by Matteo Bandello (*Novelle,* 1554), is set in Verona during the reign of Bartolomeo della Scala, Dante's patron. But of course Shakespeare had not read the great Italian writers of the *trecento*, Dante, Petrarch and Boccaccio, although Petrarch, whose *canzoni* to Laura are among the greatest sonnets ever written, is mentioned in *Romeo and Juliet* (2.4.39). And Shakespeare knew of Boccaccio through Chaucer, whose *Troilus and Criseyde* left its mark on *Romeo and Juliet* just as 'The Knight's Tale', later dramatized by Shakespeare and Fletcher in *The Two Noble Kinsmen*, did on *A Midsummer Night's Dream*.[1]

Brooke's Tragical History of Romeus and Juliet

Whether or not Shakespeare was familiar with any of the Italian and French sources – da Porto, Bandello or Boaistuau's French translation of Bandello – he had almost certainly read the story of 'Rhomeo and Julietta' from William Painter's *Palace of Pleasure* (1567). Above all he based his play on Arthur Brooke's *Tragical History of Romeus and Juliet*. This poem of 3,020 lines of fourteeners, roughly the same length as Shakespeare's play, was written in 1562, reprinted in 1582 by Tottel and reissued again in 1587. Brooke's version distils information from all its predecessors into a poem that bursts with exciting detail which neither its so-called 'poulter's measure' metre nor its prefatory moralizing can diminish. It is to *Romeo and Juliet* what Plutarch's *Life of Antonius* is to *Antony and Cleopatra*. Frank Kermode notes that

> To read Brooke with the play in mind is to be struck
> repeatedly by the easy skill with which Shakespeare
> has transformed the tale into a dramatic action,

---

1 Ann Thompson notes that Romeo and Juliet 'had been placed alongside Troilus and Criseyde as "patterns" of love' as recently as 1583 in Brian Melbancke's Euphuistic *Philotimus* (Thompson, 94–5).

altering and compressing to make a sharp theatrical point, telescoping events, expanding such characters as the Nurse and Mercutio, cutting material and inventing new episodes . . . considered in relation to its source, [it] is one of the dramatist's most brilliant transformations.

(Riv², 1102)

Its influence on Shakespeare has been extensively studied at least since J.J. Munro's edition of Brooke (1908), most notably by Geoffrey Bullough, who sees Brooke as one of C.S. Lewis's 'drab' writers, that is, not a Sidney, Spenser or Marlowe, but a second division writer of note (Bullough, 1.276–83). Bullough points out that the story was popular in Elizabethan times, hence presumably Brooke's interest in it, and he quotes from a masque by George Gascoigne written to celebrate the alliance through marriage of two great Catholic families, the Montagues and Dormers, in 1575. One of Lord Montague's daughters was the mother of the 3rd Earl of Southampton (Ard², 31), as Shakespeare, who dedicated *Venus and Adonis* and *Lucrece* to Southampton, may well have known. The Gascoigne masque featured a boy actor who wore a token in his cap:

This token which the *Mountacutes* did bear always, for that
They covet to be known from Capels where they pass,
For ancient grudge which long ago 'tween these two houses was.[1]

Bullough sees Brooke as a 'serious-minded Protestant moralist' (1.275) because of his sententious address 'To the Reader'.[2]

---

1 That the play and events from the life of the Earl of Southampton may overlap here was first mooted by M.C. Bradbrook in *Shakespeare: The Poet in his World* (1978). Gibbons draws attention to this (Ard², 31–2), noting also Gascoigne's use of the phrase 'ancient grudge', which occurs in the Prologue of *Romeo and Juliet*.

2 There are two addresses 'To the Reader'; the first one, quoted here, is in prose and dates from 1562. All citations from Brooke follow Bullough, although I have modernized spelling throughout.

After extolling the 'glorious triumph of the continent man upon the lusts of wanton flesh', Brooke affirms that he is writing his poem with a view to improving humankind morally by example:

> And to this end (good reader) is this tragical matter written, to describe unto thee a couple of unfortunate lovers, thralling themselves to unhonest desire, neglecting the authority and advice of parents and friends, conferring their principal counsels with drunken gossips, and superstitious friars (the naturally fit instruments of unchastity) attempting all adventures of peril, for the attaining of their wished lust, using auricular confession (the key of whoredom and treason) for furtherance of their purpose, abusing the honourable name of lawful marriage, the cloak the shame of stolen contracts, finally, by all means of unhonest life, hasting to most unhappy death.

Brooke's friars are whoremongers and traitors who use the seal of confession to further their own nefarious ends, in this case to aid and abet the course of true love. But in *Romeo and Juliet* the Friar is blameless, and we have the Prince's reassurance that he has always been a 'holy man' (5.3.270). Brooke further blackens his friar morally by giving him a shady lascivious past, noting that in his youth he used his cell for secret sexual assignations. This is 'trusty Laurence' secret cell' (1264), which is well hidden and equipped with a bed, because here 'he was wont in youth his fair friends to bestow' (1274). But the same friar, who is seventy years old (2843), is simultaneously called a 'friendly friar in this distress'. By the end of the poem, he has become 'that good barefooted friar' who 'many times he worthily did serve / The commonwealth and in his life was never found to swerve' (2997–8) and he is cleared of all blame. The moralizing tone of the preface is finally overwhelmed by the power and drive of the narrative and the pervasive eroticism of the poem.

Tybalt, Mercutio and Paris

In Brooke's poem, the Capulets' 'old accustomed feast' (1.2.19) is part of the Christmas revels (see 1.5.28n.) and the story of Romeo and Juliet stretches over nine months before the final tragedy. Juliet's wedding date to Paris is fixed, with curious precision, for 10 September (Brooke, 2072). The 'Argument' notes that after being married 'in shrift' by a friar, 'Young Romeus climbs fair Juliet's bower by night. / Three months he doth enjoy his chief delight' (4–5), until 'Tybalt's rage' and his subsequent death lead to Romeo's banishment.[1] Tybalt's role in *Romeo and Juliet* is one of the shortest – he has only four lines more than Balthasar and six fewer than Montague – but it is crucial to the plot, his presence vastly more important than the number of lines.[2] In Shakespeare he is there from the start, a dangerous firebrand and Romeo's sworn enemy. He at once spots Romeo at the feast when Romeo speaks in praise of Juliet, thereby casting a menacing shadow over his wooing of her. In Brooke, Romeus has been married for a while ('The summer of their bliss doth last a month or twain', 949) before the encounter with Tybalt, which moreover builds up momentum over nearly eighty lines before Tybalt is killed (956–1034). In 3.1 of *Romeo and Juliet*, the young men clash instantly and Romeo kills Tybalt in a fit of rage. In the poem, the scene starts with a reference to the Prince's inability to control the two rogue households of Montague and Capulet. The feud is compared to a fire that is forever smouldering, with the slightest spark able to reignite it. 'At holiest times, men say, most heinous

---

1 The 'rage' of Tybalt brings to mind the wrath of Achilles in Homer's *Iliad*, which is likewise announced at the start of the poem. Brooke may be conscious of this, as his account of the fight between Romeo and Tybalt suggests, particularly the epic simile used about Romeo's anger: 'Right as the forest boar . . . Or as a lion wild . . . Such seemed Romeo . . . Tybalt slain' (1023–34).

2 In his memoir, Franco Zeffirelli recalls explaining this to Michael York, a superb Tybalt who had voiced concern about being cast in such a small speaking part: ' "Not Romeo . . . Mercutio?" "No, Tybalt. But you won't regret it. Even with only twenty-four lines, it will be a major role when you see what we will do." He agreed because he trusted me' (*Zeffirelli*, 225–6).

crimes are done' (959), and so it comes that on Easter Monday retainers of the Montagues and those of the Capulets, led by Tybalt, collide. In essence this scene corresponds to the first scene of *Romeo and Juliet*. Romeus, walking with friends, hears the fracas and rushes to stop the mêlée: 'Part, friends, said he, part friends, help, friends, to part the fray' (999), appealing to Tybalt to do the same. Instead Tybalt savagely attacks Romeus, who then kills his kinsman of a few months in retaliation and self-defence; nearly 'five months' separate the equivalents of 2.6 and 3.5 in Brooke (2052).

Romeus' intervention corresponds to Benvolio's in the play; Benvolio does not feature in Brooke. Romeo's other confidant, Mercutio, does, but not nearly as prominently as in Shakespeare. Brooke's account of the fight and Tybalt's death, the subsequent appearance of the Prince and the exiling of Romeus correspond to 1.1 and 3.1 in the play. The absence of Mercutio from Romeus' circle of friends is striking, not least because the seeds of Shakespeare's Mercutio are unmistakably there, and Brooke almost seems to hint that Mercutio and Romeus are meant for each other's company when he rhymes them, sitting as they are on either side of Juliet: 'At th'one side of her chair her lover Romeo, / And on the other side there sat one called Mercutio' (253–4). It is the only time that Romeus is 'Romeo' in Brooke, and the cameo scene of Mercutio and Romeus flanking Juliet at the Capulet dance inspired the highly wrought lyricism of the sonnet in 1.5.92–105 and the prominence in it of hands. The passage is key to both Shakespeare's Mercutio and the way the relationship of the lovers is presented in the play. In Brooke the two friends are rivals wooing Juliet, each holding one of her hands. Mercutio, Brooke writes, was 'courteous of his speech, and pleasant of device / Even as a lion would among the lambs be bold, / Such was among the bashful maids, Mercutio to behold' (256–8). This is Shakespeare's Mercutio, joker about women, love and sex, and happiest when in the free and easy company of his friends. Mercutio's exuberance and his pivotal role in the play, Horatio to Romeo's Hamlet, make him a memorable triumph. For Coleridge, 'Mercutio is a man possessing all the elements of a poet: the whole world was, as it were, subject to his law of association' (Coleridge, 144). He captured the essence of Shakespeare's character better than most when he rhapsodically wrote:

> O how shall I describe that exquisite ebullience and overflow of youthful life, wafted on over the laughing wavelets of pleasure and prosperity . . . Wit ever wakeful, fancy busy and procreative, courage, an easy mind that, without cares of its own, was at once disposed to laugh away those of others and yet be interested in them – these and all congenial qualities, melting into the common copula of all, the man of quality and the gentleman, with all its excellencies and all its faults.
>
> (Coleridge, 135)

The greater the tragedy of his passing, then, even though he provoked it and even though his death provides Romeo with a just reason to kill Tybalt, not unlike Hamlet's reflexive slaying of Claudius on discovering that the point of Laertes' sword was poisoned.

Unfortunately for Brooke's Mercutio's wooing of Juliet, his hands are unnaturally cold, icier than glaciers, which is why she prefers Romeus: 'Then she with tender hand his tender palm hath pressed' (267). When a shrinking Romeus fails to respond, she tells him, 'O blessed be the time of thy arrival here', upon which she 'to her love drew so near / And so within her mouth her tongue he glued fast, / That no one word could scape her more' (280–2). This is the origin of the famous kisses in 1.5, which have attracted a great deal of critical attention, as full-frontal, onstage kissing was rare in the Elizabethan theatre. And of course a boy actor would have played Juliet in the full glare of the Puritans, self-appointed guardians of morality, monitoring the stage, ever ready to use its statutory single-sex character against it.[1] Shakespeare borrowed the lovers' hands from Brooke as he did almost every other detail but, as this brief scrutiny of Tybalt and Mercutio also demonstrates, his attitude to the source is far from supine even though he seems to have had a copy of the poem on his desk when writing the play. (See Fig. 3.)

Shakespeare recast the roles of Tybalt and Mercutio for dramatic reasons. In *Romeo and Juliet*, the antagonism between Romeo and Tybalt implodes when Romeo is the cause of Tybalt's humiliation at the hands of Juliet's bilious father. Tybalt's death, like Mercutio's, coincides with Romeo's wedding day; a few short hours separate these events. The irony is palpable and coruscating, even though the lovers seem to have no memory of the deaths of Tybalt and Mercutio during their wedding night in 3.5. The situation is compounded by the fact that the plot to speed up the marriage of Juliet to Paris is hatched at the very time that she and Romeo are consummating their marriage. Moreover, Juliet's father breaks the news of the impending alliance with Paris to her within minutes of her parting from Romeo. In Brooke, Juliet's mother worries about her daughter's prolonged grief over Tybalt and begins to suspect that her sixteen-year-old child harbours longings for marriage. So the Capulets decide to marry her to assuage her grief, and the right man is just to hand: County Paris, who 'was one inflamed with her desire', the son of an earl and of all the suitors the one her father liked best (1881–3). Whereas Brooke introduces Paris only here, more than halfway through the poem, Shakespeare presents him to us as Juliet's suitor before we see her and before Romeo meets her. The rival suitor appears earlier than the suitor, which adds to the tension, since Juliet's father is clearly interested in Paris' proposal and holds off only because of her age and because he wants Paris to be sure; at the feast Paris

---

1 In Jonson's *Bartholomew Fair*, Zeal-of-the-Land Busy evokes the injunction against cross-dressing in Deuteronomy to excoriate the players even though they are forced into transvestism by laws forbidding women to act on a public stage.

3 Romeo (Leonardo DiCaprio) holding the hand of Juliet (Claire Danes) in Baz Luhrmann's film *William Shakespeare's Romeo + Juliet*, 1996

will be able to compare Juliet and her peers, those other stars of Verona. Moreover, Paris' suit is urged to Juliet during her first scene in the play. It is Shakespeare's idea to invite Paris to the revels to see Juliet among her equals. It is also Shakespeare who takes Paris into the graveyard to be killed by Romeo, thus turning Romeo into a killer just as he is about to sacrifice himself for love of Juliet. The fact that Shakespeare moreover makes Paris a sympathetic character whose dying wish is to buried next to Juliet makes this even more surprising. Shakespeare is steeped in Brooke in the last scene of the play, but in the source Paris does not enter the cemetery; and it is Peter who accompanies Romeus, whence Shakespeare's using Peter's name in a Q2 stage direction (5.3.21.1) when in fact he means Balthasar.

Shakespeare's treatment of Brooke is mostly sequential, that is, the scenes of the play follow the broad narrative sweep of the poem, at times paraphrasing Brooke (e.g. Nurse's 'Lady, you sleep so long, the earl will raise you by and by' (2408) becomes 'Sleep for a week, for the next night, I warrant, / The County Paris hath set up his rest / That you shall rest but little', 4.5.5–7). He even tracks Brooke in the use of long speeches: Juliet's soliloquy in 4.3, the Friar's reprimand of Romeo in 3.3 and the Friar's report in 5.3 all correspond to protracted passages in the source, in spite of the fact that, unlike Brooke's poem, the play is acutely pressured for time and is driven by dramatic dialogue and pace.

PERFORMING LOVE

The range of adaptations in different genres that *Romeo and Juliet* has inspired across language and cultural barriers is without parallel. Stanley Wells notes that

> the existence and popularity of symphonic, operatic, balletic, filmic and other offshoots is relevant to the performance history of the play itself because

they create images that superimpose themselves on the Shakespearian text, forming expectations in the imaginations of the play's interpreters and audiences which subtly affect our response to efforts to translate that text into performance.

(Wells, 'Challenges', 4)

Such is the lyricism and romantic appeal of *Romeo and Juliet* that people have long wondered whether the story might not after all have emerged out of Shakespeare's own life. In John Madden's film *Shakespeare in Love* (1998), the life of the dramatist and the story of the play are closely synchronized, with Joseph Fiennes, a glamorous Will Shakespeare, and Gwyneth Paltrow, the beautiful Viola de Lesseps, doubling as Romeo and Juliet. The Stoppard–Norman screenplay is a brilliant fantasy and deservedly takes its place in the pantheon of films and productions inspired by *Romeo and Juliet*.

From London (c. 1596) and Cambridge (c. 1598–1601) to Douai (1694–5)

The performance history of *Romeo and Juliet* is in truth exceptional. As Hazlitt put it in his prefatory remarks to the 1819 Oxberry theatrical edition of the play, 'Of all Shakespeare's plays, this is perhaps the one that is acted, if not the oftenest, with most pleasure to the spectator'. It is impossible to do justice to its riches and inventiveness, and there is something affecting about the loyalty the play continues to inspire among all generations.[1] It did so from the start, as Marston's early reference to 'Curtain plaudities' suggests. We can only guess who played which parts then, with the exception of Will Kemp's

---

1   In *Romeo and Juliet: Shakespeare in Production* (2002), James N. Loehlin offers a wide-ranging survey of the fortunes of *Romeo and Juliet* on the stage and in film; the sometimes line-by-line annotations of the play in the theatre make it an invaluable resource. His work is complemented by Russell Jackson's important study of productions of *Romeo and Juliet* at Stratford-upon-Avon since 1945 (Jackson). In 'The film versions of *Romeo and Juliet*', *SS 49* (1996), Anthony Davies estimates that there may be up to sixty-one film versions and adaptations of *Romeo and Juliet*.

appearance as Peter. The other roles may have been played by Richard Burbage (Romeo) and Master Robert Goffe (Juliet), with, perhaps, Shakespeare as the Prince, Thomas Pope as Mercutio and William Sly as Tybalt (Halio, *Guide*, 97). This is necessarily speculative, based on what we think we know about the personnel of the Lord Chamberlain's Men in the period, although there cannot be much doubt about the casting of Burbage as Romeo, as he was the star of the company. If a 1596 date for *Romeo and Juliet* is correct, then Burbage would have been a 28-year-old Romeo to Goffe's Juliet. Robert Goffe (probably not the 'Goughe' in the list of principal actors in the 1623 Folio) is thought to have played most of Shakespeare's early female leads (Cam², 28). We do not know anything about his age, but we may assume that he was a teenager at the time, if such an extrapolation is justified by what we happen to know about other players of women's roles in Shakespeare.[1] Juliet's is one of the most demanding female parts in the canon. The scope of her role may owe something to the fact that *Romeo and Juliet* is flanked by several of Shakespeare's comedies. Women rule the roost in Shakespearean comedy, and *Romeo and Juliet* is driven by the same boy–girl dynamic as the comedies. The first two acts of the play burst with what David Bevington calls 'the ecstasy of falling in love', young men's 'adolescent camaraderie' and plenty of bawdry, cumulatively suggesting that 'Shakespeare has no interest in adhering to the strictures of neo-Aristotelian theorists insisting that tragedy not be adulterated with comedy',[2] a genre traditionally more tightly structured and formulaic than tragedy, pulling towards order while tragedy strains towards chaos.

---

1 In 'How old were Shakespeare's boy actors?', David Kathman remarks that 'Of the forty-plus named actors known to have played female roles for adult companies, those whose age we can determine were all between twelve and twenty-two years old, with the normal range being roughly thirteen to twenty-one'. Kathman notes that Richard Sharpe was between seventeen and twenty-one when he played the Duchess of Malfi, and that 'The very youngest boys seem to have played only minor parts, but boys across the entire rest of the age range can be found playing demanding lead female roles'.

2 Bevington, in Claire McEachern (ed.), *The Cambridge Companion to Shakespearean Tragedy* (2002), 54–5.

Some two or three years after the first London performances of *Romeo and Juliet* the bright young things at Cambridge were quoting it. In *1 Return from Parnassus*, the second part of a trilogy of university plays performed at St John's College, Cambridge, between 1598 and 1601, Ingenioso addresses his patron, the foolish Gullio:

> INGENIOSO   . . . We shall haue nothinge but pure
>   Shakspeare, and shreds of poetrie that he hath
>   gathered at the theators.
> GULLIO   Pardon mee moy mitressa, ast am a
>   gentleman the moone in comparison of thy
>   bright hue a meere slutt, Anthonies Cleopatra
>   a blacke browde milkmaide, Hellen a dowdie.
> INGENIOSO   Marke Romeo and Juliet; o monstrous
>   theft, I thinke he will runn through a whole
>   book of Samuell Daniells.
>
> (*Parnassus*, 183–4)

That Shakespeare's poetry was 'gathered at the theatres' rather than by reading in a study makes the point: they know Shakespeare's dramatic verse and are quoting heard lines from memory. Behind Gullio's lines lie Mercutio's from 2.4, when he teases Romeo about his romantic hyperboles:

> Now is he for the numbers that Petrarch flowed in.
> Laura to his lady was a kitchen wench – marry, she
> had a better love to berhyme her – Dido a dowdy,
> Cleopatra a gipsy, Helen and Hero hildings and
> harlots, Thisbe a grey eye or so, but not to the
> purpose. Signor Romeo, *bonjour*: there's a French
> salutation to your French slop.
>
> (2.4.38–45)

The spoof address 'Pardon mee moy mitressa' looks suspiciously like a parody of French ('moy' = '*moi*', i.e. 'me' in French), inspired perhaps by Mercutio's 'French salutation' (Riv[2],

1961).[1] Gullio's reference to a lunar comparison probably recalls Romeo's offer in the balcony scene to swear 'by yonder blessed moon' (2.2.107), suggesting that the scene was famous from its earliest performances. The use of 'slut' in *Parnassus* may echo another Shakespeare play, *As You Like It*, which contains Shakespeare's first two uses of that word (but may be too late for the *Parnassus* plays), although 'sluttish' occurs earlier, in *Venus and Adonis* (983), in the sonnets (55.4) and above all in Mercutio's Queen Mab speech, in which Q1 and Q2 closely agree: 'This is that very Mab / That plaits the manes of horses in the night, / And bakes the elf-locks in foul sluttish hairs' (1.4.88–90), Mercutio explains in one of the key passages of this 'brilliant scherzo' (Kermode, 55). From the start, it seems, Mercutio's stage presence was making itself felt, since two out of three allusions in *Parnasssus* arise from his speeches.

Given the convergence of Q1 and Q2 in the passages to which *Parnassus* alludes, the source for these echoes could be either of the two quartos. This needs noting because Q1 is in all likelihood a touring text (see pp. 34, 105), that is, an abridged version of the play that may have been used by the company at some point when they were playing away from London in the summer of 1596. The version that would have been used in the main playing spaces in London would probably have been Shakespeare's original draft of the play, his manuscript or holograph, which subsequently became Q2. In other words, the Cambridge students may have heard Q1 rather than Q2 unless they descended upon the capital at some point to see *Romeo and Juliet* and other plays.

As soon as the play became available in print, and particularly after the publication of the First Folio in 1623, a wider audience arose well beyond the reach of London theatres. The First

---

1 There may be a long-range echo, too, of Barabas's farcical French in Marlowe's *Jew of Malta*, when he enters in 4.4 disguised as a French musician with 'Must tuna my lute for sound' and '*Pardonnez-moi*, be no in tune yet', using both final *a* to mark French phonetics and 'Pardon me' or 'moi' (*The Jew of Malta*, 4.4.29ff., in David Bevington and Eric Rasmussen (eds), *Christopher Marlowe: Doctor Faustus and Other Plays*, 1995).

Folio emancipated Shakespeare from performance. Now the plays would be enjoyed by anyone who could read, none more so perhaps than *Romeo and Juliet*. The two young lovers are the only characters mentioned by name in the commendatory verses of the Folio, where the poet and translator Leonard Digges refers admiringly to the 'passions of Juliet and her Romeo', putting Juliet first just as Shakespeare does in the last line of the play.

The Bodleian First Folio of Shakespeare's plays tells an interesting tale about *Romeo and Juliet* and students in seventeenth-century Oxford. For forty years after its publication the volume remained chained to the shelves of the library for use by students; in 1664, the university, it seems, traded it in for a Third Folio of the poet's works. When the copy of the First Folio eventually found its way back to its old home in 1905, its *Romeo and Juliet* pages were the most worn. It may have been the students' favourite play; the most handled page of all was the lovers' poignant parting at dawn in 3.5 (Duncan-Jones, *Ungentle*, 282–4).

In 1662 Samuel Pepys saw a version of *Romeo and Juliet* at Lincoln's Inn Fields Theatre, directed, perhaps, by William Davenant.[1] Henry Harris played Romeo while Juliet was acted by Mary Saunderson, probably the first female Juliet ever on the English stage, with Thomas Betterton, her future husband, as Mercutio. Pepys attended a performance on 1 March, 'the first time it was ever acted. But it is the play of itself the worst that

---

1 William Davenant's connection to Shakespeare, as probable godson if not illegitimate offspring, was first mentioned by John Aubrey in his *Brief Lives* (1681). Aubrey knew Davenant, and reports that in his cups and among 'his most intimate friends' Davenant would boast 'that it seemed to him that he writ with the very spirit that did Shakespeare, and seemed contented enough to be thought his son. He would tell them the story as above [in which way his mother had a very light report, whereby she was called a whore]'; see *ODNB* Davenant, Sir William.
  Versions of *Romeo and Juliet* were performed in Nördlingen in 1604 and in Dresden in 1626; see Albert Cohn, *Shakespeare in Germany in the Sixteenth and Seventeenth Centuries* (1865). The 1626 version is recognizably based on Shakespeare's play, but the dialogue is almost entirely rewritten as prose. With the parting at dawn in 3.5 of Shakespeare's play cf. e.g. the following: 'JULIET Dearest, it is not the morning, it is the pale moon. / ROMEO Oh, could I but hope that that moon would shine a whole month, it were a comfort to us; for the sun brings us nothing but grief and suffering. / JULIET Alas, it is the dawn . . . '. The entire text is reproduced by Cohn, 304–406.

I ever heard in my life, and the worst acted that ever I saw these people do; and I am resolved to go no more to see the first time of acting, for they were all of them out more or less.'[1] It may have been the fact that it was an under-rehearsed première (being 'out' means not having mastered the lines) as much as the play that put Pepys off, although it is hard to imagine that Betterton and his fellow actors would have put in an unprofessional performance. In his theatrical history *Roscius Anglicanus* (1708), the prompter John Downes relates an egregious slip during performance:

> There being a fight and scuffle in this play between the House of Capulet and House of Paris, Mrs Holden, acting his [Paris'] wife, entered in a hurry, crying 'O my dear count!' She inadvertently left out 'o' in the pronunciation of the word 'count', giving it a vehement accent put the house into such a laughter that London Bridge at low water was silence to it. This tragedy of *Romeo and Juliet* was made some time after into a tragi-comedy by Mr James Howard, he preserving Romeo and Juliet alive so that when the tragedy was revived again 'twas played alternately, tragical one day and tragic-comical another, for several days together.

Ten years later, Dryden, unlike Pepys, enjoyed the play, noting that '*Shakespear* show'd the best of his skill in his *Mercutio*, and he said himself, that he was forc'd to kill him in the third Act, to prevent being kill'd by him.'[2] He meant, presumably, that Mercutio threatens to run away with the play at the expense of the love interest, although Romeo rather than Juliet would be in danger of being overwhelmed by the presence beyond 3.1 of a character of Falstaffian vitality. In some ways Mercutio is a foil to Romeo,

---

1   *The Diary of Samuel Pepys,* ed. Robert Latham and William Matthews, vol. 3 (1970), 39.

2   'Defence of the Epilogue. Or, *An Essay on the* Dramatique Poetry *of the last Age*', in John Loftis and David Stuart Rhodes (eds), *The Works of John Dryden*, vol. 11 (1978), 215.

the obverse of romantic love, of worshipping young women when in fact sex is a great equalizer; as Mercutio is keen to tell us, one woman will do as well as the next. Harley Granville-Barker, who returned the plays to the theatre from their nineteenth-century luxuriance, was acutely aware of Mercutio's appeal on stage: 'One or two of Mercutio's jokes are too outrageous for modern public usage; they will create discomfort among a mixed audience. But this full-blooded sensuality is . . . set very purposefully against Romeo's romantic idealism, and the balance and contrast must not be destroyed' (Granville-Barker, 34). In his counterblast to romance, Mercutio is as effective and untrustworthy as Falstaff in his critique of power in the *Henry IV* plays, close contemporaries of *Romeo and Juliet*.

The year 1679 saw the appearance of Thomas Otway's *The History and Fall of Caius Marius*, a play heavily indebted to Shakespeare's tragedy, whose place on the stage it would effectively usurp for the next six decades. Otway's Plutarchan drama, set during the Roman civil wars which opposed the plebeian leader Marius to the patricians Sulla and Metellus, includes the secret marriage of Metellus' daughter Lavinia to Young Marius. The influence of Shakespeare's *Romeo and Juliet* is pervasive: the Lavinia and Young Marius subplot owes much to Shakespeare's play; at times only the names are changed, as in: 'O Marius, Marius, wherefore art thou Marius?'. Otway's most enduring departure from Shakespeare was to allow his lovers to survive long enough after Marius ingests poison to share one last exchange before dying. The scene is more Antony and Cleopatra than Romeo and Juliet. Shakespeare's timing of the lovers' deaths, the fact that they just miss each other, has long troubled audiences.

Romeo and Juliet is among the 1694–5 transcripts of six Shakespeare plays that originated with the English College at Douai, near Reims.[1] Although there is no record of performances

---

1 The plays are *Romeo and Juliet, As You Like It, Julius Caesar, The Comedy of Errors, Twelfth Night* and *Macbeth*.

at Douai, these were in all probability 'originally prepared for some kind of theatrical production, most probably of an amateur nature . . . The *Romeo and Juliet* and *As You Like It* transcripts are by many years the earliest examples we possess of acting versions of these plays' (Cam², 164–5). The English of the Douai *Romeo and Juliet* was extensively modernized; it was provided with a cast list and cut to a length of 2,004 lines – 1,048 lines shorter than Q2, with 216 lines fewer than Q1, and trailing Garrick's *Romeo and Juliet* by 83 lines. The English College had played a key role in the Catholic struggles of the Elizabethan and Jacobean periods. Changes to the text such as 'Friar' to 'Father' point to a Catholic hand. One wonders whether the young seminarians of Douai were as keen on *Romeo and Juliet* as earlier generations of students at Oxford and Cambridge had been; this is, after all, the ultimate play of teenage anguish.

From Garrick (1748) to Berlioz (1839) and Cushman (1845)

The next recorded performance of *Romeo and Juliet* was an amateur one in New York in 1730; it was the first ever production of a Shakespeare play in America, preceding by some twenty years the arrival of Lewis Hallam's London Company of Comedians who, among other plays, put on *Romeo and Juliet* (in David Garrick's adapted text).[1] Such was the play's appeal in America that in 1869 Edwin Booth chose it to open his magnificent new theatre in New York, with himself, aged thirty-six, as Romeo opposite Juliet played by Mary McVicker, whom he married that same year.[2] Two years later, in 1871, Horace Howard Furness published the first New Variorum Edition of Shakespeare, which he dedicated to 'The Shakspere Society of Philadelphia'.

---

1 Halio, *Guide*, 104. The producer of the 1730 New York performance was a doctor by the name of Joachimus Bertrand, who played the Apothecary, jesting that he 'hoped his performance of this role would "be kindly taken and looked upon as a great condescension in a physician"' (cited in Loehlin, 44).

2 In 1864 Booth's younger brother, John Wilkes Booth, had played Romeo to huge acclaim less than a year before assassinating President Abraham Lincoln.

Mindful of the great Cambridge edition of Shakespeare by J. Glover, W.G. Clark and W.A. Wright (1863), to whose labours Furness paid fulsome tribute, the New Variorum marked the beginning of scholarly editing of Shakespeare. That the first volume in the (still ongoing) series should be *Romeo and Juliet* testifies to the seemingly timeless appeal of the play.

In 1744 the maverick Theophilus Cibber staged an adaptation of the play at the Little Theatre in the Haymarket. The cast was a family affair. Cibber, who was forty-one, played Romeo to his fourteen-year-old daughter Jenny's Juliet (she is probably the actress closest in age to Juliet ever to have played the role on the public stage), while his sister Charlotte acted Nurse. Garrick thought it the worst show he had ever seen. Cibber grafted parts of Otway's text on to *Romeo and Juliet*, as did Garrick (and later J.P. Kemble) after him, letting Romeo live long enough to share one last exchange with Juliet. In his version (1748, revised 1750), as well as purging the text of some of the seamier puns and jokes, Garrick raised Juliet's age to almost eighteen, and, following Otway, he wrote in a new parting scene for the lovers. The popular success of the scene spoke for itself, but when he was challenged about the change he defended it in the name of authenticity. The original in Bandello's *Novelle*, Garrick noted, all along had Juliet wake for Romeo, but Shakespeare missed this because it was overlooked by an unreliable French or English translation that he used. If only Shakespeare had read Bandello in the original this would not have happened; and, Garrick points out, Otway is a precedent. It struck Garrick as odd that 'so great a dramatic genius did not work up a scene from it of more nature, terror and distress' (Branam, 176). It is hard to gainsay Garrick's point, although Shakespeare's Juliet has so far outgrown Romeo by the end of the play that it seems entirely right that her final act of courage, a 'Roman' suicide unlike his gentler poisoning, should linger in our minds' eyes rather than a maudlin, however heart-wrenching, leave-taking of the two.

Garrick's dramatic instincts were finely honed; he could eloquently take issue with Shakespeare when it suited him to do so, or argue on both sides of the dramatic fence, as he did with his decision to retain Rosaline, Romeo's first love, in 1748 and then to drop her altogether in 1750. Such was Shakespeare's insight into human nature, he noted, that he knew that the young (i.e. young men) were deeply fickle, so that the presence of a first love helps characterize Romeo as a typical youth.[1] But two years later he ruefully noted that the court of public opinion had decided otherwise and Rosaline had to go; which of course involved some major rewriting of bits of dialogue and of scenes like 1.5. If Garrick caved in to misconceived public opinion, this was probably due to the rivalry in 1750 between Drury Lane (Garrick and Anne Bellamy as Romeo and Juliet; see Fig. 4) and the defection to Covent Garden of Spranger Barry and Susannah Cibber, who had both been directed in *Romeo and Juliet* in 1748 by Garrrick. The two rival productions of *Romeo and Juliet* opened on the same night (28 September 1750).[2]

Between 1750 and 1800 *Romeo and Juliet* was performed some four hundred times, which made it the most popular play of Shakespeare's during that period; this was largely thanks to Garrick and Barry, who continued to star in the role of Romeo for a number of years in the two theatres that dominated the London scene, Drury Lane and Covent Garden (see Fig. 5).[3] Whatever reservations eighteenth-century and neo-classical writers may have harboured about the play's puns and breaches of decorum – Pope, for example, cut most of the dialogue

---

1   Coleridge similarly noted that Romeo's infatuation with Rosaline attests to Shakespeare's grasp of psychology: 'it marks strongly the fineness of his insight into the nature of the passions that Romeo is introduced already love-bewildered. The necessity of loving creating an object for itself . . . The difference in this respect between men and women – it would have displeased us that Juliet had been in love or fancied herself so' (Coleridge, 6).

2   This was the so-called 'battle of the Romeos' (Loehlin, 12–20).

3   According to Charles B. Hogan, *Romeo and Juliet* is ranked thirteenth among the most performed of Shakespeare's plays in the period 1701–50, but occupies first place between 1751 and 1800, ahead of *Hamlet*, *Richard III* and *Macbeth* (Hogan, 1.460ff., 2.716ff.).

4 David Garrick and Anne Bellamy as Romeo and Juliet, engraving by Benjamin Wilson, 1753

Mr Barry and Miss Nossiter,
in the Characters of Romeo and Juliet.
Act 2.d Scene 2.d

5   Spranger Barry and Maria Isabella Nossiter as Romeo and Juliet, from an
engraving by William Eliott, 1759

between Romeo and Mercutio in 2.4 – or the candid portrayal of the sexual longings of a teenage girl, the theatres loved the play and carried on producing it regardless (see Fig. 6).

Not that its passage through the nineteenth century would be much smoother. Thus, while Coleridge championed Mercutio, he also noted that in the play as a whole 'the poet is not . . . entirely blended with the dramatist – at least, not in the degree to be afterwards noticed in *Lear, Hamlet, Othello,* or *Macbeth*' (lecture of 1811–12: Coleridge, 147–8). In 1817, Hazlitt, who had attended Coleridge's famous lectures on Shakespeare, wrote in reaction against the Bowdlers' *Family Shakespeare* of 1807, which proved remarkably effective in presenting to the age a morally cleansed version of the plays. Hence his decision to quote Juliet's opening lines from 3.2 ('Gallop apace, you fiery-

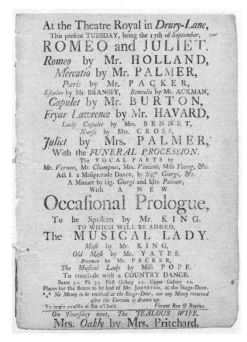

6   Playbill for *Romeo and Juliet*, Theatre Royal, Drury Lane, 1756

footed steeds') in full, to rescue Shakespeare's words from prissy censorship:

> We the rather insert this passage here, inasmuch as we have no doubt it has been expunged from the Family Shakespeare. Such critics do not perceive that the feelings of the heart sanctify, without disguising, the impulses of nature. Without refinement themselves, they confound modesty with hypocrisy.
>
> (Hazlitt, 253)

Unlike their predecessors, and indeed their Victorian successors, the Romantics were ready to accept Shakespeare as raw and flawed, if necessary – as a wild and untutored genius and the better for it. It is a pity, then, that no Garrick emerged to carry the Romantic torch on to the stage.

But if no actors and actresses in the early years of the nineteenth century could quite measure up to the landmark Romeos (and Juliets) of the second half of the eighteenth century, it was not for lack of trying by Kemble (who used Garrick's text largely), his sister Sarah Siddons and Edmund Kean. As James N. Loehlin notes, 'The major English Shakespeareans of the Victorian period – Macready, Samuel Phelps, Charles Kean and Henry Irving – were all better suited to tragic kingship than to the youthful ardour of Romeo' (Loehlin, 21). Nevertheless, Kean was not without admirers, notably Hazlitt, who wrote of Romeo's scene with the Friar in 3.3 that 'Perhaps one of the finest pieces of acting that ever was witnessed on the stage is Mr Kean's manner of doing this scene and his repeating of the word *Banished*. He treads close indeed upon the genius of his author' (Hazlitt, 106). This highly charged, melodramatic scene also elicited her best acting in the role of Romeo from Charlotte Cushman.

The performance of Garrick's adaptation of Shakespeare at the Odéon in Paris in 1827, with Charles Kemble and Harriet Smithson (Berlioz's future wife), inspired Hector Berlioz to compose his '*symphonie dramatique*', *Roméo et Juliette*, a sumptuous Beethovenian tribute to Shakespeare's play. The piece premiered in 1839 and was admired by Wagner, who sent Berlioz the full score of *Tristan und Isolde* (influenced by the Part II *adagio* of the symphony), with a warm dedication. Berlioz poured his musical soul into a work so inextricably associated with his own life. Commenting on Berlioz's favourite movement of the symphony, Stanley Wells notes that in the '*Scène d'amour*',

> long-breathed phrases accompanied by rhythmical pulsations speak eloquently of passionate yearning . . . Berlioz's musical depiction of the gradual dispersal of the masquers into the night, apparently strumming their guitars and humming snatches of half-remembered song, is not only theatrical as well as musical in its effect but appeared to be reflected, whether consciously or not, in one of the more sensitively directed episodes of Michael Bogdanov's production with the dying away of the sounds of motor bikes as revellers left the Capulets' ball.[1]

By common consent, the most successful Romeo of the nineteenth-century theatre was Charlotte Cushman, an American who played Romeo to her sister Susan's Juliet at the Haymarket Theatre in December 1845 (see Fig. 7); her first runs as Romeo had been in America in 1837. Cushman's range was impressive: not only did she play an admired Lady Macbeth and Viola hard on the heels of a Romeo who was by all accounts stunning, but she proceeded to play Hamlet, first on tour in England and Ireland in 1847, and then in New York and Boston in 1851.[2] For *Romeo and Juliet* she reverted, controversially, to what was essentially Shakespeare's play, after the lengthy reign

---

1 Wells, 'Challenges', 4. The *Times* reviewer (7 December 1839), however, singled out the '*Scène d'amour*' and the '*Nuit sereine*' as relative weaknesses in what he otherwise judged to be a 'noble symphony' and Berlioz's 'finest work' to date.
2 See Tony Howard, *Women as Hamlet: Performance and Interpretation in Theatre, Film and Fiction* (Cambridge, 2007), 48–56.

7   Charlotte and Susan Cushman as Romeo and Juliet in 3.5, from a
    nineteenth-century daguerreotype

of Garrick's text. The elusive Rosaline, who had so offended
Romantic readers of the play – Romeo in love *twice*? – staged a
comeback, and Romeo and Juliet no longer enjoyed the luxury
of a prolonged exchange before dying. The *Times* reviewer
of 30 December 1845 waxed rhapsodic in his acclamation of
Charlotte Cushman's performance. She was, he noted, the best
Romeo in years, and whereas for a long time Romeo had been a
'convention', hers was 'a creative, a living, breathing, animated,
ardent, human being'. The most effusive accolades flowed from
the Irish dramatist James Sheridan Knowles, who thought that
'every scene exhibited the same truthfulness' (Stebbins, 63).

Cushman's sister's Juliet too received her share of plaudits. One of the few concessions to the heroine's androgynous stage presence was the excision from Juliet's 'What's Montague? It is nor hand nor foot, / Nor arm nor face nor any other part / Belonging to a man' (2.2.40–2) of 'nor any other part', a mild piece of bawdry which evidently would not work for Miss Cushman. Interestingly, the phrase does not feature in Q2. As an exclusive Q1 reading it may have entered *Romeo and Juliet*'s rich textual history as a piece of theatrical improvisation in the first place, given the performance pedigree of Q1. Only since Malone has the reading appeared in standard editions of the play. Not that Cushman was unduly worried about her gender, if a story told about her female Romeo in Boston during the 1851–2 season can be credited. In the middle of one of the most intimate moments between Romeo and Juliet, a member of the audience sneezed derisively. Cushman at once chaperoned her Juliet off the stage before returning to the footlights to announce 'in a clear, firm voice, "Some man must put that person out, or I shall be obliged to do it myself"'. The recreant was expelled to cheers from the audience while Cushman recalled her companion 'and proceeded with the play as if nothing had happened'.[1]

From Gounod (1867) and Tchaikovsky (1870/80) to Gielgud and Prokofiev (1935)

In his 1867 opera *Roméo et Juliette*, Charles Gounod, with librettists Michel Carré and Jules Barbier, followed Garrick in not allowing Roméo and Juliette to die separately. After three hours of luscious music and grand choruses he granted them one final rapturous duet in the Capulets' crypt, with Roméo temporarily oblivious to the poison he had swallowed only a few moments earlier. In Roméo's 'O, ma femme! O, ma bien aimée', Gounod evokes the lovers' memory of their parting at dawn. On the point of dying together, she from a self-inflicted stab wound, they commend their souls to God. Whereas in Shakespeare the

---

1   Clara Erskine Clement, *Charlotte Cushman* (1882), 67–8.

lovers have three duets, the first a mere fourteen lines long, in Gounod they share four, including Roméo's soaring aria 'Je te le dis, je t'adore' in Act 2 during the balcony scene. The opera is remarkably loyal to the play while trying to tighten its plot, as when the dying Tybalt urges his uncle to marry Juliette to Paris. As the bride is led to the altar by her father, to comply with her cousin's last wish, she collapses. By a fine stroke of irony Nurse (probably 'Angelica' in Shakespeare) is here called Gertrude, after Hamlet's mother, showing quite how aware Gounod and his librettists were of Shakespeare's works. Three years later came the third nineteenth-century musical adaptation of *Romeo and Juliet*, Pyotr Ilyich Tchaikovsky's 1870 symphonic poem, the 'Fantasy Overture' *Romeo and Juliet* (revised extensively in 1880). Its rich, surging sounds hauntingly evoke doomed love, recalling the oceanic music of Wagner's *Tristan und Isolde*, but without sacrificing the delicate touches that are quintessentially Tchaikovsky's.

The most remarkable *Romeo and Juliet* in late Victorian England was Henry Irving's 1882 production at the Lyceum, because of its ostentatious tableaux and the partnering of two legendary actors, Irving and Ellen Terry (see Fig. 8). References to Juliet's age were cut from the text as a 36-year-old Ellen Terry played opposite Irving, aged forty-four.[1] Could the great actor who excelled at Shylock, Richard III and Hamlet put on 'the fresh, spontaneous, youthful ardour' of Romeo? Apparently not, by the almost universal agreement of those who saw it. So attention focused on the staging instead. According to Bram Stoker, author and manager of Irving's Lyceum Theatre, 'perhaps the greatest and most romantic love-story that ever was written, is one which not only lends itself to, but demands, picturesque setting' (Stoker, 93). Among the more notable features of this *Romeo and Juliet* was the splitting of the last

---

1   In the 1976 RSC production by Trevor Nunn and Barry Kyle, a 37-year-old Ian McKellen played Romeo to Francesca Annis's 31-year-old Juliet. Their perform-ances were distinctive but they seemed at times to be acting against a text insistent on the lovers' youth.

8 Ellen Terry and Fanny Stirling as Juliet and Nurse, in Henry Irving's Lyceum production, 1882

scene into two parts, set into outside and inside the Capulet tomb. The *Times* reviewer of 9 March 1882, keen to be generous to the country's pre-eminent actors, praised the authenticity of the set's Verona, its apt costumes, true to what modern knowledge had decided 'mediaeval Italians' looked like, the handsome curtain ('a curtain of wonderful beauty, by the way') and the excellence of lesser roles such as Mercutio's (William Terriss; see Fig. 9) and Nurse's (Fanny Stirling).

John Gielgud was Ellen Terry's great-nephew, so his 1935 production of *Romeo and Juliet* at the New Theatre continued a family tradition. Its cast included the 28-year-old Laurence Olivier as Romeo (later Mercutio), Gielgud as Mercutio (then

9   William Terriss as Mercutio, in Henry Irving's Lyceum production, 1882

Romeo), Peggy Ashcroft (also twenty-eight) as Juliet (see Fig. 10), Edith Evans as Nurse, Glen Byam Shaw as Benvolio and a young Alec Guinness in the part of the Apothecary. The main players were all older than the parts demanded, with Juliet twice the age of Shakespeare's child heroine. According to Ashcroft, for whom the 1935 Gielgud production marked her first time in the role of Juliet,

> it wasn't until the last production, when I had learned something about how I wanted to approach the part, that I felt I achieved the 'fourteen year-old', and that I realized, for instance, the value

10   Laurence Olivier and Peggy Ashcroft in the balcony scene, in John
      Gielgud's New Theatre production, 1935

of the balcony scene coming straight out of the
ballroom scene (even though Romeo has his long
soliloquy just before it). Instead of it being what you
might be led to think of as a languishing moonlight
scene, gazing at the sky, it's a girl who is almost out
of breath with excitement, who rushes out into the
air. Anyway, that is how I found the way to play the
balcony scene, after the third go at it.[1]

The swapping of roles by Gielgud and Olivier was the
production's most distinctive feature, one that was piquantly
enhanced by their polarized ways of speaking the verse.
Whereas later generations of theatre-goers and of course film
audiences too thought that Gielgud's elocution was at times
mannered, in 1935 it was Olivier who was taken to task, for

1   Peggy Ashcroft, 'Playing Shakespeare', *SS 40* (1988), 13.

being populist in his elocution. He wanted his Shakespeare to sound modern, he insisted, and in later years he felt that he was proved right: in 1944 he filmed Henry V to huge acclaim, pentameters tripping off his tongue with muscular clarity. He was evidently more suited to Henry V and Hamlet than to the delicate lyricism of Romeo's lines. One of the oldest adages about *Romeo and Juliet*, one which every director and every actor in the part of either lover has to tackle, is that once actors are old enough to understand the play's rhetoric they are usually too old to play the lovers' parts.[1] If the critics in general preferred Gielgud's Romeo to Olivier's, on the grounds that he better understood and conveyed the play's poetry, Gielgud himself paid generous tribute to Olivier in the part, acknowledging that while he himself was 'more lyrically successful' than Olivier at delivering Mercutio's Queen Mab speech, Olivier was 'infinitely romantic' as Romeo, with his pose beneath Juliet's balcony perfectly capturing the essence of the character.[2]

Ashcroft and Evans were generally admired, and Evans would reprise her role in Peter Hall's 1961 RSC production opposite Dorothy Tutin's winsome Juliet (Jackson, 63–4).[3] Ashcroft's Juliet was an English rose. The *Times* reviewer of 18 October 1935 lauded her acting because in her interpretation 'art and temperament seem perpetually to be moving hand in hand. Her performance is memorable for the exquisite naturalness with which it holds the character to the plane of poetry.' As for the staging, the balcony was unusually prominent and more of the action was played in the dark than is required by the text,

---

1   Kenneth S. Rothwell notes similarly about Leonardo DiCaprio and Claire Danes, who played the young lovers in Baz Luhrman's 1996 *William Shakespeare's Romeo + Juliet*, that 'Like all youthful Romeos and Juliets, they are accused of not being up to the challenge. Rex Reed thought that neither "has a clue to what they are saying, or what Shakespeare is all about" ' (Rothwell, 231).

2   John Gielgud and John Miller, *Acting Shakespeare* (1997; first published in 1992 as *Shakespeare – Hit or Miss*), 42.

3   The *Times* reviewer praised Tutin's 'radiant Juliet' for speaking the poetry as poetry while yet emerging as a believable, romantic and impetuous young girl, 'very much a creature of flesh and blood'.

although most key scenes in *Romeo and Juliet* are set at night. There were very few cuts, except for the second chorus (2.0) and Peter and the musicians in 4.5; performances lasted three hours.[1]

That same autumn of 1935, Sergei Prokofiev was putting the finishing touches to his ballet *Romeo and Juliet* at the Bolshoi's retreat of Polenovo. The work is an exquisite rendering of Shakespeare's masterpiece. It premiered in Brno in the former Czechoslovakia in 1938. On its first night at the Royal Opera House in London, the ballet, choreographed by Kenneth MacMillan, enjoyed forty-three curtain calls; to date it has played over four hundred times at Covent Garden alone, while the English National Opera's production, choreographed by Rudolf Nureyev, has also achieved international fame (see Fig. 11). According to David Nice, 'it is in the lovers' music alone that Prokofiev reaches new heights of lyrical directness'. This supreme lyricism turns the balcony scene into magic, 'the great horn-led Andante amoroso for the balcony scene, a remarkable feat of sustained lyricism which grows out of Prokofiev's most poetic night-pictures, strings finally returning to their muted, magical starting-point'.[2] Like Garrick and Gounod, Prokofiev originally proposed a happy ending for the ballet, to the extent that Juliet would wake just in time to dance a few last movements with Romeo. But, as Prokofiev later recalled, 'our own Shakespeare scholars proved more papal than the pope' in opposing this change; Shakespeare's 'libretto', it seems, however heart-breaking and resistant of sentimentality, was deemed to be infallible. If the Kirov objected to a less bleak finale, it may have done so because a happier ending would pander to a bourgeois mentality; fine for the imperial Mariinksy, but inappropriate for the socialist Kirov.

1   See Halio, *Guide*, 105.
2   David Nice, 'Prokofiev's Shakespearean ballet', The Royal Ballet *Romeo and Juliet*, Royal Opera House programme, 2007, 33.

11 Lynn Seymour as Juliet with Christopher Gable as Romeo in Prokofiev's *Romeo and Juliet*, Royal Ballet, 1965

From West Side Story *(1957) to Old Pronunciation* *Shakespeare (2004)*

When the ballet star Mikhail Baryshnikov named Fred Astaire as the dancer he admired most in the world, he was acknowledging the cheek-by-jowl existence of classical dance and the musical comedies that Astaire graced with his breath-taking virtuoso steps. *West Side Story* is a masterly musical adaptation of *Romeo and Juliet* set in the very neighbourhood of New York City that would twenty years later become the site of the Metropolitan Opera House and the Lincoln Center. It started life on Broadway in 1957 and was filmed in 1961, with Natalie Wood as Maria (= Juliet) and Richard Beymer as Tony (= Romeo). Leonard Bernstein composed the music and Stephen Sondheim the lyrics. Whereas in Shakespeare the causes of the two houses' hatred remain a mystery, here two teenage gangs, one white (the Jets), the other Puerto Rican (the Sharks), fight a turf war fuelled by racial tension. In keeping with the artful modern transposition of Shakespeare's play, the fire escape of a sanitized slum tenement of New York becomes the balcony where Tony and Maria first declare their love for each other ('Tonight'). The sweltering heat of New York City in late summer echoes Shakespeare's Italian July backdrop and allows Maria to wait for Tony on the roof of her apartment block, gracefully dancing alone in anticipation, a ballerina Juliet waiting for Romeo in 3.2. The curved top of the fire escape on which she and Tony confess their love to each other prominently projects onto the roof, a poignant reminder of what was, just before Chino joins her to tell her that her lover has killed her brother (see Fig. 12). The energy, colour and atmosphere of *West Side Story* make it the outstanding adaptation of Shakespeare's play, huge differences between them notwithstanding, with Tony of the Jets killing Maria's brother Bernardo, not her cousin as in Shakespeare, and Maria surviving to mourn her boyfriend when he is slain by Chino in revenge. The parents of the teenagers are almost

12　Maria (Natalie Wood) on the fire escape, in *West Side Story*, directed by Robert Earle Wise, 1961

entirely absent, which renders the lovers' predicament even more poignant. They are orphans in the storm and rebels with little cause in a Manhattan steeped as much in the art of Edward Hopper as in music and Shakespeare.

The age of Zeffirelli (1960–8)

Franco Zeffirelli directed *Romeo and Juliet* for the Old Vic in 1960, with Judi Dench (Juliet), John Stride (Romeo) and Alec McCowen (Mercutio). The set was meant to evoke a medieval city on the verge of the Renaissance, Zeffirelli responding to the distinctly Italian atmosphere of the play. In line with a certain historical *verismo*, his actors, male and female, wore their hair long as young people do in paintings of the period. The underlying intention was to subvert the traditions of florid sentimentality that had grown up around the lovers' story: 'The balcony scene was the very centre of the sort of Norma Shearer/Leslie Howard approach I was determined to demolish' (*Zeffirelli*, 163). Zeffirelli was aiming for authenticity, if necessary at the expense of the verse. Although some of the classically trained actors like Dench were acutely aware of the liberties taken with the language and text – which was cut drastically by about a third (*c.* 1,000 lines) – the production, after a shaky start, ran for a remarkable two years, from October 1960 to 1962.

Presented as a play which involved long-haired children rebelling against their parents over love and sex, it is hard to imagine a classic work more suitable than *Romeo and Juliet* for inaugurating the decade of youth culture and hippies. This marked a time when the young turned on their parents over conflicts such as the Vietnam war, which reached its climax in the Tet offensive of 1968, the very year Zeffirelli's film of *Romeo and Juliet* appeared. Zeffirelli's two versions of *Romeo and Juliet*, the Old Vic 1960 production and his 1968 film of the play, are as much part of the 1960s as the rock musical *Hair* (Broadway and London, 1968) or Kenneth Tynan's counter-culture nude revue *Oh! Calcutta!* (1970).[1] Writing in the *Observer* about the production, Tynan noted that Zeffirelli's characters were 'precisely life-like, and we watched them living, spontaneously and unpredictably'. That vitality without Shakespeare's exact words, the play as supreme pantomime, has arguably been the most distinctive feature of its afterlife. *Romeo and Juliet* without words, as ballet and music, has been as successful and acclaimed as Shakespeare's *Romeo and Juliet*, but of course, paradoxically so, because Shakespeare's words and dramatic art shaped the story by breathing magical sounds into it.[2] In a long review essay in *Shakespeare Survey*, John Russell Brown defended the Old Vic production against the charge of destroying the 'poetry' of the play, pointing to Zeffirelli's flair for compressing speech and action on the stage and his fine ear for cadences and rhythm:

> The greatest innovation of his production lay in unifying words and stage-business, in making the actors' speech as lively and fluent as their physical action. The result was that the dialogue did not appear the effect of study and care, but the natural idiom of the characters in the particular situations . . . many speeches were tuned with musical exactness . . . For example, when Romeo called 'Peace, peace!' at the climax of the Queen Mab speech, Mercutio's 'True' followed quickly and flatly, and then, changing the key, 'I talk of dreams . . .' was low and quiet, rapt in mood. This director knows more about musical speech than most of those working in our theatres today.
>
> (Brown, 149–50)

1   The revue's title is a pun on *O quel cul t'as!* ('O, what an arse you have!'), not a refer-ence to Kolkata in West Bengal.
2   In answer to the question why *Romeo and Juliet* is 'one of the world's best-loved stories', Northrop Frye replies 'Mainly, we think, because of Shakespeare's word magic' (Bloom, 164).

Brown singled out Juliet's soliloquy as one of the production's failings, which may be why the speech is missing from Zeffirelli's 1968 film. It is the Everest of the play; Tynan calls it 'the mighty obstacle of the potion speech' (Tynan, 33).[1]

In her Groucho interview, Olivia Hussey, who played Juliet in Zeffirelli's film, recalls how she was asked to do this scene for her audition. Her performance in it got her the part even though all that survives in the finished film is 'Love, give me strength', which is not even in that scene but instead comes from the last lines in 4.1 when Juliet leaves the Friar with 'Love give me strength, and strength shall help afford. / Farewell, dear father'. According to Hussey, Zeffirelli remarked, 'we have to keep this film flowing – moving forward . . . We have to make it one line, so that it just doesn't take away from the whole feeling of love that Romeo and Juliet have.' Later she learnt that, apparently, Zeffirelli did not shoot the philtre lines because 'If she does this potion scene, it will – she'll get all the attention. The film won't be Romeo and Juliet – it will be "did you see Olivia Hussey in that scene?".'[2]

One of the charges levelled against Zeffirelli's Old Vic production had been that Romeo showed too little sympathy for Paris, whom he kills in front of Juliet's bier (Zeffirelli removed Paris from Act 5 of the film). Shakespeare ensures that Romeo does not know until it is too late that the person he fought and killed was Paris, one who was 'writ with me in sour misfortune's book' (5.3.82). Paris and Romeo attract almost identical book metaphors of cover and text, appearance and essential self, through Juliet's mother (1.3.80–95) and through Juliet who, in response to the news that Tybalt has been slain by Romeo, exclaims 'Was ever book containing such vile matter / So fairly bound?' (3.2.83–4). Henceforth Romeo and Paris are forever conjoined in the universal book of the dead. The presence

---

1 Tynan (32) thought that even Claire Bloom, 'the best Juliet I have ever seen', failed to rise to the challenge of the speech in the 1952 Old Vic production.

2 *Olivia Hussey: Romeo and Juliet*, http://www.grouchoreviews.com/interviews/229.

of Paris in the last scene poses real problems for directors of the play, as Romeo's slaying of his rival threatens to detract from the channelling of our sympathy for the lovers; just as it would be hard to imagine Antony and Cleopatra sharing their final moments with another suitor or lover, or with children.[1] Rather than two dead young lovers, the last scene of the play delivers three, with Paris called a 'Good gentle youth' and 'boy' in the text just before his death (5.3.59, 70). Which is why in the 1869 production in New York Booth turned Paris' death into an act of self-defence by Romeo (the evidence of the text notwithstanding), while in the 2000 RSC *Romeo and Juliet* Michael Boyd portrayed Paris as a sinister sexual predator who posed a threat to Juliet.

Zeffirelli's film of *Romeo and Juliet* became the greatest Shakespeare box-office success before Luhrmann's, winning two Academy Awards and being nominated for Best Director and Best Picture. Zeffirelli, notoriously prodigal with his sponsors' money, had to fight hard to secure the necessary funding from Paramount. In the footsteps of his flamboyant master Luchino Visconti, and in the style of grand opera (notably *La Traviata*, which he went on to film in 1983), he believed that lushness and beauty could validate his chosen milieux, whether the salons of Paris in the 1840s, the streets of Renaissance Verona or the ballrooms of the rich. How to stage the lovers' first encounter in 1.5.92ff., with its pressing demand for privacy and the intense intimacy of its rhetoric in the thick of a party, poses the greatest problem of choreography in the play. There are no stage directions in either quarto to give guidance. In Brooke's poem, the lovers are seated on chairs at the edge of the party, with Romeo holding Juliet's hand. In Zeffirelli's film, Romeo catches Juliet's eye while dancing the morisco. He then walks

---

1 Instead, Eros, Iras and Charmian act as their loyal choruses in death. In the preface to his 1678 *All for Love*, a rewriting of *Antony and Cleopatra*, Dryden rued the fact that, unlike Shakespeare, he introduced Octavia and her children into the play: 'I had not enough considered, that the compassion she moved to herself and children was destructive to that which I reserved for Antony and Cleopatra.'

around the outer side of the dance hall and, from behind a pillar, clasps her hand, having previously noticed 'her place of stand' (1.5.49). Their sonnet and kissing happen behind the pillar in total privacy until Juliet is called by Nurse to see her mother (Luhrmann handles this almost identically). A camera is needed to zoom in on the lovers and move them centre screen, with the party muted or turned up as required (as in the famous dance of Burt Lancaster with Claudia Cardinale in Visconti's *Il Gattopardo*).[1]

For the shoot Zeffirelli moved cast and crew to Tuscania, in the vicinity of Rome, the main set for the film, and then on to Pienza, near Siena, and to Gubbio. This time, perhaps recalling some of the anxiety over the unconventional looks of his Old Vic cast, particularly a Romeo who did not seem to fit with audiences' preconceptions of a romantic lead, he cast the play in such a way that its actors have since themselves become the paradigm. Until 1968 Romeo as matinée idol had meant the Olivier of the 1935 production, his mixed reception in the part notwithstanding.[2] Now Zeffirelli chose two unknown teenagers. At a second audition he picked the talented Olivia Hussey for Juliet because of her expressive eyes and delicate, gently oval features. Her beauty and accomplished acting became a key to the film's success (*Zeffirelli*, 226). She was fifteen years old when filming started, and was partnered by the seventeen-year-old Leonard Whiting as Romeo. The star cast included John McEnery as a brilliantly neurotic Mercutio, Michael York as Tybalt and Milo O'Shea as a most effective friar confidant. The chemistry between the lovers and their sheer beauty blended in

---

1 One option open to theatre directors is to empty the stage of all but the two lovers, as Richard Eyre did in his 1994 Royal Opera House *Traviata*, in which the other guests at the ball leave Alfredo and Violetta to it by waltzing audibly and visibly offstage. Giuseppe Verdi's masterpiece invites multiple comparisons with *Romeo and Juliet* and was brilliantly evoked by Adrian Noble in his 1995 production for the RSC, when Verdi's famous *brindisi* played offstage at the start of the Capulets' party.
2 In the film, Olivier speaks the Chorus' opening lines 1–8 and part of the Prince's epilogue (5.3.305–6 and 309–10). He is not seen or acknowledged in the credits.

perfectly with the production's broader visual effects, delivered to the audience by a superb use of the Italian locations.

The price entailed, inevitably perhaps, the shedding of some of Shakespeare's poetry and nearly two-thirds of Shakespeare's lines. Of course the visuals compensated for the loss of some of the rhetoric. This had already happened in Q1, in which detailed stage directions repeatedly do the work of the corresponding lines of verse and prose in Q2 by anticipating dialogue or reflecting it, as in Nurse's entry '*wringing her hands*', which clearly links to Juliet's question, 'Why dost thou wring thy hands' (3.2.31.1, 36). Film, with its use of close-ups, is a medium that Shakespeare never imagined, but it is impossible not to approve of Zeffirelli's use of zooms, and particularly of Olivia Hussey's face and eyes, which respond with imperious intelligence to the camera. Her ability to project wonder, innocence and intelligence is rendered more affecting by the fact that her parents' marriage, the film implies, may be a charade. As in Lurhmann later, so here too there is a hint that Juliet's mother may be closer to her nephew Tybalt than she ought to be; certainly she and her husband are estranged, and the film hints that this is due to the fact that they married when she was too young,[1] thereby gesturing knowingly to a passage where Juliet's mother implies that she was even younger than her daughter when she married (1.3.72–4). This affectionate view of youth informs the fight between Tybalt and Mercutio, mere frisky horseplay rather than the dangerous stand-off in Shakespeare. Zeffirelli's fight in 3.1 is exuberant fooling about by young men brimming over with testosterone, a far cry from the violence in the play. In the end, and by cutting Juliet's soliloquy and Paris' death, Zeffirelli's 1968 *Romeo and Juliet* is gloriously sentimentalized by the same director who eight years earlier had followed in Peter Brook's steps by aiming to authenticate the story and remove some of its soft focus. The

---

1   On 'And too soon marred are those so early married' (1.2.13), Capulet and his wife briefly glance at each other across their house's courtyard with, on her part, aloofness approaching disdain, on his a flitter of sorrow. In the film she is the wife of an elderly husband.

now famous nude scene in 3.5 made visual the hidden text of Juliet's metaphors and similes in 3.2. The scene was artfully crafted to enhance the lovers' continuing innocence even after they have consummated their marriage.[1]

The Zeffirelli film reached an international audience of millions and may mark the start of global Shakespeare. On the world stage it outscored the legendary Olivier film of *Henry V* of 1944, which had similarly been nominated for several Academy Awards, including Best Picture. Filming Shakespeare had come of age. It seemed inconceivable that anyone else would stray into *Romeo and Juliet* after the Zeffirelli triumph; as it happened it would take a generation before the play was filmed once again.

Bogdanov and Luhrmann: from Alfa Romeo to Clockwork Orange *Shakespeare and beyond (1986–)*

In the meantime, the play continued as a staple of the theatrical repertoire all over the world. Productions included the RSC's 1976 Nunn–Kyle *Romeo and Juliet* (see Fig. 13) and, above all, the same company's 1986 version. This was directed by Michael Bogdanov, the founder that year of the English Shakespeare Company, and would be as seminal as it was iconoclastic. After his spectacular *Taming of the Shrew* (1979), which had plunged the audience into the play through its Induction and featured Jonathan Pryce as Petruchio on a motorbike, Bogdanov's *Romeo and Juliet* was bound to be cause for excitement. Even before the audience were fully seated, the stage was animated with young men weaving in and out on roller blades. There was little surprise when Romeo and Benvolio rode on a powerful bike in 1.2. The *Guardian*'s chief reviewer, Michael Billington, dubbed the production 'Alfa Romeo and Juliet' (10 April 1986) because

---

1 John Sutherland notes that 'It complicates one's reactions that Juliet is one of the few heroines ('maids') that Shakespeare shows us in a patently post-coital state . . . It is not just ears that have been pierced [3.5.3], we may deduce. Juliet, we may calculate, has lost her maidenhead at Lolita's age – and with much of Ms Dolores Haze's [i.e. Lolita's] zest. She is that goodly thing, as Margaret archly puts it in *Much Ado About Nothing*, "a maid and stuffed" ' (John Sutherland, *Henry V: War Criminal?* (2000), 55).

13   Francesca Annis and Ian McKellen as the lovers, in the 1976 RST
      production directed by Trevor Nunn and Barry Kyle

Tybalt, played by a charismatic Hugh Quarshie, drove on to the
stage in a red Alfa Romeo convertible, a Giulietta (!) Spider,
one of the production's numerous inventive touches which
included the idea of putting the two friars on bikes, with Friar
John introduced in 2.3, much earlier than in Shakespeare.[1] The

---

1   The famous Alfa Romeo badge was, appropriately, not visible but the colour, wheel
    spokes and shape of model gave it away. A grainy VHS recording of the 1986 produc-
    tion can be inspected in the Shakespeare Birthplace Trust Record Office.

cast starred Sean Bean as Romeo, Niamh Cusack as Juliet and Michael Kitchen as Mercutio.

The production trod a fine line between hip and gimmick. In early performances Romeo committed suicide by using a hypodermic needle (later this reverted to the traditional dagger), while Mercutio, a jaded rocker, sported a guitar and shared Alka-Seltzers with Benvolio (Mercutio dissolved his in a glass of wine). The Prince was a Mafia don, and the antagonism between the two clans was fuelled by class and money, with the Capulets a *nouveau riche* family, the Montagues old money. This last had the merit of conferring additional bite to Tybalt's line at 1.5.53, 'This by his voice should be a Montague', a real problem for any director. Kitchen's Mercutio must rate as the best since John McEnery's in the 1968 Zeffirelli production. His delivery of the Queen Mab speech while cradling, if not exactly rocking to sleep, a Romeo somewhat bigger than himself was as funny as it was touching. A speech that is viewed too often as a set piece cut loose from the rest of the play here blended in perfectly with the construction of the character of Mercutio. Even the slight scene of Mercutio and Benvolio clamouring for Romeo while the latter is hiding from them (2.1) turned into a gem, as Benvolio buttoned up his fly after urinating while Mercutio's bottle of champagne popped and sprayed just as he reached the climax of his risqué jokes about Rosaline's adjacent demesnes (2.1.20). The choreography of Mercutio and Nurse in 2.4 was also brilliantly executed, as was the fateful clash in 3.1 between Mercutio and Tybalt. Tybalt's love for his convertible was exploited to comic effect; the whole scene appeared to be modelled on the gladiatorial contests in Stanley Kubrick's *Spartacus*, with the chain-wielding Tybalt as *lanista*. The bonnet of his prized car eventually became his final resting-place (see Fig. 14).

Bogdanov's *Romeo and Juliet* was an inspired populist production. For the purist there was much to deplore, not least the liberties taken with the text.[1] Mostly these were cuts: Potpan's offstage brief moment of glory (1.5.1–15) was removed and, much more radically, Bogdanov openly followed Peter Brook's 1947 production (see Fig. 15) by cutting straight from Juliet's suicide (5.3.170) to the *padrone* Prince speaking the first eight lines of the opening chorus of the play. These were, moreover, transposed into the past tense: 'we laid our scene . . . broke to new mutiny . . . made civil hands unclean . . . took their life . . . Did with their death bury their parents' strife'. As Graham Holderness points out, the unveiling of the lovers' statues by the families cynically served to emphasize their wealth at least as much as to express sorrow for their untimely passing (Holderness, 22).

The excitement of Bogdanov's RSC production would be hard to match. But a mere ten years later it was, by what is, arguably, the greatest Shakespeare film ever. In 1996, twenty-eight years after Zeffirelli, Baz Luhrmann's film *William Shakespeare's Romeo + Juliet* appeared from 20th Century Fox. It was an instant hit with audiences, doing for the millennial generation of teenagers what Zeffirelli's film had done for the baby boomers. It has become 'commercially the most successful of all films based on Shakespeare' (*OxCom*, 402). Its startling '+' instead of 'and' or ampersand to link the lovers' names underlines the extent to which the two are united above all in death, '+' signifying a coffin as well as the traditional obituary symbol for 'rest in peace' (*requiescat in pace*).[2] The film is a punk rock opera bursting with vitality, violence, noise and camp humour. It is littered with visual quotations from Shakespeare's text in an otherwise radically modernized version of the play, and set in a volatile, ethnically mixed (echoes of *West Side Story*) downtown

---

1 Thus, Nicholas Shrimpton, reviewing the production for *Shakespeare Survey*, remarked that at times the gimmicks made 'Shakespeare's text look like an intrusive nuisance', with the production lacking 'a real sense of either love or death. It offered instead a busy slice of life, full of tricks and tableaux, but void of tragic purpose' (*SS 40*, 1988, 179–80).

2 The cross becomes the *t* of 'take their life' in the opening credits, and when the title of the film first appears on screen the '+' is bloody.

14 The stand-off in 3.1, with Tybalt (Hugh Quarshie), Mercutio (Michael Kitchen), Benvolio (Martin Jacobs) and the convertible Alfa Romeo, in the 1986 RST production directed by Michael Bogdanov

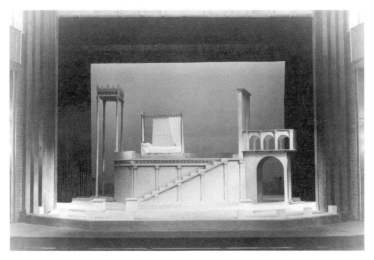

15 The Capulets' home, in the 1947 RST production directed by Peter Brook

Los Angeles, with the Montagues and Capulets as two rival business, if not gangland, families; whereas Shakespeare's play is convulsed with daggers and swords, Luhrmann's film groans under a load of guns, and the Capulet mansion, redolent of *Scarface* according to the film's producers, is guarded by heavily armed men straight out of *The Godfather*. The film is a heady brew of *Clockwork Orange* (Stanley Kubrick, 1971), *Roma* (Federico Fellini, 1972) and *Boyz n the Hood* (John Singleton, 1991). It unapologetically feeds off the pop culture of the day: thus Queen Mab is the name of an ecstasy pill (its crest a red heart pierced by an arrow) which is swallowed by the masked gatecrashers at the Capulets' party, itself a manic travesty of the 'feast' in Shakespeare's play.[1]

During the opening sequence the audience is plunged into combustible chaos when Capulets and Montagues clash head-on at a petrol station located on one of the busiest thoroughfares of Mexico City. The encounter, which climaxes in a fireball, is also extremely funny, notably when the nuns of the Ladies' College escape just in time before the Capulets and Montagues spot one another. This is hip hop Shakespeare, a surrealist dystopia in which Mexico City, Miami Beach, Los Angeles, Vera Cruz beach and San Francisco double as Verona while Mantua is a barren wasteland of trailer homes. A giant statue of Christ towers over the psychedelic city of the film, a distorted echo of the golden statues promised at the end of *Romeo and Juliet*, hovering over the very space where the madnesses of love and hate are waging war.[2]

The performances by Benvolio, Tybalt, Mercutio and the wider supporting cast are scintillating. Miriam Margolyes's Hispanic Nurse vies for attention with a brilliant cameo by Diane Venora as Gloria Capulet, Juliet's slapper mother and

1 Barbara Hodgdon talks of the film's 'postmodern aesthetic' in '*William Shakespeare's Romeo + Juliet:* everything's nice in America?', *SS 52* (1999), 88–98.
2 According to the makers of the film (1996 DVD, '*Special Features*'), the Jesus statue serves to remind the audience of the fact that in Elizabethan England, Church and state were inextricably interwoven.

Tybalt's mistress, dolled up as Cleopatra for the ball, while Pete Postlethwaite's Friar Laurence is peerless. Leonardo DiCaprio (Romeo) was twenty-two when the film opened, a new James Dean, while Claire Danes (Juliet) was seventeen. Both were older than Zeffirelli's lovers. The lyricism of the relationship against a background of frenzied violence is explored with a series of exquisite shots, from the lovers in the pool in 2.2 to them under the sheets in 3.5. No sooner has Juliet collapsed dead over Romeo than the final strains of the *Liebestod* from *Tristan und Isolde* are heard ebbing away.[1] The film's greatest concession to tenderness is when Luhrmann, like Garrick, has Juliet wake before Romeo dies. He is still alive, if barely, when she kisses him in the vain hope of catching some residual poison from his lips. Romeo's last line in Shakespeare's text 'Thus with a kiss I die' (5.3.120) is here spoken by Romeo *after* Juliet has kissed him.[2] This is nothing short of a brilliant recasting of the text and proves Luhrman's assertion that he and his writers felt that the chief purpose of their visuals was to illuminate the text; which is why they went so far as to have the opening chorus spoken twice, once by the broadcaster and then in the voiceover, to get audiences used to the language.

The 2004 Old Pronunciation (OP) *Romeo and Juliet* in Tim Carroll's production at the Globe Theatre in London was a milestone in the history of professional British Shakespeare performances.[3] For the first time in four hundred years an entire Shakespeare play was done in the phonology of the period, under the auspices of David Crystal, one of the country's foremost phoneticians, who trained at University College London under

1 On the simultaneous uses of classical and modern music, see 'The film score as cultural expression', in Samuel Crowl, *Shakespeare and Film* (New York, 2008), 116–18.

2 The line is, of course, thus lost at 120; the transfer robs Romeo of a crucial exit line which ends with 'die', just as Juliet's does at 170, 'a wonderful parallel, stressing both their common mortality and sexual consummation' (GWW, personal communication). The film is particularly free in its treatment of Shakespeare's text in Act 5.

3 In the 1940s, an OP *Hamlet* was staged at Yale by the Yale Dramatic Association (the Dramat) under the guidance of Helge Kökeritz, author of a seminal study of early modern English, *Shakespeare's Pronunciation* (New Haven, 1953).

A.C. Gimson, himself a student and disciple of Daniel Jones, the original of Shaw's Henry Higgins in *Pygmalion* (and in the musical *My Fair Lady* by Alan Jay Lerner and Frederick Loewe). It seemed entirely fitting that the play chosen for this audacious experiment should be Shakespeare's most popular play, *Romeo and Juliet*. The genesis and performances of the 2004 OP *Romeo and Juliet* are narrated in a riveting book by Crystal, *Pronouncing Shakespeare: The Globe Experiment* (2005). In it he retraces his steps from the mandatory question 'How do you know?', about the sound systems of Shakespeare's English, to the nerve-racking days of the actors' first encounters with the International Phonetic Alphabet (known as IPA and familiar to foreign learners of English), to first rehearsals and final performances with appropriate audience responses.

The production was scheduled to run for three days, from Friday to Sunday, embedded in a standard run of the play. It went remarkably well. The actors may not always have hit quite the right shading of vowel sound, but they were superbly relaxed, as was the audience. The easier aspects of Elizabethan speech were all in place: 'squirrel' was 'skirrel', 'quarrel' 'korrel' and 'quote' became 'cote' (Shakespeare spelled it 'cote' in foul papers at 1.4.31) while 'one' sounded like 'un' and 'I' leaned towards 'oi'. Ten minutes into the show it all felt entirely 'normal'. Even the noise of helicopters overhead on the Saturday afternoon and the pouring rain on the Sunday failed to dent its enthusiastic reception (Crystal, *Pronouncing*, 138–9). Juliet (Kananu Kirimi) was perfectly at home in this novel language and sounded every inch a tragic heroine in love. In her own words, 'Juliet felt less self-conscious and more front-footed . . . She was bolder, more muscular, and that seemed to give her a greater freedom, even when alone . . . Juliet's word play came to seem less intellectual and thought-based, more about pleasure than intelligence' (145–6). The three OP performances in June were highly successful, and some of the younger audiences felt that these Shakespearean characters spoke like them. They did not, of course; at least they did not speak in cockney, which is what these particular young theatre-goers thought they were doing. But it was different. It was not canonical and it diverged radically from received pronunciation (RP), commonly associated with the BBC and establishment culture, sounding rural to a lay, or even trained, ear. It reminded one of the actors of Devon English, while the *Shakespeare Survey* reviewer, Michael Dobson, who commended the 'attempt to give the play in a reconstruction of Elizabethan pronunciation as well as of Elizabethan clothing', nevertheless felt that he was listening to a 'mix of stage Irish, stage West Country and stage West Indian'.[1] Of course OP is like no version of English now current, although it more closely approximates regional accents and those marking post-vocalic *r* (such as Scots and American) than RP. The fact that on Shakespeare's stage actors spoke a *mélange* of their own regional accents and of cockney – Shakespeare's own pronunciation would have blended Warwickshire English with London speech – served to enhance the authenticity of the performance.

The same 2004 Globe production of *Romeo and Juliet* proved brilliantly inventive about the famous staging crux of Juliet's tomb in Act 5 which had also deeply exercised Henry Irving. Here, and in the full glare of daylight, Romeo kills Paris on a stone slab above the trap door before descending into the vault carrying his rival. Then, as Crystal points out, the perspective alters 'as the stage back doors open and Juliet's tomb is wheeled into view to take its place above the stone slab, with Paris now lying at the front of it. One moment we are above the ground; the next below.'[2] Throughout the last scene, the body of Paris lay out of sight of the lovers but in full view of the audience. Shakespeare chose to have Paris present in this scene against

---

1   Michael Dobson, 'Shakespeare performances in England, 2004', *SS 58* (2005), 289.
2   Crystal, *Pronouncing*, 152. In the 2009 Globe production, Paris and Romeo enter from a gallery above the stage, with Romeo prising open a trap door to gain access to a spiral staircase leading down to the main stage, the Capulet vault with Juliet on her bier. He fatally wounds Paris on the gallery before they both crash down the stairs so that Paris expires on the main stage as Shakespeare's dialogue requires.

the authority of his source, arguably his most controversial innovation and one widely rejected by directors, though not at the Globe. The handling of other scenes, like 3.5, which starts on the balcony before shifting down to the main stage so that Juliet is discovered by her mother in bed, also displayed to advantage the spatial intelligence of Tim Carroll's understanding of the text in relation to the Elizabethan stage.

THE TEXTS: Q1 (1597) AND Q2 (1599)

A printed version of *Romeo and Juliet* first appeared in 1597 under the title '*AN* EXCELLENT conceited Tragedie of Romeo and Iuliet, As it hath been often (with great applause) plaid publiquely, by the right Honourable the L. of *Hunsdon* his Seruants. LONDON, Printed by Iohn Danter. 1597.' (see Fig. 16). This is Q1, a so-called 'bad' quarto (A.W. Pollard) of which five copies survive. The British Library copy of *Romeo and Juliet* Q1 (BL C.34.k.55) is reproduced in facsimile on pp. 341–417, but all references are to the 2000 Malone Society Reprint of Q1 (MSR). Q1 has played a key role in all editions of the play since Pope first used it as a check on Q2.

The fact that Q1 was not entered on the Stationers' Register 'says nothing about Danter's right to print and publish the play or about the way he acquired the manuscript from which he had Q1 printed' (MSR, vi–vii). Two different printers were involved: John Danter, who was responsible for A–D (pp. 1–30: 1.1.1–2.3.78, MSR; *c.* 40% of the play), and Edward Allde, for E–K (pp. 31–77: 2.3.79–end, MSR; *c.* 60%). They printed their respective parts of text in different type fonts; Allde's was smaller – yielding 36 lines per page compared to Danter's 32 – which may be the reason why, if the manuscript was cast-off for the two printers to work on it simultaneously, he started using ornaments from sig. G2^v on, to fill up space that had been over-allocated (MSR, vii). Danter's running title was '*The most*

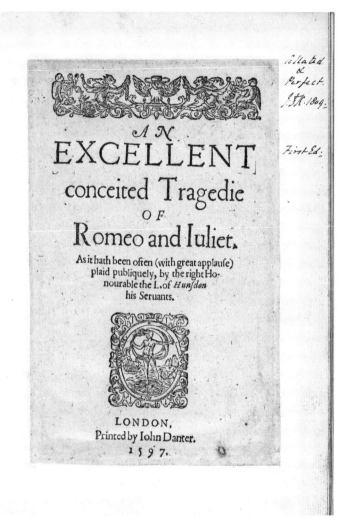

The handwritten annotations on the title page read:

> Collated
> &
> Perfect.
> J.H. 1809.

> First Ed:

A N
EXCELLENT
conceited Tragedie
O F
Romeo and Iuliet.

As it hath been often (with great applause)
plaid publiquely, by the right Honourable the L. of *Hunsdon*
his Seruants.

LONDON,
Printed by Iohn Danter.
1 5 9 7.

16   *Romeo and Juliet*, Q1, title-page (BL C.34.k.55)

excellent Tragedie, of Romeo and Iuliet.', while Allde's contracts to '*The excellent Tragedie of Romeo and Iuliet.*'

The second printed text appeared two years later, in 1599. It was another quarto (Q2), advertised as 'THE MOST EXcellent and lamentable Tragedie, of Romeo and *Iuliet. Newly corrected, augmented, and amended:* As it hath bene sundry times publiquely acted, by the right Honourable the Lord Chamberlaine his Seruants. LONDON Printed by Thomas Creede, for Cuthbert Burby, and are to be sold at his shop neare the Exchange. 1599.' (see Fig. 17). Shakespeare's autograph lies behind Q2, and the text was set by two compositors, A and B, with A setting everything except K3^v, L3^v, L4^r, L4^v and M1^r (Cantrell & Williams, 113). Thirteen copies are extant.

With an extra 688 lines, Q2 is longer than Q1 by some 22 per cent; the two quartos share only 800 lines where their texts closely correspond. The issue of length is more than usually important here because the Prologue (spoken by 'Chorus' in Q2) in both quartos keenly holds out the prospect of 'two hours' traffic', a promise which may be more readily kept by Q1 than Q2. In 1609 a third quarto, a reprint of Q2, appeared, followed, probably in 1622, by Q4 which, on the eve of the publication of the 1623 Folio, reprinted Q3, itself the basis for the First Folio, though 1623 F also refers to Q4.[1] While Q4 is essentially a reprint of Q3, it contains a number of corrections which indicate that the corrector may have had access to a copy of Q1, since Q4 and Q1 agree on a number of readings.[2] Q4's corrections mostly relate to speech prefixes and stage directions, suggesting that they were the work of an intelligent press corrector rather than of someone who had access to papers or authorial corrections

---

1   John Jowett, following Reid ('Quarto'), notes that F was set from Q3 and that 'Q4 was not yet available'; he gives 1623 as the publication of Q4 (Jowett, *RJ*, 289).

2   Lynette Hunter argues that Q4 is the product 'of an editor working just like a modern editor on the text itself' and that Q4 treats Q1 'as a reliable text' (Lynette Hunter, 'Why has Q4 *Romeo and Juliet* such an intelligent editor?', in Maureen Bell (ed.), *Re-constructing the Book: Literary Texts in Transmission* (2001), 9–21).

THE
MOST EX=
cellent and lamentable
Tragedie, of Romeo
and *Iuliet*.

Newly corre&ted, augmented, and
amended:

As it hath bene fundry times publiquely a&ted, by the
right Honourable the Lord Chamberlaine
his Seruants.

LONDON
Printed by Thomas Creede, for Cuthbert Burby, and are to
be fold at his fhop neare the Exchange.
1599.

17   *Romeo and Juliet*, Q2, title-page (BL C.12.g.18)

(see pp. 339–40). Of the later folios, F2 (1632), F3 (1664) and F4 (1685), each reprints its immediate predecessor.

Nurse's italics and Capulet's Wife's speech prefixes

Among the 800 lines that correspond in Q1 and Q2, 85 were set in Q2 from a copy of Q1. The Q1 text starts at 1.2.51 after Romeo's 'Your plantain leaf is excellent for that' and ends at 1.3.35 with Nurse's 'To bid me trudge'. A copy of Q1 was evidently to hand when Q2 was printed, but at no point, it seems, were the printers of Q2 therefore tempted to jettison their manuscript copy and revert to Q1 altogether. The two quartos were clearly perceived to be discrete enterprises, the more so since the extra lines ('augmented') promised by the title-page overtly acknowledge the lesser scale of Q1. And of course the foul papers were the property of a different stationer, Burby. The reason for falling back on Q1 for setting 85 lines was bound to rest with the state of foul papers; either text was missing, or else for some reason the text was not usable. As Pollard noted with reference to Shakespeare's somewhat expansive longhand in *Sir Thomas More*, he averaged about 49 lines per side in manuscript, which may rule out the obvious scenario of a mislaid manuscript leaf of 98 lines.[1] The most striking feature of the Q1 lines in Q2 is that they follow Q1's practice of setting Nurse's lines in italics. Moreover, Q2 continues to do so to the end of the scene, beyond 35, where the two quartos part company and Q2 reverts to foul papers. Nowhere else in Q2 are Nurse's lines in italic (in Q1 her lines are in italic again in the equivalent of 1.5, but not after that). It seems reasonably clear that her role for Q1 was written out in an Italian hand (Greg, *Editorial*), which may rule out Shakespeare, who used secretary hand in *Sir Thomas More*. In 1.3, Nurse's

---

1 A.W. Pollard, 'Variant settings in *II Henry IV*', *TLS*, 21 October 1920, 680. But at 98 lines per leaf, and assuming that this count is standard for Shakespeare, only 13 lines, *c.* 6 per side, separate Nurse's Q1 text from a manuscript leaf. The missing leaf may still be the most obvious, if not entirely neat and satisfactory, solution to the question of Nurse's Q1 presence in the Q2 text.

lines are set out as prose. Hosley does likewise, but most major editions since Capell have used verse.[1] In Q2, Nurse's speeches revert to standard type in 95 and 104. The italics in Nurse's lines after 35 imply that Q1 was consulted throughout the scene, although it is also possible that the Q2 compositor simply carried on the practice he inherited from Q1. The reason why Nurse's lines at 95 and 104 are not in italics is because they come from foul papers and are absent from Q1. Nurse's last line in 1.3 of Q1 is 79: 'Nay, he's a flower, in faith, a very flower'; both Q1 and Q2 have this in italics.

The different speech prefixes (SPs) for Capulet's Wife in 1.3 (see List of Roles, 3n.) cast an interesting light on the status of the texts behind 1.3. Shakespeare calls her 'Old Lady' ('*Old La.*') six times in SPs in the scene just when her conversation with Juliet asserts instead that she is around twenty-six years old. The very lines (72–4) about herself as a teenage mother are headed by the SP '*Old La.*'. The 'Old Lady' SPs suggest that when Shakespeare wrote this scene the contrast of youth (Juliet) and age (Juliet's mother and Nurse) was of foremost interest to him. The first of the six 'Old Lady' SPs occurs at 50, and SP 'Old Lady' continues until her very last line, when the SP for Capulet's Wife changes to 'Mother' ('*Mo.*'). Her earlier SPs in this scene are '*Wife.*'; all occur before 36, the point at which setting Q2 from holograph resumes after 85 lines of setting from Q1. It seems highly likely, then, that Shakespeare used 'Old Lady' SPs throughout this scene (except for 'Mother' at 104). According to Williams, the SPs for Capulet's Wife on B4^v of Q2 (1.3.40–82) provide 'almost mandatory evidence for a manuscript source resuming at this point' (Cantrell & Williams, 125). The entire final section of this scene, 80–106, is drastically cut in Q1 and does not include Juliet's mother's last line.

---

1   Levenson (Oxf^1, 170) notes that the language here treads a fine experimental line between verse and prose. She agrees with Wells's observation that in Nurse's speeches prose rhythms are deliberately 'counterpointed against a verse structure' (Stanley Wells, 'Juliet's nurse: the uses of inconsequentiality', in P. Edwards, I.-S. Ewbank and G.K. Hunter (eds), *Shakespeare's Styles*, Cambridge, 1980).

Shakespeare's handwriting and what it has left us

The root cause of some of the most contested readings in the play seems to be Shakespeare's longhand, as in the phonetic spelling 'cote' (for 'quote', 1.4.31).[1] *Romeo and Juliet*'s 'cote deformities' recalls 'His faces owne margent did coate such Amazes' in Q1 of *Love's Labour's Lost* (2.1.245), another printed text of foul paper pedigree which, like *Romeo and Juliet*, purports to be 'Newly corrected and augmented'. The extent to which Shakespeare's longhand bears on readings is well illustrated by Mercutio's 'pronounce' and 'dove' at 2.1.10. Both are Q1 readings, for Q2's 'prouaunt' and 'day', with Q2's 'prouaunt' for 'pronounce' probably stemming from minim confusion and the virtually identical secretary *c* and *t* being mistaken for each other. As we know from *Sir Thomas More* and other foul papers using words ending in *-ce*, Shakespeare's spelling practice is to drop the final *e*, hence 'obedyenc' (6.47; 'obedienc' at 107 and 129), 'insolenc' (92), 'offyc' (112) and frraunc (143) in *Sir Thomas More*.[2] And as for Q2's 'day' instead of 'dove', Mercutio (unlike Tybalt) did not overhear Romeo comparing Juliet to a 'snowy dove' (1.5.47), but we did, and recall that doves were sacred to Venus, whose chariot they drew. In the light of its repeated uses in the play, 'dove' is undoubtedly the correct reading here and must have stood in Shakespeare's papers. Similarly 'day' is likely to be a misreading of the longhand behind Q2, since *o* and *a* confusion is a known characteristic of Shakespeare's handwriting (see Q1

---

1   Shakespeare and his contemporaries frequently, but not invariably, pronounced the *qu* segment *k* (as in king) after French usage; so that Banquo is 'Banco' or 'Banko' in Simon Forman's account of his visit to the Globe in 1611 (Riv[2], 1966–7) and Jaques in *As You Like It* is 'jakes' = lavatory, as Ajax = 'a jakes' in *Troilus and Cressida*. But Mistress Quickly would never be 'Kickly', while 'quondam Quickly' in *H5* 2.1.79 might just be 'kondam Quickly' rather than 'kwondam Quickly', by analogy with 'quondam king' (*3H6* 3.1.23) and 'quondam carpet-mongers' (*MA* 5.2.31) (in both, *qu* seems to alliterate with *k*).

2   See John Jowett (ed.), *Sir Thomas More* (2011). *OED* jaunt *n.*[1] 1 and *OED* jaunce both cite 'jaunt' at *RJ* 2.5.26. Q2–3 have 'jaunce', while Q4 and F read 'jaunt', which is probably correct. Q2 'jaunce', as a noun rather than a verb (see 'jauncing' at 2.5.52), may be the result of another *c* for *t* misreading of copy; see Williams, 113.

'cure' *vs.* Q2 'care' at 4.1.45 and 'solid'/'sullied'/'sallied' in *Hamlet* 1.2.129).[1] The reading 'pilot' (Q1) for Q2's evidently erroneous 'Pylat' (2.2.82) reinforces the impression that the similarity of these two vowels in Shakespeare's longhand was a recurring source of confusion. Q1's 'pilot' follows on from Juliet's question about 'direction' to the Capulets' orchard and anticipates the sea image which follows (83–4), the suggestion being that Juliet is the port to which Romeo steers his bark. Not only does 'pilot' provide another instance of misread *o* and *a*, it also suggests further that Shakespeare used a long-looped downward *y* for *i*.[2] Compositor A of Q2 *Romeo and Juliet* did, however, realize that 'Pylat' was a noun and not the name of the Roman governor of Judaea, Pilate, which is why he did not use italics as he did systematically elsewhere for proper nouns. Finally, still in the context of 'dove' and 'day', the letters *v* (though written *u* in manuscript) and *y* are readily confused in secretary hand, which may have contributed to the compositors' problems.

The foul paper character of Q2 is evident in 'permissive' stage directions (e.g. '*Enter three or four Citzens . . . five or six maskers . . . their wives and all . . . Enter Madam and Nurse . . . Enter Mother . . . Enter Father*') and in a string of demonstrable false starts. Shakespeare (who reportedly never blotted a line, as his friend Ben Jonson acerbically recounted, but as the editors of the First Folio agreed) crossed out and rewrote plenty if he

---

1   Here 'cure' seems right, with Juliet desperately pleading for help, hence the pleonasm of 'cure' and 'help'. Ard[2] notes that only 'care' in the sense of 'oversight with a view to protection' would be acceptable, while also referring to proverbial 'past cure past care' and Shakespeare's inversion of it in *LLL* 5.2.28: 'Great reason: for past care is still past cure.'

2   Similarly uncorrected 1608 Q *King Lear*, set from Shakespeare's foul papers, reads 'my rackles', which the press reader rejected and changed to and equally doubtful 'my wracke'. Folio *King Lear* deciphered the manuscript accurately as 'miracles', the problem arising from *y* for *i* and writing that was not always joined up; see Weis, *Lear*, 57–8.

was, as is generally held, Hand D of *Sir Thomas More*.[1] Hand D shares many of the idiosyncrasies of spelling and pronunciation that are a distinctive feature of foul paper pedigree quartos such as Q2 of *Romeo and Juliet*, the 1600 Quarto of *2 Henry IV* or the 1608 Pied Bull Quarto of *King Lear*. Shakespeare's blottings in the *Romeo and Juliet* manuscript produced some striking first and second thoughts, notably Capulet's 'Earth hath swallowed all my hopes but she, / She is the hopeful lady of my earth', two lines retained in most editions in spite of the fact that in the context of the play they contradict each other and that only the second line can be right, so that 'She is the hopeful lady of my earth' (1.2.14) is Shakespeare's rewriting of 'Earth hath swallowed all my hopes but she'. Neither line occurs in Q1, and Williams drops both.[2] Shakespeare's deletions in *Sir Thomas More* are forceful, but here they seem to be light-touch, or else he forgot to mark them altogether since the compositors set both lines.

Second thoughts: Queen Mab and others

Mercutio's Queen Mab speech poses similar problems of first and second thoughts, revision and perhaps marginalia in manuscript, in addition to problems of a more practical nature to do with setting the text. Thus, after the first line of verse ('O, then I see Queen Mab hath been with you'; 1.4.53), the 37 lines of Mercutio's 43-line speech on 'Queen Mab' that follow are set as prose in Q2 and as verse for the remaining four lines. It is in verse throughout Q1, which all editions since Pope's have

---

1   In *Timber, or Discoveries*, Jonson wrote, 'I remember the players have often mentioned it as an honour to Shakespeare that in his writing, whatsoever he penned, he never blotted out line. My answer hath been would he had blotted a thousand, which they thought a malevolent speech'; Heminge and Condell, in their address 'To the Great Variety of Readers' in the First Folio, noted that Shakespeare's 'mind and hand went together, and what he thought he uttered with that easiness that we have scarce received from him a blot in his papers'.

2   Williams argues that in this instance Shakespeare discarded both his first and second drafts. 'Both lines are metrically' irregular and 'The two lines do not rhyme as a couplet in a sequence of dialogue which is otherwise completely rhyming, nor has either line a rhyming complement' (Williams, 104–5).

followed. The prose in Q2, up to and including 'bodes', the last word in 91, occurs entirely on C2^r, after which the prose ceases and is replaced by verse on C2^v. Since the speech must have been written out as verse in Shakespeare's foul papers, the prose of Q2 may reflect problems experienced by the compositor when setting this passage on the inner forme. There are no obvious issues with crowding on any of the other signatures of inner forme, so that whatever caused the compositor of Q2 to set as prose here is probably traceable to an aspect of this speech in his copy.[1] We can be reasonably certain that the setting as prose on C2^r shows a corrected state of C2, even though no uncorrected C2 has turned up. The sample of extant copies of Q2 is small (thirteen altogether), and a compositorial error, the omission of at least three key lines, was probably spotted early on in the run so that there would only ever have been very few uncorrected copies of C2; too few perhaps, statistically, for any to survive in the thirteen Q2s.[2]

Since Daniel (1875; first suggested by William Nanson Lettsom: see Williams, 110) some editors have shifted up the three lines 'Her chariot . . . coachmakers' (59–61, the 'empty hazelnut' block) to follow 58 ('Over men's noses as they lie asleep') rather than have them occur, as they do in Q2, after 69 ('Pricked from the lazy finger of a maid'). The fact that these three lines are absent from Q1, which otherwise affords an excellent text (Q1 and Q2 are close here), may suggest that they are an addition or revision (a case for preferring Q1 over Q2 in the Queen Mab speech is made by Thomas ('Links') and by Erne (66). It is possible that some marginalia, spotted too late in the printing process by the compositor, triggered the setting as prose here and that this was the 'empty hazelnut' block, which

---

1 Illuminating hypotheses about the setting of Q2, whether by formes or seriatim, are found in Cantrell & Williams and Cam², 209–10.

2 Cam², 210. Thomas's assertion that Q2's italics and its repetition of Q1 misprints and common errors (see e.g. 1.2.65) demonstrate that Q2 was printed from 'an uncorrected copy of Q1' begs the question of the three uncorrected lines in Q2 (Thomas, 'Links', 113).

was then inserted into the wrong place in the passage. On the other hand, the Queen Mab speech clearly works well without the lines (as in Q1) and it also, at a stretch, works with them in their Q2 place. The phrase 'in this state' (70) would seem to refer to travelling in state in a coach created by the fairies' chief coachmaker. Instead of 'state', Q1, which runs on from 'the lazy finger of a maid', has 'sort'. Q2's 'state' may be a revised reading after the insertion of the Q2-only chariot, to reflect the mock-grandeur of Queen Mab who now rides a coach, a prestigious, novel and of course aristocratic form of transport in the mid-1590s (*OED* state *sb.* 17c glosses 'in state: with great pomp and solemnity; with a great train; with splendid or honorific trappings and insignia' and cites this example). If the lines stand where Q2 has them, then everything before them becomes a crescendo towards the hazelnut chariot.[1]

Q2's two versions of grey-eyed morn chasing away darkness, the first one, attributed to Romeo, at the end of 2.2, the second, given to the Friar at the start of 2.3 (of the four shared lines only the second couplet differs), occur immediately after the misattribution of 2.2.186 to Juliet, who has two consecutive speech prefixes. There were evidently problems with the manuscript here. A third version of the lines is found in Q1, this one closer to the Friar's than to Romeo's. The straining for lyrical effect in this quartet of lines seems laboured and descriptive rather than evocative, and its contested attribution suggests that it was problematic from the start. In cautious support of giving the lines to Romeo and not the Friar is Williams's observation that their rendering in *England's Parnassus* (*c.* 1600) quotes Romeo's and not the Friar's version, while substituting 'streams' for 'streaks' (Williams, 120–1).

---

1   Further instances of second thoughts in the Mab speech are the courtiers' knees and noses: see 1.4.77n.

The clearest instance of second thoughts in Q2 may be the lines referring to carrion flies corresponding to 3.3.40ff., where Q2 reads (my italics):

This may flies do when I from this must fly.	[a]
And sayest thou yet that exile is not death?	[b]
But Romeo may not, he is banished.	[c]
Flies may do this, but I from this must fly;	[d]
They are free men, but I am banished.	[e]

Only one of lines [a] and [d] can be retained in an edited version of the play. The reason for preferring [d] is because lines [c] and [d] also occur verbatim in Q1, so that [c] followed by [d] was performed in 1597. Furthermore, 43, which ends in 'death', has been shifted down to follow the second 'banished', in immediate anticipation of the various means of death proposed to the Friar by a desperate Romeo (see further Williams, 128–9).

From Q1 to Q2

The presence of [c] and [d] in Q1 determines the choice between two lines in Q2, one of which is almost certainly a rewriting. The relationship between the two quartos is key to any scholarly edition of *Romeo and Juliet*. While the New Bibliography downgraded the importance of Q1 as a 'bad quarto' and a memorially reconstructed or 'pirated' text, it has recently been powerfully rehabilitated in a major new edition by Lukas Erne, which makes the strongest case yet for seeing Q1 as a legitimate version of the play in its own right, a text cut for touring purposes. New writing, perhaps by Shakespeare, is thought to exist alongside undoubted traces of memorial reconstruction, as when characters garble speeches by mixing up passages from different parts of the texts, a characteristic feature of someone trying to recall a speech but an impossible mistake for a compositor.[1] Erne goes so far as to suggest that the publication in 1599 of Q2 may have come about as a direct consequence of the commercial success of Q1.[2]

That the two quartos are closely linked, and that Q2 was set in the full knowledge of the existence of Q1 – indeed, the presence of Q1 in the Q2 printing-house – is beyond doubt (Jowett, *RJ*, 289). In addition to the 85 shared lines, there may be further local instances of Q1 being used by the compositors of Q2, one of them occurring in the same passage as the already cited 'pronounce'/'prouaunt' crux which probably arose from Q2's failure to decipher Shakespeare's longhand correctly (see p. 181). As Gibbons notes, though, the idiosyncratic use of a colon in *Abraham: Cupid* (2.1.13) in both Q1 and Q2 suggests that Q1 influenced Q2 here at the very point where the compositor of Q2 was struggling with his manuscript: 'Here, then, a bibliographical link between Q1 and Q2 is accompanied by an adjacent manuscript link between Q2 and foul papers.' Consequently the question arises why compositor A, if he set with Q1 and foul papers to hand at the same time, did not correct his text to 'pronounce' and 'dove', particularly since he was scrupulous when setting the 85 Q1 lines in Q2. As Cantrell and Williams demonstrate in their seminal study of the setting of Q2, with reference to the speech prefixes in the 85 Q1/Q2 lines, while Compositor A has his 'personal preferences in the spelling of speech prefixes [as with e.g. 'ROMEO' and 'JULIET'], he is greatly influenced by his copy and follows it exactly 28 times out of 33' (Cantrell & Williams, 113–14).

1   Gibbons (Ard[2], 4–8) compares the two versions of Mercutio's dying speech in Q1 and Q2 (3.1.98–105) and Benvolio's apologia (3.1.166–71), highlighting the extent to which each time Q1 is a paraphrase with echoes of Shakespeare: 'Q1 substitutes pedestrian hack-writing in regular dull rhythm . . . The Q1 version recalls the rough shape and length of the speech, recognizes its dramatic function, but does not reproduce the words' (Ard[2], 6).

2   Conversely, Q2 may have been produced to supersede Q1, an unsatisfactory version of the play, as seems to have been the case with Q2 of *Hamlet* and also with *Love's Labour's Lost* (even though Q1 *LLL* is lost).

The hypothesis that Q1 was a performance text 'redacted' for the provinces from the foul papers (Farley-Hills) has the merit of recognizing that the Q1 memorial theories alone do not satisfactorily account for the demonstrable links between the two quartos. It also explains the rationale for stage directions like the one that follows 1.1.57 in Q1, which supplants the dialogue in Q2 (this particular SD is discussed on p. 113). What this leaves unanswered is the scale of the divergence between the two texts and Q1's failure to cut in obvious places when at the same time it appears to omit some of the most strikingly lyrical passages. Also, the two quartos diverge widely in the last two acts to the point where it is hard to imagine that Q1 was to hand when Q2 was being printed.

Q2 *Romeo and Juliet* is one of Shakespeare's most prunable texts: the Friar's homilies and the musicians suggest themselves. And yet Q1, which shrinks Juliet's great soliloquy in 3.2 to four lines (and even those are misquoted, or misremembered), preserves the musicians as well as the Friar's long exegetic narrative, which most productions cut. Furthermore, the Friar's 41 lines in Q1 5.3 (229–69) differ almost entirely from the 40 corresponding lines in Q2, except for the last four. One of these, the penultimate line in Q1, is identical to the text in Q2, while the others are close enough to be demonstrably related. Hence Halio's argument that the redactor of Q1 was Shakespeare himself, abridging with an eye on a two-hour performance while at the same time rewriting extensively (Halio, 'Contexts'). While this view has merit, it begs the wider question why Shakespeare would do so when he had, probably only just recently, finished writing the play.

One such revision of foul papers in Q1 would be the lovers' meeting in the Friar's cell in 2.6. The rhetoric of the scene differs strikingly between the two quartos, while the dramatic action is structured similarly but not identically. In both, Romeo enters, Juliet follows and they leave together with the Friar to get married. In Q2, Juliet enters and greets the Friar first, who replies by referring her to Romeo; unless of course she flies into Romeo's arms and they are kissing while she greets the Friar, which would give his retort a benign barb. Q1 does not leave this to chance. Juliet's first word in the scene is 'Romeo', to which he replies, 'My Juliet, welcome'. The scenic design of Q1 is more narrowly focused; it is a true performance text. But both texts move swiftly, which is why the Q1 SD '*Enter* JULIET *somewhat fast, and embraces* ROMEO.' can be seamlessly grafted on to the text in Q2. The scene is only eight lines longer in Q2 than in Q1. The lovers' vows in Q2 contain some of the play's richest conceits:

ROMEO

    Ah, Juliet, if the measure of thy joy
    Be heaped like mine, and that thy skill be more
    To blazon it, then sweeten with thy breath
    This neighbour air, and let rich music's tongue
    Unfold the imagined happiness that both
    Receive in either by this dear encounter.

JULIET

    Conceit more rich in matter than in words
    Brags of his substance, not of ornament.
    They are but beggars that can count their worth,
    But my true love is grown to such excess,
    I cannot sum up sum of half my wealth.

                              (2.6.24–34)

In these tropes resonate the rhetorical artistry of Shakespeare's sonnets and the musical cadences of the verse of *The Merchant of Venice*. Sidney Thomas, however, sees it differently and compares these lines ('verbal triflings and coldly brilliant conceits') unfavourably to their equivalent in Q1 which, he claims, 'contains lines of extraordinary lyric beauty and dramatic effectiveness. Few things in the undoubtedly Shakespearian portions of the play surpass it in ecstatic fervour' (Thomas, 'Chettle', 10). Certainly the reading 'So light of foot ne'er hurt the trodden flower. / Of love and joy, see, see the sovereign power' compares well with the corresponding passage in Q2.[1]

Similarly with Paris' tribute to Juliet in Q1's version of 5.3.12–17, which starts with a line almost identical to Q2's: 'Sweet flower, with flowers I strew thy bridal bed' (cf. Q2's 'Sweet flower, with flowers thy bridal bed I strew'), before diverging from foul papers to imagine Juliet as an angel in heaven:

> Sweet tomb that in thy circuit dost contain
> The perfect model of eternity.
> Fair Juliet, that with angels dost remain
> Accept this latest favour at my hands,
> That living honoured thee, and being dead
> With funeral praises do adorn thy tomb.

Thomas concedes that these lines do not 'sound' like Shakespeare and concludes that they are the work of an 'editor commissioned by John Danter . . . to tidy up the manuscript'. This editor, he concludes, may have been Henry Chettle, the supposed author too of the famous 'literary' Q1 stage directions (Thomas, 'Chettle'; see also Jowett, 'Chettle'). Even if it is granted that parts of Q1 were rewritten or added with poetic gusto and flair, Erne is correct in noting that in general 'poetic passages were affected far more than others when Shakespeare's original version was cut' (Erne, 26). The cutting back in Q1 of Juliet's role by some 40 per cent also points this way. Q1 is faster and more action-packed than Q2. It is impossible to be sure how it came about, but Erne's inclusive view of its genesis, a creative

---

1 An agnostic position ('No disinterested evaluation of the above two scenes [2.6 in Q1 and Q2] can prefer the one to the other') is adopted by Lene B. Petersen in *Shakespeare's Errant Texts: Textual Form and Linguistic Style in Shakespearean 'Bad' Quartos and Co-authored Plays* (Cambridge, 2010), 134. Petersen sees in Q1 characteristic traits of oral-formulaic composition, more commonly associated with Homeric and Anglo-Saxon poetry; thus, for example, the truncated version in Q1 of Juliet's 3.2 opening lines 'conveniently serves to illustrate how descriptive and lyrical segments are usually bound for exclusion in oral-memorial derivation' (87).

combination of abridging and remembering with a view to performance, recommends itself on multiple fronts.[1]

Q1's stage directions: a record of performance or 'literary' ornaments?

At first sight, suitability for performance would seem to be the guiding principle and distinctive characteristic of the famous Q1 stage directions, which feature in every mainstream modern edition of the play. Of the ones which follow, only two (1.1.57 and 3.5.0) have not been adopted in this edition. The major Q1 stage directions are as follows (see also pp. 339–40).

1.1.57:	[*They draw, to them enters Tybalt, they fight, to them the Prince, old Montague, and his wife, old Capulet and his wife, and other Citizens and part them.*]
1.5.122:	*They whisper in his ear.*
2.4.129:	*He walks by them and sings.*
148:	*She turns to Peter her man.*
2.6.15:	*Enter* JULIET *somewhat fast, and embraceth* ROMEO.
3.1.89:	*Tybalt under Romeo's arm thrusts Mercutio in and flies.*
3.2.31:	*Enter* NURSE *wringing her hands, with the ladder of cords in her lap.*
3.3.107:	*He offers to stab himself, and* NURSE *snatches the dagger away.*
161:	NURSE *offers to go in and turns again.*
3.5.0:	[*Enter Romeo and Juliet at the window.*]
42:	*He goeth down.*
67:	*She goeth down from the window.*
159:	*She kneels down.*

---

1   Erne (19) refers to Humphrey Moseley's claim in the 1647 Beaumont and Fletcher Folio that 'When these comedies and tragedies were presented on the stage, the actors omitted some scenes and passages (with the authors' consent) as occasion led them; and when private friends desired a copy, they then (and justly too) transcribed what they acted.'

235:   *She looks after Nurse.*

4.3.58:   *She falls upon her bed within the curtains.*

4.5.48:   *All at once cry out and wring their hands.*

95:   *They all but the Nurse go forth, casting rosemary on her and shutting the curtains.*

5.1.11:   *Enter* BALTHASAR *his man booted.*

5.3.11:   PARIS *strews the tomb with flowers.*

21:   *Enter* ROMEO *and* BALTHASAR, *with a torch, a mattock, and a crow of iron.*

44:   ROMEO *opens the tomb.*

139:   *Friar stoops and looks on the blood and weapons.*

147:   *Juliet rises.*

170:   *She stabs herself and falls.*

Are these stage directions by Shakespeare or are they instead, as John Jowett argues, by Henry Chettle, 'Danter's ex-partner as stationer and his continuing associate', who worked for Danter as assistant and compositor until 1596–7 (Jowett, *RJ*, 288, after Thomas, 'Chettle')? Including the Q1 stage directions in edited texts confers on them an authority that they may not possess. The assumption that has traditionally underpinned such editorial decisions is that the stage directions reflect theatrical practice of the period.[1] This is hardly contentious; even if the stage directions were primarily 'literary', they would still reflect what someone with experience of the stage in the mid-1590s thought were appropriate stage directions. It is not clear at what point these stage directions entered the manuscript that became Q1: whether they were present from the start or whether they were written in after one particular performance or a set of performances before the manuscript was handed over to Danter for printing; or whether they entered the text of Q1 much

---

1   According to Hoppe, the 'common trait' of all the Q1 stage directions is that they arise less from a before-stage view of the performance than from an onstage point of view. In other words, although some of them might be the result of a spectator's observation, many others display an actor's-eye view and all are explainable on that basis (Hoppe, *Quarto*, 79–80).

The most excellent Tragedie,

1 I the heades of their Maides, or the Maidenheades,
take it in what fence thou wilt.

2 Nay let them take it in fence that feele it, but heere
comes two of the *Mountagues.*

Enter two Seruingmen of the Mountagues.

1 Nay feare not me I warrant thee.

2 I feare them no more than thee, but draw.

1 Nay let vs haue the law on our fide, let them begin
firft. Ile tell thee what Ile doo, as I goe by ile bite my
thumbe, which is difgrace enough if they fuffer it.

2 Content, goe thou by and bite thy thumbe, and ile
come after and irowne.

1 *Moun:* Doo you bite your thumbe at vs?

1 I bite my thumbe.

2 *Moun:* I but i'ft at vs?

1 I bite my thumbe, is the law on our fide?

2 No.

1 I bite my thumbe.

1 *Moun:* I but i'ft at vs?   *Enter Beneuolio.*

2 Say I, here comes my Mafters kinfman.

They draw, to them enters Tybalt, *they fight, to them the*
Prince, old Mountague, *and his wife,* old Capulet *and*
his wife, and other Citizens and part them.

Prince: Rebellious fubiects enemies to peace,
On paine of torture, from thofe bloody handes
Throw your miftempered weapons to the ground,
Three Ciuell brawles bred of an airie word,
By the old *Capulet* and *Mountague,*
Haue thrice difturbd the quiet of our ftreets.
If euer you difturbe our ftreets againe,
                                                       Your

18   *Romeo and Juliet*, Q1, A4v (TLN 52–82) (BL C.34.k.55)

Fig. 18 Sig. A4ᵛ of Q1, set by Danter, shows one of the two major Q1 stage directions *not* adopted in this edition: '*They draw, to them enters Tybalt, they fight, to them the Prince, old Montague, and his wife, old Capulet and his wife, and other Citizens and part them.*' (1.1.57). In Q2, this simply reads '*They fight*', followed by a further 20 lines of dialogue before the Prince enters at 1.1.78. Q1's stage direction translates into onstage action the exchanges between Tybalt and Benvolio and the comedy ensuing on the entries of the Montague and Capulet parents. This shortcut through action is symptomatic of a script closely aligned to performance. Unlike Q2's, the speech prefixes of Q1 are simply '*1*' and '*2*' for Q2's Samson and Gregory (Gregory is named in the text of both quartos, Samson is not) and '*1 Moun:*' for Abraham of the Montagues. In both quartos, two Montague retainers enter at 1.1.31, but in Q2 only Abraham speaks, whereas in Q1 both '*1 Moun:*' and '*2 Moun:*' spar with the Capulets. In addition to using a long descriptive stage direction, Q1 further foreshortens the dialogue before and after the Montagues' entrance at 31.

Q2 serves as copy-text here, as it does throughout except for the lines set in Q2 from Q1 (1.2.51–1.3.35). The only major editorial decision in this passage concerns the setting as verse or prose of Benvolio's first speech in the play from Q2 (62–3). It appears as prose in Q2, but can in fact be divided into 'Part, fools' (prose) followed by a perfect pentameter, 'Put up your swords, you know not what you do'. With regard to dramatic rhythm this is effective and revealing about the play's rhetorical strategies: its first verse line after the opening chorus is spoken by a character trying to impose order on chaos. The play repeatedly, though not invariably, uses verse as a marker of authority and control. Having Benvolio speak verse agrees with his formal speech patterns elsewhere. It is, too, Benvolio who explains, and tries to mitigate, Romeo's part in the death of Tybalt in 3.1 when he ends his account with 'This is the truth, or let Benvolio die' (3.1.177). His last word in the play, 'die', is also Romeo's and Juliet's final utterance (in Q1, but not Q2, Benvolio's death is reported by Montague at the same time as the death of Romeo's mother). While the speech prefixes for Q2 are easy to follow, they vary considerably: thus Gregory is '*Grego.*', '*Greg.*', '*Gre.*', while Samson is '*Samp.*', '*Sam*', '*Să*', '*Sam.*' and Abraham '*Abram.*' and '*Abra.*'. The spellings of SPs – the Q2 ones probably stood in Shakespeare's manuscript – largely reflect the whim of the author. Nevertheless, they were important enough to the author to be written in rather than left indeterminate as they are in Q1, even though they are not needed or used in the dialogue.

later.[1] If Chettle added them to the manuscript in the printing-house, he must have done so to the whole manuscript before it was shared out for printing, unless he was on equally good professional terms with Allde and Danter. This hypothetical promptbook manuscript, with Chettle's stage directions, would then have been cast off for separate printing by formes so that Danter and Allde could work on it simultaneously.[2] As it is, only two of the Q1 stage directions occur in the Danter section, while the vast majority of them, including all the well-known ones, happen after Danter's stint came to an abrupt end when his two presses were impounded for printing an unauthorized book and were 'defaced and made unserviceable for printing'.[3] Jowett argues that the stage directions 'are connected with the printing-house' because of 'a significant correspondence between their locations within the text' and 'certain mechanical adjustments made by the compositors to use up surplus space' (Jowett, 'Chettle', 54). In other words, Allde's use of ornaments, to compensate for the mismatch between his smaller typeface and the casting-off, and the use of elaborate stage directions are related. This rather reduces the stage directions to the status of space fillers and, according to Jowett, part of a redesign, one which resembles Chettle's practice elsewhere in his own plays. The fact that the stage directions repeatedly appear to anticipate or respond to words on the page – see '*wringing her hands*' at

1 Hoppe, *Quarto*. Halio envisages a scenario in which Shakespeare 'first wrote out a full draft of his play . . . Since the draft was too lengthy for playhouse performance, a shorter draft was made, with further revisions as well as cuts, including numerous tinkerings with individual words or phrases. This became the acting version of the play, from which the promptbook was prepared. This revised, second draft was then printed in 1597 in the first quarto' (Halio, *Guide*, 7).

2 Greg, *Folio*, 231–2. See J.A. Lavin, 'John Danter's ornamental stock', *SB*, 23 (1970), 29–34. Contrary to Hoppe's assertion that Q1 was set seriatim, 'shortages, recurrence, and distribution of type, as well as habits of spelling and the use of spacing materials, indicate that both A–D and E–K were cast off and set by formes' (MSR, viii). The hypothesis of casting-off for simultaneous printing by Danter and Allde, however, presumably assumes that Allde was always going to be one of two chosen printers rather than being brought in as a direct result of the seizing of Danter's press.

3 The raid by the Stationers' Company on Danter's shop happened sometime during Lent, 9 February–27 March 1597.

3.2.31 or 'PARIS *strews the tomb with flowers.* PARIS Sweet flower, with flowers thy bridal bed I strew', 5.3.11–12) – may indeed support the view that the stage directions were written by someone looking at the text in front of him. Rather than being a record of performance, they may constitute the most exciting padding in the textual history of Shakespeare's plays. Their interest and value is not significantly diminished by this, since whoever wrote them bears witness to the theatre of the time and was involved in the production of theatrical manuscripts. The stage directions are either an eye-witness record of actual performance, or imagined performance cues by a contemporary who knew the text of Q1 in manuscript and realized, when Allde started his stint of printing, that the ornaments needed complementing by further fillers. The Q1 stage directions may in that sense be untested, aspirational rather than actual, but they have proved their worth in the theatre since and continue to intrigue and fascinate.

EDITORIAL PROCEDURES

This edition is based on Q2, with the 85 lines of 1.2.51–1.3.35 reprinted from Q1. Along with Q3–4, F, F2 and a number of later editions, Q1 has been collated throughout with regard to lines that it shares or nearly shares with Q2. Q1's readings carry considerable authority and a number of them are adopted in this edition, with the most important listed in Appendix 1. The 800 lines in which the texts of Q1 and Q2 are intimately linked have been collated throughout. So have a number of readings from passages in which Q1 and Q2 diverge too widely for full collation while yet sporadically producing almost identical lines in different parts of a scene. Other lines of Q1 which are divergent from Q2 while engaging essentially the same dramatic action (for example in the opening scene) are collated as *var. Q1*, following editorial tradition; as opposed to *not in Q1* which identifies specific gaps where Q1 and Q2 might be expected to offer identical readings because of the surrounding text. Since Q3, Q4 and F all follow one another and Q2, the collations privilege Q2–4, F; Q1 is always last, hence the template *Q2–4, F; var.* [*or 'not in'*] *Q1*, except for the 85 lines of 1.2.51–1.3.35, where the standard collation is *Q1–4, F*. In a number of instances Q1 and Q4 agree on superior readings to Q2–4, F. The textual note then has Q1 first, hence *Q1, Q4*. The importance of Q1 for *Romeo and Juliet* scholarship is reflected in the decision to reproduce it in facsimile in Appendix 2.

All quotations are in modern spelling throughout the edition, with two exceptions: readings from Q1 and Q2 in the commentary are given in original spelling for clarity; and original spelling is retained in the passage from *1 Return from Parnassus* quoted on p. 55, to avoid distorting the representation of a French accent.

ROMEO AND JULIET

LIST OF ROLES

CAPULETS

JULIET	*a thirteen-year-old girl from Verona, only child of the rich Capulet*
CAPULET	*her father*
CAPULET'S WIFE	*her mother*
COUSIN CAPULET	*a relative of her father's*
NURSE	*Juliet's wet-nurse* 5
PETER	*Nurse's man*
TYBALT	*Juliet's cousin*
Tybalt's Page	
PETRUCHIO	*a follower of Tybalt*
SAMSON	*a Capulet retainer* 10
GREGORY	*another Capulet retainer*
SERVINGMEN	*in the Capulet household*

MONTAGUES

ROMEO	*sole son and heir of the Montague family*
MONTAGUE	*Romeo's father*
MONTAGUE'S WIFE	*Romeo's mother* 15
BENVOLIO	*Romeo's cousin*
BALTHASAR	*Romeo's man*
ABRAHAM	*a Montague retainer*
SERVINGMEN	*in the Montague household*

THE PRINCE'S KINDRED

PRINCE Escalus	*governor of Verona* 20
MERCUTIO	*his kinsman, and friend of Romeo's*
County PARIS	*another kinsman, suitor to Juliet*
Paris' Page	
Mercutio's Page	

OTHERS

CHORUS	25
CITIZENS	*of Verona*
FRIAR LAURENCE	*a Franciscan*
FRIAR JOHN	*another Franciscan*
Apothecary	*of Mantua*

Three WATCHMEN   30

Three MUSICIANS,
Simon Catling, Hugh Rebeck
and James Soundpost

Attendants, Masquers, Torchbearers, Guests and Gentlewomen

LIST OF ROLES Rowe first gave the characters in 1709, although the 1694 Douai MS (see pp. 59–60) provides a partial list.

1 JULIET At 13 years of age (1.2.9), Juliet is the youngest of Shakespeare's heroines. In the sources she is 16 or 18. The word 'thirteen' never occurs in the play, whereas *fourteen* does six times, always with reference to Juliet's age. She is 'Julietta' in the title of William Painter's novella in book 2 of *The Palace of Pleasure* (1567). Her name may have been anglicized to make it chime with her July birthday. She speaks exclusively in verse and has the second-longest part in the play after Romeo. She is the Capulets' only child (3.5.165). Shakespeare's only other Juliet is Claudio's pregnant betrothed, Juliet (also called 'Julietta', as in Italian 'Giulietta'), in *Measure for Measure*; see also List of Roles, 20n.

2 CAPULET called 'Cappelletti' (da Porto; Capelletti in Bandello) in the Italian sources. He is called 'father' five times in Q2 3.5. The SDs of Q1 refer to him as '*old* Capulet' (3x), '*olde Capolet*' (4x), '*Capolet*' (1x) and '*Oldeman*' (2x). He is *old Capulet* twice in the text. He appears to be at least in his 50s (1.5.30–9), an elderly father of a young daughter. The Capulets and the rival Montagues seem to be upper bourgeoisie rather than nobility (the latter represented by Paris and the Prince). However, the Prologue's *alike in dignity* (1) could imply that they are nobility (*OED* dignity 2), with *dignity* Shakespeare's rendering of Brooke's 'two ancient stocks, which Fortune high did place / Above the rest, indued with wealth, and nobler of their race, / Loved of the common sort, loved of the Prince alike' (Brooke, 25–7).

3 CAPULET'S WIFE Rowe's SP 'Lady Capulet' for Juliet's mother features in several modern editions of the play, including Ard[2] and Cam[2]. The 21 uses in Q2 SPs and SDs of 'Lady' are descriptive of gender, not rank. Juliet's mother is called 'Wife' 14 times (including four uses in SDs and SPs in the Q1 section) and 'Mother' on 17 occasions in SDs and SPs; and she is once called '*Madame*' in a SD in 3.5. Given the problems with the character's double entry in that scene (at 3.5.36 and 3.5.64), the single '*Madame*' (at 3.5.36) may be an anticipatory mistake, as the next spoken word in the text is also 'Madam', Nurse's address to Juliet. On a statistical count of occurrences in Q2, the editorial SP ought to be either 'Lady' or 'Mother', since that is primarily what Shakespeare calls her in the presumed MS that lies behind Q2. Short of using two different SPs, it seems safest, if not entirely satisfactory, to use 'Capulet's Wife' throughout even if, on the page, that obscures her role as mother in those crucial scenes where she is portrayed primarily in that relationship. In performance, of course, the SPs do not matter.

Juliet's mother would seem to be a mere 26 years old, since she claims to have had Juliet before she was 14 herself (1.3.73). However, she refers to her *old age* at the end of the play (5.3.207).

4 COUSIN CAPULET He and Juliet's father last danced in a masque at the wedding of Lucentio over 30 years earlier (1.5.33–9). His minute part in the play consolidates the sense of the Capulets' ball being a family affair. The guest list (1.2.63–71) includes other members of the extended Capulet family.

5 NURSE Shakespeare inherited the character from Brooke. Nurse may be an older woman with only four teeth left (1.3.14; she is an 'ancient dame' in Brooke, 344), although her daughter Susan was Juliet's contemporary, which is why Nurse was Juliet's wetnurse. Her name may be 'Angelica', because Capulet's instruction at 4.4.5 could hardly be addressed to his wife, the only other character present apart from Nurse. Findlay (217) suggests that the name 'Angelica' serves to underline her 'nurturing, comforting role within the Capulet household'.

6 PETER a part probably written for the comic actor Will Kemp, as the Q1 text at 4.4.16 and a Q2 SD at 4.5.99 suggest. Kemp had recently played Falstaff in the two *Henry IV* plays and would play Dogberry in *Much Ado*. 'Peter' first appears as Romeo's man (not Nurse's) in Matteo Bandello's *Le novella del Bandello* (1554): see 5.3.21.1–2n., and Bullough, 1.271–2.

7 TYBALT a character invented by Luigi da Porto in his *Istoria novellamente ritrovata di due nobili amanti* (pub. *c*. 1530; see Bullough, 1.270, 276). Da Porto calls him 'Tebaldo Cappelletti', but his mocking title 'Prince of Cats' comes from Thomas Nashe's *Have With You*: 'not *Tibault* or *Isegrim*, Prince of Cats, were ever endowed with the like Title' (Nashe, 3.51). It was probably the fortuitous occurrence in Nashe of a feline character with the identical name to that of Juliet's cousin that prompted Shakespeare to graft this epithet on to Brooke's Tybalt. Tybalt may be Rosaline's brother, as they are respectively called *my brother's child* (3.1.148) and *My fair niece* (1.2.69).

10 SAMSON a braggart retainer of the Capulet household, named after the biblical Samson, a hero of Herculean strength (Judges, 13–16). The Bible's spelling of the name is adopted here, following Oxf. Samson speaks the first line of the play after the Chorus. His name is only given in the first SD of 1.1 ('*Sampson*') and in SPs of 1.1. In Q1 Samson and Gregory are simply identified as '*1*' and '*2*'. Oxf¹ (143) suggests that Samson's and Gregory's names 'may enhance the servants' mock-heroic postures'.

11 GREGORY His name is the first word in the play after the Prologue. Unlike the other retainers of the two houses, he is twice mentioned in the dialogue (1.1.1 and 60). While 'Gregory' may seem incongruously English in Verona, it perhaps serves to advertise the Catholic setting of the play (see also *abbey wall* at 2.4.179): the name would have been associated above all

with Pope Gregory XIII (1572–85), the great reformer of the calendar. Cf. 'Gregory' and other English names in an Italian household in *TS* 4.1.

13 ROMEO Romeo is the *only son* (1.5.136) and probably the only offspring of the Montagues. His role is the longest in the play. He is called 'Romeus' in Brooke, although there is one occurrence of 'Romeo' to rhyme with 'Mercutio' (Brooke, 253). He is 'Romeo Montecchi' in da Porto and Bandello. Shakespeare switches back to the Italian 'Romeo', perhaps following Painter's title 'Rhomeo and Julietta', but the use of this form also enables him to exploit the euphonies and rhyming possibilities in English of the *o* vowel, not available from the masculine Latin ending -*eus*. Romeo's age is not given; he is probably a teenager like Juliet (though see 5.3.59). In Bandello, Romeo is between 20 and 21 years old, and reputedly the most handsome and courteous of all the youth of Verona.

14 MONTAGUE father of Romeo, called 'Montecchi' in da Porto

15 MONTAGUE'S WIFE She speaks only three lines in the play (all in the first scene) and dies of a broken heart the same night as her son. Rowe first substituted 'Lady Montague' for Q2's 'M.*Wife*.2.' and '*Wife*.'; Q1 has '*M:wife*.' and '*Wife:*'.

16 BENVOLIO a Montague whose name is Shakespeare's invention. Benvolio calls Montague *uncle* (1.1.141) and he and Romeo address each other as *cousin* (1.1.158, 202). The name derives from the Italian 'ti voglio bene', i.e. 'I am well disposed towards you', or even 'I love you' (in contrast to Malvolio, the name Shakespeare gives to the killjoy in *Twelfth Night*). We first see him confronting Tybalt (perhaps a significant act: see Ard², 39: 'the man of good will' taking on 'the embodiment of violent aggression'). Our last glimpse of him is towards the end of 3.1, where he is loyally defending Romeo against Juliet's mother's demand for revenge. In Q1 'young Benvolio' dies the same

night as his aunt, Romeo's mother; see 5.3.210n. and Appendix 4.

17 BALTHASAR Shakespeare introduced the name for the part in the play, though it is not, of course, his invention. The name, which is also found in *Comedy of Errors, Merchant of Venice* and *Much Ado*, occurs once only in the text of *RJ*, even though the character speaks nearly 30 lines in the final act.

18 ABRAHAM a Montague retainer, who enters with an anonymous companion in the opening scene. Abraham's name does not occur in the text. It only exists in the Q2 SPs '*Abram.*' and '*Abra.*'. In Q1 he is referred to as '*1 Mount:*'.

20 PRINCE Escalus His name is the first to occur in Brooke's poem (Brooke, 13). In the play it features only once, in a SD (1.1.78.1). The audience never discovers that he is named anything other than 'Prince', the word used for him in the dialogue. Shakespeare used 'Escalus' again in *Measure for Measure*, where the name is the first word in the play (possibly punning on 'scales' of justice); the name does not feature in the sources of *Measure for Measure* (Bullough, 2.415).

Escalus is an anglicized version of the patronym 'della Scala'. The story of Giulietta Cappelletti and Romeo Montecchi in da Porto and Bandello is set in Verona during the reign of Bartolomeo della Scala – patron of Dante Alighieri, the author of the *Divina Commedia*, the greatest medieval poem about the converging of human and divine love.

21 MERCUTIO kinsman to Prince Escalus and a friend of Romeo's. In da Porto

he is called 'Marcuccio', and described as a man 'who by nature had very cold hands, in July as in January', a curious detail which Brooke, but not Shakespeare, paraphrases: 'A gift he had that nature gave him in his swathing band, / That frozen mountain ice was never half so cold / As were his hands' (260–2). In English the name chimes with 'mercurial', which may have been Shakespeare's intention; *OED* defines a 'mercurial' individual as one 'born under the influence of the planet Mercury . . . a lively, quick-witted, or volatile person', an apt characterization of Mercutio.

22 County PARIS called 'County Paris' (seven times in the text, once in a SD) or 'Sir Paris' (twice). In the Luhrmann film he attends the Capulets' fancy dress party as the all-American astronaut Dave Paris, *Time* magazine's Bachelor of the Year. There may be an echo of Homer in the name 'Paris' for Romeo's rival for Juliet; see 3.3.73n.

23 *Paris'* Page the only one of the play's three pages to have a speaking part

25 CHORUS The Chorus disappears from the play after introducing Act 2 (or speaking the envoi of Act 1)

27 FRIAR LAURENCE the third largest part after those of Romeo and Juliet, though Friar Laurence is prone to homilies which are frequently curtailed in performance

30 Three WATCHMEN Q2 uses the SPs '*Watch.*', '*Chief. watch.*', '*3. Watch.*' and '*Wat.*' to describe the various watchmen. Q1 similarly deploys four different SPs: '*Watch:*', '*Cap:*', '*1.*' and '*Capt:*'.

121

THE MOST EXCELLENT
AND LAMENTABLE
TRAGEDY OF ROMEO
AND JULIET

THE PROLOGUE

[*Enter* CHORUS.]

CHORUS

Two households, both alike in dignity,
In fair Verona, where we lay our scene,
From ancient grudge break to new mutiny,
Where civil blood makes civil hands unclean.
From forth the fatal loins of these two foes   5
A pair of star-crossed lovers take their life,
Whose misadventured piteous overthrows

Prol.1–14 The choric sonnet is modelled on the 'Argument' in Brooke, although the rhyming structure of the source's sonnet is Italian rather than English. In the 1996 Luhrmann film, 1–12 are read as a news item on television; 6–12 are then repeated, to foreground the key paradox of *take their life*. In the 1968 film by Zeffirelli, Laurence Olivier speaks lines 1–8 and part of the Prince's epilogue (5.3.305–6, 309–10); he is not seen, or acknowledged in the credits.

1 **dignity** worth, honourable status (see Brooke, 25–6)
2 **fair Verona** See pp. 16, 18, 28, 43–4.
3 **ancient grudge** old feud
   break erupt
4 **civil blood** the blood of citizens
6 **star-crossed** thwarted by the influence of malign stars (cited under *OED* star *sb.*[1] 20)
7 **misadventured** hapless (cited in *OED*)

TITLE] *Q2–4;* THE TRAGEDIE OF ROMEO and IVLIET *F;* An EXCELLENT conceited Tragedie *OF* Romeo and Iuliet. *Q1   Running title*] Rowe; *The most lamentable Tragedie / of Romeo and Iuliet. Q2–4; The most excellent Tragedie, / of Romeo and Iuliet / sigs A3ᵛ–D4ᵛ (Danter), [followed by] The excellent Tragedie / of Romeo and Iuliet / sigs E1ʳ–K4ʳ (Allde) Q1; The Tragedie of Romeo and Iuliet. F*   THE PROLOGUE] *Q2–4, F, Q1*   0.1] *Capell;* Corus. *Q2;* Chorus. *Q3–4; not in Q1*   1 households, both] *Q2–4;* houshold Frends *Q1*   6 take] *Q2–4;* tooke *Q1*   7 misadventured] *Q2–4; misaduentures Q1*

123

Doth with their death bury their parents' strife.
The fearful passage of their death-marked love,
And the continuance of their parents' rage,   10
Which but their children's end naught could remove,
Is now the two hours' traffic of our stage;
The which, if you with patient ears attend,
What here shall miss, our toil shall strive to mend.   [*Exit.*]

[1.1]   *Enter* SAMSON *and* GREGORY, *with swords*
              and bucklers, of the house of Capulet.

SAMSON   Gregory, on my word, we'll not carry coals.

GREGORY   No, for then we should be colliers.

SAMSON   I mean, an we be in choler, we'll draw.

GREGORY   Ay, while you live, draw your neck out of collar.

---

8   **Doth** The southern third person plural (Abbott, 332, 334), used repeatedly by Shakespeare, here creates an effective assonance with *death*.
9   **passage** trajectory
     death-marked doomed
12 **two hours'** See pp. 24, 95, 116.
     traffic business (cited under *OED sb.* 3)
14 probably 'What may be deficient in this performance [for *here shall miss* Q1 reads 'here we want', i.e. here we lack] we will do our best to improve in future ones'; Cam² compares *MND* 5.1.415–16; *here*, spelled 'heare' in Q2, may play on 'ear' and 'hear'.
1.1 The time is about 9 a.m. on a Sunday morning in the middle of July, the location a street in Verona (158–9; 3.4.18).
0.1 SAMSON *and* GREGORY See List of Roles, 10n., 11n.
1   **carry coals** allow ourselves to be insulted, literally, do dirty work (cited under OED coal *sb.* 12); the expres-

sion was proverbial (Dent, C464). The dialogue proceeds swiftly from coals to word-play on *collier(s)*, *choler* (anger) and *collar* (halter, spelled 'choller' in Q2), three near homophones meaning different things. A sexual undertone to the phrase *carry coals* may be suggested by its association with 'privy lodging' and sex in John Webster's *Duchess of Malfi*: 'To see her in the shameful act of sin . . . with some strong-thighed bargeman . . . or else some lovely squire / That carries coals up to her privy lodgings' (2.5.41–5). Colliers had a bad reputation for cheating in Shakespeare's time, hence the 'foul collier' in *TN* 3.4.119.
3   **an** if
4   **draw . . . collar** keep clear of the hangman's noose; to 'slip the collar' was proverbial (Dent, N69). Gregory cautions Samson against committing a capital offence by drawing his weapon too eagerly.

---

8 Doth] *Q2–4; var. Q1;* Do *Rowe*   14 miss] *Q2–4; want Q1*   mend] *Q2–4; amend Q1*   SD] *Capell; not in Q2–4, Q1*   1.1] F *(Actus Primus. Scoena Prima.); not in Q2–4, Q1*   0.1–2] *Q2–4, F; Enter 2. Seruing-men of the* Capolets. *Q1*   1 on] *Q2–4;* A *F; of Q1*   3 an] *Q2–4 (*and*); if F, Q1*   4 of] *Q2–3; of the Q4, Q1;* o'th *F*   collar] *F, Q1;* choller *Q2–3;* Coller *Q4*

SAMSON   I strike quickly being moved.   5

GREGORY   But thou art not quickly moved to strike.

SAMSON   A dog of the house of Montague moves me.

GREGORY   To move is to stir, and to be valiant is to stand;
therefore, if thou art moved, thou runn'st away.

SAMSON   A dog of that house shall move me to stand. I   10
will take the wall of any man or maid of Montague's.

GREGORY   That shows thee a weak slave, for the weakest
goes to the wall.

SAMSON   'Tis true, and therefore women, being the
weaker vessels, are ever thrust to the wall; therefore   15
I will push Montague's men from the wall and thrust
his maids to the wall.

GREGORY   The quarrel is between our masters and us
their men.

SAMSON   'Tis all one. I will show myself a tyrant: when   20
I have fought with the men, I will be civil with the
maids, I will cut off their heads.

---

5 **moved** provoked, but the primary meaning of 'move' (to stir) is preserved in the word-play on *move*, *stir* and *stand* that follows in 8–9.

8 **stand** face the enemy. The Capulet and Montague retainers speak in prose ('proletarian prose' according to Kermode, 53) throughout this scene.

11 **take the wall** commandeer the best and cleanest place on the pavement, the one closest to the wall and furthest from the gutter; taking the wall was an assertion of superiority or contempt and therefore an insult.

12–13 **weakest . . . wall** a proverbial expression then as now (Dent, W185), with Gregory pretending not to follow the drift of Samson's talk about taking the wall

14–17 The word-play on *wall* deepens into something more sinister than mere social provocation. Prompted by Gregory's *weak* (12), Samson boasts that he will push the Montague men away from the wall but their women against it, to assault them sexually (hence *thrust* rather than 'push').

21 **civil** Editors sometimes emend to Q1's 'cruel', since that is what Samson really means, but he has already displayed a degree of sarcastic wit by pretending to surrender the wall to the Montague maids while meaning the exact opposite; *civil* renders the barbed flavour of the needling raillery about violence and sex between Samson and Gregory.

7 Montague] *Theobald (after Brooke); Mountague Q2–4, F;* the *Montagues Q1*   8–9] *Pope, var. Q1; verse Q2–4, F*   14 'Tis] *Q2–4;* Thats *Q1; not in F*   21 civil] *Q2–3, F;* cruel *Q4; var. Q1*   22 I will] *Q2–4;* and *F; var. Q1*

GREGORY   The heads of the maids?

SAMSON   Ay, the heads of the maids, or their maidenheads,
take it in what sense thou wilt.   25

GREGORY   They must take it in sense that feel it.

SAMSON   Me they shall feel while I am able to stand, and
'tis known I am a pretty piece of flesh.

GREGORY   'Tis well thou art not fish; if thou hadst, thou
hadst been poor john. Draw thy tool, here comes of   30
the house of Montagues. [*They draw.*]

Enter two other Servingmen
[*, one of them* ABRAHAM, *of the house of Montague*].

SAMSON   My naked weapon is out. Quarrel, I will back
thee.

GREGORY   How, turn thy back and run?

SAMSON   Fear me not.   35

---

26 'Those who experience it will know
whether you mean beheading or having sex.' Samson, of course, means
sex, hence his boast in the next line
about his manhood. Gregory's refusal
to take his meaning provokes the
sexual bragging of 27–8.

30 **poor john** literally, a salted and dried
fish, usually hake, eaten during Lent
– hence lacking the sap and juice of
Samson's self-professed sexual prow-
ess and hardly likely to *stand*; also
used as a general term of abuse in
the period. Gregory's gratuitous taunt
casts aspersions on Samson's virility
just as he goaded Samson earlier about
his cowardice.
    tool with a bawdy pun; see *naked
weapon* in 32.

30–1 **of the . . . Montagues** a use of the
so-called partitive genitive, a genitive
used to define the part by the whole,

the whole here being 'the house of
Montagues'. Williams notes that this
is rare in Shakespeare, but cites 'there
be of them that will themselves laugh'
from *Ham* (Ard² has 'be of them' at
3.2.38) and refers to Numbers, 13.20,
23 as examples of its common usage in
the King James Bible (Williams, 101).
The pointed indefiniteness is intended
to be contemptuous.

31.1–2 *The two men who enter here have
been identified to the audience only as
Montagues; readers know that one of
them is Abraham, because his name
appears as '*Abram.*' in SPs. In Q1 he is
merely '*1 Moun:*', and his second line
(44) goes to his companion, '*2 Moun:*'.

32 **naked weapon** a sword drawn from
its scabbard (termed *vagina* in Latin,
as Shakespeare undoubtedly knew),
with an obvious sexual allusion

35 'Do not doubt me.'

26 in] *Q1, Q4; not in Q2–3, F*   30 of] *Q2–4, F;* two of *Q1*   31 house] *Q2–4, F; not in
Q1*   Montagues] *Q2–4;* the *Mountagues F, Q1*   SD] *this edn*   31.1–2] *this edn; Enter two other seruing
men. Q2–4, F; Enter two Seruingmen of the* Mountagues. *Q1; Enter Abraham and Balthasar. / Rowe*

GREGORY No, marry, I fear thee!

SAMSON Let us take the law of our sides; let them begin.

GREGORY I will frown as I pass by and let them take it as
they list.

SAMSON Nay, as they dare. I will bite my thumb at them, 40
which is disgrace to them if they bear it.

ABRAHAM Do you bite your thumb at us, sir?

SAMSON I do bite my thumb, sir.

ABRAHAM Do you bite your thumb at us, sir?

SAMSON *[aside to Gregory]* Is the law of our side if I say 45
'Ay'?

GREGORY *[aside to Samson]* No.

SAMSON No, sir, I do not bite my thumb at you, sir, but I
bite my thumb, sir.

GREGORY Do you quarrel, sir? 50

ABRAHAM Quarrel, sir? No, sir.

SAMSON But if you do, sir, I am for you. I serve as good
a man as you.

ABRAHAM No better.

SAMSON Well, sir. 55

[*Enter* BENVOLIO.]

---

37 **of our sides** on our side (Abbott, 175)
40 **bite my thumb** Cotgrave glosses *'faire la nique'* as 'To mock by . . . putting the thumbnail into the mouth and with a jerk (from the upper teeth) make it to knack (that is pop)'. In his pamphlet *The Dead Term* (1608), Thomas Dekker describes behaviour in the walks of St Paul's Church: 'What swearing is there, what shouldering, what justling, what jeering, what biting of thumbs, to beget quarrels' (Var, 8–9).
54 **No better** The Nunn–Kyle prompt-book for the RSC's 1976 *RJ* has Tybalt enter here 'on 1st gallery R[ight] with

Page', in time for Gregory to spot him before Benvolio's entry after 55.
55.1 Benvolio is first identified in the text 10 lines after his entry (65). The SD and Gregory's comment at 56–7 appear to be in contradiction here, since Benvolio is a Montague, not a Capulet. Williams (142) suspects a slip by Shakespeare, while Evans (Cam²) argues that Gregory refers to Tybalt 'who is seen approaching'. In Q1 the scene of the fight is compressed into a three-line SD. In the 1947 RSC production Peter Brook cut *Here . . . kinsmen* (56–7) to avoid confusion.

41 disgrace] *Q2, Q1;* a disgrace *Q3–4, F*   45, 47, 56 SDs] *Capell*   of] *Q2–4, F;* on *Q1*   52 But] *Q2–4; not in F, Q1*   54 better.] *Q2–4;* better? *F*   55 SD] *Capell*

127

GREGORY [*aside to Samson*]   Say 'better'. Here comes one
of my master's kinsmen.

SAMSON   Yes, better, sir.

ABRAHAM   You lie.

SAMSON   Draw if you be men. Gregory, remember thy   60
washing blow. *They fight.*

BENVOLIO [*Draws.*]   Part, fools!
Put up your swords, you know not what you do.

Enter TYBALT.

TYBALT
What, art thou drawn among these heartless hinds?
[*Draws.*] Turn thee, Benvolio, look upon thy death.   65

BENVOLIO
I do but keep the peace. Put up thy sword,
Or manage it to part these men with me.

TYBALT
What, drawn and talk of peace? I hate the word
As I hate hell, all Montagues and thee.

---

61 **washing** swashing (the reading in
Q4), slashing. This is Shakespeare's
only use of the word, while 'swashing'
too occurs only once in the canon
('a swashing and a martial outside',
AYL 1.3.116). Ard² compares
Golding's 1567 translation of Ovid's
Metamorphoses: 'Astyages . . . Did with
a long sharp arming sword a washing
blow him give' (Ovid, *Met.*, 5.252).
62–3 These lines are printed as prose
in Q and F. Benvolio's first two lines
try to impose order on chaos through
cadence (Oxf¹ hears 'prose with verse
rhythms').
63 **swords** Luhrmann zoomed in here

on Benvolio's brandished weapon, a
9mm automatic with the brand name
SWORD.
63.1 Tybalt is not named in the text
until 107.
64 **heartless hinds** cowards; literally,
timid or cowardly (*heartless*) female
deer of three years, or else hinds without their stags. Benvolio should take on
a worthy adversary, a proper hart/stag
like Tybalt. Brooke spells 'hart' when
the Benvolio character advises Romeus
to find himself another love: 'Yet in
some other place bestow thy witless
wandring hart' (132); see also 182n.
67 **manage** use

58 sir] *Q2–4; not in F, Q1*   61 washing] *Q2–3, F; swashing Q4; not in Q1*   SD] *Q2–4, F; They draw,
to them enters* Tybalt, *they fight, to them the Prince, old* Mountague, *and his wife, old* Capulet *and his
wife, and other Citizens and part them. Q1*   62 SD] *Oxf*   63] *Capell; prose Q2–4, F*   64–5] *Pope; prose
Q2–4, F*   65 SD] *this edn*   68 drawn] *Q2–4; draw F; not in Q1*

Have at thee, coward.   [*They fight.*]   70

Enter three or four Citizens *with clubs or partisans.*

CITIZENS

Clubs, bills and partisans! Strike, beat them down,
Down with the Capulets, down with the Montagues!

Enter old CAPULET *in his gown, and his* WIFE.

CAPULET

What noise is this? Give me my long sword, ho!
CAPULET'S WIFE

A crutch, a crutch! Why call you for a sword?

Enter old MONTAGUE *and his* WIFE.

CAPULET

My sword, I say. Old Montague is come,   75
And flourishes his blade in spite of me.
MONTAGUE

Thou villain Capulet! – Hold me not, let me go.

70.1 **Citizens** In Q2 they enter as
'*Citizens*' but speak as officers (SP
'*Offi.*').
   partisans The partisan was a long-
handled spear with a symmetrical
double-edged blade; it was commonly
carried ceremonially as a badge of
office by civic guards.
71 **bills** The bill combined an axe-blade,
a spike and a hook, carried high on
a handle; it was commonly used by
constables of the watch.
72.1 *gown* here probably robe of
office rather than dressing-gown or
nightgown (*pace* Var, Cam²); a nightgown would hardly tally with the

information provided at 159, where
the time is given as shortly before
9 a.m. Rather than signalling that
Capulet was woken from his rest,
the gown is a symbol of magistracy
(cf. *KL* 4.6.160–1), a piquant detail
because it implies that the feud
entails a betrayal of the family heads'
civic duty.
73 **long sword** a heavy two-handed
sword, commonly used in battle and
comically inappropriate for the aged
Capulet, as his wife immediately
points out in the next line
75 SP See List of Roles, 2n.
77 **Hold . . . go** addressed to his wife

70 SD] *F (Fight.); not in Q2–4*   70.1] *Q2–4, F; var. Q1*   71 SP] *Williams (Steevens); Offi. Q2–4,
F*   72.1] *Q2–4, F; var. Q1*   74 SP] *Oxf; Wife. Q2–4, F; Lady Capulet / Rowe*   74.1] *Q2–4, F (after
76); var. Q1*

MONTAGUE'S WIFE

Thou shalt not stir one foot to seek a foe.

Enter PRINCE Escalus *with his train.*

PRINCE

Rebellious subjects, enemies to peace,
Profaners of this neighbour-stained steel –　　　　　80
Will they not hear? What ho, you men, you beasts,
That quench the fire of your pernicious rage
With purple fountains issuing from your veins;
On pain of torture, from those bloody hands
Throw your mistempered weapons to the ground　　　85
And hear the sentence of your moved prince.
Three civil brawls bred of an airy word,

---

78 The pressure of the action here is alleviated by a timely bit of domestic comedy as Montague's wife, just like Capulet's, stands up confidently to her choleric husband and reins him in.

78 SP See List of Roles, 15n.

78.1 **Escalus** See List of Roles, 20n.

80 'unnatural desecrators of what should be deep and instinctive bonds, using steel to shed the blood of fellow citizens' (hence *neighbour-stained*). The Latin root meaning of the word 'profane' (*pro fano*, literally, 'in front of the temple') have been known to educated members of the audience; the word's associations with worship are recalled at 1.5.92–3.
　　neighbour-stained neighbour-stainèd

81 **Will . . . hear?** The implication is either that his reproof is falling on deaf ears or that he cannot make himself audible above the din of the fighting, hence his exasperated *What ho*, commanding silence; *they* refers to the brawlers and perhaps also to the two elderly couples.

83 **fountains** One of Verona's claims to

be among the best towns in Lombardy was its 'store of springs', according to Brooke (7).

85 **mistempered** Instead of being tempered in icy water to harden the steel (as in Othello's 'sword of Spain, the ice-brook's temper', *Oth* 5.2.251), the brawlers' swords are perversely tempered in the tepid blood of their fellow Veronese. The broader meanings of ill-tempered and undisciplined, contemptuous of the common good, are also implied.

86 **moved** movèd; angry and provoked; see 5.

87 **Three** The uses of *Three* and *thrice* (89) are Shakespeare's. Brooke merely notes that the Prince finally ran out of patience after various futile attempts to cajole the opposing factions into making peace. Shakespeare commonly uses *thrice* as a ritual hyperbole, as in Venus' addressing Adonis as 'Thrice fairer than myself' (*VA* 7), or Henry V telling Falstaff that the grave gapes for him 'thrice wider than for other men' (*2H4* 5.5.54).
　　airy unsubstantial, imaginary

---

78 SP] *Oxf;* M. *Wife*.2. *Q2–4; 2. Wife F; Lady Capulet / Rowe　* one] *Q2–4;* a *F; not in Q1　* 78.1] *Q2–4, F; var. Q1　* PRINCE Escalus] *Cam (after Brooke); Prince* Eskales *Q2–4, F; the Prince Q1　* 87 brawls] *Q2–4, Q1;* Broyles *F*

By thee, old Capulet, and Montague,
Have thrice disturbed the quiet of our streets
And made Verona's ancient citizens   90
Cast by their grave-beseeming ornaments,
To wield old partisans in hands as old,
Cankered with peace, to part your cankered hate.
If ever you disturb our streets again,
Your lives shall pay the forfeit of the peace.   95
For this time all the rest depart away.
You, Capulet, shall go along with me,
And, Montague, come you this afternoon,
To know our farther pleasure in this case,
To old Freetown, our common judgement-place.   100
Once more, on pain of death, all men depart.
                Exeunt [all but Montague, his Wife and Benvolio].

MONTAGUE

Who set this ancient quarrel new abroach?
Speak, nephew, were you by when it began?

90 **ancient** elderly, venerable
91 **grave-beseeming ornaments** sober and solemn attire; with probable word-play on *grave* meaning 'tomb' (cf. Mercutio's 'you shall find me a grave man' at 3.1.100). The 'grave citizens' of Pisa (*TS* 1.1.10, 4.2.95) or the 'potent, grave, and reverend signiors' of *Oth* 1.3.76 suggest that *grave* was a conventional tag.
92–3 The *hands* of the town fathers have grown serenely rusty at fighting (*Cankered with peace*), but now they need to abuse their same frail hands once again to bear arms to quell this corrosive feud.
92 **partisans** See 70.1n.
100 **Freetown . . . judgement-place**

In Brooke, 'Freetown' (translating Painter's 'Villafranca') is Capulet's castle (Brooke, 2258), but in the play Capulet lives in a house in Verona, enclosed by a walled orchard (2.1.5). As a traditional Solomonic place of judgement, *Freetown* is fittingly called *old*, meaning venerable, long established.
102 **abroach** afoot; cf. the phrase 'to broach something with someone', i.e. to bring something up as a matter of interest or concern. But old Montague's specific choice of words reflects the bristling of swords and halberds on the stage just then ('to broach' means 'to pierce, stab, thrust through' (*OED* broach *v.*[1]).

93 part your] *Q2–3, F;* party our *Q4; not in Q1*   99 farther] *Q2, Q4, Q1;* Fathers *Q3, F*   101 SD *all . . . Benvolio*] *Rowe subst.*   102 SP] *Q2–4, F; M: wife. Q1*   new] *Q2–4, F;* first *Q1*

BENVOLIO

Here were the servants of your adversary
And yours, close fighting ere I did approach.   105
I drew to part them. In the instant came
The fiery Tybalt, with his sword prepared,
Which, as he breathed defiance to my ears,
He swung about his head and cut the winds
Who, nothing hurt withal, hissed him in scorn.   110
While we were interchanging thrusts and blows
Came more and more, and fought on part and part,
Till the Prince came, who parted either part.

MONTAGUE'S WIFE

O where is Romeo, saw you him today?
Right glad I am he was not at this fray.   115

BENVOLIO

Madam, an hour before the worshipped sun
Peered forth the golden window of the east,
A troubled mind drive me to walk abroad,

104–13 The primary purpose of these apparently redundant lines is to create an image of Tybalt as a fire-breathing dragon whose sword whooshes as it cuts through the air. His speaking part is the smallest by far of the major characters'. Q1 cuts straight from 103 to an enquiry after Romeo by his mother (114), thus missing the chance to name Tybalt at this point.

105 **close fighting** locked in combat

107 **fiery Tybalt** the first mention of Tybalt by name

110 **Who** Invulnerable *winds* are here personified: they mocked (*hissed*) Tybalt's fencing antics.
nothing hurt withal not in any way injured

112 **on . . . part** on either side

114 **Romeo** the first reference to Romeo in the play, seven lines after the men-

tion of Tybalt. Romeo's mother's lines soften the tone of the play and shift its focus away from the feud to the love plot. Benvolio reciprocates by adopting the rhetoric of a sonneteer (104ff., 116ff.).

118 **troubled mind** Benvolio too is suffering from lover's melancholia (124), which means that he is well equipped to be Romeo's sentimental sparring-partner.
drive a permissible form of the past tense which, though rare, occurs elsewhere in the poetry and drama of the period and was deemed to be the 'purest' form of the past tense. Var (15–16) draws an analogy with the use of 'writ' for 'wrote', common in Shakespeare; past tense *drive* would be pronounced with a short vowel as 'driv'. The change to 'drave' in the

106–13] *Q2–4, F; not in Q1*   109 swung] *Pope;* swoong *Q2;* swong *Q3–4, F*   111 thrusts] *Q2–3, F;* thrust *Q4*   114 SP] *Oxf;* M. *Wife.* 2. *Q2–4, F, Q1; Lady Montague / Rowe*   115 I am] *Q2, Q1;* am I *Q3–4, F*   118 drive] *Q2;* draue *Q3–4, F;* drew *Q1*

Where underneath the grove of sycamore
That westward rooteth from this city side,   120
So early walking did I see your son.
Towards him I made, but he was ware of me
And stole into the covert of the wood.
I, measuring his affections by my own,
Which then most sought where most might not be
    found,   125
Being one too many by my weary self,
Pursued my humour, not pursuing his,
And gladly shunned who gladly fled from me.

MONTAGUE

Many a morning hath he there been seen,
With tears augmenting the fresh morning's dew,   130
Adding to clouds more clouds with his deep sighs.
But all so soon as the all-cheering sun
Should in the farthest east begin to draw

later quartos and in Folio suggests that
Shakespeare's usage may already have
been archaic or old-fashioned.
abroad out of doors, away from home
119 **sycamore** The three references by
Shakespeare to this common English
tree (see also *LLL* 5.2.89, *Oth* 4.3.39),
distinguished by vigorous growth and
a huge shade-giving dome, all connect
it to lovelornness. This suggests that
its use follows its name ('sick-amor'
= lovesick); the tree itself is neither
particularly beautiful nor associated
otherwise with romance.
120 **westward** Romeo is seen by Benvolio
in a grove of sycamores to the west
(the direction of sunset) before sun-
rise. Our first reported glimpse of him
is at dawn.
122–8 Benvolio's artfully lyrical verse
underlines the distance the play has
travelled from the violent prose of its
beginning.

122 **ware** aware, conscious (cited in *OED*)
123 **covert . . . wood** not unlike the
'neighbour thicket' by the sycamore in
LLL 5.2.94 in which Boyet hides from
the royal party
127 **humour** This alludes to the chief
humoral fluids (blood, choler, melancholy, phlegm) of Galenic and
Hippocratic medicine; their distribution and balance were thought to
govern people's physical and mental
constitutions and dictate their moods.
Black . . . humour (139), also known
as melancholy, one of the cardinal
humours, was traced to an excess of
black bile.
132 **all-cheering** bringing comfort to
everyone who sees it
133–4 **draw . . . bed** Aurora is the goddess of dawn in Roman mythology.
In Homer the 'rosy-fingered' dawn
reportedly blushes because every
morning Phoebus Apollo surprises her

119 sycamore] *F (Sycamour), Q1 (Sicamoure);* Syramour *Q2–4*   127 humour] *Q2, Q4;* honour
Q3, F, Q1

The shady curtains from Aurora's bed,
Away from light steals home my heavy son,   135
And private in his chamber pens himself,
Shuts up his windows, locks fair daylight out
And makes himself an artificial night.
Black and portentous must this humour prove,
Unless good counsel may the cause remove.   140

BENVOLIO

My noble uncle, do you know the cause?

MONTAGUE

I neither know it nor can learn of him.

BENVOLIO

Have you importuned him by any means?

MONTAGUE

Both by myself and many other friends;
But he, his own affections' counsellor,   145
Is to himself – I will not say how true –
But to himself so secret and so close,
So far from sounding and discovery
As is the bud bit with an envious worm
Ere he can spread his sweet leaves to the air,   150

rising from the bed of the old sea god Neptune. *RJ* features more dawns than any other Shakespeare play, though the word 'dawn' itself first occurs in *H5* 4.1.271.

135 **heavy son** *heavy* = melancholic, depressed. The adjective connects back to *light* meaning both not heavy and luminous, hence the related play on *son* and 'sun', with Romeo the *son* behaving like the setting sun by shutting out the light in his room.

136 **private** alone, solitary
  pens shuts in (as in a pen)

139 **Black . . . humour** See 127n.

141 **uncle** See List of Roles, 16n.

143 **importuned him** asked him persist-

ently, pressed him for an answer

146 Romeo is anything but true to his usual gregarious, sociable self.

147 **secret . . . close** extremely secretive; the figure of speech is a hendiadys: two virtual synonyms are used in conjunction for emphasis, a rhetorical strategy repeated in *sounding and discovery* in the next line.

148 **sounding** being accessible to having his thoughts fathomed (line cited under *OED vbl sb.*[2] b); cf. Suffolk's description of Gloucester as a man who is 'Unsounded yet and full of deep deceit' (*2H6* 3.1.57). The point is that Romeo is impervious to his father's probings.

142 learn] *Q2–4, F, Q1;* learn it *Rowe*   144 other] *Q2–4;* others *F; not in Q1*   145 his] *Q3–4, F;* is *Q2; not in Q1*

Or dedicate his beauty to the same.
Could we but learn from whence his sorrows grow,
We would as willingly give cure as know.

Enter ROMEO.

BENVOLIO

See where he comes. So please you, step aside.
I'll know his grievance, or be much denied.   155

MONTAGUE

I would thou wert so happy by thy stay
To hear true shrift. Come, madam, let's away.

Exeunt [Montague and his Wife].

BENVOLIO

Good morrow, cousin.

ROMEO   Is the day so young?

BENVOLIO

But new struck nine.

ROMEO   Ay me, sad hours seem long.
Was that my father that went hence so fast?   160

BENVOLIO

It was. What sadness lengthens Romeo's hours?

ROMEO

Not having that which, having, makes them short.

---

151 **same** Pope changed to 'sun', an imaginative emendation rendered more plausible by the apparent confusions of *a* and *u* in Shakespeare's hand and the common minim error of *m* and *n*. Several major editions follow Pope.

153 **give cure** help restore to health

155 **I'll . . . grievance** I'll find out why he is so distressed (cited under *OED* grievance *sb.* 2).

156 **by thy stay** through staying behind, but also by being a prop and affording support, a meaning that was com-

mon in English particularly during the second half of the 16th century (*OED* stay *sb.*²)

157 **true shrift** full revelation (of what is troubling him so)

158 **cousin** kinsman rather than specifically cousin, the two of them being members of the wider Montague clan; *cousin* is used loosely in the period.
so young This implies that the hours seemed so long to him that he cannot believe that it should only be nine in the morning.

151 same] *Q2–4, F;* sun *Pope² (Theobald); not in Q1*   153.1] *Q2–4, F*   157 SD *Montague . . . Wife*] *Capell subst.*

135

BENVOLIO   In love?

ROMEO   Out.

BENVOLIO   Of love?   165

ROMEO

    Out of her favour where I am in love.

BENVOLIO

    Alas, that love, so gentle in his view,

    Should be so tyrannous and rough in proof.

ROMEO

    Alas, that love, whose view is muffled still,

    Should without eyes see pathways to his will.   170

    Where shall we dine? O me, what fray was here?

    Yet tell me not, for I have heard it all.

    Here's much to do with hate, but more with love.

    Why then, O brawling love, O loving hate,

    O anything of nothing first create,   175

---

167 **love . . . view** a reference to Cupid's mild and meek appearance (as a nude putto)

168 **in proof** when tried and tested; as in the expression 'the proof of the pudding' (see also 208, *proof of chastity*)

169 **view is muffled** Cupid is blindfolded because love is irrational. A famous Renaissance painting of Cupid by Lucas Cranach the Elder shows him removing his blindfold as he rises from a volume of Plato's works, to signify that philosophy can impart true vision to love (see Panofsky, 106, plate 57).

    still always

170 probably an allusion to the proverbial assertion that 'Love will find a way' in spite of being blind (Dent, L531)

171 **dine** have our midday meal; *supper* at the Capulets' is referred to three times in the scenes which follow.

172 **heard it all** probably a weary expression of Romeo's sense of *déjà vu*, thus distancing him from the feud's

irrational hatreds, rather than meaning that he could hear the din of the brawl in his grove of sycamores

173–80 These lines contain a string of oxymorons intended to show up the subjectivity of lovers, whose imagination can turn everything into its opposite as in *cold fire* or *sick health*. Romeo is keeping Benvolio at bay with a parody of lovers' artificial discourse, to forestall his question about the identity of his beloved at 197.

175 **anything . . . nothing** The two words are antonyms, like *loving* and *hate* in the preceding line, with a play on the proverbial saying that 'Nothing can come of nothing' (Dent, N285, cites *KL* 1.1.90).

    *create** Most editors follow Q1's reading 'create' rather than Q2's 'created' because it yields a perfect pentameter, rhymes with *hate* and is grammatically permissible in the period. Abbott (342) notes that words like 'miscreate', 'create' and 'consecrate' which are

---

163, 165 love?] *Rowe;* loue. *Q2–4, F, Q1*   175 create] *Q1;* created *Q2–4, F*

O heavy lightness, serious vanity,
Misshapen chaos of well-seeming forms,
Feather of lead, bright smoke, cold fire, sick health,
Still-waking sleep that is not what it is.
This love feel I that feel no love in this.   180
Dost thou not laugh?

BENVOLIO   No, coz, I rather weep.

ROMEO

Good heart, at what?

BENVOLIO   At thy good heart's oppression.

ROMEO

Why, such is love's transgression.
Griefs of mine own lie heavy in my breast,
Which thou wilt propagate to have it pressed   185
With more of thine. This love that thou hast shown
Doth add more grief to too much of mine own.

'directly derived from Latin participles . . . may themselves be regarded as participial adjectives without the addition of d'; see e.g. 'And the issue there create / Ever shall be fortunate' (*MND* 5.1.391–2). Past participle 'created' seems halting and clunky and has a supernumerary syllable (for an ingenious defence of it, see Oxf[1], 156).

177 a striking metaphor contrasting with the stock oxymorons of thwarted love, complementing the primal 'anything of nothing' of 175
*well-seeming Q4's reading, adopted in all major editions of the play, suggests that either the letter *m* or a tilde in foul papers was omitted by the compositor. Q1 has 'best seeming', which also makes good sense.
179 **Still-waking** forever wakeful
180 i.e. this is the kind of inner turmoil that I suffer as a lover while all along my love is not reciprocated.
181 **coz** cousin (see 158n.)

182 **heart** Q2 spells 'hart' for *heart* here. While punning on 'hart' (stag) and 'heart' (the seat of love) is not uncommon in Shakespeare (see 64, and *TN* 1.1.16–23), what is meant is 'heart', *Good heart* being an intimate form of address. It may be that 'hart' was a variant Shakespearean spelling for 'heart'. In Q2, and counting compounds like 'heartsick', 'hart' is used 17 times while 'heart' occurs on 24 occasions.
oppression burden
184–6 **Griefs . . . thine** 'I harbour too many sorrows of my own already for you to add to them by weeping over me'; this train of thought is expanded further in the next sentence.
185 **to . . . pressed** by 'oppressing' my heart further. Benvolio is accused by Romeo of wanting to multiply (*propagate*) his sorrows rather than relieve them by trying to comfort him (cited under *OED* propagate).

177 well-seeming] *Q4;* welseeing *Q2–3, F;* best seeming *Q1*   179 Still-waking] *F2;* Still waking *Q2–4, F, Q1*   181 Dost] *Q5;* Doest *Q2–4, F, Q1*   184 mine] *Q2–3, F, Q1;* my *Q4*

Love is a smoke made with the fume of sighs;
Being purged, a fire sparkling in lovers' eyes;
Being vexed, a sea nourished with loving tears.   190
What is it else? A madness most discreet,
A choking gall and a preserving sweet.
Farewell, my coz.

BENVOLIO   Soft, I will go along;
An if you leave me so, you do me wrong.

ROMEO

Tut, I have lost myself. I am not here.   195
This is not Romeo, he's some otherwhere.

BENVOLIO

Tell me in sadness, who is that you love?

ROMEO

What, shall I groan and tell thee?

BENVOLIO   Groan? Why, no,
But sadly tell me who.

---

189 **purged** The word next occurs after Romeo's and Juliet's first kiss at 1.5.106. Here it is linked to the all-consuming effect of *fire* (passion), the specific image evoking smoke (*fume of sighs*) driven out by flames.

190 **vexed** troubled or suffering (rather than in the modern sense of annoyed) **loving tears** Q1 has 'a louers teares' here, while Pope's reading, 'lovers' tears', has found favour with some editors. By picking up the participle *sparkling* (189), Q2's construction creates an effective, cross-line syntactic chiasm (*fire sparkling . . . loving tears*). Tears which swell a sea of sorrows are more powerful symbols than passive tears shed by lovers' eyes.

192 The sweet and sour antithesis occurs again in Juliet's lines in 2.5.23–4.

193 **Soft** the equivalent of modern 'Wait a moment'

194 **An if** if

195–6 Romeo claims that he cannot leave Benvolio because he has already gone: the real Romeo resides with Rosaline (*some otherwhere*); cf. *TGV* 1.1.65. Ard[2] compares Brooke's 'And whilst I talked with him, himself he hath exiled, / Out of himself' (419–20).

195 **Tut** a mild exclamation of impatience

197 **in sadness** seriously, in earnest. Not unlike the melancholy Antonio asking Bassanio about the lady from Belmont (*MV* 1.1.119–210), Benvolio suggests that, however 'sad' he may be, Romeo should tell him the name of his love, while Romeo pretends to take the phrase literally by offering to *groan* as part of his response (198). The play on *sadness* continues to 202.

199 Benvolio fails to coax Rosaline's name from Romeo, and the first scene ends without her name having been mentioned.

---

190 loving] *Q2–4, F;* a louers *Q1;* lovers *Pope*   195 Tut] *Q2–4, F, Q1;* But *F3–4*   lost] *Q2–4, F, Q1;* left *Daniel 1875*   197 who is that] *Q2–4, F;* whome she is *Q1;* who she is *Pope*   198–9] *Hanmer; Q2–4, F line* thee? / who? /

ROMEO

A sick man in sadness makes his will;   200
A word ill urged to one that is so ill.
In sadness, cousin, I do love a woman.

BENVOLIO

I aimed so near when I supposed you loved.

ROMEO

A right good markman, and she's fair I love.

BENVOLIO

A right fair mark, fair coz, is soonest hit.   205

ROMEO

Well in that hit you miss. She'll not be hit
With Cupid's arrow. She hath Dian's wit,
And in strong proof of chastity well armed
From love's weak childish bow she lives uncharmed.

200–1 The lines are spoken in gently mocking reproof of Benvolio's urging Romeo to tell him the truth, whether he be sad or not; *sadness*, Romeo notes, is the state of mind of dying people, and that is how sick he is too.

203 **I . . . near** I guessed as much (*OED* aim *v.* 3); *aimed* and *markman* (204) evoke the mythopoeic iconography of Cupid, the baby archer god of love; cf. 'Cupid all arm'd: a certain aim he took / At a fair vestal' (*MND* 2.1.157ff.) and 2.5.8.

204 **markman** a now obsolete form of 'marksman'

205 **fair mark** with a sexual pun, *mark* meaning vulva (Oxf[1], 159); cf. 'target' in *AC* 1.3.83, where Antony swears by his 'sword' and Cleopatra replies by her 'target'.

206 **Well . . . miss** Editors commonly insert a comma after *Well*, but there is none in Q2, and Q1 has 'But in that hit you misse'. Using a comma here turns Romeo's *Well* into a conversational pause marker rather than an adverbial

qualifier of just how badly off the mark Benvolio is. Romeo does not mean 'As it happens, you are off the mark', but 'You are far (or *Well*) off the mark with that comment', because although his beloved is indeed fair she seems impervious to love's blandishments.

207 **Dian's wit** the intelligence or *nous* of the goddess of hunting and chastity, Diana; perhaps also with an allusion to Queen Elizabeth, the most famous virgin in the land, who had been celebrated for this by, amongst others, Spenser (see Ard[2], 92) and, more obliquely, Shakespeare in *MND* 2.1.158–64

208 **proof** armour

209 From the perspective of Romeo's beloved, Romeo's infatuation is mere child's play with bow and arrows, without any power to bewitch.
uncharmed While Q1's 'vnharm'd' captures the sense of remaining free (pristine and virginal) from love's wounds, *uncharmed* evokes the magic of love.

200 A . . . makes] *Q2–3, F;* Bid a . . . make *Q4, Q1*   204 markman] *Q2–3, F (*mark man*);* markeman *Q4, Q1;* marks-man *F3*   206 Well] *Q2–3, F;* Well, *Q4;* But *Q1*   209 uncharmed] *Q2–4, F;* vnharm'd *Q1*

She will not stay the siege of loving terms,   210
Nor bide th'encounter of assailing eyes,
Nor ope her lap to saint-seducing gold.
O, she is rich in beauty, only poor
That when she dies, with beauty dies her store.

BENVOLIO

Then she hath sworn that she will still live chaste?   215

ROMEO

She hath, and in that sparing makes huge waste,
For beauty starved with her severity,
Cuts beauty off from all posterity.
She is too fair, too wise, wisely too fair,
To merit bliss by making me despair.   220
She hath forsworn to love, and in that vow
Do I live dead that live to tell it now.

BENVOLIO

Be ruled by me, forget to think of her.

ROMEO

O teach me how I should forget to think!

---

210 **stay** endure; anticipating *Nor bide* in 211
211 She is not willing to receive Romeo, knowing that he will try to woo her eye-to-eye.
212 an allusion to Jupiter's seduction of Danaë in a shower of gold; the story is related in Ovid's *Metamorphoses*, Book 6.
saint-seducing gold i.e. sumptuous gifts
213–14 **rich . . . store** i.e. the only flaw in her beauty is that with her death beauty itself will vanish because in her person she distilled the quintessence of female comeliness.
215 Benvolio's question follows on logically from Romeo's telling him that his

beloved will not be wooed.
216 **in . . . waste** By being so niggardly (*sparing*) in her attitude to love and sex, she wastes her opportunity to propagate her beauty.
219–21 **She . . . love** Romeo claims that Rosaline is not deliberately driving him to distraction by rejecting his love because that would implicate her in the mortal sin of despair; rather, she has abjured love altogether. His language is laced with religious terms, a common rhetorical feature of the hyperbolic language of courtly love.
221–2 **in . . . now** i.e. he is alive but only as a living-dead person, because his true life is his love and that has been killed by Rosaline's vow of chastity.

211 bide] *Q2–4;* bid *F; var. Q1*   212 ope] *Q2–4, Q1;* open *F*   213 rich in beauty,] *Q3–4, F, Q1;* rich, in bewtie *Q2*   214 beauty dies her] *Q2–4, F, Q1;* her dies Beauty's *Theobald*   216 makes] *Q4;* make *Q2–3, F; not in Q1*

BENVOLIO

    By giving liberty unto thine eyes.   225

    Examine other beauties.

ROMEO   'Tis the way

    To call hers, exquisite, in question more.

    These happy masks that kiss fair ladies' brows,

    Being black, puts us in mind they hide the fair.

    He that is strucken blind cannot forget   230

    The precious treasure of his eyesight lost.

    Show me a mistress that is passing fair,

    What doth her beauty serve but as a note

    Where I may read who passed that passing fair?

    Farewell, thou canst not teach me to forget.   235

BENVOLIO

    I'll pay that doctrine, or else die in debt.   *Exeunt.*

[1.2]   *Enter* CAPULET, County PARIS *and a* Servingman.

CAPULET

But Montague is bound as well as I,

---

227 to inspire examination of her outstanding beauty even further (since
the contrast with other women will
foreground hers the more)

229 **puts** put; but perhaps the singular
is used because the primary phrase
governing the verb here is *Being black*
(Abbott, 336).

230 **strucken** struck or stricken. This
irregular participial formation
(Abbott, 344) reflects 'strooken' in
Q2–4 and F, an idiosyncratic phonetic
spelling which Shakespeare uses on
a number of occasions. The *Harvard
Concordance* lists 55 instances of
'strook' and six of 'strooken'.

232 **mistress** 'lady-love' (Cam[2])

235 For Henry Irving this was the 'key-

note of the play' (Stoker, 93).

236 Benvolio vows that he will suc-
ceed in teaching Romeo the lesson
(*doctrine*) to forget his love by looking at other women; and should he
fail to do so he will die his friend's
debtor, having defaulted on his
promise.

1.2 Sunday afternoon (1.1.98) in a street
near the Capulets' house

0.1 **County** count; as in County Palatine
in *MV* 1.2.44
Servingman so named in Q1; he is
termed '*the Clowne*' in Q2, which may
suggest that the role is imagined as a
comedy part.

1 **bound** bound over, obliged to keep the
peace

226–7] *Pope; Q2–4, F line* beauties. / more. /   **1.2]** *Capell*   0.1] *Rowe subst.; Enter* Capulet, *Countie*
Paris, *and the Clowne. Q2–4, F; Enter Countie* Paris, *old* Capulet. *Q1*   1 But] *Q2;* And *Q4; not in*
Q3, F, Q1

In penalty alike, and 'tis not hard, I think,
For men so old as we to keep the peace.

PARIS

Of honourable reckoning are you both,
And pity 'tis you lived at odds so long.   5
But now, my lord, what say you to my suit?

CAPULET

But saying o'er what I have said before:
My child is yet a stranger in the world;
She hath not seen the change of fourteen years.
Let two more summers wither in their pride   10
Ere we may think her ripe to be a bride.

PARIS

Younger than she are happy mothers made.

CAPULET

And too soon marred are those so early married.
She is the hopeful lady of my earth.
But woo her, gentle Paris, get her heart.   15
My will to her consent is but a part,

---

4 **reckoning** value
9 **fourteen years** See List of Roles, 1n.
This is the first of several references
to Juliet's extreme youth. Her 16 years
in Brooke may lie behind Capulet's
suggestion to Paris that his child ought
to wait for two more years before
marrying.
10–11 **summers . . . ripe** Capulet's
imagery perversely connects the summers' withering to Juliet's maturing
towards marriage.
13 ***married** Q1's reading recollects
the proverbial jingle, 'The maid that
soon married is, soon marred is' (from
Puttenham; see Tilley, M701, on
'marrying is marring'). Q2's 'made' is
preferred by most editions.
14 Most editions follow Q2 here and

reproduce 'Earth hath swallowed all
my hopes but she, / She is the hopeful
lady of my earth', which would seem
to imply that Juliet once had brothers
and sisters (see Hosley, 'Children').
But Capulet flatly contradicts this
later with 'this only child' (3.5.165).
Given the pattern of first and second
thoughts in Q2, it is likely that 'She is
the hopeful lady of my earth' constitutes Shakespeare's rewriting of 'Earth
hath swallowed all my hopes but she'.
Lines 13 and 14 are the only pair not
to rhyme as a couplet in Capulet's long
speech; see pp. 4, 102.
hopeful i.e. in whom my hopes are
vested
15–18 This hardly accords with Capulet's
treatment of Juliet in 3.5.

13 married] *Q1;* made *Q2–4, F*   14] *this edn;* Earth hath swallowed all my hopes but she, / Shees the
hopefull Lady of my earth: / *Q2–4, F; not in Q1*   14 She is] *Q4;* Shees *Q2–3, F; not in Q1*

And, she agreed, within her scope of choice
Lies my consent and fair according voice.
This night I hold an old accustomed feast,
Whereto I have invited many a guest   20
Such as I love; and you among the store
One more, most welcome, makes my number more.
At my poor house look to behold this night
Earth-treading stars that make dark heaven light.
Such comfort as do lusty young men feel   25
When well-apparelled April on the heel
Of limping winter treads, even such delight
Among fresh fennel buds shall you this night
Inherit at my house. Hear all, all see,
And like her most whose merit most shall be;   30
Which, on more view, of many mine being one,
May stand in number, though in reckoning none.

19 **an . . . feast** In the source this is a Christmas banquet, whereas here it is a summer ball or revels; see 1.5.28.

24 The image anticipates the hyperbole of Juliet's eyes outshining the brightest lights in the night-time firmament (1.5.43–5); it was perhaps inspired by Philip Sidney's popular and highly experimental sonnet cycle *Astrophil and Stella* ('star lover and star').

26–7 **When . . . treads** Cf. *Son* 98: 'When proud-pied April, dressed in all his trim, / Hath put a spirit of youth in everything.'

28 **fennel** a contested Q2 reading (Q1 has 'female'). In support of *fennel*, Williams (104–5) adduces John Lyly's *Sappho and Phao* (1584): 'little things catch little minds, and fancy is a worm that feedeth first upon fennel' (Lyly, *Sappho*, 2.390). The image of young women as *fennel buds* may have been inspired by the fragrancy of fennel, and the vernal colour of its yellow flowers suits the 'well apparelled April' of 26; Durham (120) notes that 'Fennel was thrown in the path of brides, and it was especially the flower of newly married couples'.

29 **Inherit** receive (cited under *OED v.* 3)

31–2 Capulet seems to suggest that among the bevy of fair women at the feast Juliet may well occupy pride of place as the daughter of the house (*one* = 'one of many' and 'number one'), but she may not turn out to be the most deserving of Paris' love. The word *reckoning* can mean the 'mode of regarding a matter' (*OED vbl sb.* 7a) as well as 'counting'; see Oxf[1], which wrestles with the complexity of the couplet and concludes that it is possible that in this instance 'rhetoric and wordplay have confounded meaning'.

17 agreed] *Q2; agree Q3–4, F; not in Q1*   28 fennel] *Q2–4, F; female Q1, F2–4*   31 on] *Q4; one Q2–3, F; not in Q1*

Come, go with me. [*to Servingman*] Go, sirrah, trudge
  about
Through fair Verona; find those persons out
Whose names are written there, and to them say   35
My house and welcome on their pleasure stay.

Exeunt [Capulet and Paris].

SERVINGMAN   Find them out whose names are written
here! It is written that the shoemaker should meddle
with his yard and the tailor with his last, the fisher
with his pencil and the painter with his nets, but I am   40
sent to find those persons whose names are here writ,
and can never find what names the writing person
hath here writ. I must to the learned. In good time!

Enter BENVOLIO *and* ROMEO.

BENVOLIO

Tut, man, one fire burns out another's burning,
One pain is lessened by another's anguish.   45
Turn giddy and be holp by backward turning.
One desperate grief cures with another's languish.
Take thou some new infection to thy eye,
And the rank poison of the old will die.

---

33 **trudge** walk ponderously; with menial
connotations

38–40 **It . . . nets** a parody of a passage
from the Epistle Dedicatory of Lyly's
Euphues, the Anatomy of Wit: 'The
shoemaker must not go above his
latchet, nor the hedger meddle with
anything but his bill' (Lyly, *Works*,
1.180); see also Tilley, 1926. The sexual innuendoes in *meddle with* (Partridge
glosses as 'to coït'), *yard* and *pencil* are
characteristic of the play.

43 **In good time** because just then
Benvolio and Romeo, among the
learned (they are literate), enter, the

answer to his prayers

44–55 Benvolio and Romeo continue their
discussion from the end of the first scene,
ignoring the illiterate Servingman. That
opposites drive one another other out
is a commonplace (cf. e.g. Dent, F277,
G446, P457); the lines echo the impact
on Romeus of his first sight of Juliet in
Brooke's poem (particularly 206–10). It
is symptomatic of the play's patterned
rhetoric that the first six lines (44–9)
form an English sonnet sestet.

46 **holp** helped; a participle formation
with the final *-en* ('holpen') dropped
(Abbott, 343)

33 SD] *Staunton (Capell)*   36 SD] *Rowe; Exeunt. Q1; Exit. Q2–4, F*   37–8 written here] *Q1*; written.
Here *Q2–4, F*   45 One] *Q3–4, F, Q1*; On *Q2*   48 thy] *Q2, Q1*; the *Q3–4, F*

ROMEO

Your plantain leaf is excellent for that.   50

BENVOLIO

For what, I pray thee?

ROMEO   For your broken shin.

BENVOLIO

Why, Romeo, art thou mad?

ROMEO

Not mad, but bound more than a madman is;

Shut up in prison, kept without my food,

Whipped and tormented and – Good-e'en, good
  fellow.   55

SERVINGMAN Godgigoden. I pray, sir, can you read?

ROMEO

Ay, mine own fortune in my misery.

SERVINGMAN Perhaps you have learnt it without book.

But I pray, can you read anything you see?

ROMEO

Ay, if I know the letters and the language.   60

SERVINGMAN Ye say honestly. Rest you merry.

ROMEO Stay, fellow, I can read. (*He reads the letter.*)

50–1 The *plantain leaf* is a traditional herbal ointment applied to wounds as balm (cited under *OED* plantain *sb.*[1]). Romeo evokes it here in jesting banter as a remedy for Benvolio's shin, which he anticipates breaking because Benvolio urges him to cast his eye on another beauty (thereby daring to doubt Romeo's devotion to Rosaline). Costard similarly suggests plantain as a salve for a head with a broken 'shin': 'no salve, sir, but a plantain!' (*LLL* 3.1.71).

51–1.3.35 **For . . . trudge** The next 81 lines of Q2 were set from Q1; see pp. 98–9.

55 **Good-e'en** good evening; used as a form of salutation any time after noon (rather like modern Italian *buona sera*)

56 **Godgigoden** 'God give you good even', which according to *OED* is 'variously mutilated' to 'God dig-you-den' in *LLL* 4.1.42, 'give ye good-e'en' (*TGV* 2.1.90), *God ye good den* (2.4.106) and *Godgigoden* (3.5.172).

61 **Rest you merry** Misconstruing Romeo's quip about letters and language as a literal acknowledgement of illiteracy, the Servingman excuses himself with a traditional parting formula, which he repeats at 82.

62 SD *letter* i.e. Capulet's guest-list, misleadingly called 'Letter' in Q2

51–1.3.35] *These lines in Q2 were set from Q1.*   55 Good-e'en] *Q1–4, F (*Godden*)*   58–9] *Q1; Q2–4, F line* book: / see? /

> *Signor Martino and his wife and daughters;*
> *County Anselm and his beauteous sisters;*
> *The lady widow of Vitruvio;*   65
> *Signor Placentio and his lovely nieces;*
> *Mercutio and his brother Valentine;*
> *Mine uncle Capulet, his wife and daughters;*
> *My fair niece Rosaline, and Livia;*
> *Signor Valentio and his cousin Tybalt;*   70
> *Lucio and the lively Helena.*
> A fair assembly. Whither should they come?

SERVINGMAN   Up.

ROMEO   Whither? To supper?

63–71 These lines are set as verse, following Dyce. Williams (105) notes that comparable lists of names feature as verse in *H5* 4.8.93–101. The list (not in the sources) contains the first mention of Mercutio and the first by name of Rosaline. By having Romeo read the guest-list, Shakespeare ensures that the first time Rosaline's name is spoken it comes from Romeo's lips. Her name is usually marked in performance by some form of recognition. In the 1986 Bogdanov production the list became a set of invitation cards which Romeo and Benvolio read out to each other using tone of voice to poke fun at epithets such as *beauteous*.

63 *Signor* first changed from French 'Seigneur' to Italian 'Signior' by Rowe. The source is not much help in determining why Shakespeare might have wanted to use the French rather than the Italian form of address since it offers only a general invitation to all the best people in Verona; see Brooke, 159–62.

73 **Up** The servant's laconic response

to Romeo's question may be no more than a direction, but it is clearly inadequate (up where?), hence Romeo's repeating the question, specifying *supper*. The servant has just had to memorize Romeo's list of names, his straining to keep up with the reading usually a rich seam of comedy in performance. His unhelpful reply may be retaliation by brevity.

74 Williams, following Capell, suspects textual corruption and suggests leaving out *To supper?*, reading it as a memorial anticipation of the question 'Sups the fair Rosaline' 10 lines further down. Q punctuates 74 with a single question mark at the end of the line, thereby turning Romeo's reply into a reference to a supper to which he has not yet been invited and about which he knows nothing. Inserting a question mark after *Whither* as in F resolves the issue up to a point. Benvolio's *thither* at 86 picks up the *Whither* of Romeo's question just as his *Sups* (84) does Romeo's *supper*.

63–71] *Dyce (Capell); prose Q1–4, F (passim italics except for proper names)*   63, 66, 70 *Signor] Rowe subst.; Seigneur Q1–4, F*   63 *daughters] Q1–4; daughter F*   64 *Anselm] Q1–4, F; Anselmo Dyce² (Capell)*   65 *Vitruvio] F3; Vtruuio Q1–4, F; Utruvio Q5*   69 *and] Q1; not in Q2–4, F*   71 *lively] Q1–4, F; lovely Rowe*   74 Whither? To supper?] *Q1–4 (Whither [Whether Q1] to supper?), F; Whither? / SERVINGMAN To supper Theobald (Warburton); Whither? / SERVINGMAN To our house Capell*

SERVINGMAN   To our house.   75
ROMEO   Whose house?
SERVINGMAN   My master's.
ROMEO   Indeed, I should have asked thee that before.
SERVINGMAN   Now I'll tell you without asking. My
   master is the great rich Capulet, and if you be not of   80
   the house of Montagues, I pray come and crush a cup
   of wine. Rest you merry.   [*Exit.*]
BENVOLIO

   At this same ancient feast of Capulet's
   Sups the fair Rosaline whom thou so loves,
   With all the admired beauties of Verona.   85
   Go thither, and with unattainted eye
   Compare her face with some that I shall show,
   And I will make thee think thy swan a crow.
ROMEO

   When the devout religion of mine eye
   Maintains such falsehood, then turn tears to fires,   90
   And these who, often drowned, could never die,
   Transparent heretics, be burnt for liars.
   One fairer than my love! The all-seeing sun
   Ne'er saw her match since first the world begun.

---

81 **crush** drink, quaff (cited under *OED*
   v. 7)
86 **unattainted** unprejudiced (cited
   under *OED ppl. a.*)
88 **swan a crow** a proverbial expression (Dent, S1028). The counterpoint
   between white and black anticipates
   the imagery of Romeo's first sight
   of Juliet in 1.5, down to the use of
   the word 'crow': 'So shows a snowy
   dove trooping with crows / As
   yonder lady o'er her fellows shows'
   (1.5.47–8).

89–94 While applying devotional imagery
   to romantic love was not unusual, the
   conceit of Romeo's eyes as two hardy
   heretics (*often drowned* but never dying)
   that deserve burning at the stake for
   apostasy if they betray their first love
   verges on the metaphysical (John
   Donne deploys just such mystical conceits in his poem 'The Canonization').
   The lines form a sestet (*ababcc*), as does
   Benvolio's reply.
90 ***fires** after Pope, who changes 'fire' in
   Q and F to *fires*, to rhyme with 'liars'

78 thee] *Q1;* you *Q2–4, F*   82 SD] *F; not in Q1–4*   90 fires] *Pope;* fire *Q1–4, F*

BENVOLIO

Tut, you saw her fair none else being by,   95
Herself poised with herself in either eye.
But in that crystal scales let there be weighed
Your lady's love against some other maid
That I will show you shining at this feast,
And she shall scant show well that now seems best.   100

ROMEO

I'll go along no such sight to be shown,
But to rejoice in splendour of mine own.   [*Exeunt.*]

[1.3]   *Enter* CAPULET'S WIFE *and* NURSE.

CAPULET'S WIFE

Nurse, where's my daughter? Call her forth to me.

NURSE

Now by my maidenhead at twelve year old,
I bade her come. What, lamb! What, ladybird!

95–100 Benvolio's sestet follows a different rhyme scheme (*eeffgg*) from Romeo's and from the one he himself used at 44–9. Romeo's first rhyme *eye/ die* (89, 91) recalls the rhyme at 48–9, and *eye* occurs again in the *a* rhyme of Benvolio's next sestet at 95–6.

95 **Tut** See 1.1.195n. This is Benvolio's second tutting; the other two tuts in the play are uttered by Romeo and Mercutio.

97 **that crystal scales** The conjunction of singular and plural (*that . . . scales*) is permissible in Elizabethan usage. The metaphor of eyes as *Transparent heretics* (92) and *crystal scales* underlines how much *RJ* is a play about gazing, with eyes the portals of the soul.

102 **splendour . . . own** Romeo claims that, far from dispelling Rosaline from

his mind, the sight of other women will further bring home to him her superior beauty, which will fill him with joy.

1.3 Sunday evening (101–2) in the private apartments of the Capulets' house. The scene is largely Shakespeare's invention.

2 **by . . . old** Nurse is certain that she was still a virgin at the age of 12 but cannot vouch for it beyond that. Juliet loses her virginity at the age of 13.

3 **bade her** told her to
ladybird Nurse's use of *ladybird* has been suspected of being a slip, since the word could apparently denote a wanton, but *OED* lists it only as a term of endearment, citing this passage. Nurse adores her young charge, who is a substitute daughter.

---

97 that] *Q1–4, F;* those *Rowe*   98 lady's love] *Q1–4, F;* Lady–love *Theobald;* lady love *Capell*   maid] *Q1, F;* maide: *Q2;* maid, *Q3–4*   100 she . . . well] *Q1–4;* she shew scant shell, well, *F (var.);* she shew scant shell, well, *F (var.1);* she shall scant shell, well, *F (var.2);* shele shew scant, well, *F2*   seems] *Q1–2;* shewes *Q3–4, F*   102 SD] *Pope*   **1.3**] *Capell*   1+ SP] *Oxf; Wife. Q1–4, F; Lady Capulet / Rowe*   2–79] *Nurse's lines are in italics, except for proper names Q1–4*   2–4] *Johnson;* prose *Q1–4, F*   3 bade] *Q1–3, F (*bad*);* had *Q4*

God forbid, where's this girl? What, Juliet!

Enter JULIET.

JULIET   How now, who calls?   5
NURSE   Your mother.
JULIET
        Madam, I am here. What is your will?
CAPULET'S WIFE
        This is the matter. – Nurse, give leave awhile,
        We must talk in secret. Nurse, come back again.
        I have remembered me, thou's hear our counsel.   10
        Thou knowest my daughter's of a pretty age.
NURSE
        Faith, I can tell her age unto an hour.
CAPULET'S WIFE
        She's not fourteen.
NURSE   I'll lay fourteen of my teeth,
        And yet, to my teen be it spoken, I have but four,
        She's not fourteen. How long is it now   15
        To Lammastide?
CAPULET'S WIFE   A fortnight and odd days.

---

4   Juliet's first entrance in the play is comically delayed by her stubborn, headstrong unwillingness to be torn away from whatever she was doing.
8   **give leave** a request for privacy
10 **thou's** colloquial contraction of 'thou shalt' (cited under Abbott, 461), with 'shall' used here for 'will' (Abbott, 315) or 'must' (cf. 1.5.75)
11 **pretty age** Juliet is of an age where certain issues can be discussed, notably County Paris' courtship of her.
13 **lay** wager, bet (*OED v.*[1] 12a)
14–15   **teen . . . fourteen** playing on *four* (Nurse's teeth) and *teen* (= sorrow),

adding up to the not quite *fourteen* years of Juliet and anticipating the *teen* awaiting Juliet.
16 **Lammastide** a harvest festival starting on 1 August. The linking of Juliet's birth to Lammastide and its association with reaping and first corn fits with the promise of bounty and fruitful marriage. The calendar references and discussion of Juliet's age signal, for the second time, her extreme youth (see 1.2.8–11), and provide the play with a setting towards the middle of July, 'A fortnight and odd days' short of 31 July.

8 SP] *Oxf; W: Q1; Wife. Q2–4, F; Lady Capulet / Rowe*   8–11] *Capell; prose Q1–4, F*   13–16 I'll . . . Lammastide] *Steevens; prose Q1–4; mislined verse F (*teeth, / spoken, / fourteen. / tide? /)
14 teen] *Q1–4, F; teeth F2*

NURSE

Even or odd of all days in the year,
Come Lammas Eve at night shall she be fourteen.
Susan and she, God rest all Christian souls,
Were of an age. Well, Susan is with God;   20
She was too good for me. But as I said,
On Lammas Eve at night shall she be fourteen,
That shall she, marry! I remember it well.
'Tis since the earthquake now eleven years,
And she was weaned, I never shall forget it,   25
Of all the days of the year upon that day.
For I had then laid wormwood to my dug,
Sitting in the sun under the dovehouse wall.
My lord and you were then at Mantua.

17ff. Coleridge (146) suggests that Nurse's essentially 'uncultivated mind' causes her to recollect the past 'wholly by coincident images' rather than by 'certain regular trains of cause and effect'.

17 **Even or odd** a comically pedantic correction by Nurse of Juliet's mother's *odd days*, meaning a few

19 **Susan** Nurse's daughter has an oddly Protestant English name for a Veronese baby. Shakespeare uses 'Susan' twice only, both times in this play, the other Susan being the servant girl Susan Grindstone (see 1.5.9). 'Susan' was a relative newcomer among English names at the time. Among the first Susans in Stratford-upon-Avon was Shakespeare's own daughter Susanna, who was coincidentally 13 years old when Q1 of *RJ* was being printed. Similarly, Nurse's daughter Susan would have been 13 if she had lived, since she was born at the same time as Juliet: see pp. 5, 38–9.

24 A tantalizing passage of Shakespeare's invention, and commonly used to justify different dates for the play; see pp. 36–7.

25–63 These lines are inspired by a col-

ourful passsage of gossip in Brooke (650ff.), in which Nurse tells Romeo that, as Juliet's wet-nurse, she frequently, gently, smacked the baby Juliet's bottom before immediately kissing it better: 'And gladder then was I of such a kiss forsooth / Than I had been to have a kiss of some old lecher's mouth. / And thus of Juliet's youth began this prating nurse / And of her present state to make a tedious long discourse' (650–3).

25 **weaned** Juliet's weaning on the day of the earthquake sounds a foreboding note. Nurse draws attention to it with 'Of all the days of the year' (26).

27 **wormwood** absinth, a bitter-tasting plant extract used medicinally and to flavour drinks. Nurse applied it to her nipple so that Juliet would reject it (cited in *OED*).
    dug nipple

28 **dovehouse** dovecote

29 **Mantua** Shakespeare gets his Italian geography right here, since Verona and Mantua are neighbouring towns (in *Two Gentlemen of Verona*, *Taming of the Shrew* and *The Tempest* he does

17–49] *Capell; prose Q1–4, F*   18 shall] *Q1, Q3–4, F; stal Q2*   23 That] *Q1–3, F; then Q4*

Nay, I do bear a brain. But as I said,   30
When it did taste the wormwood on the nipple
Of my dug and felt it bitter, pretty fool,
To see it tetchy and fall out with the dug!
'Shake', quoth the dovehouse. 'Twas no need, I trow,
To bid me trudge.   35
And since that time it is eleven years,
For then she could stand high-lone; nay, by th' rood,
She could have run and waddled all about,
For even the day before she broke her brow.
And then my husband – God be with his soul,   40
'A was a merry man – took up the child:
'Yea,' quoth he, 'dost thou fall upon thy face?
Thou wilt fall backward when thou hast more wit,

not). The curious detail of Juliet's parents' stay in Mantua on the day she ceased to be a baby rhymes with Romeo's exile later in the same city after their wedding night. As infant and teenage wife she is alone on two of the most important days of her life.

30 Nay . . . brain The phrase is spoken perhaps in response to expressions of impatience by her interlocutors, who are wondering where this garrulous monologue is leading. Having made her point, Nurse launches back into tales of little Juliet with renewed vigour.

31–3 The use here of *it* for Juliet is affectionately diminutive; she is a baby rather than a little girl: see *pretty fool* at 32.

34 'Shake' The dovecote did not, of course, speak but shook from the tremor, which caused Nurse to make a speedy getaway from its wall (in case it collapsed on top of her).
I trow 'Believe you me' (*OED v.* 4b); a mild colloquial expletive, one of

Nurse's assertive mannerisms; see also 2.5.61.

35 trudge leave, get out; see also 1.2.33n.; a ponderous walk is befitting to Nurse, whom Juliet later calls *lame* (2.5.4).

36 At this point in the text Q2 switches back to Shakespeare's MS after setting from Q1.

37 high-lone 'quite alone, without support' (cited in *OED*)
by th' rood 'by Christ's cross' (see similarly *Ham* 3.4.13)

38 could have was able to

39 broke her brow cut her forehead (when she fell); as if being weaned on the day of the earthquake were not ominous enough (cited under *OED* break *v.* 5b). Nurse relates all these as trivial domestic incidents, but they stack up against Juliet's prospects of happiness.

41 'A he; with the ellipsis fitting Nurse's rushed speech (Abbott, 402)

43 fall backward a ribald innuendo by Nurse's husband

33 with the] *Q2–4, F; with Q1;* wi'th' *Riv²*   36 eleven] *Q2–4 (a leuen), F (a eleuen), Q1 (a leauen)*   37 high-lone] *Q2 (hylone), Q1 (high lone); a lone Q3; alone Q4, F*

Wilt thou not, Jule?' And by my holidam,
The pretty wretch left crying and said 'Ay'.   45
To see now how a jest shall come about!
I warrant, an I should live a thousand years,
I never should forget it. 'Wilt thou not, Jule?' quoth he,
And, pretty fool, it stinted and said 'Ay'.

CAPULET'S WIFE

Enough of this, I pray thee, hold thy peace.   50

NURSE

Yes, madam, yet I cannot choose but laugh,
To think it should leave crying and say 'Ay';
And yet, I warrant, it had upon it brow
A bump as big as a young cockerel's stone;
A perilous knock, and it cried bitterly.   55
'Yea,' quoth my husband, 'fall'st upon thy face?
Thou wilt fall backward when thou comest to age,
Wilt thou not, Jule?' It stinted and said 'Ay'.

JULIET

And stint thou too, I pray thee, Nurse, say I.

NURSE

Peace, I have done. God mark thee to his grace,   60

---

44 **holidam** holiness (*OED* gives halidom). See similarly 'By my halidom'
in *TGV* 4.2.132, which Ard² glosses
as 'bless me'. The word was popularly
thought to be compounded of 'holy'
and 'dame' (= the Virgin Mary), in
which case it could be glossed as 'by
our Lady' (Crystal, *Words*, gives 'what
I hold holy' for 'holidam').
45 **wretch** little creature; playfully depre-
ciative (cited under *OED sb.* 2e)
46 i.e. the remark made in jest by Nurse's
husband has now come true, since
Juliet is to be married.
47 **an** if; and again at 62
49 **stinted** stopped (crying)

50 SP Capulet's Wife is abruptly called
'*Old La.*' here in Q2. Up until this
point she has been '*Wife*' four times
in this scene (at 1, 8, 13, 16), all of
them occurring before 36, the point
where Q1 and MS reconnect; see
p. 99.
53 **it brow** *it* = its (Abbott, 228); see
similarly 'That it's had it head bit off
by it young' (*KL* 1.4.207).
54 **stone** testicle
59 **say I** Juliet echoes Nurse's previous
line and her *said 'Ay'*.
60 **God . . . grace** 'May God single you
out as a specially favoured person';
grace here = favour

44 Jule] *Q2–4, F; Iuliet Q1* 46 now] *Q2–4, F; not in Q1* 47 should] *Q2, Q1; shall Q3–4, F
(shall)* 48 Jule] *Q2–4, F; Iuliet Q1; Iulet F* 50–8] *Q2–4, F; not in Q1* 50 SP] *Oxf; Old La. Q2–4,
F; not in Q1* 58 Jule] *Q2–4, F; Iuliet Q1* 60–3] *Pope; prose Q2–4, F, Q1*

Thou wast the prettiest babe that e'er I nursed.
An I might live to see thee married once,
I have my wish.

CAPULET'S WIFE

Marry, that 'marry' is the very theme
I came to talk of. Tell me, daughter Juliet,   65
How stands your dispositions to be married?

JULIET

It is an honour that I dream not of.

NURSE

An honour! Were not I thine only nurse,
I would say thou hadst sucked wisdom from thy teat.

CAPULET'S WIFE

Well, think of marriage now. Younger than you,   70
Here in Verona, ladies of esteem,
Are made already mothers. By my count,
I was your mother much upon these years
That you are now a maid. Thus then in brief:
The valiant Paris seeks you for his love.   75

NURSE

A man, young lady; lady, such a man

---

62 **once** some day
64 **Marry** an interjection common at the
   time (*OED int.* b)
66 **stands . . . dispositions** The accord
   of singular verb and plural noun is
   permissible in the English of the
   period and 'extremely common in the
   Folio' (Abbott, 333).
67, 68 ***honour** the reading in Q1,
   whereas Q2–4 and F, followed by
   some modern editions, have 'houre';
   see p. 339.
68–9 **Were . . . teat** more of Nurse's
   earthy humour, implying with pride
   – while pretending otherwise – that it

was from her milk that Juliet drew her
natural intelligence.
69 **thy teat** i.e. the teat from which you
   sucked as a baby
70–2 **Younger . . . mothers** Juliet is old
   enough to have a baby, according to
   her mother, whose reference to *ladies
   of esteem* suggests that in the Verona of
   the play well-bred women marry young.
72 **By my count** spoken in jest, perhaps,
   because the sentence that follows
   would make her 26 years old, oddly
   contrasting with her use of *old age* at
   5.3.207; see List of Roles, 3n., and
   pp. 4–5.

61 wast] *Q2–4, F; wert Q1*   62 An] *Q2–4, F; not in Q1*   I might] *Q2–4, F; might I Q1*   live] *Q2–4,*
F; but liue Q1   64 SP] *Oxf; Old La. Q2–4, F; Wife: Q1*   66 dispositions] *Q2–4; disposition F; not*
in Q1   67, 68 honour] *Q1; houre Q2–4 (houre 68), F*   68–9] *Pope; prose Q2–4, F, Q1*   68 thine]
Q2–3, F; not in Q4; thy Q1   70 SP] *Oxf; Old La. Q2–4, F; Wife: Q1*   76–7] *Pope; prose Q2–4, F, Q1*

As all the world – why, he's a man of wax.

CAPULET'S WIFE

Verona's summer has not such a flower.

NURSE

Nay, he's a flower, in faith, a very flower.

CAPULET'S WIFE

What say you, can you love the gentleman?   80
This night you shall behold him at our feast.
Read o'er the volume of young Paris' face,
And find delight writ there with beauty's pen;
Examine every married lineament,
And see how one another lends content;   85
And what obscured in this fair volume lies
Find written in the margent of his eyes.
This precious book of love, this unbound lover,
To beautify him only lacks a cover.
The fish lives in the sea, and 'tis much pride   90

77 **of wax** used here in emphatic commendation (cited under *OED* wax *sb.*[1]). Ard[2] quotes from *Euphues and his England*: 'you make . . . your lover . . . so exquisite that for shape he must be framed in wax' (Lyly, *Works*, 2.166).

82–95 *Read* leads ponderously to finding, examining and seeing the hidden treasures of Paris, whose inner rich self (the *golden story*) needs an equally beautiful outer binding (*gold clasps*), Juliet; she will be the cover to Paris' book. Pope harshly called the lines 'ridiculous'. Juliet later compares Romeo's face to a book when learning the news of Tybalt's death: 'Was ever book containing such vile matter / So fairly bound?' (3.2.83–4).

84–5 'Note how harmoniously joined up his features are and how they complement one another' (cited under *OED* married *a.* 2).

85 **content** contènt; satisfaction through mutual complementing as well as giv-

ing substance one to the other

87 **the margent . . . eyes** the marginal annotations which his eyes are in relation to the main body of the volume that is Paris' face (*OED* margent *sb.* 1 glosses 'A commentary, summary, or annotation in the margin of a text' and cites this line). If Juliet desires to know more than is revealed by Paris' face, she should gaze into his eyes. The conceit of Paris' eyes as an additional, if 'marginal', source of knowledge underlines the difference between this laboured ritual and the spontaneity of love at first sight.

89 **him** The personal pronoun can apply freely to the book or the lover or, as here, to both.

90–1 To say that fish live in the sea is to affirm that they are in their element, hence the implied thought that it is the most natural thing in the world for a beautiful wife (*fair without*) to be the exterior cover of a noble and great-hearted man (*fair within*). Juliet's

78, 80, 97 SPs] *Oxf; Old La. Q2–4, F; Wife. Q1*   80–96] *not in Q1*   84 married] *Q2; seuerall Q3–4, F*

154

For fair without the fair within to hide.
That book in many's eyes doth share the glory
That in gold clasps locks in the golden story.
So shall you share all that he doth possess,
By having him, making yourself no less.   95

NURSE

No less? Nay, bigger – women grow by men.

CAPULET'S WIFE

Speak briefly, can you like of Paris' love?

JULIET

I'll look to like, if looking liking move,
But no more deep will I endart mine eye
Than your consent gives strength to make it fly.   100

Enter Serving[man].

SERVINGMAN   Madam, the guests are come, supper served
up, you called, my young lady asked for, the Nurse
cursed in the pantry, and everything in extremity. I
must hence to wait; I beseech you follow straight.   [*Exit.*]

CAPULET'S WIFE

We follow thee. Juliet, the County stays.   105

---

mother asserts that since women's physical beauty and men's inner nobility perfectly reflect and complement each other, her daughter should look favourably on Paris' suit.

96 **bigger** pregnant

98 Juliet's use of *look* picks up the undercurrent of eyes and physical attraction from her mother's lines, but her use of future tense and conditional clause do not augur well for Juliet and Paris.

99 **endart** cited in *OED*, the prefix *en–* acting as intensifier. Juliet compares

her eyes' power to Cupid's arrows, which sink into lovers' hearts and drive them mad; cf. *MND* 3.2.440–1, where Cupid is called 'a knavish lad' who makes 'poor females mad'. Juliet's confident asseveration that she will love according to parental *consent* and rules is profoundly ironic in retrospect.

103 **cursed** because she should be helping out in the pantry rather than gossiping with Juliet and her mother, as all hands are required for the party preparations

96 Nay, bigger –] *F* (nay bigger:); Nay, bigger *Q2–4*   99 endart] *Q2–4, F;* engage *Q1*   100 it] *Q1, Q4; not in Q2–3, F*   100.1] *Q2–4 (Enter Seruing.), F (Enter a Seruing man.); Enter Clowne. Q1*   104 SD] *F*   105 SP] *Oxf; Mo. Q2–4, F*

NURSE

Go, girl, seek happy nights to happy days.   *Exeunt.*

[1.4]   *Enter* ROMEO, MERCUTIO, BENVOLIO,
              with five or six other Masquers, Torchbearers.

ROMEO

What, shall this speech be spoke for our excuse,
Or shall we on without apology?

BENVOLIO

The date is out of such prolixity.
We'll have no Cupid hoodwinked with a scarf,
Bearing a Tartar's painted bow of lath,   5

1.4 Sunday evening at dusk (1.2.19, 1.4.43), a street outside the Capulets' house (the scene is not in the sources)

0.1–2 Mercutio enters the play here, probably not masked (29–30). He is among the invited guests to the Capulets' party along with his brother Valentine, a 'ghost' character (see 1.2.67). Mercutio is not identified by name until 95, by which time he has delivered the Queen Mab speech and ribbed Romeo about love and sex. The masquers and torchbearers are probably different people (see Romeo's 'Give me a torch', 11), even though the SD in Q2, which separates them only by a comma, might suggest otherwise. Altogether some 12 or 13 people seem to enter here.

1–2 The topic of conversation has now shifted away from Rosaline and the beauty of other women to the traditional greeting of the masquers. Romeo's *excuse* or *apology* probably refer to the custom of a presenter introducing the masquers to their host at parties.

3 'Such long-windedness (*prolixity*) is no longer fashionable.'

4 Cupid . . . scarf another reference

to the proverbially blind Cupid, the implication being that Romeo and Benvolio should dispense with conventional Cupids as much as with outdated introductions.

5 Tartar's . . . bow a reference to the Mongols ('Tartars'), whose legendary archers and horsemen conquered large parts of Asia and Eastern Europe under their leader Genghis Khan in the 13th century. The Tartar bow was much more powerful than the one favoured by English archers (Ard²). Cupid's *Tartar's . . . bow* is a sign of love's power, cruelty and lightning speed; Puck's claim to be 'Swifter than arrow from the Tartar's bow' (*MND* 3.2.101) proves that Shakespeare can trust his audience to recognize his bow and arrow as the epitome of speed. References to 'Tartar limbo', reputedly 'worse than hell' (*CE* 4.2.32), 'flinty Tartar's bosom' (*AW* 4.4.7) and 'Tartars never train'd / To offices of tender courtesy' (*MV* 4.1.32–3) suggest that he also associated Tartars with cruelty.

lath literally, a narrow piece of wood; here, 'the material of a counterfeit weapon' (cited under *OED sb.* 2)

1.4] Steevens   0.1–2] Q2–4, F; *Enter Maskers with* Romeo *and a Page. Q1*   3 SP] Q2–4, F, Q1; *Mer. (Capell)*

Scaring the ladies like a crow-keeper;
Nor no without-book prologue, faintly spoke
After the prompter, for our entrance.
But let them measure us by what they will,
We'll measure them a measure and be gone.   10

ROMEO

Give me a torch. I am not for this ambling,
Being but heavy I will bear the light.

MERCUTIO

Nay, gentle Romeo, we must have you dance.

ROMEO

Not I, believe me. You have dancing shoes
With nimble soles, I have a soul of lead   15
So stakes me to the ground I cannot move.

MERCUTIO

You are a lover; borrow Cupid's wings,
And soar with them above a common bound.

---

6 **crow-keeper** either someone guarding cornfields from rooks, or a scarecrow; probably the former, and denoting a rustic profession associated with lowly status and, by Shakespeare, with clumsiness, as in Lear's 'That fellow handles his bow like a crow-keeper' (*KL* 4.6.87–8). The result is the same, namely, to send young females scattering in a flurry.

7–8 *These two lines have been imported into Q2 from Q1 since the time of Pope. They connect with the young men's decision not to be formally presented to their hosts. Conflating the admission to the Capulets' party with the theatrical entrance of an actor fits perfectly with the local context; the non-existent presenter of the masquers merges into a spurned Prologue before a play (*without-book*) who does not even know his lines and therefore has to parrot the prompter. Benvolio vows that the two of them will forgo fakery or artifice and instead be true to themselves.

9–10 with a pun on *measure* meaning dance (*OED* measure *sb.* 15); i.e. they will dance a bit and then leave while pretending not to care how they are received.

11 **ambling** dancing, moving about gaily, light-footed, anticipating the pun on *light* in the following line

12 **heavy** heavy-hearted, with a *soul of lead* (15)

16 **stakes ... ground** fastens me to the ground as if by a stake (cited under *OED v.*[1] 3c)

18 **soar ... bound** leap much higher than is normal; *bound* picks up *ground* from 16 in a cross-line internal rhyme.

7–8] *Q1; not in Q2–4, F*   16 move] *Q2–4, F; stirre Q1*

ROMEO

I am too sore empierced with his shaft
To soar with his light feathers, and so bound   20
I cannot bound a pitch above dull woe;
Under love's heavy burden do I sink.

MERCUTIO

And to sink in it should you burden love,
Too great oppression for a tender thing.

ROMEO

Is love a tender thing? It is too rough,   25
Too rude, too boisterous, and it pricks like thorn.

MERCUTIO

If love be rough with you, be rough with love;
Prick love for pricking, and you beat love down.
Give me a case to put my visage in,
A visor for a visor! What care I   30

19–20 **I . . . feathers** prompted by the reference to Cupid's wings, which are replicated in the feathers that allow his arrows to *soar* and render *sore*. By hitting their target they paralyse the lover who, now *sore*, can no longer *soar*.

19 **empierced** empiercèd; transfixed

21 **pitch** the height from which a bird of prey swoops down on its quarry (*OED* pitch *sb.*[2] 21a), prompted by *soar* in the preceding line, which sets up an opposition between *soar* and *bound*, predicated on their possible identical meanings. The image of young men soaring prior to pouncing on young women graphically renders the predatory nature of sex. Images from hawking also shape the relationship of Kate and Petruchio in *The Taming of the Shrew.*

23 SP *In Q2 the SP for this speech (23–4) is '*Horatio.*', a name that clearly stood in Shakespeare's MS. Williams suggests that 'Horatio' may be the name of one of the masquers (GWW, private communication).

23–4 For an analogous image, see Donne's mystical love and sex lyric 'Air and Angels' (15–18): 'Whilst thus to ballast love I thought, / And so more steadily to have gone, / With wares which would sink admiration, / I saw I had love's pinnace overfraught'.

26 **boisterous** painfully rough (cited in *OED*)

28 Mercutio turns Romeo's innocent reference to the pricking of thorns into a piece of bawdy persiflage, advising Romeo to use his 'prick' and thus lay love to rest. On 'prick' and sex in the period, cf. 'pricked thee out for women's pleasure' (*Son* 20.13) and see *OED*, which cites a 1592 usage, 'The pissing boy lift up his prick'.

29 **case** mask

30 **visor . . . visor** more raillery by Mercutio, this time self-deprecating his looks by alluding to the proverb 'A well-favoured visor will hide her ill-favoured face' (Dent, V92)

20 so bound] *Q2–4;* to bound *F; not in Q1*   23 SP] *Q4; Horatio. Q2–3; Hora. F*

What curious eye doth quote deformities?
Here are the beetle brows shall blush for me.

BENVOLIO

Come, knock and enter, and no sooner in
But every man betake him to his legs.

ROMEO

A torch for me. Let wantons light of heart   35
Tickle the senseless rushes with their heels,
For I am proverbed with a grandsire phrase:
I'll be a candleholder and look on,
The game was ne'er so fair, and I am dun.

MERCUTIO

Tut, dun's the mouse, the constable's own word.   40

31 **curious** closely observant and discriminating (*OED a.* 3 quotes this line and glosses 'Careful or nice in observation or investigation, accurate'). The image is of a supercilious fop scrutinizing people's appearance for faults.
quote deformities point out blemishes

32 **beetle brows** The mask he has just borrowed has prominent heavy eyebrows. The phrase is commonly suggestive of a lowering or sullen appearance, a look which is part of Mercutio's devil-may-care act (*OED* cites first usage of 'beetle-browed' in Langland, 1362).

34 **betake . . . legs** start to dance

35 **A torch** Romeo repeats his earlier request for a torch, adamant that he will not dance. The dancers and torchbearers linger outside the Capulets' house in spite of Benvolio's urging them to knock and enter.

36 an erotically suggestive circumlocution for dancing. Straw rushes were used on the floor in well-to-do Elizabethan homes on festive occasions (and at the coronation of Henry V in *2H4* 5.5.1).

37 **proverbed** furnished with a proverbial phrase (this is the only example *OED* cites under proverb *v.* 2)
grandsire phrase sage or venerable old saying; the following line is a paraphrase of the proverb 'He that worst may must hold the candle' (Dent, C40), and applies to Romeo's self-imposed austerity.

39–40 Dent compares proverbial 'When Play (game, jest) is best it is time to leave' (P399). Romeo's point is that he is not in a festive mood but *dun*, i.e. dingy and brown, the opposite of fair (see 'dun' versus 'white' in *Son* 130); hence merrymaking, dancing and courting (*The game*) are not for him. There is a further pun on 'done' = finished: because of Rosaline, Romeo has 'done' with all that romantic nonsense.

40 **dun's the mouse** The phrase is perhaps attributed to the constable because it may have meant 'Peace; be still' (Malone, Var, 58), 'Be quiet, lie low'. It recalls the proverbial expression 'When all candles be out all cats be gray', because at night it is impossible to tell villains and upright people apart.

31 quote] *Q3–4, F;* cote *Q2;* coate *Q1*   34 betake] *Q2, Q4, F;* betakes *Q3*   39 dun] *Q3–4;* dum *Q2;* done *F, Q1*

If thou art dun, we'll draw thee from the mire
Or, save your reverence, love, wherein thou stickest
Up to the ears. Come, we burn daylight, ho!

ROMEO

Nay, that's not so.

MERCUTIO   I mean, sir, in delay

We waste our lights, in vain light lights by day.   45

Take our good meaning, for our judgement sits

Five times in that ere once in our five wits.

ROMEO

And we mean well in going to this masque,

---

41 In the period, 'Dun' could be a proper
name for a horse, rather like 'Dobbin'
later. Behind Mercutio's line lies the
proverbial expression 'Dun is in the
mire', which means 'things are at a
stand-still or deadlock' (*OED* dun *sb.*[1],
which cites 39–41). 'Dun is in the
mire' also seems to have been an old
Christmas game in which a log would
take the place of the cart-horse Dun
and be dumped in the middle of the
room, from where the revellers would
try to retrieve it, the trick being to
make the game last until everyone had
had a chance to pull and tug and with
as many falls on toes as possible (Var,
58–9).

42 **save your reverence** 'begging your
pardon'; corresponding to modern
'Pardon my French', suggesting
that Mercutio is about to give an
obscene synonym for *mire*, namely
human waste (see *OED* sir-reverence
= 'Human excrement', citing Robert
Greene, 1592: 'His face . . . and his
Necke, were all besmeared with the
soft sirreuerence, so as he stunk').
Instead, Mercutio says *love*, while
implying that Romeo might as well be
up to his neck in faecal matter.

43 **burn daylight** a proverbial phrase for

lighting candles during daylight hours.
He means that they are wasting time as
surely as if they were wastefully using
candles during the day.

45 ***light . . . day*** Punctuation and text
here follow Williams, who shifts the
comma from its place in Q2, after *in
vain*, to before it, thus providing at one
stroke 'an easy and natural reading'
(109). The crux lies in Q2's dittograph
'lights lights', which in Q1 is 'like
Lampes' and which Johnson changed
to 'like lights'. Shedding a single *s* in
the first 'lights' turns the plural noun
into an optative verb and renders the
line perfectly intelligible.

46 **good meaning** intended sense
(implying: 'which you, Romeo, know
full well even though you pretend not
to')

46–7 ***for . . . wits*** This perhaps means
that there is better sense (*judgement*) in
plain speaking (*good meaning*) than in
the joint effort of the five senses and
our mental faculties. Mercutio is tiring
of the battle of wits between Romeo
and himself and proposes a truce now
that he has had his sallies thrown back
at him. Q2 has 'fine' for *five*, probably
a turned letter in the forme of type (for
five wits see 2.4.72n.).

---

42 your] *F; you Q2–4;* this *Q1*   45 waste . . . light lights] *Williams;* waste our lights in vaine, lights
lights *Q2–4, F;* burne our lights by night, like Lampes *Q1;* waste our lights in vain, like lights
Johnson   47 five] *Malone (Wilbraham);* fine *Q2–4, F;* right *Q1*

But 'tis no wit to go.
MERCUTIO   Why, may one ask?
ROMEO
I dreamt a dream tonight.
MERCUTIO   And so did I.   50
ROMEO
Well, what was yours?
MERCUTIO   That dreamers often lie.
ROMEO
In bed asleep while they do dream things true.
MERCUTIO
O, then I see Queen Mab hath been with you.
She is the fairies' midwife, and she comes
In shape no bigger than an agate stone   55
On the forefinger of an alderman,
Drawn with a team of little atomi
Over men's noses as they lie asleep.

49 **no wit** bad judgement (because of the feud between their families); playing on Mercutio's claim that *good meaning* (as in Romeo's *we mean well*) is the seat of sound judgement

50 **a dream** We never learn what Romeo's dream was about other than that it was a foreboding of things to come, hence his anxiety about the Capulets' party.

51 **lie** tell untruths and/or lie in bed

53–95 **O . . . she** After the first line of verse, the 37 lines of Mercutio's 42½-line speech on 'Queen Mab' that follow are set as prose in Q2, with the closing 4½ lines as verse. Q1 has verse throughout.

53 **Mab** On *Mab* as a contraction of 'Samaab' (one of the chief earthly 'spirits of the east') in Nashe's *Pierce Penilesse*, see Holmer, 'Nashe', 66–8.

55–6 **agate . . . alderman** The *agate* denotes Mab's microscopic size, while the choice of stone may allude to the agate worn in a seal ring as a symbol of office by aldermen like Shakespeare's father, when he was 'bailiff' or mayor of Stratford-upon-Avon. For Q2's 'Alderman', Q1 has 'Burgomaster', which also means mayor (cf. German 'Bürgermeister'; see also *1H4* 2.1.75).

57 **with** by (Abbott, 193)

*little atomi** the smallest possible particles, *little* acting as an intensifier since *atomi* by itself means 'a diminutive or tiny being' (cited under *OED* atomy *sb.*[1]). Shakespeare uses 'atomy' to describe the skeletal anatomy of the beadle in *2H4* 5.4.29. Holmer ('Nashe', 64) suspects the influence of Nashe's 'the Sunne hath *Atomi*' from *Christ's Tears over Jerusalem* (1593).

53 O] *Q2–4, F;* Ah *Q1*   you.] *Q2–4, F;* you. / *Ben:* Queene Mab whats she? / *Q1*   54–91] *Q1;* prose *Q2–4, F*   55 an] *Q2–4, Q1; not in F*   56 alderman] *Q2–4, F;* Burgomaster *Q1*   57 atomi] *Q1;* ottamie *Q2;* atomies *Q3–4, F*   58 Over] *Q2–4, F;* A thwart *Q1*

161

Her chariot is an empty hazelnut
Made by the joiner squirrel or old grub,   60
Time out o'mind the fairies' coachmakers;
Her wagon-spokes made of long spinners' legs,
The cover of the wings of grasshoppers,
Her traces of the smallest spider web,
Her collars of the moonshine's watery beams,   65
Her whip of cricket's bone, the lash of film,
Her wagoner a small grey-coated gnat,
Not half so big as a round little worm
Pricked from the lazy finger of a maid.
And in this state she gallops night by night   70

59–61 *The absence from Q1 of these lines may suggest that they are an addition or revision in Q2 (see pp. 103–4). The reason for shifting the three lines about Mab's chariot up from their position in Q2–4 is that otherwise 62ff. describe something which does not yet exist.

60 **grub** A 'grub' is a caterpillar, maggot or, in this case, a woodworm; *squirrel* and *grub* are the *fairies' coachmakers* because they provide the nuts and bore holes in them.

62 **spinners'** This probably refers to spiders, although the crane-fly, better known by its popular name of daddy-long-legs, is supported by some editors (e.g. Oxf[1]).

63 **cover** This seems to refer to the gossamer sides of the chariot (cited under *OED sb.*[1] 1); it is hard to account for it if the *empty hazelnut* lines are left where they are in Q2 (see 59–61n.).

65 The insubstantial yokes (*collars*) of the imaginary team drawing Mab's gossamer chariot are made of liquid lunar beams, fantastical like the rest of it.

66 **film** gossamer

67 **wagoner** charioteer

69 **Pricked** removed with a pin or needle (cited under *OED* prick v. 16). Q1 has the blander 'Pickt', but *Pricked* is more dramatic and suggestive.
lazy . . . maid alluding to the folklore belief that idle maids grow worms in their fingers. Var (64) quotes Beaumont's *The Woman Hater* (*c.* 1606), 3.1: 'Keep thy hands in thy muff and warm the idle worms in thy fingers' ends'. Editors commonly prefer Q1's 'maide' over Q2's 'man', which may stem from a misreading of MS, perhaps 'maie' for maiden. But 'maie' for 'maid' occurs nowhere else in the canon, so this line of reasoning may not be secure (Williams, 111).

70–94 On the links between this and Chaucer's *The Parlement of Foules*, see Thompson, 78–9.

70 **in this state** in such pomp and solemnity. The phrase may refer to travelling in state in a coach created by the fairies' chief coachmaker; *OED* (state *sb.* 17c) cites this line and glosses 'in state: with great pomp and solemnity; with a great train; with splendid or honorific trappings and insignia'.

59–61] *Daniel 1875; after 69 Q2–4, F; not in Q1*   64 Her] *Q2–4, F;* The *Q1*   66 film] *F2;* Philome *Q2–4, F;* filmes *Q1*   69 Pricked] *Q2–4, F;* Pickt *Q1*   maid] *Q1;* man *Q2–4, F*   70 state] *Q2–4, F;* sort *Q1*

Through lovers' brains, and then they dream of love;
On courtiers' knees, that dream on curtsies straight;
O'er lawyers' fingers, who straight dream on fees;
O'er ladies lips, who straight on kisses dream,
Which oft the angry Mab with blisters plagues,   75
Because their breaths with sweetmeats tainted are.
Sometime she gallops o'er a courtier's nose,
And then dreams he of smelling out a suit;
And sometime comes she with a tithe-pig's tail,
Tickling a parson's nose as 'a lies asleep;   80
Then he dreams of another benefice.
Sometime she driveth o'er a soldier's neck,
And then dreams he of cutting foreign throats,
Of breaches, ambuscados, Spanish blades,
Of healths five fathom deep; and then anon   85

75–6 **blisters . . . are** Sweetmeats are artificial and deceitful, intended to hide stale breath and decay, even perhaps venereal infection; cf. the definition of 'whore' as 'Sweet-meats which rot the eater; in man's nostril / Poisoned perfumes' (Webster, *The White Devil*, 3.2.80–1).

77 **courtier's nose** A mere five lines earlier, *courtiers' knees* and *curtsies* were visited by Queen Mab, but now it is the turn of their noses and lawsuits to attract her attention. The two separate references to courtiers may suggest that one of them was marked for deletion. Q1 reads 'Lawyers lap' for *courtier's nose* and omits the *lawyers' fingers* of 73, which is why it can bring in the lawyer here without creating its own repetition (two lawyers for two courtiers). It also avoids the replication of *nose* (in Q2 both the courtier's and the parson's noses are mentioned) but it then introduces its own duplicate

reference to lips since *ladies' lips* have already been mentioned at 74.

79 **tithe-pig's tail** A *tithe-pig* was a pig paid in settlement of the tithe or tenth part of all produce pledged to the Church. At the mere thought of a tithe-pig the comfortably fed parson warms to the idea of a further lucrative Church living (*benefice*, 81) with perks.

84 **breaches, ambuscados** gaps in a defensive wall, ambushes
Spanish blades The best-tempered swords were famously made of Toledo steel.

85 **healths . . . deep** drinking of toasts even if the cups were 30 feet (*five fathom*) deep, enough for him to drown in. Silence in *2 Henry IV* pledges to drain his cup 'a mile to th' bottom' (5.3.52). Var (65) quotes Dekker and Webster's *Westward Ho*, 5.1.20–1: 'Troth sir, my master and Sir *Gozlin* are guzzling: they are dabbling together fathom deep.'

---

72 On] *Q2–4, F*; O'er *Q1*   73 dream] *Q2–4*; dreamt *F*   74 on] *Q3–4, F, Q1*; one *Q2*   76 breaths] *Q1*; breath *Q2–4, F*   78 dreams] *Q2, Q4, F, Q1*; dreame *Q3*   79 a] *Q2–4, Q1*; *not in F*   80 parson's] *Q3–4, F, Q1*; Persons *Q2*   as 'a] *Q2–4, F*; that *Q1*   81 he dreams] *Q2–4, F*; dreames he *Q1*

Drums in his ear, at which he starts and wakes,
And being thus frighted, swears a prayer or two
And sleeps again. This is that very Mab
That plaits the manes of horses in the night,
And bakes the elf-locks in foul sluttish hairs,   90
Which once untangled much misfortune bodes.
This is the hag, when maids lie on their backs,
That presses them and learns them first to bear,
Making them women of good carriage.
This is she –
ROMEO   Peace, peace, Mercutio, peace,   95
Thou talk'st of nothing.
MERCUTIO   True, I talk of dreams,
Which are the children of an idle brain,
Begot of nothing but vain fantasy,
Which is as thin of substance as the air,
And more inconstant than the wind who woos   100
Even now the frozen bosom of the north,
And, being angered, puffs away from thence,

---

89 **plaits** intertwines, braids into knots, in a mischievous and aberrant manner, anticipating the next line, which may allude to a disease associated with poverty and lack of hygiene

90 ***bakes the elf-locks** clots hair into a tangled mass of knotted locks, a condition (in humans) for which elves were popularly blamed. It is now known chiefly by its medical name of *plica* or *plica polonica*. The affliction may be linked to venereal infection, hence *foul sluttish*. It was a common superstition that disentangling *elf-locks* brought bad luck. See also Edgar's 'My face I'll grime with filth, / Blanket my loins, elf all my hair in knots' (*KL* 2.3.180–1).

92–4 Mab inspires erotic dreams in virginal young women while they are asleep. She embraces (*presses*) them and teaches (*learns*) them to *bear* lovers which inevitably leads them to bear children and thus become mothers and matrons, 'women of good carriage'; which in turn conjures up a vision of young women with their lovers on top.

95–6 **she – . . . nothing** For the full stop after *she* in Q and F most editors substitute a dash. Mercutio is in full flow when Romeo jumps in with *nothing*, with a probable *double entendre* on *nothing* meaning vagina, following on from Mab's visitation of the maids and from the *tender thing* (the same as 'nothing') of 24–5.

99 **as thin . . . air** proverbial (Dent, A92)

100 **inconstant . . . wind** proverbial (Dent, W412)

86 ear] *Q2–4, Q1;* eares *F* 90 bakes] *Q2–4, F;* plats *Q1;* cakes *Pope* elf-locks] *Q1, Q4;* Elklocks *Q2–3, F*

Turning his side to the dew-dropping south.

BENVOLIO

This wind you talk of blows us from ourselves;

Supper is done, and we shall come too late.   105

ROMEO

I fear too early, for my mind misgives;

Some consequence, yet hanging in the stars,

Shall bitterly begin his fearful date

With this night's revels, and expire the term

Of a despised life closed in my breast   110

By some vile forfeit of untimely death.

But he that hath the steerage of my course

Direct my suit. On, lusty gentlemen.

BENVOLIO

Strike, drum.

---

103 **Turning his side** Q2's 'side' (Q1 has 'face') is endorsed widely by modern editors. It fits well with the pathetic fallacy of imagining the wind as a rebuffed agent, turning from the ice maiden of the north to the deliquescent sensuality of the south. The word 'dew' occurs repeatedly, alone and compounded, in Shakespeare, associated with tears as well as life-dispensing and regenerative liquid and fresh beauty; see Romeo's tears 'augmenting the fresh morning's dew' (1.1.130), 'the morning silver melting dew' in *Luc* (24), Puck's 'dew-drops' which are pearls (*MND* 2.1.14–15) and 'the morn and liquid dew of youth' in *Ham* 1.3.40.

104 Benvolio reminds Mercutio of the fact that he is himself full of hot air, not unlike the winds blowing from the south, and that this is sweeping them off course (*from ourselves*), their destination being the Capulets' party.

107 **consequence** momentous event (*OED sb.* 6)

109–11 **expire ... term ... forfeit** All

three words are legal jargon pertaining to the law of contract.

110 **despised** despisèd

112 **he** In the context of destiny and star-crossed love, it is tempting to interpret *he* as the Deity, in which case modern usage would require capital 'H', although none of the Qs and Fs uses a capital (Var and Penguin do). But Romeo probably means 'Love', as Williams (111) argues, referring to the exchange between Romeo and Juliet in the balcony scene. To Juliet's 'By whose direction found'st thou out this place?' Romeo replies 'By love, that first did prompt me to enquire. / He lent me counsel' (2.2.79–81).

113 **suit** A number of editors follow Q1 here which reads 'saile' for Q2's 'sute', because 'sail' ties in well with the nautical metaphors of *steerage* and puffing winds. But 'suit' occurs twice in Brooke (68, 79) and is almost certainly the reading of the MS behind Q2. Romeo is prepared to attend the party because at the Capulets' that night 'Sups the fair Rosaline' (1.2.84).

103 side] *Q2–4, F;* face *Q1*   113 suit] *Q2–4, F;* saile *Q1*

[1.5] *They march about the stage, and*
Servingmen *come forth with napkins.*

HEAD SERVINGMAN Where's Potpan, that he helps not to
take away? He shift a trencher, he scrape a trencher!

1 SERVINGMAN When good manners shall lie all in one or
two men's hands, and they unwashed too, 'tis a foul
thing.   5

HEAD SERVINGMAN Away with the join-stools, remove
the court-cupboard, look to the plate. Good thou, save
me a piece of marchpane and, as thou loves me, let the
porter let in Susan Grindstone, and Nell, Anthony
and Potpan.   10

2 SERVINGMAN Ay, boy, ready.

HEAD SERVINGMAN You are looked for, and called for,

1.5 Sunday night (1.2.19) in the ballroom
of the Capulets' house. The action
in Q2 is continuous here (as at 2.2
below), but most editors mark a new
scene; this edition follows that pattern
for convenience of reference. Q1 cuts
straight from the end of the previous
scene to Capulet's welcome, as do most
performances.

1 Potpan The name describes a menial
kitchen hand who scours pots and pans
(which he is failing to do here). *OED*
compares Grumio's 'Now, were not I a
little pot and soon hot' (*TS* 4.1.5).

2 take away They are clearing up after
supper in readiness for the dance.
He . . . trencher Potpan ought to get
on with these chores, the exclamation
mark denoting an invitation for him to
do so; a *trencher* is a wooden plate or
platter.

3–5 It is a deplorably *foul thing* that only
one or two of the kitchen staff have
manners at all and theirs are tarnished
by dirty hands; since Latin for hand
is '*manus*', the few with *manners* have
dirty *manus*.

6 join-stools fitted together by joiners
and hence superior to ordinary stools

7 court-cupboard 'a moveable side-
board or cabinet used to display
plate, etc.' (cited in *OED*); the plate
in it is a status symbol, a sign of the
Capulets' affluence, as plate started
to supersede wooden trenchers in
prosperous English homes during
the second half of the 16th century
(Ard², 113).
plate tableware, including silver and
china

8 marchpane marzipan, a sweet con-
sisting of a thick paste of almonds, egg
whites and sugar (cited in *OED*)

9 Susan Grindstone See 1.3.19n.

1.5] *Steevens* 0.1–2, 1–15] *Q2–4, F; not in Q1* 0.1–2] *Ard²; They . . . Napkins. Enter* Romeo. *Q2–4;*
They . . . their napkins. Enter Seruant. F 1 SP] *this edn; Ser. Q2–4, F* 1–5] *Pope; 3–4 prose Q3–4;*
as verse Q2 1–2] *Pope; Q2–4, F line* away? / Trencher. / 3–5] *Q3–4, F; Q2 lines as irregular verse*
hands / thing / 3 SP] *this edn; 1. Q2–4, F* 6 SP] *this edn; Ser. Q2–4, F* 8 loves] *Q2–4;* lovest
F 11 SP] *this edn; 2. Q2–4, F* 12 SP] *this edn; Ser. Q2–4, F*

asked for, and sought for, in the great chamber.

3 SERVINGMAN   We cannot be here and there too. Cheerly,   14
boys, be brisk awhile, and the longer liver take all.   *Exeunt.*

Enter [CAPULET, CAPULET'S WIFE, JULIET, TYBALT,
NURSE, County PARIS, COUSIN CAPULET, *Tybalt's Page,
Attendants and*] *all the Guests and Gentlewomen to
the Masquers.*

CAPULET

Welcome, gentlemen. Ladies that have their toes
Unplagued with corns will walk a bout with you.
Ah, my mistresses, which of you all
Will now deny to dance? She that makes dainty,
She, I'll swear, hath corns. Am I come near ye now?   20
Welcome, gentlemen. I have seen the day
That I have worn a visor and could tell
A whispering tale in a fair lady's ear,
Such as would please. 'Tis gone, 'tis gone, 'tis gone.

14 **cannot . . . too** proverbial (Dent, H438.1)
  Cheerly a cry of encouragement
15 **longer . . . all** proverbial (Dent, L395)
17 **corns** bunions, painful malformations of the large toes of either foot. Capulet is joking, of course, but bunions were a blemish, hence the idea that any woman present who pretends to be too modest to dance must have imperfect feet.
  *walk a bout literally, engage in a tilt or contest, but here meaning take a turn on the dance floor. Oxf¹, citing Brissenden, suggests that the use of *walk* may point to 'the graceful pavane', because in that dance couples can 'be side by side with hands linked at arm's length and the steps

involve turns back and forth, retreats and advances, so that it is ideal for highlighting dramatic conversation'. In *Much Ado*, Don Pedro invites Hero to 'walk a bout' with him, to which she replies, 'So you walk softly, and look sweetly, and say nothing, I am yours for the walk; and especially when I walk away' (2.1.76–9).
19 **makes dainty** pretends to be bashful, 'acts coy' (Oxf¹)
20 **come near ye** struck a chord with you, found you out; the phrase is proverbial (Dent, N56.1) and may be the cue to Romeo's party to approach Capulet.
21 **I . . . day** proverbial (Dent, D81.1)
23 **A whispering tale** intimate and insinuating words to seduce a woman

14 SP] *this edn;* 3. *Q2–4, F*   14–15] *Pope; Q2–4, F line* boyes, / all. /   15 SD] *Q2–4, F; They retire behind. / Malone*   15.1–4] *this edn; Enter all . . . Maskers. Q2–4, F; Enter old* Capulet *with the Ladies. Q1*   17 walk] *Q2–4, F;* haue *Q1*   a bout] *Pope;* about *Q2–4, F, Q1*   20 ye] *Q2–3, F;* you *Q4, Q1*

You are welcome, gentlemen. Come, musicians, play.　　25
　　　　　　　Music plays and they dance.
A hall, a hall! Give room and foot it, girls.
More light, you knaves, and turn the tables up,
And quench the fire, the room is grown too hot.
Ah, sirrah, this unlooked-for sport comes well.
Nay, sit, nay, sit, good cousin Capulet,　　　　　　30
For you and I are past our dancing days.
How long is't now since last yourself and I
Were in a masque?

COUSIN CAPULET　　　By'r Lady, thirty years.

CAPULET

What, man, 'tis not so much, 'tis not so much:
'Tis since the nuptial of Lucentio,　　　　　　　35

---

26 **A . . . hall** a common cry to clear space for a dance, to *give room* (cited under *OED* hall)

27 **knaves** servants (said here without opprobrious intent)

turn . . . up i.e. turn the tables upside down and move them out of the dancing space (cited under *OED* turn *v.* 81c)

28 **quench the fire** Shakespeare seems to have forgotten that the dance takes place on a late July night, and the following day is moreover asserted to be hot (3.1.2). Instead he is thinking of Brooke's calendar: 'The weary winter nights restore the Christmas games / And now the season doth invite to banquet townish dames. / And first in Capel's house' (155ff.).

29 **sirrah** addressed in banter by an expansive Capulet to his cousin

unlooked-for unexpected (by his guests); but the dancing affords a chance to Capulet and Cousin Capulet

to catch up, as their dancing days are over.

comes well is welcome

30 **cousin** See 1.1.158n. on *cousin* = kinsman; he is probably the '*uncle Capulet*' of the invitation letter (1.2.68), the paterfamilias bid to the feast with his wife and daughters.

31 **past . . . days** proverbial (Dent, D118)

33–40 **thirty . . . ago** So Juliet's father is in his 50s. Since the son is now 30, Lucentio's wedding was probably 31 years earlier. Shakespeare may be playing with a 13/31 chiasm: Juliet's age and the 31 years since that other wedding when the old men were young; on 13, see pp. 2–5, 38–9.

35 **nuptial** wedding; the reference to the 'nuptials' of Theseus and Hippolyta in *MND* 1.1.1 suggests that the word was applied to aristocratic weddings or those of the upper bourgeoisie, such as the Capulets and Montagues of Verona.

---

25 gentlemen. Come,] *Rowe subst.;* gentlemen come, *Q2;* gentlemen, come *Q3–4, F; not in Q1* SD] *Q2–4, F; not in Q1* 26 A . . . hall] *Q2–4;* A Hall, Hall *F; not in Q1* 27 knaves *Q2–4, F; Cos: Q1;* CAPULET'S COUSIN *Oxf* 33 By'r Lady] *Q2–4, F (*Berlady*);* By Ladie *Q1* 34+ SP] *(1.) Capu. Q2–4; 1. Capu., Cap. F; Cap:, Ca: Q1* 35 Lucentio,] *F, Q1; Lucientio: Q2–4*

Come Pentecost as quickly as it will,
Some five-and-twenty years, and then we masqued.

COUSIN CAPULET

'Tis more, 'tis more, his son is elder, sir,
His son is thirty.

CAPULET   Will you tell me that?
His son was but a ward two years ago.   40

ROMEO [*to a Servingman*]
What lady's that which doth enrich the hand
Of yonder knight?

SERVINGMAN   I know not, sir.

ROMEO
O, she doth teach the torches to burn bright.

36 **Pentecost** a time traditionally associated with renewal, salvation and Maying, hence the Whitsun festivals; cf. 'for at Pentecost, / When all our pageants of delight were played' (*TGV* 4.4.156–7).

38 **elder** older

39 **Will . . . that** a rhetorical question expressing incredulity

40 **but a ward** a mere child (cited under *OED* ward *sb.*[2] 7)

41–2 **What . . . knight** Romeo's first sight of Juliet notes her hand in that of another masquer during a formal courtly dance, hence *measure* (49) and his noting her position after the dance. His paean to her beauty suggests that, unlike him, she is not masked. Brooke describes her as being 'right fair of perfect shape / Which Theseus or Paris would have chosen to their rape' (197–8).

42 **yonder** the first of the play's five *yonders* and five *yonds*, all but two (a *yond* each from Paris at 5.3.3 and Friar Laurence at 5.3.125) spoken by Romeo and Juliet. They long for union in the teeth of separation, hence perhaps the multiple uses of this gently mournful, sonorous word signifying distance.

knight 'Paris, no doubt' (Sprague, 299; and Oxf[1] notes that 'productions since the early nineteenth century have often introduced him [Paris] as Juliet's partner in dance or conversation'); but Juliet's dance partner is not identified in the text. In the 1978 BBC film Juliet (Rebecca Saire) dances with her cousin Tybalt (Alan Rickman).

I . . . sir He does not know probably because he is a torchbearer of Romeo's party (Cam[2]).
The part-line is omitted in Q1.

43–52 The harmony of sound created by the monosyllabic rhymes here anticipates the perfect symbiosis of the lovers, but is rudely interrupted by Tybalt's jarring *Montague* (53).

43–8 Juliet is seen in terms of a black and white conceit, a visual counterpoint as important in the play's metaphoric textures as youth and age. The reference to *torches* flows from Brooke's 'With torch in hand a comely knight did fetch her forth to dance' (246). It grounds Romeo's image in the setting of the Capulets' ball; in the *chiaroscuro* of the party this is all Romeo sees of her, but the imagery launched at this

36 Pentecost] *Q1;* Pentycost *Q2–4, F*   38 SP] *Williams;* 2. Capu. *Q2–4;* 2. Cap. F; Cos: *Q1*   sir] *Q2–4, F;* far *Q1*   39 SP] *Q1 (Cap.);* 1. Capu. *Q2–4;* 3. Cap. F   41 SD] *Capell (to a Servant)*   lady's] *Pope;* Ladies *Q2;* Ladie is *Q3–4, F, Q1*

169

It seems she hangs upon the cheek of night
As a rich jewel in an Ethiop's ear,   45
Beauty too rich for use, for earth too dear.
So shows a snowy dove trooping with crows
As yonder lady o'er her fellows shows.
The measure done, I'll watch her place of stand
And, touching hers, make blessed my rude hand.   50
Did my heart love till now? Forswear it, sight,
For I ne'er saw true beauty till this night.

TYBALT

This by his voice should be a Montague.
Fetch me my rapier, boy.   *[Exit Page.]*
                         What, dares the slave

point suffuses this play of nights and dawns and the spaces in between.

44 **hangs . . . night** Cf. 'which like a jewel hung in ghastly night, / Makes black night beauteous, and her old face new' (*Son* 27.11–12).

45 **Ethiop** Night is personified here as an *Ethiop* with Juliet as a lustrous pendant; cf. *TGV* 2.6.25–6.

46 This continues the image of Juliet as an ornament too precious to be worn, of such worth that all earth cannot afford her, reinforcing the idea of an ethereal presence not best suited to the sublunary world of *use* and the deterioration of beauty.

47 **snowy dove** The white *dove* offsets Juliet from the *crows* that the other young beauties become in the image. The contrast recalls Benvolio's promise to make Romeo 'think thy swan [Rosaline] a crow' (1.2.88); for *dove* Q1 has a swan ('So shines a snow-white Swan trouping with Crowes'), but this does not rhyme with 'love' (see e.g. 2.1.10) and would apply the same image to Juliet and Rosaline.

49 **measure** dance

stand halt and rest (cited under *OED* stand *sb.*[1] 2a). According to Brooke, Romeo is waiting for Juliet to return

from the dance: 'The whilst our Romeus a place had warily won / Nigh to the seat were she must sit, the dance once being done' (249–50), Juliet 'turned to her chair with pleasant cheer'. She was glad when Romeo approached her and sat 'At th'one side of her chair', while on the other side 'there sat one called Mercutio' (251–4).

50 **rude** coarse, compared to Juliet's; see 92ff.

51–2 Cf. Marlowe's famous line from *Hero and Leander*, 'Who ever lov'd, that lov'd not at first sight?' (1.176; quoted in *AYL* 3.5.82).

51 **Forswear it** 'Break your oath' (of undying love to Rosaline).

53 **by his voice** Tybalt seems to mean 'accent' by *voice*, thus implying that Montagues and Capulets speak differently. Tybalt's recognition and angry reaction (53–8) are invented by Shakespeare.

Montague the first word not to rhyme after five couplets and the very name that Juliet later wishes he did not possess

54 **rapier** sharp light sword

slave here a bilious term of contempt (as in Lear's abuse of Oswald with 'you slave, you cur', *KL* 1.4.79)

47 snowy] *Q2–3; F;* snowe *Q4;* snow-white *Q1*   52 ne'er] *Q2–4;* neuer *F, Q1*   54 SD] *Collier*[2]

Come hither, covered with an antic face,   55
To fleer and scorn at our solemnity?
Now by the stock and honour of my kin,
To strike him dead I hold it not a sin.

CAPULET

Why, how now, kinsman, wherefore storm you so?

TYBALT

Uncle, this is a Montague, our foe,   60
A villain that is hither come in spite
To scorn at our solemnity this night.

CAPULET

Young Romeo is it?

TYBALT   'Tis he, that villain Romeo.

CAPULET

Content thee, gentle coz, let him alone.
'A bears him like a portly gentleman   65
And, to say truth, Verona brags of him
To be a virtuous and well-governed youth.
I would not for the wealth of all this town
Here in my house do him disparagement.
Therefore be patient, take no note of him.   70
It is my will, the which if thou respect,
Show a fair presence and put off these frowns,
An ill-beseeming semblance for a feast.

TYBALT

It fits when such a villain is a guest.

---

55 **antic face** fantastical mask
56 **fleer and scorn** the second hendiadys (*fleer = scorn*) applied to Romeo (the earlier one was his father's description of him as 'so secret and so close' at 1.1.147)
57 **stock . . . kin** pedigree and respect due to my ancestors (another hendiadys)
61 **in spite** with hostile intent

65 i.e. his demeanour is that of a proper/ handsome (*portly*) gentleman.
67 **well-governed** commendably in control of himself, disciplined
69 **disparagement** dishonour
72 **presence** demeanour (*OED sb.* 5)
73 **ill-beseeming semblance** unsuitable expression

55 antic] *Q1 (*Anticke*); anticque *Q2;* antique *Q3–4, F   59, 75, 120 SPs, 81 SP2] *Capu. Q2–4; Cap. F; Ca: Q1   65 'A] *Q2–4, F;* he *Q1   68 this] *Q2–4, Q1;* the *F*

I'll not endure him.

CAPULET   He shall be endured.   75
What, goodman boy, I say he shall, go to!
Am I the master here or you? Go to!
You'll not endure him? God shall mend my soul,
You'll make a mutiny among my guests,
You will set cock-a-hoop, you'll be the man!   80

TYBALT
Why, uncle, 'tis a shame.

CAPULET   Go to, go to,
You are a saucy boy. Is't so indeed?
This trick may chance to scathe you, I know what.
You must contrary me! – Marry, 'tis time,
Well said, my hearts. – You are a princox, go,   85
Be quiet, or – More light, more light! – For shame,
I'll make you quiet. – What, cheerly, my hearts!

TYBALT
Patience perforce with wilful choler meeting

---

75 **endure him** tolerate his presence
shall must
76 **goodman boy** a double insult: *goodman* denotes a rank below that of a gentleman and *boy* is the equivalent of 'whippersnapper'. Old Capulet forcefully reprimands Tybalt for his lack of courtesy towards a guest and his failure to respect his seniors and betters.
78 **God . . . soul** proverbial (Dent, G173.1)
79 **mutiny** discord (*OED sb.* 2)
80 **set cock-a-hoop** start a riot by removing all conventional restraint; to *set cock-a-hoop* literally means to remove the tap (the *cock* or stopcock) from the barrel and put it on top of the *hoop* (a metonym for barrel) to let the ale flow unchecked so that everyone becomes intoxicated. *OED* cites this line and Dent gives the expression as proverbial (C493).
you'll . . . man 'You are the one to

sort this, are you indeed!'
82 **saucy boy** impudent fellow
Is't so indeed 'Is this how things stand?' (i.e. with you telling me how to run my own household)
83 **This . . . you** Your inappropriate behaviour (*trick*) will injure (*scathe*) you. There may be a more specific implied threat to Tybalt's financial expectations from Capulet as punishment for this defiance (Cam², Oxf¹).
84 **contrary** contràry; cross, oppose
85 **princox** insolent pup (cited under *OED* princox)
86 **More . . . light!** probably after Brooke's 'But brighter than the sun the waxen torches shone / That, mauger what he could, he was espied of everyone' (173–4), the moment the unmasked Romeo is recognized
88–91 The switch to rhyming couplets after the blank verse of Tybalt's clash with Capulet sounds a chilling note of

---

79 my] *Q2–4, Q1;* the *F*   80 set] *Q2–3, F, Q1;* set a *Q4*

Makes my flesh tremble in their different greeting.
I will withdraw, but this intrusion shall,   90
Now seeming sweet, convert to bitt'rest gall.   *Exit.*

ROMEO

If I profane with my unworthiest hand
This holy shrine, the gentle sin is this:
My lips, two blushing pilgrims, ready stand
To smooth that rough touch with a tender kiss.   95

premeditation and is ominously placed directly before the first exchange between Romeo and Juliet. Dent has 'Patience perforce' as proverbial (P111).

89 **different greeting** collision of opposites (*Patience* and *choler*)

90–1 **this . . . gall** i.e. Romeo's trespass will turn present pleasure and happiness to deepest sorrow. Some productions err in having Tybalt overhear the start of Romeo and Juliet's exchange and thus hate Romeo even more for presuming to woo his cousin.

92–109 Staging the lovers' first encounter, with the intense intimacy of its rhetoric in the thick of a dance, poses a major problem of choreography (Brooke has them seated on chairs at the edge of the party while Romeus holds Juliet's hand). In the Zeffirelli film, Romeo catches Juliet's eye while dancing the morisco, before walking around the outer side of the dance hall and, from behind a pillar, clasping her hand. They commune and kiss unseen by anyone other than the camera until Nurse's summons at 110. Zeffirelli's orchestration is closely followed by Luhrmann.

92–105 The 14 lines between the lovers form a sonnet: Romeo speaks the first quatrain (*abab*), Juliet the second (*cbcb*), and both end in *kiss*. They share the sestet, but he has two more lines than she and also concludes the

sonnet. The final couplet coincides with the lovers' closing lips.

92 **profane** defile, but with the specific meaning of trespassing on something sacred: Juliet is an object of spiritual worship to Romeo, hence *shrine* and *sin* (93); see also 1.1.80n.

unworthiest hand The prominence of hands here and in the lines which follow is inspired by Brooke's account (259ff.) of Mercutio and Romeus each holding Juliet's hand as she sits between them. Mercutio seizes 'fair Juliet's snowish' right hand in his – it is colder than 'frozen mountain ice' – while in 'his trembling hand her left hath loving Romeus caught', at which point 'she with tender hand his tender palm hath pressed' (267), a line that Shakespeare remembers in 95 (*tender*) and particularly in 99 (*palm*).

93 **holy shrine** Juliet's hand which at 50 he hoped to touch

93–5 **the gentle . . . kiss** The reason for my touching your hand, and thus possibly committing an affectionate error (*gentle sin*), is to be allowed to kiss better your hand where mine touched it.

94 **two blushing pilgrims** This continues the imagery of shrines and atonement while playing on the colour of his lips, which are *blushing* at his boldness in taking Juliet's hand and at the prospect of kissing her.

95 **rough touch** by his *rude hand* (50)

91 bitt'rest] *Q2 (* bittrest*); bitter *Q3–4, F, Q1* SD] *Q2–4, F; not in Q1* 93 sin] *Q2–4, F, Q1; fine *Theobald (Warburton)* 94 ready] *Q1; did readie *Q2–4, F*

JULIET

Good pilgrim, you do wrong your hand too much,
Which mannerly devotion shows in this,
For saints have hands that pilgrims' hands do touch,
And palm to palm is holy palmers' kiss.

ROMEO

Have not saints lips and holy palmers too?   100

JULIET

Ay, pilgrim, lips that they must use in prayer.

ROMEO

O then, dear saint, let lips do what hands do –
They pray; grant thou, lest faith turn to despair.

JULIET

Saints do not move, though grant for prayers' sake.

96–9 Juliet artfully deflects Romeo's suggestion that she may need kissing to make up for his hand's *rough touch*. She does not want to be seen to be won too easily and thus seem *light* (cf. 2.2.99).

96 **Good pilgrim** used in an affectionate, and perhaps gently ribbing, way by Juliet, to signal that she is prepared to play along with his particular ritual of courtship (cf. *dear saint* in 102). In a number of productions, from Henry Irving's (1882) to Gielgud's (1935) and Peter Brook's (1947), Romeo has worn white pilgrim's robes, presumably because of this line and his arch reference to his lips as *blushing pilgrims*. **you . . . your** Juliet's use of the formal second person pronoun *you* and the possessive *your* contrasts with Romeo's more intimate and bolder *thou* (103) and *thine* (106). She uses *thou* for the first time when she is alone at her window (2.2.33), and follows it with another *thou* and two *thy*s.

97 **Which mannerly devotion** 'the seemly worship of which', with a witty quibble on the root meaning of *mannerly* (see 3–4n.)

98–9 The hands of saints are relics which

pilgrims touch for their salvation; so his hand would be free to touch hers even if she were the exalted object of his fantasy. Indeed, she explains, not without gently mocking, the touching of the palms of saints and pilgrims (*palmers*) constitutes an appropriate *kiss* in such a holy context (cited under *OED* palmer *sb¹*).

99 **palm to palm** the suppliant's hand against the hand of the sacred relic, after Brooke's 'Then she with tender hand his tender palm hath pressed' (267); alluding, perhaps, to the custom of pilgrims to the Holy Land bringing back palm branches as tokens of their visit. Brooke's double 'tender' turns in the play into a line-long quibble on *palm* and *palmers*, the 'tender' having migrated up to 95 to become the promise of a *tender kiss*.

102 **do . . . do** i.e. join in prayer, or, as lips, in a kiss

103–4 **thou . . . though** In witty repartee she inverts his *grant thou* to *though grant* and teases out the opposite conclusion from his saintly metaphor, that saints can give without surrendering themselves. Their sway happens in mysterious ways through interceding with the godhead.

98 that] *Q2–4, F;* which *Q1*   104 prayers'] *Warburton;* praiers *Q2–4, F; var. Q1*

ROMEO

Then move not while my prayer's effect I take.   105

[*Kisses her.*]

Thus from my lips by thine my sin is purged.

JULIET

Then have my lips the sin that they have took.

ROMEO

Sin from my lips? O trespass sweetly urged!

Give me my sin again.   [*Kisses her.*]

JULIET   You kiss by th' book.

NURSE

Madam, your mother craves a word with you.   110

[*Juliet moves towards her mother.*]

---

105 **prayer's effect** the reward for my prayer, i.e. a passive kiss, in that she will stay still

105 SD *The editorial placing of the SD at the end of the sonnet, after the final couplet, thus interrupting Romeo's two-line speech, seems preferable to the alternate editorial placement after 104. Sprague notes that while Juliet was kissed 'fully on the mouth' in an 1876 production by Ernesto Rossi, this was unusual. Duncan-Jones concurs ('Full-frontal kisses were rare in Shakespeare's theatre'), noting that 'Shakespeare's clear indication here that the audience see Romeo kissing Juliet on the lips, twice, at their very first meeting, is excitingly bold' (Duncan-Jones, 'Pilgrims').

106 **sin** continuing the image of Juliet as a saint

107 Saints were thought to purge offenders' sins by interceding with Christ for Him to take upon Himself their trespasses.

108 **trespass sweetly urged** a *trespass* since his kisses are a *sin* according to

the metaphorical language they have been using, and *sweetly urged* (seductively argued) because Juliet does so with maidenly modesty, with a play also on the sweetness of the kiss

109 SD *Several editions have a second kiss here, making it precede Juliet's 'You kiss by th' book', which thus becomes a direct comment on Romeo's kisses. Williams suggests that, if a second kiss is allowed, it ought to occur after Juliet's *by th' book* because of a cross-scenic echo between Nurse's entry here, interrupting the lovers' kiss, and her rushing into the newly-weds' bedroom to tell them that Juliet's mother is on her way up (Williams, 'Edit', 119–21).

109 **by th' book** according to the rules (cited under *OED* book 15); Juliet teasingly reproves Romeo for triumphing over her reticence with his elaborate courtly wooing. See *cunning* below (2.2.101), when Juliet rejects the rhetorical ritual dance of lovers for plain, honest expression of sentiment.

110 **craves** entreats (cited under *OED v.* 2)

---

105 prayer's] *Capell;* praiers *Q2–4, F, Q1*   SD] *Rowe (opp. 103)*   106 thine] *Q2–4, F;* yours *Q1*   109 SD] *Capell*   by th' book] bith booke *Q2–4; F;* by the booke *Q1*   110 SD] *Oxf*

ROMEO

What is her mother?

NURSE   Marry, bachelor,

Her mother is the lady of the house,

And a good lady, and a wise and virtuous.

I nursed her daughter that you talked withal.

I tell you, he that can lay hold of her   115

Shall have the chinks.

ROMEO   Is she a Capulet?

O dear account! My life is my foe's debt.

BENVOLIO

Away, be gone, the sport is at the best.

ROMEO

Ay, so I fear; the more is my unrest.

CAPULET

Nay, gentlemen, prepare not to be gone;   120

We have a trifling foolish banquet towards.

     They whisper in his ear.

---

111 **What** Who

    bachelor young man, with the additional senses here of being unmarried and being on the bottom rung of the social ladder of the better class of people

114 **talked withal** spoke to. In Bogdanov's production, Nurse paused disapprovingly before saying *talked withal*, knowingly stressing *talked* to indicate that she had witnessed their illicit kissing.

115 **lay . . . her** get her, carry her off home as his wife

116 **have the chinks** be rich; literally, have pieces of ready money, from the sound ('chink') made by rattling coins striking one another (cited under *OED* chink *sb.*[3] 3). The phrase is an appropriately slangy one for Nurse.

117 **dear account** heavy reckoning;

his very reason for living now lies in the hands of his enemy, Juliet Capulet, whose debtor he therefore is. Shakespeare here closely follows Brooke, 325.

118 **the sport . . . best** proverbial (Dent, P399: 'When play (game, jest) is best it is time to leave'); see also 1.4.10.

121 **banquet** 'A course of sweetmeats, fruit, and wine, served either as a separate entertainment, or as a continuation of the principal meal . . . a dessert' (*OED sb.*[1] 3)

    towards coming up (dessert is held up by Capulet as an inducement to stop his guests from leaving)

121 SD *i.e. they take their leave discreetly. In Q1 this is sandwiched between 119 and a line reading 'I pray you let me intreat you. Is it so?'. The rhythm of the dialogue suggests that

121 SD] *Q1; not in Q2–4, F; Maskers excuse themselves with a bow. / Capell; They signal to Capulet that they must leave Oxf[1]*

Is it e'en so? Why then, I thank you all.
I thank you, honest gentlemen, good night.
More torches here! Come on then, let's to bed.
Ah, sirrah, by my fay, it waxes late. 125
I'll to my rest. *Exeunt [all but Juliet and Nurse].*

JULIET

Come hither, Nurse. What is yond gentleman?

NURSE

The son and heir of old Tiberio.

JULIET

What's he that now is going out of door?

NURSE

Marry, that I think be young Petruchio. 130

JULIET

What's he that follows here, that would not dance?

this Q1 SD should be inserted after 'intreat you' and as a prompt for 'Is it so?'. It marks a pragmatic shortcut to clear the revellers off the stage, the whispering being their excuses, accepted by Capulet, for leaving in spite of his *banquet* and entreaties. '*They*' refers to the *gentlemen* (120), the masquers.

122 **Is . . . so?** spoken in response to the message about his guests leaving the party, which Capulet closes down with *let's to bed* (124), thereby emptying the stage of all except Juliet and Nurse.

124 **More torches here** i.e. to show the revellers safely out

125 **sirrah** perhaps muttered to himself, or else to one of the servants
by my fay truly (literally, 'by my faith')

127 **yond gentleman** Juliet pretends to be interested in two other young men first to throw Nurse off the scent before asking after Romeo. In Brooke too, Juliet, a 'young and wily dame',

was 'careful . . . what way were best devise / To learn his name', asking Nurse about two other guests as decoy before enquiring after Romeus (Brooke, 341–50).

131 **would not dance** In 1.4 Romeo vowed not to dance, to be instead 'a candleholder and look on' (14–22, 38), which Juliet confirms. His encounter with Juliet happens at 'her place of stand' (49), tempting though it is to imagine that they dance together during the sonnet because dance = harmony. In Brooke, Romeus is identified by Juliet not as the guest who would not dance but as 'he with visor in his hand, / That yonder doth in masking weed beside the window stand' (351–2). Olivier danced with Vivien Leigh in his 1940 Broadway *RJ*, and in Zeffirelli's film the lovers' raised hands met during the pavane; in this respect most performances go against the authority of the text.

126 SD] *Malone; Exeunt. Q1; not in Q2–4, F* 129 of] *Q2–3, F, Q1; of the Q4* 131 here] *Q2–4, F; there Q1*

NURSE

I know not.

JULIET

Go ask his name.   [*Nurse moves away.*]
                        If he be married,
My grave is like to be my wedding bed.

NURSE [*returning*]

His name is Romeo, and a Montague,   135
The only son of your great enemy.

JULIET

My only love sprung from my only hate,
Too early seen unknown, and known too late!
Prodigious birth of love it is to me
That I must love a loathed enemy.   140

NURSE

What's tis, what's tis?

JULIET   A rhyme I learnt even now

---

132 **I know not** Flora Robson's Nurse
(BBC, 1955) knew his name because
she overheard the row over Romeo
between Tybalt and Capulet. Nurse
may not want to tell Juliet because a
love affair with a Montague would
inevitably lead to tragedy (the Friar
takes the opposite view at 2.3.86–8).
In Zeffirelli, 1968, Nurse goes up to
Tybalt who, disdainfully, tells her that
it is Romeo.

133 SD In the Garrick–Kemble text of
1814 Nurse exits after *name* and re-
enters after *wedding bed* (135 SD).

133–4 **If . . . bed** a dark premonition,
shared by the audience who remember
the Chorus' reference to the young
lovers' *death-marked love* (Prol.9)

133 **married** marrièd

136 **The only son** See List of Roles, 13n.

137–40 Juliet's spontaneous outburst
about her feelings almost gives her
away to Nurse and forces her to explain

her *rhyme* as best she can, as not a
substantive statement but something
akin to a nursery rhyme (141–2).

137 Juliet's first and sole love is inspired
by someone descended from the only
object of hate in her life, the Montagues.

138 She loved at first sight before she
knew who he was, and now that she
knows she cannot go back.

139 **Prodigious** portentous

140 **loathed** loathèd

141 **tis . . . tis** 'a common dialect or
subliterary pronunciation of "this"'
(Williams, 11)

141–2 **A rhyme . . . withal** Responding
to Nurse's *What's tis*, Juliet deflects
suspicion away from Romeo by
pretending that she learnt the *rhyme*
(i.e. 137–40) from one of her dancing
partners, thus presumably ruling out
Romeo whom, a few short moments
earlier (131), she identified as the one
who refused to dance.

133 SD] *this edn*   134 wedding] *Q2–4, Q1*; wedded *F*   135 SD] *Oxf*   141 tis . . . tis?] *Q2–4*; this?
. . . this? *F*; *this? . . . that? Q1*   learnt] *Q2–4, Q1*; learne *F*

Of one I danced withal.
One calls within 'Juliet'.
NURSE   Anon, anon!
Come, let's away, the strangers all are gone.   *Exeunt.*

[2.0]   [*Enter*] CHORUS.

CHORUS
Now old desire doth in his deathbed lie,
And young affection gapes to be his heir;
That fair for which love groaned for and would die,
With tender Juliet matched is now not fair.
Now Romeo is beloved and loves again,   5
Alike bewitched by the charm of looks,

---

143 **strangers** guests (*OED* guest 2a)
2.0 Johnson noted that the second
Chorus was pointless, because it failed
to advance the action, merely relating
'what is already known, or what the
next scenes will show', doing so moreover 'without adding the improvement
of any moral sentiment' (*Johnson on
Shakespeare*, 236). Some editions (e.g.
Riv², Cam²) have the second Chorus
close Act 1. Q2 places it after the
exit of Juliet and Nurse and before
Romeo's entry alone. It is commonly
omitted in performance.
1 **old desire** i.e. Romeo's love for
Rosaline
   doth The use of an emphatic, if
redundant, *doth* enables a perfect *lie/
die* rhyme.
2 **gapes** longs, yearns (*OED v.* 4b);
evocative of hungry heirs waiting
open-mouthed to be fed their inherit-
ance. The Chorus is using the image to
bring home the strength of feeling of
Romeo's new love.
3 **That fair** i.e. the *fair Rosaline* of

1.2.84; with *fair* artfully echoing *heir*
from the preceding line, an instance
of the play's characteristic cross-line
rhyming, here suggesting a seamless
join between the loves
   for . . . for The alliterative repetition
of *for* renders the line metrically regular and gives it a more natural cadence,
thus overriding the syntactic violation
of the single verb attracting the same
preposition twice.
4 **matched** compared (cited under *OED*
match *v.*¹ 8a)
5 **loves again** reciprocates her love
(*again* = in return), hence *matched* in
4 (cf. the 'marriage of true minds' of
Son 116)
6 'both equally engrossed in each other's
beauty'. *Alike* comes from Brooke, 487:
'But each of them alike did burn in
equal flame'. Both *bewitched* and *charm*
are used here primarily in their modern
senses, although in the 1590s they were
freighted with the sinister *double entendres* of magic and witchcraft.
   bewitched bewitchèd

---

143 all are] *Q2–3, F;* are all *Q4; not in Q1* **2.0**] *Rowe* 0.1, 1–14] *Q2–4, F; not in Q1* 0.1] *Cam;*
Chorus. Q2–4, F 4 matched] *Q3–4, F;* match *Q2*

But to his foe supposed he must complain,
And she steal love's sweet bait from fearful hooks.
Being held a foe, he may not have access
To breathe such vows as lovers use to swear,   10
And she as much in love, her means much less
To meet her new beloved anywhere.
But passion lends them power, time means, to meet,
Tempering extremities with extreme sweet.   *[Exit.]*

[2.1]   *Enter* ROMEO *alone.*

ROMEO

Can I go forward when my heart is here?
Turn back, dull earth, and find thy centre out.
[Withdraws.]

Enter BENVOLIO *with* MERCUTIO.

BENVOLIO

Romeo, my cousin Romeo, Romeo!

---

7 **foe supposed** Because their families
are sworn enemies their offspring
assume that they are also such.
complain make lamentation
8 The image of Juliet snatching happiness in love from baited hooks comes
from Brooke where, after her first
encounter with Romeus, she wonders
whether he might not 'with friendly
speech' like a 'traitor lie in wait, / As oft
the poisoned hook is hid, wrapped in
the pleasant bait?' (387–8); *sweet* recalls
Juliet's *sweetly urged* trespass (1.5.108).
9 **access** accèss
14 softening or mitigating their harsh predicament with moments of utter bliss;
with a quibble on 'temper' (the process

of hardening steel; see 3.1.117n.) and
extremities
2.1 Early Monday morning (1.5.120–5;
2.1.39–40), a street outside the
Capulets' orchard
2 a self-deprecatory exhortation by
Romeo to himself (*dull earth*) to retrace
his steps to Juliet (*centre*). The expression 'as dull as earth' was proverbial
(Dent, E27.2).
3 Some editors follow Q1 here and delete
the third *Romeo* to produce a regular
pentameter rather than the alexandrine
of Benvolio's and Mercutio's combined
lines in Q2. The Q2 text can be made
to scan as a five-beat line given its scope
for elision and contraction.

14 SD] *Theobald*   **2.1]** *Hanmer*   2 SD] *Ard²; Exit. / Rowe; leaps the Wall. / Capell; He turns
back and withdraws. Oxf*   2.1] *Q2–4, F; Enter Benuolio Mercutio. Q1*   3 Romeo, Romeo] *Q2–4, F;
Romeo Q1*

MERCUTIO   He is wise
And, on my life, hath stol'n him home to bed.
BENVOLIO
He ran this way and leapt this orchard wall.   5
Call, good Mercutio.
MERCUTIO   Nay, I'll conjure too.
Romeo, humours, madman, passion, lover,
Appear thou in the likeness of a sigh,
Speak but one rhyme and I am satisfied,
Cry but 'Ay me', pronounce but 'love' and 'dove',   10

4   **stol'n him** discreetly taken himself
off; with *him* as ethical dative
home to bed He never goes home to
bed during this night.
5   **orchard wall** the first reference to the
walled orchard – the wall's height is
noted at 2.2.63 – underneath Juliet's
window; in Brooke the orchard is 'a
garden plot' which 'fronted full upon
her leaning place, / Where she is wont
to show her heart by cheerful friendly
face' (451–4). The term 'balcony' does
not occur in either play or poem.
The character 'Wall' in the Pyramus
and Thisbe interlude in *MND* is a
burlesque version of the Capulets'
orchard's enclosure.
6 SP *Although the half-line *Nay . . . too*
is given to Benvolio in Q2, Q1 has
Mercutio cut in here and speak, which
makes excellent dramatic sense. He
uses the word 'conjure' three more
times, at 16, 17 and 26, and is henceforth Romeo's sparring partner and
Tybalt's chief adversary.
7   **humours . . . lover** Romeo distils all
these: he is possessed with humours
(a lover's caprices or, as we might say,
hormones or testosterone) to the point
of becoming irrational and an addict

to romantic love; cf. Orsino, another
figure in thrall to the notion of love
(see *TN* 1.1.1–15).
10 **Ay me** a common sigh of lovers; *Ay*
rhymes with the self, 'I', thus wit-
tily providing the *one rhyme* Mercutio
requests. Behind it lies Latin '*ohi
me*' or '*heu me*'. Not only are 'Ay'
and 'I' homophones, but *Ay me/*'I
me' can be a semantically tautological rhyme of 'I' nominative and
'I' accusative.
*__pronounce . . . 'dove'__ 'pronounce'
and 'dove' are Q1 readings for Q2's
probably erroneous 'prouaunt' and
'day', 'prouaunt' stemming from
minim confusion and the virtually
identical secretary-hand *c* and *t* being
mistaken for each other. Similarly,
'day' is likely to be a misreading of
the longhand behind Q2, since *o* and
a confusion is a known characteristic
of Shakespeare's handwriting (cf. 'or'
and *arse* at 38) and the letters *v* and *y*
are easily mixed up in secretary hand
(see also *pilot* at 2.2.82). Romeo has
already compared Juliet to a *snowy
dove* (1.5.47) and doves are sacred
to Venus whose chariot they draw (see
2.5.7).

3–4 He . . . bed] *F, Q1 subst.; one line in Q2–4*   6 SP] *Q1, Q4; not in Q2–3, F (part-line completes
Benvolio's speech)*   7–21] *Q2–4, F; prose Q1*   7 madman] *Q2–3, F, Q1;* madam *Q4*   lover] *Q2–4, F;*
liver *Q1*   9 one] *Q3–4, F, Q1;* on *Q2*   10 Cry] *Q2–4, Q1;* Cry me *F*   pronounce] *Q1, Q4;* prouaunt
Q2–3, F; Couply *F2;* couple *Rowe*   dove] *Q1;* day *Q2–3, F;* die *Q4*

Speak to my gossip Venus one fair word,
One nickname for her purblind son and heir,
Young Abraham Cupid, he that shot so trim
When King Cophetua loved the beggar maid –
He heareth not, he stirreth not, he moveth not;   15
The ape is dead and I must conjure him.
I conjure thee by Rosaline's bright eyes,
By her high forehead and her scarlet lip,
By her fine foot, straight leg, and quivering thigh
And the demesnes that there adjacent lie,   20
That in thy likeness thou appear to us.

11 **my gossip Venus** The playfully intimate reference to Venus (*gossip* here
meaning a familiar friend; *OED sb.* 2a)
implies that Mercutio excels at venery.
It is probably inspired by Brooke, who
introduces Mercutio as the top predator in the sexual jungle: 'Even as a
lion would among the lambs be bold,
/ Such was among the bashful maids
Mercutio to behold' (257–8).

12 **purblind** completely blind (cited in
OED)
   *heir another Q1 reading which is
almost certainly correct, for Q2's 'her'

13 **Abraham Cupid** an oxymoron since
Cupid is a boy (whom Berowne,
anticipating the use of *purblind* here,
calls 'This whimpled, whining, purblind, wayward boy', *LLL* 3.1.174),
whereas Abraham is the archetypal
Old Testament patriarch. The visual
collision of youth and old age, of
biblical patriarch and baroque *putto*,
in *Abraham Cupid* connects with the
wider motifs of opposites attracting and repelling each other here.
Oxf¹ compares *Abraham Cupid* with
'Signor Junior' in *LLL* 3.1.175, which
Woodhuysen glosses as 'senior junior',
citing Hibbard on Cupid as 'the oldest
of the classical deities, since it was love

that brought order out of chaos, and
simultaneously the youngest of them, a
mere boy' (see also Williams, 113–14).
   *shot so trim hit the mark so accurately. Q1's reading 'trim' is probably what Shakespeare wrote because
it echoes the line 'The blinded boy that
shoots so trim' from the ballad of King
Cophetua. Shakespeare knew the ballad
well and alludes to it in three other plays
from the mid-1590s (*LLL* 1.2.104ff.,
4.1.65ff.; *R2* 5.3.79; *2H4* 5.3.99). Q2's
compositor probably misread as 'true'
through minim confusion. Oxf¹ retains
Q2's 'true', arguing that the line in the
play is deeply anomalous anyway.

14 **Cophetua** Cophètua

15 The consciously archaic *-eth* forms of
the third person singular accord with
the parodic tone of Mercutio's appeal to
Romeo to give his friends a sign of life.

16 **ape** fool, used here affectionately; cf.
'Jollity for apes and grief for boys'
(*Cym* 4.2.194).

20 **demesnes** female genitals (cited under
OED 6). Mercutio has picked out her
forehead, lip, foot and leg before hom-
ing in on her sexuality. The bawdy ribbing characterizes Mercutio and injects
a measure of comic relief into the
romantic excess that concludes Act 1.

12 heir] *Q1, Q4;* her *Q2–3, F*   13 Abraham] *Q2–4, F, Q1;* auburn *Theobald;* Adam *Steevens
(Upton)*   trim] *Q1;* true *Q2–4, F*   15 stirreth] *Q2, Q4, F;* striueth *Q3; not in Q1*   16 and] *Q2–4;
om. F; not in Q1*   17 thee] *Q2, Q4, F, Q1;* the *Q3*

BENVOLIO

An if he hear thee thou wilt anger him.

MERCUTIO

This cannot anger him. 'Twould anger him
To raise a spirit in his mistress' circle
Of some strange nature, letting it there stand   25
Till she had laid it and conjured it down –
That were some spite. My invocation
Is fair and honest. In his mistress' name
I conjure only but to raise up him.

BENVOLIO

Come, he hath hid himself among these trees   30
To be consorted with the humorous night.
Blind is his love, and best befits the dark.

MERCUTIO

If love be blind, love cannot hit the mark.
Now will he sit under a medlar tree,

22 **An if** If indeed (a double conditional, with *An* = if; Abbott, 105); Benvolio's emphasis turns the line into a perfect iambic pentameter.
23–7 **'Twould . . . spite** i.e. for somebody else to possess Rosaline would cause Romeo upset.
24 **raise** cause an erection
   spirit ghost
   circle vagina; cf. Nerissa's 'ring' in the last line of *The Merchant of Venice*.
25 **strange** i.e. other than Romeo
   letting . . . stand allowing it to stay upright (erect)
26 until she has caused it to detumesce (by ejaculation). Mercutio is graphically explicit in his sexual persiflage at Romeo's expense.
27 **spite** injury, harm
   invocation i.e. summoning of him; *invocation* scans with five syllables rather than modern four. Cf. Jaques' gloss on the nonce word 'ducdame' as

'a Greek invocation, to call fools into a circle' (*AYL* 2.5.56).
28–9 **In . . . him** quibbling on (a) producing Romeo from his hiding place and (b) making him have an erection
31 **be consorted with** keep the company of, as in 'for aye consort with black-browed night' (*MND* 3.2.386); see also 3.1.44.
   humorous damp and capricious (cited in *OED*)
34 **medlar** slang for the female genitals, derived from the medlar fruit's appearance (cited under *OED* medlar 3a). The medlar is a tart-tasting apple-like fruit with a gaping tip (see 38n. on *open-arse*). It is eaten raw after lengthy ripening, or used for making jelly and wine. Shakespeare was familiar with its particular qualities, hence 'you'll be rotten ere you be half ripe, and that's the right virtue of the medlar' in Rosalind's grafting lesson (*AYL* 3.2.117–18).

25 there stand] *Q2–4;* stand *F;* there to stand *Q1*   27–9] *Capell; Q2–4, F line* spight. / name / him. / ; *prose Q1*   28 In] *Q2;* and in *Q3–4, F, Q1*   30 these] *Q2–4, F;* those *Q1*

And wish his mistress were that kind of fruit   35
As maids call medlars when they laugh alone.
O Romeo, that she were, O, that she were
An open-arse, thou a poperin pear!
Romeo, good night, I'll to my truckle-bed;
This field-bed is too cold for me to sleep.   40
Come, shall we go?
BENVOLIO   Go then, for 'tis in vain
To seek him here that means not to be found.
                              Exeunt [Benvolio and Mercutio].

36 When young women are alone they call
  medlars 'open-arses' (see 38), they
  are then less bound by social
  conventions of modesty; cf. *Ham*
  4.7.176–9.
37–8 Mercutio's most salacious
  innuendo in the play invites us to
  imagine Romeo as a pear to Rosaline's
  medlar.
38 *open-arse* medlar, in popular
  parlance. Q2 reads 'open, or' and
  Q1 'open *Et caetera*'; the latter is
  evidently a euphemism, while Q2's
  'or' may misread MS 'arse'. Cotgrave
  glosses French *Neffle* as 'a medlar,
  or Open-arse', and the bawdy names
  for the fruit are found in Chapman's
  Bussy d'Ambois ('right openars-
  es . . . Farewell medlar', 3.2.244–7)
  and in John Davies's *The Scourge
  of Folly* ('To loathe a medlar, being
  an open-taile', epigramme 23). Wells
  notes that ripe medlars are called
  fruit de trou de cul in French (literally, 'arsehole fruit') and suspects
  that 'Mercutio is accusing Romeo
  of wishing to take Rosaline anally'
  (*Sex*, 157).

poperin pear an allusion to the
  resemblance of a pear to male genitals
  (cited under *OED* poppering *sb.*). The
  pear's name derives from the Flemish
  town of Poperinghe near Ypres, while
  the triple *p* alliteration of *poperin
  pear* entails a thrusting onomatopoeia
  obvious from the sexual play on 'pop
  'er in'.
39 truckle-bed a low bed on castors,
  usually reserved for children, and
  pulled out for use from under an
  adult high or standing-bed. Mercutio
  is jesting when he evokes an image of
  himself cosily tucked away in a child's
  bed at home while Romeo is out
  in the field.
40 field-bed a bed out in the open (cited
  in *OED*). The word itself comes from
  Brooke: Nurse, not unlike Pandarus
  in *Troilus and Criseyde*, brings the
  married young lovers to a bed, saying, 'Lo, here a field (she showed
  a field-bed ready dight [made up])
  / Where you may, if you list, in
  arms revenge yourself by fight'
  (897–8).
  sleep sleep in

38 open-arse] *Riv²;* open, or *Q2–3, F;* open & catera, and *Q4;* open *Et caetera Q1;* open-arse or
Hosley; open-arse and *Wilson–Duthie;* open arse and *Williams*   42 SD] *Ard²;* Exit. *Q2–3; Exeunt.*
Q4, F; not in Q1

[2.2]

ROMEO [*Comes forward.*]
He jests at scars that never felt a wound.
But soft, what light through yonder window breaks?
It is the east, and Juliet is the sun.
Arise, fair sun, and kill the envious moon,
Who is already sick and pale with grief   5
That thou her maid art far more fair than she.
Be not her maid, since she is envious;
Her vestal livery is but sick and green,

2.2 Early Monday morning (1.5.120–5; 2.1.39–40) leading up to dawn (2.2.188–9) in the Capulets' orchard, in front of the window of Juliet's bedroom

1 SD *The action is continuous here, but most editors mark a new scene as they do at 1.5 above. Romeo has not left the stage, the location is the same, and his *wound* (1) rhymes with Benvolio's *found* in the preceding line, the couplet split by a scene break. 'What value is there in an act-pause after Capulet's supper, between Romeo's first meeting with Juliet and the balcony-scene?', Granville-Barker asks rhetorically with reference to conventional act and scene divisions imposed on the flux of the play (32). The situation is not entirely dissimilar to the merging of 1.4 and 1.5, where characters onstage at the end of 1.4 walk on to the set of 1.5 (see 1.5n.).

2 But soft 'Hold on, now.'
light meaning both the light in the window and Juliet herself, as the following lines' lunar and solar metaphors make clear
window This would have been a window in the tiring-house, the *aedes mimorum* above the stage, fronting the audience. The two specific references to this space in Q1's SDs, both from 3.5 when the newly wed lovers part at dawn, read '*window*', although most productions use a balcony. Williams

(144) notes that 'the architecture of the Elizabethan theater, dividing the lovers, visually reinforces the division of the families'.

3–10 The comparison of Juliet to a vestal virgin, chaste as the moon but bright as the sun, is launched by Romeo's first glimpse of light in her bedroom above.

3–4 Juliet . . . moon The moon borrows its pale reflected light from the sun, hence her jealousy of the bigger star and now too of Juliet who, merely by being, turns darkness into light. Juliet's luminous aura links her to dawn and the rising sun, a metaphor that grounds her later terror of the dark as she anticipates waking in the sombre Capulet vault.

6 her maid i.e. as a chaste virgin

8 vestal livery pale and virginal appearance. The use of *vestal* comes from the revered virgin priestesses of the temple of the goddess Vesta in Rome, sacred guardians of the fire of the hearth; their punishment for fornication was burying alive, a fate that Juliet dreads above all others as she prepares to swallow the draught prepared by the Friar (4.3.33–5). Shakespeare probably alludes to the 'vestal' Queen Elizabeth in Oberon's account of Cupid taking aim at 'a fair vestal, throned by the west' only to see his 'fiery shaft / Quenched in the chaste beams of

---

2.2] *Hanmer*   1 SD] *Spencer subst.*   6 art] *Q2–3, F, Q1;* at *Q4*   8 sick] *Q2–4, F;* palc *Q1*

And none but fools do wear it. Cast it off.

[Enter JULIET *aloft.]*

It is my lady, O, it is my love!　　　　　　　　　　　　　　10
O, that she knew she were!
She speaks, yet she says nothing. What of that?
Her eye discourses, I will answer it.
I am too bold, 'tis not to me she speaks.

the watery moon', with the 'imperial votress' passing on unaffected, 'fancy-free' (*MND* 2.1.155–64).

sick and green a reference to 'green-sickness', then the name for a form of anaemia affecting teenage girls at puberty. It characteristically causes missed or irregular periods and pale or greenish complexions. Romeo prays that Juliet will not live as a devotee of lunar virginity or a nun, but give herself to life (see also *green-sickness carrion* at 3.5.156).

9　**none . . . it** i.e. only fools stay virgins. The contrast between fulfilled womanhood and fruitless virginity (spelled out in e.g. *MND* 1.1.65–90) was a commonplace, tempered, however, by the virginal condition of the Queen, which meant that it was probably unwise to criticize virginity too harshly.

9.1　*Several editions, and productions from Garrick to the 1978 BBC *RJ*, have Juliet enter after 2.2.1 (even earlier in Oxf[1], after 2.1.42) and thus prompt Romeo's paean to her as the rising sun, even though it is only at 10 that he actually recognizes that it is she. Williams sees a natural progression between the invitation to the *sun* (Juliet) to rise (2–9) and the trope becoming incarnate in the dramatic action of 10 when she appears: 'This sequence – anticipation before illumi-

nation – has a parallel in V.iii.84–91 where Romeo describes the radiance from Juliet (ll. 84–6) before he sees her (l. 91)' (Williams, 144). Wells argues that the SD should come earlier because 'she *is* the light that he sees' (*Sex*, 159). Brooke conflates Juliet's appearance with the light of the moon: 'Impatient of her woe, she hapt to lean / one night / Within her window, and anon the moon did shine so bright' (467–8).

11　a part-line which in Q2 follows 10 on the same line, which is why Greg concluded that there was duplication here (*Editorial*, 61); 10 and 11 are both missing from Q1 in a passage which is otherwise close to Q2.

12　**She . . . nothing** Juliet has appeared in her 'window' (see Q1 3.5.0) to collect herself after her heady encounter with Romeo; her initial silence allows him to pay her a rhapsodic tribute in the form of a metaphysical conceit about her eyes and cheeks.

13　**eye . . . I** Juliet is gazing up at the sky, which causes Romeo to imagine her eyes as two stars on a visit to the heavens (see 15–17n.); simultaneously, though, he is playing on the homophony of *eye* and *I*, meaning that if *Her eye/*'her I' speaks, then his *I* will answer. Her first words in this scene, '*Ay me*' (25), recollect Mercutio's teasing at 2.1.10.

9.1] *Hosley; after 3 Rowe; after 1 Capell; after 2.1.42 SD Oxf[1]*　10–11] *Johnson; one line in Q2–4, F; not in Q1*

Two of the fairest stars in all the heaven,   15
Having some business, do entreat her eyes
To twinkle in their spheres till they return.
What if her eyes were there, they in her head?
The brightness of her cheek would shame those stars
As daylight doth a lamp. Her eyes in heaven   20
Would through the airy region stream so bright
That birds would sing and think it were not night.
See how she leans her cheek upon her hand.
O, that I were a glove upon that hand,
That I might touch that cheek!
JULIET   Ay me.

15–17 Two of heaven's finest constellations are otherwise engaged and therefore ask Juliet's sparkling eyes to replace
them temporarily in the firmament.
16 **some business** an errand (Oxf¹)
17 **spheres** the orbits of the fixed stars
which propose trading places with
Juliet's eyes. Cam² notes that 'In the
Ptolemaic system each of the seven
planets was fixed in a hollow crystal-
line sphere, which revolved concentri-
cally at different distances around the
centre (the Earth)'.
19–20 **The brightness . . . lamp** The
second of 12 references to cheeks in
the play picks up the first, in which
Juliet's stellar beauty lit up the *cheek of
night* (1.5.44), whereas now the lustre
of her own cheeks outshines the stars,
against all expectation and convention.
This metaphysical conceit prepares
the ground for the image of her eyes
setting the night-time skies ablaze in
the lines which follow.
20 *****eyes** the reading of Q1, whereas Q2
has 'eye', perhaps recalling the *eye* of
13, although by now *eye* has explicitly
become *eyes* in the lines intervening
between 13 and 21.
21 **airy region** intangible spaces of the sky
stream perhaps a rhetorical remi-

niscence of Marlowe's Faustus seeing Christ's blood streaming in an
apocalyptic firmament (*Doctor Faustus*,
A-text, ed. David Scott Kastan, 2005,
5.2.74).
22 The confusion of lark and nightingale
at the lovers' parting at dawn in 3.5 is
foreshadowed here.
23–4 **hand . . . hand** After a perfect
bright / night rhyme, the anticipated
accord with *hand* ominously does not
happen; instead *hand* is made to rhyme
with itself.
23 The audience is invited to gaze at Juliet
with Romeo and note her pensive pose,
which at this point is intensely melodramatic; the use of *leans* comes from
Juliet's 'leaning place' in Brooke (454),
and clearly implies that Shakespeare
envisages her window to have a sill,
imagining it perhaps as one of the
grand ornate windows befitting the
house of a rich merchant like Capulet
that he would have known from Italian
paintings.
24 **O . . . glove** The erotic potential of
gloves wrapped around the object of
desire was not lost on the glover's son
from Stratford-upon-Avon.
25 **Ay me** here an ingenuous, melancholy
expression of love

16 do] *Q3–4, F, Q1;* to *Q2*   20 eyes] *Q1;* eye *Q2–4, F*   23 how] *Q2–4, F; var. Q1*

ROMEO   She speaks.   25
O speak again, bright angel, for thou art
As glorious to this night, being o'er my head,
As is a winged messenger of heaven
Unto the white-upturned wondering eyes
Of mortals that fall back to gaze on him   30
When he bestrides the lazy-puffing clouds
And sails upon the bosom of the air.

JULIET
O Romeo, Romeo, wherefore art thou Romeo?

26–32 The double comparison of Juliet to an *angel* and 'a winged messenger of heaven', marvelled at by sublunary mortals, compresses angelology with classical mythopoeia, angels being *winged* just like the gods' messenger Hermes. Romeo's paean to Juliet in her presence, but not within her hearing, allows him to voice ever more extravagant imaginative projections of her without slipping into the anticommunal form of a soliloquy. With Juliet at her window and Romeo in the orchard below, the staging visually reinforces Romeo's comparison of Juliet to an angel high above him (see Bevington, *Action*, 111–12, on vertical mappings of space in *RJ*, and Thomson, 230ff., on the 'integration of the visual and verbal'). Karin Beier's lovers (1993) spoke their duet while perching precariously on swings (Hortmann, 470–1).

27–32 This may allude to a passage in Ovid's *Metamorphoses* where anglers, shepherds and ploughmen gaze up in wonder as Daedalus and Icarus fly high up in the air on their escape from Crete, thinking themselves gods able to travel through the skies (Ovid, *Met.*, 8.292–6). Shaheen (75–6) refers to Christ's ascension into heaven in Acts, 1.9–11.

28 **winged** wingèd

29 **white-upturned . . . eyes** upturnèd; eyes directed upwards so that their whites show (cited under *OED*

upturned 1a)

31 **bestrides** anticipating the apocalyptic vision of 'an emperor Antony' whose legs, like a colossus, 'bestrid the ocean' (*AC* 5.2.81) – a metaphor inspired by the angel in Revelation, 10.1, whose legs are pillars of fire, an image immortalized in a famous woodcut by Albrecht Dürer. The epic scope and dynamism of the image contrast the supine star-gazers with the energetic motion of heaven's messenger. Applied to the 13-year-old Juliet the image is provocatively 'overblown'.

lazy-puffing clouds racks of cloud that languidly swell (cited under *OED* lazy *a.* 4); *puffing*, the indubitable reading of Q2 (see also *puffs* at 1.4.102), anticipates the swelling of *sails* and *bosom* (32). Q1's more passive 'lasie pacing', i.e. 'lazy-passing' or 'lazy-pacing', is adopted in several editions. Q1 paints the clouds as a still life; in Q2 they gather and stack in a dynamic skyscape in a manner altogether more reflective of Romeo's kinetic rhetoric which has Juliet's eyes *stream* through the sky in the preceding trope. Hosley defends *puffing* ('Corrupting', 19).

32 **bosom** surface (*OED sb.* 2), but with the literal meaning implicit too, in the spherical shape of a breast

33ff. **thou . . . thy** The familiar pronouns and possessives convey an artless passion.

31 lazy-puffing] *Q2–4, F (*lazie puffing*); lasie pacing *Q1; lazy passing *Ulrici (Collier)*

Deny thy father and refuse thy name,
Or if thou wilt not, be but sworn my love,   35
And I'll no longer be a Capulet.

ROMEO

Shall I hear more, or shall I speak at this?

JULIET

'Tis but thy name that is my enemy.
Thou art thyself, though not a Montague.
What's Montague? It is nor hand nor foot,   40
Nor arm nor face nor any other part
Belonging to a man. O be some other name!
What's in a name? That which we call a rose
By any other word would smell as sweet;
So Romeo would, were he not Romeo called,   45
Retain that dear perfection which he owes
Without that title. Romeo, doff thy name,
And for thy name, which is no part of thee,
Take all myself.

ROMEO   I take thee at thy word.
Call me but love and I'll be new baptized.   50

---

34 **Deny thy father** the most unlikely
thing he could do because it would
make him a bastard. By denying their
parentage they are reborn in each
other's love, henceforth their sole
source of shared selfhood.
   thy name i.e. the patronymic
'Montague'

43 **rose** chosen for its scent and because
its vowel is identical with the first (and
stressed) syllable of *Romeo*; the expression 'as sweet as a rose' is proverbial
(Dent, R178). See also 2.4.204.

44 **word** Most editions accept Q2's reading 'word' here, but some editors have
argued in favour of Q1's 'name', because
persons or things are said to be known
by their 'names' and not their 'words'.
In support of *word*, Williams (115) cites
the play on 'name' and 'word' by the
Clown during his banter with Viola: 'I
would therefore my sister had had no
name . . . her name's a word, and to
dally with that word might make my
sister wanton' (*TN* 3.1.16–19).

46 **dear** precious
   owes possesses, owns (*OED v.* I 1a)

47 **title** appellation, name (*OED sb.* 4)
   doff get rid of, cast off (cited under
   OED v. 3)

50 **new baptized** renamed (cited under
   OED v. 3), but chiming with the strand
   of Christian mysticism that underpins
   the play's romantic imagery (see 114n.)

40–2] *Malone;* Whats *Mountague?* it is nor hand nor foote, / Nor arme nor face, ô be some other name
/ Belonging to a man. / *Q2–4, F;* Whats *Mountague?* / It is nor hand nor foote, / Nor arme, nor face,
nor any other part. / *Q1* 44 word] *Q2–4, F;* name *Q1*

189

Henceforth I never will be Romeo.

JULIET

What man art thou that thus bescreened in night
So stumblest on my counsel?

ROMEO   By a name
I know not how to tell thee who I am.
My name, dear saint, is hateful to myself,   55
Because it is an enemy to thee.
Had I it written, I would tear the word.

JULIET

My ears have yet not drunk a hundred words
Of thy tongue's uttering, yet I know the sound.
Art thou not Romeo, and a Montague?   60

ROMEO

Neither, fair maid, if either thee dislike.

JULIET

How cam'st thou hither, tell me, and wherefore?
The orchard walls are high and hard to climb,
And the place death, considering who thou art,

---

52 **bescreened** hidden from sight (cited in *OED*)
53 **stumblest on** chances upon (cited under *OED v.* 1b)
   counsel private musings
58 **drunk . . . words** Juliet finds Romeo's *words* intoxicating and, thirsty for more, she is counting them (he has spoken 59 words to her so far in this scene).
59 **tongue's** a physically charged word here coming immediately after *drunk* and because they kissed only a few minutes earlier. Although language is naturally articulated in the mouth by the tongue, the dramatic context may suggest a reference back to the lovers' kissing.
   uttering Malone compared with this 'His ear to drink her sweet tongue's

utterance' in *Edward III* (2.1.2), a play from the 1590s published in quarto by Cuthbert Burby in 1596 (close in time to *RJ*) on which Shakespeare may have collaborated with Marlowe.
61 **if . . . dislike** if you dislike either; *dislike* here being used grammatically the way modern English might use 'displease', so that 'it dislikes thee' means you don't like it (Abbott, 220)
62–5 'This scene should be compared with that of Miranda and Ferdinand [*Tem* 3.1] – how fine the variety on the same air', Coleridge noted about these lines and the 'balcony' scene generally (Coleridge, 136).
63–73 Brooke refers to 'your deadly foes, my kinsmen' tearing Romeus apart, 'like lions wild' (491–7).

53–4] *F; Q2–4 line* counsell? / am: /   58 yet not] *Q2–4, F;* not yet *Q1*   59 thy tongue's uttering] *Q2–4, F;* that tongues vtterance *Q1;* that tongue's uttring *Pope*   61 maid . . . dislike] *Q2–4, F;* Saint . . . displease *Q1*   62 cam'st] *F, Q1;* camest *Q2–4*

If any of my kinsmen find thee here.　　　　　65

ROMEO

With love's light wings did I o'erperch these walls,
For stony limits cannot hold love out,
And what love can do, that dares love attempt;
Therefore thy kinsmen are no stop to me.

JULIET

If they do see thee, they will murder thee.　　　　　70

ROMEO

Alack, there lies more peril in thine eye
Than twenty of their swords. Look thou but sweet,
And I am proof against their enmity.

JULIET

I would not for the world they saw thee here.

ROMEO

I have night's cloak to hide me from their eyes,　　　　　75
An but thou love me, let them find me here.
My life were better ended by their hate
Than death prorogued, wanting of thy love.

JULIET

By whose direction found'st thou out this place?

ROMEO

By love, that first did prompt me to enquire.　　　　　80
He lent me counsel, and I lent him eyes.

---

66 **o'erperch** fly over (Onions; cited in *OED*). Like Cupid, Romeo has acquired wings to carry him ever closer to Juliet (after Brooke's 'so light . . . he leapt the wall', 830). The scene's spatial orchestration, with Juliet elevated above Romeo, consolidates the upward-soaring aspiration and idealism of the relationship; see p. 188.
73 **proof against** impervious, invulnerable to (cited under *OED a.*[1] a)
75 **night's cloak** anticipating 3.2.10–16, where Juliet, yearning for night,

addresses it as a *sober-suited matron* wearing a *black mantle*. Shakespeare gleaned this from Brooke, where Romeus pays nightly visits to Juliet's window to catch a glimpse of her 'when on earth the night her mantle black hath spread' (457).
78 **prorogued** proroguèd; adjourned, deferred
wanting of lacking
81 **eyes** Cupid can now see, thanks to Romeo whom he 'counselled' to fall in love and who therefore becomes blind.

65 kinsmen] *Q3–4, F, Q1;* kismen *Q2*

I am no pilot, yet wert thou as far
As that vast shore washed with the farthest sea,
I should adventure for such merchandise.

JULIET

Thou knowest the mask of night is on my face,   85
Else would a maiden blush bepaint my cheek
For that which thou hast heard me speak tonight.
Fain would I dwell on form, fain, fain deny
What I have spoke; but farewell, compliment.
Dost thou love me? I know thou wilt say 'Ay',   90
And I will take thy word; yet, if thou swear'st,
Thou mayst prove false. At lovers' perjuries,
They say, Jove laughs. O gentle Romeo,
If thou dost love, pronounce it faithfully,
Or if thou think'st I am too quickly won,   95
I'll frown and be perverse and say thee nay,
So thou wilt woo, but else not for the world.
In truth, fair Montague, I am too fond,

---

82 ***pilot** a marine navigator; follows on from Juliet's question about *direction* (79) to the Capulets' orchard and anticipates the ensuing sea image. Juliet is the harbour and merchandise towards which Romeo steers his course; see p. 101.

83–4 The *vast shore* and *farthest sea* may allude to the far-flung, legendary kingdom of Colchis from where Jason the Argonauts snatched the Golden Fleece with the help of Colchis' royal princess, Medea, whom he subsequently betrayed. Shakespeare knew this story from Ovid (*Met.*, 7.263–89) and uses it in *Tem* 5.1.33–50 and *MV* 1.1.169–76.

86 **bepaint** colour (cited in *OED*)

88 **Fain** gladly
   dwell on form linger over ceremony

89 **compliment** modest formalities

90 '**Ay**' used again here to pick up the sense 'I' as well as meaning 'yes'; the second half of the line starts with *I*, ends with *'Ay'*, and is followed immediately by modulations of *I/Ay* in the next line. The collapsing of *I* and *Ay* between Romeo and Juliet underlines their mutuality.

92–3 **At . . . laughs** from Ovid's *Ars Amatoria*, 1.633: '*Iuppiter ex alto periuria ridet amantum*' ('Jove laughs at lovers' perjuries'; the line has become proverbial, Dent, J82).

93 **gentle** 'The epithet applies to Romeo's birth, manners, and disposition' (Oxf[1], 212) and anticipates the *tassel-gentle* at 159.

97 **else** otherwise

98 **fond** affectionate

---

82 pilot] *Q1, Q3–4, F;* Pylat *Q2*   83 washed] *Q1, Q4;* washeth *Q2;* washet *Q3, F*   89 compliment] *Q2–4, F;* complements *Q1*   90 love me? I] *Q2–4;* Love? I *F;* love me? Nay I *Q1*   93 laughs] *Q2–4;* laught *F;* smiles *Q1*

And therefore thou mayst think my haviour light.
But trust me, gentleman, I'll prove more true   100
Than those that have more cunning to be strange.
I should have been more strange, I must confess,
But that thou overheard'st, ere I was ware,
My true-love passion. Therefore pardon me,
And not impute this yielding to light love,   105
Which the dark night hath so discovered.

ROMEO

Lady, by yonder blessed moon I vow,
That tips with silver all these fruit-tree tops –

JULIET

O swear not by the moon, th'inconstant moon,
That monthly changes in her circled orb,   110
Lest that thy love prove likewise variable.

ROMEO

What shall I swear by?

JULIET   Do not swear at all,

---

99 **light** wanton
101 ***have more cunning** are more
adept, studied or artful at being reticent or reserved; *cunning* is the reading
of Q1 (Q2 has 'coying'), while Brooke
applies *cunning* to Juliet torn by grief
over Romeus' banishment and Tybalt's
death (1080).
  strange reserved, not familiar (cited
under *OED a.*[11] b)
103 **ware** aware, conscious (of your presence) (see 1.1.122n.)
105 **impute** attribute, ascribe
106 **Which** referring back to *yielding* in
105
  discovered discoverèd
107 **blessed** blessèd; happy, fortunate,
but also in bliss, perhaps because the

moon is full (*circled orb*, 110), hence
its silver tipping the trees on this midsummer night. For Romeo the moon
may be *blessed* also for being beheld by
Juliet's eyes.
108 **tips with silver** The image serves to
create a magical, lyrical mood for the
lovers' meeting; cf. the moon 'Decking
with liquid pearl the bladed grass' in
MND 1.1.211.
109 **th'inconstant moon** By monthly
growing and decreasing the moon is
constant only in change; its mutability
was proverbial (Dent, M1111).
110 ***circled orb** an unwitting sexual
innuendo since Mercutio's talk of raising spirits in Rosaline's *circle* (2.1.24)
still resonates in our ears.

---

99 haviour] *Q1;* behauiour *Q2–4, F*   101 cunning] *Q1;* coying *Q2–3, F;* more coying *Q4;* more
coyning *F2;* the coyning *Williams*   104 true-love] *Q2–4 (*truloue*);* true Loues *F, Q1*   107 blessed]
Q2–4, Q1; om. F   vow] *Q2–4, F;* swear *Q1*   108 tops –] *Rowe;* tops. *Q2–4, F, Q1*   110 circled] *Q1,
Q3–4, F;* circle *Q2*

Or if thou wilt, swear by thy gracious self,
Which is the god of my idolatry,
And I'll believe thee.

ROMEO   If my heart's dear love –   115

JULIET

Well, do not swear. Although I joy in thee,
I have no joy of this contract tonight;
It is too rash, too unadvised, too sudden,
Too like the lightning which doth cease to be
Ere one can say 'it lightens'. Sweet, good night.   120
This bud of love by summer's ripening breath
May prove a beauteous flower when next we meet.
Good night, good night; as sweet repose and rest
Come to thy heart as that within my breast.

ROMEO

O, wilt thou leave me so unsatisfied?   125

JULIET

What satisfaction canst thou have tonight?

ROMEO

Th'exchange of thy love's faithful vow for mine.

JULIET

I gave thee mine before thou didst request it,

---

113 **gracious** charming and attractive, but glancingly alluding to the more spiritual, Protestant meaning, 'possessed of grace'. The use of the word is particularly pertinent in the light of the Catholic phrase that follows in the next line.

114 **god . . . idolatry** the exalted object of my worship. Romeo and Juliet inhabit a Roman Catholic world; some of their well-wrought tropes are archly couched in its language.

117 **contract** contràct; 'formal agreement for marriage; betrothal' (*OED sb.* 3b, which cites '[Time] trots hard with

a young maid, between the contract of her marriage and the day it is solemnized', *AYL* 3.2.307–9)

119 **lightning** Cf. Hermia and Lysander on 'The course of true love' all too often being rendered 'Brief as the lightning in the collied night' (*MND* 1.1.145).
doth cease The use of emphatic *doth* is a rhetorical feature of the play, although here it may be a metrical filler; see also *did call*, 170.

121 **bud of love** lyrically playing on the idea of their love's growth and blossoming

113 gracious] *Q2–4, F;* glorious *Q1*   115 heart's dear] *Q2–4, F;* true harts *Q1*

194

And yet I would it were to give again.

ROMEO

　　Wouldst thou withdraw it? For what purpose, love?　　130

JULIET

　　But to be frank and give it thee again;
　　And yet I wish but for the thing I have.
　　My bounty is as boundless as the sea,
　　My love as deep; the more I give to thee,
　　The more I have, for both are infinite.　　　　　　135
　　I hear some noise within. Dear love, adieu.
　　　　[*Nurse calls within.*]
　　Anon, good Nurse! – Sweet Montague, be true,
　　Stay but a little, I will come again.　　　　　　[*Exit.*]

ROMEO

　　O blessed, blessed night! I am afeared,
　　Being in night, all this is but a dream,　　　　　140
　　Too flattering-sweet to be substantial.

　　　　　[*Enter* JULIET *above.*]

JULIET

　　Three words, dear Romeo, and good night indeed.

131 **frank** open and sincere (*OED a.*² 3a), but also bounteous (Oxf¹)

133–4 **bounty . . . deep** artfully reprising Romeo's marine imagery (82–4); the boundlessness and depth of the sea are proverbial (Dent, S169.1, 3). Ard² quotes Rosalind telling Celia, 'O coz . . . that thou didst know how many fathom deep I am in love! But it cannot be sounded' (*AYL* 4.1.195–8).

139 **blessed** blessèd; now night is apostrophized by Romeo in the same terms as the moon.

140–1 Romeo voices doubts similar to those expressed by the quartet of lovers in *MND* 4.1.186–217 as they wake; on the edge of consciousness, they compare the events of the night to 'far-off mountains turned into clouds'. The line scans relatively easily, with quadrisyllabic *substantial*, as 'Too flàttering-swèet to bè substàntiàl'.

141 ***flattering-sweet** after Theobald; see *silver-sweet*, 165.

142 **Three words** here used generically, as in *Three civil brawls* (1.1.87)

136 SD] *Rowe; Cals within. F; not in Q2–4, Q1*　138 SD] *Rowe*　141 flattering-sweet] *Theobald;* flattering sweete *Q2–4, F;* flattering true *Q1*　141.1] *Rowe subst.; Enter. F2*　142 dear] *Q2–4, F;* good *Q1*

If that thy bent of love be honourable,
Thy purpose marriage, send me word tomorrow
By one that I'll procure to come to thee,   145
Where and what time thou wilt perform the rite,
And all my fortunes at thy foot I'll lay,
And follow thee my lord throughout the world.

NURSE [*within*]

Madam!

JULIET

I come, anon! – But if thou meanest not well,   150
I do beseech thee –

NURSE [*within*]   Madam!

JULIET   By and by, I come! –
To cease thy strife and leave me to my grief.
Tomorrow will I send.

ROMEO   So thrive my soul –

JULIET

A thousand times good night.   [*Exit.*]

ROMEO

A thousand times the worse to want thy light.   155

143–53 **If . . . send** after Brooke, 533–44,
which includes the word 'wanton'
(541) used by Shakespeare in 177
143 **bent** inclination (*OED sb.*[2] 5)
145 **one** i.e. Nurse
    procure induce; cf. 'What unac-
    customed cause procures her hither?'
    (3.5.67). While Juliet's use of the word
    is free from any taint of corruption,
    procure commonly resonates with illicit
    sex and secret assignations, hence its
    painful aptness when applied to Nurse,
    who turns from trusted confidante and
    duenna to *Ancient damnation* (3.5.236).
151 **By and by** at once
152 **strife** endeavour, but Q4's 'sute'

('suit') should be noted, since 'suit'
occurs twice in the passage in Brooke
that Shakespeare used: in 'unlawful suit'
(541) and, more importantly, in Juliet's
exhortation, 'and now your Juliet you
beseeks / To cease your suit, and suffer
her live among her likes' (543–4), the
lines which lie directly behind 152.
Shakespeare read 'cease your suit' but
wrote *cease thy strife*, and then recalled
strife in *thrive* in the following line, in
a manner characteristic of this play's
patterns of cross-line rhymes and asso-
nances, a kind of phonic stichomythia.
Here as elsewhere his use of Brooke is
creatively eclectic.

146 the] *Q2–4, F;* that *Q1* rite] *Q2–3, F, Q1 (*right*);* rights *Q4* 148 lord] *F, Q1;* L. *Q2–3;* Loue
Q4 149, 151 NURSE [*within*] Madam!] *Capell; Within*: Madam. *F;* Madam. *opp.* world *148 and* come
151 Q2–4; not in Q1 152 strife] *Q2–3, F;* sute *Q4; not in Q1* 154 SD] *F; not in Q2–4, Q1* 155
light] *Q2–3, F;* sight *Q4; not in Q1*

Love goes toward love as schoolboys from their books,
But love from love toward school with heavy looks.

Enter JULIET *again.*

JULIET

Hist, Romeo, hist! O, for a falconer's voice
To lure this tassel-gentle back again –
Bondage is hoarse and may not speak aloud,   160
Else would I tear the cave where Echo lies
And make her airy tongue more hoarse than mine
With repetition of my 'Romeo'.

ROMEO

It is my soul that calls upon my name.
How silver-sweet sound lovers' tongues by night,   165
Like softest music to attending ears.

158 **Hist** a call for attention, to enjoin people to listen, with a sibilant ono-matopoeia (*OED* hist *int.* gives first recorded usage as 1617)

158–9 **O . . . again** Juliet's hawking metaphor infuses a predatory dimension into the lovers' mutual idealizing. A gentler version of the trope occurs in her penultimate speech in this scene, where she compares Romeo to *a wanton's bird* (177).

159 **tassel-gentle** tercel-gentle, a male peregrine falcon, '*gentle* because nobler than the goshawk' (Ard²), and applied to Romeo by an adoring Juliet

160 Thraldom to the spell of love makes Juliet whisper (see *hoarse*), but she also speaks in hushed tones to protect Romeo from her family. Following on from the bond between hawk and falconer, she turns her domestic predicament into an image of loving submission, of voluntary *Bondage* to Romeo, whom she called her *lord*

at 148 and to whom she henceforth gives fealty.

161–3 'Else I would rip through the cavernous chamber where Echo resides and force Echo to repeat (echo) the name of Romeo until she in turn is hoarse' (even though Echo is a spirit whose very nature is defined by repetition). In Ovid, the nymph Echo inhabited a body before she fell passionately in love with Narcissus (Ovid, *Met.*, 3.429–642). Her speech had already shrunk to repeating others' last words, a punishment by Juno for Echo's concealing Jupiter's adulteries. When Narcissus failed to requite her love she withered away, wandering in the woods and hiding in lonely caves, until finally she was just an *airy tongue*.

165–6 a string of sibilants and melodious vowels in two perfect pentameters; the 'silver' sound or tongue of music was proverbial (Dent, M1319.1); cf. 4.5.125–38.

156 toward] *Q2–4;* towards *F;* to *Q1*   157.1] *Q2–4, F; not in Q1*   160 not] *Q2–3, F, Q1; om. Q4*   162 more . . . mine] *Q4;* more hoarse, then *Q2–3, F;* as hoarse as mine *Q1*   163 Romeo] *Q2–4, F;* Romeos name. *Romeo? Q1;* Romeo's name. *Steevens;* Romeo's name. Romeo! *Oxf*   164 soul] *Q2–3, F, Q1;* loue *Q4*

197

JULIET

    Romeo!

ROMEO   My nyas?

JULIET   What o'clock tomorrow

    Shall I send to thee?

ROMEO   By the hour of nine.

JULIET

    I will not fail. 'Tis twenty year till then.

    I have forgot why I did call thee back.   170

ROMEO

    Let me stand here till thou remember it.

JULIET

    I shall forget to have thee still stand there,

    Remembering how I love thy company.

ROMEO

    And I'll still stay to have thee still forget,

    Forgetting any other home but this.   175

JULIET

    'Tis almost morning. I would have thee gone,

    And yet no farther than a wanton's bird,

---

167 ***nyas** fledgling, untrained hawk; the word continues the hawking imagery and appropriately applies it to the teenage Juliet now outside the nest (her bedroom). Q2's 'Neece' cannot be right, but given Shakespeare's use elsewhere of medial *y* for *i* may reflect 'nyec' in MS. This is Shakespeare's only 'nyas', although he refers to 'eyasses' (an eyas = a nyas) in the Folio version of *Ham* 2.2.335 (Ard³).

169 **year** years; cf. 1.3.2, where Nurse uses the singular of *year* colloquially for plural; here the uninflected usage is poetic rather than dialectal.

170 **did call** another use by Juliet of emphatic 'do' (see also 119)

171–4 **till . . . still** a string of arch *double entendres* playing on the different meanings of *still*. Romeo's offer to stay until Juliet remembers elicits the response that, since she so loves his company, she will continue to forget, if doing so means that he will therefore always (*still*) stay; to which he replies that he will stay *still* so as not to jolt her memory.

177 **wanton's** naughty child's; cf. 'As flies to wanton boys are we to the gods, / They kill us for their sport' (*KL* 4.1.38–9). Juliet compares herself to a wanton boy with a pet bird kept on a silken thread and given some little leeway to move freely before being reined in by its possessive master who imprisons it for love. Juliet's trope is inspired by her trapped predicament; see also *KL* 5.3.8–9.

167 My nyas?] *Wilson–Duthie (*My Niess?*); My Neece. *Q2–3, F; My Deere. *Q4; Madame. *Q1; My sweete. *F2* What] *Q2–4, F;* At what *Q1*   169 year] *Q2;* years *Q3–4, F, Q1*   172 forget to] *Q2, Q1;* forget, to *Q3–4, F* thee] *Q2, Q4, F, Q1;* the *Q3*   177 farther] *Q2–4;* further *F, Q1*

That lets it hop a little from his hand,
Like a poor prisoner in his twisted gyves,
And with a silken thread plucks it back again,   180
So loving-jealous of his liberty.

ROMEO

I would I were thy bird.

JULIET   Sweet, so would I,
Yet I should kill thee with much cherishing.
Good night, good night. Parting is such sweet sorrow
That I shall say goodnight till it be morrow.   185

ROMEO

Sleep dwell upon thine eyes, peace in thy breast;
Would I were sleep and peace, so sweet to rest.

[Exit Juliet.]

The grey-eyed morn smiles on the frowning night,

179 **twisted gyves** interlaced shackles or fetters, perhaps alluding also to the twisting motions of a prisoner struggling in vain to free himself, the point being that the bird on a *silken thread* (180) is as surely snared as a prisoner in harsh shackles.

181 **his** its (Abbott, 228)

184–5 **sorrow . . . morrow** Equating parting with pain and mourning is proverbial (Dent, P82.1).

186–7 Romeo's couplet seems spoken in response to Juliet's, even though Q2 gives 186 to Juliet. This must be a mistake, since in Q2 two identical SPs ('*Iu.*') appear in succession. Williams takes issue with Hosley's assigning *Parting . . . morrow* (184–5) to Romeo and *Sleep . . . rest* to Juliet. He notes that Juliet's couplet and *Good night* are fitting for her, as she has repeatedly wished Romeo good night in this very scene (Williams, 119).

188–91 The quartet survives in two distinct versions in Q2, the first one given to Romeo (as here) and the second attributed to the Friar, though the lines hardly fit with the Friar's meditation on medicinal herbalism. For Romeo, they constitute his response to Juliet's *morning* (176) and *morrow* (185) and anticipate her famous evocation of the horses of the sun at the start of 3.5. Williams (120–1) refers to the presence of these lines in *England's Parnassus* (*c.* 1600) and notes that the text quoted is the first (Romeo) version in Q2, with the exception of 'streams' for 'streaks'.

188 Romeo is talking about first light on a beautiful July morning, not the *glooming* at the end of the play when 'The sun for sorrow will not show his head' (5.3.306). Dent has 'grey-eyed morning' as proverbial (M1168.1). The respective personifications of morning and night, smiling and frowning, reflect victory and defeat as night yields to day.

178 his] *Q2–4, F;* her *Q1*   179 gyves] *Q2 (*giues)   180 silken] *Q2–4, F;* silke *Q1*   plucks] *Q2–4, F;* puls *Q1*   184] *Q1; Q2, Q4 line* night. / sorrow, / ; *Q3, F line* night. / *Ro.* . . . sorrow, /   186 SP] *Q1, Q4;* Iu. *Q2–3, F*   187 SD] *this edn (GWW); after 185 Pope*   188–91] *Q2–3, F; var. in Q1, Q4; see 2.3.1 t.n.*

199

Chequering the eastern clouds with streaks of light,
And darkness, fleckled, like a drunkard reels   190
From forth day's pathway made by Titan's wheels.
Hence will I to my ghostly sire's close cell,
His help to crave and my dear hap to tell.   *Exit.*

[2.3]   *Enter* FRIAR [LAURENCE] *alone, with a basket.*

FRIAR LAURENCE
Now, ere the sun advance his burning eye
The day to cheer and night's dank dew to dry,

189 **Chequering** variegating, diversifying with a different colour or shade (cited under *OED* chequer); cf. the 'chequered shadow on the ground' cast on the woodland floor by leaves that above it 'quiver with the cooling wind' in *Tit* 2.2.14–15. The lovers, obsessed with 'I' and 'eye', inhabit a world of subjective perception rather than objective reality.

190–1 Darkness is compared to a drunk lurching out of the track of the chariot of the sun god (Helios, Titan or Hyperion) so as not to be struck down by its surge.

190 **fleckled* 'Marked with little flecks or spots; dappled; also of a person: freckled' (cited in *OED*)

192–3 The lines are prompted by Brooke's 'To Friar Laurence will I wend, to learn his sage advice / He is my ghostly sire' (558–9).

192 **ghostly** spiritual; *ghostly* occurs in *ghostly father* at 2.3.41 and twice in *ghostly confessor* (2.6.21, 3.3.49).
*sire's Brooke's 'sire' (559) has been accepted by a number of editors (e.g.

Ard[2], Cam[2]) in preference to Q2's 'friar' (Q1 has 'fathers'); in secretary hand, long *s* and *f* are easily misread, though *s* and *fr* less so.

close cell perhaps a long-range reminiscence of a later passage in Brooke where Romeus seeks refuge in 'trusty Laurence's cell . . . a secret place . . . Where he [Laurence] was wont in youth, his fair friends to bestow' (1263–73).

193 **dear hap** good fortune

2.3 First light on Monday (1) in the herb garden of an abbey in Verona

1–26 The Friar's lines here, and elsewhere, are frequently pruned in performance.

1–18 after Brooke, 565–74

1 **advance** raise

2 The *d* alliteration sets the tone for the Friar's stylized language which rhymes, with studied monotony, for 26 lines. This artificial mode of expression may serve to highlight the limitations of the Friar's role as the moral guardian of order.

dank damp

189 Chequering] *Q2–3, F;* Checking *Q4, Q1*   190 fleckled] *Q3, F;* fleckted *Q2;* flecked *Q1; not in Q4*   192 sire's] *Delius;* Friers *Q2–4;* Fries *F;* fathers *Q1*   2.3] *Hanmer*   0.1] *Q2–4 subst., F; Enter Frier Francis. Q1*   1 FRIAR LAURENCE Now] *F2, Rowe; Fri.* The grey-eyed morne smiles on the frowning night, / Checking the Easterne clowdes with streaks of light: / And fleckeld darknesse like a drunkard reeles, / From forth daies path, and *Titans* burning wheeles: / Now *Q2–4, F, Q1 subst.; see 2.2.188–91 t.n.*

I must up-fill this osier cage of ours
With baleful weeds and precious-juicèd flowers.
The earth that's nature's mother is her tomb,   5
What is her burying grave, that is her womb;
And from her womb children of divers kind
We sucking on her natural bosom find,
Many for many virtues excellent,
None but for some, and yet all different.   10
O, mickle is the powerful grace that lies
In plants, herbs, stones and their true qualities,
For naught so vile that on the earth doth live
But to the earth some special good doth give,
Nor aught so good but, strained from that fair use,   15
Revolts from true birth, stumbling on abuse.

---

3   **up-fill** fill up (cited under *OED v.*)
    osier i.e. made of willow twigs
    cage basket (cited under *OED sb.* 4a)
    ours the shared property of the
    Franciscans rather than the Friar's own
    (Cam²), or else perhaps an indicator of
    a folksy way of talking, complementing
    his use of *mickle* (11)
4   **baleful** deadly or noxious (cited in
    OED)
    precious-juiced precious-juicèd; full
    of natural goodness (cited in *OED*)
5–6   Earth and nature constantly recy-
    cle through the processes of rotting
    and manure, rebirth and growth.
    The rhyme of *womb* and *tomb*, with
    the words differentiated by a single
    consonant, instances the flimsy divide
    between life and death, one of the
    key motifs in this play of opposites,
    thresholds and crossings-over. (Dent,
    E28.1, has earth as the common
    mother of all as proverbial.)
7   **children** plants and herbs, the pro-
    duce of nature (see 12)
9–18   This passage develops the idea that
    there are no plants that do not pos-
    sess at least some benign power, while

granting at the same time that some
plants, when misused, can have the
opposite effect.
11   **mickle** archaic word meaning great
    or much, characteristic of Spenser's
    The Faerie Queene; used here perhaps
    to mark the Friar's idiom as elderly
    and rural. He refers to his *old life* at
    5.3.267, after Brooke, who calls him
    'old man' (598; see also 2117–20).
    grace 'efficacy', 'wholesome quality'
    (cited under *OED sb.* 13), rather than
    carrying a particular spiritual resonance
13   another archaism, this time of sen-
    tence construction, expecting us to fill
    in missing 'there is' after *For*
    naught nothing
15–16   Even intrinsically beneficient
    plants can be wrenched from their
    true nature to become poisonous (pro-
    verbial; see Dent, N317).
15   **aught** anything
    strained perverted. *OED* strain *v.¹* d
    cites the line and glosses 'strain': 'To
    apply or use (a thing) beyond its prov-
    ince', in this case the quality of *fair use*.
16   **stumbling on abuse** falling into a
    perversion of itself

---

12 plants, herbs] *Q2–4, F;* hearbes, plants *Q1*   15 aught] *Q2–4, F;* nought *Q1*

Virtue itself turns vice, being misapplied,
And vice sometime by action dignified.

Enter ROMEO.

Within the infant rind of this weak flower
Poison hath residence and medicine power,   20
For this, being smelled, with that part cheers each
    part,
Being tasted, stays all senses with the heart.
Two such opposed kings encamp them still
In man as well as herbs, grace and rude will,

17–18 Each thing, including moral being, can be twisted into its opposite (just as medicinal plants can turn to poison); the couplet prepares the ground for the analogy between plants and humankind in 24.

18 'Depraved behaviour is sometimes excused (*dignified*) in the name of *action*'; or else the Friar may mean that occasionally the end is made to justify the means, alluding perhaps to the Florentine historian and politician Machiavelli, whom Shakespeare evokes in *3H6* 3.2.193.

18.1 Romeo enters here in Q2 and thus overhears, perhaps in respectful silence, the Friar's reflections on the contrary qualities of his flowers, a poignant, dramatically effective moment since he may be distilling the potion Juliet takes (see 22). Listening to the Friar discursing on poison and medicine may also prompt Romeo to seek out the apothecary later (Dessen, *Recovering*, 65–6). Q1 does not mark an entry for Romeo. Pope placed his entry after 26, making him speak the moment he appears. In Peter Brook's 1947 production, Romeo entered running at 21, crept up on the Friar and covered his eyes while he spoke 22–7.

Bogdanov had him come in after *heart* (22), but annotates his entry 'Romeo (off)' in the promptbook, to indicate that he is heard but not yet seen.

19 **infant** newly grown

20 The alliterative epanalepsis of *Poison* and *power* artfully reflects the paradoxical ability of the fragile flower to do harm and good in equal measure.

21 **that part** i.e. its scent

22 **stays . . . heart** induces cardiac arrest with all the senses paralysed; *with* here meaning 'together with'. The Friar may be referring to *digitalis*, a medication prepared from foxglove, or else to deadly nightshade, also known as belladonna and used in medicine. A number of editors follow Q1 'slaies' and write 'slays' for *stays*. Williams (122) notes that the compositor's ligature case for *st/sl* 'is more than once foul', instancing '*shall/*stal' (1.3.18) and another occurrence of '*stay/slay*' at 4.1.72.

23 **opposed** opposèd; dual and antagonistic
   still always

24 **grace . . . will** godliness – with man sharing in the divine through *grace* – and, at the same time, the animal instincts – the spirit and bodily instincts, the *opposed kings* of 23

18 sometime *Q2–4, F;* sometimes *Q1*   18.1] *Q2–4, F; not in Q1; after 26 Pope*   19 weak] *Q2–4, F;* small *Q1*   22 stays] *Q2;* slaies *Q3–4, F, Q1*   senses] *Q2, Q4, F, Q1;* sence *Q3*   23 kings] *Q2–4, F;* foes *Q1*

And where the worser is predominant   25
Full soon the canker death eats up that plant.

ROMEO

Good morrow, father.

FRIAR LAURENCE   *Benedicite.*

What early tongue so sweet saluteth me?
Young son, it argues a distempered head
So soon to bid good morrow to thy bed.   30
Care keeps his watch in every old man's eye,
And where care lodges, sleep will never lie;
But where unbruised youth with unstuffed brain
Doth couch his limbs, there golden sleep doth reign.
Therefore thy earliness doth me assure   35
Thou art uproused with some distemperature;
Or if not so, then here I hit it right,

26 **the canker ... plant** A man ruled by his instincts or passions rots from within just as cankered plants do.

27 *Benedicite* 'Bless you.'

28 **early tongue** like an early bird, that is up betimes in the morning

29 **distempered** sick, physically and mentally out of sorts, suffering an imbalance in the bodily 'humours' of blood, phlegm, choler and melancholy (also known as black choler); hence the King in *Hamlet* is reportedly 'marvellous distempered ... with choler' (3.2.293–6), while Hamlet's schoolfriends try to discover the reason for his melancholy, his 'cause of distemper' (3.2.328–29); see also *TN* 1.5.89–91. Variations on 'temper' and cognates occur at different points of *RJ*, including the surprising use of *distemperature* at 36 so shortly after *distempered*; see also *mistempered* (1.1.85) and *temper* at 3.1.117.

30 **good morrow** used here as a parting exchange rather than a greeting

31–2 i.e. care is the natural prerogative of old age as opposed to youth.

33 **unbruised** unbruisèd; untouched by the buffetings of life
unstuffed not burdened, free from worries (cited under *OED ppl. a.*)

34 **couch** rest; the use of the word in *AC* 4.4.52 ('Where souls do couch on flowers') may suggest that for Shakespeare *couch* evokes luxuriance and comfort, here of youth sleeping soundly.
golden sleep on the linking of *golden* and *youth*, see the dirge in *Cymbeline*, 'Fear no more the heat o' th' sun', in which 'lads and girls' are said to be 'golden' (4.2.258–63); sleep is repeatedly 'golden' in Shakespeare as e.g. in *1H4* 2.3.40. 'Morning sleep is golden' is proverbial (Dent, S525.1).

36 **uproused** stirring abroad (cited under *OED ppl. a.*)
distemperature troubled state of mind (cited in *OED*)

37 **here** with this; i.e. with the thought which follows, that Romeo has not been to bed at all

27 father] *Q2–4, F;* to my Ghostly Confessor *Q1*   28 sweet] *Q2–4, F;* soone *Q1*   32 will] *Q2–4, F;* can *Q1*   34 doth reign] *Q2–4, F;* remaines *Q1*   36 with] *Q2–4, F;* by *Q1*

Our Romeo hath not been in bed tonight.

ROMEO

That last is true, the sweeter rest was mine.

FRIAR LAURENCE

God pardon sin! Wast thou with Rosaline?   40

ROMEO

With Rosaline, my ghostly father? No,

I have forgot that name and that name's woe.

FRIAR LAURENCE

That's my good son; but where hast thou been then?

ROMEO

I'll tell thee ere thou ask it me again.

I have been feasting with mine enemy,   45

Where on a sudden one hath wounded me

That's by me wounded. Both our remedies

Within thy help and holy physic lies.

I bear no hatred, blessed man, for lo,

My intercession likewise steads my foe.   50

FRIAR LAURENCE

Be plain, good son, and homely in thy drift;

---

39 **sweeter rest** a rest more pleasant than sleep, with *sweeter* hinting at sex, hence Friar Laurence's next line
41 **ghostly** See 2.2.192n.
42 **woe** The irony in this use of one of the play's key words (*woe, woes, woeful* occur 29 times altogether) becomes clear when *woe* rhymes with *Romeo* in the final couplet of the tragedy. For a similarly pointed play on *woe*, see Paris at 3.4.8: 'These times of woe afford no times to woo.'
44 **thou** Romeo's use of the familiar *thou* to address the Friar, like Juliet's use of *thou* and *thy* at 2.2.33–4, creates an intimate, if not conspiratorial atmosphere between them.
46–7 **Where ... wounded** Romeo and Juliet were *wounded* because pierced

by Cupid's arrow at the same time, a rhetorical way of saying that the two of them are equally smitten. The banter of the next three lines continues the trope of wounding and foes.
47 **Both our remedies** the cure for both of us
48 **holy physic** sacred healing powers as a priest able to confer the sacrament of marriage
49 **lo** a jocular interjection to draw attention to something; obs., survives in 'lo and behold'.
50 **intercession** prayer, plea
steads profits (cited in *OED*)
foe i.e. Juliet
51 **plain ... homely** hendiadys used for emphasis

---

38 in bed] *Q2–4, F;* a bed *Q1*   39 That] *Q2–4, F;* The *Q1*   40 Wast] *Q2–4, F;* wert *Q1*   46 a sudden] *Q2–4, F;* the sodaine *Q1*   51 good] *Q2–4, F;* my *Q1*   and] *Q2–4, Q1;* rest *F*

Riddling confession finds but riddling shrift.

ROMEO

Then plainly know, my heart's dear love is set
On the fair daughter of rich Capulet.
As mine on hers, so hers is set on mine,   55
And all combined, save what thou must combine
By holy marriage. When, and where, and how
We met, we wooed and made exchange of vow,
I'll tell thee as we pass; but this I pray,
That thou consent to marry us today.   60

FRIAR LAURENCE

Holy Saint Francis, what a change is here!
Is Rosaline, that thou didst love so dear,
So soon forsaken? Young men's love then lies
Not truly in their hearts but in their eyes.
Jesu Maria, what a deal of brine   65
Hath washed thy sallow cheeks for Rosaline!
How much salt water thrown away in waste

---

52 **Riddling** spoken in riddles, enigmatic
    shrift absolution (*OED sb.* 2)
56 **combined** conjoined
59 **pass** go along
61 **Saint Francis** Francis is evoked here
because Laurence is a Franciscan. The
saint from Assisi loved birds and is
their patron saint. Birds feature at
strategic points in *RJ*, notably the
lark and nightingale at the parting of
the young lovers at dawn (3.5) and in
Juliet's imagining Romeo as a captive
bird pet (2.2.177). Shakespeare may
have known Francis's hymn to the sun
and its universal blessing of creation
(see pp. 16–17).
63–4 **Young . . . eyes** Young men love
too much by sight and appearance
(hence, the Friar implies, fickleness
like Romeo's is only to be expected).

'Love comes by looking (in at the
eyes)' is proverbial (Dent, L501).
65 **Jesu Maria** a distinctly Catholic
exclamation or mild oath; 'Jesu' is used
twice more in the play, by Mercutio
at 2.4.29 and by Nurse at 2.5.29, in
line with the play's Italian setting of
friars' cells and abbeys (see *abbey wall*
at 2.4.179). Shakespeare nowhere else
refers to the Virgin as *Maria* (Cam[2]).
    brine salt water, i.e. tears; spelled out
in the next line
66 **sallow** brownish in complexion (cited
in *OED*). Romeo's hopeless love of
Rosaline and lack of sleep caused his
skin to turn yellow and, perhaps, his
cheeks to be hollow (*sallow* and 'shal-
low' are virtually homophones; in the
theatre an audience could be trusted to
pick up both meanings).

---

57 When, and where] *Q2–4, F;* where, and when *Q1*   58 vow] *Q2–4, F;* vowes *Q1*   59 we] *Q2–4, F;*
I *Q1*   67 thrown] *Q2–4, F;* cast *Q1*

To season love that of it doth not taste.
The sun not yet thy sighs from heaven clears,
Thy old groans yet ringing in mine ancient ears.   70
Lo, here upon thy cheek the stain doth sit
Of an old tear that is not washed off yet.
If e'er thou wast thyself and these woes thine,
Thou and these woes were all for Rosaline.
And art thou changed? Pronounce this sentence then: 75
Women may fall when there's no strength in men.

ROMEO

Thou chid'st me oft for loving Rosaline.

FRIAR LAURENCE

For doting, not for loving, pupil mine.

ROMEO

And bad'st me bury love.

FRIAR LAURENCE   Not in a grave
To lay one in, another out to have.   80

ROMEO

I pray thee, chide me not. Her I love now
Doth grace for grace and love for love allow;
The other did not so.

---

68 i.e. the salt of his tears in vain
seasoned a love that could not be
tasted because it was not love at all,
hence his readiness to trade it in for
another love (*OED* cites 67–8 under
season *v.*).

69 His *sighs* are like vapours or mists that
the sun in due course burns up.

70 **ringing in** haunting (cited under
OED ring *v.*¹)

73–4 'If you really were yourself then and
these were indeed your lamentations,
they were all over Rosaline.'

75 **sentence** maxim

76 If men are as inconstant as Romeo
has just proved to be, then women's

natural changeability and susceptibil-
ity can be excused.

80 This alludes to the practice of adding
bodies to graves that are already occupied, as in Donne's poem 'The Relic':
'When my grave is broke up again /
Some second guest to entertain / . . .
And he that digs it, spies / A bracelet
of bright hair about the bone' (1–2,
5–6). The image, in clear anticipation
of the onstage action of the play's
last Act, conjures up a reversion of
funeral practice, of digging up a grave
not only to bury a dead body but to
resurrect one too.

82 **grace** favour (*OED*)

68 it] *Q2–4, F;* loue *Q1*   70 yet ringing] *Q2–3, F;* yet ring *Q4;* ring yet *Q1*   mine] *Q2;* my *Q3–4, F,*
Q1   71 Lo, here] *Q2–4, F;* And loe *Q1*   73 wast thyself] *Q2–4, F;* wert thus *Q1*   81 me] *Q2–4, F;*
not in Q1   Her] *Q2–4, F;* she *Q1*

FRIAR LAURENCE   O, she knew well
Thy love did read by rote, that could not spell.
But come, young waverer, come, go with me.   85
In one respect I'll thy assistant be,
For this alliance may so happy prove,
To turn your households' rancour to pure love.

ROMEO
O, let us hence, I stand on sudden haste.   89

FRIAR LAURENCE
Wisely and slow, they stumble that run fast.   *Exeunt.*

[**2.4**]   *Enter* BENVOLIO *and* MERCUTIO.

MERCUTIO   Where the devil should this Romeo be? Came
he not home tonight?

BENVOLIO
Not to his father's; I spoke with his man.

MERCUTIO
Why, that same pale, hard-hearted wench, that
Rosaline,

84 **Thy . . . rote** The Friar suggests
Romeo's love for Rosaline was illiterate
and that it was his callow (*by rote =*
unthinking) understanding of love that
kept her away (*OED* rote *sb.*²); illiteracy
and reading are a running joke in the
play. Cf. proverbial 'Read not before
you learn to spell' (Dent, R38). Cam²
adduces 'Who will read must first learn
spelling' from *Astrophil and Stella*.
85 **waverer** because he is emotionally
fickle (cited in *OED*)
86–8 This recollects the Friar's thought
in Brooke, 607–10, that 'this marriage
might appease' the strife between the
two warring families.
88 **rancour** bitter hatred
89 **stand** insist (*OED* stand *v.* 74e cites

this line and glosses 'to give oneself to,
practise')
90 proverbial (Dent, F141, H198, R211),
a version of the Latin dictum *festina
lente* = hurry on slowly, as the most
assured way of reaching one's destination (see also 2.6.15n.)
stumble See also 5.3.122.
2.4 Around noon (108–9; 2.5.1, 10–11).
When Nurse enters at 97.1 it has gone
noon, although only a few minutes of
playing time separate Romeo's dawn
interview and Nurse's entry.
2 **tonight** last night
4 **pale** Rosaline's pallor (real or attributed)
suggests a lack of blood and passion, as
does her *hard-hearted* imperviousness;
she is called *white* at 14.

84 that] *Q2–4, F; and Q1* 85 go] *Q2–3, F, Q1; and goe Q4* 89–90] *Q2–4, F; not in Q1* 90 SD]
Q2–4, F; opp. 89 Q1 **2.4**] *Hanmer* 0.1] *Q2–4, F; Enter Mercutio, Benuolio. Q1* 1–2] *Q2–4, F;
Capell lines* be! / night? / 1 devil] *Q2–4, F (deule Q2, deu'le Q3–4, deu le F); not in Q1* 4–5]
Q2–4, Q1; prose F

Torments him so that he will sure run mad.   5

BENVOLIO

Tybalt, the kinsman to old Capulet,

Hath sent a letter to his father's house.

MERCUTIO   A challenge, on my life.

BENVOLIO   Romeo will answer it.

MERCUTIO   Any man that can write may answer a letter.   10

BENVOLIO   Nay, he will answer the letter's master, how he
dares being dared.

MERCUTIO   Alas, poor Romeo, he is already dead, stabbed
with a white wench's black eye, run through the ear
with a love song, the very pin of his heart cleft with   15
the blind bow-boy's butt-shaft – and is he a man to
encounter Tybalt?

BENVOLIO   Why, what is Tybalt!

MERCUTIO   More than Prince of Cats. O, he's the

---

6   **kinsman** The reminder about
Tybalt's kinship with the Capulets
serves to bring the audience back to
the factional feud. The Friar's hope
for peace a few lines earlier still rings
in the audience's ears.

7   **a letter** the second of four letters in
the play (see 1.2.62 SD). This one
also provokes a joke about literacy and
illiteracy.

8   **challenge** summons to a duel
on my life 'I bet you'

9   **answer** accept; anticipating the quibble on *answer* in the next lines

11–12 **how . . . dared** how forcefully he
will respond to being thus provoked

13–16 **Alas . . . butt-shaft** Mercutio
suggests that Romeo's inner being has
been sapped by Rosaline's *black eye*,
transfixed with love poetry and pierced
by an arrow from Cupid's bow. The
fencing terms of stabbing, running
through and cleaving also belong to
love's combats.

15   **pin** stud in the centre of a target used
in archery (cited under *OED sb.*¹), here
the inner core of his heart; hitting or
cleaving the pin was proverbial (Dent,
P336), but with different meanings
attaching to it. For a much saucier use
of 'cleaving the pin' in the context of
'upshoot', 'pricks' and 'rubbing', see
Ard³, *LLL* 4.1.135n.

16   **blind bow-boy's** i.e. Cupid's
butt-shaft a strong, unbarbed arrow
used for archery practice; Shakespeare's
only other use of the word occurs
in *LLL* 1.2.168, in a passage which
resembles this one by similarly using
technical terms from duelling.

19   **Prince of Cats** probably derived from
Tybert (a near homophone of Tybalt),
prince of cats in the medieval folklore
collection *Reynard the Fox*. The title
'Prince of Cattes' for Tybalt (*'Tibault'*)
is first used by Nashe in *Have With
You* (Nashe, 3.51); see also List of
Roles, 21n.

6–7] *Q1; prose Q2–4, F*   6 kinsman] *Q3–4, F, Q1;* kisman *Q2*   14 run] *Q2–4, F;* shot *Q1*   18 SP] *F,
Q1; Ro. Q2; Rom. Q3–4*   19 Cats] *Q2–4, F;* cattes I can tell you *Q1*

courageous captain of compliments: he fights as you   20
sing pricksong, keeps time, distance and proportion.
He rests his minim rests, one, two, and the third
in your bosom; the very butcher of a silk button,
a duellist, a duellist, a gentleman of the very first

20 **courageous . . . compliments** The
c alliteration mimes the rapid thrusting and stabbing of Tybalt's fencing;
captain of compliments means that he
is supremely accomplished primarily
in points of ceremony pertaining to
duelling, i.e. he fights foppishly by the
book but lacks flair and substance.
he fights Q1 here reads 'Catso, he
fights', which not only recalls the
'Cats' of the mock title bestowed upon
Tybalt but calls him '*cazzo*' ('prick' in
Italian): Tybalt is King of Cats and
Chief Prick.
21 **pricksong** music so called because
it was sung from written or 'pricked'
notes (*cantus precatus*) rather than from
memory (*OED* defines 'prick' as 'a
mark or dot in musical notation').
According to Mercutio, Benvolio
sings by the book just as Tybalt fights
by it, with pedantic precision and
without inspiration (he disparagingly
calls Tybalt a fighter by 'the book of
arithmetic' in 3.1.104).
distance 'A definite interval of space
to be observed between two combat-
ants' in fencing (cited under *OED
sb.* 5b)
proportion cadence or rhythm to be
observed in the rules of duelling
22 **rests . . . rests** observes pauses as
precise as minims; a minim in musical
notation is half a whole note, hence of
very short duration (cited under *OED*
minim). Tybalt has perfect fencing
rhythm, timing his thrusts and parries
like a musician.
22–3 **third . . . bosom** After two well
timed feints Tybalt will strike home

and hit his target.
23 **butcher . . . button** This may
recollect the cleft stud of the pin
of Romeo's heart (15); Tybalt, like
Cupid, can deftly strike his oppo-
nent right through the heart, hence
the *silk button* (on a doublet). Ard²
sees a more specific reference to the
most famous practitioner of the new
school of fencing in Blackfriars, Rocco
Bonetti. He died in 1587, allegedly of
wounds received in a duel from one
Austen Baggar, who had challenged
him with the words, 'thou that takest
upon thee to hit any Englishman with
a thrust upon any button'. Bonetti's
successor Vincentio Saviolo wrote a
fencing manual, *Vincentio Saviolo his
Practice* (1595), which Shakespeare
used in *RJ* (Holmer, 'Draw') and in
AYL 5.4.99–101.
24 **duellist** one well practised at duels.
This is only the second recorded
instance of the word in the period,
suggesting that Mercutio's repetition
of it deliberately pokes fun at it as
new-fangled, affected or modish.
24–5 **a gentleman . . . house** one of
the best people in town, spoken here
sarcastically because the proverbial
phrase, 'a gentleman of the first head',
is a catcall meaning hardly a gentleman
at all (Dent, G66). Dent (26) suggests
that a pause before *house* would bring
the insult home to the audience. Also,
house may quibble on fencing school,
or 'college', as Bonetti's academy was
known; Mercutio may be mocking
Tybalt's pedigree, traceable to a mere
fencing school.

20 he] *Q2–4, F;* Catso, he *Q1*   22 his minim rests] *Q2–4 (*minum*);* his minum *F;* me his minum
rest *Q1*

209

house, of the first and second cause. Ah, the immortal   25
passado, the *punto reverso*, the hay!

BENVOLIO   The what?

MERCUTIO   The pox of such antic, lisping, affecting
fantasticoes, these new tuners of accent! By Jesu, a
very good blade, a very tall man, a very good whore!   30

---

25 **first . . . cause** terminology from
duelling; *The Book of Honour and Arms*
by Sir William Segar (1590) offers a
definition of first and second causes:
'whensoever one man doeth accuse
another of such a crime as meriteth
death, in that case the combat ought be
granted. The second cause of combat
is honour, because among persons of
reputation, honour is preferred before
life' (quoted in Cam²).

immortal famous, but with a pun on
immortal meaning beyond mortality;
in other words the *passado* can kill its
target.

26 *passado* a thrust while stepping
forward; *OED* cites this line, but
attributes the first English usage to
Saviolo's manual ('You may with much
suddenness make a *passata* with your
left foot'; see 23n.).

punto reverso or, technically, *punta
riversa* = 'A thrust made with the point
of the sword and typically delivered
from the executant's left side with the
palm up' (*OED*), as opposed to *punta
dritta*, where the palm is down in the
normal position

the hay 'a home-thrust', from the
Italian *hai* (meaning 'you have it',
second person singular of have/
avere); *OED* hay *sb.*⁵ cites this as the
first recorded usage, hence Benvolio's
failure to understand what Mercutio
means. (All but a handful of *OED* first
usages from *RJ* record 1592 as the
play's date and need to be seen in that
context; where this is not the case, as
at 29 below, the different date is given.

See pp. 33–43.)

28 **antic** clownish or fantastical
lisping mannered
affecting affected

29 ***fantasticoes** (Q1) absurd and irrational fools. *OED* gives this reference
under 'fantastico' as the first of only
two recorded usages (*RJ*, 1597), but
overlooks Thomas Nashe's *Have With
You* ('follow one of these new-fangled
Galiardos and *Senior Fantasticos*',
Nashe, 3.31), which is probably where
Shakespeare encountered it. Most
editors follow Crow's conjecture,
'phantasimes', accepting his suggestion that the compositor of Q2, which
has 'phantacies', overlooked a tilde in
the MS, or that perhaps the MS was
not clearly enough marked up.

new . . . accent fellows who give
a spurious vocal tone to a way of
speaking, i.e. by *lisping* and *affecting*
(cited under *OED* tuner b). Mercutio
pillories Tybalt's faddish behaviour as
posturing. The train of thought here
may have been inspired by Nashe's
'amorous *Villanellas* and *Quipassas*',
which follow immediately after his
reference to '*Fantasticos*' (Nashe, 3.31).

29–30 **By . . . whore** Mercutio is being
sarcastic. His use of *very* corresponds
to modern (colloquial) 'some' as in
'some good blade!', where it means
the opposite of a good fighter and
gentleman.

30 **blade** metonymic for swordsman and
here, contemptuously, a gallant (cited
under *OED sb.* 11a)
tall valiant (*OED a.* 3)

---

28 antic] *Pope;* antique *Q2–4, F;* limping antique *Q1*   29 fantasticoes] *Q1;* phantacies *Q2–4, F;*
phantacimes *Williams (Crow)*   accent] *Q2–4, F;* accents *Q1*   By Jesu] *Q2–4, Q1;* Jesu *F*

Why, is not this a lamentable thing, grandsire, that we
should be thus afflicted with these strange flies, these
fashion-mongers, these pardon-me's who stand so
much on the new form that they cannot sit at ease on
the old bench? O, their bones, their bones!   35

Enter ROMEO.

BENVOLIO   Here comes Romeo, here comes Romeo!
MERCUTIO   Without his roe, like a dried herring. O
flesh, flesh, how art thou fishified! Now is he for the

31 **grandsire** a jaunty form of address
since Benvolio is a mere youth
32 **strange flies** outlandish parasites; cf.
'how the poor world is pestered with
such water-flies' (*TC* 5.1.33–4) and
Hamlet's calling Osric a 'water-fly', a
person of no account (*Ham* 5.2.69).
33 **pardon-me's** foppish and affected
gallants aping the French
stand insist
34 **new form** the latest etiquette; but
form also means 'A long seat without
a back, a bench' (*OED* form II 17).
Mercutio's point is that they are so
concerned with the latest fad that they
can barely bear to sit on a bench when
in fact the *new form* is no more than an
old bench.
35 **bones** mocks the mincing protests of
modish gallants; also perhaps (Ard[2])
playing on the French pronunciation
of 'bones' (*bons* = plural of 'good')
while suffering from the 'malady of
France' also known as 'the Neapolitan
bone-ache', syphilis
37 **Without his roe** i.e. as Romeo without 'Ro', which is 'meo' = 'miaow';
another of Mercutio's feline jokes,
provoked this time by Benvolio's
calling out Romeo's name, maybe

paradoxically stressing its last syllable. In the play's rhetoric the Prince
of Cats (Tybalt) is pitted against a
mere pussycat (Romeo), who is
drained, moreover, of all his vital
juices.
dried herring shotten herring, a fish
that has spawned; in Romeo's case, a
young man without his sperm (*roe*),
hence dry. *OED* roe[2] cites this line
and notes that hard roe is the spawn
of the female and soft roe the sperm
of the male. Since Romeo has been
out all night, Mercutio suggests that
he must have been having intercourse
with Rosaline and is therefore a lesser
man, reduced, post-coital, spermless
and exhausted, a mere *herring*, usually
a term of contempt in Shakespeare.
The phrase as 'As lean (lank) as a
shotten herring' is proverbial (Dent,
H447).
38 **fishified** turned into fish as in
dried herring (the first recorded
usage in English, according to *OED*
fishify, which cites this line), the
point being that Romeo (*flesh*) has
become fish through intercourse
(Shakespeare repeatedly associates sex
with fish).

33 pardon-me's] *F, Q1;* pardons mees *Q2;* pardon mees *Q3;* pardona-mees *Q4;*   pardonnez-moy's
Theobald; pardona-mi's *Cam*

numbers that Petrarch flowed in. Laura to his lady
was a kitchen wench – marry, she had a better love   40
to berhyme her – Dido a dowdy, Cleopatra a gypsy,
Helen and Hero hildings and harlots, Thisbe a grey
eye or so, but not to the purpose. Signor Romeo,
bonjour: there's a French salutation to your French
slop. You gave us the counterfeit fairly last night.   45

39 **numbers** verses (*OED* number *sb.* 17a
cites *LLL* 4.3.54: 'These numbers will
I tear and write in prose')
Petrarch . . . Laura The Italian
poet Petrarch (Francesco Petrarca,
1304–74) was the author of a famous
series of idealizing sonnets celebrating
his love for Laura.
flowed in composed with such fluency
to compared to
40 **better love** because Petrarch was a
better poet than Romeo
41 **beryhme** praise in rhymes, with a
quibble on Petrarch's collection *Rime*
41–2 **Dido . . . Thisbe** All five of these
women were tragic legendary lovers:
Dido, Queen of Carthage, sheltered
Aeneas and became his lover, committing suicide when he abandoned her
(*Aeneid*, books 1–6); Cleopatra was the
lover of Caesar and Antony, and she too
killed herself (see *AC*); Helen of Troy
was the most beautiful woman in the
world, whose abduction by Paris precip-
itated the Trojan war; Hero, a priestess
of Aphrodite, fell in love with a young
man who drowned in the Hellespont
while trying to visit her, upon which she
plunged to her death out of grief (see
Marlowe, *Hero and Leander*); Thisbe,
another legendary doomed lover (Ovid,
Met., book 4), is now best known from
Shakespeare's burlesque of Pyramus
and Thisbe (*MND*).
41 **dowdy** shabbily dressed woman (cited
in *OED*)
gypsy a byword for hussy or slut
well before the first recorded usage in
OED (1632); aphetic for 'Egyptian'.

In *Antony and Cleopatra*, the Romans
claim that Antony's love for Cleopatra
turns him into a version of Venus'
doting husband Vulcan, 'the bellows
and the fan / To cool a gipsy's lust',
1.1.9–10).
hildings trash, good-for-nothings,
worthless people (*OED sb.* 2)
harlots strumpets
42–3 **a grey eye** here used, perhaps
paradoxically, as an abusive comparison, because grey eyes, according to
Malone, could be a compliment: 'a *grey*
eye undoubtedly meant what we now
denominate a *blue* eye' (quoted Var,
124). *OED* grey 3 similarly compares
'Her eyes are grey as glass' (*TGV*
4.4.190), which suggests that grey eyes
could be an attribute of female comeliness. See also *grey-eyed morn* at 2.2.188.
43 **not . . . purpose** no matter
44–5 **French slop** *slop* = breeches;
French ones were wide and loose, as
in the 'round hose [bought] in France'
worn by the 'oddly . . . suited' young
Falconbridge in *MV* 1.2.71.
45 **gave . . . counterfeit** tricked us by
giving us the *slip*, as Mercutio explains
in his next line responding to Romeo,
who pretends to take *counterfeit* in its
usual meaning of imitation; the *slip*
was a counterfeit coin (*OED sb.*⁴). Cf.
Thersites, 'If I could ha' remembered
a gilt counterfeit, thou wouldst not
have slipped out of my contemplation'
(*TC* 2.3.23–4). Cam² notes that in *The
Unfortunate Traveller* Nashe similarly
plays on 'counterfeit' = slip and 'giving the slip' (Nashe, 2.258).

40 was a] *Q2–4, F;* was but a *Q1*

ROMEO   Good morrow to you both. What counterfeit did
     I give you?

MERCUTIO   The slip, sir, the slip, can you not conceive?

ROMEO   Pardon, good Mercutio, my business was great,
     and in such a case as mine a man may strain courtesy.   50

MERCUTIO   That's as much as to say, such a case as yours
     constrains a man to bow in the hams.

ROMEO   Meaning to curtsy.

MERCUTIO   Thou hast most kindly hit it.

ROMEO   A most courteous exposition.   55

MERCUTIO   Nay, I am the very pink of courtesy.

ROMEO   Pink for flower.

MERCUTIO   Right.

ROMEO   Why, then is my pump well flowered.

---

48 **conceive** understand, grasp

49–50 **my . . . courtesy** 'I had serious
affairs to transact so my failure to
observe my friends' sensibilities may
be excusable.'

51 **case** ostensibly chaffing word-play by
Mercutio on Romeo's *case*, *strain* and
courtesy, quibbling on *case* = female
genitals; cf. the malapropism 'Jenny's
case' (genitive/genital) in *MW* 4.1.54,
and *2H4* 2.1.29, where the Hostess
complains about her 'case so openly
known to the world'.

52 **bow . . . hams** *hams* meaning the
upper thighs, used in curtsying, with
a play on sexual activity

53 **curtsy** Romeo pretends not to get his
friend's bawdy drift.

54 **kindly** graciously, but with a quibble
on 'according to sexual nature'
   hit it 'got it', but spoken with heavy
irony since *hit* can mean to copulate
(Partridge compares 'to bang')

56 **pink** 'The most excellent example of
something; the embodiment or model
of a particular quality' according to
OED pink *sb.*⁵, which cites this line and

interprets it as an extended and figurative use of 'pink' meaning 'flower',
hence Romeo's riposte, *Pink for flower*,
the correct idiom being 'flower of
courtesy'.

59 **pump** a dancing shoe of delicate
fabric. Romeo is wearing his 'pumps'
because he has been up all night and
has not changed since the Capulets'
feast. *OED* *sb.*² cites the usage in
61.
   well flowered because it is pink,
but also perhaps alluding to flowers
fashionably studded on dancing shoes,
or ribbons, as when Bottom instructs
his fellow actors to smarten up for
their court performance: 'Get your
apparel together, good strings to your
beards, new ribbons to your pumps'
(*MND* 4.2.33–4). Shakespeare's other
two uses of pumps, in *TS* 4.1.120 and
MND 4.2.34, point to a link between
ribbons, pink and dancing shoes. If a
bawdy meaning (as in modern slang
'to pump') is intended, it could be the
spark for the sexual jokes launched by
Mercutio's use of *goose* at 73.

49 Pardon, good Mercutio] *Q2–4;* Pardon *Mercutio F;* I cry you mercy *Q1*

MERCUTIO Sure wit, follow me this jest now till thou hast   60
worn out thy pump, that when the single sole of it is
worn, the jest may remain, after the wearing, solely
singular.

ROMEO O single-soled jest, solely singular for the
singleness!   65

MERCUTIO Come between us, good Benvolio, my wits
faints.

ROMEO Swits and spurs, swits and spurs, or I'll cry a
match.

MERCUTIO Nay, if our wits run the wild goose chase, I   70
am done, for thou hast more of the wild goose in one

---

60 **Sure wit** 'how clever of you';
Mercutio pretends to be impressed by
Romeo's response to his *pink* joke and
challenges him to use his pumps to follow through with the *jest*. Mercutio's
repartee recalls Romeo's earlier verbal
duel with Benvolio over Rosaline.
me ethical dative (see Abbott, 220)

61–3 **that . . . singular** so that after the
verbal sparring has run its course – the
time it takes for pumps to wear out
– the witticism will yet stand self-
contained, a *jest* that does not require
its original context to work

61 **single sole** Pumps were heelless slip-
ons, rather like ballet shoes, hence
single-soled (64) and quickly worn out.

64 **single-soled jest** a threadbare (i.e.
poor) joke; this is Shakespeare's only
use of this compound adjective, which
OED first records in Nashe's *Have
With You*: 'not in the pantofles of his
prosperitie . . . but in the single-soald
pumpes of his aduersitie' (Nashe,
3.38).

64–5 **solely . . . singleness** remarkable
only for its simplicity, its obvious sil-
liness (cited under *OED* singleness 3)

66 **Come between us** i.e. as his second

in their duel of wits, but perhaps
anticipating, with tragic irony, the
later 'came you between us' (3.1.105),
when Romeo has unwittingly caused
Mercutio's death by stepping *between*
him and Tybalt.

68 **Swits and spurs** 'Come on'; from
the combined action of a *Swits* (riding
whip) and *spurs*. *OED* switch *sb.* cites
this line and glosses 'at full speed,
in hot haste'. *Swits* may have been
prompted by *Sure wit* and may contract
'such wits'. Dent has Switch (swits)
and spur(s) as proverbial (S1046).

68–9 **I'll . . . match** I'll call a halt to
the contest (which is what Mercutio
invited him to do anyway).

70 **run . . . chase** take a wrong course
(proverbial; Dent, W390); in modern
English, sending someone on a wild
goose chase means to post them on a
fool's errand (*OED* 'wild goose chase'
cites the entire sentence *Nay . . . five*).

71 **more . . . goose** more talent for
nonsense; hence Mercutio's mock-
magnanimous surrender (*I am done*),
since he is bound to lose this contest of
folly to the more than five times more
foolish Romeo.

---

60 Sure wit] *Q2–4, F;* Well said *Q1*   62 solely] *Q2–4* (soly), *Q1* (solie); sole – *F*   66–7 wits faints]
Q2–4, F; wits faile *Q1;* wit fains *F2;* wits faint *Q5*   70 our] *Q2–4, F;* thy *Q1*   71 am] *Q2–4, F;*
haue *Q1*

of thy wits than, I am sure, I have in my whole five.
Was I with you there for the goose?

ROMEO Thou wast never with me for anything, when
thou wast not there for the goose.　　　　　　　　　　　75

MERCUTIO I will bite thee by the ear for that jest.

ROMEO Nay, good goose, bite not.

MERCUTIO Thy wit is a very bitter sweeting, it is a most
sharp sauce.

ROMEO And is it not then well served in to a sweet goose?　80

MERCUTIO O here's a wit of cheveril, that stretches from
an inch narrow to an ell broad.

ROMEO I stretch it out for that word 'broad' which, added

---

72 **five** The five wits are either the bodily
senses (hence five) or else the mental
faculties in general (*OED* wit *sb.* 3 b).

73 **Was . . . goose?** 'Did I hit the mark
there with my reference to nonsense?'
The word *goose* also means women
(cf. 'silly goose') and can carry sexual
connotations, as in the allusion in *KL*
2.2.81–2 to 'Winchester geese' = pros-
titutes (Onions), who were thus called
in London because they plied their
trade in the shadow of the palace of the
Bishop of Winchester in Southwark
(Partridge compares Pandarus' 'galled
goose' at *TC* 5.11. 53).

74–5 Romeo retorts that nonsense or the
chasing of women could always be
trusted to ensure Mercutio's presence.

76 **bite . . . ear** a mocking gesture of
tenderness

77 **good goose** a contradiction in terms,
as *bitter sweeting*, 78
goose, bite not proverbial (Dent,
G349) and 'used as a jocular cry for
mercy from an unimpressive oppo-
nent' (Ard²)

78 **sweeting** a sweet-flavoured apple rendered *bitter* by Romeo's tart wit (cited
under *OED* *sb.*¹); affectionate term of
address

79 **sharp sauce** Apple sauce is the tra-

ditional accompaniment for cooked
goose (Ard²). Onions glosses 'saucy' as
'wanton, lascivious'; see also Angelo's
reply to Isabella: 'Their saucy sweetness that do coin heaven's image / In
stamps that are forbid' (*MM* 2.4.45–6).

80 **served . . . goose** The line is proverbial: 'Sweet meat must have sour sauce'
(Dent, M839), but with a sexual quibble
on *sauce* and *goose* in that *a sharp sauce*
(semen?) is just what the *sweet goose*,
the girl in the brothel, needs. The use
of *served in*, with a barely concealed
obscene innuendo, underpins this.

81–2 **cheveril . . . broad** Like kid leather, renowned for its elasticity, Romeo's
wit can be stretched all the way from a
single inch to 45 inches (the length of
an *ell*). Romeo, according to Mercutio,
makes a little wit go a long way. The
saying 'He has a conscience like a
cheveril's skin (cheveril conscience)' is
proverbial (Dent, C608).

83 **I . . . 'broad'** i.e. Romeo will meet
(*stretch it out*) Mercutio on his own
terms by extending his wit to the word
'*broad*', which perhaps means loose or
bawdy here (*OED* broad 6c cites North's
Plutarch: 'To sport one with another,
without any broad speeches or uncomely
jests'); or perhaps it just means 'silly'.

---

74 wast] *Q2–4, F;* wert *Q1*　80 is] *Q2–4, F;* was *Q1*　then well] *Q2;* well *Q3–4, F, Q1*　in to] *Q2–4,*
Q1; into *F*

to the goose, proves thee far and wide – a broad goose.

MERCUTIO Why, is not this better now than groaning   85
for love? Now art thou sociable, now art thou Romeo,
now art thou what thou art, by art as well as by nature,
for this drivelling love is like a great natural that runs
lolling up and down to hide his bauble in a hole.

BENVOLIO Stop there, stop there!   90

MERCUTIO Thou desirest me to stop in my tale against
the hair.

BENVOLIO Thou wouldst else have made thy tale large.

MERCUTIO O, thou art deceived. I would have made it
short, for I was come to the whole depth of my tale   95
and meant indeed to occupy the argument no longer.

84 **broad goose** 'silly goose'; spoken affectionately here
86–7 **Now . . . nature** The real Romeo is back at last, jousting verbally with male companions; in such badinage and bawdy their natures and wits (*art*) properly coincide.
88 **drivelling** childish, pathetic (cited under *OED ppl. a. 2*)
  great natural veritable fool
89 **lolling** with his tongue protruding (like a village idiot)
  bauble . . . hole A *bauble* is a sceptre with a fantastical carved fool's head of the kind traditionally carried by court jesters as emblems of office: see 'An idiot holds his bauble for a god' (*TA* 5.1.79). The image is of a madman thinking that he can hide his folly by burying his stick, while the idea of burying a sceptre in a hole also suggests intercourse; cf. 'And I would give his wife my bauble, sir, to do her service' (*AW* 4.5.27–8).
91–6 Mercutio follows through the innuendoes of *bauble* and *hole* (89) with puns on *tale*/'tail', telling Benvolio not to interrupt him now that he is nearly inside his woman. Benvolio's reply, that

Mercutio should not be a bore with an ever longer story (93), is countered by the latter's retort that, far from pursuing a longer *tale*/'tail', he was looking forward to shortening it by detumescence (as in *made it short*) after penetrating as deeply as he could. With the use of *occupy* here, cf. 'God's light, these villains will make the word as odious as the word "occupy", which was an excellent good word before it was ill sorted' (*2H4* 2.4.143–5). Ben Jonson deplored the twisting of the word's innocent meaning by impure minds: 'Many out of their own obscene apprehensions refuse proper and fit words; as occupy, nature, and the like' (*Discoveries*, 8.610); Crystal, *Words*, glosses 'occupy' as 'fornicate, have sexual dealings [with]'.
91–2 **against the hair** contrary to my natural inclination; the more common phrase is 'against the grain'. Mercutio bawdily quibbles on the meaning of pressing on pubic hair during intercourse.
96 **argument** The word may be used in a sexual sense here, given its close link to *occupy*; Oxf[1] glosses *argument* as vagina.

95 for] *Q2–4, Q1; or F*

216

ROMEO   Here's goodly gear!

Enter NURSE *and her man* [PETER].

A sail, a sail!

MERCUTIO   Two, two, a shirt and a smock.

NURSE   Peter!   100

PETER   Anon.

NURSE   My fan, Peter.

MERCUTIO   Good Peter, to hide her face, for her fan's the
   fairer face.

NURSE   God ye good morrow, gentlemen.   105

MERCUTIO   God ye good den, fair gentlewoman.

NURSE   Is it good den?

MERCUTIO   'Tis no less, I tell ye, for the bawdy hand of
   the dial is now upon the prick of noon.

---

97 **goodly gear** a mocking reference to
Nurse's attire, a hint perhaps at her size
and flamboyant poor taste, or else the
last sally in the duel of wits between
Romeo and Mercutio and thus the
young men's swaggering tribute to pria-
pism, with *gear* = genital equipment.

97.1 There are nine occasions in Q2 where
an entry SD like Nurse's and Peter's here
occurs after the character who enters has
been remarked upon by those already
onstage so that 'Neither order can be
considered wrong' (Williams, 144).

98 **A sail** because her skirts are overblown and billowing so that she gives
the impression of a ponderous ship
sailing along. This dimeter stands
suspiciously isolated. It is given to
Romeo in Q2 and Mercutio in Q1.
Williams suggests that, for 'literary or
dramatic considerations', it might be
better attributed to Benvolio.

99 **shirt . . . smock** Both undergarments
are metonyms, for Peter and Nurse

respectively, hence *two*; in Q1 this line
is spoken by Benvolio.

102–3 **fan . . . face** Cf. 'To see him walk
before a lady and to bear her fan!'
(*LLL* 4.1.144).

106 **God . . . den** good evening; used after
12 noon (see 1.2.56n.), and employed
here by Mercutio in response to Nurse's
good morning. Her rising to the bait
helps Shakespeare pace, punctuate and
control the dramatic action of the play.
Nurse is abstracted, thinking that it is
morning when it is already noon.

109 **prick of noon** The indentations or
marks dividing the circumference of the
dial are called pricks, hence the *hand of
the dial* that rests on the *prick of noon* can
be called *bawdy* (cited under *OED* prick
sb. 2). It has taken Nurse three hours to
seek out Romeo when Juliet is expecting
her back within half an hour of sending
her at 9 a.m. (2.5.1–2). Mercutio's *noon*
is confirmed by Juliet's exasperations at
Nurse's lateness (2.5.9–11).

97.1] *Q2–4, Q1; after* 96 F   98 A sail, a sail!] *Q2–4, F; Mer.* A saile, a saile, a saile. *Q1*   99 SP]
Q2–4, F; Ben: Q1   103 Good] *Q2–4, F; doo good Peter Q1*   fairer face] *Q2–4, F; fairer of the two
Q1*   108 ye] *Q2; you Q3–4, F, Q1*

NURSE Out upon you! What a man are you?   110

ROMEO One, gentlewoman, that God hath made, himself
to mar.

NURSE By my troth, it is well said: 'for himself to mar',
quoth 'a? Gentlemen, can any of you tell me where I
may find the young Romeo?   115

ROMEO I can tell you, but young Romeo will be older
when you have found him than he was when you
sought him. I am the youngest of that name, for fault
of a worse.

NURSE You say well.   120

MERCUTIO Yea, is the worst well? Very well took, i'faith,
wisely, wisely.

NURSE If you be he, sir, I desire some confidence with
you.

110 **What** what kind of

111–12 **himself to mar** i.e. his to ruin;
although God made Mercutio, it is the
latter's privilege to unmake himself,
presumably through bad behaviour.
If there were no comma after *made*
(there is none in Q1), the joke would
be that Mercutio was a man whom
God self-indulgently made for the
sake of unmaking him; but this may
be a strained reading. The phrases
'man . . . that God hath made' and
making and marring are partly proverbial (Dent, M162, 48).

114 **'a** he

114–15 **where . . . Romeo** This is an
odd question since Nurse identified
Romeo for Juliet at the Capulets'
party the previous night. It could be
a loose end (Spencer) or, Oxf¹ suggests, Romeo's masked state at the ball
may be why she does not recognize
him. Irving had Romeo with his back
turned to Nurse 'in easy conversation
with Benvolio' until he spoke the line
'I am the youngest of that name . . .'
(Sprague, 303). Conversely she may
just be hoity-toity and feign not to
engage closely with them.

116–17 **older . . . him** a truism and
mimicking Nurse's use of *young
Romeo* (115)

118–19 **for . . . worse** proverbial (Dent,
F106), here with a deliberate play
on *worse* when he means 'better', as
in contemporary usage 'for lack of a
better'; cf. French *pour faute de mieux*,
which suggests that the idiom behind
Romeo's was probably indeed 'for fault
of a better'.

123 **some confidence** a few words apart,
but commonly thought to be a malapropism for 'conference', by analogy with Dogberry's 'confidence' for
'conference' in *MA* 3.5.2 or Mistress
Quickly's in *MW* 1.4.160 – both characters are notorious for this kind of
language misuse.

111 himself] *Q2–4, F;* for himselfe *Q1*   113 well said] *Q2–4, Q1;* said *F*   115 the young] *Q2–4, F;*
yong *Q1*   123 If you] *Q2–3, F, Q1;* If thou *Q4*

BENVOLIO   She will indite him to some supper.   125
MERCUTIO   A bawd, a bawd, a bawd! So ho!
ROMEO   What hast thou found?
MERCUTIO   No hare, sir, unless a hare, sir, in a lenten pie,
   that is something stale and hoar ere it be spent.
    He walks by them and sings.
    An old hare hoar, and an old hare hoar   130
      Is very good meat in Lent.
    But a hare that is hoar is too much for a score
      When it hoars ere it be spent.
   Romeo, will you come to your father's? We'll to dinner
   thither.   135

---

125 She will make an assignation with him for the evening meal. Q1 has 'inuite', but *OED* indite cites this instance as a catachresis of 'invite'; 'indite' for 'invite' is used by Mistress Quickly in *2H4* 2.1.27.

126 **bawd** procuress; *bawd* also means hare in dialectical usage (cited under *OED sb.*²). Cam² fine-tunes the dialectical provenance to the North Midlands and thus close to Shakespeare's Warwickshire.

So ho! a hunting cry after spotting the hare, hence Romeo's question about the quarry in 127, pretending to play along

128–9 Mercutio's lines may be prompted by the earlier jesting about *hair* and *tale* (91–6) or else by the *bawd/hare* quibble. After a cheeky survey of Nurse, he decides that if she is a *hare* she is at best a mouldy (*stale*) or musty one (*hoar*), fit only for a *lenten pie*, which traditionally contained no meat (*OED* lenten *sb.* and *a.* B3 cite this line); in other words she is useless for sex. He is ribbing Nurse about her

age, but his use of *hoar*, a homophone of 'whore' (*stale* also means prostitute; *OED sb.*³), introduces more bawdy into his statement.

129 SD *Dessen and Thomson (245) cite '*walks by, reading*' (John Ford, *The Broken Heart*, 1.3.50), '*walk by musing*' (Philip Massinger, *A New Way to Pay Old Debts*, 2.3.60) and '*walking by, and practising his postures*' (Massinger, *The Maid of Honour*, 1.2.7).

130–3 a piece of extemporized nonsense to show off Mercutio's verbal pyrotechnics and joke about old hares and whores, not unlike the '*Genitivo, horum*' conjugations of *MW* 4.1.53–9. The lines are set out here as in Q1 and Oxf¹, but most editions set as six lines, breaking up 130 and 132 after the first *hoar*.

132–3 another *non sequitur*: a mouldy hare is not worth any money paid for it (*score* meaning tally as in the expression 'keeping score'), if it is mouldy before it is eaten (*spent*).

134 **dinner** the main meal of the day, taken at midday

---

125 indite] *Q2–4, F*; inuite *Q1*   some supper] *Q2–4, F*; supper *Q1*   127 What] *Q2–4, F*; Why what *Q1*   found] *Q2–4, F*; found man *Q1*   129 spent] *Q2–4, F*; eaten *Q1*   SD] *Q1; not in Q2–4, F*   130–3] *Q1 subst.; Q2–4, F line* lent. / spent. / ; *Capell lines* hoar, / hoar / Lent. / hoar / score / spent. /   132 that is] *Q2–4, F*; thats *Q1*   133 When it hoars] *Q2–4, F*; if it hore *Q1*

ROMEO I will follow you.

MERCUTIO Farewell, ancient lady, farewell lady, [*singing*]
    'lady, lady'.   *Exeunt Mercutio and Benvolio.*

NURSE I pray you, sir, what saucy merchant was this that
    was so full of his ropery?   140

ROMEO A gentleman, Nurse, that loves to hear himself
    talk and will speak more in a minute than he will stand
    to in a month.

NURSE An 'a speak anything against me, I'll take him
    down, an 'a were lustier than he is, and twenty such   145
    jacks, and if I cannot, I'll find those that shall. Scurvy
    knave! I am none of his flirt-gills, I am none of his

---

137 **ancient lady** old lady, spoken to
tease Nurse who is definitely not a
'lady' (cited under *OED* ancient)

138 **'lady, lady'** from the ballad of
Susanna, licensed in 1592 under the
title 'The goodly and constant wife
Susanna', the source also of Sir Toby's
'There dwelt a man in Babylon, Lady,
Lady' in *TN* 2.3.79–80. The stanza
in question goes 'There dwelt a man
in Babylon / Of reputation great by
fame, / He took to wife a fair woman,
/ Susanna she was called by name; / A
woman fair and virtuous; / Lady, lady'
(quoted in Thomas Percy's *Reliques of
Ancient English Poetry* (1766), 1.160).
Mercutio's humming of a refrain from
the ballad of Susanna after calling
Nurse *lady*, mockingly connecting
'her ladyship' with the lady Susanna,
reverberates poignantly in the text
since Nurse's dead daughter was called
Susan (see pp. 5, 37–9). Oxf¹ prefers
'an older, more popular balled, "The
Pangs of Love and Lovers" ', but this
does not seem to have been used by
Shakespeare elsewhere.

139 **saucy merchant** impudent fellow,
with *merchant* a term of disrespect
here (Ard²)

140 **ropery** 'trickery, knavery, roguery'
(cited in *OED*). As rope was slang
for penis, *ropery* may also mean
intercourse; Q1 has 'roperipe', that is
someone fit for hanging.

141–2 **loves . . . talk** proverbially said
about a fool who would be well advised
to keep quiet (Dent, L563)

142–3 **stand to** be able to deliver,
but with a pun on erection, which
Nurse unwittingly continues in her
next speech with her vow to *take him
down.*

144 **An 'a** if he

144–5 **take him down** as in taking
down a peg, cutting down to size
but, as *lustier* makes clear, causing
him to lose his erection by more
vigorous sex than he bargained
for

146 **jacks** knavish fellows; see also 3.1.11,
4.5.140.

146–7 **Scurvy knave** worthless fellow; cf.
'The Moor's abused by some most vil-
lainous knave . . . some scurvy fellow'
(*Oth* 4.2.141–2).

147 **flirt-gills** young wanton wenches,
more commonly known as gill-flirts,
gill deriving from the name Gillian
(cited in *OED*)

---

137 SD] *Cam²*   138 SD] *Ard²; Exeunt. Q2–4; Exit. Mercutio, Benuolio. F; Exeunt Benuolio, Mercutio.*
Q1 139 I pray] *Q2–4, F; Marry farewell. Pray. Q1* 140 ropery] *Q2–4, F; roperipe Q1; Roguery*
F4 144 An 'a speak] *Q2–4, F; If hee stand to Q1* 147 flirt-gills] *Q2–3, F, Q1; Gil-flurts Q4*

skains-mates. (*She turns to Peter, her man.*) And thou
must stand by too and suffer every knave to use me at
his pleasure!   150

PETER I saw no man use you at his pleasure; if I had, my
weapon should quickly have been out. I warrant you,
I dare draw as soon as another man, if I see occasion
in a good quarrel and the law on my side.

NURSE Now, afore God, I am so vexed that every part   155
about me quivers. Scurvy knave! Pray you, sir, a word;
and, as I told you, my young lady bid me enquire you
out. What she bid me say I will keep to myself. But first
let me tell ye, if ye should lead her in a fool's paradise,
as they say, it were a very gross kind of behaviour, as   160
they say, for the gentlewoman is young and therefore,
if you should deal double with her, truly it were an
ill thing to be offered to any gentlewoman, and very
weak dealing.

---

148 **skains-mates** 'cut-throat fellows'
(Crystal, *Words*), 'ribald companion,
with a connotation of sexual sport'
(Partridge); *OED* cites the line, noting
that the meaning and origin of the
word are uncertain.

148 SD *Peter has only spoken one word
so far, *Anon* (101), which is also his
last word in the scene, at 208; the two
sentences of 151–4 are his only ones
in the scene.

149–50 **use . . . pleasure** She means pok-
ing fun at her with impunity, but *use* (like
stand, see 142–3n.) is ambiguous and
its bawdy double meaning is exploited
by Shakespeare in Peter's reply.

151 **use . . . pleasure** have (or attempt to
have) intercourse with you

151–2 **my weapon** a quibble on the
dual meaning of weapon as sword and
prick; see 1.1.32.

153 **occasion** an opportunity

155–64 more of Nurse's somewhat
inconsequential, circular and repeti-

tive talk (ironically contrasting with
her insistence on *a word*), already
much in evidence during her chat
with Juliet and her mother in 1.3. The
comedy is enhanced by the fact that
she advertises her intention not to
pass on Juliet's message while urging
Romeo not to seduce and abandon
Juliet ('lead her in a fool's paradise').

155 **vexed** cross

156 **quivers** trembles

157–8 **enquire you out** find you

159 **in** into
fool's paradise 'A state of illusory
happiness or good fortune' (*OED*); the
expression is proverbial (Dent, F523).

162–4 **deal . . . dealing** This passage
is characteristic of Nurse's voluble
excess, which includes not listening, as
the next line and Romeo's subsequent
exasperation make clear.

162 **deal double** treat her dishonestly

164 **weak** underhand, lacking in moral
fibre

148 SD] *Q1; not in Q2–4, F* 159 in] *Q2–4, F;* into *Q1*

ROMEO Nurse, commend me to thy lady and mistress. I 165
    protest unto thee –

NURSE Good heart, and i'faith I will tell her as much.
    Lord, Lord, she will be a joyful woman.

ROMEO What wilt thou tell her, Nurse? Thou dost not
    mark me. 170

NURSE I will tell her, sir, that you do protest, which, as I
    take it, is a gentlemanlike offer.

ROMEO

    Bid her devise some means to come to shrift this
        afternoon,

    And there she shall at Friar Laurence' cell

    Be shrived and married. Here is for thy pains. 175

NURSE No, truly, sir, not a penny.

ROMEO Go to, I say you shall.

NURSE

    This afternoon, sir? Well, she shall be there.

ROMEO

    And stay, good Nurse, behind the abbey wall.

    Within this hour my man shall be with thee 180

---

166 **protest** vow, solemnly promise

170 **mark me** pay attention to what I say

173 'Ask her to think up a plan to come to confession this afternoon'; after Brooke's 'On Saturday, quod he, if Juliet come to shrift, / She shall be shrived and married' (633–4). Q2's fourteener – the metre of Brooke's poem – occurs just at the point where the play reconnects with Brooke; Shakespeare seems unconsciously to have picked up the rhythm and cadence of his source here. **come to shrift** go to confession (cited under *OED* shrift)

174 **Laurence' cell** On the use of 'zero genitive' for nouns ending in a sibilant or before words starting with one, or both as here (*-ce/ce-*), see Hope, 38–9.

175 **Be shrived** be confessed and receive absolution and penance (cited under *OED* shrive)

    Here . . . pains He offers her a tip for acting as go-between, *pains* meaning labour; in Brooke, Romeus presents Nurse with six 'crowns of gold', which she eagerly accepts with a low bow (667–70). When she reports back to Juliet about her visit she fails to mention the taking of the gold: 'Nothing was done or said, that she hath left untold, / Save only one, that she forgot the taking of the gold' (691–2).

178 **shall** will

180 **man** manservant

---

165 SP] *Q2–4, Q1; Nur. F* 172 offer] *Q2–4, F; proffer Q1* 173] *Q2–3, F; prose Q4; Delius lines* devise / afternoon; / ; Bid her get leaue to morrow morning *Q1* 179 And stay] *Q2–4;* stay thou *F, Q1*

And bring thee cords made like a tackled stair,
Which to the high topgallant of my joy
Must be my convoy in the secret night.
Farewell, be trusty, and I'll quit thy pains.
Farewell, commend me to thy mistress.   185

NURSE

Now God in heaven bless thee! Hark you, sir.

ROMEO

What sayst thou, my dear Nurse?

NURSE

Is your man secret? Did you ne'er hear say
'Two may keep counsel, putting one away'?

ROMEO

'Warrant thee, my man's as true as steel.   190

NURSE   Well, sir, my mistress is the sweetest lady. Lord,
Lord, when 'twas a little prating thing – O, there is a
nobleman in town, one Paris, that would fain lay knife

---

181 **tackled stair** rope-ladder ('corden ladder' in Brooke, 813), anticipating the naval image in the next line
182 **topgallant** summit; literally, the head of the topmast (cited in *OED*); continues the cluster of nautical words (*sail, merchant, ropery*) since Nurse's arrival on the scene. The lovers' relationship is again spatially mapped, with Romeo once more, even if only in an anticipatory metaphor, reaching up towards Juliet.
183 **convoy** means of transport, path (cited in *OED*); 'conduct' in Q1 may be an early attempt at interpreting the more difficult reading *convoy*.
   secret night still silence of the night (cited under *OED* secret *a*. 2b)
184 **quit** reward, repay (from 'requite')
186 **Hark you** 'listen here'
188–9 set as a couplet here, after Rowe (Q2 has prose)
188 **secret** able to keep a confidence

189 proverbial (Dent, T257), meaning that the only way two people can keep counsel is if one of them gets rid of the other; in other words it is a dangerous thing to receive a confidence.
190 **as . . . steel** as trustworthy and reliable as steel (proverbial; Dent, S840); another comparison that connects human qualities to weaponry, consolidating the ever-present threat of violence in the play
192 **prating** chattering (in a childish manner)
193–4 **lay knife aboard** pay court, with a view to marrying her. The expression was proverbial (Dent, K157.1), but several meanings resonate in the phrase, including boarding her with his *knife*, his *gear* (as at 97), his penis. To 'lay aboard' means to run alongside a ship to board her (*OED* lay *v.*[1] 25d); cf. 'I lost mine eye in laying the prize aboard' (*2H6* 4.1.25). A number of

184 quit] *Q2;* quite *Q3–4, F, Q1*   188–9] *Rowe; prose Q2–4, F; not in Q1*   190 'Warrant] *Q2–4, F;* I warrant *F2; not in Q1*   man's] *Q2–4;* man *F; not in Q1*

aboard, but she, good soul, had as lief see a toad, a
very toad, as see him. I anger her sometimes and tell   195
her that Paris is the properer man, but I'll warrant
you, when I say so she looks as pale as any clout in the
versal world. Doth not rosemary and Romeo begin
both with a letter?

ROMEO Ay, Nurse, what of that, both with an 'R'.   200

NURSE Ah, mocker, that's the dog's name. 'R' is for
the – no, I know it begins with some other letter, and
she hath the prettiest sententious of it, of you and
rosemary, that it would do you good to hear it.

ROMEO Commend me to thy lady.   205

NURSE Ay, a thousand times.   [*Exit Romeo.*]
Peter!

---

editions cite Crofts's tracing the idiom
to the custom of diners in taverns
taking along their own knives to mark
their place and secure their helpings.

194 **as lief** as gladly
a toad Toads were proverbially a hateful sight (Dent, T361).

196 **properer** more suitable
warrant assure

197 **pale . . . clout** proverbial, *clout*
meaning cloth (Dent, C446); *OED sb.*[1]
4 cites *Tottel's Miscellany* (1557): 'No
life I fele in fote nor hand, As pale as
any clout'. Cf. also 'I should forget my
son, / Or madly think a babe of clouts
were he' (*KJ* 3.3.57–8).

198 **versal** universal (cited in *OED*); the
phrase *versal world* is proverbial (Dent,
W876.1).
rosemary and Romeo yet more
play on Romeo's name; rosemary, a
fragrant evergreen herb, was used at
weddings (see Nurse's reference to
you and rosemary, 203–4) and at funer-
als for remembrance. See 4.5.79–80,
and cf. Ophelia's mad distributing of

flowers: 'There's rosemary, that's for
remembrance. Pray you, love, remember' (*Ham* 4.5.169–70).
with a with the same

201–4 The joke is that Nurse takes *R* and
'arr' (i.e. snarling like a dog) to be related
(*OED* arr *v.*[2] cites Nashe: 'They arr and
bark at night against the moon', 3.254).
Her sense of the match of object and
name is exclusively onomatopoeic as she
is illiterate: dogs arr and are therefore
called R! Cam[2] quotes Persius calling R
the dog letter ('*canina littera*') and Ben
Jonson writes 'R is the dog's letter and
hurreth in the sound' (*English Grammar*,
8.491), to 'hurr' meaning to snarl but
also to trill a letter. Shakespeare is similarly thinking of the front-rolled Italian
r rather than the burred English one.
Nurse here reveals that Juliet engaged
in affectionate word-play about *rosemary*
and *Romeo*, just as she did with *rose* and
Romeo in 2.2.

201 **the dog's name** proverbial; 'R is the
dog's letter' (Dent, R1)

204 **do . . . it** proverbial (Dent, G320.1)

---

194 lief] *Q2–4, F (*leeue*); not in Q1*   see a] *Q2–4;* a see *F; not in Q1*   195 anger her] *Q2–3, F;*
angerer *Q4; not in Q1*   201 dog's name] *Q3–4, F;* dog, name *Q2; not in Q1*   201–2 for the – no]
Delius (Ritson); for the no *Q2–4, F;* for Thee? No *Theobald (Warburton);* not for thee, *Hanmer;* for
thee? no *Capell;* for the nonce, *Steevens; not in Q1*   206 SD] *Rowe*

PETER Anon.
NURSE Before, and apace.   *Exeunt.*

[2.5]   *Enter* JULIET.

JULIET

The clock struck nine when I did send the Nurse;
In half an hour she promised to return.
Perchance she cannot meet him. That's not so.
O, she is lame! Love's heralds should be thoughts,
Which ten times faster glides than the sun's beams,   5
Driving back shadows over louring hills.
Therefore do nimble-pinioned doves draw love,
And therefore hath the wind-swift Cupid wings.
Now is the sun upon the highmost hill

209 'Go on ahead, and briskly.'
2.5 Shortly after noon (10–11) on
Monday in Juliet's bedroom
1–2 Both *nine* and *half an hour* point to
the urgent time-scheme of the play.
4 **lame** Juliet is impatient for Nurse
to return; exasperated, given the
importance of her message to Romeo,
about arranging for their marriage, she
assumes that Nurse must be *lame* not
to be quicker about it.
4–6 **thoughts . . . hills** The image of
clouds' shadows flitting across the
landscape evokes Romeo's *lazy-puffing
clouds* (2.2.31); 'as swift as thought' is
proverbial (Dent, T240).
5 **faster . . . beams** probably proverbial
(Dent, S992.1, 995.1)
   glides Singular accord with a plural
subject is permissible in the period
(Abbott, 333).
6 dispersing clouds that hover darkly
over hills; with *louring hills* cf. *R3* 1.1.3.
7 **nimble-pinioned** 'swift-winged'
(Crystal, *Words*)

doves draw love 'silver doves' pull
the 'light chariot' of Venus as she
leaves the world in *VA* 1190–4 (cf. *Tem*
4.1.94–5: 'Cutting the clouds towards
Paphos and her son / Dove-drawn
with her'). The words *love* and *dove*
form a suggestive internal cluster in
the play: Mercutio rhymes them at
2.1.10 before referring to Venus, and
doves feature significantly in the way
the lovers are presented.
8 **wind-swift** as swift as the wind
(proverbial; Dent, W411)
9–11 This pinpoints the time of Nurse's
entry at 17.1 to midday, the *high-
most hill* (first *OED* usage). Cam[2]
compares Golding's *Metamorphoses*,
3.84–6: 'Now first the morning way
/ Lies steep upright, so that the
steeds . . . have much ado to climb
against the hill' and also *Son* 7.5–10:
'And having climbed the steep-up
heavenly hill . . . from high-most pitch
with weary car / Like feeble age he
reeleth from the day'.

209] *Q2–4, F; Peter,* take my fanne, and goe before. *Q1*   SD] *F subst.; Exit. Q2–4; Ex. omnes.*
Q1   **2.5**] *Hanmer*   3 Perchance] *Q2–4, F;* Perhaps *Q1*   4 lame] *Q2–4, F;* lazie *Q1*   heralds] *Q2–4,
Q1;* Herauld *F*

Of this day's journey, and from nine till twelve   10
Is three long hours, yet she is not come.
Had she affections and warm youthful blood,
She would be as swift in motion as a ball;
My words would bandy her to my sweet love,
And his to me.   15
But old folks, many feign as they were dead,
Unwieldy, slow, heavy and pale as lead.

Enter NURSE [*and* PETER].

O God, she comes. O honey Nurse, what news?
Hast thou met with him? Send thy man away.   19

NURSE

Peter, stay at the gate.   [*Exit Peter.*]

JULIET

Now, good sweet Nurse – O Lord, why lookest thou sad?
Though news be sad, yet tell them merrily.
If good, thou shamest the music of sweet news
By playing it to me with so sour a face.

NURSE

I am aweary, give me leave awhile.   25

14 **bandy her** carry her at speed like a tennis ball whipped ('bandied') by Juliet's racket and returned by his stroke, with a submerged allusion perhaps to lovemaking

15 Rowe's splitting the original, hypermetrical 15 into 15 and 16 not only yields a perfect couplet (16–17) but conjoins the lovers in a stark pronominal union, rendered the more effective by the dimeter.

16 **feign** pretend to be
   as as if

17 **pale as lead** because of the dull bluish-grey colour of lead (cf. 'Pale as thy smock', *Oth* 5.2.271); the phrase is proverbial (Dent, L133.1, 134, 135).

18 **O God** one of several apostrophes to the Deity by Juliet. Her earlier reference to *Jove* (2.2.92–3) followed Ovid.
   honey sweet, used here adjectivally; honey was the standard sweetener in Shakespeare's day, and Juliet is humouring Nurse.

22 **them** *news* could be either plural or singular (Cam²).

11 Is three] *Q3–4;* Is there *Q2;* I three *F; not in Q1*   15–16] *Rowe; M.* And . . . dead, *Q2–3;* And . . . dead *Q4; F lines* folkes, / dead, / *; not in Q1*   17.1 *and* PETER] *Theobald*   20 SD] *Theobald*   23 shamest] *Q2–3;* sham'st *Q4, F; not in Q1*   25 aweary] *Q2–4, F;* wearie *Q1*

226

Fie, how my bones ache. What a jaunt have I!

JULIET

I would thou hadst my bones and I thy news.

Nay, come, I pray thee, speak, good, good Nurse,
  speak.

NURSE

Jesu, what haste! Can you not stay a while?

Do you not see that I am out of breath?   30

JULIET

How art thou out of breath when thou hast breath

To say to me that thou art out of breath?

The excuse that thou dost make in this delay

Is longer than the tale thou dost excuse.

Is thy news good or bad? Answer to that,   35

Say either, and I'll stay the circumstance.

Let me be satisfied, is't good or bad?

NURSE Well, you have made a simple choice. You know
not how to choose a man. Romeo? No, not he. Though
his face be better than any man's, yet his leg excels all   40
men's; and for a hand and a foot and a body, though
they be not to be talked on, yet they are past compare.
He is not the flower of courtesy, but I'll warrant him

---

26 *****jaunt** fatiguing journey (cited in
   OED)
   have I have I had
29 **Jesu** not yet banned at this date and,
   outside *RJ*, used exclusively in the
   history plays, particularly in the *Henry
   IV*s
   you The more formal pronoun is used
   consistently by Nurse when addressing
   Juliet, while the 13-year-old uses the
   familiar *thou*, *thee*, *thy* to her servant,
   in conformity with the etiquette of the
   day in which social class overrides age.
36 **stay the circumstance** wait for the
   detail (see *without circumstance*, 5.3.181)

38 **simple** foolish; Nurse picks up Juliet's
   formal dichotomy of *good* and *bad*
   while ignoring the substance of her
   question.
39–42 **Though . . . compare** Nurse's
   comic tautological nonsense sets Juliet
   further on edge.
43 **flower of courtesy** This recalls
   Mercutio's joke about being 'the very
   pink of courtesy' (2.4.56).
43–4 **I'll . . . lamb** effectively a *non
   sequitur* after *flower of courtesy* since
   gentleness could be thought to be part
   of *courtesy*; 'as gentle as a lamb' is
   proverbial (Dent, L34).

26 jaunt] *Q1, Q4, F;* iaunce *Q2–3* I] *Q2;* I had *Q3–4, F, Q1* 40 leg excels] *Q2–4;* legs excels *F; not
in Q1* 41 a body] *Q2–3, F;* body *Q4;* a baudie *Q1*

as gentle as a lamb. Go thy ways, wench, serve God.
What, have you dined at home?   45

JULIET

No, no. But all this did I know before.
What says he of our marriage, what of that?

NURSE

Lord, how my head aches! What a head have I!
It beats as it would fall in twenty pieces.
My back a' t'other side, ah, my back, my back!   50
Beshrew your heart for sending me about
To catch my death with jauncing up and down.

JULIET

I'faith, I am sorry that thou art not well.
Sweet, sweet, sweet Nurse, tell me, what says my love?

NURSE

Your love says, like an honest gentleman,   55
And a courteous, and a kind, and a handsome,
And, I warrant, a virtuous – Where is your mother?

JULIET

Where is my mother! Why, she is within.
Where should she be? How oddly thou repliest!
'Your love says, like an honest gentleman',   60
'Where is your mother!'

NURSE   O God's Lady, dear,

---

44 **Go . . . ways** 'Lucky you!'
   wench a term of endearment for a young woman (*OED sb.* c)
   serve God 'Be good.'
45 **dined** had your midday meal
49 **as** as if
51 **Beshrew your heart** a mild and humorous imprecation on Juliet's romantic heart for sending Nurse on this 'back-breaking' trip (cf. *MA* 5.1.55)
52 **jauncing** prancing about (cited under *OED* jaunce *v.*)

55 **honest** honourable
58–61 The lines are regularized here as blank verse following Rowe. Q2 sets the first line as a fourteener, for no apparent reason, unless the lines immediately before, 55–7, were indeed inspired by Brooke (679–82), in which case Q2's fourteener would be the second instance in the play of Shakespeare slipping into the metre of his main source (see also 2.4.173).
61 **O God's Lady** 'by the Virgin Mary'

44 as a] *Q2–4;* a *F; not in Q1*   46 this] *Q2–4;* this this *F; not in Q1*   50 ah] *Q2–4 (*a*);* o *F; not in Q1*   52 jauncing] *Q2–3;* iaunting *Q4, F; not in Q1*   53 not well] *Q2–4;* so well *F; not in Q1*   58–9] *Rowe; Q2–4 line* be? / repliest: / ; *F lines* Mother? / be? / repli'st: / ; *var. Q1*

Are you so hot? Marry come up, I trow.
Is this the poultice for my aching bones?
Henceforward do your messages yourself.

JULIET

Here's such a coil! Come, what says Romeo?   65

NURSE

Have you got leave to go to shrift today?

JULIET

I have.

NURSE

Then hie you hence to Friar Laurence' cell;
There stays a husband to make you a wife.
Now comes the wanton blood up in your cheeks;   70
They'll be in scarlet straight at any news.
Hie you to church; I must another way,
To fetch a ladder by the which your love
Must climb a bird's nest soon when it is dark.
I am the drudge and toil in your delight,   75
But you shall bear the burden soon at night.
Go, I'll to dinner. Hie you to the cell.

JULIET

Hie to high fortune! Honest Nurse, farewell.   *Exeunt.*

---

62 **hot** eager, with a teasing intimation of unbecoming sexual passion
Marry come up a proverbial expression of indignant or amused surprise (Dent, M699.2)
I trow here meaning 'surely' (*OED v.* 4b glosses 'I suppose')
63 **poultice** soothing dressing (Shakespeare's only usage of the word)
65 **coil** ado, fuss; cf. 'I am not worth this coil that's made for me' (*KJ* 2.1.165).
68 **hie** hasten, go quickly (also at 72, 77, 78)
70 **wanton blood** Juliet is starting to blush.
71 **at any** at the slightest

74 **bird's nest** i.e. Juliet's bedroom; the idiom 'to climb a bird's nest' may have been proverbial (Dent, N124.1).
75 'I am a mean labourer and hack, and I labour for your pleasure.'
76 **bear the burden** assume responsibility for what will ensue; but also suggesting that Juliet will experience the weight of Romeo's body during love-making (cf. *AC* 1.5.22).
soon at night tonight (proverbial; Dent, S639.1)
78 **Hie** suggests both speed and Juliet's spontaneous joy through something akin to 'hurrah', echoing Nurse's *Hie* of 77

74 climb] *Q2, Q4, Q1;* climde *Q3, F*

[2.6]   *Enter* FRIAR [LAURENCE] *and* ROMEO.

FRIAR LAURENCE
So smile the heavens upon this holy act
That after-hours with sorrow chide us not.

ROMEO
Amen, amen, but come what sorrow can,
It cannot countervail the exchange of joy
That one short minute gives me in her sight.   5
Do thou but close our hands with holy words,
Then love-devouring death do what he dare,
It is enough I may but call her mine.

FRIAR LAURENCE
These violent delights have violent ends
And in their triumph die, like fire and powder   10
Which, as they kiss, consume. The sweetest honey
Is loathsome in his own deliciousness,
And in the taste confounds the appetite.
Therefore love moderately; long love doth so;

2.6 Monday afternoon (2.4.173) in Friar
Laurence's cell
1 **smile the heavens** may the heavens
bless, *smile* being an optative
holy act marriage, which *The Book of
Common Prayer* (1549, etc.) calls 'holy
matrimony . . . an honourable state'
2 **after-hours** in times to come (*OED*
after 8a)
3 **come . . . can** whatever sorrow may
come in the future
4 **countervail** match in value
exchange The word continues the
trading image launched by *countervail*,
but also points to the harmony and
mutuality of the pair.
6 **close** join together
7 The drumbeat of *d* and the heavy
stress on *death* anticipate the prominence accorded *die* by the caesura in

10, the rhetoric consolidating the aura
of death that surrounds the young
lovers' relationship.
love-devouring death proverbial: 'Death devours all things' (Dent,
D138.1)
9 **violent ends** perhaps condensing the
proverbial expressions 'Such beginning such end' and 'Nothing violent
can be permanent' (Dent, B262,
N321)
10 **die** with a hidden allusion to orgasm
(hence *consume*), one of the meanings
of the word *die* in the period
11–12 **sweetest . . . loathsome** probably proverbial, as in 'Too much honey
cloys the stomach' (Dent, H560)
loathsome cloying
his its
13 **confounds** ruins

2.6] *Hanmer*   0.1] *Rowe; Enter Frier and Romeo Q2–4, F; Enter Romeo, Frier. Q1*   12 loathsome]
Q2–3, F; lothsomnesse Q4; not in Q1

Too swift arrives as tardy as too slow.   15

Enter JULIET *somewhat fast, and embraces Romeo.*

Here comes the lady. O, so light a foot
Will ne'er wear out the everlasting flint;
A lover may bestride the gossamers
That idles in the wanton summer air,
And yet not fall, so light is vanity.   20

JULIET

Good even to my ghostly confessor.

FRIAR LAURENCE

Romeo shall thank thee, daughter, for us both.
[*Romeo kisses her.*]

JULIET

As much to him, else is his thanks too much.
[*She returns his kiss.*]

15 See 2.3.90n. Q1's following SD dramatically clashes with the instruction to Romeo not to rush, showing up the futility of the Friar's advice when faced with young love's passion.
15.1 *Dessen and Thomson (82) note that 'embrace' is widely used in SDs and can be combined with 'kiss' (see 22 SD), examples including '*Embracing and kissing mutually*' (Massinger, *The Roman Actor*, 3.2.128) and '*they embrace, making a mutual show of compliment*' (Thomas Killigrew, *The Conspiracy*, G1ʳ).
16–17 **so . . . flint** This is presumably spoken indulgently and with humour, since the heaviest of steps could never wear out the hardest stone; the expression 'as hard as a stone (flint, rock)' is proverbial (Dent, S878) and is commonly alluded to in Shakespeare's

plays (Dent also refers to *2H4*, *Tit*, *JC*, *KL*).
18 **gossamers** fine threads of cobweb (cited in *OED*)
19 **idles . . . air** float languidly in the playful breeze of summer (on plural and singular accord, see Abbott, 333)
20 **so . . . vanity** a stern moral admonition by the Friar after he too has momentarily succumbed to Juliet's presence and lapsed into a poetic tribute to lovers walking on air. Ard² refers to 'vanity' in Ecclesiastes, 1.2 ('all is vanity') and 2.1: 'I said in mine heart, Go to now, I will prove thee with mirth, therefore enjoy pleasure: and, behold, this also is vanity.' See also 'Up, vanity! / Down, royal state!' (*2H4* 4.5.120–1).
21 **confessor** cònfessor
22 i.e. Romeo's greeting kiss, customary at the time, will do for both.

15.1] *Q1; Enter* Iuliet. *Q2–4, F*   22 SD] *Cam² subst.*   23 is] *Q2–3; in Q4, F; not in Q1*   SD] *Cam² subst.*

ROMEO

Ah, Juliet, if the measure of thy joy
Be heaped like mine, and that thy skill be more   25
To blazon it, then sweeten with thy breath
This neighbour air, and let rich music's tongue
Unfold the imagined happiness that both
Receive in either by this dear encounter.

JULIET

Conceit more rich in matter than in words   30
Brags of his substance, not of ornament.
They are but beggars that can count their worth,
But my true love is grown to such excess,
I cannot sum up sum of half my wealth.

FRIAR LAURENCE

Come, come with me, and we will make short work,   35
For, by your leaves, you shall not stay alone
Till holy church incorporate two in one.   [*Exeunt.*]

24–5 **if . . . mine** 'if you have your fill
(see *heaped*) of happiness as I do'
26 **blazon it** celebrate it in language
(cited under *OED v.*)
27 **neighbour** surrounding
28 **both** both lovers
30–1 Juliet gently reproves Romeo for
his extravagant rhetoric, asserting
that sound ideas (*Conceit*) thrive
on substance rather than style
(*ornament*).
32 Cf. Cleopatra's 'There's beggary
in the love that can be reckoned'
(*AC* 1.1.15).
34 **sum up . . . wealth** reckon the
amount of even half my love (*wealth*)
(cited under *OED* sum); cf. 'See
Beauty's total sum summed in her face'

in sonnet 85 of *Astrophil and Stella*.
35 **make short work** get on with it
quickly
37 SD *At this not-quite-halfway point
in the play, productions (e.g. Zeffirelli,
1968) frequently break for the interval.
The 1935 Gielgud production placed
the intermission after the death of
Mercutio but allowed a mere 12 minutes (Halio, *Guide*, 107); Dessen notes
the loss of 'immediacy and ironic
punch' of Juliet's opening lines of 3.2
if they are separated by an interval
from the tragic events of 3.1 (Dessen,
Rescripting, 97). The Elizabethan
theatre played continuously, usually
for two hours (Gurr & Ichikawa, 24,
and see Prol.12).

24 SP] *Q2–4; Fri. F; not in Q1*   27 music's] *Q4, F; musicke Q2–3; not in Q1*   33 such] *Q2–4; such
such F; not in Q1*   34 sum of] *Q2–3; some of Q4, F; not in Q1*   37 SD] *Q1 (Exeunt omnes.)*

[3.1]   *Enter* MERCUTIO, BENVOLIO,
                         [*Mercutio's Page*] *and Men.*

BENVOLIO

I pray thee, good Mercutio, let's retire;
The day is hot, the Capels are abroad,
An if we meet we shall not scape a brawl,
For now, these hot days, is the mad blood stirring.

MERCUTIO Thou art like one of these fellows that, when   5
he enters the confines of a tavern, claps me his sword
upon the table and says 'God send me no need of
thee!'; and by the operation of the second cup draws
him on the drawer, when indeed there is no need.

BENVOLIO Am I like such a fellow?   10

MERCUTIO Come, come, thou art as hot a jack in thy
mood as any in Italy; and as soon moved to be moody,
and as soon moody to be moved.

3.1 Late Monday afternoon, an hour or so after the marriage of Romeo and Juliet (114–15).

2 **hot** a key word, literally and figuratively, in this play of July dog days, levelled in this scene at Benvolio (11) and Mercutio (162), and elsewhere at Juliet (2.5.62) and Capulet (3.5.175).
Capels The abbreviated form of the surname occurs in Brooke and is used in the text of the play, generally, it seems, for scansion reasons (though once in a Q2 SD), with *Capel, Capel's* and *Capels* all occurring. See also 4.1.112.
abroad at large

3–4 This is set as prose in Q2, but the lines scan as verse, which fits better with Benvolio's desire to observe order and decorum.

3 **An if** indeed; see also *an* for 'if' at 15, 30, 40 and 46.
scape escape

4 **mad blood** hot temper

5–29 Mercutio's comical sketch of Benvolio as a boisterous roaring boy hardly applies to him. It is, however, a pretty good likeness of Mercutio himself, as Benvolio points out (30–2); and Mercutio will shortly die in a fight he himself provoked.

6 **confines** boundary, four walls (cited in *OED*)
claps me throws; with *me* an ethical dative, used for emphasis (cited in *OED*)

8 **by the operation** after the intoxicating effect

9 **him** ethical dative
drawer tapster in a tavern; with a punning backward glance at *draws him* (cited in *OED*)

11 **jack** fellow, rowdy knave (*OED sb.*[1] 2a); cf. 'A madcap ruffian and a swearing Jack' (*TS* 2.1.281).

11–12 **in thy mood** when you are angry

12 **moved** provoked

13 **moody ... moved** angry for being provoked

3.1] *Rowe*   0.1] *Q2–4, F; Enter Benuolio, Mercutio. Q1*   0.2 *Mercutio's Page*] *this edn*   2 Capels are] *Q1; Capels Q2–3; Capulets Q4, F*   3–4] *Rowe; prose Q2–4, F; not in Q1*   5 these] *Q2–4, F; those Q1*   9 him] *Q2–4, F; it Q1*

BENVOLIO   And what to?

MERCUTIO   Nay, an there were two such, we should have   15
none shortly, for one would kill the other. Thou – why,
thou wilt quarrel with a man that hath a hair more
or a hair less in his beard than thou hast. Thou wilt
quarrel with a man for cracking nuts, having no other
reason but because thou hast hazel eyes. What eye   20
but such an eye would spy out such a quarrel? Thy
head is as full of quarrels as an egg is full of meat,
and yet thy head hath been beaten as addle as an egg
for quarrelling. Thou hast quarrelled with a man for
coughing in the street, because he hath wakened thy   25
dog that hath lain asleep in the sun. Didst thou not fall
out with a tailor for wearing his new doublet before
Easter, with another for tying his new shoes with old
riband, and yet thou wilt tutor me from quarrelling!

BENVOLIO   An I were so apt to quarrel as thou art, any   30
man should buy the fee-simple of my life for an hour
and a quarter.

MERCUTIO   The fee-simple? O simple!

21–2 Thy . . . meat proverbial (Dent, K149)

22 meat yolk or white, or both (*OED sb.* 5)

23 addle muddled and fatuous (cf. addle-headed)

27 doublet A *doublet* was a close-fitting jacket.

27–8 before Easter because new fashions were not supposed to be exhibited during Lent, the period of austerity and penitence extending from Ash Wednesday to Easter Eve and applying to diet and clothing alike. Mercutio's point is that Benvolio will use the slightest pretext for picking a fight.

29 riband ribbon (cited in *OED*)

30 apt disposed (cited under *OED a.* 4b); the word is pointedly taken up by Tybalt at 40.

31 fee-simple absolute possession; the word is a common law concept deriving from the tenure in perpetuity of land ('fee' = heritable estate in land).

31–2 an . . . quarter because that is about as long as he would last if he spoiled for fights the way Mercutio does; buying *the fee-simple* of someone's life is to kill him, literally by taking his tenure.

33 O simple! 'How naïve (or feeble) of you!'

---

29 tutor] *Q2–4, F;* forbid *Q1*   from] *Q2–4, F;* of *Q1;* for *Pope*

Enter TYBALT, PETRUCHIO *and others.*

BENVOLIO By my head, here comes the Capulets.

MERCUTIO By my heel, I care not.   35

TYBALT

Follow me close, for I will speak to them.

Gentlemen, good-e'en, a word with one of you.

MERCUTIO And but one word with one of us? Couple it
with something, make it a word and a blow.

TYBALT You shall find me apt enough to that, sir, an you   40
will give me occasion.

MERCUTIO Could you not take some occasion without
giving?

TYBALT Mercutio, thou consortest with Romeo.

MERCUTIO 'Consort'? What, dost thou make us minstrels?   45
An thou make minstrels of us, look to hear nothing

33.1 PETRUCHIO Petruchio was spotted by
Nurse and Juliet leaving the Capulets'
party (1.5.129–30), but he may speak
only two words in the play; see 90n.

34 comes For singular accord with third
person plural subject, see also 2.6.19
(and Abbott, 333).

35 By my heel an expression of contempt; for Mercutio, *heel* is the most
the Capulets rate, as opposed to
Benvolio's *head.*

37 good-e'en used here like Italian *buona
sera* for any time after lunch, suggesting that Shakespeare was familiar with
this Italian locution

38 And used here for emphasis (Abbott,
99)

39 make . . . blow proverbial (Dent,
W763)

40–1 an . . . occasion 'if you give me a
legitimate cause' (for fighting)

42–3 take . . . giving Mercutio is challenging Tybalt to have the courage
to fight without seeking a pretext to

keep on the right side of the law; he is
accusing him of being a coward.

44 consortest keep company; but Mercutio
pretends to interpret the word as a slight
by suggesting that Tybalt is accusing him
of forming part of a band of musicians,
a 'consort' (*OED v.* 7 glosses 'consort'
with 'To combine in musical harmony;
to play, sing or sound together'). Since
musicians were frequently thought to be
effete, *consortest* may contain a taunt of
homosexuality. *OED v.* 5c first records
'consort = have intercourse with' in
1600, but Mercutio's stung response
suggests that the meaning may have
been around earlier. In Joe Calarco's
all-male *Shakespeare's Romeo and Juliet*
(1997), *consortest* was interpreted by an
adolescent Mercutio in love with Romeo
as a homophobic slur (Loehlin, 166).

45 minstrels 'mincing musicians', an
insult comparable perhaps to modern
slang 'fairy', following on from
consortest

but discords. Here's my fiddlestick, here's that shall
make you dance. Zounds, 'consort'!

BENVOLIO

We talk here in the public haunt of men.
Either withdraw unto some private place,   50
Or reason coldly of your grievances,
Or else depart. Here all eyes gaze on us.

MERCUTIO

Men's eyes were made to look, and let them gaze.
I will not budge for no man's pleasure, I.

Enter ROMEO.

TYBALT

Well, peace be with you, sir, here comes my man.   55

MERCUTIO

But I'll be hanged, sir, if he wear your livery.
Marry, go before to field, he'll be your follower;
Your worship in that sense may call him 'man'.

---

47 **fiddlestick** horsehair bow; pointing
to his rapier, he indicates to Tybalt
that this is the stick he prefers to use
to make Tybalt skip, with perhaps
an obscene innuendo in *fiddlestick*,
to cast back his homosexual taunt
at Tybalt.

48 **Zounds** euphemistic contraction of
'by God's wounds', used in oaths
(*OED*) or interjections (Onions);
deemed highly offensive and removed
from Folio versions of plays such as
Titus Andronicus, *1 Henry IV* and
Othello while surviving in quartos of
the same; see Taylor.

49 **public haunt** i.e. a public square

51 **reason coldly** discuss soberly

55–6 **my man . . . livery** For Tybalt,
my man means the person he was
looking for, Romeo. Mercutio's reply

puns on *man* = manservant, someone
who would be expected to wear the
livery of the Capulets, with a play
on *livery*/'liver', because 'white liver'
was a term for cowardice (cf. *MV*
3.2.83–6). Mercutio is taunting Tybalt
by insinuating that Romeo, unlike
Tybalt, decliner of challenges, would
never be a coward and therefore can
hardly be his man.

57 **go . . . field** 'Go on ahead of him into
the arena (*field*) for your duel, if you
dare, as he will follow you.'

57–8 **he'll . . . 'man'** 'He will certainly
follow you there, only too eager to
accept your challenge; that is the only
way he will ever be your "*man*".'

58 **Your worship** sarcastically defer-
ential address to Tybalt as *King of
Cats* (76)

48 Zounds, 'consort'!] *Q2–4; Come consort. F; Consort Zwounes consort? Q1*

236

TYBALT

Romeo, the love I bear thee can afford
No better term than this: thou art a villain.   60

ROMEO

Tybalt, the reason that I have to love thee
Doth much excuse the appertaining rage
To such a greeting. Villain am I none,
Therefore farewell; I see thou knowest me not.

TYBALT

Boy, this shall not excuse the injuries   65
That thou hast done me; therefore turn and draw.

ROMEO

I do protest I never injuried thee,
But love thee better than thou canst devise
Till thou shalt know the reason of my love.
And so, good Capulet, which name I tender   70
As dearly as mine own, be satisfied.

MERCUTIO

O calm, dishonourable, vile submission!

---

59 **love** i.e. hatred, *love* being spoken sarcastically, unlike the *love* of Romeo's reply (61); Q1 here reads 'hate'.
afford yield

60 **villain** rogue and peasant; impugning Romeo's honour and social standing

61 **the reason** They are now kinsmen, since Romeo married Tybalt's cousin Juliet only an hour ago.

62–3 **appertaining . . . greeting** anger that properly befits such an offensive salutation as *villain*

64 **I . . . not** This further alludes to the idea that if only Tybalt knew Romeo's new status he would not insult him.

65 **Boy** a deliberate insult; cf. 'He calls me boy' (*AC* 4.1.1) and 'thou boy of tears' (*Cor* 5.6.100).
injuries Tybalt is referring to Romeo's

uninvited appearance at the Capulets' feast, which resulted in Tybalt's being humiliatingly reproved by Juliet's father.

67 **injuried** injured; from 'to injury = to injure' (*OED* injure 3). By adopting the rarer form of the verb, at the cost arguably of an extra syllable in the line (but not if *never* is 'ne'er'), Romeo directly echoes Tybalt's *injuries*: he is striving for harmony and adjusts his language to accord with Juliet's cousin's.

68 **devise** imagine (cited under *OED v.* 10)

70 **which . . . tender** 'a name which I value and hold dear' (*OED* tender *v.*² 3)

71 **satisfied** contented

---

59 love] *Q2–4, F;* hate *Q1*   67 injuried] *Q2;* iniured *Q3–4, F, Q1*   68 love] *Q2–4, Q1;* lou'd *F*
71 mine] *Q2;* my *Q3–4, F; not in Q1*

Alla stoccado carries it away.   [*Draws.*]
Tybalt, you rat-catcher, will you walk?

TYBALT   What wouldst thou have with me?   75

MERCUTIO   Good King of Cats, nothing but one of your
nine lives. That I mean to make bold withal and, as
you shall use me hereafter, dry-beat the rest of the
eight. Will you pluck your sword out of his pilcher
by the ears? Make haste, lest mine be about your ears   80
ere it be out.

TYBALT   I am for you. [*Draws.*]

ROMEO

Gentle Mercutio, put thy rapier up.

MERCUTIO   Come, sir, your *passado*! [*They fight.*]

---

73 *stoccado a thrust with a rapier ('*stoccata*'), from Saviolo's Italian fencing
vocabulary (Holmer, 'Draw', 168). The
correctly declined form '*stoccata*' is
given by Ard² and Cam². Shakespeare's
only other use is 'your passes, stoc-
cadoes, and I know not what' (*MW*
2.1.202–3), which suggests that
he wrote '*stoccado*', unaware of the
required gender accord in Italian (see
similarly '*passado*' for *passata* at 2.4.26).
carries it away has the advantage;
'carry the day' is proverbial (Dent,
C100.1). Cf. Hamlet's question 'Do
the boys carry it away?' (*Ham* 2.2.357).

74 **rat-catcher** As *King of Cats* (76) he is
a prime ratter (cited in *OED*).
will you walk? Mercutio calls Tybalt
back as he prepares to leave (*walk*
away) rather than challenging him to
walk out of sight for a duel. Oxf¹ notes
that instead of responding to Romeo's
offer of a truce by striking at him, as
he does in Brooke, Tybalt fights only
after being goaded by Mercutio.

76 **King of Cats** See 2.4.19n.

77 **nine lives** proverbial (Dent, C154)
make bold withal take liberties
with, kill

77–9 **as . . . eight** 'Depending on how
you behave towards me – after I
have scotched one of your lives –
I will soundly thrash (*dry-beat*) the
remaining eight.' Mercutio's bombast
is a taunt, particularly if *dry-beat*
implies, as Cam² surmises, a social
stigma, perhaps in response to
Tybalt's insult of *villain*: rather than
fighting Tybalt in a duel Mercutio
threatens to beat him as if he were a
servant.

79 **pilcher** scabbard; literally, an outer
garment of skin or leather; a dismissive
term, perhaps suggesting that Tybalt's
sword is housed cheaply in a second-
rate scabbard, fitting for a coward, not
a gentleman. This is Shakespeare's
only use of the word (cited under *OED*
pilch *sb.*). Q1 has 'scabard'.

80 **by the ears** reluctantly (*ears* was used
figuratively to refer to the hilt of the
sword); Mercutio is taunting Tybalt
with cowardice, being slow to draw his
sword.

83 **put . . . up** i.e. lower it; cf. 'Keep up
your bright swords, for the dew will
rust them' (*Oth* 1.2.59).

84 *passado* See 2.4.26n.

---

73 *Alla stoccado*] *Q1; Alla stucatho Q2–4, F; Alla stoccata Knight*   SD] *Capell*   79 pilcher *Q2–4;*
scabbard *Q1*   82 SD] *Rowe subst.*   84 SD] *Rowe subst.*

ROMEO [*Draws.*]

Draw, Benvolio, beat down their weapons.   85
Gentlemen, for shame, forbear this outrage.
Tybalt, Mercutio, the Prince expressly hath
Forbid this bandying in Verona streets.
Hold, Tybalt! Good Mercutio!

Tybalt under Romeo's arm thrusts Mercutio in and flies.

PETRUCHIO   Away, Tybalt!   90

MERCUTIO   I am hurt.

A plague a' both houses! I am sped.
Is he gone and hath nothing?

BENVOLIO   What, art thou hurt?

MERCUTIO

Ay, ay, a scratch, a scratch. Marry, 'tis enough.   95
Where is my page? Go, villain, fetch a surgeon.   [*Exit Page.*]

ROMEO

Courage, man, the hurt cannot be much.

---

86 **forbear this outrage** refrain from this disorderly behaviour

88 **bandying** violent wrangling

89 SD *Many productions (e.g. Hall, Zeffirelli 1968, Nunn–Kyle) stage the fight between Tybalt and Mercutio as a game of high jinks which accidentally results in death. Dessen and Thomson ('thrust', 229–30) compare '*thrust himself through with his sword*' from *Locrine*, 2110.

90 ***PETRUCHIO Away, Tybalt!** The words are given here as a line rather than a SD. In Q2 the line is centred and stands, without SP, as '*Away* Tybalt', reversing standard conventions by italicizing the adverb rather than the name. Williams argues that *Away, Tybalt!* constitutes dialogue

rather than direction, noting that the Q2 compositor who set this never uses 'Away' for 'exit' elsewhere. Also, at 134 Benvolio urges Romeo to flee with *Romeo, away*, and at several points in Q2 'prefixes for the speeches of unimportant characters' are omitted (Williams, 'New').

92 **plague . . . houses** Mercutio's imprecation *plague* probably follows Brooke's description, after Tybalt's death, of the feud between the two houses as 'This common plague' (Brooke, 1051). **a'** on

sped finished, dispatched (*OED* speed *v.* 7b)

95 **scratch** i.e. by the *King of Cats*

96 **villain** here an imperious address to a servant

---

85 SD] *this edn*   88 Forbid] *Q2–4;* Forbidden *F; not in Q1*   this] *Q2; not in Q3–4, F, Q1*   89 SD] *Q1; not in Q2–4, F*   90 PETRUCHIO Away, Tybalt!] *Williams (Greg);* Away Tybalt. *Q2–4;* Exit Tybalt. *F; not in Q1*   92 a' both] *Q2–4;* a both the *F;* on your *Q1;* of both the *F2;* o'both your *Dyce*   96 SD] *Capell*

MERCUTIO   No, 'tis not so deep as a well, nor so wide as a
church door, but 'tis enough, 'twill serve. Ask for me
tomorrow and you shall find me a grave man. I am   100
peppered, I warrant, for this world. A plague a' both
your houses! Zounds, a dog, a rat, a mouse, a cat, to
scratch a man to death! A braggart, a rogue, a villain,
that fights by the book of arithmetic! Why the devil
came you between us? I was hurt under your arm.   105
ROMEO
I thought all for the best.
MERCUTIO
Help me into some house, Benvolio,
Or I shall faint. A plague a' both your houses!
They have made worms' meat of me.
I have it, and soundly too. Your houses!   110

Exit [with Benvolio].

98 **so . . . well** probably proverbial (Dent,
W260.1)
98–9 **a church door** Mercutio may be
thinking of his funeral here (Ard²). Q1
has 'barne doore' but makes him visu-
alize his burial explicitly when he says,
in lines not in Q2, 'I shall be fairely
mounted vpon foure mens shoulders:
For your house of the *Mountagues* and
the *Capulets*'.
99 **'twill serve** it will do
100 **a grave man** because he will be
buried (with a sardonic pun on *grave*)
101 **peppered** ruined; Falstaff claims to
have 'peppered' two of the men in
buckram (*1H4* 2.4.184).
warrant guarantee
102 *****Zounds** See 48n.; Mercutio's second (and last) use of this word.
dog . . . cat See 3.3.30–1 and 'Why
should a dog, a horse, a rat have life
/ And thou no breath at all?' (*KL*
5.3.305–6).
104 **fights . . . arithmetic** Tybalt stands

accused by Mercutio of being a per-
nickety fighter, lacking finesse or imagination; to receive a fatal blow from
him is therefore particularly galling
and humiliating. With this derogatory
use of *arithmetic*, cf. Iago's description
of Cassio as 'a great arithmetician'
(*Oth* 1.1.18).
109–10 Set as in Q2, even though 109
is incomplete, fittingly so perhaps as
Mercutio is transmogrifying into a
corpse and will shortly be less than
whole; 110 is his last line in the play
and, while decasyllabic, does not
scan as a pentameter. Q2 punctuates 110 'I haue it, and soundly, to
your houses'.
109 **worms' meat** proverbial; cf. 'A man
is nothing but worms' meat' (Dent,
M253).
110 **I have it** I am finished; literally, I
have received it (cited under *OED*
v. 14d as first recorded usage in this
signification).

99 church] *Q2–4, F;* barne *Q1*   102 Zounds] *Q5;* sounds *Q2–4;* What *F; not in Q1*   109–10] *Q2–4,
F; Dyce lines* it, / houses! /   110 SD] *Rowe subst.; Exit. Q2–4, F; Exeunt. Q1*

ROMEO

This gentleman, the Prince's near ally,
My very friend, hath got this mortal hurt
In my behalf; my reputation stained
With Tybalt's slander – Tybalt, that an hour
Hath been my cousin. O sweet Juliet,   115
Thy beauty hath made me effeminate
And in my temper softened valour's steel!

Enter BENVOLIO.

BENVOLIO

O Romeo, Romeo, brave Mercutio is dead.
That gallant spirit hath aspired the clouds,
Which too untimely here did scorn the earth.   120

ROMEO

This day's black fate on moe days doth depend,
This but begins the woe others must end.

Enter TYBALT.

BENVOLIO

Here comes the furious Tybalt back again.

111 **ally** allỳ; kinsman (cited under *OED sb.*[1] 5)
112 **very** true (*OED a.* 6)
113 **In my behalf** for me ('in' for modern 'on')
117 Romeo's previously steely and courageous disposition (*temper*) has been softened by his marriage to Juliet. The analogy is with the hardness imparted to steel by the process of tempering, immersing white-hot steel in cold water (*OED* temper *v.* 14); cf. the 'icebrook's temper' of Othello's 'sword of Spain' (*Oth* 5.2.251); Romeo is like a blunted sword.

118 **brave** admirable (*OED a.* 3)
119 **aspired** soared up to (on this transitive use, see *OED v.* 8, which cites this line)
121–2 'The true reckoning for this day's tragic events lies in the future – this is merely the start, and worse is to come'; cf. 'But this same day / Must end that work the Ides of March begun' (*JC* 5.1.112–13). Romeo's rhyming couplet bespeaks a grim determination; its finality is taken up in the next couplet, which he shares with Benvolio.
123 **furious** fierce, aggressive, full of fighting spirit

112 got this] *Q2;* got his *Q3–4, F;* tane this *Q1*   115 cousin] *Q2–4, F;* kinsman *Q1*   118 Mercutio] *Q2–4, Q1;* Mercutio's *F*   121 moe] *Q2–4, F;* more *Q1*   122.1] *F, Q1; not in Q2–4*

ROMEO

Alive, in triumph, and Mercutio slain!
Away to heaven, respective lenity,   125
And fire-eyed fury be my conduct now.
Now, Tybalt, take the 'villain' back again
That late thou gavest me, for Mercutio's soul
Is but a little way above our heads,
Staying for thine to keep him company.   130
Either thou or I, or both, must go with him.

TYBALT

Thou wretched boy, that didst consort him here,
Shalt with him hence.

ROMEO   This shall determine that.

They fight. Tybalt falls [and dies].

BENVOLIO

Romeo, away, be gone!
The citizens are up and Tybalt slain.   135
Stand not amazed. The Prince will doom thee death
If thou art taken. Hence, be gone, away!

ROMEO

O, I am fortune's fool.

BENVOLIO   Why dost thou stay?   *Exit Romeo.*

---

124 ***Alive** after Q1. Cam² has 'Again?'
(Capell), picking up Benvolio's *again*,
which rhymes with *slain*, the last word
of Romeo's apostrophe. Oxf¹ retains
Q2 ('He gan'), while Williams argues
for 'He yare' by analogy with 'be yare
in thy preparation' (*TN* 3.3.226), since
'yare' and 'gan' are 'easily misread'.

125 **respective lenity** partial gentleness (partial because Tybalt is Juliet's
cousin) (*OED* 'respective' quotes this
line)

126 ***fire-eyed fury** incandescent rage,
as opposed to the forbearing of the
previous line; cf. 'fire-eyed maid of

smoky war' (*1H4* 4.1.113).
conduct guide

127 **take . . . again** retract the insult of
calling me 'peasant'

128 **gavest** cast at

132 **consort** accompany, attend (*OED*);
Tybalt hurls the very word at Romeo
with which he provoked Mercutio
(44–5).

135 **up** up and about

136 **amazed** bewildered and lost
doom thee death pronounce sentence of death on you

138 **fortune's fool** the fates' whipping
boy (proverbial; Dent, F617.1)

---

124 Alive] *Q1;* He gan *Q2;* He gon *Q3–4, F;* Again? *Capell;* He yare *Williams*   126 fire-eyed] *Q1;*
fier end *Q2;* fier and *Q3;* fire and *Q4, F*   128 gavest] *Q2–4;* gau'st *F, Q1*   131 Either] *Q2–4, F;* Or
Q1   133 SD *and dies*] *this edn*   138 SD] *Q2–4, F; Exeunt. Q1*

Enter Citizens.

CITIZENS

Which way ran he that killed Mercutio?
Tybalt, that murderer, which way ran he?   140

BENVOLIO

There lies that Tybalt.

CITIZEN   Up, sir, go with me.
I charge thee in the Prince's name, obey.

Enter PRINCE, *old* MONTAGUE, CAPULET,
their WIVES *and all.*

PRINCE

Where are the vile beginners of this fray?

BENVOLIO

O noble Prince, I can discover all
The unlucky manage of this fatal brawl.   145
There lies the man, slain by young Romeo,
That slew thy kinsman, brave Mercutio.

CAPULET'S WIFE

Tybalt, my cousin, O my brother's child!
O Prince, O cousin, husband, O, the blood is spilled
Of my dear kinsman! Prince, as thou art true,   150
For blood of ours shed blood of Montague.
O cousin, cousin!

---

145 **unlucky manage** tragic conduct
148 **cousin** kinsman
149 Many editors follow Capell and remove Q2's 'Cozen' for metrical reasons and because it is repeated from the previous line. Without it the line becomes a pentameter, but regularity should not necessarily override the authority of Q2 (*cousin* can be monosyllabic 'coz'). Juliet's mother

is distraught during these multiple apostrophes and her grief may cause the line to spill into a hexameter. When she speaks again she is calmer, her words are premeditated and she uses rhyming couplets (178–83).
150 **true** loyal to your word (that anyone found guilty in the future of initiating a fight between the two houses would be punished by death; see 1.1.94–5)

142 name] *Q2–4;* names *F; not in Q1*   142.1] *Q2–4, F;* Enter Prince, Capolets wife. *Q1*   148 SP] *Q2–4 (Capu. Wi.), F (Cap. Wi.); M: Q1*   149 O Prince . . . husband] *Q2–4, F;* O Prince! O husband *Capell*

PRINCE

Benvolio, who began this bloody fray?

BENVOLIO

Tybalt, here slain, whom Romeo's hand did slay,
Romeo, that spoke him fair, bid him bethink   155
How nice the quarrel was, and urged withal
Your high displeasure. All this, uttered
With gentle breath, calm look, knees humbly bowed,
Could not take truce with the unruly spleen
Of Tybalt deaf to peace, but that he tilts   160
With piercing steel at bold Mercutio's breast,
Who, all as hot, turns deadly point to point
And, with a martial scorn, with one hand beats
Cold death aside, and with the other sends
It back to Tybalt, whose dexterity   165
Retorts it. Romeo, he cries aloud
'Hold, friends, friends, part!', and swifter than his
        tongue
His agile arm beats down their fatal points,
And 'twixt them rushes; underneath whose arm
An envious thrust from Tybalt hit the life   170
Of stout Mercutio, and then Tybalt fled.

---

156 **nice** trivial, insignificant (cf. 5.2.18)
    urged withal pointed out at the same
    time
157 **high** utmost, with a reference also to
    the status of his Highness the Prince
159 **take truce** make peace
    spleen fierce temper (cited in *OED*).
    The spleen was traditionally assumed
    to be the seat of melancholy and
    morose feelings.
162 **turns . . . to point** parries sword
    with sword (*point* being a metonym of
    sword; *OED sb.*[1] II 19)
163–5 **with one . . . Tybalt** Mercutio

deflects his adversary's deadly blows
with a dagger in one hand while with
the other hand seeking to kill Tybalt,
who skilfully does the like (*Retorts*,
166) to him.
168 ***agile** nimble (after Q1; cited in
    OED)
    points swords
170 **envious** malicious, spiteful; perhaps
    also treacherous, as not according with
    the rules of fair combat since Tybalt
    struck Mercutio during the mêlée with
    Romeo (*OED a.* 2)
171 **stout** brave (*OED*)

153 bloody] *Q2–4; om. F; not in Q1*   160 Tybalt] *Q2–4;* Tybalts *F; not in Q1*   168 agile] *Q1, Q4;*
aged *Q2–3, F;* able *F2;* agent *Oxf (McKerrow)*

But by and by comes back to Romeo,
Who had but newly entertained revenge,
And to't they go like lightning, for, ere I
Could draw to part them was stout Tybalt slain,   175
And as he fell did Romeo turn and fly.
This is the truth, or let Benvolio die.

CAPULET'S WIFE

He is a kinsman to the Montague.
Affection makes him false; he speaks not true.
Some twenty of them fought in this black strife,   180
And all those twenty could but kill one life.
I beg for justice, which thou, Prince, must give:
Romeo slew Tybalt, Romeo must not live.

PRINCE

Romeo slew him, he slew Mercutio,
Who now the price of his dear blood doth owe?   185

---

172 **by and by** at once
173 **but newly** just then
   entertained considered
174 **like lightning** 'as swift as lightning'
   is proverbial (Dent, L279).
175 **stout** By applying the same martial
   epithet to Tybalt as to Mercutio,
   Benvolio further underlines their
   essential similarity, already hinted at
   in his description of their perfectly
   matched fighting.
176–7 **fly . . . die** Benvolio resumes
   rhyming just when he is hoping to save
   Romeo, a rhetorical strategy countered by Juliet's mother, who rhymes
   Montague with *not true*. The remaining
   lines of the scene are all couplets, as
   Escalus in turn attempts to impose
   order on chaos.
179 **not true** Benvolio's account of the
   fight has indeed been partial, since
   Mercutio first drew on Tybalt (contrary to 162–9). In Brooke, Mercutio

and Benvolio are absent from the
fight, as is Juliet's mother from its
aftermath; instead, 'The Montagues
do plead their Romeus void of fault,
/ The lookers on do say the fight
begun was by Tybalt' (Brooke,
1043–4).
180 **twenty** It is her turn to falsify and
   exaggerate.
   black deadly (*OED a*. II)
182 **thou** The inappropriate address
   to the Prince of the intimate second
   person pronoun conveys the despair
   and urgency of Capulet's grief-
   stricken wife, who sheds all sense of
   decorum.
185 'Who is to pay for Mercutio's
   death now that his killer is dead?',
   with *dear* (precious) acknowledging
   that Mercutio is the Prince's kinsman, as his use of *interest* at 190
   further notes; *dear blood* means vital
   fluid (Onions).

178 SP] *Q2–4, F; Mo: Q1*

MONTAGUE

Not Romeo, Prince, he was Mercutio's friend.
His fault concludes but what the law should end,
The life of Tybalt.

PRINCE   And for that offence

Immediately we do exile him hence.
I have an interest in your hates' proceeding.   190
My blood for your rude brawls doth lie a-bleeding,
But I'll amerce you with so strong a fine
That you shall all repent the loss of mine.
I will be deaf to pleading and excuses,
Nor tears, nor prayers shall purchase out abuses,   195
Therefore use none. Let Romeo hence in haste,
Else, when he is found, that hour is his last.
Bear hence this body, and attend our will.
Mercy but murders, pardoning those that kill.   *Exeunt.*

---

186 SP *The lines *Not . . . Tybalt* (186–8) are attributed mistakenly to Capulet in Q2.

187 **concludes but** only completes

190 ***your hates' proceeding** 'the actions of your nefarious family feud'. I follow Q1's reading, 'hates', here rather than Q2's 'hearts', which is retained by a number of recent editions. The word 'hate' is applied to the feud by the Prince during his first speech ('your cankered hate', 1.1.93), and by Romeo when he ruefully comments on the first fray (1.1.173).

192 **amerce** punish

195 **purchase out** redeem

198 **this body** Tybalt's body, unlike that of Mercutio who dies offstage, provides a stark foreground to the Prince's lines and the impotent fury of his Capulet aunt.

199 i.e. clemency to murderers only

begets more violent deaths. Hosley (146) cites Machiavelli's *The Prince* (ch. 17), in support of good, tough government: the Prince 'must not mind incurring the charge of cruelty for the purpose of keeping his subjects united and faithful; for, with a very few examples, he will be more merciful than those who, from excess of tenderness, allow disorders to arise, from whence spring bloodshed and rapine; for these as a rule injure the whole community, while the executions carried out by the prince injure only individuals'. Shakespeare did not need to refer to Machiavelli's expedient rules of government, but the fact that his line about mercy is spoken by a character known onstage as 'The Prince' suggests that he was well aware of Machiavelli's writings.

186 SP] *Q4; Capu. Q2; Cap: Q3, F (Cap.); La. Mont. / Theobald; not in Q1*   190 hates'] *Q1;* hearts *Q2–4, F*   194 I] *Q1, Q4;* It *Q2–3, F*   195 out] *Q2–4;* our *F;* for *Q1*   199 but] *Q2–4;* not *F*   SD] *F; Exit. Q2–4; Exeunt omnes. Q1*

[3.2]   *Enter* JULIET *alone.*

JULIET

Gallop apace, you fiery-footed steeds,
Towards Phoebus' lodging. Such a wagoner
As Phaeton would whip you to the west
And bring in cloudy night immediately.
Spread thy close curtain, love-performing night,   5
That runaways' eyes may wink, and Romeo
Leap to these arms, untalked of and unseen.

3.2 Monday evening (1–2) in Juliet's bedroom

1 Juliet's opening line recollects Marlowe's 'Gallop apace, bright Phoebus, through the sky' (*Edward II*, 4.3.43); in Brooke, 'The hastiness of Phoebus' steeds in great despite they [Romeus and Juliet] blame' (920).

fiery-footed spirited; the epithet comes from Golding, whose Phoebus' horses are 'fiery-foaming' and 'fiery-footed' (Ovid, *Met.*, 2.160, 491).

2 **lodging** probably after Brooke's 'The golden sun was gone to lodge him in the west' (1527)

wagoner charioteer; another allusion to Golding, who applies this term to Phaeton

3 **Phaeton** the son of the Sun (Phoebus Apollo); his doomed ride in his father's chariot is recounted in *Metamorphoses* 1–2. Sensing his inexperience, the horses ran riot, causing an apocalyptic trail of scorching destruction until Zeus struck Phaeton down with a thunderbolt (Ovid, *Met.*, 2.394–5). The tale of Phaeton provides a bodeful undertow to the loves of Romeo and Juliet.

4 **cloudy** dark
night The first of 11 uses of *night* in this soliloquy by Juliet, who seems mesmerized by the word; her repetition verges on the incantatory, as if

by reiteration she could conjure up night.

5 **Spread** extend (i.e. to cover and hide from view)

close curtain Curtains surrounded the four-poster beds favoured by wealthy families like the Capulets. The curtains of Juliet's bed are twice mentioned in the Q1 SDs.

love-performing night The darkness of night allows lovers to embrace and perform their sexual rituals (cited in *OED*).

6 **runaways'** fugitives', vagabonds', although the word is usually taken to refer to the bolting horses of the sun (*OED* cites a 1607 instance of 'runaways' = horses); it also looks ahead, perhaps, to Romeo on the run (he is called *runagate* at 3.5.89). Brooke (780ff.) compares Juliet's yearning to the longing for peace of soldiers, merchants and ploughmen, none of whom are mentioned by her in the play.

wink close, so as not to see

7 **Leap** rush; with this emphasis on eagerness cf. 'If Caesar please, our master / Will leap to be his friend' (*AC* 3.13.53–4). Ard[2] notes Marlowe, *Dido Queen of Carthage*: 'If thou wilt stay, / Leap in mine arms' (5.1.179–80).

arms in telling contrast to the four uses of *arm* in the fight of the final scene

3.2] *Rowe*   0.1] *Q2–4, F; Enter Iuliet. Q1*   1 SP] *F, Q1; not in Q2–4*   2 Towards] *Q2–4, F; To Q1*

Lovers can see to do their amorous rites
By their own beauties; or, if love be blind,
It best agrees with night. Come, civil night,   10
Thou sober-suited matron all in black,
And learn me how to lose a winning match,
Played for a pair of stainless maidenhoods.
Hood my unmanned blood, bating in my cheeks,
With thy black mantle, till strange love grow bold,   15
Think true love acted simple modesty.
Come, night, come, Romeo, come, thou day in night,

8–9 **Lovers . . . beauties** 'Their beauty is all the light lovers require for making love.' The phrase *amorous rites* occurs only once in Shakespeare, suggesting that he borrowed it from Marlowe's *Hero and Leander* (2.64), which may lie behind the passage generally. A number of editors compare 'dark night is Cupid's day' from *Hero and Leander*, 1.191.

9 **love . . . blind** 'Love is blind' proverbial (Dent, L506); see also 1.1.169–70, 1.4.4, 2.1.32, 2.4.16.

10 **civil** sober, grave; the fifth and last use of this adjective in the play (*OED a.* 10)

11 **Thou** Once again the intimate pronoun is used for conveying a sense of urgency while also implying that night is Juliet's confidante and guardian angel (see 18n. below).

12 **learn me** teach me, appealing to night to watch over her; 'that should learn us' in Q2 *Ham* is changed 19 years later in F to 'that should teach us', suggesting that *learn* in the sense of teach 'common in Shakespeare and still surviving in dialect, may already have been losing favour' (Harold Jenkins, Ard² *Ham* 5.2.9n.).

lose . . . match Juliet longs to be defeated and conquered (*lose*) during her sexual union with Romeo. Her

submission will be her victory; she will win either way, since Romeo's triumph will also be hers (cited under *OED* winning *ppl. a. 2*).

13 Romeo and Juliet are both virgins, hence sexually without blemish (cited under *OED* stainless *a.*); their *match* (12) concerns both their virginities.

14–15 **Hood . . . mantle** Her blood will be coursing (*bating*) through her cheeks and will make her blush while in bed with Romeo, but darkness (*thy black mantle*) will protect her from the outward signs of embarrassment (cited under *OED* bate).

14 **Hood** hide; archly following on from *maidenhoods* in the preceding line
unmanned not yet broken in, with a pun on man; the usage is taken from training hawks (cited under *OED ppl. a. 3*).

15 **till . . . bold** 'until such time that new (*strange*) love dares to assert itself'

16 an invitation to matronly night to consider that sexual consummation of real love (*true love acted*) is totally pure (*simple modesty*)

17 **Come** The word is repeated five times in four lines to convey the percussive ardour of Juliet's longing.
day in night reprising the motif of lovers seeing in the dark by their very presence (see 8–9)

9 By] *Q4;* And by *Q2–3, F*   13 maidenhoods] *Q2–3, F;* maiden-heads *Q4*   15 grow] *Q2–4, F;* grown *Rowe*

For thou wilt lie upon the wings of night
Whiter than new snow upon a raven's back.
Come, gentle night, come, loving black-browed night,   20
Give me my Romeo, and when I shall die
Take him and cut him out in little stars,
And he will make the face of heaven so fine
That all the world will be in love with night
And pay no worship to the garish sun.   25
O, I have bought the mansion of a love

18–19 Cf. the almost identical contrapuntal phrasing of Romeo's initial response to seeing Juliet at 1.5.47–8: 'So shows a snowy dove trooping with crows / As yonder lady o'er her fellows shows'; 'as black as a raven' was proverbial (Dent, R 32.2).

18 **wings of night** Personified night now assumes the guise of a guardian angel whose wings in turn lead to the startling image of the raven covered in snow. The sensation of soaring evoked by Juliet in her eager anticipation of her wedding night resonates with sexual innuendo, as do the lines which follow.

20 **loving** because she is the patron of lovers
black-browed having a dark front (cited in *OED*); cf. 'And must for aye consort with black-brow'd night' (*MND* 3.2.387).

21 **die** Sexual ecstasy in *die* may be suggested by a firework of *little stars* and Juliet's eager anticipation of her wedding night.

22 **cut . . . stars** The stellar metamorphosis of Romeo after Juliet's 'death' is Ovidian, but the image of night cutting out Romeo into miniature constellations, to spangle the heavens and outshine daylight, conjures up childhood games. Q4's 'he' (used by Niamh Cusack in Bogdanov) for *I* (21) fails

to realize that Juliet cannot articulate Romeo's death, hence her poignant use of *I* when the poetic logic of *Metamorphoses* would seem to demand 'he'. For Ovid, death is translation of matter: '*omnia mutantur, nil interit*', which Golding renders as 'Neither doth there perish aught (trust me) / In all the world but, altering, takes new shape' (Ovid, *Met.*, 15.278–9). Juliet's lyrical fantasy is an artfully displaced metaphor for the bliss that she imagines her sexual union with Romeo will induce, so that *I shall die* is almost certainly correct. Ard² refers to the apotheosis of Julius Caesar into a 'goodly shyning starre' (Ovid, *Met.*, 15.955).

25 **garish** glaring (cited in *OED*)

26 **the mansion . . . love** a body to love; with the body the shell of the soul (*OED* mansion). According to Juliet, Romeo and she are bodies longing to be *possessed* and *enjoyed* by each other. The metaphor has archly moved from a play on dark and light to one of exchange of erotic commodities. The same image is applied to her body by Imogen: 'The innocent mansion of my life, my heart' (*Cym* 3.4.69), albeit with the epithet 'innocent' (cf. 'Innogen/Imogen') before 'mansion' to underline the decorum of this image of physical desire.

19 new snow upon] *Q2–3, F;* snow vpon *Q4;* new Snow on *F2*   21 I] *Q2–3, F;* hee *Q4*

249

But not possessed it, and though I am sold,
Not yet enjoyed. So tedious is this day
As is the night before some festival
To an impatient child that hath new robes   30
And may not wear them.

Enter NURSE *wringing her hands, with the*
ladder of cords in her lap.

                                    O, here comes my Nurse,
And she brings news, and every tongue that speaks
But Romeo's name speaks heavenly eloquence.
Now, Nurse, what news? What hast thou there, the
    cords
That Romeo bid thee fetch?

NURSE   Ay, ay, the cords.   35
JULIET

Ay me, what news? Why dost thou wring thy hands?
NURSE

Ah weraday, he's dead, he's dead, he's dead!
We are undone, lady, we are undone.
Alack the day, he's gone, he's killed, he's dead.

30 **impatient child** spoken here with innocent irony, and marking the fact that Juliet is still very young, as the child's star-cutting image also suggests

31.1 *Q1's richly mimetic SD has Nurse carry the rope-ladder in a pocket in the front of her skirt (*OED* lap¹ 4b), presumably to hide it from view, hence Juliet's question, 'What hast thou there', at 34. Q2's '*Enter Nurse with cords*' states the bare facts, though the cue to Nurse's hand-wringing in

performance is explicitly provided by the text of Q2 at 36; in Q2 the more elaborate Q1 SD is redundant, while in Q1 it is needed because the line with the cue in it is missing. Dessen and Thomson (255) associate the use of wringing of hands with 'mourning or weeping women'; see also 4.5.48 SD.

37 **weraday** an expression of lament, used again by Nurse at 4.5.15; the more common form 'welladay' occurs in Q3–4 (cited in *OED*).

31 SD] *Q1; Enter Nurse with cords. Q2–4, F; Enter* NURSE *with cords wringing her hands. /*
Williams 34–5] *Hanmer; Q2–4, F line* there, / fetch *(*fetch? *F) /* cords. / ; *var. Q1* 37 weraday]
Q2; welady *Q3–4, F; not in Q1* he's . . . dead] *Q2–4, Q1 (three times);* hee's dead *(twice)* F

JULIET
> Can heaven be so envious?

NURSE   Romeo can,   40
> Though heaven cannot. O Romeo, Romeo,
> Whoever would have thought it – Romeo!

JULIET
> What devil are thou that dost torment me thus?
> This torture should be roared in dismal hell.
> Hath Romeo slain himself? Say thou but 'Ay',   45
> And that bare vowel 'I' shall poison more
> Than the death-darting eye of cockatrice.
> I am not I if there be such an 'Ay',
> Or those eyes shut that makes thee answer 'Ay'.
> If he be slain, say 'Ay', or if not, 'No'.   50
> Brief sounds determine of my weal or woe.

NURSE
> I saw the wound, I saw it with mine eyes –
> God save the mark – here on his manly breast,

---

40 **envious** spiteful

41–2 *Romeo* has two beats followed by three in 41, and three in 42, the stress pattern 'demonstrating an increasingly emotional tone' (Crystal, *Pronouncing*, 78).

45–9 Granville-Barker called Juliet's playing on 'Ay, I, eye' a 'delirium of puns', intended to lift the scene 'to a sudden height of intoxicated excitement, giving us a first and memorable taste of the Juliet of quick despair' and thus preparing the ground for her suicide in 5.3.

47 **death-darting . . . cockatrice** Killing like a cockatrice is proverbial (Dent, C496.2; cited under *OED* cockatrice). The mythic reptile, also known as the basilisk, could kill its victims with a stare; cf. 'This will so fright them both that they will kill one another by the look, like cockatrices' (*TN* 3.4.196–8) and Spenser's *Amoretti*, 49.9–10.

48–50 Ard² compares 'Ay, no. No, ay; for I

must nothing be' (*R2* 4.1.201).

48 'If your answer is "yes, Romeo has killed himself"', I will no longer be me' (because she too will then cease to be).

49 'or if you answer "yes" because Romeo's eyes are shut and he is therefore dead'

51 'Mere monosyllables (the *'Ay'* or *'No'* of the preceding line – cf. *that bare vowel* for *'Ay'* at 46) decide my happiness (*weal*) or dejection (*woe*).'

52 Nurse continues Juliet's play on *I, eye* and *Ay*. 'To see with one's own eyes' is proverbial (Dent, E266.1).

53 **God . . . mark** *OED* (*sb.*[1] 11) glosses as 'an exclamatory phrase, probably originally serving as a formula to avert an evil omen, and hence used by way of apology when something horrible, indecent, or profane has been mentioned'; cf. similarly *1H4* 1.3.56. The expression '(God) bless (save) the mark' is proverbial (Dent, G179.1).

45, 48, 49, 50 'Ay'] *Rowe;* I *Q2–4, F; not in Q1*   49 shut] *Capell;* shot *Q2–4, F; not in Q1*   51 Brief sounds] *Q5;* Briefe, sounds *Q2–4, F; not in Q1*   of my] *F, Q5;* my *Q2–4; not in Q1*

A piteous corse, a bloody piteous corse,
Pale, pale as ashes, all bedaubed in blood, 55
All in gore-blood. I sounded at the sight.

JULIET

O break, my heart, poor bankrupt, break at once!
To prison, eyes, ne'er look on liberty.
Vile earth to earth resign, end motion here,
And thou and Romeo press one heavy bier. 60

NURSE

O Tybalt, Tybalt, the best friend I had!
O courteous Tybalt, honest gentleman,
That ever I should live to see thee dead!

JULIET

What storm is this that blows so contrary?
Is Romeo slaughtered and is Tybalt dead, 65
My dearest cousin and my dearer lord?
Then, dreadful trumpet, sound the general doom,
For who is living if those two are gone?

54 **piteous** pitiful
corse corpse
55 **pale as ashes** proverbial (Dent, A339)
bedaubed spattered
56 **gore-blood** clotted, congealed blood
sounded swooned (*OED* sound *v.*⁴)
57 **bankrupt** because she is fatally
impoverished now by her loss of
Romeo (as she assumes)
59 **earth to earth** proverbial (Dent,
E30). The first earth refers to Juliet's
body, as in the language of the funeral
service, after Ecclesiastes, 12.7: 'Then
shall the dust return to the earth as it
was; and the spirit shall return unto
God who gave it.'
resign render (what was only ever
borrowed)
60 **thou** i.e. herself (as it turns out this
will be exactly her fate)
62 **honest** honourable

63 Because of her age it is unnatural that
she should have outlived him.
64 **so contrary** in such contradic-
tory directions (from Romeo's death
to Tybalt's)
67 **dreadful** awe-inspiring
trumpet . . . doom alluding to
the 'last trump', which will sound
on the Day of Judgement when 'the
dead shall be raised incorruptible' (1
Corinthians, 15.52). Juliet claims that
the fate of Romeo and Tybalt spells
the end of time.
68 Cf. Cleopatra's reaction to Antony's
death: 'O withered is the garland
of the war, / The soldier's pole is
fallen; young boys and girls / Are
level now with men; the odds is gone
/ And there is nothing left remarkable / Beneath the visiting moon'
(*AC* 4.15.66–70).

56 sounded] *Q2–4, F;* swounded *Q1* 57 bankrupt] *Q5;* banckrout *Q2–4, F; not in Q1* 60 one] *Q4;*
on *Q2–3, F; not in Q1* bier] *Q2 (*beare*), Q3–4, F (*beere*); not in Q1* 66 dearest] *Q2–4, F;* deare
loude *Q1* dearer] *Q2–4, F;* dearest *Q1* 67 dreadful] *Q2–4, F;* let the *Q1*

NURSE

Tybalt is gone and Romeo banished,
Romeo that killed him, he is banished.   70
JULIET

O God, did Romeo's hand shed Tybalt's blood?
NURSE

It did, it did, alas the day, it did.
JULIET

O serpent heart hid with a flowering face!
Did ever dragon keep so fair a cave?
Beautiful tyrant, fiend angelical,   75
Dove-feathered raven, wolvish-ravening lamb,
Despised substance of divinest show,
Just opposite to what thou justly seem'st,
A damned saint, an honourable villain.
O nature, what hadst thou to do in hell   80

---

69 **banished** banishèd; also at 70, 112, 113, 122, 124, and at 3.3.15, 19, 20, 21, 40, 42, 46, 51, 56, 57, 67

72–3 SPs *All editors here follow Q1's SPs. In Q2 Juliet speaks 72 and Nurse 73, so that Juliet answers her own question.

73–85 **O . . . palace** The idea that a fair appearance may conceal treachery is proverbial (Dent, F3); it here launches a string of paradoxes and antitheses predicated on Romeo's beauty.

73 Cf. 'look like th'innocent flower, / But be the serpent under't' (*Mac* 1.5.65–6).

75 a classic chiastic construction to vary the regular adjective/noun pattern of the next lines

76 **Dove-feathered raven* Theobald's emendation for Q2's hypermetrical 'Rauenous douefeatherd rauè' has been widely accepted (see also 85–7n., and 2.5.15n., 4.3.58n.; *Dove-feathered* is first *OED* usage). The phrase plays

on the contrasting plumages of doves and ravens (Dent, D573.2, R32.2) and pursues the motif of contrasting outer whiteness (*Dove-feathered*) and inner blackness (*raven*), doves being associated in this play with Juliet's beauty.

wolvish-ravening bloodthirsty like a wolf, with a play on *ravening/raven*. Ard[2] cites Matthew, 7.15, warning against 'false prophets, which come to you in sheep's clothing, but inwardly they are ravening wolves'.

77 echoing proverbial 'More show than substance' (Dent, S408)

Despised despisèd

78 **Just** precise

justly exactly, quibbling on the preceding use of *Just*

79 **damned* damnèd

80–2 Juliet commands nature to explain why she went to hell to implant a demon in a Romeo otherwise so glorious in physical appearance.

---

72 SP] *Q1, Q5; not in Q2–4, F*   73 SP] *Q1, F2; Nur. Q2–4, F*   serpent heart] *Q2–4, F;* serpents hate *Q1*   74 Did] *F2; Iu.* Did *Q2–4, F; not in Q1*   76 Dove-feathered raven] *Theobald;* Rauenous douefeatherd rauè *Q2–3, F;* Rauenous doue, feathred Rauen *Q4; not in Q1*   79 damned] *Q4;* dimme *Q2–3;* dimne *F; not in Q1*

When thou didst bower the spirit of a fiend
In mortal paradise of such sweet flesh?
Was ever book containing such vile matter
So fairly bound? O, that deceit should dwell
In such a gorgeous palace.

NURSE   There's no trust,   85
No faith, no honesty in men – all perjured,
All forsworn, all naught, all dissemblers.
Ah, where's my man? Give me some aqua vitae.
These griefs, these woes, these sorrows make me old.
Shame come to Romeo!

JULIET   Blistered be thy tongue   90
For such a wish! He was not born to shame;
Upon his brow shame is ashamed to sit
For 'tis a throne where honour may be crowned
Sole monarch of the universal earth.
O, what a beast was I to chide at him!   95

NURSE
Will you speak well of him that killed your cousin?

---

81 **bower** implant (cited under *OED v.*)
82 **mortal paradise** Romeo is her
heaven but because he is human he
will one day die.
83–4 **Was ... bound** recollecting Juliet's
mother's comparison of Paris' face to a
'precious book of love' (1.3.88)
85–7 ***There's ... dissemblers*** after
Capell and Ard². Q2 sets as two
hypermetrical lines: 'There's no trust,
no faith, no honestie in men, / All
periurde, all forsworne, all naught,
all dissemblers.' Oxf¹ follows, arguing
that Nurse's 'medium has often hov-
ered between verse and prose; and her
verse here, prosaic and consistently
inconsistent, contrasts effectively with
Juliet's'. Williams (127–8) proposes an

emended version of Capell with *all
perjured* and *all naught* trading places,
which renders all three lines metrical
(see t.n.).
87 **naught** wicked
all dissemblers See Balthasar's
song 'Men were deceivers ever' (*MA*
2.3.61ff.).
88 **aqua vitae** brandy (literally, 'water of
life'); see also 4.5.16.
90 **Shame** ignominy (*OED*)
Blistered ... tongue Dent compares
proverbial '(Report has) a blister on her
tongue' and 'A blister will rise upon
one's tongue that tells a lie' (R84).
91 **to shame** to suffer disgrace; Nurse
and Juliet play on the word *shame* as
noun and verb.

---

81 bower] *Q2–3;* power *Q4; not in Q1*   85–7] *Capell; Q2–4, F line* Pallace, / men, / dissemblers, / ;
Q1 lines Romeo? / There is . . . men: / forsworne. / ; *Williams lines* Pallace. / trust, / naught, /
dissemblers, /   95 at him] *Q2–4;* him *F; not in Q1*

JULIET

Shall I speak ill of him that is my husband?
Ah, poor my lord, what tongue shall smooth thy name
When I, thy three-hours' wife, have mangled it?
But wherefore, villain, didst thou kill my cousin?   100
That villain cousin would have killed my husband.
Back, foolish tears, back to your native spring,
Your tributary drops belong to woe
Which you, mistaking, offer up to joy.
My husband lives that Tybalt would have slain,   105
And Tybalt's dead that would have slain my husband.
All this is comfort. Wherefore weep I then?
Some word there was, worser than Tybalt's death,
That murdered me. I would forget it fain,
But O, it presses to my memory   110
Like damned guilty deeds to sinners' minds.
Tybalt is dead and Romeo banished;
That 'banished', that one word 'banished'
Hath slain ten thousand Tybalts. Tybalt's death
Was woe enough, if it had ended there;   115
Or, if sour woe delights in fellowship
And needly will be ranked with other griefs,
Why followed not, when she said 'Tybalt's dead',

---

98 **poor my lord** my poor lord (on trans-
posing the possessive, see Abbott, 13)
smooth thy name 'restore your
reputation from the damage (it is being
mangled) that it is now receiving' (cited
under *OED* smooth)
102 **native spring** i.e. Juliet's eyes
103–4 i.e. tears are shed for sorrow, not
for good news (since Romeo is alive).
103 **tributary** paying homage; cf. 'tributary tears' (*Tit* 1.1.162) and 'tributary
rivers' (*Cym* 4.2.36).
108 **worser** worse
109 **fain** gladly

111 **damned** damnèd
116–19 **sour . . . both** The expression
that grief enjoys company is proverbial (Dent, M1012). Juliet wishes that,
since bad news, like that of Tybalt's
death, wants more of the same for
solace, then the same it should be,
even if that means news of her parents'
deaths – anything so long as it is not
that Romeo is banished.
117 **needly** of necessity
ranked classified alongside others of
a similar kind, in a fellowship of woes
(cited under *OED v.*³)

---

106 Tybalt's] *Q2–4; Tibalt F; not in Q1*   108 word there was] *Q2; words there was Q3–4, F; not in Q1*

'Thy father', or 'thy mother', nay, or both,
Which modern lamentation might have moved?   120
But with a rearward following Tybalt's death,
'Romeo is banished' – to speak that word
Is father, mother, Tybalt, Romeo, Juliet,
All slain, all dead. 'Romeo is banished' –
There is no end, no limit, measure, bound,   125
In that word's death; no words can that woe sound.
Where is my father and my mother, Nurse?

NURSE
Weeping and wailing over Tybalt's corse.
Will you go to them? I will bring you thither.

JULIET
Wash they his wounds with tears? Mine shall be spent,   130
When theirs are dry, for Romeo's banishment.
Take up those cords. Poor ropes, you are beguiled,
Both you and I, for Romeo is exiled.
He made you for a highway to my bed,
But I, a maid, die maiden-widowed.   135
Come, cords, come, Nurse, I'll to my wedding bed
And death, not Romeo, take my maidenhead.

---

120 'which might have allowed me commonplace (*modern*; *OED* modern *a.* 4) expressions of grief (*lamentation*)' (rather than finding myself *murdered* (109) by a sorrow so overwhelming that I cannot fathom it)

121 **rearward** rearguard; coming at the end and carrying the proverbial sting in the tail, since news of Romeo's banishment is broken to her after she learns of Tybalt's death (cited under *OED* rearward *sb.*[1]). She may also play on 'ward'/'word' in a play keenly interested in testing the relationship between words, sounds and reality; cf. *words* and *woe* in 126.

126 **that word's death** The word *ban-* *ished* has infinite powers to kill and destroy.
sound express (cited under *OED v.*[1] 8b)

127 **is** are (Abbott, 335)

130–7 The rhyming couplets mark a return to a more controlled idiom after the extremes of emotion of the last lines.

135 **maiden-widowed** maiden-widowèd; 'widowed while still a maiden' (cited in *OED*)

137 **death . . . maidenhead** an anticipation of Capulet's telling Paris in 4.5 that death wed Juliet and also, more immediately, of the Friar's opening lines of the next scene

121 with] *Q2–4;* which *F; not in Q1*   136 cords] *Q2;* cord *Q3–4, F; not in Q1*

NURSE

Hie to your chamber. I'll find Romeo
To comfort you. I wot well where he is.
Hark ye, your Romeo will be here at night.   140
I'll to him; he is hid at Laurence' cell.

JULIET

O, find him, give this ring to my true knight
And bid him come to take his last farewell.   *Exeunt.*

[**3.3**]   *Enter* FRIAR [LAURENCE].

FRIAR LAURENCE

Romeo, come forth, come forth, thou fearful man.
Affliction is enamoured of thy parts,
And thou art wedded to calamity.

Enter ROMEO.

ROMEO

Father, what news? What is the Prince's doom?
What sorrow craves acquaintance at my hand   5
That I yet know not?

138 **Hie** hasten (cited under *OED* v.¹
2); see Brooke: 'Straight would I hie,
where he doth lurk, to Friar Laurence
cell' (1234). The verb 'hie' occurs
repeatedly in the poem.

139 **wot** know

3.3 Monday evening in the Friar's
cell before the setting of the watch
(147). Charlotte Cushman excelled
in this scene above all others during her acclaimed 1845 Haymarket
performance as Romeo opposite her
sister Susan's Juliet (Stebbins, 63); see
pp. 66–9.

0.1 *as in Q1, with Romeo entering after

3. In Q2, Romeo and the Friar enter
together, and while this does not pose
an insuperable obstacle for the dialogue,
it feels rather forced compared to Q1.

1 **fearful** timorous

2–3 By suggesting that *calamity* may
be destined to be Romeo's marriage
partner, the Friar continues the motif
launched by Juliet, that *death* will be
her husband (see 3.2.134–5).

2 **parts** attributes

4 **doom** sentence

5–6 **What . . . not?** 'Are there more
unknown sorrows out there that desire
to meet me?'

143 SD] *Q1; Exit. Q2–4, F*   3.3] *Rowe*   0.1] *Rowe; Enter Frier. Q1; Enter Frier and* Romeo. *Q2–4,
F*   3.1] *Q1; not in Q2–4, F*

FRIAR LAURENCE   Too familiar
Is my dear son with such sour company.
I bring thee tidings of the Prince's doom.
ROMEO
What less than doomsday is the Prince's doom?
FRIAR LAURENCE
A gentler judgement vanished from his lips: 10
Not body's death but body's banishment.
ROMEO
Ha, banishment? Be merciful, say 'death',
For exile hath more terror in his look,
Much more, than death. Do not say 'banishment'.
FRIAR LAURENCE
Hence from Verona art thou banished.   15
Be patient, for the world is broad and wide.
ROMEO
There is no world without Verona walls
But purgatory, torture, hell itself.
Hence banished is banished from the world,
And world's exile is death; then 'banished'   20
Is death mistermed. Calling death 'banished',
Thou cutt'st my head off with a golden axe
And smilest upon the stroke that murders me.

10 **vanished** parted; with a play probably on 'banished', whence the odd usage of *vanished*

15 ***Hence** Q1's reading (Q2 has 'Here') is supported by Williams, who points to *Hence banished* (19), surmising that the compositor overlooked a tilde over *e* in 'Hece' and misread *r* for *c*. He notes further the surviving tildes in *Whence* ('whēce') and *hence* ('hēce') at 78 and 165.

16 **Be patient** Forbear; following Brooke's 'With patience arm thyself' (1223). The idea that the world is wide is proverbial (Dent, W895).

17 **without** beyond

18 **Verona walls** the walls of Verona; on the use of nouns as pre-modifiers instead of present-day English genitive, see Hope (59), who compares 'here in Philippi fields' (*JC* 5.5.19).

19 **banished . . . banished** banishèd . . . banished

20 **world's exile** exile from the world, with the stress on the second syllable (*exìle*)

20, 21 **banished** banishèd; also at 40, 42, 46, 51, 56, 57

21 **mistermed** wrongly named

14 Much . . . death] *Q2–4, F;* Than death it selfe *Q1*   15 Hence] *Q1;* Here *Q2–4, F*

FRIAR LAURENCE

O deadly sin, O rude unthankfulness!
Thy fault our law calls death, but the kind Prince,   25
Taking thy part, hath rushed aside the law,
And turned that black word 'death' to banishment.
This is dear mercy, and thou seest it not.

ROMEO

'Tis torture and not mercy. Heaven is here
Where Juliet lives, and every cat and dog   30
And little mouse, every unworthy thing,
Live here in heaven and may look on her,
But Romeo may not. More validity,
More honourable state, more courtship lives
In carrion flies than Romeo. They may seize   35
On the white wonder of dear Juliet's hand
And steal immortal blessing from her lips,
Who even in pure and vestal modesty
Still blush, as thinking their own kisses sin.

24 **rude unthankfulness** uncivil ingratitude
25 **Thy fault . . . death** 'The official penalty for your misdeed is death.'
26 **rushed aside** forcefully suspended (cited under *OED v.*²)
28 **dear** precious, rare
29–30 **'Tis . . . lives** Coleridge (138) annotates 'All deep passions are a sort of atheists, that believe no future', a brilliant *aperçu* that captures the scale of the young lovers' defiance.
30–1 **every . . . thing** See 3.1.102 above.
33 **validity** soundness; virtually part of a hendiadys with *honourable state* in the next line. Cf. 'Of violent birth but poor validity' (*Ham* 3.2.184).
34 **courtship** behaviour befitting a courtier (cited as first instance under *OED* 2)
35–7 **flies . . . lips** This recalls the flea of Donne's poem of that name, where the insect's privileged access, however repugnant to the beloved, becomes the central plank of the poet's seductive stratagem.
36 **white wonder** Pale skin was a sign of upper-class origin, proof that a person was not engaged in manual or outdoor work such as farming.
37 **immortal** because heaven is where Juliet abides (29–30)
38 **vestal** virginal; see 2.2.8.
39 Juliet's lips kiss innocently as she lies asleep with her mouth closed, hence their redness (as they *blush*); *Still* = always.

26 rushed] *Q2–4, F, Q1;* push'd *(Capell);* brush'd *Collier*²   37 blessing] *Q2–4, F;* kisses *Q1*

But Romeo may not, he is banished.   40
Flies may do this, but I from this must fly;
They are free men, but I am banished:
And sayest thou yet that exile is not death?
Hadst thou no poison mixed, no sharp-ground knife,
No sudden mean of death, though ne'er so mean,   45
But 'banished' to kill me? Banished!
O Friar, the damned use that word in hell;
Howling attends it. How hast thou the heart,
Being a divine, a ghostly confessor,
A sin-absolver, and my friend professed,   50
To mangle me with that word 'banished'?

FRIAR LAURENCE
Thou fond mad man, hear me a little speak.

ROMEO
O, thou wilt speak again of banishment.

FRIAR LAURENCE
I'll give thee armour to keep off that word,
Adversity's sweet milk, philosophy,   55

40–3 The text of Q2 at this point affords the clearest signs of second thoughts (see pp. 104–5).

41 Romeo envies the very insects around Juliet – to him they become *free men* (42) – because they are allowed into her presence.

43 **sayest thou yet** do you still maintain

45 **mean . . . mean** method . . . base

47 **damned** damnèd

49 **ghostly** See 2.2.192n.
   confessor cònfessor

51 **mangle me** do me violence (cf. Juliet's use of the same word at 3.2.99)

52 **fond** foolish and doting

55 Philosophy should be Romeo's defence

against this reversal of fortune, the Friar enjoins him (he urged patience at 16). Lines 56–7 may be inspired by Boethius' *Consolation of Philosophy*, a text whose ideas Shakespeare was probably familiar with from Chaucer's *Troilus and Criseyde*. The phrasing anticipates 'Sweet are the uses of adversity' (*AYL* 2.1.12), while milk as a metaphor of benign healing is most powerfully expressed in the 'milk of human kindness' in *Mac* 1.5.17. Cam[2] compares Brooke, 1393–4: 'Virtue is always thrall, to troubles and annoy, / But wisdom in adversity finds cause of quiet joy.'

40–3] *Cam (Steevens);* This may flyes do, when I from this must flie, / And sayest thou yet, that exile is not death? / But . . . banished. / Flies . . . flie: / They . . . banished. / *Q2–4;* This may Flies doe, when I from this must flie, / And saist thou yet, that exile is not death? / But *Romeo* may not, hee is banished. / *F;* But *Romeo* may not, he is banished. / Flies may doo this, but I from this must flye. / *Q1*   43 sayest] *Q2;* say'st *Q3–4, F; not in Q1*   48 Howling] *Q2–4, Q1;* Howlings *F*   52 Thou] *Q1, Q4;* Then *Q2–3, F*   a little] *Q2–4; om. F; not in Q1*

To comfort thee though thou art banished

ROMEO

Yet banished? Hang up philosophy!

Unless philosophy can make a Juliet,

Displant a town, reverse a prince's doom,

It helps not, it prevails not. Talk no more.   60

FRIAR LAURENCE

O, then I see that mad men have no ears.

ROMEO

How should they, when that wise men have no eyes?

FRIAR LAURENCE

Let me dispute with thee of thy estate.

ROMEO

Thou canst not speak of that thou dost not feel.

Wert thou as young as I, Juliet thy love,   65

An hour but married, Tybalt murdered,

Doting like me and like me banished,

Then mightst thou speak, then mightst thou tear thy
    hair

And fall upon the ground as I do now,

57–60 **Hang . . . not** Cf. Leonato's repu-
diating the consolations of philosophy
at *MA* 5.1.34–8.

57 **Hang up philosophy** 'Let philosophy
go hang'; but specifically referring to
hanging up as unused, or unwanted,
the spiritual *armour* (54) offered by the
Friar as comfort.

59 **Displant** uproot, dislodge, remove
from its foundations (cited under *OED
v.* 2)

61 **no ears** after Brooke, 1316–17: 'For
Romeus so vexed is, with care and with
despair, / That no advise can pierce,
his close forstopped ears.'

62 **when that** when (Abbott, 287)

63–4 **dispute . . . feel** Cf. Macduff's
countering Malcolm's invitation to

'Dispute' his children's murder 'like a
man' with 'I shall do so; / But I must
also feel it as a man' (*Mac* 4.3.219–21).

63 **estate** situation

64 **that** that which (Abbott, 244)

66 **An hour** i.e. a short period of time
but no more than, merely (*OED adv.*
6a)
murdered murderèd

67 **banished** banishèd

68–9 Stage action here can be deduced
from the dialogue, with *Arise* in 71
confirming that Romeo throws himself to the ground just as he says
he does. With *tear thy hair* and the
lines which follow immediately, cf.
Brooke, 1291ff.: 'his golden locks
he tore'.

---

61 men] *Q1, Q3–4, F;* man *Q2*   62 that] *Q2, Q1; not in Q3–4, F*   63 dispute] *Q2–4, Q1;* dispaire
F   64 that] *Q2–4, F;* what *Q1*   65 I, Juliet thy] *Q2–4, Q1;* Iuliet my *F*

Taking the measure of an unmade grave. *[Falls.]*   70
    Nurse knocks [within].

FRIAR LAURENCE

Arise, one knocks. Good Romeo, hide thyself.

ROMEO

Not I, unless the breath of heartsick groans
Mist-like infold me from the search of eyes. *Knock*

FRIAR LAURENCE

    Hark how they knock. – Who's there? – Romeo, arise,
Thou wilt be taken. – Stay awhile! – Stand up.   75
    [Loud knock]
Run to my study. – By and by! – God's will,
What simpleness is this? – I come, I come! *Knock*
Who knocks so hard? Whence come you? What's
    your will?

                    Enter NURSE.

NURSE

Let me come in and you shall know my errand.
I come from Lady Juliet.

FRIAR LAURENCE   Welcome then.   80

---

70 He pretends to measure out his grave
by falling down; another mawkish gesture by Romeo, still following Brooke:
'and with his breast doth beat the trodden ground . . . He rises eft . . . He
falleth down again' (1294–6).
70 SD2 *as in Q1, where Nurse is onstage
but outside the Friar's cell
73 **Mist-like infold** This may allude to
the rescue of Paris by Aphrodite in
the plain of Troy: the goddess 'caught
up Paris / easily, since she was divine,
and wrapped him in a thick mist / and
set him down again in his own per-

fumed bedchamber' (*Iliad*, 3.380–2,
trans. Richmond Lattimore, Chicago,
1951). Shakespeare probably knew his
fellow-playwright George Chapman's
loose translation of the *Iliad*, which
was circulating in MS before it was
published in 1598 under the title *The
Seven Books of the Iliads*.
76 **study** private room; *OED sb.* 8a cites
JC 2.1.7: 'Get me a taper in my study,
Lucius'.
    By and by! 'now, at once!'
77 **simpleness** foolish behaviour (on
Romeo's part) (cited under *OED* 3)

70 SD] *this edn; He falls upon the ground. Oxf* SD2] *Q1, Q4 subst.; Enter Nurse, and knocke. Q2–3,
F (knockes)* 73 SD] *Q4, F; They knocke. Q2–3; var. Q1* 75 SD] *Cam²; Slud knock. Q2–3; Knocke
again. Q4; Knocke. F; She knockes againe. Q1* 77 SD] *Q2–4, F; not in Q1* 78.1] *Q2–4, F; not in Q1*

NURSE

O holy Friar, O, tell me, holy Friar,
Where is my lady's lord, where's Romeo?

FRIAR LAURENCE

There on the ground, with his own tears made drunk.

NURSE

O, he is even in my mistress' case,
Just in her case. O woeful sympathy,   85
Piteous predicament! Even so lies she,
Blubbering and weeping, weeping and blubbering.
Stand up, stand up, stand an you be a man.
For Juliet's sake, for her sake, rise and stand!
Why should you fall into so deep an O?   90

Romeo rises.

ROMEO

Nurse –

NURSE   Ah, sir, ah, sir, death's the end of all.

ROMEO

Spakest thou of Juliet? How is it with her?
Doth not she think me an old murderer,
Now I have stained the childhood of our joy
With blood removed but little from her own?   95
Where is she, and how doth she, and what says

---

83 **made drunk** rendered senseless
84 **case** predicament, plight, but admit-
ting the possibility of a pun on *case* =
genitals
85 **woeful sympathy** The lovers are perfectly mutual (as implied by *sympathy*)
in their grief.
88–90 Nurse urges Romeo to *rise* like
a man, and continues with a play on
stand = have intercourse and *O*, the
universal sound of lamentation as well
as a quibble on *O* = vagina.

88 **an** if
91 **death's . . . all** proverbial (Dent,
D142.1)
92 **Spakest thou** Did you speak; identical in Q1, but F reads 'Speak'st',
which marks the elision that the metre
requires.
93 **old** seasoned, well practised
94 **childhood . . . joy** infancy of our
happiness
95 **but little** i.e. because Tybalt is her
first cousin

---

82 Where is] *Q1*; Where's *Q2–4, F*   85–6 O . . . predicament] *Q2–4, F, Q1; attributed to the Friar by*
Steevens² (Farmer)   90 SD] *Q1 subst. (He rises.); not in Q2–4, F*   92 Spakest] *Q2–4, Q1;* Speak'st
F   93 not she] *Q2–4, F;* she not *Q1*

263

My concealed lady to our cancelled love?

NURSE

O, she says nothing, sir, but weeps and weeps,
And now falls on her bed, and then starts up,
And Tybalt calls, and then on Romeo cries,   100
And then down falls again.

ROMEO   As if that name,
Shot from the deadly level of a gun,
Did murder her, as that name's cursed hand
Murdered her kinsman. O, tell me, Friar, tell me,
In what vile part of this anatomy   105
Doth my name lodge? Tell me, that I may sack
The hateful mansion.

He offers to stab himself, and Nurse snatches the dagger away.

FRIAR LAURENCE   Hold thy desperate hand!
Art thou a man? Thy form cries out thou art.
Thy tears are womanish, thy wild acts denote
The unreasonable fury of a beast.   110

---

97 **concealed** secretly wedded; with the stress falling on the first syllable, perfectly anticipating *cancelled* = annulled (the legal use because the Prince's banishment is tantamount to an annulment of their wedding)

100 **on Romeo cries** calls out to Romeo; Cam² glosses 'exclaims against', i.e. criticizes, not a likely response from Juliet (*OED v.* 17 gives both readings).

102 **deadly level** lethal aiming; as in levelling (= aiming) a gun at someone (cited under *OED* level *sb.* 9)

103 **cursed** cursèd

105–7 **In . . . mansion** With this metaphor of body and building, cf. Juliet's 'mansion of a love' at 3.2.26.

107–57 **Hold . . . coming** Friar Laurence's 51-line harangue of

Romeo, the longest speech in the play, telescopes 128 lines by the Friar in Brooke (1353–480). It is usually shortened in performance (Garrick, for example, cut it by 30 lines); see pp. 31–2.

108–12 after Brooke, 1353–8: 'Art thou, quoth he, a man? thy shape saith so thou art: / Thy crying and thy weeping eyes, denote a woman's heart, / . . . I stood in doubt . . . / If thou a man, or woman wert, or else a brutish beast.'

109 **Thy tears** further performer's clues embedded in the dialogue
*denote indicate (*OED* 3 cites as first instance)

110 **unreasonable** irrational, like beasts (cited in *OED*); cf. 'a beast that wants discourse of reason' (*Ham* 1.2.150).

97 cancelled] *Q2–4, Q1;* conceal'd *F*   100 calls . . . cries] *Q2–4, F;* cryes . . . calles *Q1*   101–2] *Rowe; Q2–4, F line* again. / gun, /; *var. Q1*   102 deadly] *Q2–4, Q1;* dead *F*   107 SD] *Q1; not in Q2–4, F*   109 denote] *Q1, Q4, F;* deuote *Q2–3*

Unseemly woman in a seeming man,
And ill-beseeming beast in seeming both!
Thou hast amazed me. By my holy order,
I thought thy disposition better tempered.
Hast thou slain Tybalt? Wilt thou slay thyself,   115
And slay thy lady that in thy life lives,
By doing damned hate upon thyself?
Why rail'st thou on thy birth, the heaven and earth,
Since birth, and heaven, and earth, all three do meet
In thee at once, which thou at once wouldst lose?   120
Fie, fie, thou sham'st thy shape, thy love, thy wit,
Which, like a usurer, abound'st in all,
And usest none in that true use indeed
Which should bedeck thy shape, thy love, thy wit.
Thy noble shape is but a form of wax,   125
Digressing from the valour of a man;
Thy dear love sworn but hollow perjury,
Killing that love which thou hast vowed to cherish;

111–12 His crying like a woman in the *form* (shape; 108) of a man turns him into a freakish hermaphrodite; cf. *TN* 2.2.33.

113 **amazed** filled with consternation (*OED v.* 3)

114 **disposition** character, temperament, frame of mind
tempered compounded of the right mix and proportions (*OED v.* 4)

117 **doing . . . thyself** i.e. committing suicide; the use of *damned* reminds us of the doctrine of suicide as mortal sin.
damned damnèd

118 **birth** parentage (since he wants to kill the Montague part in himself)

119–20 Suicide would cause him to forfeit everything: his good name and reputation (*birth*), his soul (*heaven*) and his life (*earth*).

122–4 While having an abundance of manly good looks, the pledged love of Juliet and natural intelligence, he hoards them like an usurer rather than putting them to good and proper use. The three cardinal blessings bestowed on Romeo by nature, *shape*, *love* and *wit*, are further dissected in the lines which follow.

124 **bedeck** adorn

125 **form of wax** insubstantial mould, without the proper hard core befitting a man, one that will melt away the moment masculine virtues are required; a use of *wax* diametrically opposed to Nurse's commendation of County Paris as a *man of wax* (1.3.77). Dent compares proverbial 'Soft wax will take any impression' (W136).

126 **Digressing** deviating (cited under *OED v.* 2)

116 that . . . lives] *F4;* that . . . lies *Q2–4, F;* too, that liues in thee *Q1*   118 rail'st] *F;* raylest *Q2–4; not in Q1*   121 sham'st] *F;* shamest *Q2–4; not in Q1*

Thy wit, that ornament to shape and love,
Misshapen in the conduct of them both,   130
Like powder in a skilless soldier's flask
Is set afire by thine own ignorance,
And thou dismembered with thine own defence.
What, rouse thee, man! Thy Juliet is alive,
For whose dear sake thou wast but lately dead: 135
There art thou happy. Tybalt would kill thee,
But thou slew'st Tybalt: there art thou happy.
The law that threatened death becomes thy friend
And turns it to exile: there art thou happy.
A pack of blessings light upon thy back,   140
Happiness courts thee in her best array,
But like a mishaved and sullen wench
Thou pouts upon thy fortune and thy love.
Take heed, take heed, for such die miserable.
Go, get thee to thy love as was decreed.   145
Ascend her chamber, hence, and comfort her,

130 **Misshapen** distorted, but here probably meaning something like misdirected, in view of the simile which follows in 132–3; word-play on *shape* is clearly intended too.

131 **skilless** clumsy, lacking the necessary skill to deal safely with powder

132 The explosive imagery recalls the Friar's earlier dread of the incendiary violence of the young lovers' passion, that like fire and powder they will be destroyed at the moment of consummation (2.6.11).
   ignorance lack of wisdom (because of his quick temper)

133 **dismembered** torn to shreds
   with . . . defence with what should

safeguard you from harm, i.e. your natural intelligence (*wit*), which you have allowed to be *Misshapen* (129–30)

134 **rouse thee** get up

135 **dear** precious
   lately dead The Friar mocks Romeo's overwrought lover's antics.

136 **There** in that
   happy fortunate

139 **exile** exile (see 20n.)

142 **mishaved** mishavèd; badly behaved (Q1 has 'misbehaude')

143 ***pouts upon** sulk at; on this verbal inflection after *thou*, see Abbott, 340; see also 3.5.110.

145 **decreed** decided

137 slew'st] *F*; slewest *Q2–4, Q1* (sluest)   happy.] *Q2–4, F*; happy too, *Q1*   138 becomes] *Q2–4*; became *F*; *not in Q1*   139 turns] *Q2, Q4*; turne *Q3*; turn'd *F*; *not in Q1*   140 of blessings] *Q2, Q4, Q1*; of blessing *Q3*; or blessing *F*   light] *Q2–3, F*; lights *Q4, Q1*   142 mishaved] *Q2–3*; mishaped *F*; misbehau'd *Q4, Q1*   143 pouts upon] *Q4* (powts vpon); puts vp *Q2–3*; puttest vp *F*; frownst vpon *Q1*

But look thou stay not till the watch be set,
For then thou canst not pass to Mantua,
Where thou shalt live till we can find a time
To blaze your marriage, reconcile your friends,   150
Beg pardon of the Prince and call thee back
With twenty hundred thousand times more joy
Than thou went'st forth in lamentation.
Go before, Nurse. Commend me to thy lady
And bid her hasten all the house to bed,   155
Which heavy sorrow makes them apt unto.
Romeo is coming.

NURSE

O lord, I could have stayed here all the night
To hear good counsel. O, what learning is!
My lord, I'll tell my lady you will come.   160

ROMEO

Do so, and bid my sweet prepare to chide.
Nurse offers to go in and turns again.

NURSE

Here, sir, a ring she bid me give you, sir.

---

147 **look . . . not** make sure you do not stay

till . . . set as late as the posting of the guard at dusk (because the city gates will be locked at night and he would be trapped in Verona). Shakespeare here follows Brooke, who notes that the guard was 'discharged' and the gates of the city 'set open' early in the morning, in time for Romeus to slip away safely then; see 166ff.

148 **Mantua** the first reference to Mantua as the place of Romeo's exile. The Prince banned him from Verona but did not decree a place. The Friar's choice may be determined by its proximity to Verona. Juliet's parents stayed in Mantua the day she was weaned: see 1.3.29n.

150 **blaze** proclaim openly in a celebratory fashion (*OED v.*²)

friends i.e. kinsmen, Romeo's Montague and Capulet relatives now that he is married to Juliet

151–3 **call . . . lamentation** See Brooke, 1447–8.

158–9 Nurse's comment is as much for the audience's benefit as for Romeo's, acknowledging the inordinate length of the Friar's speech but defending it by drawing attention to its attempt at edification and comfort (*good counsel*).

161 **chide** reprove me (for killing her cousin)

151 the] *Q2, Q4;* thy *Q3, F; not in Q1*   158 all the] *Q2–4;* all *F;* all this *Q1*   161 SD] *Q1; not in Q2–4, F*   162 bid] *Q2–3, F;* bids *Q4;* bad *Q1*

Hie you, make haste, for it grows very late.   *Exit.*

ROMEO

How well my comfort is revived by this.

FRIAR LAURENCE

Go hence, good night, and here stands all your state: 165
Either be gone before the watch be set,
Or by the break of day disguised from hence.
Sojourn in Mantua. I'll find out your man,
And he shall signify from time to time
Every good hap to you that chances here.   170
Give me thy hand. 'Tis late. Farewell. Good night.

ROMEO

But that a joy past joy calls out on me,
It were a grief so brief to part with thee.
Farewell.   *Exeunt [severally].*

[**3.4**]   *Enter old* CAPULET, *his* WIFE *and* PARIS.

CAPULET

Things have fallen out, sir, so unluckily,
That we have had no time to move our daughter.
Look you, she loved her kinsman Tybalt dearly,

---

163 **Hie you** hasten
164 **comfort** feeling of consolation, reas-
    sured state of mind (cited under *OED*
    sb. 5b)
165 **here . . . state**: 'This (*here* = herein,
    in this) sums up how things stand:'
167 **disguised** after Brooke, whose Romeus
    flees Verona 'Clad like a merchant ven-
    turer, from top even to the toe' (1734);
    Oxf¹ notes that 'The play never estab-
    lishes whether Romeo flees in disguise'.
168 **Sojourn** stay
    man personal servant; i.e. Balthasar,
    who first enters with Romeo at 5.1.11.1,
    and is there called 'Romeo's man' in the

SDs of both Q1 and Q2; see also 5.1.12.
169 **signify** report
170 **hap** event
173 **grief so brief** With this internal
    rhyme, cf. *woe* and *woo* at 3.4.8.
    brief hastily; on the use of adjectives
    for adverbs, see Abbott, 1.
3.4 The Capulets' home during the night
    of Monday to Tuesday (5, 7, 18, 34)
2   **move** 'propose the matter to' (Cam²)
3   **Look you** 'Mind this', 'Listen here';
    the only use in the play of this mildly
    colloquial imperative, which signals an
    affectionate note of friendship between
    the two men (cf. *my friend* at 3.5.192).

---

163 SD] *Q1 (Exit Nurse.); not in Q2–4, F*   167 disguised] *Q3–4, F; disguise Q2; not in Q1*   174 SD
Exeunt] Q2–4, F; not in Q1   severally] this edn   **3.4]** *Rowe*   0.1] *Q2–4, F; Enter olde Capolet and his
wife, with County Paris. Q1*

And so did I. Well, we were born to die.
'Tis very late; she'll not come down tonight.   5
I promise you, but for your company
I would have been abed an hour ago.

PARIS

These times of woe afford no times to woo.
Madam, good night; commend me to your daughter.

CAPULET'S WIFE

I will, and know her mind early tomorrow.   10
Tonight she's mewed up to her heaviness.

Paris offers to go in and Capulet calls him again.

CAPULET

Sir Paris, I will make a desperate tender
Of my child's love. I think she will be ruled
In all respects by me; nay, more, I doubt it not.
Wife, go you to her ere you go to bed,   15
Acquaint her here of my son Paris' love,
And bid her, mark you me, on Wednesday next –
But soft, what day is this?

PARIS   Monday, my lord.

CAPULET

Monday! Ha, ha. Well, Wednesday is too soon.

---

4 **born to die** proverbial (Dent, B140.2)
5 **'Tis very late** a further time marker (and again at 7 and 18); *very late* occurs again at 34 and earlier at 3.3.163; see pp. 24–33.
10 **know** will know
11 **mewed up to** shut away inside, with an allusion, probably, to the cooping up of a hawk (*OED v.*³ 4; see also 2.2.158–9) and a play on 'mewling' = wailing, whining (cf. *AYL* 2.7.144).
     heaviness dejection
12 **desperate tender** bold offer
16 **here** now; a temporal *here* rather than

a spatial one
son son-in-law; used here reassuringly to suggest to Paris that in Capulet's mind he is already a member of the family
17 **mark you me** attend to what I say
18 **But soft** 'wait a minute'
18–20 **Monday . . . Thursday** The close plotting of the week continues, and the screw is turned ever more tightly.
19 **Ha, ha** as in 'hums and ha's' or 'humming and hawing' *(OED int.* and *sb.²* 3), mere sounds to express a moment of reflection (rather than laughter)

10 SP] *Oxf; La. Q2–4; Lady. F; not in Q1*   11 she's] *Q2* (shees*); she is Q3–4, F; not in Q1*   SD] *Q1; not in Q2–4, F*   13 be] *Q3–4, F, Q1; me Q2*   16 here of] *Q2* (*here, of*)*, Q3–4, F; with Q1*

A' Thursday let it be, a' Thursday, tell her,   20
She shall be married to this noble earl.
Will you be ready? Do you like this haste?
We'll keep no great ado, a friend or two,
For, hark you, Tybalt being slain so late,
It may be thought we held him carelessly,   25
Being our kinsman, if we revel much.
Therefore we'll have some half a dozen friends
And there an end. But what say you to Thursday?

PARIS

My lord, I would that Thursday were tomorrow.

CAPULET

Well, get you gone, a' Thursday be it then.   30
Go you to Juliet ere you go to bed;
Prepare her, wife, against this wedding day.
Farewell, my lord. Light to my chamber, ho!
Afore me, it is so very late that we   34
May call it early by and by. Good night.   *Exeunt.*

[3.5]   *Enter* ROMEO *and* JULIET *aloft at the window.*

20 **A', a'** on (see Abbott, 23); see also 30 and 3.5.161.

22 **haste** an ominous word in this context, particularly in the light of the Friar's prediction that those that *run fast* are fated to *stumble* (2.3.90)

23 **ado . . . two** another internal rhyme

25 **held him carelessly** did not respect his memory

28 **there an end** proverbial (Dent, E113.1)

32 **against** in readiness for
wedding day The irony is that Romeo and Juliet are just then consummating their marriage upstairs. In Brooke the

equivalent scene to 3.4 happens after Romeus and Juliet have parted (= after *RJ* 3.5.59).

34 **Afore me** 'goodness me!'

3.5 Break of day (6–7) on Tuesday morning in Juliet's bedroom

0.1 *The scene starts on the upper level ('*aloft*'), at the window of Juliet's *chamber* (39). At 42 Romeo descends to the main stage, as to the orchard below, and at 59 he makes his exit. Juliet's mother enters on to the main stage, now imagined as Juliet's chamber, '*from within*' at 64 and is joined by Juliet, who descends from her window at 67.

23 We'll keep] *Q3–4, F;* Well, keepe *Q2;* Wee'le make *Q1*   34–5] *Theobald subst.; Q2–4, F line* and by, / Goodnight. / ; *Q1 lines* late, / and by. /   34 very] *Q2–4;* very very *Q1; om. F*   35 Good night] *Q2–4, F; not in Q1*   3.5] *Rowe*   0.1] *Cam² subst.;* Enter Romeo and Juliet aloft. *Q2–4, F;* Enter Romeo *and* Iuliet at the window. *Q1*

JULIET

Wilt thou be gone? It is not yet near day.
It was the nightingale, and not the lark,
That pierced the fearful hollow of thine ear.
Nightly she sings on yond pomegranate tree.
Believe me, love, it was the nightingale.   5

ROMEO

It was the lark, the herald of the morn,
No nightingale. Look, love, what envious streaks
Do lace the severing clouds in yonder east.
Night's candles are burnt out, and jocund day

1–36 Romeo and Juliet's duet in these lines is in effect an aubade, a traditional song of lovers' parting at dawn – Donne's 'The Sun Rising' and 'Break of Day' are among the most expressive of the genre. Cam[2] refers to Ovid's *Amores*, 1.13, in which the lover pleads with Aurora to delay the onset of dawn because, in Marlowe's translation, he lies in the 'tender arms' of his love and 'birds send forth shrill notes from every bough' (Marlowe, 438).

1 **Wilt . . . gone?** Juliet's speaking first after consummation may reflect the shifting of the centre of gravity from him to her until, in the final line of the play, their tale becomes that 'of Juliet and her Romeo', the possessive pronoun underlining quite how submerged his story has become in hers (5.3.310). On the other hand she may be responding to Romeo's telling her that he has to leave; that is, the characters could be in the midst of a conversation when we join them.

2 **lark** skylark; to stir with the lark is proverbial, as in *TS* Ind.2.45, *H5* 3.7.32 and *R3* 5.3.57. The lark is 'tuneable' in *MND* 1.1.183 and merrily warbling in *WT* 4.3.9 ('The lark, that tirra-lira chants'). The nightingale's distinctive habit of singing at night is alluded to in *MV* 5.1.104–6: 'The

nightingale, if she should sing by day / When every goose is cackling, would be thought / No better a musician than the wren!'. Cam[2] (202), following Lever, detects the influence of a passage from John Eliot's *Orthoepia Gallica* (1593) starting 'Harke, harke, tis some other bird sings now. / Tis a blacke-bird or a Nightingale' (p. 149).

3 **pierced** because even the liquid and melodious song of the nightingale is an unwelcome sound breaking into their idyll
   fearful apprehensive

4 **pomegranate tree** an exotic plant in Shakespeare's England. Lafew's telling Parolles 'You were beaten in Italy for picking a kernel out of a pomegranate' implies that Shakespeare associated pomegranates with Italy (*AW* 2.3.254–5). The fruit features prominently in one of his favourite sources, the erotic Song of Songs (Song of Solomon, 6.7, 11).

8 **severing** parting

9 **Night's candles** the stars of heaven; cf. 'There's husbandry in heaven; / Their candles are all out' (*Mac* 2.1.5–6).
   jocund playful, sprightly (*OED* cites this line, and the next one under 'tiptoe')

Stands tiptoe on the misty mountain tops.   10
I must be gone and live, or stay and die.

JULIET

Yond light is not daylight; I know it, I.
It is some meteor that the sun exhales
To be to thee this night a torchbearer
And light thee on thy way to Mantua.   15
Therefore stay yet; thou need'st not to be gone.

ROMEO

Let me be ta'en, let me be put to death.
I am content so thou wilt have it so.
I'll say yon grey is not the morning's eye,
'Tis but the pale reflex of Cynthia's brow;   20
Nor that is not the lark whose notes do beat
The vaulty heaven so high above our heads.
I have more care to stay than will to go.
Come, death, and welcome! Juliet wills it so.
How is't, my soul? Let's talk; it is not day.   25

10 **tiptoe** on tiptoe, poised to advance
11 **die** perhaps with an intended sexual
  innuendo: if he stays he will remain in
  Juliet's bed and die again in her arms,
  before being captured and put to death
  by the Prince.
12 **I . . . I** one of Juliet's distinctive speech
  mannerisms; see *I, ay, eye* at 3.2.45–9.
13 **meteor** a refulgent natural phenom-
  enon, radiating light to guide Romeo
  safely to Mantua in the dark
  exhales Meteors or shooting stars were
  thought to be made of vapours drawn
  from the earth by the sun (*OED* cites this
  line under both 'exhale' and 'meteor').
19 **say . . . grey** more internal rhyming;
  and cf. *grey-eyed morn* at 2.2.188.
20 **reflex** reflèx
  Cynthia's brow the forehead of the
  moon, personified here poetically as
  the goddess *Cynthia* (another name for
  Diana)

21 **beat** batter (with sounds); cf. 'with
  what loud applause / Didst thou beat
  heaven with blessing Bolingbroke'
  (*2H4* 1.3.91–2).
22 **vaulty** suggesting that the heavens
  resound with birdsong; the idiom
  probably derives from a famous lay by
  Guillaume Du Bartas by way of Eliot's
  Ortho-epia Gallica (Lever, 81–2).
23–6 Rhyming resumes briefly here with
  Romeo's *go/so*, followed by Juliet's
  away, which picks up his *day* across
  the speech boundary, signalling a
  perfect unison of husband and wife.
  The effects of harmonious sound
  patterns are artfully challenged
  a mere seven lines later where her
  grows is answered by him with *woes*
  (35–6).
23 **have more care** would much rather
  (*care* = solicitude)
25 **my soul** addressed to Juliet

10 mountain] *Q2, Q1;* Mountaines *Q3–4, F*   13 exhales] *Q3–4, F, Q1;* exhale *Q2;* exhaled *Hosley*   19
the] *Q3–4, F, Q1;* the the *Q2*   20 brow] *Q2–4, F, Q1;* bow *Collier²*   21 the lark] *Q2–4, Q1;* Larke *F*

JULIET

It is, it is! Hie hence, be gone, away!
It is the lark that sings so out of tune,
Straining harsh discords and unpleasing sharps.
Some say the lark makes sweet division;
This doth not so, for she divideth us.   30
Some say the lark and loathed toad change eyes.
O, now I would they had changed voices too,
Since arm from arm that voice doth us affray,
Hunting thee hence with hunt's-up to the day.
O, now be gone! More light and light it grows.   35

ROMEO

More light and light, more dark and dark our woes.

Enter NURSE *hastily.*

NURSE   Madam!
JULIET   Nurse?
NURSE

Your lady mother is coming to your chamber.   39

---

26 **Hie** hurry
28 'uttering in song unmelodious and inharmonious sounds, and grating notes without proper pitch'; cf. 'I never heard / So musical a discord' (*MND* 4.1.117).
29 **division** a rapid sweet melody (*OED* 7a*)*; the song smoothes over the transition between night and day through musical accompaniment.
30 **she** Like the nightingale, Juliet's lark is female.
31 **lark . . . eyes** Cf. 'Sweet are the uses of adversity / Which like the toad, ugly and venomous, / Wears yet a precious jewel in his head' (*AYL* 2.1.12–14).
    loathed loathèd
    change exchange
32 **changed voices** because the croak-

ing of the toad would jar less with this painful parting than the melodious song of the lark, which heralds Romeo's dawn departure
33–6 See 23–6n.
33 **affray** frighten away; from French *effrayer* (cited in *OED*)
34 **hunts-up** a song to serenade the new bride the morning after her wedding night; originally a song played to rouse huntsmen at dawn (see *Cym* 2.3.20–1: 'Hark, hark, the lark at heaven's gate sings / And Phoebus gins arise').
36.1 *This Q1 SD is clearly correct since only Nurse enters. Nurse's warning to Juliet, 'Be wary, look about' (40), reminds us of the fact that she knows Romeo is with Juliet.

35 light it] *Q2–4, Q1;* itli ght *F*   36.1] *Q1 (after 59); Enter Madame and Nurse. Q2–4, F*

The day is broke. Be wary, look about.   [*Exit.*]

JULIET

Then, window, let day in and let life out.

ROMEO

Farewell, farewell. One kiss, and I'll descend.

He goeth down.

JULIET

Art thou gone so, love, lord, ay husband, friend?

I must hear from thee every day in the hour,

For in a minute there are many days.   45

O, by this count I shall be much in years

Ere I again behold my Romeo.

ROMEO

Farewell.

I will omit no opportunity

That may convey my greetings, love, to thee.   50

JULIET

O, think'st thou we shall ever meet again?

---

40 **look about** 'be careful'; proverbial (Dent, L427.1)

42 SD *as in Q1. The scene in Juliet's bedroom that follows after 67 was almost certainly played out on the main stage, with Romeo's descent here and Juliet's at 67 both marked explicitly in Q1, consolidating the illusion that the stage is her upstairs bedroom. In Act 4 Juliet is discovered on the same bed, which probably doubled as her last resting place in the Capulet vault. The staging challenges posed by the changes in location during this scene are discussed in Cam² (31) and by Loehlin (193ff.); see pp. 94, 116.

43 **ay** an intensifier, equivalent to 'yes, indeed', since *husband* marks the most important bond between them.

After considering various alternatives, including 'aye = ever', 'alas' and 'ah', Williams (131) notes that 'It can only be the affirmative, though that is always spelled "I" in Q2; perhaps when it stands before a noun as an intensifier (as it does here uniquely) it takes this form to avoid ambiguity'.

44–5 **every . . . days** Juliet's topsy-turvy measuring of time results in a conceit that makes her urge Romeo to consider the fact that for her every minute spent apart from him needs to be counted as *many days*, hence her assertion in the next two lines that she will be old before she sees him again.

46 **count** method of calculating; see *by my count* at 1.3.72.

much in years ancient

---

40 SD] *Theobald*   42 SD] *Q1; not in Q2–4, F*   43 love . . . friend?] *Q2–4, F;* my Lord, my Loue, my Frend? *Q1;* Love, Lord, ah Husband, Friend, *F2*   51 think'st] *Q2, Q1;* thinkest *Q3–4, F*

ROMEO

I doubt it not, and all these woes shall serve
For sweet discourses in our times to come.

JULIET

O God, I have an ill-divining soul!
Methinks I see thee now, thou art so low,   55
As one dead in the bottom of a tomb.
Either my eyesight fails, or thou look'st pale.

ROMEO

And trust me, love, in my eye so do you.
Dry sorrow drinks our blood. Adieu, adieu!   *Exit.*

JULIET

O Fortune, Fortune, all men call thee fickle.   60
If thou art fickle, what dost thou with him
That is renowned for faith? Be fickle, Fortune,
For then I hope thou wilt not keep him long,
But send him back.

Enter CAPULET'S WIFE [*from within*].

CAPULET'S WIFE   Ho, daughter, are you up?

52–3 **all . . . come** Dent compares proverbial 'The remembrance of past sorrows (dangers) is joyful' (R73).

54 **ill-divining soul** foreboding spirit (cf. 'O my prophetic soul!', *Ham* 1.5.41)

55 **so low** because he is on the bottom rungs of the rope-ladder

59 **Dry . . . blood** The image of thirsty sorrow draining the teenage lovers like a feasting vampire derives from the popular belief that sorrows and sighs sucked away one's life-blood. Ard[2] compares Oberon's 'sighs of love, that costs the fresh blood dear' (*MND* 3.2.97) and Cam[2] cites 'blood-sucking sighs' (*3H6* 4.4.22). Dent has 'Sorrow is dry' as proverbial (S656).

60 **thee** Juliet's addressing Fortune with the familiar second person pronoun conveys the intensity of her feeling. Fortune is proverbially changeable (Dent, F606).

61–4 **If . . . back** an artful conceit in which Juliet urges Fortune to continue to be fickle – commonly her greatest fault in the eyes of the world – because then she will have no time for the likes of Romeo who are loyal and faithful (and will therefore restore him to Juliet presently)

64 **you** The force of Juliet's mother's *you* and *your* when addressing her daughter fits with her worrisome (*unaccustomed*, 67) early visit on this Tuesday morning. Her weaving in and out of *you* and

53 times] *Q2;* time *Q3–4, F, Q1*   54 SP] *Q4, F, Q1; Ro. Q2–3*   57 look'st] *F, Q1;* lookest *Q2–4*   64 SD] *this edn; Enter Mother. Q2–4, F; Enter Juliets Mother, Nurse. Q1; Enter Mother* [LADY CAPULET *below*]. *Cam*[2]   64, 68 SP1, 69, 78, 80 SP2, 87 SPs] *Oxf; La. Q2–4; Lad. F; Moth: Q1*

JULIET

Who is't that calls? It is my lady mother. 65
Is she not down so late, or up so early?
What unaccustomed cause procures her hither?
She goes down from the window.

CAPULET'S WIFE

Why, how now, Juliet?

JULIET   Madam, I am not well.

CAPULET'S WIFE

Evermore weeping for your cousin's death?
What, wilt thou wash him from his grave with tears? 70
An if thou couldst, thou couldst not make him live;
Therefore have done. Some grief shows much of love,
But much of grief shows still some want of wit.

JULIET

Yet let me weep for such a feeling loss.

CAPULET'S WIFE

So shall you feel the loss, but not the friend 75

---

thou while trying to comfort Juliet over Tybalt's death shows an acute awareness of the function of register in her speech, from the cajoling uses of *thou* in 70–1 to the sterner tone of 75–6. In Brooke she uses the formal 'you' throughout the equivalent scene (1787ff.).

66 **down so late** still up (from the night before)

67 **procures** induces (cited under *OED v.* 2c); see 2.2.145n.

69 **weeping** Juliet weeps throughout this scene (see *conduit* at 129), in which Q2 again provides explicit instructions about its characters' appearances and actions. In Brooke the lines behind Juliet's mother's about excessive grief are spoken to Nurse (1205ff.).

70 **wash** remove (cited under *OED v.* 15a)

71 **An . . . couldst** even if you could
thou couldst not . . . live after

Brooke: 'You cannot call him back with tears, and shriekings shrill' (1797)

72–3 **Some . . . wit** spoken in mild reproof to Juliet, whom her mother instructs to mourn in moderation because, according to her, unrestrained grief always (*still*) exhibits lack of judgement. Capulet's Wife recalls Brooke, echoing both Nurse's attempt to console Juliet (1211–12) and Juliet's mother's exhortation to her daughter to consider that Tybalt 'is in bliss', that his death was 'God's appointed will' (1794–8). Dent compares proverbial 'To lament the dead avails not and to the living it is hurtful' (D126).

74 **feeling** deeply felt, hurtful

75–6 **So . . . for** 'You will thus indeed experience his loss but not him' (in other words, her grief is excessive and self-indulgent).

65 It is] *Q2–4, Q1;* Is it *F*   67 hither] *Q2, Q4, F;* either *Q3*   67 SD] *Q1 (after 40);* not in *Q2–4, F*   75, 84 SPs] *Oxf;* La. *Q2–4;* Lad. *F;* not in *Q1*

Which you weep for.

JULIET   Feeling so the loss,
I cannot choose but ever weep the friend.

CAPULET'S WIFE
Well, girl, thou weep'st not so much for his death
As that the villain lives which slaughtered him.

JULIET
What villain, madam?

CAPULET'S WIFE   That same villain Romeo.   80

JULIET [*aside*]
Villain and he be many miles asunder.
– God pardon him! I do, with all my heart,
And yet no man like he doth grieve my heart.

CAPULET'S WIFE
That is because the traitor murderer lives.

JULIET
Ay, madam, from the reach of these my hands.   85
Would none but I might venge my cousin's death!

CAPULET'S WIFE
We will have vengeance for it, fear thou not.
Then weep no more. I'll send to one in Mantua,
Where that same banished runagate doth live,

---

77 **ever** forever
   weep mourn for
79 **which** who (Abbott, 265)
81 Juliet's impromptu response, wishing
   that Romeo and all things villainous
   or harmful be as far apart as possible,
   nearly gives her away (cited under
   OED asunder *adv*.) The lines which
   follow resonate with *double entendres*
   and culminate in Juliet's open defiance
   at 121–3.
83 ***no . . . heart** The punctuation of Q2,
   'no man like he, doth greeue my heart',
   is without parallel in Shakespeare. Most
   editions omit the comma after *he* (on

'he' for 'him', see Abbott, 206, and
Hope, 84), but Williams suggests 'no
man like, he doth grieve my heart', thus
'placing the emphasis on Romeo, as the
subject of the main clause, rather than
on "no man". The ambiguity, to be
sure, derives from Juliet's deception.'
86 **venge** avenge
89 **runagate** fugitive
   doth live Romeo has only just left
   Juliet's bedroom to head for Mantua.
   The town was suggested to Romeo
   by the Friar in the presence of Nurse,
   who seems to have shared this information with Juliet's mother.

81 SD] *Hanmer*   82 him] *Q4; not in Q2–3, F, Q1*   83 like he doth] *Q5;* like he, doth *Q2–4, F;* like,
he doth *Williams; not in Q1*   84 murderer] *Q2; not in Q3–4, F, Q1*

Shall give him such an unaccustomed dram   90
That he shall soon keep Tybalt company;
And then I hope thou wilt be satisfied.

JULIET

Indeed, I never shall be satisfied
With Romeo till I behold him. Dead –
Is my poor heart so for a kinsman vexed.   95
Madam, if you could find out but a man
To bear a poison, I would temper it,
That Romeo should, upon receipt thereof,
Soon sleep in quiet. O, how my heart abhors
To hear him named and cannot come to him,   100
To wreak the love I bore my cousin
Upon his body that hath slaughtered him.

CAPULET'S WIFE

Find thou the means and I'll find such a man.
But now I'll tell thee joyful tidings, girl.

JULIET

And joy comes well in such a needy time.   105

---

90 **Shall** who shall (Abbott, 244)
unaccustomed dram unfamiliar (i.e.
poisonous) draught
94 **him. Dead** – Juliet is anxious not
to give herself away to her mother,
as she wishes to have a hand in the
plot against Romeo only to thwart it.
Most editions punctuate *Dead* either
with a single dash in front of it or by
bracketing it with dashes. In Q2 'him'
is followed by a full stop, an extra
space and 'Dead' with a capital letter
('him.   Dead'), suggesting a pause
between them in foul papers. We are to
imagine Juliet speaking the truth – that
she longs to see Romeo – and then,
at the last minute, salvaging the situation by adding *Dead* but, unwilling
to wish Romeo dead, finally adding a

phrase (95) to which *Dead* may also be
attached.
95 **vexed** afflicted
97 **temper** mix, to produce a truly
lethal cocktail, but Juliet plays on the
meaning of *temper* = render free from
excess: if she moderates the poison she
can render it harmless.
99 **sleep in quiet** Juliet's *poison* (97) will
be a mere sleeping draught; ironically,
the Friar's potion, which puts her
into a death-like trance, precipitates
Romeo's swallowing the apothecary's
lethal liquid.
100 **and . . . him** while it is unable to
reach him
101 **wreak** avenge (cited under *OED v.*
5b)
105 **needy** lacking cheer, desolate

90 unaccustomed] *Q2–3, F;* accustom'd *Q4*   94 him. Dead –] *this edn;* him. Dead *Q2–4, F;* him,
dead *Q1;* him – Dead *Rowe;* him – dead – *Pope*   103 SP] *Oxf; Mo. Q2–4, F; Iul: Q1*   104 tidings]
Q2–3, F; tiding *Q4;* newes *Q1*

What are they, beseech your ladyship?

CAPULET'S WIFE

Well, well, thou hast a careful father, child,
One who, to put thee from thy heaviness,
Hath sorted out a sudden day of joy
That thou expects not, nor I looked not for.   110

JULIET

Madam, in happy time; what day is that?

CAPULET'S WIFE

Marry, my child, early next Thursday morn,
The gallant, young and noble gentleman,
The County Paris, at Saint Peter's church
Shall happily make thee there a joyful bride.   115

JULIET

Now by Saint Peter's church and Peter too,
He shall not make me there a joyful bride!
I wonder at this haste, that I must wed
Ere he that should be husband comes to woo.
I pray you tell my lord and father, madam,   120
I will not marry yet; and when I do, I swear
It shall be Romeo, whom you know I hate,
Rather than Paris. These are news indeed!

---

107 **careful** solicitous; applied in Brooke to both Juliet's mother (1786) and her father (1892) in the passage behind these lines

108–10 This is only partly the reason why her father wants to give her away in such hurried fashion. He also wishes to impress Paris with a *desperate tender* (3.4.12) and assert his authority over Juliet (3.4.13–14). Prospero, father of the second-youngest daughter in Shakespeare (Miranda is 14), proceeds more cautiously, hoping that her heart will follow where his plans lead: 'It

goes on, I see, / As my soul prompts it' (*Tem* 1.2.420–1).

108 **put . . . heaviness** distract you from your sorrow

109 **sorted out** selected (*OED v.*[1] 14a)
sudden imminent

110 **expects** On inflecting -*ts* for euphony with second person singular of words ending in -*t*, see Abbott, 340, and 3.3.143 above; Cam[2] compares 'counterfeits' at 131.

111 **in happy time** 'how fortunate!'

112 **Marry** an expression of surprise (*OED int.*), used here for emphasis

---

106 beseech] *Q2–3, F;* I beseech *Q4; not in Q1*   107 SP] *Oxf; M. Q2–3, F; Mo. Q4, F; Moth: Q1*   111 that] *Q2–4, Q1;* this *F*   112 SP] *Oxf; M. Q2–3; Mo. Q4, F; Moth: Q1*   115 happily] *Q2, F;* happly *Q3–4; not in Q1*   there] *Q2–4, Q1; not in F*

CAPULET'S WIFE

Here comes your father; tell him so yourself,
And see how he will take it at your hands.   125

Enter CAPULET *and* NURSE.

CAPULET

When the sun sets, the earth doth drizzle dew,
But for the sunset of my brother's son
It rains downright.
How now, a conduit, girl? What, still in tears,
Evermore showering? In one little body   130
Thou counterfeits a bark, a sea, a wind,
For still thy eyes, which I may call the sea,
Do ebb and flow with tears. The bark thy body is,
Sailing in this salt flood; the winds thy sighs,
Who, raging with thy tears and they with them,   135
Without a sudden calm will overset
Thy tempest-tossed body. How now, wife,

---

126 **earth ... dew** Cf. 'But as the earth doth weep, the sun being set' (*Luc* 1226) and *CE* 5.1.311–13, where 'drizzle' is followed closely by 'conduit', as it is here.
129 **conduit** spring, fountain; after Brooke's 'So that my pained heart by conduits of the eyne, / No more henceforth (as wont it was) shall gush forth dropping brine' (1805–6)
130 **showering** weeping (cited under *OED v.* 3c)
130–7 **In ... body** Prompted by his daughter's sighs and floods of tears, Capulet compares her to a ship buffeted by stormy winds. His simile is a heavy-handed attempt at comforting his child, as ineffectual as his wife's belief that only Romeo's death could atone for

Tybalt's and assuage Juliet's grief.
132 **still** all the time
133 **The bark ... is** The nautical metaphor may be inspired by Brooke's extended comparison of Romeus to a tempest-tossed bark making for its 'desired port' in the hours leading up to his wedding night: 'Thy steerless ship (O Romeus) ... wreck thy sea-beaten bark' (800–8); see also 1.4.112, 2.4.182.
135 **Who** which (Abbott, 264)
136 **Without ... calm** i.e. unless you calm down and stop these tears and sighs
overset capsize; continuing the nautical trope of Juliet's body (cited under *OED v.*[11] b). Capulet means that she will make herself ill with grief.
137 **tempest-tossed** tempest-tossèd

---

124 SP] *Oxf; M. Q2–3; Mer. Q4; Mo. F; Moth*: *Q1*   125.1] *Q2–4, F; Enter olde Capulet. Q1*   126 earth] *Q2–3, F; Ayre Q4; not in Q1*   128–9] *Q4, F; one line in Q2–3; not in Q1*   131 counterfeits a] *F;* counfeaits. A *Q2;* counterfaits: A *Q3;* counterfeits, a *Q4;* resemblest a *Q1*   135 thy] *Q2–4; the F; not in Q1*

Have you delivered to her our decree?

CAPULET'S WIFE

Ay, sir, but she will none, she gives you thanks.

I would the fool were married to her grave.   140

CAPULET

Soft, take me with you, take me with you, wife.

How will she none? Doth she not give us thanks?

Is she not proud? Doth she not count her blessed,

Unworthy as she is, that we have wrought

So worthy a gentleman to be her bride?   145

JULIET

Not proud you have, but thankful that you have.

Proud can I never be of what I hate,

But thankful even for hate that is meant love.

CAPULET

How, how, how, how, chopped logic? What is this?

'Proud' and 'I thank you', and 'I thank you not',   150

And yet 'not proud'? Mistress minion, you,

Thank me no thankings nor proud me no prouds,

But fettle your fine joints 'gainst Thursday next

To go with Paris to Saint Peter's church,

---

141 **take . . . you** speak so that I can understand you (first *OED v.* 59b usage)

143 **proud** delighted **her** herself

144 **wrought** prevailed upon

145 **bride** bridegroom (*OED sb.*[1] 2)

148 **thankful . . . love** i.e. grateful, though even for something hateful (marriage to Paris) because it was meant as an act of love

149 **chopped logic** sophistry; referring to Juliet's play on *thankful, hate* and *love* in 146–8 (*OED* chop-logic cites this line, but Williams argues instead for a verbal usage, *OED* chop *v.*[2] 8); Dent gives 'to chop logic' as proverbial (L412).

151 **Mistress minion** 'spoiled little madam'

152 **Thank . . . thankings . . . proud . . . prouds** given as proverbial locutions by Dent, X1.0 ('X me no x')

153 **fettle . . . joints** brace your dainty limbs (spoken sarcastically) **'gainst** in readiness for

139 SP] *Oxf; La. Q2–4; Lady. F; Moth: Q1* gives] *Q3–4, F;* giue *Q2; not in Q1*   145 bride] *Q2;* Bridegroome *Q3–4, F; not in Q1*   147 hate] *Q2–4, Q1;* haue *F*   149 How . . . how] *Q2 (*How, how, howhow*);* How now, how now *Q3–4, F (*How, now, how now*); not in Q1*   chopped] *Q2–4, F;* chop *Q1*   151] *Q2–4; om. F; var. Q1*

Or I will drag thee on a hurdle thither.   155
Out, you green-sickness carrion! Out, you baggage,
You tallow-face!
CAPULET'S WIFE   Fie, fie, what, are you mad?
JULIET
Good father, I beseech you on my knees,
Hear me with patience but to speak a word.
She kneels down.
CAPULET
Hang thee, young baggage, disobedient wretch!   160
I tell thee what: get thee to church a' Thursday
Or never after look me in the face.
Speak not, reply not, do not answer me.
My fingers itch. Wife, we scarce thought us blessed
That God had lent us but this only child,   165
But now I see this one is one too much,

---

155 **on a hurdle** The image carried a
particular resonance at a time when
traitors were dragged to their deaths
tied to hurdles; for Capulet his
daughter's defiance constitutes an act
of treachery. In Brooke her father
reminds Juliet of the power of life
and death wielded over their children
by Roman patriarchs 'if children did
rebel' (1951–5).

156 **green-sickness** See 2.2.5, 8 above;
Ard² compares Polonius' 'Pooh, you
speak like a green girl' (*Ham* 1.3.100).
carrion corpse; used here contemptuously: to Capulet a disobedient daughter is worthless and, to him, dead even
though living.
baggage strumpet

157 **tallow-face** paleface; a term of
abuse, hurled at Juliet because of her
extreme pallor, perhaps with the added
slur that her looks hardly justify her
pride and that she should therefore

be especially thankful for Paris' offer
of marriage
Fie . . . mad addressed to Capulet by
his wife, who is shocked by the feroc-
ity of his language; cf. *too hot* at 175
below. Much of the detail of Capulet's
harangue of Juliet is Shakespeare's
invention, although in Brooke Capulet
is called 'old man' and 'testy father'
and has a violent temper: 'Then she
[Juliet] that oft had seen the fury of
her sire' (1995).

158–9 The dialogue of Q2 characteristically contains the information that
the shorter Q1 provides as a SD; see
3.2.31.1n.

161 **a'** on

164 **itch** i.e. to strike her; *fingers itch* is
proverbial (Dent, F237).

165 See pp. 4, 102, 142.

166 **this . . . much** Dent compares proverbial 'To be one too many (too many
by one)' (O62.1).

157 You] *Q2–4, F*; out you *Q1*   SP] *Oxf; La. Q2–4; Lady. F; not in Q1*   159 SD] *Q1; not in Q2–4,
F*   160, 170, 176 SP] *Q1; Fa. Q2–4, F*

And that we have a curse in having her.
Out on her, hilding!

NURSE   God in heaven bless her!
You are to blame, my lord, to rate her so.

CAPULET
And why, my Lady Wisdom? Hold your tongue,   . 170
Good Prudence, smatter with your gossips, go.

NURSE
I speak no treason.

CAPULET   O, Godgigoden!

NURSE
May not one speak?

CAPULET   Peace, you mumbling fool!
Utter your gravity o'er a gossip's bowl,
For here we need it not.

CAPULET'S WIFE   You are too hot.   175

CAPULET
God's bread, it makes me mad.
Day, night, hour, tide, time, work, play,

168 **hilding** jade, hussy
169 **rate** upbraid
170–1 **Lady Wisdom ... Good Prudence**
    A modern version of these two would
    be 'meddlesome Madam Wiseacre'.
171 **smatter** prattle (cited under *OED*
    v. 2b)
172 **Godgigoden** a mild expression of
    annoyance (Q2 = 'Godigeden'), liter-
    ally, 'God give ye good evening', with
    the added meaning of 'and now kindly
    be on your way'; see 1.2.56n.
173 **mumbling** prattling (*OED v.* 2a)
174 **gravity** 'crumbs of wisdom' (spoken
    sarcastically)
    o'er ... bowl while dining with your

fellows
176 **God's bread** a mild oath: 'by the
    body (*bread*) of Christ'
176–8 set as in Q2, but a number of editors
    follow Hoppe and tidy up the metre
    on the basis that *hour, tide, time* can
    be deleted as first thoughts that were
    subsequently rejected (see Williams,
    132, and Ard²). Oxf¹, on the other hand,
    robustly defends Q2, arguing that the
    roughness of the metre in Q2 'along
    with the disrupted list of oppositions,
    effectively conveys the impression of an
    infuriated Capulet threatening to spin
    out of control'. The corresponding line
    in Q1 is also irregular.

171 gossips] *Q2–4, Q1;* gossip *F*   172 CAPULET O] *Q1 (Cap:* Oh*);* Father, ô *Q2–3;* Fa. O *Q4;* Father,
O *F*   173 SP1] *Q4; not in Q2–3, F, Q1*   SP2] *Q2–4, F (Fa.); not in Q1*   174 bowl] *Q2–4, Q1;* bowles
F   175 SP] *Oxf; Wi. Q2–4; La. F; Mo: Q1*   177–8] *Q2–4, F;* Day, night, early, late, at home, abroad,
/ Alone, in company, waking or sleeping, / Still my care hath beene to see her matcht. / *Q1;* Day,
night – work, play – / Alone, in company – still my care hath been / To have her matched; / *Hoppe*

Alone, in company, still my care hath been
To have her matched; and having now provided
A gentleman of noble parentage,   180
Of fair demesnes, youthful and nobly ligned,
Stuffed, as they say, with honourable parts,
Proportioned as one's thought would wish a man,
And then to have a wretched puling fool,
A whining mammet, in her fortune's tender,   185
To answer 'I'll not wed, I cannot love,
I am too young, I pray you pardon me'.
But an you will not wed, I'll pardon you!
Graze where you will, you shall not house with me.
Look to't, think on't; I do not use to jest.   190
Thursday is near. Lay hand on heart, advise.
An you be mine, I'll give you to my friend;
An you be not, hang, beg, starve, die in the streets,
For, by my soul, I'll ne'er acknowledge thee,
Nor what is mine shall never do thee good.   195
Trust to't, bethink you; I'll not be forsworn.   *Exit.*

JULIET

Is there no pity sitting in the clouds
That sees into the bottom of my grief?

---

178 **still** always
181 **demesnes** estates and lands
nobly ligned 'ligned' is a 16th-century
spelling of modern 'lined', as in family
lines (cf. 'aligned'). According to Brooke,
Paris would soon inherit a fortune, 'his
fathers wealth is such. / Such is the
nobleness, and honour of the race, /
From whence his father came' (1966–8).
182 **Stuffed** brim-full; Dent compares
proverbial 'To be stuffed with virtues
(good parts)' (S945.1).
184 **puling** wailing (cited in *OED*)
185 **mammet** mere weakling
in . . . tender 'when good fortune
presents itself to her on a plate'

188 **an** if
I'll pardon you! spoken with irony
and mock magnanimity
189 **Graze** feed (like a cow on open pas-
ture); Dent (P380) compares proverbial 'To graze on the plain (common)'.
190–1 **I . . . advise** closely following
Brooke: 'Advise thee well, and say thou
art warned now, / And think not that I
speak in sport' (1983–4).
191 **Lay . . . heart** 'Consider very carefully'; the modern phrase 'hand on
heart' means a pledge of faith.
192 **An . . . mine** if you are indeed my
daughter
195 See Brooke, 1977–8.

---

181 ligned] *Ard²* *(Jenkins);* liand *Q2;* allied *Q3–4, F;* trainde *Q1;* lianc'd *(Capell);* limb'd *Hosley;*
lined *Oxf*   195 never] *Q2–3, F;* ever *Q4, Q1*

O sweet my mother, cast me not away!
Delay this marriage for a month, a week,   200
Or if you do not, make the bridal bed
In that dim monument where Tybalt lies.

CAPULET'S WIFE

Talk not to me, for I'll not speak a word,
Do as thou wilt, for I have done with thee.   *Exit.*

JULIET

O God! O Nurse, how shall this be prevented?   205
My husband is on earth, my faith in heaven.
How shall that faith return again to earth,
Unless that husband send it me from heaven
By leaving earth? Comfort me, counsel me.
Alack, alack, that heaven should practise stratagems   210
Upon so soft a subject as myself.
What sayst thou? Hast thou not a word of joy?
Some comfort, Nurse.

NURSE   Faith, here it is.
Romeo is banished, and all the world to nothing
That he dares ne'er come back to challenge you;   215
Or if he do, it needs must be by stealth.
Then, since the case so stands as now it doth,
I think it best you married with the County.
O, he's a lovely gentleman!

201–2 **bridal . . . lies** This is the very place destined for her and Romeo.

206 **faith in heaven** i.e. her solemn marriage vows (*faith*; *OED sb.* 8) are divinely sanctioned (and cannot therefore be dissolved by earthly power).

207–9 **How . . . earth?** i.e. she could be free again to wed again only if Romeo died.

211 **soft** tender and unequal

213–35 **Faith . . . done** See Brooke,

2299–312: 'And County Paris now she praiseth ten times more . . . But greatly did these wicked words the lady's mind disease, / But ay she hid her wrath, and seemed well content, / When daily did the naughty nurse new arguments invent'.

214 **all . . . nothing** betting everything against naught

215 **challenge** claim; Nurse implies that Romeo will hardly risk his life for her.

203 SP] *Oxf; Mo. Q2–4, F; Moth: Q1*   213–14] *F; Q2–4 line* Nurse. / nothing, / *; var. Q1*   216 by] *Q2–3, F; my Q4; not in Q1*   219 he's] *Q2–4, F (* hees*); he is Q1*

Romeo's a dishclout to him. An eagle, madam   220
Hath not so green, so quick, so fair an eye
As Paris hath. Beshrew my very heart,
I think you are happy in this second match,
For it excels your first; or if it did not,
Your first is dead, or 'twere as good he were   225
As living here and you no use of him.

JULIET
Speak'st thou from thy heart?

NURSE
And from my soul too, else beshrew them both.

JULIET   Amen.

NURSE   What?   230

JULIET
Well, thou hast comforted me marvellous much.
Go in, and tell my lady I am gone,
Having displeased my father, to Laurence' cell,
To make confession and to be absolved.   234

220 **dishclout** mere rag (a term of contempt). Dent (D380.1) compares proverbial 'not worth a dish-clout (cloth)', cites Nashe's *Unfortunate Traveller* ('He makes a dishcloth of his own country in comparison of Spain'; Nashe, 2.301) and further adduces 'Canonizing . . . the contemptiblest world's dishclout for a relic' in *Have With You* (Nashe, 3.54).

220–1 **eagle . . . eye** Eagles are proverbially sharp-sighted (Dent, E4.1, E6).

221 **green** the reading of Q2–4 and F, rendering Hanmer's emendation 'keen' less plausible, even though it would be a more obvious reading in the context of eagles' eyes. Shakespeare seems to suggest that Paris is blessed with exceptional physical beauty: his *eye* (a metonym for the whole person) exceeds even the fresh (*green*) and sharp (*quick*) eye of an eagle.

quick lively, full of vitality

222 **Beshrew** 'devil take'; a mild imprecatory expression

225–6 **or . . . him** 'He might as well be dead for all the good he can do you now since you are here' (and he is banned hence).

227 Cf. proverbial 'What the heart thinks the tongue speaks' (Dent, H334).

229 **Amen** The word here expresses Juliet's contempt for Nurse's mendacity of heart and soul.

231 **marvellous much** wonderfully well; on the adverbial use of the adjective here, see Abbott, 1.

226 here] *Q2–4, F; not in Q1;* hence *Hanmer*   227 Speak'st] *Q2, Q1;* speakest *Q3–4, F*   228 else] *Q2;* or else *Q3–4, F, Q1*

NURSE

Marry, I will, and this is wisely done.   *Exit.*

Juliet looks after Nurse.

JULIET

Ancient damnation! O most wicked fiend!

Is it more sin to wish me thus forsworn,

Or to dispraise my lord with that same tongue

Which she hath praised him with above compare

So many thousand times? Go, counsellor,   240

Thou and my bosom henceforth shall be twain.

I'll to the Friar to know his remedy.

If all else fail, myself have power to die.   *Exit.*

[4.1]   *Enter* FRIAR [LAURENCE] *and* County PARIS.

FRIAR LAURENCE

On Thursday, sir? The time is very short.

PARIS

My father Capulet will have it so,

And I am nothing slow to slack his haste.

FRIAR LAURENCE

You say you do not know the lady's mind?

Uneven is the course; I like it not.   5

---

235 SD2 *As 'it is rare to have an SD
when neither speech nor movement
is required' (Ann Thompson, private
communication), this descriptive SD
may illustrate the surmised literary (as
opposed to theatrical) pedigree of Q1's
SDs; see pp. 109–14.

236 **Ancient damnation!** 'wicked old
creature!'

241 **my bosom** my most secret thoughts
twain strangers to each other

242 **remedy** with the final stressed vowel
a diphthong rhyming with *die*; see also
4.1.67.

4.1 Tuesday afternoon in Friar Laurence's

cell, probably, because of the usual
time of shrift (see 2.4.173–5). On the
other hand morning, immediately after
3.5, is also a possibility because Juliet
desperately needs the Friar's advice.

2 **father** father-in-law (first *OED* usage)

3 **I . . . haste** 'I am not going to hang
back in case I slow him down' (since
Capulet's haste suits Paris, who is
eager to be married).
slack delay (cited in *OED*)

5 **Uneven** not smooth (*OED a.* 4a cites
this as first figurative use); cf. 'The
course of true love never did run
smooth' (*MND* 1.1.134).

235 SD1] *Q1, Q4; not in Q2–3, F*   SD2] *Q1 subst.; not in Q2–4, F*   236 wicked] *Q2–4, F;* cursed
Q1   237 Is it] *Q2–4, Q1;* It is *F*   4.1] *Rowe*   0.1] *Q2–4, F; Enter Fryer and Paris. Q1*

PARIS

    Immoderately she weeps for Tybalt's death,
    And therefore have I little talked of love,
    For Venus smiles not in a house of tears.
    Now, sir, her father counts it dangerous
    That she do give her sorrow so much sway,   10
    And in his wisdom hastes our marriage
    To stop the inundation of her tears,
    Which, too much minded by herself alone,
    May be put from her by society.
    Now do you know the reason of this haste.   15

FRIAR LAURENCE [*aside*]

    I would I knew not why it should be slowed.
    – Look, sir, here comes the lady toward my cell.

Enter JULIET.

PARIS

    Happily met, my lady and my wife.

JULIET

    That may be, sir, when I may be a wife.

PARIS

    That may be must be, love, on Thursday next.   20

JULIET

    What must be shall be.

---

8 **Venus . . . tears** 'There is no scope for love in a grieving household'; but also alluding to the planet Venus, since each of the twelve zodiacal parts of heaven is called a 'house', and the lovers are *star-crossed* (Prol.6). Mahood (71–2) argues that, astrologically, Venus is not found in mournful parts of the heavens and compares Spenser's 'When oblique Saturn sat in the house of agonies' (*Faerie Queene*, 2.9.52).

11 **hastes** haste = 'chiefly literary' form for *hasten* (*OED*)
    marriage (three syllables)

12 **inundation** 'overflowing, superabundance' (cited in *OED*)

13–14 i.e. she might drown in grief on her own whereas companionship (*society*) may help dispel it.

21 **What . . . shall be** proverbial (Tilley, M1331)

7 talked] *Q1* (talkt); talke *Q2–4, F*   10 do] *Q2;* doth *Q3–4, F, Q1*   16 SD] *Theobald*   17 toward] *Q2;* towards *Q3–4, F;* to *Q1*   17.1] *Q2–4, F; Enter Paris. Q1 (after 16)*

FRIAR LAURENCE   That's a certain text.

PARIS

Come you to make confession to this father?

JULIET

To answer that, I should confess to you.

PARIS

Do not deny to him that you love me.

JULIET

I will confess to you that I love him.   25

PARIS

So will ye, I am sure, that you love me.

JULIET

If I do so, it will be of more price

Being spoke behind your back than to your face.

PARIS

Poor soul, thy face is much abused with tears.

JULIET

The tears have got small victory by that,   30

For it was bad enough before their spite.

PARIS

Thou wrong'st it more than tears with that report.

JULIET

That is no slander, sir, which is a truth,

And what I spake, I spake it to my face.

PARIS

Thy face is mine, and thou hast slandered it.   35

---

a certain text undoubtedly true

26 **ye** Paris switches from *you* to *ye*, perhaps to create an internal *ye/me* rhyme, thus archly conjoining himself and Juliet rhetorically. Hope notes that the strict distinction in Old English between 'ye' and 'you' had broken down in Early Modern English; though not quite, because 'ye' for 'you' could also be used in entreaties and appeals; Abbott (236) compares 'I do beseech ye, if you bear me hard' (*JC* 3.1.157). In his next line (29), Paris more pointedly uses the familiar *thy*, an intimacy which Juliet does not reciprocate, while his adieu again has *ye* (42).

27 **price** worth

29 **abused** wronged (first *OED* usage)

31 **spite** injury (*OED*)

33 no] *Q2–3, F, Q1; om. Q4*   34 my] *Q2–4, Q1;* thy *F*

JULIET

It may be so, for it is not mine own.
Are you at leisure, holy father, now,
Or shall I come to you at evening mass?

FRIAR LAURENCE

My leisure serves me, pensive daughter, now.
My lord, we must entreat the time alone.   40

PARIS

God shield I should disturb devotion!
Juliet, on Thursday early will I rouse ye;
Till then, adieu, and keep this holy kiss.   *Exit.*

JULIET

O, shut the door, and when thou hast done so,
Come weep with me, past hope, past cure, past help.   45

FRIAR LAURENCE

O Juliet, I already know thy grief;
It strains me past the compass of my wits.
I hear thou must, and nothing may prorogue it,

36 **not mine own** because her face
belongs to her husband, Romeo. Juliet
is turning Paris' logic of the one flesh
of Christian marriage ('Thy face is
mine') against him; on the 'undividable,
incorporate' oneness of marriage see
further 2.6.37, and cf. *CE* 2.2.110–46.
38 **evening mass** In spite of *OED*'s
observation 'that mass was not (nor-
mally) celebrated in the evening', mass
was sometimes said then (Shaheen, 80).
Cam² cites a Catholic evening mass at
6 o'clock in the London lodgings of the
Portuguese ambassador in 1576.
39 **pensive** sorrowful (*OED*). In Brooke,
Juliet is called 'pensive wight' as she
heads upstairs to her chamber to take
the Friar's draught (2317), heavily burdened by 'inward woe' but bravely not
letting it show 'by her outward look'.
40 **entreat . . . alone** request you to
grant us privacy (by leaving)

41 **shield** forbid (*OED v.* 5)
43 **holy kiss** probably a standard, cheek-
to-cheek kiss of formal leave-taking
44 **thou** After Paris' departure Juliet
switches from formal *you* to the familiar *thou*, the Friar in turn using *thy*
(46) in this scene of intense emotional
pressure.
45 *****cure** after Q1; some editions prefer
Q2's 'care'. Shakespeare's *u* and *a* are
a notorious source of confusion (see
pp. 100–1). Here *cure* seems right as
Juliet pleads desperately for assistance,
hence the pleonasm of *cure* and *help*. Ard²
notes that 'care' would only be possible
in the sense of 'oversight with a view to
protection' and refers to proverbial 'past
cure past care' and *LLL* 5.2.28: 'Great
reason: for past care is still past cure'.
47 **compass . . . wits** scope of my
comprehension
48 **prorogue** postpone

40 we] *Q2–4, Q1;* you *F*   43 SD] *Q2–4; Exit Paris. F, Q1*   45 cure] *Q1;* care *Q2–4, F*   47 strains]
Q2–4; streames *F; not in Q1*

On Thursday next be married to this County.

JULIET

Tell me not, Friar, that thou hearest of this,   50
Unless thou tell me how I may prevent it.
If in thy wisdom thou canst give no help,
Do thou but call my resolution wise,   [*showing her knife*]
And with this knife I'll help it presently.
God joined my heart and Romeo's, thou our hands;   55
And ere this hand, by thee to Romeo's sealed,
Shall be the label to another deed,
Or my true heart with treacherous revolt
Turn to another, this shall slay them both.
Therefore, out of thy long-experienced time   60
Give me some present counsel, or behold,
'Twixt my extremes and me this bloody knife
Shall play the umpire, arbitrating that
Which the commission of thy years and art
Could to no issue of true honour bring.   65
Be not so long to speak. I long to die,
If what thou speak'st speak not of remedy.

FRIAR LAURENCE

Hold, daughter, I do spy a kind of hope,

---

54 **knife** Cam[2] notes that 'Elizabethan ladies sometimes wore small household knives at their girdles' (see Duncan-Jones, 'Dagger', 314–15).
   help it presently resolve my predicament at once (by committing suicide)
57 **label** codicil or supplementary clause; one that would cancel the previous contract (referred to in *sealed*), her marriage to Romeo (cited in *OED*)
59 **them both** i.e. her heart and hand
60 **long-experienced time** wisdom gathered over many years
61 **present** instant
62 **bloody knife** after Brooke, where

Juliet defies her mother's choice of Paris as her husband with 'Else will I pierce my breast, with sharp and bloody knife' (1915); *bloody* here means cruel or 'possessing the power to draw blood'.
63 **arbitrating** settling by arbitration (first *OED* usage)
64 **commission . . . art** authority invested in you by your age and wisdom (*OED* commission *sb.*[1] 5)
65 **issue** resolution
66 **so long** so slow
66–7 **die . . . remedy** See 3.5.242–3 and 242n.
68 **spy** glimpse

53 SD] *this edn*   54 with this] *Q2–4;* with' his *F; not in Q1*   56 Romeo's] *Q2–4;* Romeo *F; not in Q1*

Which craves as desperate an execution
As that is desperate which we would prevent.   70
If rather than to marry County Paris
Thou hast the strength of will to slay thyself,
Then is it likely thou wilt undertake
A thing like death to chide away this shame,
That cop'st with death himself to scape from it;   75
An if thou dar'st, I'll give thee remedy.

JULIET

O bid me leap, rather than marry Paris,
From off the battlements of any tower,
Or walk in thievish ways, or bid me lurk
Where serpents are. Chain me with roaring bears,   80
Or hide me nightly in a charnel-house,
O'ercovered quite with dead men's rattling bones,
With reeky shanks and yellow chapless skulls;
Or bid me go into a new-made grave,
And hide me with a dead man in his shroud,   85

---

69 **craves** demands
69–70 **as . . . prevent** Dent compares
proverbial 'A desperate disease must
have a desperate cure' (D357).
79 **thievish ways** paths infested by
robbers
80 **Chain . . . bears** This alludes to the
popular Elizabethan pastime of bear-
baiting, in which mastiffs were set on
a bear tied to a post; see 'They have
tied me to a stake; I cannot fly, / But
bear-like I must fight the course' (*Mac*
5.7.1–2).
81 **charnel-house** a small building adjacent to a church in which were gathered
skulls and bones from older graves now
needed for newly deceased bodies. Just
such a structure rose against the north
side of the chancel of Holy Trinity
church in Stratford-upon-Avon. The
famous inscription on Shakespeare's

tomb ('Good friend for Jesus' sake forbear, / To dig the dust enclosed here')
may warn against the transfer of his
body into such a place.
83 ***chapless** without a lower jaw or
chap (*OED* cites as first instance); see
similarly *Ham* 5.1.84.
85 ***shroud** The reading *shroud* is supplied
by 1622 Q4 to complete Q2's 'And hide
me with a dead man in his'; Q1 reads
'Or lay me in tombe with one new
dead'. Malone's conjecture of 'tomb'
for *shroud* (Malone, 10.133), adopted by
Williams, duplicates *grave* at 84; Juliet
may instead be imagining gradations of
horror, from live burial in a fresh grave
to the grotesque prospect of sharing
a male corpse's winding sheet. As she
prepares to swallow the Friar's draught,
she twice refers to Tybalt, mangled and
festering in *his shroud* (4.3.43, 52).

---

72 slay] *Q1, Q4;* stay *Q2–3, F*   73 is it] *Q2–4, F;* Tis *Q1*   76 dar'st] *Q2* (darest), *F;* dearest
Q3–4; doost *Q1*   78 off] *Q1;* of *Q2–4, F*   any] *Q2–4, F;* yonder *Q1*   81 hide] *Q2–4, F;* shut *Q1*
83 chapless] *Q1, Q4;* chapels *Q2–3, F*   85 shroud] *Q4;* graue *F; not in Q2–3; var. Q1;* tomb *Williams*

Things that, to hear them told, have made me tremble,
And I will do it without fear or doubt,
To live an unstained wife to my sweet love.

FRIAR LAURENCE

Hold then: go home, be merry, give consent
To marry Paris. Wednesday is tomorrow.   90
Tomorrow night look that thou lie alone.
Let not the Nurse lie with thee in thy chamber.
Take thou this vial, being then in bed,
And this distilling liquor drink thou off,
When presently through all thy veins shall run   95
A cold and drowsy humour, for no pulse
Shall keep his native progress, but surcease.
No warmth, no breath, shall testify thou livest.
The roses in thy lips and cheeks shall fade
To wanny ashes, thy eyes' windows fall   100
Like death, when he shuts up the day of life.
Each part, deprived of supple government,

88 **unstained** See *stainless* at 3.2.13; 'stain' is a key word in the play.

89 **merry** anticipating its near homophone *marry* in the next line, i.e. merry to marry

94 **distilling** The participle is present and active, i.e. the narcotic will course through Juliet's body. Q1's 'distilled' describes the drug itself rather than its action; in the phrase 'known and feeling sorrow' (*KL* 4.6.218) the participle is both present and past, i.e. 'known and realized sorrows' (Abbott, 372).

96 **cold and drowsy** heavy and sluggish (Q1 has 'dull and heauie slumber'); cf. 'the dead and drowsy fire' (*MND* 5.1.378).
humour See 1.1.127n.

97 **native** natural (Onions)
surcease stop; cf. 'If th'assassination / Could trammel up the consequence,

and catch / With his surcease, success' (*Mac* 1.7.2–4).

98 *breath after Q1; Q2's 'breast' could be a compositorial anticipation of *testify*.

100 *wanny pale; a widely accepted editorial emendation for Q2's 'Too many'. Williams notes that the likely presence in foul papers of 'Too' for *To* probably caused the reading of 'many'. Q4's 'paly' seems to echo Brooke's comparison of the smouldering feud between the houses to dormant 'sparkles of their wrath' that lie 'raked up, in ashes pale and dead' (957).

100–1 **eyes' . . . death** eyelids close as if you were dead

101 **day of life** Cf. 'The death of each day's life' (*Mac* 3.2.37).

102 **supple government** ready control of body's movements (first *OED* supple 3c usage)

86 told] *Q2–4, F;* namde *Q1*   92 the] *Q2;* thy *Q3–4, F, Q1*   94 distilling] *Q2–4, F;* distilled *Q1*
98 breath] *Q1, Q3–4, F;* breast *Q2*   100 To wanny] *Hoppe (Kellner);* Too many *Q2–3;* Too paly *Q4;*
To many *F; not in Q1*   thy] *Q2;* the *Q3–4, F; not in Q1*   101 shuts] *Q2–4;* shut *F; not in Q1*

Shall stiff and stark and cold appear like death,
And in this borrowed likeness of shrunk death
Thou shalt continue two-and-forty hours,   105
And then awake as from a pleasant sleep.
Now, when the bridegroom in the morning comes
To rouse thee from thy bed, there art thou dead.
Then, as the manner of our country is,
In thy best robes, uncovered on the bier,   110
Thou shalt be borne to that same ancient vault
Where all the kindred of the Capulets lie.
In the meantime, against thou shalt awake,
Shall Romeo by my letters know our drift,
And hither shall he come. And he and I   115
Will watch thy waking, and that very night
Shall Romeo bear thee hence to Mantua.
And this shall free thee from this present shame,
If no inconstant toy nor womanish fear
Abate thy valour in the acting it.   120

JULIET

Give me, give me, O, tell not me of fear!

103 **stiff and stark** utterly rigid; *stark* = 'rigid', 'stiff' (first *OED* usage)
104 **shrunk death** because of the shrivelled appearance of corpses
105 **two-and-forty hours** a tantalizing figure in the light of the sliding time-scheme of the action, at odds with the actual events; see pp. 30–1.
109–10 **manner . . . bier** after Brooke, 2523–5
111–12 This is preceded in Q2 by the line 'Be borne to buriall in thy kindreds graue', probably a first draft of 111–12; see pp. 102–5.
112 **Capulets** The minor metrical

irregularity may be resolved by eliding the *u*, i.e. 'Cap'lets'. Cam² surmises that Shakespeare wrote 'Capels'.
113 **against** in anticipation of the time when
119 **inconstant toy** capricious whim (*OED* toy 4a). The phrases *inconstant toy* and *womanish fear* derive from the corresponding speech by the Friar in Brooke: 'Cast off from thee at once the weed of womanish dread' (2145) and 'That no inconstant toy thee let thy promise to fulfil' (2190).
womanish fear Dent tentatively compares proverbial 'To fear is womanish' (W724.1).

110 In] *Q3–4, F; not in Q1* bier,] *Hanmer;* Beere, / Be borne to buriall in thy kindreds graue: / *Q2–4, F* 111 shalt] *Q3–4, F;* shall *Q2; not in Q1* 115 And he] *Q3–4;* an he *Q2; not in F, Q1* 116 waking] *Q3–4;* walking *Q2; not in F, Q1* 119 toy] *Q2–3, F;* joy *Q4; not in Q1* 121 not me] *Q2–3, F;* me not *Q4; not in Q1* fear] *Q2–4;* care *F; not in Q1*

FRIAR LAURENCE

Hold! Get you gone, be strong and prosperous
In this resolve; I'll send a friar with speed
To Mantua, with my letters to thy lord.

JULIET

Love give me strength, and strength shall help afford.   125
Farewell, dear father.   *Exeunt.*

[**4.2**]   *Enter* Father CAPULET, CAPULET'S WIFE,
               NURSE *and* Servingmen, *two or three.*

CAPULET

So many guests invite as here are writ.   [*Exit Servingman.*]
Sirrah, go hire me twenty cunning cooks.

SERVINGMAN You shall have none ill, sir, for I'll try if
they can lick their fingers.

CAPULET How canst thou try them so?   5

SERVINGMAN Marry, sir, 'tis an ill cook that cannot lick
his own fingers; therefore, he that cannot lick his
fingers goes not with me.

CAPULET   Go, be gone.   [*Exeunt Servingmen.*]
We shall be much unfurnished for this time.   10
What, is my daughter gone to Friar Laurence?

NURSE   Ay, forsooth.

---

123 **resolve** determination (first *OED*
usage)
4.2 Late Tuesday evening (35–6, 39) in
the Capulets' house
1 **as . . . writ** See 1.2.35; the same illiterate servant is probably involved.
2 **twenty cunning cooks** hardly the
humble affair with 'no great ado, a friend
or two . . . some half a dozen friends'
(3.4.23, 27) proposed earlier out of
respect for the dead Tybalt (see Cam²).

cunning expert
3 **none ill** no bad ones
try establish
4 **lick their fingers** referring to the
proverbial expression for a good cook
who, as the Servingman's next reply
makes clear, is happy to taste his own
food (Dent, C636)
10 **unfurnished** unprovided (cited in
OED)

126 SD] *Q1, Q4; Exit. Q2–3, F*   **4.2**] *Rowe*   0.1–2] *Q2–4, F subst. (*Mother*); Enter old Capolet, his Wife, Nurse, and Seruingman. Q1*   1+ SP] *The first 7 SPs in Q2 for Capulet are Ca., Capu., Ca., Cap., Ca., Ca., Cap.*   1 SD] *Capell subst.*   9 SD] *this edn; Exit Servingman. Q1; not in Q2–4, F*

CAPULET

Well, he may chance to do some good on her.
A peevish self-willed harlotry it is.

Enter JULIET.

NURSE

See where she comes from shrift with merry look.   15

CAPULET

How now, my headstrong, where have you been
    gadding?

JULIET

Where I have learnt me to repent the sin
Of disobedient opposition
To you and your behests, and am enjoined
By holy Laurence to fall prostrate here   20
To beg your pardon. Pardon, I beseech you;
Henceforward I am ever ruled by you.
    She kneels down.

CAPULET

Send for the County, go tell him of this.
I'll have this knot knit up tomorrow morning.

JULIET

I met the youthful lord at Laurence' cell   25

---

14 **peevish   self-willed   harlotry**
contrary, headstrong little madam;
'good-for-nothing' (Ard²), 'silly girl,
hussy' (Cam²). Glendower applies
the identical phrase to his daughter
in *1H4* 3.1.196–7. *OED* harlotry 4
glosses as 'a term of opprobrium for
a woman'.

16 **gadding** aimlessly wandering about

17 **me** ethical dative

repent For a similarly transitive use,
see Lysander's 'Content with Hermia?
No; I do repent / The tedious minutes I with her have spent' (*MND*
2.2.111–12).

24 **tomorrow   morning** By advanc-
ing the marriage from Thursday
to Wednesday, Capulet further
compounds its already overhasty
character.

14 self-willed] *Q2–4* (selfwield); selfe-wild *F, Q1*   17 me] *Q2–3, F; not in Q4, Q1*   22 SD] *Q1; not
in Q2–4, F*

And gave him what becomed love I might,
Not stepping o'er the bounds of modesty.

CAPULET

Why, I am glad on't, this is well. Stand up;
This is as't should be. Let me see – the County!
Ay, marry, go, I say, and fetch him hither.   30
Now, afore God, this reverend holy friar,
All our whole city is much bound to him.

JULIET

Nurse, will you go with me into my closet,
To help me sort such needful ornaments
As you think fit to furnish me tomorrow?   35

CAPULET'S WIFE

No, not till Thursday; there is time enough.

CAPULET

Go, Nurse, go with her; we'll to church tomorrow.

Exeunt [Juliet and Nurse].

CAPULET'S WIFE

We shall be short in our provision.
'Tis now near night.

CAPULET   Tush, I will stir about,

---

26 **becomed** becomèd; becoming. *OED*
adduces only this example from *RJ* as
illustration, hence the surmise that it
may be a coinage (Ard²); see *distilling*
at 4.1.94, the obverse of here where
a rare past participle functions as
present participle.
29 **This . . . be** proverbial (Dent, S398.1)
31–2 after Brooke, 2249–50
32 **bound** beholden
33–5 In Brooke, Juliet says 'Unto my
closet fare I now, to search and to
choose out / The bravest garments
and the richest jewels there / Which
(better him to please) I mind on
Wednesday next to wear' (2234–6).

While the marriage is not brought
forward in Brooke, it is nevertheless
planned for Wednesday as it becomes
in the play too.
33 **closet** private chamber
34 **sort** choose
35 **furnish me** provide me with
39 **near night** Shakespeare is taking
liberties with the time-scheme here,
since Juliet has only just returned
from the Friar's cell. The repeated
foreshortening of time ratchets up the
tension.
Tush 'an exclamation of impatient
contempt or disparagement' (*OED*)
stir about busy myself

---

31 reverend holy] *Q2–4, F*; holy reuerent *Q1*   36, 38 SPs] *Oxf*; *Mo. Q2–4, F*; *Moth*: *Q1*   37, 39 SPs]
Q1 (Capo:); *Fa. Q2–4, F*   37 SD] *Q2–4, F (Exeunt)*; *Exeunt Nurse and Iuliet. Q1*

And all things shall be well, I warrant thee, wife.   40
Go thou to Juliet, help to deck up her.
I'll not to bed tonight. Let me alone,
I'll play the housewife for this once.   [*Exit Capulet's Wife.*]
                                   What, ho!
They are all forth. Well, I will walk myself
To County Paris to prepare up him   45
Against tomorrow. My heart is wondrous light
Since this same wayward girl is so reclaimed.   *Exit.*

[**4.3**]   *Enter* JULIET *and* NURSE.

JULIET

Ay, those attires are best. But, gentle Nurse,
I pray thee leave me to myself tonight,
For I have need of many orisons
To move the heavens to smile upon my state,
Which, well thou knowest, is cross and full of sin.   5

                  Enter CAPULET'S WIFE.

CAPULET'S WIFE

What, are you busy, ho? Need you my help?

JULIET

No, madam, we have culled such necessaries

41 **deck up** 'clothe in rich or ornamental garments . . . array, attire, adorn'; see also 'I thought thy bride-bed to have decked, sweet maid, / And not have strewed thy grave' (*Ham* 5.1.245–6).

45 **prepare up him** get him ready

46 **Against** in anticipation of

4.3 Tuesday night (2, 10) in Juliet's bedroom

1 **attires** after Brooke ('set on my attire'), whose lines 2325–33 Juliet follows closely. The scene is heavily indebted to Brooke, notably to Juliet's 54-line complaint beginning 'What, is there any one beneath the heavens high, / So much unfortunate as I?' (2349–402).

3 **orisons** prayers

4 This compresses three lines from Brooke: 'Unto the heavenly minds . . . That they so smile upon the doings of tomorrow' (2327–9).

5 **cross** refractory, obstinate

7 **culled** gathered, gleaned

43 SD] *this edn*   45 up him] *Q2–4;* him up *F; not in Q1*   47 SD] *Q2–3; Exeunt. Q4, Q1; Exeunt Father and Mother. F*   4.3] *Rowe*   5 knowest] *Q2–4;* know'st *F; not in Q1*   5.1] *Oxf; Enter Mother. Q2–4, F, Q1*   6, 12 SPs] *Oxf; Mo. Q2–4, F; Moth: Q1*

As are behoveful for our state tomorrow.
So please you, let me now be left alone,
And let the Nurse this night sit up with you,   10
For I am sure you have your hands full all
In this so sudden business.
CAPULET'S WIFE   Good night.
Get thee to bed and rest, for thou hast need.
JULIET
Farewell.   .   *Exeunt [Capulet's Wife and Nurse].*
          God knows when we shall meet again.
I have a faint cold fear thrills through my veins,   15
That almost freezes up the heat of life.
I'll call them back again to comfort me.
Nurse! – What should she do here?
My dismal scene I needs must act alone.
Come, vial.   20
What if this mixture do not work at all?
Shall I be married then tomorrow morning?
No, no! This shall forbid it. Lie thou there.
          [Lays down a knife.]
What if it be a poison which the Friar

---

8 **behoveful** needful, expedient
our state my condition. Juliet's use
of *our* rather than 'my' is proud and
communal, befitting a bride from one
of the great houses of Verona, and
affirms her apparent sense of duty
when in reality she means 'my condition', that of a young woman ready to
defy her parents.
11 **you ... full** Dent sees as proverbial
(H114).
12 **business** (three syllables)
15–58 The 'mighty obstacle of the potion
speech' (Tynan, 33) is frequently cut in
performance (e.g. Zeffirelli, 1968). It is

resounding proof of Shakespeare's
belief in the acting abilities of his boy
performers.
15–16 This recollects the narcotic of
4.1.94–7; according to Brooke, Juliet
broke into 'A sweat as cold as mountain
ice . . . the moisture hath wet every
part of hers' (2390–1).
19 **dismal** calamitous (*OED a.* 3 cites as
first instance)
21 after Brooke, 2361–2
24–9 Juliet's sudden suspicion of the
Friar is not in the source, even though
its portrayal of him is morally more
ambiguous than the play's.

14 SD] *Oxf (after 13); Exeunt. Q2–4, F; Exit. Q1*   16 life] *Q2–4;* fire *F; not in Q1*   20–1 Come . . .
all?] *Hanmer;* one line in *Q2–4, F*   22] *Q2–4, F;* Must I of force be married to the Countie? *Q1*   23
SD] *Johnson subst.*

Subtly hath ministered to have me dead,   25
Lest in this marriage he should be dishonoured,
Because he married me before to Romeo?
I fear it is, and yet methinks it should not,
For he hath still been tried a holy man.
How if, when I am laid into the tomb,   30
I wake before the time that Romeo
Come to redeem me? There's a fearful point.
Shall I not then be stifled in the vault, .
To whose foul mouth no healthsome air breathes in,
And there die strangled ere my Romeo comes?   35
Or if I live, is it not very like
The horrible conceit of death and night,
Together with the terror of the place,
As in a vault, an ancient receptacle
Where for this many hundred years the bones   40
Of all my buried ancestors are packed,
Where bloody Tybalt, yet but green in earth,
Lies festering in his shroud, where, as they say,
At some hours in the night spirits resort –
Alack, alack, is it not like that I,   45
So early waking, what with loathsome smells,
And shrieks like mandrakes torn out of the earth,

25 **Subtly** cunningly, treacherously (cf.
'super-subtle Venetian', *Oth* 1.3.357)
ministered dispensed
29 **still been tried** always proved to be
(*OED* try 7a)
30–5 after Brooke, 2370–7
32 **redeem** save
34 **healthsome** wholesome
37 **conceit** imagining
39 **receptacle** rèceptàcle, as required by
the metre; cf. receptacle = tomb in *Tit*
1.1.92, 2.3.235.
42–3 after Brooke, 2380–2
42 **bloody** covered in blood
green in earth 'just buried' (*OED* green

10d gives as first and only instance)
46 **loathsome smells** after Brooke,
'loathsome stink' (2371)
47–8 **mandrakes . . . mad** This alludes
to the popular superstition that the
poisonous mandrake plant (mandragora), whose forked roots were fabled to
evoke the human form, shrieked when
pulled out of the earth, causing madness. Juliet's reference to *mandrakes*
(not in Brooke) as she is about to
swallow the drugged draught flows
from the plant's narcotic and medicinal properties. Cleopatra requests
mandragora as a drug to 'sleep out this

40 this] *Q2;* these *Q3–4, F; not in Q1*

That living mortals, hearing them, run mad –
O, if I wake, shall I not be distraught,
Environed with all these hideous fears,   50
And madly play with my forefathers' joints,
And pluck the mangled Tybalt from his shroud
And, in this rage, with some great kinsman's bone,
As with a club, dash out my desperate brains?
O, look, methinks I see my cousin's ghost   55
Seeking out Romeo that did spit his body
Upon a rapier's point. Stay, Tybalt, stay!
Romeo, Romeo, Romeo, here's drink. I drink to thee.
She falls upon her bed within the curtains.

[4.4]   *Enter* CAPULET'S WIFE *and* NURSE *with herbs.*

CAPULET'S WIFE

Hold, take these keys and fetch more spices, Nurse.

great gap of time' (*AC* 1.5.5) and Iago
remarks 'Not poppy, nor mandragora,
/ Nor all the drowsy syrups of the
world / Shall ever medicine thee to
that sweet sleep' (*Oth* 3.3.330–2). Ard²
compares *2H6* 3.2.310 and Webster's
Duchess of Malfi, 2.5.1–2.
49 *wake after Q4 (Q2 has 'walke'),
  which again provides a superior reading; see Appendix 1.
50 **Environed** environèd; surrounded,
  hemmed in
53 **rage** frenzy
  great venerable
58 The apostrophes of this hypermetric
  Q2 line may hide a false start, or *here's
  drink* may be a submerged SD in a
  MS in which the boundaries between
  SDs and text are blurred on several
  occasions (see pp. 84, 101).
58 SD Curtains formed part of the trappings of wealthy Elizabethan beds and

are needed to screen Juliet from view
during the next scene. The action
is continuous from 4.3 to 4.4 and
from 4.4 to 4.5. It seems that in early
performances – as reflected in Q1s
SDs – the curtains remained open
(Nurse shuts them at 4.5.95 SD).
Juliet's 'dead' body is visible on her
bed, therefore, throughout 4.4. Dessen
(*Recovering*, 190) and Gurr (*Playing*,
22) compare Desdemona's bed in Folio
Oth 5.2. The tomb in 5.3 is probably
the same space (*pace Playing*, 24: 'for
all the symbolic attractiveness of making the marriage bed into the funeral
bier, my own inclination is towards the
trapdoor').

4.4 The time stretches from 3 a.m. (4) to
dawn (20) on Wednesday, the proposed
wedding day of Paris and Juliet. The
location is the Capulets' kitchens; the
scene is Shakespeare's invention.

49 O] *Q2–3, F;* Or *Q4, F2; not in Q1*   wake] *Q4;* walke *Q2–3, F; not in Q1*   51 joints] *Q2–3, F;*
joynes *Q4;* bones *Q1*   57 a] *Q2–4;* my *F;* his *F2; not in Q1*   58] *Q2–4, F; Romeo* I come, this doe
I drinke to thee. *Q1*   58 SD] *Q1; not in Q2–4, F*   **4.4**] *Rowe*   0.1] *this edn;* Enter Lady of the house
and Nurse. *Q2–4, F;* Enter Nurse with hearbs, Mother. *Q1*   1 SP] *Oxf;* La. *Q2–4;* Lady. *F;* Moth: *Q1*

NURSE

They call for dates and quinces in the pastry.

Enter CAPULET.

CAPULET

Come, stir, stir, stir. The second cock hath crowed,
The curfew bell hath rung, 'tis three o'clock.
Look to the baked meats, good Angelica;   5
Spare not for cost.

NURSE   Go, you cotquean, go,

Get you to bed. Faith, you'll be sick tomorrow
For this night's watching.

CAPULET

No, not a whit. What, I have watched ere now
All night for lesser cause, and ne'er been sick.   10

CAPULET'S WIFE

Ay, you have been a mouse-hunt in your time,
But I will watch you from such watching now.

Exeunt Capulet's Wife and Nurse.

2   **pastry** 'place where pastry is made'
    (Onions)
3   **second cock** Cocks were said to crow
    at midnight, at 3 a.m. (as here) and an
    hour before dawn.
4   **curfew bell** used loosely here for the
    matin bell that rings at first light
5   **baked meats** pastries, pies
    Angelica probably Nurse's name
    rather than his wife's (see List of
    Roles, 5n.). Capulet's folksy address
    reflects his buoyant mood, and he jests
    with a servant he had earlier called a
    mumbling fool (3.5.173).

6   **cotquean** male busybody playing
    at housewife; spoken to Capulet in
    banter by Nurse (first *OED* 3 usage)
8   **watching** staying awake (see 9, 12)
11 **mouse-hunt** tomcat, prowler, chaser
    of women; spoken by his wife claim-
    ing to remember a young, firebrand
    Capulet; 'mouse' was a widely used
    term of endearment: see *Ham* 3.4.185.
    Dent compares proverbial 'Cat after
    kind, good mouse hunt' (C136).
12 **I . . . now** 'I propose to keep an eye
    (*watch*) on your nocturnal antics
    (*watching*) from now on.'

2.1] *Q2–4, F (Enter old Capulet.); Enter Oldeman. Q1*   4 three] *Q2–4, F;* foure *Q1*   6 SP] *Q2–4, F,
Q1; La. Cap. / Singer (Jackson)*   10 lesser] *Q2;* lesse *Q3–4, F; not in Q1*   12 SD] *Q2–4, F (Exit
Lady and Nurse.); not in Q1*

CAPULET

A jealous-hood, a jealous-hood!

Enter three or four with spits and logs and baskets.

Now, fellow, what is there?

1 SERVINGMAN

Things for the cook, sir, but I know not what.

CAPULET

Make haste, make haste.   [*Exit 1 Servingman.*]

Sirrah, fetch drier logs.   15

Call Peter; he will show thee where they are.

2 SERVINGMAN

I have a head, sir, that will find out logs

And never trouble Peter for the matter.

CAPULET

Mass, and well said! A merry whoreson, ha!

Thou shalt be loggerhead.   [*Exit 2 Servingman.*]

Good faith, 'tis day!   20

---

13 **jealous-hood** (probably) jealousy, with -*hood* as a suffix denoting a state of being, as in 'childhood', 'knighthood' or 'manhood'. The hyphenated spelling follows *OED* (first *OED* usage) and derives from 1685 F4. All earlier editions have two discrete words, 'jealous hood'.

13.1 Dessen and Thomson ('basket', 20) generally link baskets in SDs with country people and 'poor and simple figures' such as the Clown in *Titus Andronicus* or Old Gobbo in *The Merchant of Venice*. Friar Laurence (who enters with a basket at 2.3) is both a country person and the custodian of the abbey's herb garden and pharmacy, hence his basket.

16 **Peter** Q1 calls Peter 'Will' here, while at 4.5.99.1 Q2 reads '*Enter Will Kemp*'. The slips in Q1 (an early acting version) and Q2 (foul papers) suggest that the actor Will Kemp played Nurse's man Peter; see pp. 36, 310, 322.

19 **Mass** 'by the Mass' (a mild imprecation)

20 **loggerhead** blockhead; literally, foreman of loggers. The servant's boast to have a head for logs (17) also makes him a numbskull, according to Capulet. *OED* cites *LLL* 4.3.200 and glosses 'A thick-headed or stupid person; a blockhead' (*OED* 1a).
**faith* Q4's widely accepted reading for Q2's 'father'. While *faith* (like 'truth') is common in assertive exclamations, there is no precedent for 'father'.

13] *Capell; one prose line in Q2–4; F lines* jealoushood, / there? / ; *Q1 lines* sirra? / there? /   13 SD] *Q2–4, F (after* there?*); Enter Seruingman with Logs & Coales. Q1 (after 11)*   fellow] *Q2–4, F;* sirra *Q1*   what is] *Q2–4;* what *F*   14 SP] *Capell subst.; Fel. Q2–4, F; Ser: Q1*   15 SD] *Capell*   16 Peter] *Q2–4, F;* Will *Q1*   17 SP] *Capell subst.; Fel. Q2–4, F; Ser: Q1*   20 SD] *Cam²*   faith] *Q4;* father *Q2–3, F; not in Q1*

The County will be here with music straight,
For so he said he would.   *Play music.*
                    I hear him near.
Nurse! Wife! What, ho! What, Nurse, I say!

Enter NURSE.

Go waken Juliet; go and trim her up.
I'll go and chat with Paris. Hie, make haste,   25
Make haste. The bridegroom, he is come already.
Make haste, I say.   [*Exeunt Capulet and Servingmen.*]

[4.5]

NURSE [*Goes to curtains.*]

Mistress, what, mistress! Juliet! Fast, I warrant her,
    she –
Why, lamb, why, lady! Fie, you slug-a-bed!
Why, love, I say! Madam! Sweetheart! Why, bride!
What, not a word? You take your pennyworths now.
Sleep for a week, for the next night, I warrant,   5
The County Paris hath set up his rest

---

21 **straight** at once
27 SD In Q2 no exit is marked for either
   Capulet or Nurse. Some editors do
   not mark a scene break here, on the
   grounds that Q1 and Q2 point to
   continuous action, with Juliet's bed
   onstage, though recessed, throughout.
   A number of productions either cut
   the scene altogether or carefully stage
   its action around the bed; see Loehlin
   (220) on Bogdanov (using a revolve),
   Hands (a balcony) and Boyd (servants
   tossing props across Juliet's bed).
4.5 Dawn on Wednesday morning
   (4.4.20; 4.5.1ff.) in Juliet's bedroom
1–64 The scene repeatedly echoes
   Brooke, 2408–61 ('Lady, you sleep so
   long, (the Earl) will raise you by and

by . . . The woeful news how Juliet
was sterved [had died] in her bed').
1 SD *In Brooke, Nurse enters Juliet's
   bedroom at dawn, 'unshut the door, for
   she the key did keep' (2405).
1 **Fast** soundly asleep
2 **slug-a-bed** lazybones, late sleeper
   (*OED* cites as first instance)
4 **take your pennyworths** make the
   most of your bargain (cited under
   OED pennyworth 3a). Dent gives proverbial 'To take one's pennyworths of
   the pillow' (P219.2).
6 **set . . . rest** staked his all; developing
   the money metaphor of *pennyworths*:
   rest = the stakes held in reserve in
   primero – once they are lost the game
   is over; probably proverbial (Dent,

22 SD] *Q2–4, F (after 20); not in Q1*   26–7] *F; one line in Q2–4*   27 SD] *Rowe*   **4.5**] *Pope*   1 SD]
this edn; Nurse goes to curtains. / Spencer (as 0.1)

That you shall rest but little. God forgive me,
Marry and amen. How sound is she asleep.
I needs must wake her. Madam, madam, madam!
Ay, let the County take you in your bed. 10
He'll fright you up, i'faith. Will it not be?
What, dressed, and in your clothes, and down again?
I must needs wake you. Lady, lady, lady!
Alas, alas, help, help! My lady's dead!
O weraday that ever I was born! 15
Some aqua vitae, ho! My lord, my lady!

Enter CAPULET'S WIFE.

CAPULET'S WIFE
   What noise is here?
NURSE   O lamentable day!
CAPULET'S WIFE
   What is the matter?
NURSE   Look, look! O heavy day!
CAPULET'S WIFE
   O me, O me, my child, my only life!
   Revive, look up, or I will die with thee. 20
   Help, help, call help!

Enter CAPULET.

R86.1). Nurse is jokingly warning Juliet that Paris will give her little rest in bed once they are married.
10 **take** find, surprise
11 **fright** frighten, scare (*OED* fright *v.* 2 *trans.* b cites this line as first instance)
  Will . . . be proverbial (Dent, B112.2)
12 **down again?** lying in bed once more (after getting dressed)?
15 **weraday** an expression of lament; see 3.2.37.

that . . . born proverbial (Dent, B140.1)
16 **aqua vitae** brandy; see 3.2.88. This is Nurse's second request in the play for spirits, here probably to revive Juliet rather than to comfort herself.
17 **lamentable** làmentable; from Brooke, 2459
19 **only** See Brooke's 'her only comfort dead' (2428).

9 needs must] *Q2;* must needs *Q3–4, F;* must *Q1*   15 weraday] *Q2;* weleaday *Q3;* weladay *Q4, F;* Alack the day *Q1*   16.1] *F, Q1 (Enter Mother.); not in Q2–4*   17 SP1, 19 SP] *Oxf; Mo. Q2–4, F; not in Q1*   18 SP1] *Oxf; Mo. Q2–4, F; Moth: Q1*   21.1] *Q2–4, F (Enter Father.); Enter Oldeman. Q1*

CAPULET

> For shame, bring Juliet forth; her lord is come.

NURSE

> She's dead, deceased, she's dead, alack the day!

CAPULET'S WIFE

> Alack the day, she's dead, she's dead, she's dead.

CAPULET

> Ha, let me see her. Out, alas, she's cold.   25
> Her blood is settled and her joints are stiff.
> Life and these lips have long been separated.
> Death lies on her like an untimely frost
> Upon the sweetest flower of all the field.

NURSE

> O lamentable day!

CAPULET'S WIFE   O woeful time!   30

CAPULET

> Death that hath ta'en her hence to make me wail,
> Ties up my tongue and will not let me speak.

Enter FRIAR [LAURENCE] *and the* County PARIS.

FRIAR LAURENCE

> Come, is the bride ready to go to church?

CAPULET

> Ready to go, but never to return.
> O son, the night before thy wedding day   35
> Hath death lain with thy wife. There she lies,

---

23 **alack the day** an exclamation of regret (*OED int.* b cites this as first instance in this sense)

26 **settled** become set, ceased to flow; exactly as the Friar predicted (at 4.1.95–6) (*OED v.* 22 cites as first instance)

28–9 Cf. 'A fair young maid, scarce fourteen years of age, / The sweetest flower in Cytherea's field, / Cropp'd from the pleasures of the fruitful earth' (Marlowe, *The Jew of Malta*, 1.2.375–7).

22+ SP] *Q1; Fa. Q2–4, F (Fat. at 59)* 24 SP] *Oxf; M. Q2–3, F; Mo. Q4; Nur: Q1 (at 18)*
30 SP2] *Oxf; Mo. Q2–4, F; not in Q1* 32.1] *Q2–3 (Enter Frier and the Countie.), F, Q1 (Enter Fryer and Paris.); Enter* Frier *and the Countie, with the Musitians.* Q4 36 There] *Q2–4, F;* see, where *Q1*

Flower as she was, deflowered by him.
Death is my son-in-law, death is my heir,
My daughter he hath wedded. I will die
And leave him all; life, living, all is death's.   40

PARIS

Have I thought long to see this morning's face,
And doth it give me such a sight as this?

CAPULET'S WIFE

Accursed, unhappy, wretched, hateful day!
Most miserable hour that e'er time saw
In lasting labour of his pilgrimage!   45
But one, poor one, one poor and loving child,
But one thing to rejoice and solace in,
And cruel death hath catched it from my sight.
    All at once cry out and wring their hands.

NURSE

O woe, O woeful, woeful, woeful day!
Most lamentable day, most woeful day   50
That ever, ever I did yet behold!
O day, O day, O day, O hateful day!
Never was seen so black a day as this.
O woeful day, O woeful day!

PARIS

Beguiled, divorced, wronged, spited, slain!   55

---

39 Cf. 5.3.102–5.
41 *long Q1's reading (Q2 has 'loue') is widely preferred by editors; *thought long* means 'long looked forward to'.
45 **lasting labour** 'unceasing toil' (Ard²) **pilgrimage** weary journey
47 **solace** find comfort
48 **catched** caught, an optional past participle form in Early Modern English
49–54 Wells ('Challenges', 9) detects echoes of 'the world of Pyramus

and Thisbe' here. Coleridge (139) remarked that it was 'difficult to understand what *effect*, whether that of pity or laughter, Shakespeare meant to produce – the occasion and the characteristic speeches are so little in harmony'.

55 **divorced** divorcèd
   wronged wrongèd
   spited treated spitefully (first *OED* usage)

41 long] *Q1, Q3–4, F;* loue *Q2*   43 SP] *Oxf; Mo. Q2–4, F; Moth: Q1 (at 19)*   46 loving] *Q2–4, F;* living *Johnson²; not in Q1*   48 SD] *Q1 (after 36–40, var.); not in Q2–4, F*

Most detestable death, by thee beguiled,
By cruel, cruel thee quite overthrown.
O love, O life, not life but love in death.

CAPULET

Despised, distressed, hated, martyred, killed!
Uncomfortable time, why cam'st thou now   60
To murder, murder our solemnity?
O child, O child, my soul and not my child!
Dead art thou, alack, my child is dead,
And with my child my joys are buried.

FRIAR LAURENCE

Peace, ho, for shame! Confusion's cure lives not   65
In these confusions. Heaven and yourself
Had part in this fair maid; now heaven hath all,
And all the better is it for the maid.
Your part in her you could not keep from death,
But heaven keeps his part in eternal life.   70
The most you sought was her promotion,
For 'twas your heaven she should be advanced.
And weep ye now, seeing she is advanced
Above the clouds, as high as heaven itself?
O, in this love you love your child so ill   75
That you run mad seeing that she is well.
She's not well married that lives married long,

56 **detestable** dètestàble
59 **distressed** distressèd
60 **Uncomfortable** sorrow-inducing
64 **buried** burièd
65–83 The Friar's forceful harangue, not in Shakespeare's sources, presses home the Pauline logic of Christian consolation, that death has no sting but marks the start of life everlasting.
65 **Confusion's cure** remedy of this calamity
   *cure See 4.1.45n.

66 **confusions** commotions; uncontrolled laments
71 **promotion** elevation to a higher social status
73 **advanced** raised
75 **this love** i.e. the love that you are exhibiting just now, which makes you weep when she has achieved heavenly bliss, more than anything you ever imagined for her
76 **she is well** Dent compares proverbial 'He is well since he is in heaven' (H347); see also *Mac* 4.3.176–9.

59 SP] *Fat. Q2–4, F; var. Q1*   65 cure] *Theobald;* care *Q2–4, F; not in Q1*   72 should] *Q2–4;* shouldst *F; not in Q1*

But she's best married that dies married young.
Dry up your tears, and stick your rosemary
On this fair corse, and, as the custom is,   80
And in her best array, bear her to church;
For though fond nature bids us all lament,
Yet nature's tears are reason's merriment.

CAPULET

All things that we ordained festival
Turn from their office to black funeral: 85
Our instruments to melancholy bells,
Our wedding cheer to a sad burial feast,
Our solemn hymns to sullen dirges change;
Our bridal flowers serve for a buried corse,
And all things change them to the contrary.   90

FRIAR LAURENCE

Sir, go you in and, madam, go with him.
And go, Sir Paris. Everyone prepare
To follow this fair corse unto her grave.
The heavens do lour upon you for some ill;
Move them no more by crossing their high will.   95

> *They all but the Nurse go forth, casting rosemary*
> *on [Juliet] and shutting the curtains.*

---

79 **rosemary** here a traditional symbol
of remembrance; see 2.4.198n. on
rosemary and Romeo.
82 **fond nature** our natural loving
instincts
83 **nature's . . . merriment** 'Our hearts
may weep but our minds cause us to
rejoice.'
84 **ordained** ordainèd
festival befitting a feast; cf. 'this
blessed day / Ever in France shall be
kept festival' (*KJ* 3.1.1–2).
87 **feast** after Brooke, 2446
88 **hymns . . . dirges** Brooke has 'And

hymn into a dirge' (2510).
94 **lour** look darkly; see *R3* 1.1.3.
95 SD *Dessen and Thomson (184)
note that the Q1 SD here 'sets up
a complex effect involving wedding,
death and remembrance', because of
the associations of rosemary which,
as a stage property, is linked primarily to weddings. They compare
'with rosemary, as from a wedding'
(John Fletcher, *The Woman's Prize*, 2)
and 'with rosemary as from church'
(Marston *et al.*, *The Insatiate Countess*,
1.1.141).

81 And in] *Q2–4, F;* In all *Q1;* All in *Rowe*   82 fond] *F2;* some *Q2–4, F; not in Q1*   us all] *Q2–4;* all
vs *F; not in Q1*   95 SD] *Q1; Exeunt manet. Q2–3; Exeunt manent Musici. Q4; Exeunt. F*

Enter Musicians.

1 MUSICIAN

Faith, we may put up our pipes and be gone.

NURSE

Honest good fellows, ah, put up, put up,
For well you know this is a pitiful case.

1 MUSICIAN

Ay, by my troth, the case may be amended.

                     Exit [*Nurse. Musicians make to leave*].

Enter PETER.

PETER   Musicians, O musicians, 'Heart's ease', 'Heart's   100
ease'! O, an you will have me live, play 'Heart's ease'.

1 MUSICIAN   Why 'Heart's ease'?

PETER   O musicians, because my heart itself plays 'My

95.1 The Musicians (96ff.) were regularly
cut in productions (Zeffirelli left them
out in 1960) – they are not in the
source – until Peter Hall restored them
in 1961.

96–141 The planned serenade gives the
impression of an afterthought; see
Williams, 136, and Cam². It turns
into a form of charivari, poignantly
discordant, with Peter in vain trying to
chivvy the musicians into playing by
singing himself.

96 put . . . pipes leave off, desist playing
(proverbial, Dent, P345); see Nashe's
Summers Last Will and Testament: 'we
were as good even put up our pipes,
and sing merry, merry, for we shall get
no money' (Nashe, 3.263). The term
pipes here does not necessarily mean
wind instruments; rather, the presence
of Simon Catling (127) suggests that
the band includes at least one lutenist
or player of a stringed instrument (the

First Musician is twice called 'fiddler'
in Q2–4 SPs).

99 case . . . amended He pretends to
mistake *pitiful case* (98) as referring to
the battered case of his instrument.

99.1 *Q2 has '*Enter Will Kemp*', giving
the name of the actor rather than the
role. Kemp appears similarly in the
SPs of *MA* 4.5 and is, perhaps, intended by the use of *William* for one of the
drawers in a SD in *2H4* 2.4 (although
he probably played Falstaff, which
might suggest that another William,
Shakespeare, played the drawer).

100 'Heart's ease' a popular country
dance of the time; the lyrics are lost
but the tune survives in *The English
Dancing Master* (1651) by John
Playford; see Sternfeld, 102.

101 an if

103–4 'My . . . full' an allusion, probably, to another song from the period.
Q4's adding 'of woe' after *full* may

95.1] *Q1; not in Q2–4, F*   96 SP] *Capell; Musi. Q2–4; Mu. F; not in Q1*   99 SP] *Capell; Fid. Q2–4;
Mu. F; 1. Q1*   by] *Q3–4, F, Q1; my Q2*   SD] *this edn; Exit omnes. Q2; Exeunt omnes. Q3–4; Exit. Q1
(opp. 98); not in F*   99.1] *Q4, F; Enter Will Kemp. Q2–3; Enter Servingman. Q1*   100 SP] *Q2–4, F;
Ser. Q1*   102 SP] *Capell; Fidler. Q2–4; Mu. F; not in Q1*

heart is full'. O, play me some merry dump to comfort
me.   105

MUSICIANS   Not a dump we! 'Tis no time to play now.

PETER   You will not then?

1 MUSICIAN   No.

PETER   I will then give it you soundly.

1 MUSICIAN   What will you give us?   110

PETER   No money, on my faith, but the gleek. I will give
      you the minstrel.

1 MUSICIAN   Then will I give you the serving-creature.

PETER   Then will I lay the serving-creature's dagger on
      your pate. I will carry no crotchets. I'll re you, I'll fa   115
      you. Do you note me?

1 MUSICIAN   An you re us and fa us, you note us.

2 MUSICIAN   Pray you put up your dagger and put out
      your wit.

PETER   Then have at you with my wit! I will dry-beat you   120

point to a song printed much later, 'A
pleasant new Ballad of two Lovers',
the first stanza of which ends, 'Heigh-
ho! my heart is full of woe'.
104 dump A *dump* is a plaintive tune,
hence *merry dump* is an oxymoron.
109 soundly thoroughly; with a quibble
on 'sound' = play music, launching a
series of musical *double entendres*
111 gleek gibe (*OED*); to give someone the gleek means to mock them.
The only other occurrence of *gleek*
is Bottom's 'Nay, I can gleek upon
occasion' (*MND* 3.1.141).
111–12 give . . . minstrel call you
worthless vagabonds, or mincing
musicians (cf. 3.1.45n.)
113 serving-creature lowly born fellow,
with *creature* a more offensive term
than now
115 carry no crotchets put up with

your fancy musical conceits (*OED*
crotchet 9); in music a crotchet is a
quarter-note.
115–16 re . . . fa you i.e. teach you a
minstrelsy lesson (mocking the musicians by turning the second and fourth
note of the musical scale, *re* and *fa*,
into verbs)
117 An if
   note us get our drift; with a further
quibble on musical 'note'
118 put up sheathe (cf. *Oth* 1.2.59)
118–19 put out . . . wit draw (show, display) your wit (instead, after putting
away your dagger!)
120 SP *after Q4; Q2 and Q3 attribute
the challenge *Then . . . wit* to the
Second Musician, but this is hard to
reconcile with his attempts to calm
matters down.
120 dry-beat soundly thrash (cf. 3.1.78)

104 full] *Q2–3, F;* full of woe *Q4*   104–5 O . . . comfort me] *Q2–4; not in F; var. Q1*   108 SP]
Hoppe; Minstrels. Q2–4; Mu. F; 1. Q1; I. M. / *Capell*   110, 117, 128 SPs] *Capell; Minst. Q2; Min.
Q3–4; Mu. F; 1. Q1*   113 SP] *Capell; Minstrel. Q2; Min. Q3–4; Mu. F; 1. Q1*   114 lay] *Q2–3,
F;* say *Q4; not in Q1*   118, 130 SPs] *2. M. Q2–4, F; 2. Q1 (130 only)*   120 Then . . . wit!] *Q4; given
to Second Musician Q2–3, F*

with an iron wit and put up my iron dagger. Answer
me like men.
> When griping griefs the heart doth wound
> And doleful dumps the mind oppress,
> Then music with her silver sound –   125

Why 'silver sound'? Why 'music with her silver
sound'? What say you, Simon Catling?

1 MUSICIAN   Marry, sir, because silver hath a sweet sound.

PETER   Prates! What say you, Hugh Rebeck?

2 MUSICIAN   I say 'silver sound', because musicians sound   130
for silver.

PETER   Prates too! What say you, James Soundpost?

3 MUSICIAN   Faith, I know not what to say.

PETER   O, I cry you mercy! You are the singer. I will say

123–5 a madrigal by Richard Edwardes,
printed in *The Paradise of Dainty
Devices* (1576). Its second line
('And . . . oppress') is supplied by Q1,
while the fourth ('With . . . redress')
follows at 138. The song is slightly misquoted; the correct reading is: 'Where
griping grief the heart was wound /
And doleful dumps the mind oppress,
/ There music with her silver sound
/ Is wont with speed to give redress.'
123 **griping** painful, distressing (Onions)
124 The second line of the song is imported from Q1 because Q2 gives lines 1, 3
and 4, while oddly missing out the second line which, through *doleful dumps*,
provides the most direct link between
the song and the surrounding text.
125ff. **silver . . . sweet**   proverbial,
according to Dent (M1319.1;
S458.1). Ard[2] refers to a passage in
Nashe's *Unfortunate Traveller*, which
Shakespeare seems to recollect with
regard to *silver sound* and also *pipes* (96):
'This silver-sounding tale made such
sugared harmony in his ears that . . . he
could have found in his heart to have

packed up his pipes and to have gone
to heaven without a bait' (Nashe, 2.222)
127 **Catling** literally, a string of catgut,
made for a violin, lute or other stringed
instrument
129 **Prates** 'He is talking rubbish.' Q1's
'Pretie' for *Prates* (Q2) is preferred by
Williams, who spells 'Pratie', a 16th-
century spelling of 'pretty'.
Rebeck A rebec is a medieval stringed
instrument, predecessor of the fiddle;
in 'L'Allegro', Milton hears 'the merry
bells ring round, / And the jocund
rebecks sound'.
132 **Soundpost** another musical name, a
soundpost being 'A small peg of wood
fixed beneath the bridge of a violin or
similar instrument, serving as a support for the belly and as a connecting
part between this and the back' (*OED*)
134 **cry you mercy** beg your pardon
(spoken sarcastically)
singer Peter suggests that as a singer
the Third Musician cannot be expected just to *say* something (spoken with
mock-deference, Peter continuing to
taunt the minstrels).

123–5] *Q1; long verse line Q2–4; prose F*   124] *Q1; not in Q2–4, F*   129 Prates!] *Q2;* Pratest, *Q3, F;*
Pratee, *Q4;* Pretie, *Q1*   132 Prates] *Q2;* Pratest *Q3, F;* Pratee *Q4;* Prettie *Q1*   133 SP] *3. M. Q2–4;*
3. Mu. F; 3. Q1   134–6] *prose var. Q1, Pope; Q2–4, F line* singer. / sound, / sounding: /

for you. It is 'music with her silver sound' because   135
musicians have no gold for sounding.
       Then music with her silver sound
       With speedy help doth lend redress.   *Exit.*

1 MUSICIAN What a pestilent knave is this same!
2 MUSICIAN Hang him, jack! Come, we'll in here, tarry   140
for the mourners, and stay dinner.   *Exeunt.*

[5.1]   *Enter* ROMEO.

ROMEO

If I may trust the flattering truth of sleep,
My dreams presage some joyful news at hand.
My bosom's lord sits lightly in his throne,
And all this day an unaccustomed spirit
Lifts me above the ground with cheerful thoughts.   5
I dreamt my lady came and found me dead –
Strange dream that gives a dead man leave to think –
And breathed such life with kisses in my lips
That I revived and was an emperor.

---

139 **pestilent** confounded, bothersome
  (*OED* 4)
140 **jack** knave
141 **stay** wait for
5.1 Wednesday afternoon (18) in a street
  in Mantua, after the funeral of Juliet
  in Verona and Balthasar's ride to
  Mantua
1–2 **sleep ... dreams** These words
  remind the audience of the fact Romeo
  has spent the night of Tuesday to
  Wednesday parted from Juliet; with
  his apprehensiveness about the meaning of dreams, cf. Bottom's 'rare
  vision' (*MND* 4.1.204ff.).
2 **presage** foretell

3 'My master, Love, resides happily in
  my heart.' Cam² compares 'Yield up,
  O Love, thy crown and hearted throne'
  (*Oth* 3.3.451).
4 **spirit** i.e. 'high spirits', *unaccustomed*
  because his light-hearted mood (*lightly ... Lifts ... cheerful*) contrasts with
  his morose temper after banishment
6–9 The lines are premonitory of the
  lovers' final reunion, when Juliet's kiss
  ('I will kiss thy lips' 5.3.164) fails to
  revive Romeo; cf. *AC* 5.2.75–7.
8 **breathed ... lips** a reminiscence,
  probably, of Marlowe's 'He kiss'd her,
  and breath'd life into her lips' (*Hero
  and Leander*, 2.3)

137–8] *Johnson; one line in Q2–4; prose in F; not in Q1*   139 SP] *Capell; Min. Q2–4; Mu. F; var.
Q1*   140 SP] *Q2 (M. 2.)–4, F; 1. Q1*   141 SD] *Q1, Q4; Exit. Q2–3, F*   **5.1]** *Rowe*   1 truth] *Q2–4,
F; Eye Q1*   4 this] *Q2–4; thisan F; not in Q1*   unaccustomed] *Q2–4; vccustom'd F; not in Q1*
7 dream ... gives] *Q2–3, F; dreames ... giues Q4; dreames ... giue Q1*

Ah me, how sweet is love itself possessed,   10
When but love's shadows are so rich in joy.

Enter BALTHASAR, *Romeo's man, booted.*

News from Verona! How now, Balthasar,
Dost thou not bring me letters from the Friar?
How doth my lady? Is my father well?
How doth my Juliet? That I ask again,   15
For nothing can be ill if she be well.

BALTHASAR
Then she is well and nothing can be ill.
Her body sleeps in Capel's monument,
And her immortal part with angels lives.
I saw her laid low in her kindred's vault,   20
And presently took post to tell it you.
O, pardon me for bringing these ill news,
Since you did leave it for my office, sir.

ROMEO
Is it e'en so? Then I defy you, stars.

10 **possessed** as opposed to fancied or imagined, with a sexual innuendo (see 'mansion of a love . . . not possessed . . . Not yet enjoyed' (3.2.26–8)
11 **shadows** intimations
11.1 *Q1's '*booted*' highlights Balthasar's post-haste arrival from Verona. Dessen and Thomson compare '*booted and spurred*', also in the context of hurry, having 'posted all night' (Robert Greene, *Friar Bacon and Friar Bungay*); see also Dessen, 'Q1', 108.
15 *my Juliet Pope's reading for Q2's 'my Lady *Iuliet*' (Q1 has 'How fares my *Iuliet*') renders the line metrical by jettisoning what may be a compositor's duplication of *lady* from the previous line (Williams).

20 **laid low** i.e. in the vault
21 **presently took post** set off at once with post-horses
22 **these . . . news** Plural accord with *news* was common in the period.
23 **for my office** as my duty
24 **e'en** Q2's spelling 'in' to mark the contraction to a single syllable may be a Shakespearean spelling; see similarly *AC* 4.15.77, also set from MS or fair copy of it (*TxC*, 549).
*defy Q1's reading, first adapted by Pope and preferred by most editors, is supported by Brooke: after killing Tybalt, Romeus 'On Fortune . . . railed . . . blamed all the world and all he did defy' (1343–7).

11.1] *Q1 subst. (Enter Balthasar his man booted.); Enter* Romeos *man.* Q2–3 *(man.* Q2), F; *Enter* Romeos *man* Balthazer. Q4   15 doth my Juliet] *Pope;* doth my Lady *Iuliet* Q2–4, F; fares my *Juliet* Q1   17, 27 SPs] *Q1 (Balt.); Man.* Q2–4, F   19 lives] Q2–4; liue F; dwell Q1   24 e'en] *Collier;* in Q2; euen Q3–4, F, Q1   defy you] *Pope;* denie you Q2–4, F; defie my Q1

314

Thou knowest my lodging. Get me ink and paper,   25
And hire post-horses. I will hence tonight.

BALTHASAR

I do beseech you, sir, have patience.
Your looks are pale and wild, and do import
Some misadventure.

ROMEO   Tush, thou art deceived.
Leave me, and do the thing I bid thee do.   30
Hast thou no letters to me from the Friar?

BALTHASAR

No, my good lord.

ROMEO   No matter. Get thee gone,
And hire those horses. I'll be with thee straight.

Exit [Balthasar].

Well, Juliet, I will lie with thee tonight.
Let's see for means. O mischief, thou art swift   35
To enter in the thoughts of desperate men.
I do remember an apothecary,
And hereabouts 'a dwells, which late I noted,
In tattered weeds, with overwhelming brows,
Culling of simples. Meagre were his looks,   40
Sharp misery had worn him to the bones,

25 **ink and paper** In Brooke, 'Romeus, the while, with many a deadly thought, / Provoked much, hath caused ink and paper to be brought' (2603–4).
26 **post-horses** horses kept at inns for hire by travellers (after Brooke, 2612); see 21 above.
27 **patience** patiènce (three syllables)
28 **import** betoken
29 **Tush** See 4.2.39n.
    deceived mistaken; he is not, of course, but is misled by Romeo here, and again at 5.3.30–2.

34 **lie with** sleep next to and die together with; cf. 'die and lie with Juliet' and 'by his lady's lie' (5.3.290, 303).
35 **see for means** consider how
37 **apothecary** someone who sells medicinal drugs
37–79 after Brooke, 2567–88
38 **'a** he
39 **weeds** rags
    overwhelming conspicuous, protruding
40 **Culling of simples** picking medicinal herbs
41 **Sharp** acute

33 SD] *Q1; Exit. Q2–4; Exit Man. F (after Lord. 32)*   38 'a] *Q2–4; om. F; not in Q1*

315

And in his needy shop a tortoise hung,
An alligator stuffed, and other skins
Of ill-shaped fishes; and about his shelves
A beggarly account of empty boxes,   45
Green earthen pots, bladders and musty seeds,
Remnants of packthread and old cakes of roses
Were thinly scattered to make up a show.
Noting this penury, to myself I said
'An if a man did need a poison now,   50
Whose sale is present death in Mantua,
Here lives a caitiff wretch would sell it him'.
O, this same thought did but forerun my need,
And this same needy man must sell it me.
As I remember, this should be the house.   55
Being holiday, the beggar's shop is shut.
What, ho, apothecary!

Enter Apothecary.

APOTHECARY   Who calls so loud?
ROMEO
Come hither, man. I see that thou art poor.

---

42 **needy** bare, poorly stocked (see *beg-garly* at 45 and *penury* at 49); the word 'needy' = poverty-stricken is twice applied to the apothecary in Brooke (2573, 2575).

43 **alligator** Shakespeare's only use of *alligator* – 'crocodile' occurs five times in the canon (*2H6, Ham, Oth* and twice in *AC*) – originates in Nashe's *Have With You*: 'the next rat he seized on he made an anatomy of . . . and after hanged her over his head in his study, instead of an apothecary's crocodile or dried alligator' (Nashe, 3.67); see p. 39.

45 **beggarly account** pitifully small number; see 'his boxes were but few' (Brooke, 2568).

47 **packthread** strong twine for tying up packs or bundles
cakes of roses rose-cakes, petals compressed in the form of a cake to be used as perfume; old rose-cakes like the apothecary's presumably turn fetid. *OED* 'rose-cake' records first usage by John Florio in 1598.

51 **Whose . . . death** i.e. anyone caught selling the poison is instantly put to death.

52 **caitiff** miserable

56 **holiday** one of Shakespeare's additions to Brooke; see p. 29.

57.1] *Q1, F; not in Q2–4*   58 SP] *Q3–4, F, Q1; kom. Q2*

Hold, there is forty ducats. Let me have
A dram of poison, such soon-speeding gear   60
As will disperse itself through all the veins,
That the life-weary taker may fall dead,
And that the trunk may be discharged of breath
As violently as hasty powder fired
Doth hurry from the fatal cannon's womb.   65

APOTHECARY

Such mortal drugs I have, but Mantua's law
Is death to any he that utters them.

ROMEO

Art thou so bare and full of wretchedness,
And fearest to die? Famine is in thy cheeks,
Need and oppression starveth in thy eyes,   70
Contempt and beggary hangs upon thy back,
The world is not thy friend, nor the world's law;
The world affords no law to make thee rich,
Then be not poor, but break it and take this.

APOTHECARY

My poverty but not my will consents.   75

---

59 **forty ducats** i.e. an impressive number of gold coins; Brooke has 'fifty crowns of gold' (2577), while Boisteau gives 50 ducats (in Painter, 241). Ard² suggests that Shakespeare remembered the 40 ducats from *CE* 4.3.80, 93; see also 'My daughter! O my ducats! . . . my ducats, and my daughter!' (*MV* 2.8.15–17).

60 **dram** a small liquid measure (one-eighth of an ounce), hence a small draught. In *Ham* 1.34.36–7, 'dram' is the infinitesimal unit with which to contrast 'all the noble substance of a doubt'.
soon-speeding fast-acting ('speeding gere' in Brooke, 2585)

61 **disperse itself** circulate

62 **life-weary taker** i.e. person committing suicide

63 **trunk** body as well as corpse, *trunk* anticipating that the body will be defunct presently; Cam² notes that 'trunk' also can mean cylindrical shape, as in the tube of a gun, and compares the *fatal cannon's womb* at 65.

67 **any he** any man
utters sells

68 **bare** naked, exposed; cf. *KL* 3.4.105–6.

70 **Need and oppression** poverty and unjust treatment; probably a hendiadys like *Contempt and beggary* in the next line

71 **hangs . . . back** are wrapped about you like a cloak

66, 75, 77 SPs] *F, Q1; Poti. Q2; Po(ti.) Q3–4*   69 fearest] *Q2–4;* fear'st *F;* doost thou feare *Q1*
70 starveth in] *Q2–4, F; var. Q1;* stareth in *Rowe*

ROMEO

    I pay thy poverty and not thy will.

APOTHECARY

    Put this in any liquid thing you will

    And drink it off; and if you had the strength

    Of twenty men, it would dispatch you straight.

ROMEO

    There is thy gold, worse poison to men's souls,   80

    Doing more murder in this loathsome world

    Than these poor compounds that thou mayst not sell.

    I sell thee poison; thou hast sold me none.

    Farewell, buy food, and get thyself in flesh.

                                 [Exit Apothecary.]

    Come, cordial and not poison, go with me   85

    To Juliet's grave, for there must I use thee.   *[Exit.]*

[5.2]   *Enter* FRIAR JOHN.

FRIAR JOHN

    Holy Franciscan friar, brother, ho!

               Enter FRIAR LAURENCE.

FRIAR LAURENCE

    This same should be the voice of Friar John.

    Welcome from Mantua. What says Romeo?

    Or if his mind be writ, give me his letter.

---

76 *pay Q1's reading is widely preferred by editors although Oxf[1] defends Q2's 'pray'. Williams blames a similar rogue insertion of *r* by Q2's compositor for an earlier textual crux (see 'friar'/*sire* at 2.2.192).

77–9 after Brooke, 2587–8

82 **compounds** drugs (chemical compounds)

84 **get . . . flesh** put on some weight

5.2 Wednesday evening (24) in Friar Laurence's cell in Verona

76 pay] *Q1, Q4;* pray *Q2–3,* F 81 murder] *Q2–3,* F; murthers *Q4; not in Q1* 84 SD] *Wilson–Duthie* 86 SD] *Wilson–Duthie; Exeunt Q2–4,* F, *Q1* **5.2**] *Pope* 0.1] *Q1; Enter Frier* John *to Frier* Lawrence. *Q2–4,* F, 1, 5 SPs] *Capell; Joh. Q2–4; Iohn.* F, *Q1* 1.1] *Q2–4,* F; *not in Q1* 2+ SP] *Capell; Law. Q2–4,* F; *Laur: Q1*

FRIAR JOHN

Going to find a barefoot brother out,   5
One of our order, to associate me,
Here in this city visiting the sick,
And finding him, the searchers of the town,
Suspecting that we both were in a house
Where the infectious pestilence did reign,   10
Sealed up the doors and would not let us forth
So that my speed to Mantua there was stayed.

FRIAR LAURENCE

Who bare my letter then to Romeo?

FRIAR JOHN

I could not send it – here it is again –
Nor get a messenger to bring it thee,   15
So fearful were they of infection.

FRIAR LAURENCE

Unhappy fortune! By my brotherhood,
The letter was not nice but full of charge,
Of dear import, and the neglecting it
May do much danger. Friar John, go hence,   20

5–12 after Brooke, 2488–99
5 **barefoot** Franciscans usually walked barefoot as a sign of poverty and humility, although the wearing of shoes, unlike travel on horseback, was allowed by the rules of the order.
6 **associate** Brooke records that in Italy it was the custom ('wonted guise') for Franciscans to walk in pairs (2488–90). This allowed the friars to monitor each other's behaviour.
8 **searchers** officers 'appointed to view dead bodies and to make report upon the cause of death' (*OED*)
9 **house** probably an ordinary dwelling rather than a convent as in Brooke, since the brother Friar John was

seeking out was on a charitable call to the *sick* (7) in Verona. Rule XI of the Franciscan Order warns the brothers against entering convents of nuns.
11 **Sealed up** Quarantine was a common practice at the time.
12 **speed** rapid progress
14 **here . . . again** 'I am returning it to you.'
16 **infection** (four syllables)
17 **brotherhood** order (i.e. the Franciscans)
18 **nice** trivial
   charge momentous matter
19 **dear import** grave consequence
   neglecting it failure to deliver it
20 **danger** harm

12 my] *Q2–3, F; may Q4; not in Q1*   14, 22 SPs] *Capell; John. Q2–4, F; var. Q1*   14 could] *Q2–3, F; cold Q4; var. Q1*

319

Get me an iron crow, and bring it straight
Unto my cell.

FRIAR JOHN   Brother, I'll go and bring it thee.   *Exit.*

FRIAR LAURENCE

Now must I to the monument alone.
Within this three hours will fair Juliet wake.
She will beshrew me much that Romeo   25
Hath had no notice of these accidents.
But I will write again to Mantua
And keep her at my cell till Romeo come.
Poor living corse, closed in a dead man's tomb!   *Exit.*

[5.3]   *Enter* County PARIS *and his* Page *with flowers*
          and sweet water [and a torch].

PARIS

Give me thy torch, boy. Hence, and stand aloof.
Yet put it out, for I would not be seen.

---

21 **crow** 'a crowbar, used for prying open a door or tomb' (Dessen & Thomson)
24 **this three hours** a time marker to signal that this scene takes place in the evening; *this* rather than 'these' because the period of *three hours* is taken as a unit of time; see also 5.3.176. Juliet wakes after midnight.
25 **beshrew** blame
26 **accidents** unfortunate events
29 **corse** corpse
5.3 The scene starts late on Wednesday night and finishes at dawn on Thursday; the location is Verona's churchyard, in particular the Capulet tomb, positioned centrally (Friar Laurence, standing at the edge of the cemetery, discerns Romeo's torch

'yond . . . in the Capels' monument', 125–7). The choreographic demands of this scene are complex (see Halio, *Guide*, 99), notably with regard to the positioning of minor characters. The Nunn–Kyle production used a gallery for the entries of Paris, his Page, Romeo and Balthasar, while Juliet's tomb occupied the main stage so that they had to descend to it; the prompt-book has 'Romeo jumps onto stage'; for the gallery Bogdanov substituted a balcony.
0.2 ***sweet water*** perfume. Dessen and Thomson compare '*a casting-bottle of sweet water in his hand, sprinkling himself*' (Marston, *Antonio and Mellida*, 3.2.24).
1 **stand aloof** withdraw some distance

5.3] *Rowe*   0.1 *Enter . . . water*] *Q1; Enter* Paris *and his Page. Q2–4 (*Page. Q4), F   and a torch*] *Cam²
subst.*   1 aloof] *Q2–4;* aloft *F; not in Q1*

Under yond yew trees lay thee all along,
Holding thy ear close to the hollow ground.
So shall no foot upon the churchyard tread,   5
Being loose, unfirm, with digging up of graves
But thou shalt hear it. Whistle then to me,
As signal that thou hearest something approach.
Give me those flowers. Do as I bid thee, go.

PAGE [*aside*]

I am almost afraid to stand alone   10
Here in the churchyard, yet I will adventure.   [*Retires.*]
    Paris strews the tomb with flowers.

PARIS

Sweet flower, with flowers thy bridal bed I strew,
O woe, thy canopy is dust and stones,
Which with sweet water nightly I will dew,
Or, wanting that, with tears distilled by moans.   15
The obsequies that I for thee will keep,
Nightly shall be to strew thy grave and weep.   *Page whistles.*
The boy gives warning something doth approach.
What cursed foot wanders this way tonight,
To cross my obsequies and true love's rite?   20
What, with a torch? Muffle me, night, awhile.   [*Retires.*]

---

3 *yew trees** The traditional presence of
yews in churchyards has rendered them
symbols of sadness and melancholy.
all along at full stretch
10 **stand** stay, wait (*OED v.* 16a)
11 SD2 *another Q1 SD duplicated by
the dialogue (12)
13 **canopy . . . stones** Her cover is a
gravestone rather than the festive,
richly brocaded hangings that would

have adorned Juliet's *bridal bed* (12).
14 **dew** bedew
16 **obsequies** funeral rites. Brooke refers
to 'her obsequies' (2506) in her native
town of Verona. Paris' presence in this
scene is Shakespeare's invention; see
pp. 52, 81–2, 93–4.
19 **cursed** cursèd
20 **cross** thwart
21 **Muffle** conceal, wrap in darkness

3 yond yew trees] *Pope;* yond young trees *Q2–4, F;* this Ew-tree *Q1*   4 Holding] *Q2–4, F;* keeping
Q1   8 hearest] *Q2–4, F;* hear'st *Rowe; not in Q1*   10 SD] *Capell*   11 SD1] *Capell subst.*   SD2] *Q1;*
not in Q2–4, F   17 SD] *Q2–4, F (Whistle Boy.); Boy whistles and calls. My Lord. Q1*   19 way] *Q2–4;*
wayes F; was *Q1*   20 rite] *Q2–4, F (right); rites Q1*   21 SD] *Capell*

Enter ROMEO *and* BALTHASAR *with a torch,*
a mattock and a crow of iron.

ROMEO

Give me that mattock and the wrenching iron.
Hold, take this letter. Early in the morning
See thou deliver it to my lord and father.
Give me the light. Upon thy life I charge thee,   25
Whate'er thou hearest or seest, stand all aloof,
And do not interrupt me in my course.
Why I descend into this bed of death
Is partly to behold my lady's face,
But chiefly to take thence from her dead finger   30
A precious ring, a ring that I must use
In dear employment. Therefore hence, be gone.
But if thou, jealous, dost return to pry
In what I farther shall intend to do,
By heaven, I will tear thee joint by joint   35
And strew this hungry churchyard with thy limbs.
The time and my intents are savage-wild,

21.1–2 *as in Q1; Q2 has '*Enter* Romeo *and* Peter'. Editors have suggested that 'Peter' is used in Q2 because Will Kemp doubled in the parts of Balthasar and Nurse's man Peter, and that Shakespeare forgot that Romeo addressed his 'man' as Balthasar at 5.1.12. But Brooke repeatedly calls Romeus' man 'Peter' in this final scene, which suggests that Shakespeare here inadvertently followed his source too closely; see similarly 1.5.28n.

21.1 *mattock* 'a tool similar to a pick but with a point or chisel edge at one end of the head and an adze-like blade at the other, used for breaking up

hard ground, grubbing up trees, etc.' (*OED*)

22 **wrenching iron** crowbar

26 **stand all aloof** stay well clear (cf. 'lay thee all along', 3)

27 **course** course of action

30–1 **chiefly . . . precious ring** This is a ruse to mislead Balthasar about his true reason for breaking open the Capulet tomb.

32 **dear employment** important business

33 **jealous** suspicious

36 **hungry** The cemetery greedily devours corpses; see also 45–8.

37 **savage-wild** utterly ferocious

21.1] *Q1 (after 17); Enter* Romeo *and* Peter. *Q2–3, F; Enter* Romeo *and* Balthazer *his man. Q4*   22 that] *Q2–3, F;* the *Q4;* this *Q1*   26 hearest] *Q2–4;* hear'st *F; not in Q1*   34 farther] *Q2–4;* further *F, Q1*

More fierce and more inexorable far
Than empty tigers or the roaring sea.

BALTHASAR

I will be gone, sir, and not trouble ye.   40

ROMEO

So shalt thou show me friendship. Take thou that.
[*Gives money.*]
Live and be prosperous, and farewell, good fellow.

BALTHASAR [*aside*]

For all this same, I'll hide me hereabout.
His looks I fear, and his intents I doubt.   [*Retires.*]
Romeo opens the tomb.

ROMEO

Thou detestable maw, thou womb of death,   45
Gorged with the dearest morsel of the earth,
Thus I enforce thy rotten jaws to open,
And in despite I'll cram thee with more food.

PARIS [*apart*]

This is that banished haughty Montague
That murdered my love's cousin, with which grief   50
It is supposed the fair creature died,

38–9 **fierce . . . tigers** Tigers were proverbially fierce (Dent, T287.1), more so, presumably, when they were starving (*empty*).

44 SD2 *placed here before 45 as in Q1. Noting that the tomb seems to be still closed at 73, Williams shifts the SD to follow 83, suggesting that the direction should perhaps be interpreted as 'Romeo busies himself with opening the tomb'. For a detailed discussion of this 'notorious problem' in performance, see Loehlin, 237–8.

45 **detestable** dètestàble

46 **Gorged** Death as a grisly banqueter feasting off the living is a leit-motiv in the play whose motto might be '*tempus edax rerum*' (time the devourer of things); see pp. 24–33, and see *hungry* (36) and *maw, morsel, jaws* and *food* in 45ff. See further 'O proud Death, / What feast is toward in thine eternal cell' (*Ham* 5.2.369–70).
  dearest . . . earth i.e. Juliet
48 **in despite** to spite you (because you are already stuffed full of food)
49 **haughty** proud, disdainful
51 **supposed** supposèd

40, 43 SPs] *Q1, Q4; Pet. Q2–3, F*   40 ye] *Q2;* you *Q3–4, F, Q1*   41 SD] *this edn; Gives a purse Cam²*   43 SD] *Capell*   44 SD1] *Hanmer*   SD2] *Q1; not in Q2–4, F*   49 SD *this edn (GWW)*

And here is come to do some villainous shame
To the dead bodies. I will apprehend him.
[*Steps forward.*]
– Stop thy unhallowed toil, vile Montague!
Can vengeance be pursued further than death?   55
Condemned villain, I do apprehend thee.
Obey and go with me, for thou must die.

ROMEO

I must indeed, and therefore came I hither.
Good gentle youth, tempt not a desperate man.
Fly hence and leave me. Think upon these gone,   60
Let them affright thee. I beseech thee, youth,
Put not another sin upon my head
By urging me to fury. O, be gone!
By heaven, I love thee better than myself,
For I come hither armed against myself.   65
Stay not, be gone; live, and hereafter say
A madman's mercy bid thee run away.

PARIS

I do defy thy conjuration
And apprehend thee for a felon here.

52–3 **villainous . . . bodies**   after
   Brooke, 2797–8
53 **apprehend** arrest
54 **toil** labour
   vile despicable; although Tybalt's earlier insult of *villain* (3.1.60) may also
   be recollected
56 **Condemned** condemnèd
59 **youth** a term of affection and solidar-
   ity here (also at 61, 84) for one who is
   destined to share his fate (see 81–2)
   rather than suggesting that Paris is
   younger than Romeo; his use of *boy*
   at 70 is contemptuous and spoken in
   anger; cf. 1.5.76, 82; 3.1.65.
68 **conjuration solemn entreaty, adju-
   ration; after Capell, extrapolated from

'coniurations' in Q1. Q2's 'commiration' is a nonce word, but Williams, following Mommsen, argues in favour of
'commination', the secondary meaning
of which is 'threats' (from the Latin
minari = to threaten). 'Commination'
is not found elsewhere in the canon,
while *conjuration* = entreaty occurs at
R2 3.2.23, *H5* 1.2.29 and *Ham* 5.2.38.
Williams defends 'commination' on
palaeographic grounds ('merely a matter of *r* for *n*'), noting that it is not
surprising 'to find the easier reading
['conjurations'] in the report [Q1], the
difficilior lectio concealed behind the
authoritative text [Q2]'.
69 **felon** villain

53 SD] *Cam*   60 these] *Q2–4;* those *F; not in Q1*   68 conjuration] *Capell;* coniurations *Q1;*
commiration *Q2;* commis(s)eration *Q3–4, F;* commination *Williams (Mommsen)*

ROMEO

    Wilt thou provoke me? Then have at thee, boy!   70

      They fight.

PAGE

    O Lord, they fight. I will go call the watch.   [*Exit.*]

PARIS

    O, I am slain! If thou be merciful,

    Open the tomb, lay me with Juliet.   [*Dies.*]

ROMEO

    In faith, I will. Let me peruse this face.

    Mercutio's kinsman, noble County Paris!   75

    What said my man when my betossed soul

    Did not attend him as we rode? I think

    He told me Paris should have married Juliet.

    Said he not so? Or did I dream it so?

    Or am I mad, hearing him talk of Juliet,   80

    To think it was so? O, give me thy hand,

    One writ with me in sour misfortune's book.

    I'll bury thee in a triumphant grave.

    A grave – O, no, a lantern, slaughtered youth,

    For here lies Juliet, and her beauty makes   85

    This vault a feasting presence full of light.

    Death, lie thou there, by a dead man interred.

    How oft, when men are at the point of death,

---

73 SD *A number of productions (e.g. Zeffirelli, 1968, and Luhrmann) cut Paris out of the tomb scene, because Romeo may forfeit the audience's sympathy by killing him – even if he acts in self-defence, or if Paris is a sinister sexual predator, as in Boyd's production (2000).

75 **Mercutio's kinsman** and kinsman of the Prince too; see 295.

76 **betossed** betossèd; in turmoil

83 **triumphant** resplendent

84–6 **lantern . . . light** Juliet's radiance turns the Capulet tomb into a luminescent beacon, and Paris will rest in a brightly lit banqueting hall. Light and food metaphors are reversed in the conceit, with the hungry grave transformed into a festive presence chamber (*feasting presence*) in which Juliet royally entertains.

87 **dead man** i.e. Romeo

70 SD] *Q1; not in Q2–4, F*   71] *Q4, F, Q1; line in italics as SD in Q2–3*   71 SP] *Q4; not in Q2–3; Pet. F; Boy: Q1*   SD] *Capell (Rowe)*   73 SD] *Theobald*

Have they been merry, which their keepers call
A lightening before death. O, how may I   90
Call this a lightening? O my love, my wife,
Death, that hath sucked the honey of thy breath
Hath had no power yet upon thy beauty.
Thou art not conquered. Beauty's ensign yet
Is crimson in thy lips and in thy cheeks,   95
And death's pale flag is not advanced there.
Tybalt, liest thou there in thy bloody sheet?
O, what more favour can I do to thee
Than with that hand that cut thy youth in twain
To sunder his that was thine enemy?   100
Forgive me, cousin! Ah, dear Juliet,
Why art thou yet so fair? Shall I believe
That unsubstantial death is amorous,
And that the lean abhorred monster keeps
Thee here in dark to be his paramour?   105
For fear of that I still will stay with thee
And never from this palace of dim night

89 **keepers** nurses at deathbeds; guardians or gaolers of prisoners awaiting death
90 **lightening** 'exhilaration or revival of the spirits which is supposed to occur in some instances just before death' (cited under *OED sb.*[2]). Dent sees as proverbial (L277).
92–115 Malone and Steevens see traces here of Samuel Daniel's *The Complaint of Rosamond* (1592), Steevens (Var, 280) comparing 'And nought-respecting death (the last of paines) / Placed his *pale colours* (th'*ensign* of his might) / Upon his new-got spoil' (misquoting *Complaint*, 605–7: 'When naught respecting death, the last of pains, / Placed his pale colours, th'ensign of his might, / Upon his new-got spoil before his right'), which anticipates 92–6.
94 **ensign** banner, standard

96 **advanced** advancèd
100 **sunder his** i.e. separate him off, kill his youth just as it did Paris'
102 *****Shall I believe** probably Shakespeare's second thoughts, as Q2 has 'I will beleeue, / Shall I beleeue', metre and sense requiring the first one to be deleted
103–5 **death . . . paramour** This continues the personification of death as grotesque lover; see 4.5.36ff.
104 **abhorred** abhorrèd
106 **still** always
107 *****palace** the reading of Q3 for Q2's 'pallat'. The Q2 compositor probably mistook *c* for *t* because of Shakespeare's habit of dropping *e* after final *c*; see 2.1.10n. on *pronounce . . . 'dove'*.
dim night a contrast with the *feasting presence* of 86

94 art] *Q2–4;* are *F; not in Q1*   100 thine] *Q2–4;* thy *F; not in Q1*   102 Shall I believe] *Theobald;* I will beleeue, / Shall I beleeue *Q2–4, F;* O I beleeue *Q1;* I will beleeue *Pope*   107 palace] *Q3–4, F;* pallat *Q2; not in Q1*

Depart again. Here, here will I remain
With worms that are thy chambermaids. O, here
Will I set up my everlasting rest,   110
And shake the yoke of inauspicious stars
From this world-wearied flesh. Eyes, look your last;
Arms, take your last embrace, and lips, O you
The doors of breath, seal with a righteous kiss
A dateless bargain to engrossing death.   115
Come, bitter conduct, come, unsavoury guide.
Thou desperate pilot, now at once run on
The dashing rocks thy seasick weary bark!
Here's to my love.   [*Drinks.*]
                    O true apothecary,
Thy drugs are quick. Thus with a kiss I die.   120
Falls [*and dies*].

109 **worms . . . chambermaids** The phrase may be echoed in Andrew Marvell's 'To his Coy Mistress'; Ard² compares *Ham* 4.3.20–3.

110 **set . . . rest** another ironic parallel with Paris, who was expected by Nurse to have 'set up his rest' on a night of connubial bliss with Juliet (see 4.5.6n.). Here *rest* is a poignant euphemism for death, hence *everlasting*. Dent sees the phrase as proverbial (R86.1), while acknowledging that the two uses of it in the play differ significantly (Dent, 26, n.5).

111 **yoke . . . stars** heavy burden decreed by fate

115 **dateless** everlasting; cf. 'precious friends hid in death's dateless night' (*Son* 30.6).
   engrossing surfeiting, devouring; see *Gorged* at 46.

116–18 Romeo's marine metaphor and use of *bark* recall Capulet's extended metaphor of an inconsolable Juliet as

a *tempest-tossed body* (3.5.131–7). Oxf¹ compares Brooke's 'To the Reader', 799–808, 1365–70, 1519–26, and *Astrophil and Stella*, 85.1–4; see also Thompson, 107–9.

116 **bitter** because of the disagreeable, *unsavoury*, taste of the poison, but also 'full of affliction' (*OED* 3)
   conduct i.e. the poison that will steer him to death

118 **bark** i.e. Romeo's body

120 **quick** with a pun on *quick* = alive, that is, the deadly poison transports him to the only life he now craves, a life of death, because Juliet (he believes) has gone there ahead of him. See similarly *restorative* at 166 and *Ham* 5.2.123–5, 244.
   die Loehlin (242) notes that in 'all versions of the play produced between the late seventeenth and mid-nineteenth centuries' Romeo survived long enough to have a 'substantial dialogue with Juliet in the tomb'; see pp. 53–94.

108] *Q4;* Depart againe, come lye thou in my arme, / Heer's to thy health, where ere thou tumblest in. / O true Appothecarie! / Thy drugs are quicke. Thus with a kisse I die. / Depart again, here, here, will I remain, / *Q2–3, F; not in Q1*   119 SD] *Theobald; not in Q2–4, F, Q1*   120 SD *Falls] Q1; not in Q2–4, F   and dies] this edn*

Enter FRIAR LAURENCE *with lantern, crow and spade.*

FRIAR LAURENCE

　　Saint Francis be my speed! How oft tonight

　　Have my old feet stumbled at graves. Who's there?

　　[*Balthasar comes forward.*]

BALTHASAR

　　Here's one, a friend, and one that knows you well.

FRIAR LAURENCE

　　Bliss be upon you! Tell me, good my friend,

　　What torch is yond that vainly lends his light   125

　　To grubs and eyeless skulls? As I discern,

　　It burneth in the Capels' monument.

BALTHASAR

　　It doth so, holy sir, and there's my master,

　　One that you love.

FRIAR LAURENCE　　　　　Who is it?

BALTHASAR　　　　　　　　　　　　Romeo.

FRIAR LAURENCE

　　How long hath he been there?

BALTHASAR　　　　　　　　　　Full half an hour.   130

FRIAR LAURENCE

　　Go with me to the vault.

BALTHASAR　　　　　　　　I dare not, sir.

　　My master knows not but I am gone hence,

　　And fearfully did menace me with death

120.1 *Dessen and Thomson note that
in SDs of the period the 'lantern' 'is
often linked to surreptitious activity
such as clandestine visits at night to a
graveyard or tomb'.
121 **speed** assistance, help
122 **stumbled** usually an ill omen; the
Friar warned earlier (2.3.90) that haste
leads to stumbling, and Juliet felt that
Romeo had stumbled on her private

thoughts (2.2.53). See also 'For many
men that stumble at the threshold /
Are well foretold that danger lurks
within' (*3H6* 4.7.11–12), or 'Three
times today my foot-cloth horse did
stumble, / And started when he looked
upon the Tower, / As loath to bear me
to the slaughterhouse' (*R3* 3.4.83–5).
125–7 after Brooke, 1295–6
126 **grubs** worms

120.1] *Q2–4, F; Enter Fryer with a Lanthorne. Q1*　122 SD] *this edn*　123+ SP] *Q4; Man. at 123,
128, 129, 130, 131 (Q2–3, Q1, F), 137*

328

If I did stay to look on his intents.

FRIAR LAURENCE

Stay then, I'll go alone. Fear comes upon me. 135
O, much I fear some ill unthrifty thing.

BALTHASAR

As I did sleep under this yew tree here,
I dreamt my master and another fought,
And that my master slew him. *[Exit.]*

FRIAR LAURENCE   Romeo!

Friar stoops and looks on the blood and weapons.

Alack, alack, what blood is this which stains 140
The stony entrance of this sepulchre?
What mean these masterless and gory swords
To lie discoloured by this place of peace?
Romeo! O, pale! Who else? What, Paris too,
And steeped in blood? Ah, what an unkind hour 145
Is guilty of this lamentable chance!
The lady stirs.   *Juliet rises.*

JULIET

O comfortable Friar, where is my lord?
I do remember well where I should be,
And there I am. Where is my Romeo? 150

135 **Fear** See also the Friar's line and behaviour at 159. Laurence here briefly resembles Brooke's tainted Friar rather than Shakespeare's, who is intrepid and resourceful.

136 **unthrifty** harmful

137–9 **As . . . him** Balthasar fearfully shrouds his account of what he witnessed in a dream, presumably lest his failure to intervene in the fatal fight rebound on him.

137 *****yew** See 3n.

143 **discoloured** stained (with blood, whence *gory*, 142)

145 **unkind** ùnkind, unnatural, evil

147 SD *****Juliet wakes from her drugged sleep to find herself next to Romeo and Paris, both dead, side by side. She does not acknowledge Paris' presence and fails to spot Romeo at first.

148 **comfortable** comforting, reassuring

150 **Where . . . Romeo?** As the Friar points out, Romeo is right there next to her (*in thy bosom*, 155). Juliet fails to spot him because she is still drowsy from the Friar's draught; the tentative dialogue provides the clue to her gradual awakening.

135 Fear comes] *Q2–4*; feares comes *F; var. Q1*   136 unthrifty] *Q2*; unluckie *Q3–4* (vnluckie *Q3*), *F; not in Q1*   137 SP] *Q2–4, F; not in Q1*   yew] *Pope*; yong *Q2–4, F; not in Q1*   139 SD1] *this edn*   SD2] *Q1; not in Q2–4, F*   147 SD] *Q1; not in Q2–4, F*

FRIAR LAURENCE

    I hear some noise. Lady, come from that nest

    Of death, contagion and unnatural sleep.

    A greater power than we can contradict

    Hath thwarted our intents. Come, come away.

    Thy husband in thy bosom there lies dead,   155

    And Paris too. Come, I'll dispose of thee

    Among a sisterhood of holy nuns.

    Stay not to question, for the watch is coming.

    Come, go, good Juliet. I dare no longer stay.   159

JULIET

    Go, get thee hence, for I will not away.   *Exit* [*Friar*].

    What's here? A cup closed in my true love's hand?

    Poison, I see, hath been his timeless end.

    O churl, drunk all, and left no friendly drop

    To help me after? I will kiss thy lips.

    Haply some poison yet doth hang on them   165

    To make me die with a restorative.   [*Kisses him.*]

    Thy lips are warm!

Enter Paris' Page *and* Watchmen.

CHIEF WATCHMAN

    Lead, boy. Which way?

JULIET

    Yea, noise? Then I'll be brief. O happy dagger!

---

156 **Paris too** i.e. close to Romeo; see
144.
162 **timeless** untimely, but also eternal
163 **churl** miser, niggard (*OED* 6); spoken affectionately, a final melancholy
banter, accusing Romeo of being
too niggardly to leave anything for
Juliet

164 **help me after** assist me in
committing suicide to follow
you
165 **Haply** perhaps
166 **restorative** because a kiss, though
fatal, would reunite her with him; see
quick (120).
168 SP *See List of Roles, 30n.

160 SD] *Dyce; Exit. Q2–4, F (after 159); not in Q1*   163 drunk] *Q2;* drinke *Q3–4, F, Q1*   left] *Q2–4,*
F; leaue *Q1* 166 SD] *Capell* 167.1] *this edn; Enter Boy and Watch. Q2–4, F; Enter watch. Q1 (after*
166)   168 SP] *Hoppe subst.; Watch. Q2–4, F, Q1; 1. W. / Capell*

[*Takes Romeo's dagger.*]
This is thy sheath; there rust, and let me die.   170
She stabs herself, falls [*and dies*].

PAGE
This is the place, there where the torch doth burn.
CHIEF WATCHMAN
The ground is bloody. Search about the churchyard.
Go, some of you; whoe'er you find, attach.
[*Exeunt some of the Watch.*]
Pitiful sight! Here lies the County slain,
And Juliet bleeding, warm and newly dead,   175
Who here hath lain this two days buried.

<hr>

169 SD *The dagger is probably Romeo's, because of 203–4 and Brooke, who notes that 'she with Romeus' knife, / When she awakes, herself (alas) she slaith' (Argument, 13–14). Since at least the 18th century Juliets have often resorted to weapons of their own, including hairpins (Sprague, 318–89); see also Duncan-Jones, 'Dagger', 314–15.

170 **rust** Q2's reading is supported by a number of editions, though in the past it was widely rejected in favour of Q1's 'Rest', an echo perhaps of Romeo's *everlasting rest* at 110, underlining the lovers' convergence. But *rust* picks up the bloodstained (*discoloured*) weapons of 143, and the image of the dagger 'rusting' inside Juliet is singularly and characteristically visceral (cf. e.g. 3.3.73–137). Her fervent hope is that Romeo's dagger will never again be used, that she may forever be its sole sheath, her sexually suggestive metaphor a searing parody of the only union their parents' feud will allow. With *rust* and blood here, compare 'And this thy son's blood, cleaving to my blade, / Shall rust upon my weapon till thy blood / Congealed with this do make

me wipe off both' (*3H6* 1.3.50–2).
let me die Brook (1947) cut straight from here to 305 (*A glooming peace*) and attributed the closing lines to the Chorus rather than the Prince as in Shakespeare. Bodganov cut to Escalus speaking the first eight lines of the play's transposed opening chorus, artfully adjusting its verbs into the past tense.

173 **attach** arrest

176 **this two days** The phrase suggests confusedly that the scene takes place in the early hours of Friday morning, two days on from Wednesday when Juliet was buried, thus roughly agreeing with the Friar's promise at 4.1.105 that his sleeping draught would last for 42 hours. Q1 similarly has '*Iuliet* two daies buried' and 'intoombd two dayes'. Other time pointers, however, firmly anchor the action here in the early hours of Thursday morning, implying that the Watchman is talking distractedly or generically, that is, he may mean 'only recently' or 'within the last two days'; see pp. 29–31. On *this* for 'these', see 5.2.24n.; Cam² calls *two days* a 'collective singular'.
buried burièd

169 SD] *Oxf* 170 This is] *Q2, Q4*; Tis is *Q3*; 'Tis in *F; var. Q1* rust] *Q2–4, F*; Rest *Q1* SD] *Oxf; Kils herselfe. F; She stabs herselfe and falles. Enter watch. Q1; not in Q2–4* 172 SP] *Hoppe subst.; Watch. Q2–4, F; var. Q1; 1. W. / Capell* 173 SD] *Hanmer*

Go, tell the Prince, run to the Capulets,
Raise up the Montagues. Some others search.

[Exeunt others of the Watch.]

We see the ground whereon these woes do lie,
But the true ground of all these piteous woes   180
We cannot without circumstance descry.

Enter one [of the Watch] *with Romeo's man* [BALTHASAR].

2 WATCHMAN

Here's Romeo's man. We found him in the churchyard.

CHIEF WATCHMAN

Hold him in safety till the Prince come hither.

Enter FRIAR LAURENCE *and another* Watchman.

3 WATCHMAN

Here is a friar that trembles, sighs and weeps.
We took this mattock and this spade from him   185
As he was coming from this churchyard's side.

CHIEF WATCHMAN

A great suspicion! Stay the friar too.

Enter the PRINCE *and Attendants.*

PRINCE

What misadventure is so early up,
That calls our person from our morning rest?

---

180 **ground** playing on the meanings 'earth' and 'reason (for)'
181 **circumstance** proper information **descry** perceive, discern
183 **safety** custody

186 **this churchyard's side** this side of the churchyard (Hoppe)
187 **A great suspicion** strong grounds for suspicion
Stay keep under guard

178 SD] *Capell*   181.1] *Q1 subst. (Enter one with Romets Man.); Enter Romeos man. Q2–4, F*   182
SP] *Rowe; Watch. Q2–4, F; I. Q1*   183.1] *Q2–4, F; Enter one with the Fryer. Q1*   184 SP] *Q2–4, F
(3. Watch.); I. Q1*   186 churchyard's] *Q2;* Church-yard *Q3–4, F; not in Q1*   187 SP] *Q2–4 (Chief.
watch.); Con. F; Cap: Q1; 1. W. / Capell* too] *F;* too too *Q2–4; not in Q1*   187.1] *Rowe; Enter the
Prince Q2–4, F; Enter the Prince with others. Q1*

Enter CAPULET *and his* WIFE.

CAPULET

What should it be that is so shrieked abroad?   190

CAPULET'S WIFE

O, the people in the street cry 'Romeo',
Some 'Juliet', and some 'Paris', and all run
With open outcry toward our monument.

PRINCE

What fear is this which startles in your ears?

CHIEF WATCHMAN

Sovereign, here lies the County Paris slain,   195
And Romeo dead, and Juliet, dead before,
Warm and new killed.

PRINCE

Search, seek, and know how this foul murder comes.

CHIEF WATCHMAN

Here is a friar, and slaughtered Romeo's man,
With instruments upon them fit to open   200
These dead men's tombs.

CAPULET

O heavens! O wife, look how our daughter bleeds!
This dagger hath mista'en, for lo, his house
Is empty on the back of Montague,
And is mis-sheathed in my daughter's bosom.   205

---

194 **startles** springs up; cf. 'Patience herself would startle at this letter' (*AYL* 4.3.13).

199 ***slaughtered** after Q4; Q2 reads 'Slaughter *Romeos* man'. The capital letter and lack of a participle marker suggest that the compositor thought 'Slaughter' was the name of Romeo's servant. Williams suggests that the MS may have read 'Slaughterd', which the compositor misread as 'Slaughtere', a man's name, and set without the finale *e* (GWW, private communication).

203 **house** i.e. scabbard

205 **mis-sheathed** mis-sheathèd

189.1] *Q4, F, Q1; Enter Capels Q2–3*   190 is so shrieked] *Daniel subst.;* is so shrike *Q2;* they so shrike *Q3–4, F*   191 SP] *Oxf; Wife. Q2–4, F; Moth: Q1*   193 our] *Q2–4, F;* out *F; not in Q1*   194 your] *Q2–4, F;* our *Capell*   195, 199 SPs] *Hoppe (Chief Watch); Watch. Q2–4; Wat. F; Capt: Q1; 1. W. / Capell*   199 slaughtered] *Q4, F;* Slaughter *Q2–3; not in Q1*   201 tombs.] *Q4, F;* Tombes. *Enter Capulet and his wife. Q2–3*   202 heavens!] *Q2;* heaven *Q3–4, F; not in Q1*   205 is] *Q3–4, F;* it *Q2;* it is *Q1*

CAPULET'S WIFE

O me, this sight of death is as a bell
That warns my old age to a sepulchre.

Enter MONTAGUE *[and Attendants].*

PRINCE

Come, Montague, for thou art early up
To see thy son and heir now early down.

MONTAGUE

Alas, my liege, my wife is dead tonight; 210
Grief of my son's exile hath stopped her breath.
What further woe conspires against mine age?

PRINCE

Look, and thou shalt see.

MONTAGUE

O thou untaught! What manners is in this,
To press before thy father to a grave? 215

PRINCE

Seal up the mouth of outrage for a while,
Till we can clear these ambiguities
And know their spring, their head, their true descent,
And then will I be general of your woes
And lead you even to death. Meantime forbear, 220

---

207 **warns** summons (*OED* 7a); see *R3*
1.3.39.
old age even though she appears to
be only 26 or 27 years old; see List of
Roles, 3n. She has aged instantly, ready
to die from a broken heart, matching
the fate of Romeo's mother (210).
210 **my . . . dead** a significant departure
from Brooke (or Painter), where there
is no reference to Romeo's mother's
death. In Q1 Montague says 'Dread
Soueregine, my Wife is dead to night,
/ And young *Benuolio* is deceased too'

(20.143–4). Dessen notes that in Q1
'the wiping out of the younger generation is complete' ('Q1', 113).
214 **untaught** unmannerly; addressed to
the dead Romeo for predeceasing his
father
215 **press before** hasten on ahead of
216 **outrage** angry language, fury
(Onions)
219 **general** the commander
220 **even to death** even if it should mean
death (the penalty threatened to the
families and their retainers at 1.1.95)

---

206 SP] *Oxf; Wife. Q2, F; Wi. Q3–4; not in Q1* 207.1 *Enter* MONTAGUE] *Q2–4; Enter olde Montague. Q1
and Attendants] Capell subst.* 209 now early] *Q3–4, F; now earling Q2; more early Q1* 212 mine] *Q2; my
Q3–4; var. Q1* 214 is in] *Q2–4, Q1; in is F* 216 the mouth] *Q2–3, F; the moneth Q4; your mouthes Q1*

And let mischance be slave to patience.
Bring forth the parties of suspicion.

FRIAR LAURENCE

I am the greatest, able to do least,
Yet most suspected, as the time and place
Doth make against me, of this direful murder.   235
And here I stand, both to impeach and purge,
Myself condemned and myself excused.

PRINCE

Then say at once what thou dost know in this.

FRIAR LAURENCE

I will be brief, for my short date of breath
Is not so long as is a tedious tale.   230
Romeo, there dead, was husband to that Juliet,
And she, there dead, that's Romeo's faithful wife.
I married them, and their stol'n marriage day
Was Tybalt's doomsday, whose untimely death
Banished the new-made bridegroom from this city;   235
For whom, and not for Tybalt, Juliet pined.
You, to remove that siege of grief from her,
Betrothed and would have married her perforce
To County Paris. Then comes she to me,
And with wild looks bid me devise some mean   240
To rid her from this second marriage,
Or in my cell there would she kill herself.
Then gave I her, so tutored by my art,
A sleeping potion, which so took effect
As I intended, for it wrought on her   245

---

221 **let . . . patience** 'bear your sorrows with fortitude'
222 **parties of suspicion** suspects
223 **the . . . least** the chief suspect, yet least able to help
225 **direful** terrible

226 **impeach** discredit; see similarly *MND* 2.1.214–19.
227 **condemned** condemnèd
229 **my . . . breath** the little life left me
233 **stol'n** surreptitious
237 **siege of grief** charge of pain

232 that's] *Q2–3, F;* that *Q4; var. Q1*   240 mean] *Q2;* meanes *Q3–4, F; var. Q1*

The form of death. Meantime I writ to Romeo
That he should hither come as this dire night
To help to take her from her borrowed grave,
Being the time the potion's force should cease.
But he which bore my letter, Friar John,   250
Was stayed by accident, and yesternight
Returned my letter back. Then, all alone,
At the prefixed hour of her waking
Came I to take her from her kindred's vault,
Meaning to keep her closely at my cell   255
Till I conveniently could send to Romeo.
But when I came, some minute ere the time
Of her awakening, here untimely lay
The noble Paris and true Romeo dead.
She wakes, and I entreated her come forth   260
And bear this work of heaven with patience.
But then a noise did scare me from the tomb,
And she, too desperate, would not go with me,
But, as it seems, did violence on herself.
All this I know, and to the marriage   265
Her nurse is privy; and if aught in this
Miscarried by my fault, let my old life
Be sacrificed some hour before his time
Unto the rigour of severest law.

PRINCE
We still have known thee for a holy man.   270

246 **form** semblance
247 **as** probably a redundant *as* used
with definitions of time, according to
Abbott (114), who compares 'This is
my birthday: as this very day / Was
Cassius born' (*JC* 5.1.71–2). Perhaps
as here functions rather the way 'of'
would in this same position, as in 'of
an evening' for 'one evening'.

251 **stayed** stopped
253 **prefixed** prefixèd
     hour (two syllables; see 'hower' in Q2)
255 **closely** covertly, secretly (*OED* 3
     compares 'For we have closely sent for
     Hamlet hither', *Ham* 3.1.29)
261 **patience** patìence (three syllables)
268 **his** its
270 **still** always

258 awakening] *Q2;* awaking *Q3–4, F; not in Q1*   262 scare] *Q2–4;* scarre *F; not in Q1*   265–8] *Pope;*
Q2–4, F line priuie: / fault, / time, / ; *not in Q1*   268 his] *Q2, Q1;* the *Q3–4, F*

Where's Romeo's man? What can he say to this?

BALTHASAR

I brought my master news of Juliet's death,
And then in post he came from Mantua
To this same place, to this same monument.
This letter he early bid me give his father,   275
And threatened me with death, going in the vault,
If I departed not and left him there.

PRINCE

Give me the letter; I will look on it.
Where is the County's page that raised the watch?
Sirrah, what made your master in this place?   280

PAGE

He came with flowers to strew his lady's grave,
And bid me stand aloof, and so I did.
Anon comes one with light to ope the tomb,
And by and by my master drew on him.
And then I ran away to call the watch.   285

PRINCE

This letter doth make good the Friar's words,
Their course of love, the tidings of her death.
And here he writes that he did buy a poison
Of a poor pothecary, and therewithal
Came to this vault, to die and lie with Juliet.   290
Where be these enemies? Capulet, Montague,
See what a scourge is laid upon your hate,
That heaven finds means to kill your joys with love;
And I, for winking at your discords too,
Have lost a brace of kinsmen. All are punished.   295

---

273 **in post** in haste
275 **early** i.e. first thing in the morning
284 **by and by** at once
286 **make good** bear out
289 **pothecary** aphetic form of 'apoth-ecary', probably to complete the alliterative pattern of *poison*, *poor* and *pothecary*

293 **kill . . . love** 'destroy your happi-ness through your children's love for each other'; or 'destroy your children (*joys*) through *love*' (a tragically ironic punishment for your *hate*, 292)
294 **winking . . . discords** shutting my eyes to the full gravity of your feud
295 **brace** pair (i.e. Mercutio and Paris)

CAPULET

O brother Montague, give me thy hand.
This is my daughter's jointure, for no more
Can I demand.

MONTAGUE   But I can give thee more,
For I will raise her statue in pure gold,
That whiles Verona by that name is known,   300
There shall no figure at such rate be set
As that of true and faithful Juliet.

CAPULET

As rich shall Romeo's by his lady's lie,
Poor sacrifices of our enmity.

PRINCE

A glooming peace this morning with it brings.   305
The sun for sorrow will not show his head.
Go hence, to have more talk of these sad things.
Some shall be pardoned and some punished,
For never was a story of more woe   309
Than this of Juliet and her Romeo.   [*Exeunt.*]

297 **jointure** The only marriage settlement Capulet can now offer for
   his daughter is an extended hand of
   friendship.
299 ***raise** cause to be erected; see
   Brooke: 'The bodies dead removed
   from vault where they did die, / In
   stately tomb, on pillars great, of marble raise they high' (3013–14).
301 **at . . . set** be so highly esteemed
303 i.e. Capulet will in turn provide a
   golden statue of Romeo to match
   Juliet's as he rests by her side.

305 **glooming** dark, overcast; the final
   of the play's dawns is also the most
   cheerless.
308 Brooke reports that Nurse is banished for hiding Juliet's marriage from
   her parents, whence 'a mischief great
   is grown' (2987–90), and the apothecary 'high is hanged by the throat'
   (2993). Friar Laurence, however, is
   granted a free pardon; he becomes
   a hermit and dies five years later
   (2995–3005).
   punished punishèd

299 raise] *Q4, F;* raie *Q2–3;* erect *Q1*   301 such] *Q2, Q1;* that *Q3–4, F*   303 Romeo's . . . lady's]
Q2–4; Romeo . . . Lady *F, Q1*   305 glooming] *Q2–4, F;* gloomie *Q1*   310 SD] *F (Exeunt omnes.);*
not in Q2–4, Q1

APPENDIX 1

Q1 AND Q4 READINGS

Q1 READINGS

The following is a list of significant Q1 readings accepted in this edition. The uniquely important Q1 SDs, almost all of which feature in the text, are discussed separately on pp. 110–11. Q1 SPs are not listed; neither are Q1 line arrangements adopted in the edition, nor lines imported into it from Q1 such as, for example, 1.4.7–8 or 4.5.124.

in] *Q1, Q4; not in Q2–3, F* (1.1.26)
create] *Q1;* created *Q2–4, F* (1.1.175)
married] *Q1;* made *Q2–4, F* (1.2.13)
written here] *Q1;* written. Here *Q2–4, F* (1.2.37–8)
and] *Q1; not in Q2–4, F* (1.2.69)
thee] *Q1;* you *Q2–4, F* (1.2.78)
seems] *Q1–2;* shewes *Q3–4, F* (1.2.100)
shall] *Q1, Q3–4, F;* stal *Q2* (1.3.18)
honour] *Q1;* houre *Q2–4 (houre 68), F* (1.3.67, 68)
it] *Q1 Q4; not in Q2–3, F* (1.3.100)
atomi] *Q1;* ottamie *Q2;* atomies *Q3–4, F* (1.4.57)
maid] *Q1;* man *Q2–4, F* (1.4.69)
breaths] *Q1;* breath *Q2–4, F* (1.4.76)
elf-locks] *Q1, Q4;* Elklocks *Q2–3, F* (1.4.90)
antic] *Q1 (Anticke);* anticque *Q2;* antique *Q3–4, F* (1.5.55)
ready] *Q1;* did readie *Q2–4, F* (1.5.94)
pronounce] *Q1, Q4;* prouaunt *Q2–3, F;* Couply *F2;* couple *Rowe* (2.1.10)
dove] *Q1;* day *Q2–3, F;* die *Q4* (2.1.10)
heir] *Q1, Q4;* her *Q2–3, F* (2.1.12)
trim] *Q1;* true *Q2–4, F* (2.1.13)
eyes] *Q1;* eye *Q2–4, F* (2.2.20)
pilot] *Q1, Q3–4, F;* Pylat *Q2* (2.2.82)
washed] *Q1, Q4;* washeth *Q2;* washet *Q3, F* (2.2.83)
haviour] *Q1;* behauiour *Q2–4, F* (2.2.99)
cunning] *Q1;* coying *Q2–3, F;* more coying *Q4;* more coyning *F2;* the coyning *Williams* (2.2.101)
circled] *Q1, Q3–4, F;* circle *Q2* (2.2.110)
fantasticoes] *Q1;* phantacies *Q2–4, F;* phantacimes *Williams (Crow)* (2.4.29)
jaunt] *Q1, Q4, F;* iaunce *Q2–3* (2.5.26)
Capels are] *Q1; Capels Q2–3;* Capulets *Q4, F* (3.1.2)
Alla stoccado] *Q1; Alla stucatho Q2–4, F;* Alla stoccata *Knight* (3.1.73)
Alive] *Q1;* He gan *Q2;* He gon *Q3–4, F;* Again? *Capell;* He yare *Williams* (3.1.124)
fire-eyed] *Q1;* fier end *Q2;* fier and *Q3;* fire and *Q4, F* (3.1.126)
agile] *Q1, Q4;* aged *Q2–3, F;* able *F2;* agent *Oxf (McKerrow)* (3.1.168)

hates'] *Q1;* hearts *Q2–4, F* (3.1.190)
I] *Q1, Q4;* It *Q2–3, F* (3.1.194)
Hence] *Q1;* Here *Q2–4, F* (3.3.15)
Thou] *Q1, Q4;* Then *Q2–3, F* (3.3.52)
men] *Q1, Q3–4, F;* man *Q2* (3.3.61)
Where is] *Q1;* Where's *Q2–4, F* (3.3.82)
denote] *Q1, Q4, F;* deuote *Q2–3* (3.3.109)
talked] *Q1 (*talkt*);* talke *Q2–4, F* (4.1.7)
cure] *Q1;* care *Q2–4, F* (4.1.45)
slay] *Q1, Q4;* stay *Q2–3, F* (4.1.72)
off] *Q1;* of *Q2–4, F* (4.1.78)
chapless] *Q1, Q4;* chapels *Q2–3, F* (4.1.83)
breath] *Q1, Q3–4, F;* breast *Q2* (4.1.98)
long] *Q1, Q3–4, F;* loue *Q2* (4.5.41)
defy you] *Pope;* denie you *Q2–4, F;* defie my *Q1* (5.1.24)
pay] *Q1, Q4;* pray *Q2–3, F* (5.1.76)

Q4 READINGS

Of the readings unique to Q4, seven are adopted in addition to six Q4 SPs:

well-seeming] *Q4;* welseeing *Q2–3, F;* best seeming *Q1* (1.1.177)
damned] *Q4;* dimme *Q2–3;* dimne *F; not in Q1* (3.2.79)
pouts upon] *Q4 (*powts vpon*);* puts vp *Q2–3;* puttest vp *F;* frownst vpon *Q1* (3.3.143)
shroud] *Q4;* graue *F; not in Q2–3; var. Q1;* tomb *Williams* (4.1.85)
wake] *Q4;* walke *Q2–3, F; not in Q1* (4.3.49)
faith] *Q4;* father *Q2–3, F; not in Q1* (4.4.20)
raise] *Q4, F;* raie *Q2–3;* erect *Q1* (5.3.299)

MERCUTIO] *Q4; Horatio. Q2–3; Hora. F* (1.4.23)
MONTAGUE] *Q4; Capu. Q2; Cap: Q3, F (Cap.); La. Mont. / Theobald; not in Q1* (3.1.186)
NURSE] *Q4; not in Q2–3, F, Q1* (3.5.173)
PETER] *Q4; 2. M. Q2–3, F; not in Q1* (4.5.120)
PAGE] *Q4; not in Q2–3; Pet. F; Boy: Q1* (5.3.71)
BALTHASAR] *Q4; Man. at 5.3.123, 128, 129, 130, 131 (Q2–3, Q1, F), 137 (Q2, F)* (5.3.123+)

APPENDIX 2

Q1 *ROMEO AND JULIET*

Reproduced in facsimile by courtesy of the British Library
Board (BL C.34.k.55 © The British Library Board)

Line numbering conforms to the Malone Society Reprint facsimile edition of
the copy in the Huntington Library, ed. Jill L. Levenson and Barry Gaines,
and checked by Thomas L. Berger and G.R. Proudfoot (Oxford, 2000).

A N
EXCELLENT,
conceited Tragedie
O F
R omeo and Iuliet.

As it hath been often (with great applause)
plaid publiquely, by the right Honourable the L. of *Hunsdon*
his Seruants.

LONDON,
Printed by Iohn Danter.
1 5 9 7

The Prologue.

Two houſhold Frends alike in dignitie,
(In faire Verona, *where we lay our Scene)*
From ciuill broyles broke into enmitie,
VVhoſe ciuill warre makes ciuill hands vncleane.
From forth the fatall loynes of theſe two foes,
A paire of ſtarre-croſt Louers tooke their life :
VVhoſe miſaduentures, piteous ouerthrowes,
(Through the continuing of their Fathers ſtrife,
And death-markt paſſage of their Parents rage.)
Is now the two howres traffique of our Stage.
The which if you with patient eares attend,
VVhat here we want wee'l ſtudie to amend.

The moſt excellent Tragedie of
Romeo and Iuliet.

Enter 2. Seruing-men of the Capolets.

Gʳ *Regorie,* of my word Ile carrie no coales.

2 No, for if you doo, you ſhould be a Collier.

1 If I be in choler, Ile draw.

2 Euer while you liue, drawe your necke out of the
the collar.

1 I ſtrike quickly being moou'd.

2 I, but you are not quickly moou'd to ſtrike.

1 A Dog of the houſe of the *Mountagues* moues me.

2 To mooue is to ſtirre, and to bee valiant is to ſtand
to it : therefore (of my word) if thou be mooud thou't
runne away.

1 There's not a man of them I meete, but Ile take
the wall of.

2 That ſhewes thee a weakling, for the weakeſt goes
to the wall.

1 Thats true, therefore Ile thruſt the men from the
wall, and thruſt the maids to the walls : nay, thou ſhalt
ſee I am a tall peece of fleſh.

2 Tis well thou art not fiſh, for if thou wert thou
wouldſt be but poore Iohn.

1 Ile play the tyrant, Ile firſt begin with the maids, &
off with their heads.

2 The heads of the maids?

The most excellent Tragedie,

1 I the heades of their Maides, or the Maidenheades, take it in what fence thou wilt.

2 Nay let them take it in fence that feele it, but heere comes two of the *Mountagues.*

Enter two Seruingmen of the Mountagues.

1 Nay feare not me I warrant thee.

2 I feare them no more than thee, but draw.

1 Nay let vs haue the law on our fide, let them begin firft. Ile tell thee what Ile doo, as I goe by ile bite my thumbe, which is difgrace enough if they fuffer it.

2 Content, goe thou by and bite thy thumbe, and ile come after and frowne.

1 *Moun:* Doo you bite your thumbe at vs?

1 I bite my thumbe.

2 *Moun:* I but i'ft at vs?

1 I bite my thumbe, is the law on our fide?

2 No.

1 I bite my thumbe.

1 *Moun:* I but i'ft at vs?   *Enter Beneuolio.*

2 Say I, here comes my Mafters kinfman.

They draw, to them enters Tybalt *, they fight , to them the Prince, old* Mountague, *and his wife , old* Capulet *and his wife, and other Citizens and part them.*

1 *Prince:* Rebellious fubiects enemies to peace,
On paine of torture, from thofe bloody handes
Throw your miftempered weapons to the ground.
Three Ciuell brawles bred of an airie word,
By the old *Capulet* and *Mountague,*
Haue thrice difturbd the quiet of our ftreets.
If euer you difturbe our ftreets againe,

                   Your

of Romeo and Iuliet.

Your liues fhall pay the ranfome of your fault:
For this time euery man depart in peace.
Come *Capulet* come you along with me,
And *Mountague*, come you this after noone,
To know our farther pleafure in this cafe,
To old free Towne our common iudgement place,
Once more on paine of death each man depart.

                           Exeunt.

  M: wife. Who fet this auncient quarrel firft abroach?
Speake Nephew, were you by when it began?
  Benuo : Here were the feruants of your aduerfaries,
And yours clofe fighting ere I did approch.
  VVife: Ah where is *Romeo*, faw you him to day?
Right glad I am he was not at this fray.
  Ben : Madame, an houre before the worfhipt funne
Peept through the golden window of the Eaft,
A troubled thought drew me from companie:
Where vnderneath the groue *Sicamoure*,
That Weftward rooteth from the Cities fide,
So early walking might I fee your fonne.
I drew towards him, but he was ware of me,
And drew into the thicket of the wood:
I noting his affeétions by mine owne,
That moft are bufied when th'are moft alone,
Purfued my honor, not purfuing his.
  Moun: Black and portentious muft this honor proue,
Vnleffe good counfaile doo the caufe remooue.
  Ben : Why tell me Vncle do you know the caufe?

             Enter Romeo.

  Moun: I neyther know it nor can learne of him.
  Ben : See where he is, but ftand you both afide,
Ile know his grieuance, or be much denied.

             B   *Moun*

The most excellent Tragedie,

Mount: I would thou wert so happie by thy stay
To heare true shrift, Come Madame lets away.
 Benuo: Good morrow Cosen.
 Romeo: Is the day so young?
 Ben : But new stroke nine.
 Romeo: Ay me, sad hopes seeme long.
Was that my Father that went hence so fast?
 Ben : It was, what sorrow lengthens *Romeos* houres?
 Rom: Not hauing that, which hauing makes them
 Ben : In loue.   (short.
 Ro: Out.
 Ben: Of loue.
 Ro : Out of her fauor where I am in loue.
 Ben : Alas that loue so gentle in her view,
Should be so tyrranous and rough in proofe.
 Ro : Alas that loue whose view is muffled still,
Should without lawes giue path-waies to our will:
Where shall we dine? Gods me, what fray was here?
Yet tell me not for I haue heard it all,
Heres much to doe with hate, but more with loue,
Why then, O brawling loue, O louing hate,
O anie thing, of nothing first create!
O heauie lightnes serious vanitie!
Mishapen *Caus* of best seeming thinges,
Feather of lead, bright smoke, cold fire, sicke health,
Still waking sleepe, that is not what it is:
This loue feele I, which feele no loue in this.
Doest thou not laugh?
 Ben: No Cose I rather weepe.
 Rom: Good hart at what?
 Ben: At thy good hearts oppression.
 Ro: Why such is loues transgression,
            Griefes

of Romeo and Iuliet.

Griefes of mine owne lie heauie at my hart,
Which thou wouldſt propagate to haue them preſt
With more of thine, this griefe that thou haſt ſhowne,
Doth ad more griefe to too much of mine owne:
Loue is a ſmoke raiſde with the fume of ſighes
Being purgde, a fire ſparkling in louers eyes:
Being vext, a ſea raging with a louers teares.
What is it elſe? A madnes moſt diſcreet,
A choking gall, and a preſeruing ſweet. Farewell Coſe.

Ben: Nay Ile goe along.
And if you hinder me you doo me wrong.

Ro: Tut I haue loſt my ſelfe I am not here,
This is not *Romeo*, hee's ſome other where.

Ben: Tell me in ſadnes whome ſhe is you loue?

Ro: What ſhall I grone and tell thee?

Ben: Why no, but ſadly tell me who.

Ro: Bid a ſickman in ſadnes make his will,
Ah word ill vrgde to one that is ſo ill.
In ſadnes Coſen I doo loue a woman.

Ben: I aimde ſo right, when as you ſaid you lou'd.

Ro: A right good mark-man, and ſhee's faire I loue.

Ben: A right faire marke faire Coſe is ſooneſt hit.

Ro: But in that hit you miſſe, ſhee'le not be hit
With *Cupids* arrow, ſhe hath *Dianaes* wit,
And in ſtrong proofe of chaſtitie well arm'd:
Gainſt *Cupids* childiſh bow ſhe liues vnharm'd,
Shee'le not abide the ſiedge of louing tearmes,
Nor ope her lap to Saint ſeducing gold,
Ah ſhe is rich in beautie, only poore,
That when ſhe dies with beautie dies her ſtore. *Exem.*

Enter Countie Paris, *old* Capulet.
Of honorable reckoning are they both,

B 2

And

The most excellent Tragedie,

And pittie tis they liue at ods fo long:
But leauing that, what fay you to my fute?

  Capu: What fhould I fay more than I faid before,
My daughter is a ftranger in the world,
Shee hath not yet attainde to fourteene yeares:
Let two more fommers wither in their pride,
Before fhe can be thought fit for a Bride.

  Paris: Younger than fhe are happie mothers made.

  Cap: But too foone marde are thefe fo early maried:
But wooe her gentle *Paris*, get her heart,
My word to her confent is but a part,
This night I hold an old accuftom'd Feaft,
Whereto I haue inuited many a gueft,
Such as I loue: yet you among the ftore,
One more moft welcome makes the number more.
At my poore houfe you fhall behold this night,
Earth treadding ftars, that make darke heauen light:
Such comfort as doo lufty youngmen feele,
When well apparaild Aprill on the heele
Of limping winter treads, euen fuch delights
Amongft frefh female buds fhall you this night
Inherit at my houfe, heare all, all fee,
And like her moft, whofe merite moft fhalbe.
Such amongft view of many myne beeing one,
May ftand in number though in reckoning none.

  Enter Seruingman.
Where are you firra, goe trudge about
Through faire *Verona* ftreets, and feeke them out:
Whofe names are written here and to them fay,
My houfe and welcome at their pleafure ftay.

  Exeunt.

  Ser: Seeke them out whofe names are written here,
  and

of Romeo and Iuliet.

and yet I knowe not who are written here: I muſt to
the learned to learne of them, that's as much to ſay, as
the Taylor muſt meddle with his Laſte, the Shoomaker
with his needle, the Painter with his nets, and the Fiſher
with his Peaſill, I muſt to the learned.

Enter Benuolio and Romeo.

Ben: Tut man one fire burnes out anothers burning
One paine is leſſned with anothers anguiſh:
Turne backward, and be holp with backward turning,
One deſperate griefe cures with anothers languiſh.
Take thou ſome new infection to thy eye,
And the ranke poyſon of the old will die.

Romeo: Your Planton leaſe is excellent for that.

Ben : For what?

Romeo: For your broken ſhin.

Ben: Why *Romeo* art thou mad?

Rom: Not mad, but bound more than a mad man is.
Shut vp in priſon, kept without my foode,
Whipt and tormented, and Godden good fellow.

Ser: Godgigoden, I pray ſir can you read,

Rom : I mine owne fortune in my miſerie.

Ser : Perhaps you haue learned it without booke:
but I pray can you read any thing you ſee?

Rom: I if I know the letters and the language.

Seru: Yee ſay honeſtly, reſt you merrie.

Rom: Stay fellow I can read.

He reads the Letter.

SEigneur Martino *and his wife and daughters,* Countie
Anſelme *and his beauteous ſiſters, the* Ladie widdow *of*
Vtruuio, Seigneur Placentio, *and his louelie* Neeces,
Mercutio *and his brother* Valentine, *mine vncle* Capu-
let *his wife and daughters,* my *faire* Neece Roſaline *and*
Liuia.

B 2.

351

The most excellent Tragedie,

Liuia, Seigneur Valentio *and his Cosen* Tibalt , Lucio
and the liuelie Hellena.
A faire assembly, whether should they come?
  Ser: Vp.
  Ro: Whether to supper?
  Ser: To our house.
  Ro: Whose house?
  Ser: My Masters.
  Ro: Indeed I should haue askt thee that before.
  Ser: Now il'e tel you without asking. My Master is
the great rich *Capulet*, and if you be not of the house of
Mountagues, I pray come and crush a cup of wine. Rest
you merrie.
  Ben: At this same auncient feast of *Capulets*,
Sups the faire R*osaline* whom thou so loues:
With all the admired beauties of *Verona*,
Goe thither and with vnattainted eye,
Compare her face with some that I shall shew,
And I will make thee thinke thy swan a crow.
  Ro: When the deuout religion of mine eye
Maintaines such falshood, then turne teares to fire,
And these who often drownde could neuer die,
Transparent Heretiques be burnt for liers
One fairer than my loue, the all seeing sonne
Nere saw her match, since first the world begun.
  Ben: Tut you saw her faire none els being by,
Her selfe poysd with her selfe in either eye:
But in that Cristall scales let there be waide,
Your Ladyes loue, against some other maide
That I will shew you shining at this feast,
And she shall scant shew well that now seemes best.
  Rom: Ile goe along no such sight to be showne,
  But

of Romeo and Iuliet.

But to reioyce in splendor of mine owne.

Enter Capulets wife and Nurse.

Wife: Nurce wher's my daughter call her forth to
mee.

Nurce: *Now by my maiden head at twelue yeare old I
bad her come, what Lamb, what Ladie bird, God forbid,
Wher's this girle? what* Iuliet. *Enter Iuliet.*

Iuliet: How now who cals?

Nurce: Your Mother.

Iul: Madame I am here, what is your will?

Wi: This is the matter, Nurse giue leaue a while, we
must talke in secret. Nurce come back again I haue re-
membred me, thou'se heare our counsaile. Thou know
est my daughters of a prettie age.

Nurce: Faith I can tell her age vnto a houre.

Wife: Shee's not fourteene.

*Nurce: Ile lay fourteene of my teeth, and yet to my
teene be it spoken, I haue but foure, shee's not fourteene.
How long is it now to* Lammas-tide?

Wife: A fortnight and odde dayes.

*Nurce: Euen or odde, of all dayes in the yeare come
Lammas* Eue *at night shall she be fourteene.* Susan *and she
God rest all Christian soules were of an age.* Well Susan *is
with God, she was too good for me: But as I said on* Lammas Eue *at night shall she be fourteene, that shall she ma-
rie I remember it well. 'Tis since the Earth-quake nowe e-
leauen yeares, and she was weind I neuer shall forget it, of
all the daies of the yeare vpon that day: for I had then laid
wormewood to my dug, sitting in the sun vnder the Doue-
house wall. My Lord and you were then at* Mantua, *nay I
do beare a braine: But as I said, when it did tast the wormwood on the nipple of my dug, & felt it bitter, pretty foole*

to

The moſt excellent Tragedie,

to ſee it teachie and fall out with Dugge. Shake queth the
Doue-houſe tⱳas no need I trow to bid me trudge, and ſince
that time it is a leauen yeare: for then could Iuliet *ſtande*
high lone, nay by the Roode, ſhee could haue wadled vp and
downe, for euen the day before ſhee brake her brow, and then
my husband God be with his ſoule, hee was a merrie man:
Doſt thou fall forward Iuliet? *thou wilt fall backward when*
thou haſt more wit: wilt thou not Iuliet? *and by my holli-*
dam, the pretty foole left crying and ſaid I . To ſee how a
ieaſt ſhall come about, I warrant you if I ſhould liue a hun-
dred yeare , I neuer ſhould forget it , wilt thou not Iuliet?
and by my troth ſhe ſtinted and cried I.

Iuliet: And ſtint thou too, I pre thee Nurce ſay I.

Nurce: *VVell goe thy waies , God marke thee for his*
grace, thou wert the prettieſt Babe that euer I nurſt, might
I but liue to ſee thee married once, I haue my wiſh.

VVife: And that ſame marriage Nurce, is the Theame
I meant to talke of: Tell me *Iuliet,* howe ſtand you affected to be married?

Iul: It is an honor that I dreame not off.

Nurce : *An honor ! were not I thy onely Nurce, I*
would ſay thou hadſt ſuckt wiſedome from thy Teat.

VVife: Well girle, the Noble Countie *Paris* ſeekes
thee for his Wife.

Nurce: *A man young Ladie , Ladie ſuch a man as all*
the world, why he is a man of waxe.

VVife: *Veronaes* Summer hath not ſuch a flower.

Nurce: *Nay he is a flower, in faith a very flower.*

VVife: Well *Iuliet,* how like you of *Paris* loue.

Iuliet: Ile looke to like, if looking liking moue,
But no more deepe will I engage mine eye,
Then your conſent giues ſtrength to make it flie.

Enter Clowne.

of *Romeo* and *Iuliet*.

Clowne: Madam you are cald for, supper is readie,
the Nurce curst in the Pantrie, all thinges in extreamitie,
make hast for I must be gone to waite.

Enter Maskers with Romeo *and a Page.*

Ro: What shall this speech bee spoke for our excuse?
Or shall we on without Apologie.

Benuoleo: The date is out of such prolixitie,
Weele haue no *Cupid* hudwinckt with a Scarfe,
Bearing a *Tartars* painted bow of lath,
Scaring the Ladies like a crow-keeper:
Nor no withoutbooke Prologue faintly spoke
After the Prompter, for our entrance.
But let them measure vs by what they will,
Weele measure them a measure and be gone.

Rom: A torch for me I am not for this aumbling,
Beeing but heauie I will beare the light.

Mer: Beleeue me *Romeo* I must haue you daunce.

Rom: Not I beleeue me you haue dancing shooes
With nimble soles, I haue a soule of lead
So stakes me to the ground I cannot stirre.

Mer: Giue me a case to put my visage in,
A visor for a visor, what care I
What curious eye doth coate deformitie.

Rom: Giue me a Torch, let wantons light of hart
Tickle the senceles rushes with their heeles:
For I am prouerbd with a Grandsire phrase,
Ilebe a candleholder and looke on,
The game was nere so faire and I am done.

Mer: Tut dun's the mouse the Cunstables o'ld word
If thou beest Dun, weele draw thee from the mire
Of this surreuerence loue wherein thou stickst.
Leaue this talke, we burne day light here.

C   *Rom:* Nay

The most excellent Tragedie,

  Rom: Nay thats not so.   *Mer:* I meane sir in delay,
Weburne our lights by night, like Lampes by day,
Take our good meaning for our iudgement sits
Three times a day, ere once in her right wits.
  Rom: So welmeane well by going to this maske,
But tis no wit to goe.
    Mer: Why Romeo may one aske?
    Rom: I dreamt a dreame to night.
    Mer: And so did I.   *Rom:* Why what was yours?
    Mer: That dreamers often lie.   (true,
    Rom: In bed asleepe while they doe dreame things
    Mer: Ah then I see Queene Mab hath bin with you.
    Ben: Queene Mab whats she?
She is the Fairies Midwife and doth come
In shape no bigger than an Aggat stone
On the forefinger of a Burgomaster,
Drawne with a teeme of little Atomi,
A thwart mens noses when they lie asteepe,
Her waggon spokes are made of spinners webs,
The couer, of the winges of Grashoppers,
The traces are the Moone-shine watrie beames,
The collers crickets bones, the lash of filmes,
Her waggoner is a small gray coated flie,
Not halfe so big as is a little worme,
Pickt from the lasie finger of a maide,
And in this sort she gallops vp and downe
Through Louers braines, and then they dream of loue
O're Courtiers knees: who strait on curfies dreame
O're Ladies lips, who dreame on kisses strait:
Which oft the angrie Mab with blisters plagues,
Because their breathes with sweet meats tainted are:
Sometimes she gallops ore a Lawers lap,
                                              And

of Romeo and Iuliet.

And then dreames he of smelling out a sute,
And sometime comes she with a tithe pigs taile,
Tickling a Parsons nose that lies asleepe,
And then dreames he of another benefice:
Sometime she gallops ore a souldiers nose,
And then dreames he of cutting forraine throats,
Of breaches ambuscados, countermines,
Of healthes fiue fadome deepe, and then anon
Drums in his eare: at which he startes and wakes,
And sweares a Praier or two and sleepes againe.
This is that Mab that makes maids lie on their backes,
And proues them women of good cariage. (the night,
This is the verie Mab that plats the manes of Horses in
And plats the Elfelocks in foule sluttish haire,
Which once vntangled much misfortune breedes.

  Rom: Peace, peace, thou talkst of nothing.

  Mer: True, I talke of dreames,
Which are the Chi'dren of an idle braine,
Begot of nothing but vaine fantasie,
Which is as thinne a substance as the aire,
And more inconstant than the winde,
Which wooes euen now the frose bowels of the north,
And being angred puffes away in haste,
Turning his face to the dew-dropping south. (selues,

  Ben: Come, come, this winde doth blow vs from our
Supper is done and we shall come too late.

  Ro: I feare too earlie, for my minde misgiues
Some consequence is hanging in the stars,
Which bitterly begins his fearefull date
With this nights reuels, and expiers the terme
Of a dispised life, closde in this breast,
By some vntimelie forfet of vile death:

The most excellent Tragedie,

But he that hath the steerage of my course
Directs my saile, on lustie Gentlemen.

     Enter old Capulet *with the Ladies.*

  Capu: Welcome Gentlemen, welcome Gentlemen,
Ladies that haue their toes vnplagud with Corns
Will haue about with you, ah ha my Mistresses,
Which of you all will now refuse to dance?
Shee that makes d aintie, shee Ile sweare hath Corns.
Am I come neere you now, welcome Gentlemen, wel-
More lights you knaues, & turn these tables vp, (come,
And quench the fire the roome is growne too hote.
Ah sirra, this vnlookt for sport comes well,
Nay sit, nay sit, good Cosen *Capulet:*
For you and I are past our standing dayes,
How long is it since you and I were in a Maske?

  Cos: By Ladie sir tis thirtie yeares at least.

  Cap: Tis not so much, tis not so much,
Tis since the mariage of *Lucentio,*
Come *Pentecost* as quicklie as it will,
Some fiue and twentie yeares, and then we maskt.

  Cos: Tis more, tis more, his sonne is elder far.

  Cap: Will you tell me that it cannot be so,
His sonne was but a Ward three yeares agoe,
Good youths I faith. Oh youth's a iolly thing.

  Rom: What Ladie is that that doth inrich the hand
Of yonder Knight? O shee doth teach the torches to
     burne bright!
It seemes she hangs vpon the cheeke of night,
Like a rich iewell in an *Aethiops* eare,
Beautie too rich for vse, for earth too deare:
So shines a snow-white Swan trouping with Crowes,
As this faire Ladie ouer her fellowes showes.

of Romeo and Iuliet.

The meafure done, ile watch her place of ftand,
And touching hers, make happie my rude hand
Did my heart loue till now? Forfweare it fight,
I neuer faw true beautie till this night.

  Tib: This by his voice fhould be a *Mountague*,
Fetch me my rapier boy . What dares the flaue
Come hither couer'd with an Anticke face,
To fcorne and ieere at our folemnitie?
Now by the ftocke and honor of my kin,
To ftrike him dead I hold it for no fin.

  Ca: Why how now Cofen, wherfore ftorme you fo,

  Ti: Vncle this is a *Mountague* our foe,
A villaine that is hether come in fpight,
To mocke at our folemnitie this night.

  Ca: Young *Romeo*, is it not?

  Ti: It is that villaine *Romeo*.   (man,

  Ca: Let him alone, he beares him like a portly gentle·
And to fpeake truth, *Verona* brags of him,
As of a vertuous and well gouern'd youth:
I would not for the wealth of all this towne,
Here in my houfe doo him difparagement:
Therefore be quiet take no note of him,
Beare a faire prefence, and put off thefe frownes,
An ill befeeming femblance for a feaft.

  Ti: It fits when fuch a villaine is a gueft,
Ile not indure him.

  Ca: He fhalbe indured, goe to I fay, he fhall,
Am I the Mafter of the houfe or you?
You'le not indure him? God fhall mend my foule
You'le make a mutenie amongft my guefts,
You'le fet Cocke a hoope, you'le be the man.

  Ti: Vncle tis a fhame.

                          C 2   *Ca:* Goe

The most excellent Tragedie,

Ca: Goe too, you are a faucie knaue.
This tricke will feath you one day I know what.
Well faid my hartes, Be quiet :
More light Ye knaue, or I will make you quiet. (ting.

Tibalt : Patience perforce with wi full choller mee-
Makes my flesh tremble in their different greetings:
I will withdraw, but this intrusion shall
Now seeming sweet, convert to bitter gall.

Rom: If I prophane with my vnworthie hand,
This holie shrine, the gentle sinne is this:
My lips two blushing Pilgrims ready stand,
To smooth the rough touch with a gentle kisse.

Iuli: Good Pilgrime you doe wrong your hand too
Which mannerly deuotion shewes in this: (much,
For Saints haue hands which holy Palmers touch,
And Palme to Palme is holy Palmers kisse.

Rom: Haue not Saints lips, and holy Palmers too?

Iuli: Yes Pilgrime lips that they must vse in praier.

Ro: Why then faire saint, let lips do what hands doo,
They pray, yeeld thou, least faith turne to dispaire.

Iu: Saints doe not mooue though: grant nor praier
                                 forsake.

Ro: Then mooue not till my praiers effect I take.
Thus from my lips, by yours my sin is purgde.

Iu: Then haue my lips the sin that they haue tooke.

Ro: Sinne from my lips, O trespasse sweetly vrgde!
Giue me my sinne againe.

Iu: You kisse by the booke.

Nurse: Madame your mother calles.

Rom: What is her mother?

*Nurse: Marrie Batcheler her mother is the Ladie of the
house, and a good Lady, and a wise, and a vertuous. I nurst
                                                      her*

360

of Romeo and Iuliet.

her daughter that you talkt withall, I tell you, he that can
lay hold of her shall haue the chinkes.

Rom: Is she a *Mountague*? Oh deare account,
My life is my foes thrall.

Ca: Nay gentlemen prepare not to be gone,
We haue a trifling foolish banquet towards.

They whisper in his eare.

I pray you let me intreat you- Is it so?
Well then I thanke you honest Gentlemen,
I promise you but for your company,
I would haue bin a bed an houre agoe:
Light to my chamber hoe.

Exeunt.

Iul: Nurse, what is yonder Gentleman?
Nur: *The sonne and heire of old* Tiberio.
Iul: Whats he that now is going out of dore?
Nur: *That as I thinke is yong* Petruchio. (dance?
Iul: Whats he that followes there that would not
Nur: *I know not.*
Iul: Goe learne his name, if he be maried,
My graue is like to be my wedding bed.
Nur: His name is Romeo and a Mountague, *the onely
sonne of your great enemie.*
Iul: My onely Loue sprung from my onely hate,
Too early seene vnknowne and knowne too late:
Prodigious birth of loue is this to me,
That I should loue a loathed enemie.
Nurse: *VVhats this? whats that?*
Iul: Nothing Nurse but a rime I learnt euen now of
one I dancst with.
Nurse: *Come your mother staies for you, Ile goe along
withyou.*

Exeunt.

Enter

The most excellent Tragedie,

Enter Romeo alone.

Ro: Shall I goe forward and my heart is here?
Turne backe dull earth and finde thy Center out.

Enter Benuolio Mercutio.

Ben: Romeo, my cofen Romeo.

Mer: Doeft thou heare he is wife,
Vpon my life he hath ftolne him home to bed.

Ben: He came this way, and leapt this Orchard wall,
Call good *Mercutio.*

Mer: Call, nay Ile coniure too.
Romeo, madman, humors, pafsion, liuer, appeare thou in
likenes of a figh: fpeek but one rime & I am fatiffied, cry
but ay me. Pronounce but Loue and Doue, fpeake to
my goffip Venus one faire word, one nickname for her
purblinde fonne and heire young Abraham: Cupid hee
that fhot fo trim when young King Cophetua loued the
begger wench. Hee heares me not. I coniure thee by
Rofalindes bright eye, high forehead, and fcarlet lip, her
prettie foote, ftraight leg, and quiuering thigh, and the
demaines that there adiacent lie, that in thy likeneffe
thou appeare to vs.

Ben: If he doe heare thee thou wilt anger him.

Mer: To this cannot anger him, marrie if one fhuld
raife a fpirit in his Miftris circle of fome ftrange fafhion,
making it there to ftand till the had laid it, and coniurde
it downe, that were fome fpite. My inuocation is faire
and honeft, and in his Miftrs name I coniure onely but
to raife vp him.

Ben: Well he hath hid himfelfe amongft thofe trees,
To be conforted with the humerous night,
Blinde in his loue, and beft befits the darke.

Mer:

of Romeo and Iuliet.

Mer : If loue be blind, loue will not hit the marke,
Now will he fit vnder a Medler tree,
And wifh his Miftris were that kinde of fruite,
As maides call Medlers when they laugh alone.
Ah *Romeo* that fhe were, ah that fhe were
An open *Et cætera*, thou a poprin Peare.
Romeo God night, il'e to my trundle bed:
This field bed is too cold for mee.
Come lets away, for tis but vaine,
To feeke him here that meanes not to be found.

Ro : He iefts at fcars that neuer felt a wound:
But foft, what light forth yonder window breakes?
It is the Eaft, and *Iuliet* is the Sunne,
Arife faire S nne, and kill the enuious Moone
That is alreadie ficke, and pale with griefe:
That thou her maid, art far more faire than fhe.
Be not her maide fince fhe is enuious,
Her veftall liuerie is but pale and greene,
And none but fooles doe weare it, caft it off.
She fpeakes, but fhe fayes nothing. What of that?
Her eye difcourfeth, I will anfwere it.
I am too bold, tis not to me fhe fpeakes,
Two of the faireft ftarres in all the skies,
Hauing fome bufines, doe ent at her eyes
To twinckle in their fpheares, till they returne.
What if her eyes were there, they in her head,
The brightnes of her cheekes would fhame thofe ftars:
As day-light doth a Lampe, her eyes in heauen,
Would through the airie region ftreame fo bright,
That birdes would fing, and thinke it were not night.
Oh now fhe leanes her cheekes vpon her hand,
I would I were the gloue to that fame hand,

D   The

The most excellent Tragedie,

That I might kisse that cheeke.

  Iul : Ay me.

  Rom: She speakes, Oh speake againe bright Angell:
For thou art as glorious to this night beeing ouer my
As is a winged messenger of heauen   (head,
Vnto the white vpturned woondring eyes,
Of mortals that fall backe to gaze on him,
When he bestrides the lasie pacing cloudes,
And failes vpon the bosome of the aire.

  Iul : Ah *Romeo, Romeo,* wherefore art thou *Romeo?*
Denie thy Father, and refuse thy name,
Or if thou wilt not be but sworne my loue,
And il'e no longer be a *Capulet.*

  Rom : Shall I heare more, or shall I speake to this?

  Iul : Tis but thy name that is mine enemie.
Whats *Mountague?* It is nor hand nor foote,
Nor arme, nor face, nor any other part.
Whats in a name? That which we call a Rose,
By any other name would smell as sweet:
So *Romeo* would, were he not *Romeo* cald,
Retaine the diuine perfection he owes:
Without that title *Romeo* part thy name,
And for that name which is no part of thee,
Take all I haue.

  Rom : I take thee at thy word,
Call me but loue, and il'e be new Baptisde,
Henceforth I neuer will be *Romeo.*

  Iu: What man art thou, that thus beskrind in night,
Doest stumble on my counsaile?

  Ro: By a name I know not how to tell thee.
My name deare Saint is hatefull to my selfe,
Because it is an enemie to thee.

of Romeo and Iuliet.

Had I it written I would teare the word.

   Iul: My eares haue not yet drunk a hundred words
Of that tongues vtterance, yet I know the found:
Art thou not *Romeo* and a *Mountague?*

   Ro: Neyther faire Saint, if eyther thee diſpleaſe.

   Iu: How camſt thou hether, tell me and wherfore?
The Orchard walles are high and hard to clime,
And the place death conſidering who thou art,
If any of my kinſmen finde thee here.

   Ro: By loues light winges did I oreperch theſe wals,
For ſtonie limits cannot hold loue out,
And what loue can doo, that dares loue attempt,
Therefore thy kinſmen are no let to me.

   Iul: If they doe finde thee they will murder thee.

   Ro: Alas there lies more perrill in thine eyes,
Then twentie of their ſwords, looke thou but ſweete,
And I am prooſe againſt their enmitie.   (here.

   Iul: I would not for the world they ſhuld find thee

   Ro: I haue nights cloak to hide thee from their ſight,
And but thou loue me let them finde me here:
For life were better ended by their hate,
Than death proroged wanting of thy loue.

   Iu: By whoſe direction foundſt thou out this place?

   Ro: By loue, who firſt did prompt me to enquire,
He gaue me counſaile and I lent him eyes.
I am no Pilot: yet wert thou as farre
As that vaſt ſhore, waſht with the furtheſt ſea,
I would aduenture for ſuch Marchandiſe.

   Iul: Thou knowſt the maſke of night is on my face,
Els would a Maiden bluſh bepaint my cheeks:
For that which thou haſte heard me ſpeake to night,
Faine would I dwell on forme, faine faine denie,

          D 2   Wha

The moſt excellent Tragedie,

What I haue ſpoke: but farewell complements.
Doeſt thou loue me? Nay I know thou wilt ſay I,
And I will take thy word: but if thou ſwearſt,
Thou maieſt proue falſe:
At Louers periuries they ſay Ioue ſmiles.
Ah gentle *Romeo*, if thou loue pronounce it faithfully:
Or if thou thinke I am too eaſely wonne,
Il'e frowne and ſay thee nay and be peruerſe,
So thou wilt wooe: but els not for the world,
In truth faire *Mountague*, I am too fond,
And therefore thou maieſt thinke my hauiour light:
But truſt me gentleman Ile proue more true,
Than they that haue more cunning to be ſtrange.
I ſhould haue bin ſtrange I muſt confeſſe,
But that thou ouer-heardſt ere I was ware
My true loues Paſsion: therefore pardon me,
And not impute this yeelding to light loue,
Which the darke night hath ſo diſcouered.
    Ro: By yonder bleſſed Moone I ſweare,
That tips with ſiluer all theſe fruit trees tops.
    Iul: O ſweare not by the Moone the vnconſtant
That monthlie changeth in her circled orbe, (Moone,
Leaſt that thy loue proue likewiſe variable.
    Ro: Now by
    Iul: Nay doo not ſweare at all,
Or if thou ſweare, ſweare by thy glorious ſelfe,
Which art the God of my Idolatrie,
And il'e beleeue thee.
    Ro: If my true harts loue
    Iul: Sweare not at al, though I doo ioy in
I haue ſmall ioy in this contract to night, (thee,
It is too raſh, too ſodaine, too vnaduiſde,
                                        Too

of Romeo and Iuliet.

Too like the lightning that doth ceafe to bee
Ere one can fay it lightens. I heare fome comming,
Deare loue adew, fweet *Mountague* be true,
Stay but a little and il'e come againe.

   Ro: O bleffed bleffed night, I feare being night,
All this is but a dreame I heare and fee,
Too flattering true to be fubftantiall.

   Iul: Three wordes good *Romeo* and good night in-
If that thy bent of loue be honourable?   (deed.
Thy purpofe marriage, fend me word to morrow
By one that il'e procure to come to thee:
Where and what time thou wilt performe that right,
And al my fortunes at thy foote il'e lay,
And follow thee my Lord through out the world.

   Ro: Loue goes toward loue like fchoole boyes from
      their bookes,
But loue from loue, to fchoole with heauie lookes.

   Iul: *Romeo, Romeo,* O for a falkners voice,
To lure this Taffell gentle backe againe:
Bondage is hoarfe and may not crie aloud,
Els would I teare the Caue where Eccho lies
And make her airie voice as hoarfe as mine,
With repetition of my *Romeos* name.
Romeo?

   Ro: It is my foule that calles vpon my name,
How filuer fweet found louers tongues in night.

   Iul: Romeo?

   Ro: Madame.

   Iul: At what a clocke to morrow fhall I fend?

   Ro: At the houre of nine.

   Iul: I will not faile, tis twentie yeares till then.
Romeo I haue forgot why I did call thee backe.

The most excellent Tragedie,

Rom: Let me stay here till you remember it.

Iul: I shall forget to haue thee still staie here,
Remembring how I loue thy companie.

Rom: And il'e stay still to haue thee still forget,
Forgetting any other home but this.

Iu: Tis almost morning I would haue thee gone,
But yet no further then a wantons bird,
Who lets it hop a little from her hand,
Like a pore prisoner in his twisted giues,
And with a silke thred puls it backe againe,
Too louing iealous of his libertie.

Ro: Would I were thy bird.

Iul: Sweet so, would I,
Yet I should kill thee with much cherrishing thee.
Good night, good night, parting is such sweet sorrow,
That I shall say good night till it be morrow.   (breast,

Rom: Sleepe dwell vpon thine eyes, peace on thy
I would that I were sleep and peace of sweet to rest.
Now will I to my Ghostly fathers Cell,
His help to craue, and my good hap to tell.

Enter Frier Francis.   (night,

Frier: The gray ey'd morne smiles on the frowning
Checkring the Easterne clouds with streakes of light,
And flecked darkenes like a drunkard reeles,
From forth daies path, and *Titans* fierie wheeles:
Now ere the Sunne aduance his burning eye,
The world to cheare, and nights darke dew to drie
We must vp fill this oasier Cage of ours,
With balefull weeds, and precious iuyced flowers.
Oh mickle is the powerfull grace that lies
In hearbes, plants, stones, and their true qualities:
For nought so vile, that vile on earth doth liue,

of Romeo and Iuliet.

But to the earth some speciall good doth giue:
Nor nought so good,but straind from that faire vse,
Reuolts to vice and stumbles on abuse:
Vertue it selfe turnes vice being misapplied,
And vice sometimes by action dignified.
Within the infant rinde of this small flower,
Poyson hath residence,and medecine power:
For this being smelt too, with that part cheares ech hart,
Being tasted slaies all sences with the hart.
Two such opposed foes incampe them still,
In man as well as herbes,grace and rude will,
And where the worser is predominant,
Full soone the canker death eats vp that plant.

    Rom: Good morrow to my Ghostly Confessor.
    Fri: Benedicite, what earlie tongue so soone saluteth
Yong sonne it argues a distempered head,   (me?
So soone to bid good morrow to my bed.
Care keepes his watch in euerie old mans eye,
And where care lodgeth, sleep can neuer lie:
But where vnbrused youth with vnstuft braines
Doth couch his limmes,there golden sleepe remaines:
Therefore thy earlines doth me assure,
Thou art vprowl'd by some distemperature.
Or if not so,then here I hit it righ
Our *Romeo* hath not bin a bed to night.

    Ro: The last was true, the sweeter rest was mine.
    Fr: God pardon sin,wert thou with *Rosaline?*
    Ro: With *Rosaline* my Ghostly father no,
I haue forgot that name,and that names woe.   (then?
    Fri: Thats my good sonne: but where hast thou bin
    Ro: I tell thee ere thou aske it me againe,
I haue bin feasting with mine enemie:

The most excellent Tragedie,

Where on the sodaine one hath wounded mee
Thats by me wounded, both our remedies
With in thy help and holy phisicke lies,
I beare no hatred blessed man: for loe
My intercession likewise steades my foe.

  Frier: Be plaine my sonne and homely in thy drift,
Ridling confession findes but ridling strift.

  Rom: Then plainely know my harts deare loue is set
On the faire daughter of rich *Capulet*;
As mine on hers, so hers likewise on mine,
And all combind, saue what thou must combine
By holy marriage: where, and when, and how,
We met, we woo'd, and made exchange of vowes,
Il'e tell thee as I passe: But this I pray,
That thou consent to martie vs to day.

  Fri: Holy S. *Francis*, what a change is here?
Is *Rosaline* whome thou didst loue so deare
So soone forsooke, so yong mens loue then lies
Not truelie in their harts, but in their eyes.
Iesu Maria, what a deale of brine
Hath washt thy sallow cheekes for *Rosaline?*
How much salt water cast away in waste,
To seafon loue, that of loue doth not taste.
The sunne not yet thy sighes from heauen cleares,
Thy old grones ring yet in my ancient eares,
And loe vpon thy cheeke the staine doth sit,
Of an old teare that is not washt off yet.
If euer thou wert thus, and these woes thine,
Thou and these woes were all for *Rosaline*,
And art thou changde, pronounce this sentence then
Women may fal, when ther's no strength in men.

  Rom: Thou chidst me oft for louing *Rosaline.*
                            Exit

of *Romeo and Iuliet*.

Fr: For doating, not for louing, pupill mine,

Rom: And badſt me burie loue.

Fr: Not in a graue,

To lay one in another out to haue,

Rom: I pree thee chide not, ſhe whom I loue now

Doth grace for grace, and loue for loue allow :

The other did not ſo.

Fr: Oh ſhe knew well

Thy loue did read by rote, and could not ſpell,

But come yong Wauerer, come goe with mee,

In one reſpeſt Ile thy aſsiſtant bee :

For this alliaunce may ſo happie proue,

To turne your Houſholds rancour to pure loue. *Exeunt.*

Enter *Mercutio, Bennolio.*

Mer: Why whats become of *Romeo* ? came he not
  home to night ?

Ben: Not to his Fathers, I ſpake with his man.

Mer: Ah that ſame pale hard hearted wench, that *Ro-*
Torments him ſo, that he will ſure run mad. (ſaline»

Mer: *Tybalt* the Kinſman of olde *Capolet*

Hath ſent a Letter to his Fathers Houſe :

Some Challenge on my life.

Ben: *Romeo* will anſwere it.

Mer: I, anie man that can write may anſwere a letter.

Ben: Nay, he will anſwere the letters maſter if hee bee
  challenged.

Mer: Who, *Romeo* ? why he is alreadie dead : ſtabd
with a white wenches blacke eye , ſhot thorough the eare
with a loue ſong, the verie pinne of his heart cleft with the
blinde bow-boyes but-ſhaft. And is he a man to encounter
Tybalt ?

Ben: Why what is *Tybalt* ?

Mer: More than the prince of cattes I can tell you. Oh
he is the couragious captaine of complements, Catſo, he

E   fights

371

The excellent Tragedie

fightes as you fing pricke-fong , keepes time dyftance and
proportion,refts me his minum reft one two and the thirde
in your bofome,the very butcher of a filken button,a Duel.
lift a Duellift,a gentleman of the very firft houfe of the firft
and fecond caufe, ah the immortall Paffado, the Punto re-
uerfo, the Hay.

   Ben: The what?

   Me: The Poxe of fuch limping antique affecting fan-
tafticoes thefe new tuners of accents. By Iefu a very good
blade,a very tall man,a very good whoore.Why ground-
fir is not this a miferable cafe that we fhould be ftil afflicted
with thefe ftrange flies: thefe fafhionmongers, thefe par-
donmees, that ftand fo much on the new forme, that they
cannot fitte at eafe on the old bench.Oh their bones , they
bones.

   Ben. Heere comes *Romeo.*

   Mer: Without his Roe,like a dryed Hering.Offefh flefh
how art thou fifhified. Sirra now is he for the numbers that
Petrarch flowdin : *Laura* to his Lady was but a kitchin
drudg,yet fhe had a better loue to berime her:Dido a dowdy Cleopatra a Gypfie,*Hero* and *Hellen* hildings and harle-
tries:*Thifbie* agray eye or fo,but not to the purpofe.Signior
Romeo bon iour,there is a French curtefie to your French
flop : yee gaue vs the counterfeit fairely yefternight.

   Rom: What counterfeit I pray you?

   Me: The flip the flip,can you not conceiue?

   Rom: I cry you mercy my bufines was great,and in fuch
a cafe as mine, a man may ftraine curtefie.

   Mer: Oh thats as much to fay as fuch a cafe as yours wil
conftraine a man to bow in the hams.

   Rom: A moft curteous expofition.

   Me: Why I am the very pinke of curtefie.

   Rom: Pinke for flower?

   Mer: Right.

   Rom: Then is my Pumpe well flour'd:

   Mer: Well faid, follow me nowe that ieft till thou haft
worn

of Romeo and Iuliet.

worne out thy Pumpe,that when the fingle fole of it is worn
the ieft may remaine after the wearing folie finguler.

Rom: O fingle foald ieft folie finguler for the finglenes.

Me. Come between vs good *Benuolio,*for my wits faile.

*Rom:*S wits and fpurres,fwits & fpurres,or Ile cry a match.

Mer: Nay if thy wits runne the wildgoofe chafe,I haue
done : for I am fure thou haft more of the goofe in one of
thy wits, than I haue in al my fiue:Was I with you there for
the goofe?

Rom: Thou wert neuer with me for any thing,when
thou wert not with me for the goofe.

Me: Ile bite thee by the eare for that ieft.

Rom: Nay good goofe bite not.

Mer: Why thy wit is a bitter fweeting,a moft fharp fauce

Rom: And was it not well feru'd in to a fweet goofe?

Mer: Oh heere is a witte of Cheuerell that ftretcheth
from an ynch narrow to an ell broad.

Rom: I ftretcht it out for the word broad,which added to
the goofe,proues thee faire and wide a broad goofe.

Mer: Why is not this better now than groning for loue?
why now art thou fociable,now art thou thy felfe, nowe art
thou what thou art,as wel by arte as nature. This driueling
loue is like a great naturall,that runs vp and downe to hide
his bable in a hole.

Ben: Stop there.

Me: Why thou wouldft haue me ftopp my tale againft
the haire.

Ben: Thou wouldft haue made thy tale too long?

Mer: Tut man thou art deceiued, I meant to make it
fhort,for I was come to the whole depth of my tale?and
meant indeed to occupie the argument no longer.

Rom: Heers goodly geare.

Enter Nurfe and her man.

Mer: A faile,a faile,a faile.

E 2   *Ben:* Two

The excellent Tragedie

Ben: Two, two, a shirt and a smocke.

Nur: *Peter,* pree thee giue me my fan.

Mer: Pree thee doo good *Peter,* to hide her face: for her fanne is the fairer of the two.

Nur: God ye goodmorrow Gentlemen.

Mer: God ye good den faire Gentlewoman.

Nur: Is it god ye gooden I pray you.

Mer: Tis no leffe I assure you, for the baudie hand of the diall is euen now vpon the pricke of noone.

Nur: Fie, what a man is this?

Rom: A Gentleman Nurse, that God hath made for himselfe to marre.

Nur: By my troth well said : for himselfe to marre quoth he? I pray you can anie of you tell where one maie finde yong *Romeo?*

Rom: I can: but yong *Romeo* will bee elder when you haue found him, than he was when you sought him, I am the yongest of that name for fault of a worfe.

Nur: Wellfaid.

Mer: Yea, is the worst well? mas well noted, wifely, wifely.

Nu: If you be he fir, I defire fome conference with ye,

Ben: O, belike fhe meanes to inuite him to fupper.

Mer: So ho. A baud, a baud, a baud.

Rom: Why what haft found man?

Mer: No hare fir, vnleffe it be a hare in a lenten pye, that is fomewhat ftale and hoare ere it be eaten.

> *He walkes by them, and fings.*

And an olde hare hore, and an olde hare hore
    is verie good meate in Lent :
But a hare thats hoare is too much for a fcore,
    if it hore ere it be fpent.

You! come to your fathers to fupper?

Rom: I will.

Mer: Farewell ancient Ladie, farewell fweete Ladie

> *Exeunt Bennolio, Mercutio.*

Nur

of Romeo and Iuliet.

Nur : Marry farewell. Pray what faucie merchant was this that was fo full of his roperipe?

Rom : A gentleman Nurſe that loues to heare himſelfe talke, and will ſpeake more in an houre than hee will ſtand to in a month.

Nur : If hee ſtand to anie thing againſt mee, I'le take him downe if he were luſtier than he is : if I cannot take him downe, Ile finde them that ſhall : I am none of his ſlurtgills, I am none of his skaines mates.

She turnes to Peter her man.

And thou like a knaue muſt ſtand by, and ſee euerie Iacke vſe me at his pleaſure.

Pet : I ſee no bodie vſe you at his pleaſure, if I had, I would ſoone haue drawen : you know my toole is as ſoone out as anothers if I ſee time and place.

Nur : Now afore God he hath ſo vext me, that euerie member about me quiuers : ſcuruie Iacke. But as I ſaid, my Ladie bad me ſeeke ye out, and what ſhee bad me tell yee, that Ile keepe to my ſelfe : but if you ſhould lead her into a fooles paradice as they ſaye, it were a verie groſſe kinde of behauiour as they ſay, for the Gentlewom an is yong. Now if you ſhould deale doubly with her, it were verie weake dealing, and not to be offered to anie Gentlewoman.

Rom : Nurſe, commend me to thy Ladie, tell her I proteſt.

Nur : Goodheart : yfaith Ile tell her ſo : oh ſhe will be a ioyfull woman.

Rom : Why, what wilt thou tell her?

Nur : That you doo proteſt : which (as I take it) is a Gentlemanlike proffer.

Rom : Bid her get leaue to morrow morning
To come to ſhrift to Frier *Laurence* cell :
And ſtay thou Nurſe behinde the Abbey wall,
My man ſhall come to thee, and bring along
The cordes, made like a tackled ſtaire,
Which to the high top-gallant of my ioy

E 3   Muſt

The excellent Tragedie

Muſt be my conduƈt in the ſecret night.
Hold, take that for thy paines.

   Nur: No, not a penie truly.

   Rom: I ſay you ſhall not chuſe.

   Nur: Well, to morrow morning ſhe ſhall not faile.

   Rom: Farewell, be truſtie, and Ile quite thy paine. *Exit*

   Nur: *Peter*, take my fanne, and goe before. *Ex. omnes.*

        Enter Iuliet.

   Iul: The clocke ſtroke nine when I did ſend my Nurſe,
In halfe an houre ſhe promiſt to returne.
Perhaps ſhe cannot finde him. Thats not ſo,
Oh ſhe is lazie, Loues heralds ſhould be thoughts,
And runne more ſwift, than haſtie powder fierd,
Doth hurrie from the fearfull Cannons mouth.

        Enter Nurſe.

Oh now ſhe comes. Tell me gentle Nurſe,
What ſayes my Loue?

   Nur: Oh I am wearie, let mee reſt a while, Lord how
my bones ake. Oh wheres my man? Giue me ſome aqu
vitæ.

   Iul: I would thou hadſt my bones, and I thy newes.

   Nur: Fie, what a iaunt haue I had: and my backe a to-
ther ſide. Lord, Lord, what a caſe am I in.

   Iul: But tell me ſweet Nurſe, what ſayes *Romeo*?

   Nur: *Romeo*, nay, alas you cannot chuſe a man. Hees
no bodie, he is not the Flower of curteſie, he is not a proper
man: and for a hand, and a foote, and a baudie, wel go thy
way wench, thou haſt it ifaith. Lord, Lord, how my head
beates?

   Iul: What of all this? tell me what ſayes he to our mariage?

   Nur: Marry he ſayes like an honeſt Gentleman, and a
kinde, and I warrant a vertuous: wheres your Mother?

   Iul: Lord, Lord, how odly thou replieſt? He ſaies like a
                         kinde

of *Romeo and Iuliet*.

kinde Gentleman, and an honeſt, and a vertuous; wheres
your mother?

Nur: Marry come vp, cannot you ſtay a while? is this
the poulteſſe for mine aking boanes? next arrant youl haue
done, euen doot your ſelfe.

Iul: Nay ſtay ſweet Nurſe, I doo intreate thee now,
What ſayes my Loue, my Lord, my *Romeo*?

Nur: Goe, hye you ſtraight to Friar *Laurence* Cell,
And frame a ſcuſe that you muſt goe to ſhrift:
There ſtayes a Bridegroome to make you a Bride.
Now comes the wanton blood vp in your cheekes,
I muſt prouide a ladder made of cordes,
With which your Lord muſt clime a birdes neſt ſoone,
I muſt take paines to further your delight,
But you muſt beare the burden ſoone at night.
Doth this newes pleaſe you now?

Iul: How doth her latter words reuiue my hart.
Thankes gentle Nurſe, diſpatch thy buſines,
And Ile not faile to meete my *Romeo*.   *Exeunt*.

Enter Romeo, Frier.

Rom: Now Father *Laurence*, in thy holy grant
Conſiſts the good of me and *Iuliet*.

Fr: Without more words I will doo all I may,
To make you happie if in me it lye.

Rom: This morning here ſhe pointed we ſhould meet,
And conſumate thoſe neuer parting bands,
Witnes of our harts loue by ioyning hands,
And come ſhe will.

Fr: I geſſe ſhe will indeed,
Youths loue is quicke, ſwifter than ſwifteſt ſpeed.

Enter Iuliet ſomewhat faſt, and embraceth Romeo.
See where ſhe comes,
So light of foote nere hurts the troden flower:
Of loue and ioy, ſee ſee the foueraigne power.

Iul: *Romeo*.

                                                   Rom:

The excellent Tragedie

Rom: My *Iuliet* welcome. As doo waking eyes
(Cloafd in Nights myfts) attend the frolicke Day,
So *Romeo* hath expected *Iuliet*,
And thou art come.

Iul: I am (if I be Day)
Come to my Sunne: fhine foorth, and make me faire.

Rom: All beauteous fairnes dwelleth in thine eyes,

Iul: *Romeo* from thine all brightnes doth arife,

Fr: Come wantons, come, the ftealing houres do paffe
Defer imbracements till fome fitrer time,
Part for a while, you fhall not be alone,
Till holy Church haue ioynd ye both in one.

Rom: Lead holy Father, all delay feemes long.

Iul: Make haft, make haft, this lingring doth vs wrong,

Fr: O, foft and faire makes fweeteft worke they fay,
Haft is a common hindrer in croffe way.   *Exeunt omnes.*

Enter Benuolio, Mercutio.

Ben: I pree thee good *Mercutio* lets retire,
The day is hot, the *Capels* are abroad.

Mer: Thou art like one of thofe, that when hee comes
into the confines of a tauerne, claps me his rapier on the
boord, and fayes, God fend me no need of thee : and by
the operation of the next cup of wine, he drawes it on the
drawer, when indeed there is no need.

Ben: Am I like fuch a one ?

Mer: Go too, thou art as hot a Iacke being mooude,
and as foone mooude to be moodie, and as foone moodie to
be mooud.

Ben: And what too ?

Mer: Nay, and there were two fuch, wee fhould haue
none fhortly. Didft not thou fall out with a man for cracking of nuts, hauing no other reafon, but becaufe thou hadft
hafill eyes ? what eye but fuch an eye would haue pickt out
fuch a quarrell ? With another for coughing, becaufe hee
wakd

of Romeo and Iuliet.

wakd thy dogge that laye a sleepe in the Sunne? With a
Taylor for wearing his new dublet before Easter: and
with another for tying his new shoes with olde ribands.
And yet thou wilt forbid me of quarrelling.

Ben: By my head heere comes a *Capolet.*

Enter Tybalt.

Mer: By my heele I care not.

Tyb: Gentlemen a word with one of you.

Mer: But one word with one of vs? You had best couple
it with somewhat, and make it a word and a blow.

Tyb: I am apt enough to that if I haue occasion.

Mer: Could you not take occasion?

Tyb: *Mercutio* thou consorts with *Romeo?*

Me: Consort. Zwounes consort: the slaue wil make fidlers of vs. If you doe sirra, look for nothing but discord: For
heeres my fiddle-sticke.

Enter Romeo.

Tyb: Well peace be with you, heere comes my man.

Mer: But Ile be hanged if he weare your lyuery: Mary
go before into the field, and he may be your follower, so in
that sence your worship may call him man.

Tyb: *Romeo* the hate I beare to thee can affoord no better words then these, thou art a villaine.

Rom: *Tybalt* the loue I beare to thee, doth excuse the
appertaining rage to such a word: villaine am I none, ther-
fore I well perceiue thou knowst me not.

Tyb: Bace boy this cannot serue thy turne, and therefore
drawe.

Ro: I doe protest I neuer iniured thee, but loue thee better than thou canst deuise, till thou shalt know the reason of
my loue.

Mer: O dishonorable vile submission. *Allastockado* caries
it away. You Ratcatcher, come backe, come backe.

Tyb: What wouldest with me?

F

Mer:

The excellent Tragedie

Mer: Nothing King of Cates, but borrow one of your nine liues, therefore come drawe your rapier out of your scabard, least mine be about your eares ere you be aware.

Rom: Stay *Tibalt*, hould *Mercutio* : *Bennolio* beate downe their weapons.

> *Tibalt vnder Romeos arme thrusts Mer-*
> *cutio, in and flyes.*

Mer: Is he gone, hath hee nothing ? A poxe on your houses.

Rom: What art thou hurt man, the wound is not deepe.

Mer: Noe not so deepe as a Well, nor so wideas a barne doore, but it will serue I warrant. What meant you to come betweene vs ? I was hurt vnder your arme.

Rom: I did all for the best.

Mer: A poxe of your houses, I am fairely drest. Sim goe fetch me a Surgeon.

Boy: I goe my Lord.

Mer: I am pepperd for this world, I am sped yfaith, he hath made wormes meate of me, & ye aske for me to morrow you shall finde me a graue-man. A poxe of your houses I shall be fairely mounted vpon foure mens shoulders : For your house of the *Mountegues* and the *Capolets* : and then some peasantly rogue, some Sexton, some base slaue shall write my Epitapth, that *Tybalt* came and broke the Princes Lawes, and *Mercutio* was slaine for the first and second cause. Wher's the Surgeon ?

Boy: Hee's come sir.

Mer: Now heele keepe a mumbling in my guts on the other side, come *Bennolio*, lend me thy hand : a poxe of your houses. *Exeunt*

Rom: This Gentleman the Princes neere Alie, My very frend hath tane this mortall wound In my behalfe, my reputation staind With *Tibalts* slaunder, *Tybalt* that an houre Hath beene my kinsman, Ah *Iuliet*

of Romeo and Iuliet.

Thy beautie makes me thus effeminate,
And in my temper foftens valors fteele.

Enter Benuolio.

Ben: Ah *Romeo Romeo* braue *Mercutio* is dead,
That gallant fpirit hath a fpir'd the cloudes,
Which too vntimely fcorn d the lowly earth.
Rom: This daies black fate,on more daies doth depend
This but begins what other dayes muft end.

Enter Tibalt.

Ben: Heere comes the furious *Tibalt* backe againe.
Rom: Aliue in tryumph and *Mercutio* flaine?
Away to heauen refpectiue lenity:
And fier eyed fury be my conduct now.
Now *Tibalt* take the villaine backe againe,
Which late thou gau'ft me:for *Mercutios* foule,
Is but a little way aboue the cloudes,
And ftaies for thine to beare him company.
Or thou,or I,or both fhall follow him.

Fight,Tibalt falles.

Ben: *Romeo* away,thou feeft that *Tibalt's* flaine,
The Citizens approach,away,begone
Thou wilt be taken.
Rom: Ah I am fortunes flaue.

Exeunt

Enter Citizens.

Watch. Wher's he that flue *Mercutio*, *Tybalt* that villaine?
Ben: There is that *Tybalt.*

F 2   *Watch:* Vp

The excellent Tragedie

Vp sirra goe with vs,

Enter Prince, Capolets wife.

Pri: Where be the vile beginners of this fray?
 Ben: Ah Noble Prince I can discouer all
The most vnlucky mannage of this brawle.
Heere lyes the man slaine by yong *Romeo,*
That slew thy kinsman braue *Mercutio,*
 M : *Tibalt,Tybalt,*O my brothers child,
Vnhappie sight? Ah the blood is spilt
Of my deare kinsman, Prince as thou art true:
For blood of ours, shed bloud of *Mountagew.*
 Pri: Speake *Bennolio* who began this fray?
 Ben: *Tibalt* heere slaine whom *Romeos* hand did slay,
Romeo who spake him fayre bid him bethinke
How nice the quarrell was.
But *Tibalt* still persisting in his wrong,
The stout *Mercutio* drewe to calme the storme,
Which *Romeo* seeing cal'd stay Gentlemen,
And on me cry'd, who drew to part their strife,
And with his agill arme yong *Romeo,*
As fast as tung crydepeace, sought peace to make.
While they were enterchanging thrusts and blows,
Vnder yong *Romeos* laboring arme to part,
The furious *Tybalt* cast an enuious thrust,
That rid the life of stout *Mercutio,*
With that he fled, but presently return'd,
And with his rapier braued *Romeo:*
That had but newly entertain'd reuenge.
And ere I could draw forth my rapyer
To part their furie, downe did *Tybalt* fall,
And this way *Romeo* fled.
 Mo: He is a *Mountagew* and speakes partiall,
Some twentie of them fought in this blacke strife:
And all those twenty could but kill one life.
           I doe

of Romeo and Iuliet.

I doo intreate sweete Prince thou'lt iustice giue,
Romeo slew *Tybalt*, *Romeo* may not liue.
  Prin : And for that offence
Immediately we doo exile him hence.
I haue an interest in your hates proceeding,
My blood for your rude braules doth lye a bleeding,
But Ile amerce you with so large a fine,
That you shall all repent the losse of mine.
I will be deafe to pleading and excuses,
Nor teares nor prayers shall purchase for abuses.
Pittie shall dwell and gouerne with vs still :
Mercie to all but murdrers, pardoning none that kill.

                                   Exeunt omnes.

                    Enter Iuliet.

  Iul : Gallop apace you fierie footed steedes
To *Phœbus* mansion, such a Waggoner
As *Phaeton*, would quickly bring you thether,
And send in cloudie night immediately.

        Enter Nurse wringing her hands, with the ladder
                of cordes in her lap.
But how now Nurse : O Lord, why lookst thou sad?
What hast thou there, the cordes?
  Nur : I, I, the cordes : alacke we are vndone,
We are vndone, Ladie, we are vndone.
  Iul : What diuell art thou that torments me thus?
  Nurs : Alack the day, hees dead, hees dead, hees dead.
  Iul : This torture should be roard in dismall hell.
Can heauens be so enuious?
  Nur : *Romeo* can if heauens cannot.
I saw the wound, I saw it with mine eyes,
God saue the sample, on his manly breast :
A bloodie coarse, a piteous bloodie coarse,
All pale as ashes, I swounded at the sight.

                F 3   *Iul :*

383

The excellent Tragedie

Iul: Ah *Romeo*, *Romeo*, what disaster hap
Hath feuer'd thee from thy true *Iuliet* ?
Ah why shou'd Heauen so much conspire with Woe,
Or Fate enuie our happie Marriage,
So soone to sunder vs by timelesse Death?

Nur: O *Tybalt*, *Tybalt*, the best frend I had,
O honest *Tybalt*, curteous Gentleman.

Iul: What storme is this that blowes so contrarie,
Is *Tybalt* dead, and *Romeo* murdered :
My deare loude cousen, and my dearest Lord.
Then let the trumpet sound a generall doome,
These two being dead, then liuing is there none.

Nur : *Tybalt* is dead, and *Romeo* banished,
Romeo that murdred him is banished.

Iul: Ah heauens, did *Romeos* hand shed *Tybalts* blood?
Nur: It did, it did, alacke the day it did.

Iul: O serpents hate, hid with a flowring face :
O painted sepulcher, including filth.
Was neuer booke containing so foule matter,
So fairly bound. Ah, what meant *Romeo* ?

Nur: There is no truth, no faith, no honestie in men,
All false, all faithles, periurde, all forsworne.
Shame come to *Romeo*.

Iul: A blister on that tung, he was not borne to shame:
Vpon his face Shame is ashamde to sit.
But wherefore villaine didst thou kill my Cousen ?
That villaine Cousen would haue kild my husband.
All this is comfort. But there ye ——————————
Worse than his death, —————faine I would forget:
But ah, it presseth to my memorie,
Romeo is banished. Ah that word Banished
Is worse than death, *Romeo* is banished,
Is Father, Mother, *Tybalt*, *Iuliet*,
All kild, all slaine, all dead, all banished.
Where are my Father and my Mother Nurse?

Nur : Weeping and wayling ouer *Tybalts* coarse.
VVil

of Romeo and Iuliet.

VVill you goe to them?

  Iul: I, I, when theirs are ſpent,
Mine ſhall he ſhed for *Romeos* baniſhment.

  Nur: Ladie, your *Romeo* will be here to night,
Ile to him, he is hid at *Laurence* Cell.

  Iul: Doo ſo, and beare this Ring to my true Knight,
And bid him come to take his laſt farewell.   *Exeunt.*

    Enter Frier.

  Fr: *Romeo* come forth, come forth thou fearfull man,
Affliction is enamourd on thy parts,
And thou art wedded to Calamitie.
    Enter Romeo.

  Rom: Father what newes, what is the Princes doome,
VVhat Sorrow craues acquaintance at our hands,
VVhich yet we know not.

  Fr: Too familiar
Is my yong ſonne with ſuch ſowre companie:
I bring thee tidings of the Princes doome.

  Rom: VVhat leſſe than doomes day is the Princes doome?

  Fr: A gentler iudgement vaniſht from his lips,
Not bodies death, but bodies baniſhment.

  Rom: Ha, Baniſhed? be mercifull, ſay death:
For Exile hath more terror in his lookes,
Than death it ſelfe, doo not ſay Baniſhment.

  Fr: Hence from *Verona* art thou baniſhed:
Be patient, for the world is broad and wide.

  Rom: There is no world without *Verona* walls,
But purgatorie, torture, hell it ſelfe,
Hence baniſhed, is baniſht from the world:
And world exilde is death. Calling death baniſhment,
Thou cutſt my head off with a golden axe,
And ſmileſt vpon the ſtroke that murders me.

  Fr: Oh monſtrous ſinne, O rude vnthankfulnes:
Thy fault our law calls death, but the milde Prince
(Taking thy part) hath ruſhd aſide the law,

                         And

The excellent Tragedie

And turnd that blacke word death to banishment:
This is meere mercie, and thou seest it not.

 Rom : Tis torture and not mercie, heauen is heere
Where *Iuliet* liues : and euerie cat and dog,
And little mouse, euerie vnworthie thing
Liue here in heauen, and may looke on her,
But *Romeo* may not. More validitie,
More honourable state, more courtship liues
In carrion flyes, than *Romeo*: they may seaze
On the white wonder of faire *Iuliets* skinne,
And steale immortall kisses from her lips;
But *Romeo* may not, he is banished.
Flies may doo this, but I from this must flye.
Oh Father hadst thou no strong poyson mixt,
No sharpe ground knife, no present meane of death,
Though nere so meane, but banishment
To torture me withall : ah, banished.
O Frier, the damned vse that word in hell :
Howling attends it. How hadst thou the heart,
Being a Diuine, a ghostly Confessor,
A sinne absoluer, and my frend profest,
To mangle me with that word, Banishment ?

  Fr : Thou fond mad man, heare me but speake a word,
 Rom: O, thou wilt talke againe of Banishment.

  Fr : Ile giue thee armour to beare off this word,
Aduersities sweete milke, philosophie,
To comfort thee though thou be banished.

 Rom : Yet Banished ? hang vp philosophie,
Vnlesse philosophie can make a *Iuliet*,
Displant a Towne, reuerse a Princes doome,
It helpes not, it preuailes not, talke no more.

  Fr : O, now I see that madmen haue no eares.
  Rom: How should they, when that wise men haue no
eyes.

  Fr : Let me dispute with thee of thy estate.
  Rom : Thou canst not speak of what thou dost not feele
               Wert

of Romeo and Iuliet.

Wert thou as young as I, *Iuliet* thy Loue,
An houre but married, *Tybalt* murdred,
Doting like me, and like me banifhed,
Then mightft thou fpeake, then mightft thou teare thy
    hayre.
And fall vpon the ground as I doe now,
Taking the meafure of an vnmade graue.

Nurfe knockes.

Fr : *Romeo* arife, ftand vp thou wilt be taken,
I heare one knocke, arife and get thee gone.
  Nu : Hoe Fryer,
  Fr : Gods will what wilfulnes is this?

Shee knockes againe.

Nur : Hoe Fryer open the doore,
Fr : By and by I come. Who is there?
Nur : One from Lady *Iuliet.*
Fr : Then come neare.
Nur : Oh holy Fryer, tell mee oh holy Fryer,
Where is my Ladies Lord? Wher's *Romeo*?
  Fr : There on the ground, with his owne teares made
drunke,
  Nur : Oh he is euen in my Miftreffe cafe.
Iuft in her cafe. Oh wofull fimpathy,
Pitteous predicament, euen fo lyes fhee,
Weeping and blubbring, blubbring and weeping:
Stand vp, ftand vp, ftand and you be a man,
For *Iuliets* fake, for her fake rife and ftand,
Why fhould you fall into fo deep an O.

He rifes.

Romeo: Nurfe,
Nur : Ah fir, ah fir. Wel death's the end of all.

              G   *Rom:*

The excellent Tragedie

Rom: Spakeſt thou of *Iuliet,* how is it with her?
Doth ſhe not thinke me an olde murderer,
Now I haue ſtainde the childhood of her ioy,
With bloud remou'd but little from her owne?
Where is ſhe? and how doth ſhe? And what ſayes
My conceal'd Lady to our canceld loue?

Nur: Oh ſhe ſaith nothing, but weepes and pules,
And now fals on her bed, now on the ground,
And *Tybalt* cryes, and then on *Romeo* calles.

Rom: As if that name ſhot from the deadly leuel of a gun
Did murder her, as that names curſed hand
Murderd her kinſman. Ah tell me holy Fryer
In what vile part of this Anatomy
Doth my name lye? Tell me that I may ſacke
The hateſull manſion?

He offers to ſtab himſelfe, and Nurſe ſnatches
the dagger away.

Nur: Ah?
Fr: Hold, ſtay thy hand: art thou a man? thy forme
Cryes out thou art, but thy wilde actes denote
The vnreſonable furyes of a beaſt.
Vnſeemely woman in a ſeeming man,
Or ill beſeeming beaſt in ſeeming both.
Thou haſt amaz'd me. By my holy order,
I thought thy diſpoſition better temperd,
Haſt thou ſlaine *Tybalt?* wilt thou ſlay thy ſelfe?
And ſlay thy Lady too, that liues in thee?
Rouſe vp thy ſpirits, thy Lady *Iuliet* liues,
For whoſe ſweet ſake thou wert but lately dead:
There art thou happy. *Tybalt* would kill thee,
But thou ſlueſt *Tybalt,* there art thou happy too.
A packe of bleſſings lights vpon thy backe,
Happines Courts thee in his beſt array:
But like a misbehaude and ſullen wench
Thou frownſt vpon thy Fate that ſmilles on thee.

Take

388

of Romeo and Iuliet.

Take heede, take heede, for such dye miserable.
Goe get thee to thy loue as was decreed:
Ascend her Chamber Window, hence and comfort her,
But looke thou stay not till the watch be set:
For then thou canst not passe to *Mantua.*
Nurse prouide all things in a readines,
Comfort thy Mistresse, hatte the house to bed,
Which heauy sorrow makes them apt vnto.

   Nur: Good Lord what a thing learning is,
I could haue stayde heere all this night
To heare good counsell. Well Sir,
Ile tell my Lady that you will come,

   Rom: Doe so and bidde my sweet prepare to childe,
Farwell good Nurse.

      Nurse offers to goe in and turnes againe.

   Nur: Heere is a Ring Sir, that she bad me giue you,
   Rom: How well my comfort is reuiud by this.

              Exit Nurse.

   Fr: Soiorne in *Mantua,* Ile finde out your man,
And he shall signifie from time to time:
Euery good hap that doth befall thee heere.
Farwell.

   Rom: But that a ioy, past ioy cryes out on me,
It were a griefe so breefe to part with thee.

      Enter olde Capolet and his Wife, with
         County Paris.

   Cap: Thinges haue fallen out Sir so vnluckily,
That we haue had no time to moue my daughter.

         G 2   Looke

The excellent Tragedie

Looke yee Sir, ſhe lou'd her kinſman dearely,
And ſo did I. Well, we were borne to dye,
Wife wher's your daughter, is ſhe in her chamber?
I thinke ſhe meanes not to come downe to night.

   Par: Theſe times of woe affoord no time to woce,
Maddam farwell, commend me to your daughter.

         Paris offers to gee in, and Capolet
              calles him againe.

   Cap: Sir *Paris*? Ile make a deſperate tender of my child,
I thinke ſhe will be rulde in all reſpectes by mee:
But ſofe what day is this?

   Par: Munday my Lord.

   Cap: Oh then Wenſday is too ſoone,
On Thurſday let it be: you ſhall be maried.
Wee'le make no great a doe, a frend or two, or ſo:
For looke ye Sir, *Tybalt* being ſlaine ſo lately,
It will be thought we held him careleſlye:
If we ſhould reuell much, therefore we will haue
Some halfe a dozen frends and make no more adoe,
But what ſay you to Thurſday.

   Par: My Lorde I wiſhe that Thurſday were to morrow.

   Cap: Wife goe you to your daughter, ere you goe to
   bed.
Acquaint her with the County *Paris* loue,
Fare well my Lord till Thurſday next.
Wife gette you to your daughter, Light to my Chamber,
Afore me it is ſo very very late,
That we may call it earely by and by.

                               Exeunt.

                                    Enter

of Romeo and Iuliet.

Enter Romeo and Iuliet at the window.

Iul: Wilt thou be gone? It is not yet nere day,
It was the Nightingale and not the Larke
That pierſt the fearfull hollow of thine eare:
Nightly ſhe ſings on yon Pomegranate tree,
Beleeue me loue, it was the Nightingale.

Rom: It was the Larke, the Herald of the Morne,
And not the Nightingale. See Loue what enuious ſtrakes
Doo lace the ſeuering clowdes in yonder Eaſt.
Nights candles are burnt out, and iocond Day
Stands tiptoes on the myſtie mountaine tops.
I muſt be gone and liue, or ſtay and dye.

Iul: Yon light is not day light, I know it I:
It is ſome Meteor that the Sunne exhales,
To be this night to thee a Torch-bearer,
And light thee on thy way to *Mantua.*
Then ſtay awhile, thou ſhalt not goe ſoone.

Rom: Let me ſtay here, let me be tane, and dye:
If thou wilt haue it ſo, I am content.
Ile ſay yon gray is not the Mornings Eye,
It is the pale reflex of *Cynthias* brow.
Ile ſay it is the Nightingale that beates
The vaultie heauen ſo high aboue our heads,
And not the Larke the Meſſenger of Morne.
Come death and welcome, *Iuliet* wils it ſo.
What ſayes my Loue? lets talke, tis not yet day.

Iul: It is, it is, be gone, flye hence away,
It is the Larke that ſings ſo out of tune,
Straining harſh Diſcords and vnpleaſing Sharpes.
Some ſay, the Larke makes ſweete Diuiſion:

G 3   Thia

391

The excellent Tragedie

This doth not so : for this diuideth vs.
Some say the Larke and loathed Toad change eyes,
I would that now they had changd voyces too :
Since arme from arme her voyce doth vs affray,
Hunting thee hence with Huntsvp to the day.
So now be gone, more light and light it growes.

 Rom : More light and light, more darke and darke our
  woes,
Farewell my Loue, one kisse and Ile descend.

He goeth downe.

 Jul : Art thou gone so, my Lord, my Loue, my Frend?
I must heare from thee euerie day in the hower :
For in an hower there are manie minutes,
Minutes are dayes, so will I number them :
Oh, by this count I shall be much in yeares,
Ere I see thee againe.

 Rom : Farewell, I will omit no opportunitie
That may conueigh my greetings loue to thee.

 Iul : Oh, thinkst thou we shall euer meete againe.

 Rom : No doubt, no doubt, and all this woe shall serue
For sweete discourses in the time to come.

 Jul : Oh God, I haue an ill diuining soule.
Me thinkes I see thee now thou art below
Like one dead in the bottome of a Tombe :
Either mine ey-sight failes, or thou lookst pale.

 Rom : And trust me Loue, in my eye so doo you,
Drie sorrow drinkes our blood : adieu, adieu. *Exit*

Enter Nurse hastely.

 Nur : Madame beware, take heed the day is broke,
Your Mother's comming to your Chamber, make all sure.
  She goeth downe from the window.

             Enter

of *Romeo and Iuliet.*

Enter Iuliets Mother, Nurse.

Moth: Where are you Daughter?
Nur: What Ladie, Lambe, what *Iuliet?*
Iul: How now, who calls?
Nur: It is your Mother.
Moth: Why how now *Iuliet?*
Iul: Madam, I am not well.
Moth: What euermore weeping for your Cofens death:
I thinke thoult wafh him from his graue with teares.
Iul: I cannot chufe, hauing fo great a loffe.
Moth: I cannot blame thee.
But it greeues thee more that Villaine liues.
Iul: What Villaine Madame?
Moth: That Villaine *Romeo.*
Iul: Villaine and he are manie miles a funder.
Moth: Content thee Girle, if I could finde a man
I foone would fend to *Mantua* where he is,
That fhould beftow on him fo fure a draught,
As he fhould foone beare *Tybalt* companie.
Iul: Finde you the meanes, and Ile finde fuch a man:
For whileft he liues, my heart fhall nere be light
Till I behold him, dead is my poore heart.
Thus for a Kinfman vext?
Moth: Well let that paffe. I come to bring thee ioyfull (newes?
Iul: And ioy comes well in fuch a needfull time.
Moth: Well then, thou haft a carefull Father Girle,
And one who pittying thy needfull ftate,
Hath found thee out a happie day of ioy.
Iul: What day is that I pray you?
Moth: Marry my Childe,

The

The excellent Tragedie

The gallant, yong and youthfull Gentleman,
The Countie *Paris* at Saint *Peters* Church,
Early next Thurfday morning muft prouide,
To make you there a glad and ioyfull Bride.

   Iul: Now by Saint *Peters* Church and *Peter* too,
He fhall not there make mee a ioyfull Bride.
Are thefe the newes you had to tell me of?
Marrie here are newes indeed. Madame I will not marrie
     yet.
And when I doo, it fhalbe rather *Romeo* whom I hate,
Than Countie *Paris* that I cannot loue.

Enter olde Capolet.

   Moth: Here comes your Father, you may tell him fo,
   Capo: Why how now, euermore fhowring?
In one little bodie thou refembleft a fea, a barke, a ftorme:
For this thy bodie which I tearme a barke,
Still floating in thy euerfalling teares,
And toft with fighes arifing from thy hart:
Will without fuccour fhipwracke prefently.
But heare you Wife, what haue you founded her, what faid
     fhe to it?

   Moth: I haue, but fhe will none fhe thankes ye:
VVould God that fhe were married to her graue.

   Capo: What will fhe not, doth fhe not thanke vs, doth
fhe not wexe proud?

   Iul: Not proud ye haue, but thankfull that ye haue:
Proud can I neuer be of that I hate,
But thankfull euen for hate that is ment loue.

   Capo: Proud and I thanke you, and I thanke you not,
And yet not proud. VVhats here, chop logicke.
Proud me no prouds, nor thanke me no thankes,
But fettle your fine ioynts on Thurfday next
To goe with *Paris* to Saint *Peters* Church,
Or I will drag you on a hurdle thether.
                        Out

of Romeo and Iuliet.

Out you greene ficknes baggage, out you tallow face.
  Iu: Good father heare me fpeake?

She kneeles downe.

  Cap: I tell thee what, eyther refolue on thurfday next
To goe with *Paris* to Saint Peters Church:
Or henceforth neuer looke me in the face.
Speake not, reply not, for my fingers ytch.
Why wife, we thought that we were fcarcely bleft
That God had fent vs but this onely chyld:
But now I fee this one is one too much,
And that we haue a croffe in hauing her.
  Nur: Mary God in heauen blefie her my Lord,
You are too blame to rate her fo.
  Cap. And why my Lady wifedome? hold your tung,
Good prudence fmatter with your goffips, goe.
  Nur: Why my Lord I fpeake no treafon.
  Cap: Oh goddegodden.
Vtter your grauity ouer a goffips boule,
For heere we need it not.
  Mo: My Lord ye are too hotte.
  Cap: Gods bleffed mother wife it mads me,
Day, night, early, late, at home, abroad,
Alone, in company, waking or fleeping,
Still my care hath beene to fee her matcht,
And hauing now found out a Gentleman,
Of Princely parentage, youthfull, and nobly trainde.
Stuft as they fay with honorable parts,
Proportioned as ones heart coulde wifh a man:
And then to haue a wretched whyning foole,
A puling mammet in her fortunes tender,
To fay I cannot loue, I am too young, I pray you pardon
    mee?
But if you cannot wedde Ile pardon you,
Graze where you will, you fhall not houfe with me,
Looke to it, thinke ont, I doe not vfe to ielt.

H

I

The excellent Tragedie

I tell yee what, Thursday is neere,
Lay hand on heart, aduise, bethinke your selfe,
If you be mine, Ile giue you to my frend:
If not, hang, drowne, starue, beg,
Dye in the streetes: for by my Soule
Ile neuer more acknowledge thee,
Nor what I haue shall euer doe thee good,
Thinke ont, looke toot, I doe not vse to iest.   *Exit*

Iul: Is there no pitty hanging in the cloudes,
That lookes into the bottom of my woes?
I doe beseech you Madame, cast me not away,
Defer this mariage for a day or two,
Or if you cannot, make my mariage bed
In that dimme monument where *Tybalt* lyes.

Moth: Nay be assured I will not speake a word.
Do what thou wilt for I haue done with thee.   *Exit*

Iul: Ah Nurse what comfort? what counsell canst thou
          giue me.

Nur: Now trust me Madame, I know not what to say,
Your *Romeo* he is banisht, and all the world to nothing
He neuer dares returne to challendge you.
Now I thinke good you marry with this County,
Oh he is a gallant Gentleman, *Romeo* is but a dishclout
In respect of him. I promise you
I thinke you happy in this second match.
As for your husband he is dead:
Or twere as good he were, for you haue no vse of him.

Iul: Speakst thou this from thy heart?

Nur: I and from my soule, or els beshrew them both.

Iul: Amen.

Nur: What say you Madame?

Iul: Well, thou hast comforted me wondrous much,
I pray thee goe thy waies vnto my mother
Tell her I am gone hauing displeasde my Father,
To Fryer *Laurence* Cell to confesse me,
And to be absolu'd.

of Romeo and Iuliet.

Nur: I will, and this is wisely done.

                  She lookes after Nurse.

Iul: Auncient damnation, O most cursed fiend.
Is it more sinne to wish me thus forsworne,
Or to dispraise him with the selfe same tongue
That thou hast praisde him with aboue compare
So many thousand times? Goe Counsellor,
Thou and my bosom henceforth shalbe twaine.
Ile to the Fryer to know his remedy,
If all faile els, I haue the power to dye.

                       Exit.

Enter Fryer and Paris.

Fr: On Thursday say ye: the time is very short,
Par: My Father *Capolet* will haue it so,
And I am nothing slacke to slow his hast.
  Fr: You say you doe not know the Ladies minde?
Vneuen is the course, I like it not.
  Par: Immoderately she weepes for *Tybalts* death,
And therefore haue I little talkt of loue.
For *Venus* smiles not in a house of teares,
Now Sir, her father thinkes it daungerous:
That she doth giue her sorrow so much sway.
And in his wisedome hasts our mariage,
To stop the inundation of her teares,
Which too much minded by her selfe alone
May be put from her by societie.
Now doe ye know the reason of this hast,
  Fr: I would I knew not why it should be slowd.

        H 2   *Enter*

The excellent Tragedie

Enter Paris.

Heere comes the Lady to my cell,

    Par: Welcome my loue, my Lady and my wife:

    Iu: That may be sir, when I may be a wife,

    Par: That may be, must be loue, on thursday next.

    Iu: What must be shalbe.

    Fr: Thats a certaine text.

    Par: What come ye to confession to this Fryer,

    Iu: To tell you that were to confesse to you.

    Par: Do not deny to him that you loue me,

    Iul: I will confesse to you that I loue him,

    Par: So I am sure you will that you loue me,

    Iu: And if I doe, it wilbe of more price,

Being spoke behinde your backe, than to your face.

    Par: Poore soule thy face is much abus'd with teares

    Iu: The teares haue got small victory by that,

For it was bad enough before their spite.

    Par: Thou wrongst it more than teares by that report,

    Iu: That is no wrong sir, that is a truth:

And what I spake I spake it to my face.

    Par: Thy face is mine and thou hast slaundred it,

    Iu: It may be so, for it is not mine owne.

Are you at leasure holy Father now:

Or shall I come to you at euening Masse?

    Fr: My leasure serues me pensiue daughter now,

My Lord we must entreate the time alone.

    Par: God sheild I should disturbe deuotion,

Iuliet farwell, and keep this holy kisse.

                           Exit Paris

    Iu: Goe shut the doore and when thou hast done so,

Come weepe with me that am past cure, past help,

    Fr: Ah Iuliet I already know thy griefe,

I heare thou must and nothiug may proroge it,

                                On

of *Romeo and Iuliet*.

On Thurſday next be married to the Countie,

   Iul: Tell me not Frier that thou hearſt of it,
Vnleſſe thou tell me how we may preuent it.
Giue me ſome ſudden counſell : els behold
Twixt my extreames and me, this bloodie Knife
Shall play the Vmpeere, arbitrating that
Which the Commiſsion of thy yeares and arte
Could to no iſſue of true honour bring.
Speake not, be briefe : for I deſire to die,
If what thou ſpeakſt, ſpeake not of remedie.

   Fr : Stay *Iuliet*, I doo ſpie a kinde of hope,
VVhich craues as deſperate an execution,
As that is deſperate we would preuent.
If rather than to marrie Countie *Paris*
Thou haſt the ſtrength or will to ſlay thy ſelfe,
Tis not vnlike that thou wilt vndertake
A thing like death to chyde away this ſhame,
That coapſt with death it ſelfe to flye from blame.
And if thou dooſt, Ile giue thee remedie.

   Iul: Oh bid me leape (rather than marrie *Paris*)
From off the battlements of yonder tower :
Or chaine me to ſome ſteepie mountaines top,
VVhere roaring Beares and ſauage Lions are :
Or ſhut me nightly in a Charnell-houſe,
VVith reekie ſhankes, and yeolow chaples ſculls :
Or lay me in tombe with one new dead :
Things that to heare them namde haue made me tremble ;
And I will doo it without feare or doubt,
To keep my ſelfe a faithfull vnſtaind VVife
To my deere Lord, my deereſt *Romeo*.

   ·*Fr* : Hold *Iuliet*, hie thee home, get thee to bed,
Let not thy Nurſe lye with thee in thy Chamber :
And when thou art alone, take thou this Violl,
And this diſtilled Liquor drinke thou off :
VVhen preſently through all thy veynes ſhall run
A dull and heauie ſlumber, which ſhall ſeaze

The excellent Tragedie

Each vitall spirit: for no Pulse shall keepe
His naturall progresse, but surcease to beate:
No signe of breath shall testifie thou liust.
And in this borrowed likenes of shrunke death,
Thou shalt remaine full two and fortie houres,
And when thou art laid in thy Kindreds Vault,
Ile send in hast to *Mantua* to thy Lord,
And he shall come and take thee from thy graue.

   Iul: Frier I goe, be sure thou send for my deare *Romeo*,
                                          Exeunt.

Enter olde Capolet, his Wife, Nurse, and
Seruingman.

  Capo: Where are you sirra?
  Ser: Heere forsooth.
  Capo: Goe, prouide me twentie cunning Cookes.
  Ser: I warrant you Sir, let me alone for that, Ile knowe
them by licking their fingers.
  Capo: How canst thou know them so?
  Ser: Ah Sir, tis an ill Cooke cannot licke his owne fin-
gers.
  Capo: Well get you gone.

          Exit Seruingman.

But wheres this Head-strong?
  Moth: Shees gone (my Lord) to Frier *Laurence* Cell
To be confest.
  Capo: Ah, he may hap to doo some good of her,
A headstrong selfe wild harlotrie it is.

                                Enter

of Romeo and Iuliet.

Enter Iuliet.

Moth: See here she commeth from Confession,
  Capo: How now my Head-strong, where haue you bin
gadding?
  Iul: Where I haue learned to repent the sin
Of froward wilfull opposition
Gainst you and your behests, and am enioynd
By holy *Laurence* to fall prostrate here,
And craue remission of so foule a fact.

She kneeles downe.

Moth: Why thats well said.
  Capo: Now before God this holy reuerent Frier
All our whole Citie is much bound vnto.
Goe tell the Countie presently of this,
For I will haue this knot knit vp to morrow.
  Iul: Nurse, will you go with me to my Closet,
To sort such things as shall be requisite
Against to morrow.
  Moth: I pree thee doo, good Nurse goe in with her,
Helpe her to sort Tyres, Rebatoes, Chaines,
And I will come vnto you presently,
  Nur: Come sweet hart, shall we goe ?
  Iul: I pree thee let vs.

Exeunt Nurse and Iuliet.

Moth: Me thinks on Thursday would be time enough,
  Capo: I say I will haue this dispatcht to morrow,
Goe one and certefie the Count thereof.
  Moth: I pray my Lord, let it be Thursday.
  Capo: I say to morrow while shees in the mood.
  Moth: We shall be short in our prouision.

Capo:

The excellent Tragedie

Capo: Let me alone for that, goe get you in,
Now before God my heart is paſsing light,
To ſee her thus conformed to our will.   *Exeunt.*

Enter Nurſe, Iuliet.

Nur: Come, come, what need you anie thing elſe?
Iul: Nothing good Nurſe, but leaue me to my ſelfe:
For I doo meane to lye alone to night.
  Nur: Well theres a cleane ſmocke vnder your pillow,
and ſo good night.   *Exit.*

Enter Mother.

Moth: What are you buſie, doo you need my helpe?
Iul: No Madame, I deſire to lye alone,
For I haue manie things to thinke vpon.
  Moth: Well then good night, be ſtirring *Iuliet*,
The Countie will be earlie here to morrow.   *Exit.*
  Iul: Farewell, God knowes when wee ſhall meete a-
    gaine.
Ah, I doo take a fearfull thing in hand.
What if this Potion ſhould not worke at all,
Muſt I of force be married to the Countie?
This ſhall forbid it. Knife, lye thou there.
What if the Frier ſhould giue me this drinke
To poyſon mee, for feare I ſhould diſcloſe
Our former marriage? Ah, I wrong him much,
He is a holy and religious Man:
I will not entertaine ſo bad a thought.
What if I ſhould be ſtifled in the Toomb?

O

of Romeo and Iuliet.

Awake an houre before the appointed time:
Ah then I feare I shall be lunaticke,
And playing with my dead forefathers bones,
Dash out my franticke braines. Me thinkes I see
My Cosin *Tybalt* weltring in his bloud,
Seeking for *Romeo*: stay *Tybalt*, stay.
Romeo I come, this doe I drinke to thee.

>   *She fals vpon her bed within the Curtaines.*

>   *Enter Nurse with hearbs, Mother.*

Moth: Thats well said Nurse, set all in redines,
The Countie will be heere immediatly.

>   *Enter Oldeman.*

Cap: Make hast, make hast, for it is almost day,
The Curfewe bell hath rung, t'is foure a clocke,
Looke to your bakt meates good Angelica.

Nur: Goe get you to bed you cotqueane. I faith you
will be sicke anone.

Cap: I warrant thee Nurse I haue ere now watcht all
night, and haue taken no harme at all.

Moth: I you haue beene a mouse hunt in your time.

>   *Enter Seruingman with Logs & Coales.*

Cap: A Ielous hood, a Ielous hood: How now sirra?
What haue you there?

Ser: Forsooth Logs.

Cap: Goe, goe choose dryer. Will will tell thee where
thou shalt fetch them.

Ser: Nay I warrant let me alone, I haue a heade I no to
                    I   choose

The excellent Tragedie

choofe a Log.

Exit.

Cap: Well goe thy way, thou fhalt be logger head,
Come, come, make haft call vp your daughter,
The Countie will be heere with muficke ftraight,
Gods me hees come, Nurfe call vp my daughter.

Nur: Goe, get you gone. What lambe, what Lady
birde? faft I warrant. What Iuliet? well, let the County take
you in your bed: yee fleepe for a weeke now, but the next
night, the Countie *Parss* hath fet vp his reft that you fhal reft
but little. What lambe I fay, faft ftill: what Lady, Loue,
what bride, what Iuliet? Gods me how found fhe fleeps: Nay
then I fee I muft wake you indeed. Whats heere, laide on
your bed, dreft in your cloathes and down, ah me, alack the
day, fome Aqua vitæ hoe.

Enter Mother.

Moth: How now whats the matter?
Nur: Alack the day, fhees dead, fhees dead, fhees dead.
Moth: Accurft, vnhappy, miferable time.

Enter Oldeman.

Cap: Come, come, make haft, wheres my daughter?
Moth: Ah fhees dead, fhees dead.
Cap: Stay, let me fee, all pale and wan.
Accurfed time, vnfortunate olde man.

Enter Fryer and Paris.

Par: What is the bride ready to goe to Church?
Cap: Ready to goe, but neuer to returne.
O Sonne the night before thy wedding day,
Hath Death laine with thy bride, flower as fhe is,
Deflowerd by him, fee, where fhe lyes,

Death

of Romeo and Iuliet.

Death is my Sonne in Law, to him I giue all that I haue,

  Par: Haue I thought long to fee this mornings face,
And doth it now prefent fuch prodegies?
Accurft, vnhappy, miferable man,
Forlorne, forfaken, deftitute I am:
Borne to the world to be a flaue in it.
Diftreft, remediles, and vnfortunate.
O heauens, O nature, wherefore did you make me,
To liue fo vile, fo wretched as I fhall.

  Cap: O heere fhe lies that was our hope, our ioy,
And being dead, dead forrow nips vs all.

          All at once cry out and wring their hands

  All cry: And all our ioy, and all our hope is dead,
Dead, loft, vndone, abfented, wholy fled.

  Cap: Cruel, vniuft, impartiall deftinies,
Why to this day haue you preferu'd my life?
To fee my hope, my ftay, my ioy, my life,
Depriude of fence, of life, of all by death,
Cruell, vniuft, impartiall deftinies.

  Cap: O fad fac'd forrow map of mifery,
Why this fad time haue I defird to fee.
This day, this vniuft, this impartiall day
Wherein I hop'd to fee my comfort full,
To be depriude by fuddaine deftinie.

  Moth: O woe, alacke, diftreft, why fhould I liue?
To fee this day, this miferable day.
Alacke the time that euer I was borne,
To be partaker of this deftinie.
Alacke the day, alacke and welladay.

  Fr: O peace for fhame, if not for charity,
Your daughter liues in peace and happines,
And it is vaine to wifh it otherwife.

          I 2   Come

The excellent Tragedie

Come sticke your Rosemary in this dead coarse,
And as the custome of our Country is,
In all her best and sumptuous ornaments,
Conuay her where her Ancestors lie tomb'd,

   Cap: Let it be so, come wofull sorrow mates,
Let vs together taste this bitter fate.

They all but the Nurse goe foorth, casting Rosemary on
her and shutting the Curtens.

Enter Musitions.

Nur: Put vp, put vp, this is a wofull case.   *Exit.*
1. I by my troth Mistresse is it, it had need be mended.

Enter Seruingman.

Ser: Alack alack what shal I doe, come Fidlers play mé
  some mery dumpe.
1. A sir, this is no time to play.
Ser: You will not then?
1. No marry will wee,
Ser: Then will I giue it you, and soundly to.
1. What will you giue vs?
Ser: The fidler, Ile re you, Ile fa you, Ile sol you.
1. If you re vs and fa vs, we will note you.
Ser: I will put vp my Iron dagger, and beate you with
my wodden wit, Come on Simon sound Pot, Ile pose you
  1 Lets heare.
Ser: When griping griefe the heart doth wound,
And dolefull dumps the minde oppresse:
Then musique with her siluer sound,
Why siluer sound? Why siluer sound?
  1. I thinke because musicke hath a sweet sound.
  Ser: Pretie, what say you Mathew mimikine?

of *Romeo* and *Iuliet.*

2. I thinke becaufe Mufitions found for filuer.

Ser: Prettie too : come, what fay you?

3. I fay nothing.

Ser: I thinke fo, Ile fpeake for you becaufe you are the Singer, I faye Siluer found, becaufe fuch Fellowes as you haue fildome Golde for founding. Farewell Fidlers, farewell.　　　　　　　　　　　　　　　　　　*Exit.*

1. Farewell and be hangd : come lets goe.　　*Exeunt.*

Enter Romeo.

Rom: If I may truft the flattering Eye of Sleepe,
My Dreame prefagde fome good euent to come,
My bofome Lord fits chearfull in his throne,
And I am comforted with pleafing dreames.
Me thought I was this night alreadie dead:
(Strange dreames that giue a dead man leaue to thinke)
And that my Ladie *Iuliet* came to me,
And breathd fuch life with kiffes in my lips,
That I reuiude and was an Emperour.

Enter Balthafar his man booted.

Newes from *Verona.* How now *Balthafar,*
How doth my Ladie? Is my Father well?
How fares my *Iuliet?* that I aske againe,
If fhe be well, then nothing can be ill.

Balt: Then nothing can be ill, for fhe is well,
Her bodie fleepes in *Capels* Monument,
And her immortall parts with Angels dwell,
Pardon me Sir, that am the Meffenger of fuch bad tidings.

Rom: Is it eu'n fo? then I defie my Starres.

I 3　　　　　　　　　　　　　　　　　　Goe

The excellent Tragedie

Goe get me ineke and paper, hyre post horse,
I will not stay in *Mantua* to night.

  Balt: Pardon me Sir, I will not leaue you thus,
Your lookes are dangerous and full of feare:
I dare not, nor I will not leaue you yet,

  Rom: Doo as I bid thee, get me incke and paper,
And hyre those horse : stay not I say.

Exit Balthasar.

Well *Iuliet*, I will lye with thee to night.
Lets see for meanes. As I doo remember
Here dwells a Pothecarie whom oft I noted
As I past by, whose needie shop is stufft
With beggerly accounts of emptie boxes:
And in the same an *Aligarta* hangs,
Olde endes of packthred, and cakes of Roses,
Are thinly strewed to make vp a show,
Him as I noted, thus with my selfe I thought:
And if a man should need a poyson now,
(Whose present sale is death in *Mantua*)
Here he might buy it. This thought of mine
Did but forerunne my need : and here about he dwels,
Being Holiday the Beggers shop is shut.
What ho Apothecarie, come forth I say.

Enter Apothecarie.

  Apo: VVho calls, what would you sir?
  Rom: Heeres twentie duckates,
Giue me a dram of some such speeding geere,
As will dispatch the wearie takers life,
As suddenly as powder being fierd
From forth a Cannons mouth.

  Apo: Such drugs I haue I must of force confesse,
But yet the law is death to those that sell them. *Rom:*

of Romeo and Iuliet.

Rom: Art thou so bare and full of pouertie,
And dooft thou feare to violate the Law?
The Law is not thy frend, nor the Lawes frend,
And therefore make no confcience of the law:
Vpon thy backe hangs ragged Miferie,
And ftarued Famine dwelleth in thy cheekes.

Apo: My pouertie but not my will confents,

Rom: I pay thy pouertie, but not thy will.

Apo: Hold take you this, and put it in anie liquid thing
you will, and it will ferue had you the liues of twenty men.

Rom: Hold, take this gold, worfe poyfon to mens foules
Than this which thou haft giuen me. Goe hye thee hence,
Goe buy the cloathes, and get thee into flefh.
Come cordiall and not poyfon, goe with mee
To *Iuliets* Graue: for there muft I vfe thee.   *Exeunt.*

Enter Frier Iohn.

Iohn: VVhat Frier *Laurence*, Brother, ho?

Laur: This fame fhould be the voyce of Frier *Iohn*,
VVhat newes from *Mantua*, what will *Romeo* come?

Iohn: Going to feeke a barefoote Brother out,
One of our order to affociate mee,
Here in this Cittie vifiting the fick,
VVhereas the infectious peftilence remaind,
And being by the Searchers of the Towne
Found and examinde, we were both fhut vp.

Law: VVho bare my letters then to *Romeo*?

Iohn: I haue them ftill, and here they are.

Law: Now by my holy Order,
The letters were not nice, but of great weight.
Goe get thee hence, and get me prefently

A₃

409

The excellent Tragedie

A ſpade and mattocke.
   Iohn: Well I will preſently go fetch thee them. *Exit.*
   Laur: Now muſt I to the Monument alone,
Leaſt that the Ladie ſhould before I come
Be wakde from ſleepe. I will hye
To free her from that Tombe of miſerie.   *Exit.*

Enter Countie Paris and his Page with flowers
and ſweete water.

   Par: Put out the torch, and lye thee all along.
Vnder this Ew-tree, keeping thine eare cloſe to the hollow
   ground.
And if thou heare one tread within this Churchyard,
Staight giue me notice.
   Boy: I will my Lord.

Paris ſtrewes the Tomb with flowers.

   Par: Sweete Flower, with flowers I ſtrew thy Bride
   bed.
Sweete Tombe that in thy circuite doſt containe,
The perfect modell of eternitie:
Faire *Iuliet* that with Angells doſt remaine,
Accept this lateſt fauour at my hands,
That liuing honourd thee, and being dead
With funerall praiſes doo adorne thy Tombe.
   Boy whiſtles and calls. My Lord.

Enter Romeo and Balthaſar, with a torch, a
mattocke, and a crow of yron.

of Romeo and Iuliet.

Par: The boy giues warning, something doth approach.
What curfed foote wanders this was to night,
To ſtay my obſequies and true loues rites?
What with a torch, muffle me night a while.

    Rom: Giue mee this mattocke, and this wrentching I-
      ron.
And take theſe letters, early in the morning,
See thou deliuer them to my Lord and Father.
So get thee gone and trouble me no more.
Why I deſcend into this bed of death,
Is partly to behold my Ladies face,
But chiefly to take from her dead finger,
A precious ring which I muſt vſe
In deare imployment. but if thou wilt ſtay,
Further to prie in what I vndertake,
By heauen Ile teare thee ioynt by ioynt,
And ſtrewe thys hungry churchyard with thy lims.
The time and my intents are ſauage, wilde.

    Balt: Well, Ile be gone and not trouble you.

    Rom: So ſhalt thou win my fauour, take thou this,
Commend me to my Father, farwell good fellow.

    Balt: Yet for all this will I not part from hence.

           Romeo opens the tombe.

    Rom: Thou deteſtable maw, thou womb of death,
Gorde with the deareſt morſell of the earth.
Thus I enforce thy rotten iawes to ope.

    Par: This is that baniſht haughtie *Mountague*,
That murderd my loues coſen, I will apprehend him.
Stop thy vnhallowed toyle vile *Mountague*.
Can vengeance be purſued further then death?
I doe attach thee as a fellon heere,
The Law condemnes thee, therefore thou muſt dye.

    Rom: I muſt indeed, and therefore came I hither,
Good youth begone, tempt not a deſperate man,

           K   Heape

The excellent Tragedie

Heape not another sinne vpon my head
By sheding of thy bloud, I doe protest
I loue thee better then I loue my selfe :
For I come hyther armde against my selfe,
  Par: I doe defie thy coniurations :
And doe attach thee as a fellon heere.
  Rom: What dost thou tempt me, then haue at thee boy.

They fight.

  Boy: O Lord they fight, I will goe call the watch.
  Par: Ah I am slaine, if thou be mercifull
Open the tombe, lay me with *Iuliet*.
  Rom: Yfaith I will, let me peruse this face,
Mercutios kinsman, noble County *Paris* ?
What said my man, when my betossed soule
Did not regard him as we past a long.
Did he not say *Paris* should haue maried
Iuliet ? eyther he said so, or I dreamd it so.
But I will satisfie thy last request,
For thou hast prizd thy loue aboue thy life.
Death lye thou there, by a dead man interd,
How oft haue many at the houre of death
Beene blith and pleasant ? which their keepers call
A lightning before death But how may I
Call this a lightning. Ah deare *Iuliet*,
How well thy beauty doth become this graue ?
O I beleeue that vnsubstanciall death,
Is amorous, and doth court my loue.
Therefore will I, O heere, O euer heere,
Set vp my euerlasting rest
With wormes, that are thy chamber mayds.
Come desperate Pilot now at once runne on
The dashing rockes thy sea-sicke weary barge:
Heers to my loue. O true Apothecary:
Thy drugs are swift: thus with a kisse I dye.
       Falls
       Enter

of Romeo and Iuliet.

Enter Fryer with a Lantborne.

How oft to night haue thefe my aged feete
Stumbled at graues as I did paffe along.
Whofe there?
   Man. A frend and one that knowes you well.
   Fr: Who is it that conforts fo late the dead,
What light is yon? if I be not deceiued,
Me thinkes it burnes in *Capels* monument?
   Man It doth fo holy Sir, and there is one
That loues you dearely.
   Fr. Who is it?
   Man: Romeo.
   Fr: How long hath he beene there?
   Man: Full halfe an houre and more.
   Fr: Goe with me thether.
   Man: I dare not fir, he knowes not I am heere:
On paine of death he chargde me to be gone,
And not for to difturbe him in his enterprize.
   Fr: Then muft I goe : my minde prefageth ill.

Fryer ftoops and lookes on the bloud and weapons.

What bloud is this that ftaines the entrance
Of this marble ftony monument?
What meanes thefe maifterles and goory weapons?
Ah me I doubt, whofe heere? what *Romeo* dead?
Who and *Paris* too? what vnluckie houre
Is acceffary to fo foule a finne?

                              Iuliet rifes.

The Lady fturres.

                  K 2   Iul:

The excellent Tragedie

Ah comfortable Fryer,
I doe remember well where I should be,
And what we talkt of: but yet I cannot see
Him for whose sake I vndertooke this hazard.

    Fr: Lady come foorth, I heare some noise at hand,
We shall be taken, *Paris* he is slaine,
And *Romeo* dead: and if we heere be tane
We shall be thought to be as accessarie,
I will prouide for you in some close Nunery.

    Iul: Ah leaue me, leaue me, I will not frō hence.

    Fr: I heare some noise, I dare not stay, come, co.ne,

    Iu': Goe get thee gone.
Whats heere a cup closde in my louers hands?
Ah churle drinke all, and leaue no drop for me.

                Enter Watch.

    Watch: This way, this way.

    Iul: I, noise? then must I be resolute.
O happy dagger thou shalt end my feare,
Rest in my bosome, thus I come to thee.
           She stabs her selfe and falles.

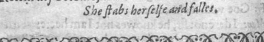

              Enter watch.

    Cap: Come looke about, what weapons haue we heere
See frends where *Iuliet* two daies buried,
New bleeding wounded, search and see who's neare,
Attach and bring them to vs presently.
          Enter one with the Fryer.

    1. Captaine heers a Fryer with tooles about him,
Fitte to ope a tombe.

    Cap: A great suspition, keep him safe,
                        Entr

of *Romeo and Iuliet*.

Enter one with Romeis Man.

1. Heeres *Romeos* Man.

Capt : Keepe him to be examinde,

Enter Prince with others.

Prin : What early mischiefe call, vs vp so soone.

Capt : O noble Prince, see here
Where *Iuliet* that hath lyen intoombd two dayes,
Warme and fresh bleeding, *Romeo* and Countie *Paris*
Likewise newly slaine:

Prin : Search seeke about to finde the murderers,

Enter olde Capolet and his Wife.

Capo : What rumor's this that is so early vp?

Moth : The people in the streetes crie *Romeo*,
And some on *Iuliet :* as if they alone
Had been the cause of such a mutinie.

Capo : See Wife, this dagger hath mistooke:
For (loe) the backe is emptie of yong *Mountague*,
And it is sheathed in our Daughters breast.

Enter olde Montague.

Prin : Come *Mountague*, for thou art early vp,
To see thy Sonne and Heire more early downe.

Mount : Dread Soueraigne, my Wife is dead to night,
And yong *Benuolio* is deceased too:
What further mischiefe can there yet be found?

Prin : First come and see, then speake.

Mount : O thou vntaught, what manners is in this
To presse before thy Father to a graue.

Prin : Come seale your mouthes of outrage for a while,
And let vs seeke to finde the Authors out
Of such a hainous and seld seene mischaunce.
Bring forth the parties in suspition,

Fr : I am the greatest able to doo least,
Most worthie Prince, heare me but speake the truth.

K 3   And

415

The excellent Tragedie

And Ile informe you how these things fell out.
Iuliet here flaine was married to that *Romeo*,
Without her Fathers or her Mothers grant:
The Nurfe was priuie to the marriage.
The balefull day of this vnhappie marriage,
VVas *Tybalts* doomefday: for which *Romeo*
VVas banifhed from hence to *Mantua*.
He gone, her Father fought by foule conftraint
To marrie her to *Paris*: But her Soule
(Loathing a fecond Contract) did refufe
To giue confent; and therefore did fhe vrge me
Either to finde a meanes fhe might auoyd
VVhat fo her Father fought to force her too:
Or els all defperately fhe threatned
Euen in my prefence to difpatch her felfe.
Then did I giue her, (tutord by mine arte)
A potion that fhould make her feeme as dead:
And told her that I would with all poft fpeed
Send hence to *Mantua* for her *Romeo*,
That he might come and take her from the Toombs,
But he that had my Letters (Frier *Iohn*)
Seeking a Brother to affociate him,
VVhereas the ficke infection remaind,
VVas ftayed by the Searchers of the Towne,
But *Romeo* vnderftanding by his man,
That *Iuliet* was deceafde, returnde in poft
Vnto *Verona* for to fee his loue.
VVhat after happened touching *Paris* death,
Or *Romeos* is to me vnknowne at all.
But when I came to take the Lady hence,
I found them dead, and fhe awakt from fleep:
VVhom faine I would haue taken from the tombe,
VVhich fhe refufed feeing *Romeo* dead,
Anone I heard the watch and then I fled,
VVhat after happened I am ignorant of.
And if in this ought haue mifcaried.

By

of Romeo and Iuliet.

By me, or by my meanes let my old life
Be facrificed fome houre before his time.
To the moft ftrickeft rigor of the Law.

Fry: VVe ftill haue knowne thee for a holy man,
VVheres *Romeos* man, what can he fay in this?

Balth: I brought my maifter word that fhee was dead,
And then he poafted ftraight ftom *Mantua,*
Vnto this Toombe. Thefe Letters he deliueredme,
Charging me early giue them to his Father.

Prin: Lets fee the Letters, I willread them ouer.
VVhere is the Counties Boy that calld the VVatch?

Boy: I brought my Mafter vnto *Iuliets* graue,
But one approaching, ftraight I calld my Mafter.
At laft they fought, I ran to call the VVatch.
And this is all that I can fay or know.

Prin: Thefe letters doe make good the Fryers wordes,
Come *Capolet*, and come olde *Mountagewe.*
VVhere are thefe enemies? fee what hate hath done,

Cap: Come brother *Mountague* giue me thy hand,
There is my daughters dowry: for now no more
Can I beftowe on her, thats all I haue.

Moun: But I will giue them more, I will erect
Her ftatue of pure golde:
That while *Verona* by that name is knowne.
There fhall no ftatue of fuch price be fet,
As that of *Romeos* loued *Iuliet.*

Cap: As rich fhall *Romeo* by his Lady lie,
Poore Sacrifices to our Enmitie.

Prin: A gloomie peace this day doth with it bring,
Come, let vs hence,
To haue more talke of thefe fad things,
Some fhall be pardoned and fome punifhed:
For nere was heard a Storie of more woe,
Than this of *Iuliet* and her *Romeo.*

FINIS.

417

APPENDIX 3

RHYME

The play's uses of rhetorical artifice, rhythm, cadence and rhyme to express the nature of love and desire count among its major literary achievements. It explores a wealth of rhymes in a manner more characteristic of comedy than of tragedy (see e.g. Ard[3] *LLL*, Appendix 4). The following table lists the chief rhymes that Shakespeare considered workable in *Romeo and Juliet*.

RHYMES IN *ROMEO AND JULIET*

Rhymes are listed in alphabetical order, including internal rhymes and words rhyming with themselves.

about / out
access / less
adieu / true
advanced / advanced
affray / day
again / complain
again / slain
ago / woo
all / brawl
alone / one
along / wrong
anguish / languish
anon / gone
armed / uncharmed
aside / denied
assure / distemperature
attend / mend
away / stay
Ay / Ay

Ay / I
banished / banished
bed / maidenhead
bed / maiden-widowed
beguiled / exiled
Benedicite / me
best / unrest
books / looks
bound / sound
brain / reign
breast / pressed
breast / rest
breath / breath
bright / night
brine / Rosaline
brings / things
burning / turning
by / eye
Capulet / debt

case / judgement-place
cell / farewell
cell / tell
chaste / waste
child / spilled
choice / voice
clears / ears
come / tomb
concealed / cancelled*
crows / shows
dark / mark
day / away
day / day
dead / buried
dead / lead
death / death
delay / day
delight / night
depend / end

418

descend / friend
die / I
die / remedy
dignity / mutiny
discreet / sweet
doom / doom
drift / shrift
ear / dear
enemy / me
excellent / different
excuses / abuses
eye / die
eye / dry
eye / fly
eye / lie
eye / spy†
fair / despair
feast / best
feast / face
feast / guest
feel / heel
fine / mine
fires / liars
flower / flower
flower / power
fly / die
foes / overthrows
forget / debt
found / wound
fray / slay
friend / end
friend / friend
give / live
glory / story
go / foe
go / so
grave / have
grow / know
grows / woes
had / dead
hand / hand
hand / stand
haste / fast
haste / last
hate / create

hate / late
he / me
head / bed
head / punishèd
heart / heart
heart / part
heir / fair
hence / intents
here / bier
here / dear
here / otherwhere
hereabout / doubt
him / him
hit / hit
hit / wit
ho / so
hoar / score
house / virtuous
how / vow
I / lie
ill / will
is / this
keep / weep
kin / sin
kind / find
lament / merriment
Lent / spent
lie / descry
lie / die
lie / enmity
lies / eyes
lies / qualities
life / strife
lineament / content
live / give
lo / foe
long / young
looks / hooks
loss / loss
love / move
love / remove
lover / cover
marred / married
marrièd / bed
masque / ask

me / be
me / enemy
me / thee
meet / sweet
meeting / greeting
Mercutio / owe
mine / combine
mine / Rosaline
misapplied / dignified
misery / see
Montague / enemy
Montague / solemnity
Montague / true
much / touch
myself / myself
name / am
next / text
night / knight
night / light
night / night
no / woe
now / allow
Nurse / corse
obey / fray
offence / hence
on / done
on / dun
one / none
oppression /
   transgression
ours / flowers
part / heart
part / part
poor / store
possess / less
pray / today
prayer / despair
predominant / plant
pride / bride
pride / hide
proceeding / a-bleeding
prove / love
prove / remove
purged / urged
rage / stage

reels / wheels
remedies / lies
remedy / die
rest / breast
right / tonight
Romeo / Romeo
Romeo / Mercutio
Rosaline / mine
sake / take
satisfied / satisfied
say / away
say / say
say / stay
scene / unclean
sea / thee
sealed / deed
see / be
set / Capulet
set / Juliet
severity / posterity
shall / gall
show / crow
shown / own
sighs / eyes
sight / night
sin / opposition
sit / yet

sits / wits
slave / face
so / foe
so / slow
sorrow / morrow
soul / low
sound / sound
spent / banishment
spite / night
stand / hand
stay / away
stays / days
still / will
stones / moans
store / more
strew / dew
strife / life
sun / begun
swear / anywhere
sword / word
thee / die
then / again
then / men
there / hair
thigh / lie
thine / Rosaline
this / kiss

today / fray
tomb / womb
tonight / rite
too / do
took / book
true / Montague
true / you
[unsatisfied / tonight]
use / abuse
vow / now
waste / taste
wedding-bed /
    maidenhead
weighed / maid
well / ill
well / spell
were / pear
wife / wife
will / ill
will / kill
will / will
woe / Romeo
wound / sound
you / adieu
you / you
young / long

* internal rhyme
† internal rhyme in a prose passage

APPENDIX 4

CASTING AND DOUBLING

There are thirty-one speaking parts in *Romeo and Juliet* if Petruchio's 'Away, Tybalt!' and the Chorus are counted in. Of these, fourteen are 'principal parts', with three boy actors required for the four female roles of Juliet, her mother, Nurse and Romeo's mother. Other (mute) women's roles at the Capulets' feast in 1.5, such as Rosaline, Livia, Helena *et al.* (1.2.63ff.), would have been acted by other members of the Lord Hunsdon's/Lord Chamberlain's Men. The shorter Q1 version of the play requires 'nine men and three boys for the principal parts, with an additional seven men and two boys for minor roles, including doubling of parts'.[1]

Given the large casting requirement of thirty-one roles and the much smaller scale of the company, doubling was essential. While the principal players could not easily double major parts, both because they were onstage much of the time and because they would have been instantly identified with their roles, other parts are relatively straightforward to double: the three musicians (4.5) and the three members of the watch (5.3) involve a straight switch, while bibliographic evidence may indicate that Nurse's servant Peter and Romeo's man Balthasar were doubled. When Balthasar is mistakenly called Peter in a Q2 SD (at 5.3.21.1), this may mean one of two things: either Shakespeare followed his source too closely (Brooke has Peter here) and forgot that he had called the character by an invented name, or else he is

---

1   Halio, *Guide*, 97–8. David Bradley gives a cast of twelve for Q1 and sixteen for Q2 (Bradley, 234). King estimates that in Q1 'nine men can play nine principal and three minor male roles', while in Q2 'Eleven men can play twelve principal and four minor parts. Three boys play three principal female roles, and the fifteen actors in principal roles speak 97% of the lines' (King, 82–3, 174–6).

called Peter in Q2 because the same actor, Will Kemp, played both Peter and Balthasar. Melchiori argues instead that Benvolio who, inexplicably, disappears from the play after 3.1, doubled as Balthasar and that the curious reference to his death in Q1 (see 5.3.210n.) is connected to his resurgence as another character here. Melchiori also notes, plausibly, that Paris' Page and the small part of Montague's Wife may have been played by the same actor, and that the Prince or Friar Laurence doubled as Chorus (Melchiori, 788, 791). His further suggestion that Paris and Tybalt were played by the same member of the cast is less convincing. It arises out of Paris' striking absence as a speaking part from the party in 1.5. He is specifically bidden to the feast by Juliet's father (1.2.21–2) and Juliet is instructed to read over the volume of his face (1.3.81–95) at the dance, yet there is nothing in Q1 or Q2 that positively places him at the feast. He is no more identified as being there than Rosaline, even though editors and directors routinely introduce both him and her at this point; Q2's inclusive 1.5 opening SD, '*Enter all the guests and gentlewomen to the masquers*', is commonly taken to include Paris and Rosaline. The expectation in the lead-up to 1.5 is clearly that Paris and Rosaline will be there to encounter Juliet and Romeo. To Melchiori, the reason for Paris' absence is 'because the actor impersonating Paris is present on the stage in I.v *in another role*', namely that of Tybalt. But in Act 5 Tybalt's corpse lies in the Capulets' vault and, though shrouded, is identified as such by Romeo a mere twenty-four lines after he has killed Paris in the same scene (5.3.97). If Tybalt is recognizable in his winding-sheet he cannot be Paris (although it could of course be another actor under the shroud).

If absence can imply doubling, as Melchiori believes it does with regard to Paris and Tybalt, then Nurse's absence after 4.5 invites speculation about her doubling in the remaining scenes, although not as a woman because the only women in the final scene, Juliet and her mother, appear with Nurse in 1.3 and could not therefore be doubled by her. It is possible that the same actor played Montague's Wife and Nurse and that Nurse's absence from the play after 4.5 is because the Nurse actor was meant to play Romeo's mother in 5.3. If so, Shakespeare changed his mind, because Montague tells us at 5.3.210 that his wife has died of grief the very night her son committed suicide. What would have been a perfect cross-play echo, the parental quartet who earlier (1.1) confronted each other now symmetrically grieving for their children, becomes a somewhat unbalanced scene marked, perhaps, by theatrical expediency, the resources the company could muster just then to put on the play. In Q1 Benvolio's death is reported immediately after that of Romeo's mother: 'Dread sovereign, my wife is dead tonight / And young Benvolio is deceasèd too.' Both actors may have been needed for roles other than those of Nurse and Benvolio. Mercutio, Tybalt and Benvolio are all available for taking on any new roles after 3.1, including the Musicians, Balthasar, the Apothecary, Friar John, the Watchmen or Paris' Page, minor characters who enter the play after 3.1. It is possible that the actor who played Mercutio also undertook either Samson or Gregory, who only speak in the opening scene. The role of Samson, the longer part of the two – he professes to 'strike quickly being moved' (1.1.5) – would suit Mercutio, with its predatory talk about women and sex; doubling here might add depth retrospectively to the character of Samson. As to which members of Hunsdon's/Chamberlain's Men played which parts, while Romeo was almost certainly Richard Burbage and Juliet, probably, Robert Goffe, attributing other roles is entirely speculative (see p. 34).

CASTING CHART[1]

Actor	Prol.	1.1	1.2	1.3	1.4	1.5	2.0	2.1
Romeo		x	x		x	x		x
Juliet				x		x		
Friar Laurence								
Capulet		x	x			x		
Nurse				x		x		
Mercutio					x	x		x
Benvolio		x	x		x	x		x
Capulet's Wife		x		x		x		
Prince		x						
Paris			x			x		
Montague		x						
Tybalt		x				x		
Balthasar								
Samson		x						
Peter								
Chief Watchman								
Chorus	x						x	
Gregory		x						
Friar John								
Paris' Page								
1 Musician								
Apothecary								
Citizens		x						
Abraham		x						
Montague's Wife		x						
2 Musician								
Cousin Capulet						x		
3 Watchman								
2 Watchman								
3 Musician								
Petruchio								

1 Roles are listed in decreasing order of length. Servingmen are not listed, but appear in a number of scenes, notably 1.2, 1.3, 1.5, 4.2 and 4.4.

	2.2	2.3	2.4	2.5	2.6	3.1	3.2	3.3	3.4
Romeo	x	x	x		x	x		x	
Juliet	x			x	x		x		
Friar Laurence		x			x			x	
Capulet						x			x
Nurse	x		x	x			x	x	
Mercutio			x			x			
Benvolio			x			x			
Capulet's Wife						x			x
Prince						x			
Paris									x
Montague						x			
Tybalt						x			
Balthasar									
Samson									
Peter			x	x					
Chief Watchman									
Chorus									
Gregory									
Friar John									
Paris' Page									
1 Musician									
Apothecary									
Citizens						x			
Abraham									
Montague's Wife									
2 Musician									
Cousin Capulet									
3 Watchman									
2 Watchman									
3 Musician									
Petruchio						x			

	3.5	4.1	4.2	4.3	4.4	4.5	5.1	5.2	5.3
Romeo	x						x		x
Juliet	x	x	x	x		x			x
Friar Laurence		x				x		x	x
Capulet	x		x		x	x			x
Nurse	x		x	x	x	x			
Mercutio									
Benvolio									
Capulet's Wife	x		x	x	x	x			x
Prince									x
Paris		x				x			x
Montague									x
Tybalt									
Balthasar							x		x
Samson									
Peter						x			
Chief Watchman									x
Chorus									
Gregory									
Friar John								x	
Paris' Page									x
1 Musician						x			
Apothecary							x		
Citizens									
Abraham									
Montague's Wife									
2 Musician						x			
Cousin Capulet									
3 Watchman									x
2 Watchman									x
3 Musician						x			
Petruchio									

ABBREVIATIONS AND REFERENCES

All quotations from *Romeo and Juliet* are keyed to this edition. Quotations from other works by Shakespeare come from individual Arden 3 volumes or, where these are not available, from *The Arden Shakespeare: Complete Works*, ed. Richard Proudfoot, Ann Thompson and David Scott Kastan (rev. edn, 2004). Unless otherwise indicated, place of publication in references is London.

ABBREVIATIONS

ABBREVIATIONS USED IN NOTES

*	identifies commentary notes in which readings differ from the text on which this edition is based
conj.	conjectured by
n.	commentary note
om.	omitted
SD	stage direction
SP	speech prefix
subst.	substantially
this edn	a reading, SD or SP first adopted in this edition
TLN	through line numbering
t.n.	textual note
var.	variant

WORKS BY AND PARTLY BY SHAKESPEARE

AC	*Antony and Cleopatra*
AW	*All's Well That Ends Well*
AYL	*As You Like It*
CE	*The Comedy of Errors*
Cor	*Coriolanus*
Cym	*Cymbeline*
E3	*King Edward III*
Ham	*Hamlet*
1H4	*King Henry IV, Part 1*
2H4	*King Henry IV, Part 2*
H5	*King Henry V*
1H6	*King Henry VI, Part 1*
2H6	*King Henry VI, Part 2*

427

3H6	*King Henry VI, Part 3*
H8	*King Henry VIII*
JC	*Julius Caesar*
KJ	*King John*
KL	*King Lear*
LC	*A Lover's Complaint*
LLL	*Love's Labour's Lost*
Luc	*The Rape of Lucrece*
MA	*Much Ado about Nothing*
Mac	*Macbeth*
MM	*Measure for Measure*
MND	*A Midsummer Night's Dream*
MV	*The Merchant of Venice*
MW	*The Merry Wives of Windsor*
Oth	*Othello*
Per	*Pericles*
PP	*The Passionate Pilgrim*
PT	*The Phoenix and Turtle*
R2	*King Richard II*
R3	*King Richard III*
RJ	*Romeo and Juliet*
Son	*Sonnets*
STM	*Sir Thomas More*
TC	*Troilus and Cressida*
Tem	*The Tempest*
TGV	*The Two Gentlemen of Verona*
Tim	*Timon of Athens*
Tit	*Titus Andronicus*
TN	*Twelfth Night*
TNK	*The Two Noble Kinsmen*
TS	*The Taming of the Shrew*
VA	*Venus and Adonis*
WT	*The Winter's Tale*

REFERENCES

EDITIONS OF SHAKESPEARE COLLATED

Alexander	*William Shakespeare: The Complete Works*, ed. Peter Alexander (1951)
Ard	*Romeo and Juliet*, ed. Edward Dowden (1900)
Ard²	*Romeo and Juliet*, ed. Brian Gibbons (1980)
Bevington	*The Complete Works of Shakespeare*, ed. David Bevington, 6th edn (London and White Plains, NY, 2009)

Bryant	*Romeo and Juliet*, ed. J.A. Bryant (New York, 1964)
Cam	*The Works of William Shakespeare*, ed. J. Glover, W.G. Clark and W.A. Wright, 8 vols (Cambridge, 1864)
Cam²	*Romeo and Juliet*, ed. G. Blakemore Evans (Cambridge, 1984)
Capell	*Mr William Shakespeare, his Comedies, Histories, and Tragedies*, ed. Edward Capell, 10 vols (1768)
Collier	*The Works of William Shakespeare*, ed. John Payne Collier, 8 vols (1842–4)
Collier²	*The Plays of Shakespeare*, ed. John Payne Collier, 8 vols (1853)
Craig	*Romeo and Juliet*, ed. W.J. Craig (Oxford, 1891)
Crofts	*Romeo and Juliet*, ed. J.E. Crofts (1936)
Daniel	*Romeo and Juliet*, ed. P.A. Daniel (1875)
Delius	*Shakespeares Werke*, ed. N. Delius, 7 vols (Elberfeld, 1854–65)
Dowden	See Ard
Durham	*Romeo and Juliet*, ed. W.H. Durham (New Haven, Conn., 1917)
Dyce	*The Works of William Shakespeare*, ed. Alexander Dyce, 6 vols (1857)
Dyce²	*The Works of William Shakespeare*, ed. Alexander Dyce, 2nd edn, 9 vols (1867)
Erne	*The first quarto of Romeo and Juliet*, ed. Lukas Erne (Cambridge, 2007)
F	*Mr William Shakespeares Comedies, Histories, and Tragedies*, The First Folio (1623)
F2	*Mr William Shakespeares Comedies, Histories, and Tragedies*, The Second Folio (1632)
F3	*Mr William Shakespeares Comedies, Histories, and Tragedies*, The Third Folio (1663, 1664)
F4	*Mr William Shakespear's Comedies, Histories, and Tragedies*, The Fourth Folio (1685)
Garrick–Kemble	*Romeo and Juliet*, with alterations by David Garrick, rev. J.P. Kemble (1814)
Halio	*Romeo and Juliet: Q1 and Q2*, ed. Jay L. Halio (Newark, Del., 2008)
Hankins	*Romeo and Juliet*, ed. J.E. Hankins (Baltimore, Md., 1960)
Hanmer	*The Works of Shakespear*, ed. Sir Thomas Hanmer, 6 vols (Oxford, 1743–4)
Hoppe	*Romeo and Juliet*, ed. H.R. Hoppe (New York, 1947)
Hosley	*Romeo and Juliet*, ed. R. Hosley (New Haven, Conn., 1954)
Houghton	*Romeo and Juliet*, ed. R.E.C. Houghton (Oxford, 1947)
Hudson	*The Complete Works of William Shakespeare*, ed. Henry N. Hudson, 11 vols (Boston, Mass., 1851–6)
Johnson	*The Plays of William Shakespeare*, ed. Samuel Johnson, 8 vols (1765)

Johnson[2]	*The Plays of William Shakespeare*, ed. Samuel Johnson, 8 vols (1771)
Kittredge	*Romeo and Juliet*, ed. George Lyman Kittredge (Boston, Mass., 1940)
Knight	*Comedies, Histories, Tragedies, and Poems of William Shakspere*, ed. C. Knight, 12 vols (1842–4)
Malone	*The Plays and Poems of William Shakespeare*, ed. Edmond Malone, 10 vols (1790)
Mommsen	*Romeo und Julia*, ed. Tycho Mommsen (Oldenburg, 1859)
Mowat–Werstine	*Romeo and Juliet*, ed. Barbara A. Mowat and Paul Werstine (New York, 1992)
MSR	Malone Society Reprints, *Romeo and Juliet 1597* (*Q1*), prepared by Jill L. Levenson and Barry Gaines, and checked by Thomas L. Berger and G.R. Proudfoot (Oxford, 2000)
Oxf	*William Shakespeare, The Complete Works*, ed. Stanley Wells and Gary Taylor, with John Jowett and William Montgomery (Oxford, 1986)
Oxf[1]	*Romeo and Juliet*, ed. Jill L. Levenson (Oxford, 2000)
Pope	*The Works of Shakespeare*, ed. Alexander Pope, 6 vols (1723–5)
Pope[2]	*The Works of Shakespeare*, ed. Alexander Pope, 8 vols (1728)
Q1	*Romeo and Juliet*, The First Quarto (1597)
Q2	*Romeo and Juliet*, The Second Quarto (1599)
Q3	*Romeo and Juliet*, The Third Quarto (1609)
Q4	*Romeo and Juliet*, The Fourth Quarto (*c.* 1622/3)
Q5	*Romeo and Juliet*, The Fifth Quarto (1637)
Riv[2]	*The Riverside Shakespeare*, ed. G. Blakemore Evans *et al.*, 2nd edn (Boston, Mass., 1997)
Rowe	*The Works of Mr William Shakespear*, ed. Nicholas Rowe, 6 vols (1709)
Singer	*The Dramatic Works of William Shakespeare*, ed. Samuel Weller Singer, 10 vols (1826)
Sisson	*William Shakespeare: The Complete Works*, ed. C.J. Sisson (1954)
Spencer	*Romeo and Juliet*, ed. T.J.B. Spencer, New Penguin Shakespeare (1967)
Staunton	*The Plays of Shakespeare*, ed. Howard Staunton, 3 vols (1860)
Steevens	*The Plays of William Shakespeare*, ed. Samuel Johnson and George Steevens, 10 vols (1773)
Steevens[2]	*The Plays of William Shakespeare*, ed. Samuel Johnson and George Steevens, 10 vols (1778)
Theobald	*The Works of Shakespeare*, ed. Lewis Theobald, 7 vols (1733)
Ulrici	*Romeo and Juliet*, ed. H. Ulrici (Halle, 1853)
Var	*Romeo and Juliet*, ed. H.H. Furness, New Variorum Shakespeare (Philadelphia, Pa., 1871)
Warburton	*The Works of Shakespear*, ed. Alexander Pope and William Warburton, 8 vols (1747)

White	*The Works of William Shakespeare*, ed. Richard Grant White, 12 vols (Boston, Mass., 1857–65)
Williams	*Romeo and Juliet*, ed. G.W. Williams (Durham, NC, 1964)
Wilson–Duthie	*Romeo and Juliet*, ed. John Dover Wilson and George Ian Duthie (Cambridge, 1955)

OTHER WORKS CITED OR USED

Abbott	E.A. Abbott, *A Shakespearian Grammar*, 2nd edn (1870)
Baldwin	T.W. Baldwin, *The Organization and Personnel of the Shakespearean Company* (Princeton, NJ, 1927)
Bandello	Matteo Bandello, *Le novelle del Bandello* (1554)
Belsey	Catherine Belsey, 'The Name of the Rose', *Yearbook of English Studies*, 23 (1993), 126–42
Bevington, *Action*	David Bevington, *Action is Eloquence: Shakespeare's Language of Gesture* (Cambridge, Mass., 1984)
Bevington, *Biography*	David Bevington, *Shakespeare and Biography* (Oxford, 2010)
Bevington, *Read*	David Bevington, *How to Read a Shakespeare Play* (Oxford, 2006)
Bevington, *Shakespeare*	David Bevington, *Shakespeare* (Oxford, 2002)
Bloom	Harold Bloom (ed.), *William Shakespeare's Romeo and Juliet* (Philadelphia, Pa., 2002)
Boaistuau	P. Boaistuau, *Histoires Tragiques extraictes des oeuvres italiens de Bandel, & mises en nostre langue Françoise* (Paris, 1559)
Bogdanov	Michael Bogdanov, *Romeo and Juliet*, 1986 RSC promptbook
Booth	Stephen Booth, 'Shakespeare's language and the language of Shakespeare's time', *SS 50* (1997), 1–17
Bradley	David Bradley, *From Text to Performance in the Elizabethan Theatre: Preparing the Play for the Stage* (Cambridge, 1991)
Branam	George C. Branam, 'The genesis of David Garrick's *Romeo and Juliet*', *SQ*, 35 (1984), 170–9
Brissenden	Alan Brissenden, *Shakespeare and the Dance* (1981)
Brook	Peter Brook, *Romeo and Juliet*, 1947 RSC promptbook
Brooke	Arthur Brooke, *The Tragical History of Romeus and Juliet, written first in Italian by Bandell, and now in English by Ar. Br.* (1562)
Brown	John Russell Brown, 'S. Franco Zeffirelli's *Romeo and Juliet*', *SS 12* (1962), 147–55
Bullough	Geoffrey Bullough (ed.), *Narrative and Dramatic Sources of Shakespeare*, 8 vols (1957–75)
Cantrell & Williams	Paul L. Cantrell and George Walton Williams, 'The printing of the Second Quarto of *Romeo and Juliet* (1599)', *SB*, 9 (1957), 107–16

Carroll	*The Two Gentlemen of Verona*, ed. William C. Carroll (2004)
Chambers	E.K. Chambers, *The Elizabethan Stage*, 4 vols (1923)
Chaucer	*The Riverside Chaucer*, ed. Larry D. Benson, 3rd edn (Boston, Mass., 1987)
Cohn	Albert Cohn, *Shakespeare in Germany in the Sixteenth and Seventeenth Centuries* (1865)
Coleridge	*Coleridge on Shakespeare*, ed. Terence Hawkes (1969)
Cotgrave	Randle Cotgrave, *A Dictionary of the French and English Tongues* (1611)
Crow	John Crow, 'Editing and emending', *Essays and Studies* (1955), 1–20
Crystal, *Pronouncing*	David Crystal, *Pronouncing Shakespeare* (Cambridge, 2005)
Crystal, *Words*	David Crystal and Ben Crystal, *Shakespeare's Words* (2002)
Cusack	Niamh Cusack, 'Juliet', in Russell Jackson and Robert Smallwood (eds), *Players of Shakespeare 2, Further Essays in Shakespearean Performance* (1988)
Daniel, *Complaint*	Samuel Daniel, *The Complaint of Rosamond*, in *Poems and a Defence of Ryme*, ed. A.C. Sprague (Cambridge, Mass., 1930)
da Porto	Luigi da Porto, *Istoria novellamente ritrovata di due nobili amanti con la loro pietosa morte intervenuta gia nella Città di Verona nel tempo del S. Bartholomeo della Scala* (Venice, c. 1530)
Davies	Anthony Davies, 'The film versions of *Romeo and Juliet*', *SS* 49 (1996), 153–62
Dekker	*Thomas Dekker: Dramatic Works*, ed. Fredson Bowers, vol. 2 (Cambridge, 1955)
Dent	R.W. Dent, *Shakespeare's Proverbial Language: An Index* (Berkeley, Calif., 1981)
Dessen, 'Q1'	Alan C. Dessen, 'Q1 *Romeo and Juliet* and Elizabethan theatrical vocabulary', in Halio, *Contexts*, 107–22
Dessen, *Recovering*	Alan C. Dessen, *Recovering Shakespeare's Theatrical Vocabulary* (Cambridge, 1995)
Dessen, *Rescripting*	Alan C. Dessen, *Rescripting Shakespeare: The Text, the Director, and Modern Productions* (Cambridge, 2002)
Dessen & Thomson	Alan C. Dessen and Leslie Thomson, *A Dictionary of Stage Directions in English Drama, 1580–1642* (Cambridge, 1999)
Donne	*John Donne: The Complete English Poems*, ed. A.J. Smith (1986)
Duncan-Jones, 'Dagger'	Katherine Duncan-Jones, ' "O happy dagger": the autonomy of Shakespeare's Juliet', *N&Q*, 45 (1998), 314–15
Duncan-Jones, 'Pilgrims'	Katherine Duncan-Jones, 'Performing sonnets: men, women and passionate pilgrims', 2009 Sam Wanamaker Lecture
Duncan-Jones, *Sonnets*	*Shakespeare's Sonnets*, ed. Katherine Duncan-Jones, rev. edn (2010)

Duncan-Jones, *Ungentle*	Katherine Duncan-Jones, *Ungentle Shakespeare: Scenes from his Life* (2001)
Dusinberre, 'Douai'	'The Douai manuscript', in *As You Like It*, ed. Juliet Dusinberre (2006), 374–97
Dusinberre, *Women*	Juliet Dusinberre, *Shakespeare and the Nature of Women*, 3rd edn, 2003
Edmondson & Wells	*Shakespeare's Sonnets*, ed. Paul Edmondson and Stanley Wells (Oxford, 2004)
Erne, *Literary*	Lukas Erne, *Shakespeare as Literary Dramatist* (Cambridge, 2003)
Evans	G.B. Evans, 'The Douai manuscript: six Shakespearean transcripts (1694–95)', *Philological Quarterly*, 41 (1962), 158–72
Farley-Hills	David Farley-Hills, 'The "Bad" Quarto of *Romeo and Juliet*', *SS 49* (1996), 27–44
Faucit	Helena Faucit, *On Some of Shakespeare's Female Characters* (Edinburgh, 1891)
Findlay	Alison Findlay, *Women in Shakespeare: A Dictionary* (2010)
Galey	Alan Galey, 'Let me be satisfied, is't good or bad? Re-evaluating the First Quarto of *Romeo and Juliet*', *Archiv für das Studium der neueren Sprachen und Literaturen* (Berlin, 2009), 272–87
Garber	Marjorie Garber, *Coming of Age in Shakespeare* (1981)
Gerard	John Gerard, *Herbal* (1597)
Gielgud	John Gielgud, *Early Stages 1921–36* (1939)
Golding	See Ovid, *Met.*
Granville-Barker	Harley Granville-Barker, *Prefaces to Shakespeare*, vol. 5 (1930)
Greg, *Editorial*	W.W. Greg, *The Editorial Problem in Shakespeare* (Oxford, 1942)
Greg, *Folio*	W.W. Greg, *The Shakespeare First Folio* (Oxford, 1955)
Gurr, *Company*	Andrew Gurr, *The Shakespeare Company, 1594–1642* (Cambridge, 2004)
Gurr, 'Date'	Andrew Gurr, 'The date and the expected venue of *Romeo and Juliet*', *SS 49* (1996), 15–25
Gurr, *Playing*	Andrew Gurr, *The Shakespearian Playing Companies* (Oxford, 1996)
Gurr & Ichikawa	Andrew Gurr and Mariko Ichikawa, *Staging in Shakespeare's Theatres* (Oxford, 2000)
GWW	George Walton Williams
Hackett	Helen Hackett, *A Midsummer Night's Dream* (2005)
Halio, *Contexts*	Jay L. Halio, *Shakespeare's Romeo and Juliet: Texts, Contexts, and Interpretation* (Newark, Del., 1995)
Halio, *Guide*	Jay L. Halio, *Romeo and Juliet: A Guide to the Play* (Westport, Conn., 1998)

Harvard Concordance	Marvin Spevack, *The Harvard Concordance to Shakespeare* (Cambridge, Mass., 1973)
Hazlitt	*The Complete Works of William Hazlitt*, ed. P.P. Howe, after A.R. Walker and Arnold Glover, 21 vols (1930–4), vol. 4
Hirrel	Michael J. Hirrel, 'Duration of performances and lengths of plays: how shall we beguile the lazy time?', *SQ*, 61 (2010), 159–82
Hobson	Harold Hobson, *Theatre* (1948)
Hogan	Charles B. Hogan, *Shakespeare in the Theatre, 1701–1800*, 2 vols (Oxford, 1952)
Holderness	Graham Holderness, *William Shakespeare: 'Romeo and Juliet'* (1990)
Holmer, 'Draw'	Joan Ozark Holmer, 'Draw, if you be men: Saviolo's significance for *Romeo and Juliet*', *SQ*, 45 (1994), 163–89
Holmer, 'Nashe'	Joan Ozark Holmer, 'No "vain fantasy": Shakespeare's refashioning of Nashe for dreams and Queen Mab', in Halio, *Contexts*, 49–82
Hope	Jonathan Hope, *Shakespeare's Grammar* (2003)
Hoppe, 'First'	H.R. Hoppe, 'The First Quarto version of *Romeo and Juliet*, II.vi and IV.v.43 ff.', *RES*, 14 (1938), 271–84
Hoppe, *Quarto*	H.R. Hoppe (ed.), *The Bad Quarto of 'Romeo and Juliet'* (Ithaca, NY, 1948)
Hortmann	Wilhelm Hortmann, *Shakespeare on the German stage: The Twentieth Century* (Cambridge, 1998)
Hosley, 'Children'	Richard Hosley, 'How many children had Lady Capulet?', *SQ*, 18 (1967), 3–6
Hosley, 'Corrupting'	Richard Hosley, 'The corrupting influence of the Bad Quarto on the received text of *Romeo and Juliet*', *SQ*, 4 (1953), 11–33
Hosley, 'Stage'	Richard Hosley, 'The use of the upper stage in *Romeo and Juliet*', *SQ*, 5 (1954), 371–9
Hulme	Hilda M. Hulme, *Explorations in Shakespeare's Language* (1962)
Irace	Kathleen O. Irace, *Reforming the 'Bad' Quartos: Performance and Provenance of Six Shakespearean First Editions* (Newark, Del., 1994)
Jackson	Russell Jackson, *Romeo and Juliet*, Shakespeare at Stratford series (2003)
Johnson on Shakespeare	*Samuel Johnson on Shakespeare*, ed. H.R. Woudhuysen (1989)
Jonson	Ben Jonson, ed. C.H. Herford and Percy Simpson, 11 vols (Oxford, 1925)
Jowett, 'Chettle'	'Henry Chettle and the first quarto of *Romeo and Juliet*', *Papers of the Bibliographical Society of America*, 92 (1998), 53–74
Jowett, *RJ*	John Jowett, '*Romeo and Juliet*', in *TxC*, 288–305

Kahn   Coppélia Kahn, 'Coming of age in Verona', in C. Lenz, C.
                    Neely and G. Greene (eds), *The Woman's Part: Feminist
                    Criticism of Shakespeare* (Chicago, Ill., 1980), 171–93
Kastan, *Book*   David Scott Kastan, *Shakespeare and the Book* (Cambridge,
                    2001)
Kastan, *Companion* David Scott Kastan (ed.), *A Companion to Shakespeare*
                    (Oxford, 1999)
Kathman   David Kathman, 'How old were Shakespeare's boy actors?',
                    SS 58 (2005), 220–46
Kermode   Frank Kermode, *Shakespeare's Language* (2000)
King   T.J. King, *Casting Shakespeare's Plays: London Actors and
                    their Roles, 1590–1642* (Cambridge, 1992)
Laoutaris   Chris Laoutaris, *Shakespearean Maternities: Crises of
                    Conception in Early Modern England* (Edinburgh, 2008)
Levenson,   Jill L. Levenson, 'Shakespeare's *Romeo and Juliet:* the places
  'Invention'   of invention', *SS 49* (1996), 45–55
Levenson,   Jill L. Levenson, *Romeo and Juliet: Shakespeare in
  Performance   Performance* (Manchester, 1987)
Lever   J.W. Lever, 'Shakespeare's French fruits', *SS 6* (1953), 82–3
Levith   Murray J. Levith, *Shakespeare's Italian Settings and Plays*
                    (Basingstoke, 1989)
Loehlin   James N. Loehlin, *Romeo and Juliet: Shakespeare in
                    Production* (Cambridge, 2002)
Lyly, *Sappho*   John Lyly, *Sappho and Phao*, ed. David Bevington
                    (Manchester, 1993)
Lyly, *Works*   *The Complete Works of John Lyly*, ed. R.W. Bond, 3 vols
                    (Oxford, 1902)
McDonald   Russ McDonald, *Shakespeare and the Arts of Language*
                    (Oxford, 2001)
Maguire   Laurie Maguire, *Shakespeare's Names* (Oxford, 2007)
Mahood   M.M. Mahood, *Shakespeare's Wordplay* (1957)
Marlowe   Christopher Marlowe, *Complete Plays and Poems*, ed. E.D.
                    Pendry and J.C. Maxwell (1976)
Marston   *The Works of John Marston*, ed. A.H. Bullen, 3 vols (1887)
Melchiori   Giorgio Melchiori, 'Peter, Balthasar, and Shakespeare's art
                    of doubling', *Modern Language Review*, 78 (1983), 777–92
Munro   *Brooke's 'Romeus and Juliet', being the original of Shakespeare's
                    'Romeo and Juliet', newly edited by J.J. Munro* (1908)
Nashe   Thomas Nashe, *Works*, ed. R.B. McKerrow, 5 vols (1904–
                    10), rev. F.P. Wilson (1958)
Nicholl   Charles Nicholl, 'Thomas Nashe', *ODNB*
Novy   Marianne Novy, *Love's Argument: Gender Relations in
                    Shakespeare* (Chapel Hill, NC, 1984)
Nunn   Trevor Nunn and Barry Kyle, *Romeo and Juliet*, 1976 RSC
                    promptbook
ODNB   *Oxford Dictionary of National Biography*

435

OED	*Oxford English Dictionary*
Onions	C.T. Onions, *A Shakespeare Glossary*, rev. Robert D. Eagleson (Oxford, 1986)
Otway	Thomas Otway, *Caius Marius*, in *Works*, ed. J.C. Ghosh, 2 vols (1932)
Ovid, *Met.*	*The xv. Books of P. Ovidius Naso, entitled Metamorphoses*, trans. Arthur Golding (1567), ed. Madeleine Forey (Harmondsworth, 2002)
Oxberry	*Romeo and Juliet, a tragedy . . . adapted to the stage by David Garrick . . . as it is performed at the Theatres Royal*, ed. William Oxberry (1819)
OxCom	*The Oxford Companion to Shakespeare*, ed. Michael Dobson and Stanley Wells (Oxford, 2001)
Painter	William Painter, *The second tome of the Palace of pleasure conteyning store of goodly histories, tragicall matters . . . Chosen and selected out of diuers good and commendable authors: by William Painter. Anno.* 1567
Panofsky	Erwin Panofsky, *Studies in Iconology: Humanistic Themes in the Art of the Renaissance* (New York, 1972)
Parnassus	*The Three Parnassus Plays (1598–1601)*, ed. J.B. Leishman (1949)
Partridge	Eric Partridge, *Shakespeare's Bawdy*, rev. edn (1968)
Paster	Gail Kern Paster, *The Body Embarrassed: Drama and the Disciplines of Shame in Early Modern England* (Ithaca, NY, 1993)
Paterson	Don Paterson, *Reading Shakespeare's Sonnets: A New Commentary* (2010)
Pepys	*The Diary of Samuel Pepys*, ed. R.C. Latham and W. Matthews, 11 vols (1970–83)
Pollard	A.W. Pollard, *Shakespeare Folios and Quartos: A Study in the Bibliography of Shakespeare's Plays* (1909)
Porter	Joseph A. Porter (ed.), *Critical Essays on Shakespeare's 'Romeo and Juliet'* (New York, 1997)
Potter	Lois Potter, 'Shakespeare in the theatre, 1660–1900', in Margreta de Grazia and Stanley Wells (eds), *The Cambridge Companion to Shakespeare* (Cambridge, 2001), 183–98
Puttenham	George Puttenham, *The Art of English Poesie* (1589)
Reid, 'Folio'	S.W. Reid, 'The editing of Folio *Romeo and Juliet*', *SB*, 35 (1982), 43–66
Reid, 'Quarto'	S.W. Reid, 'Quarto copy for Folio *Romeo and Juliet*', *The Library*, 6 (1983), 118–25
RES	*Review of English Studies*
Ritson	Joseph Ritson, *Remarks, Critical and Illustrative . . . on the Last Edition of Shakespeare* (1778)
Roberts	Sasha Roberts, *William Shakespeare: Romeo and Juliet* (1998)

Rothschild	Fleur Rothschild, 'Recovering *Romeo and Juliet*: a study of critical responses to the play from 1597', unpublished PhD thesis, King's College London (1997)
Rothwell	Kenneth S. Rothwell, *A History of Shakespeare on Screen* (Cambridge, 2004)
RSC	Royal Shakespeare Company
RST	Royal Shakespeare Theatre
Rutter	Tom Rutter, *Work and Play on the Shakespearean Stage* (Cambridge, 2008)
Saviolo	*Vincentio Saviolo his Practice, In Two Books* (1595)
SB	*Studies in Bibliography*
Shaheen	Naseeb Shaheen, *Biblical References in Shakespeare's Tragedies* (Newark, Del., 1987)
Shapiro	James Shapiro, *1599: A Year in the Life of William Shakespeare* (2005)
Shell	Alison Shell, *Shakespeare and Religion* (2010)
Sidney	*The Poems of Sir Philip Sidney*, ed. William A. Ringler, Jr (Oxford, 1962)
SP	*Studies in Philology*
Spenser	*The Poetical Works of Edmund Spenser*, ed. J.C. Smith and E. de Selincourt (Oxford, 1912)
Sprague	A.C. Sprague, *Shakespeare and the Actors* (Cambridge, Mass., 1945)
SQ	*Shakespeare Quarterly*
SS	*Shakespeare Survey*
Stebbins	Emma Stebbins, *Charlotte Cushman: her Letters and Memories of her Life* (Boston, Mass., 1879)
Sternfeld	F.W. Sternfeld, *Music in Shakespearean Tragedy* (1963)
Stoker	Bram Stoker, *Personal Reminiscences of Henry Irving*, 2 vols (1906)
Tanselle	G. Thomas Tanselle, 'Time in *Romeo and Juliet*', *SQ*, 4 (1964), 349–61
Taylor	Gary Taylor, ' "Swounds" revisited: theatrical, editorial, and literary expurgation', in Gary Taylor and John Jowett, *Shakespeare Reshaped 1606–1623* (1993), 51–106
Thomas, 'Chettle'	Sidney Thomas, 'Henry Chettle and the First Quarto of *Romeo and Juliet*', *RES*, n.s., 1 (1950), 8–16
Thomas, 'Links'	Sidney Thomas, 'The bibliographical links between the first two quartos of *Romeo and Juliet*', *RES*, 25 (1949), 110–14
Thompson	Ann Thompson, *Shakespeare's Chaucer: A Study in Literary Origins* (Liverpool, 1978)
Thompson & McMullan	Ann Thompson and Gordon McMullan (eds), *In Arden: Editing Shakespeare; Essays in Honour of Richard Proudfoot* (2003)

Thomson	Leslie Thomson, 'With patient ears attend: *Romeo and Juliet* on the Elizabethan stage', *Studies in Philology*, 92 (1995), 230–47
Tilley	M.P. Tilley, *A Dictionary of the Proverbs in England in the Sixteenth and Seventeenth Centuries* (Ann Arbor, Mich., 1950)
Tilley, '*Euphues*'	M.P. Tilley, 'A parody of *Euphues* in *Romeo and Juliet*', *Modern Language Notes* (1926), 1–8
TLS	*Times Literary Supplement*
TxC	*William Shakespeare, A Textual Companion*, ed. Stanley Wells and Gary Taylor, with John Jowett and William Montgomery (Oxford, 1987)
Tynan	Kenneth Tynan, *Curtains* (1961)
Upton	John Upton, *Critical Observations on Shakespeare* (1746)
Webster	*John Webster: The Duchess of Malfi and Other Plays*, ed. René Weis (Oxford, 1996)
Weis, *Lear*	*King Lear: A Parallel Text Edition*, ed. René Weis, 2nd rev. edn (2010)
Weis, *Revealed*	René Weis, *Shakespeare Revealed* (2007)
Wells, 'Challenges'	Stanley Wells, 'The challenges of *Romeo and Juliet*', *SS 49* (1996), 1–14
Wells, *Sex*	Stanley Wells, *Shakespeare, Sex, and Love* (Oxford, 2010)
Whittier	Gayle Whittier, 'The sonnet's body and the body sonnetized in *Romeo and Juliet*', *SQ*, 40 (1989), 27–41
Williams, 'Edit'	George Walton Williams, 'To edit? To direct? – Ay, there's the rub', in Thompson & McMullan, 111–24
Williams, 'New'	George Walton Williams, 'A new line of dialogue in *Romeo and Juliet*', *SQ*, 11 (1960), 84–7
Wilson	Thomas Wilson, *The Art of Rhetoric* (1560)
Woudhuysen	*Love's Labour's Lost*, ed. H.R. Woudhuysen (1998)
Zeffirelli	Franco Zeffirelli, *The Autobiography of Franco Zeffirelli* (New York, 1986)

PRODUCTIONS AND ADAPTATIONS

The following is a selected list of major theatrical, cinematic and musical productions and adaptations of the play, most of which are cited in the Commentary and Introduction. The standard entry gives date, venue, actors for Romeo and Juliet and, where appropriate, the name of the director (in parentheses and italics).

1597/8	The Theatre or Curtain (Marston), or Swan (Williams, 147): Richard Burbage (?), Robert Goffe (?)
1604	performance of a version of the play in Nördlingen, Bavaria
1626	performance of a version of the play in Dresden, Saxony
1662	Lincoln's Inn Fields: Henry Harris, Mary Saunderson (*William Davenant?*)

1679	Dorset Garden: Thomas Otway, *The History and Fall of Caius Marius*; William Smith (Young Marius [Romeo]), Elizabeth Barry (Lavinia [Juliet]) (*Theophilus Cibber*)
1744	Little Theatre, Haymarket: Theophilus Cibber, Jenny Cibber
1748	Drury Lane: Spranger Barry, Susannah Cibber (*David Garrick*)
1750	Covent Garden: Spranger Barry, Susannah Cibber (*John Rich*)
1750	Drury Lane: David Garrick, Anne Bellamy (*David Garrick*)
1756	Drury Lane: David Garrick, Susannah Cibber/Hannah Pritchard
1789	Drury Lane: John Philip Kemble, Sarah Siddons
1815	Drury Lane: Edmund Kean, Sarah Bartley
1827	Odéon, Paris: Charles Kemble, Harriet Smithson
1839	Odéon, Paris: Hector Berlioz, *Roméo et Juliette* (*symphonie dramatique*)
1841	Haymarket: Charles Kean, Ellen Tree
1845	Haymarket: Charlotte Cushman (Romeo), Susan Cushman (Juliet)
1851	Olympic: J. William Wallack, Helena Faucit
1866	Princess: John Nelson, Stella Colas
1867	Royal Italian Opera, London: Charles Gounod, *Roméo et Juliette* (opera)
1869	Booth's, New York: Edwin Booth, Mary McVicker (*Edwin Booth*)
1880	Pyotr Ilyich Tchaikovsky, *Romeo and Juliet* ('Fantasy Overture') (revised version, first performed at Tblisi in 1886)
1881	Court Theatre (later Royal Court): Johnston Forbes-Robertson, Helena Modjeska
1882	Lyceum: Henry Irving, Ellen Terry (*Henry Irving*)
1924	Regent: John Gielgud, Gwen Ffrangcon-Davies
1935	New Theatre: John Gielgud/Laurence Olivier, Peggy Ashcroft (*John Gielgud*)
1936	MGM film: Leslie Howard, Norma Shearer (*George Cukor*)
1940	51st Street Theatre: Laurence Olivier, Vivien Leigh
1940	Kirov, St Petersburg: Sergei Prokofiev, *Romeo and Juliet* (ballet)
1947	Shakespeare Memorial Theatre (RST Stratford): Laurence Payne, Daphne Slater (*Peter Brook*)
1952	Old Vic: Alan Badel, Claire Bloom (*Hugh Hunt*)
1955	BBC TV film: Tony Britton, Virginia McKenna (*Harold Clayton*)

1957	Winter Garden, Broadway, New York: *West Side Story*; Larry Kert (Tony [Romeo]), Carol Lawrence (Maria [Juliet]) (*Jerome Robbins*)
1958	RST Stratford: Richard Johnson, Dorothy Tutin (*Glen Byam Shaw*)
1960	Old Vic: John Stride, Judi Dench (*Franco Zeffirelli*)
1961	RST Stratford: Brian Murray, Dorothy Tutin (*Peter Hall*)
1961	United Artists film: *West Side Story*; Richard Beymer, Natalie Wood (*Robert Earle Wise*)
1968	Paramount film: Leonard Whiting, Olivia Hussey (*Franco Zeffirelli*)
1973	RST Stratford: Timothy Dalton, Estelle Kohler (*Terry Hands*)
1976	RST Stratford: Ian McKellen, Francesca Annis (*Trevor Nunn / Barry Kyle*)
1978	BBC TV film (Complete Shakespeare series): Patrick Ryecart, Rebecca Saire (*Cedric Messina*)
1986	Riverside Studios: Kenneth Branagh, Samantha Bond (*Kenneth Branagh*)
1986	RST Stratford: Sean Bean, Niamh Cusack (*Michael Bogdanov*)
1993	Düsseldorf: Matthias Leja, Caroline Ebner (*Karin Beier*)
1995	RST Stratford: Zubin Varla, Lucy Whybrow (*Adrian Noble*)
1996	20th Century Fox film: *William Shakespeare's Romeo + Juliet*; Leonardo DiCaprio, Claire Danes (*Baz Luhrmann*)
1997	John Houseman Studio Theatre, New York: *Shakespeare's Romeo and Juliet*; Greg Shamie, Daniel J Shore (*Joe Calarco*)
1998	Miramax film: *Shakespeare in Love*; Joseph Fiennes (Will Shakespeare), Gwyneth Paltrow (Viola de Lesseps) and Judi Dench (Queen Elizabeth I); screenplay by Tom Stoppard and Marc Norman (*John Madden*)
2000	RST Stratford: David Tennant, Alexandra Gilbreath (*Michael Boyd*)
2004	Shakespeare's Globe: 'Original Pronunciation' *Romeo and Juliet* (David Crystal); Tom Burke, Kananu Kirimi (*Tim Carroll*)
2006	Mokhwa Repertory Company, Barbican: Kim Byung Cheol, Kim Mun Jung (*Oh Tae-Suk*)
2009	Shakespeare's Globe: Adetomiwa Edun, Ellie Kendrick (*Dominic Dromgoole*)

INDEX

This Index covers the Introduction, Commentary and Appendices 1 and 4. Page numbers in italics refer to illustrations.

448